D0554107

The American Counterrevolution

"The Tea-Tax Tempest, or the Anglo-American Revolution" (1778). Women, blacks, and Native Americans look on as men squabble about liberty—wondering what the tempest will mean for them.

The American Counterrevolution

A Retreat from Liberty, 1783-1800

LARRY E. TISE

STACKPOLE
BOOKS

Copyright © 1998 by Stackpole Books

Published by
STACKPOLE BOOKS
5067 Ritter Road
Mechanicsburg, PA 17055

All rights reserved, including the right to reproduce this book or portions thereof in any form or by any means, electronic or mechanical, including photocopying, recording, or by any information storage and retrieval system, without permission in writing from the publisher. All inquiries should be addressed to Stackpole Books, 5067 Ritter Road, Mechanicsburg, Pennsylvania 17055.

Printed in the United States of America

10 9 8 7 6 5 4 3 2 1

FIRST EDITION

Library of Congress Cataloging-in-Publication Data

Tise, Larry E.
    The American counterrevolution : a retreat from liberty, 1783–1800
/ Larry E. Tise. — 1st ed.
      p.   cm.
    Includes bibliographical references (p.   ) and index.
    ISBN 0-8117-0100-X
    1. United States—Politics and government—1783–1800.
2. Counterrevolutions—United States—History—18th century.
3. Counterrevolutionaries—Biography.   4. Liberty—History—18th
century.   I. Title.
E302.1.T57   1998
973.4—dc21   98-21556
                                                  CIP

CONTENTS

Part Three: The Limits of Liberty

Part Four: Counterrevolution

Part Five: The Victory of Order

ILLUSTRATIONS

For me history is pilgrimage in the present, not a traipsing through the past. Hence it is impossible to separate history from everything it is that I see, feel, touch, read, encounter, hear, or imbibe. As a consequence, anything I write is but a meditation on my experiences with sources, places, and people over a given period of time. And such is this work, *The American Counterrevolution.*

This segment of life's pilgrimage began when the portion that yielded another book, *Proslavery: A History of the Defense of Slavery in America, 1701–1840* (1987), came to an end. I had researched the story of the defense of slavery through the end of the Civil War and beyond and had planned to produce the sequel volume in due time. But, at just the moment *Proslavery* appeared, a host of events converged that caused me to set aside the defense of slavery—an important piece of the gigantic American puzzle—and to turn instead to confront in some manner the entire puzzle.

First of all, my colleague Lewis Perry took a sabbatical from his history post at Vanderbilt University in 1988, and he recommended that I teach his graduate survey course on the middle period of American history. This was no small challenge for me, since I had spent the previous fifteen years doing little other than executive administration of large and demanding historical organizations. Although I was engaged in efforts to rebuild the American Association for State and Local History, also located in Nashville, I agreed to teach the course.

Fifteen years of missed reading I attempted to tackle in the space of four months. It was just as if I were again cramming for my comprehensive Ph.D. examinations at the University of North Carolina seventeen years earlier. To me, the shifts in historiography from 1973 to 1988 were mind-boggling, thrilling, and illuminating. The scope and breadth of secondary literature had grown exponentially, covering topics I could only wonder about while writing *Proslavery.* The printing of so many primary sources and the availability of photocopying and word processing capabilities far beyond those of 1973 quickly transformed me from a sidelined historian to a ravenous consumer of every piece of historical literature that fell my way or that could be carried along on my endless executive peregrinations.

Beginning with that course I have moved from immersing myself in history to a passionate desire to return to some issues and ideas in American history—

matters that began to seem clear to me, but did not appear in any of the secondary literature I could find.

The story I wanted to tell was how so many Americans systematically reconfigured the principles and values of the American Revolution into something else. How could one tell such a story, at odds with conventional wisdom and fraught with endless definitional problems, without becoming ensnared in historiographical quagmires that would kill the messenger and stifle the message?

The point of departure that transformed these questions into *The American Counterrevolution* emerged during the course of three journeys I undertook in 1989 and 1990. The first was a visit to France in June and July of 1989. Flush with all of the reading I had done for Perry's course and in France on the bicentennial of the storming of the Bastille, I decided that the occasion warranted some touristy and popular activities—visits to the Arc de Triomphe, the Eiffel Tower, the Louvre, Notre-Dame, the Bateaux Mouche, Musée d'Orsay, the Pompidou Center, the Panthéon, the Bois de Boulogne, Versailles, and whatever else American visitors have traipsed through in Paris over the past three centuries. To get myself into the mood for commemorating the fall of the Bastille, I decided to take along a copy of Simon Schama's *Citizens,* a tome virtually everyone got and many actually read that year.[1]

My journey also was inspired by the fact that I had just become the first executive director of the Benjamin Franklin National Memorial at The Franklin Institute in Philadelphia. With this in mind, I made the trip an exploration along the pathway of Franklin, who spent 1776 to 1785 as America's first Minister to France. I determined that, among other things, I would see in Paris those places known to Franklin.

From the moment my plane taxied onto the runway in Philadelphia until a return flight rejoined me to that spot some two weeks later, I was riveted to Schama's chronicle. I relived in mind and emotion every scene and act of that grand drama that was the French Revolution. At the American Embassy, the Talleyrand House, and the ambassador's residence, the then-just-appointed Ambassador Walter Curley, himself a Franklin enthusiast, displayed portrait after portrait and bust after bust of the genial Franklin, who became a French idol upon his arrival in 1776. In Passy, where Franklin lived, the former Meredith Martindale (Mrs. Olivier Frapier) showed me the footprint of Franklin's residence, its elegant gardens, and the nearby residence of John, Abigail, and John Quincy Adams, who jealously seethed over Franklin's fame and their own relative anonymity.

The site of the Bastille, cleared in 1789 of a prison more vilified than utilized, remains empty of any landmark to recall the hated bastion. But at the imposing Panthéon, model for the U.S. Capitol, lay the majestic wooden coffins of revolutionary inspiriters Voltaire and Rousseau, the crypt of Enlightenment genius Descartes, and the tombs of revolutionary martyrs Mirabeau and Marat. There one could imagine the heroic burial of these idealists who brought us the revolution that came to be the measure of all revolutions before and since. I then saw their grand deeds depicted at the Louvre in mural-sized paintings by Jacques-Louis David, himself one of the principal agents of the revolution. No one but a devoted idealogue could so accurately depict, yet also thoroughly glorify, the revolutionaries of France as they remade the world.

Everywhere were reminders of the promises of fraternity and equality, liberation and freedom, emancipation and human rights. The Bois de Boulogne, with its lakes, streams, and pathways—once a hunting preserve of kings, now parkland of the people—bespoke both royalty and liberty. The sturdy elevators of the much later Eiffel Tower soar visitors up and above the usually green and luscious Champ-de-Mars. There on August 27, 1783, Franklin observed the world's first balloon flight performed by the brothers Montgolfier. On July 11, 1791, a grand procession passed by there carrying Voltaire's remains to a dark stall in the Panthéon. But there, too, six days later, Lafayette's National Guard took on a crowd of fifty thousand citizens filled with revolutionary fervor, killing at least seventeen of them and converting the French Revolution from a crusade of ideals to a chronicle of blood.

I stood contemplating the elegant Cathedral of Notre-Dame, this masterpiece of the Middle Ages with a heroic equestrian statue of a grizzled Charlemagne in front of it. How appropriate that he should be positioned there, the warrior, the law-giver, and the unifier of Christianity and the state as the first emperor of the Holy Roman Empire. Established on December 25, 800, in the Basilica of St. Peter in Rome, Charlemagne took on the title Charles Augustus when he rose from prayer during Mass. Pope Leo III lifted a golden crown to his head and then bowed to kiss the feet of the new Emperor.[2]

For a thousand years—despite wars, plagues, assassinations, crusades, and famines—Charlemagne's creation remained fixed. But then Notre-Dame became the stage for revolution itself. On an island in the River Seine with historic divisions named Île-Saint Louis and Île Cité, these segments were renamed in 1792 "Fraternity" and "Reason." On November 10, 1793, in an unparalleled Festival of Liberty across all Paris, Notre-Dame was officially dechristianized and rebaptized as the Temple of Reason, dedicated to the Supreme Being. Just three months later the National Convention would go there to celebrate its vote to abolish slavery in all French lands and territories—making France the first colonial power to do so. Yet that happy event took place little more than a month before the onset of the Reign of Terror. Sentenced to die: 16,594. Perished in prison without trial: 12,000. Executed without trial: 12,000.[3]

It was there at Notre-Dame, too, that the revolution in France moved into a dramatic new phase when Napoléon Bonaparte on April 18, 1802, restored Roman Catholicism. It was a mere Machiavellian prelude to the dramatic moment on December 2, 1804, when Bonaparte took the crown of Holy Roman Emperor from the hands of a startled Pope Pius VII and placed it on his own head. The mantle of Charlemagne was seized, not conferred; done in Paris, not Rome; played out with theatrics, not prayer.

At the Dôme des Invalides, once a church, now a mausoleum for the overthrown, twice defeated, exiled, and bitterly-hated Emperor Napoléon, one knows by the scale and majesty of the place that one is in the presence of historical moment itself. How could a people so in love with liberty elevate to such regal scale this diminutive tyrant who spilled French blood so wantonly across the Western world—this man who not only spurned liberty, but also restored slavery in French colonies? What had brought Napoléon to a place of honor in French and Western history surpassing all others—except perhaps for that same Charlemagne whose statued visage at Notre-Dame glowers on every passerby that "thou shalt respect order," "do your duty at your station in life," and, above all, "worship God." Even "nor shalt thou ever suffer the separation of church and state."

What contrast there is in moving from Notre-Dame and the Invalides to Versailles and Fontainebleau, domestic castles and seats of government for the great Bourbon kings. The former bespeak power and glory; the latter declare opulence and lavishness on a scale barely equaled anywhere in the world. One searches the expanses for symbols that give them coherence and meaning. And despite the abundance of buildings, parks, fountains, art, and treasures, one is always brought back to the initial perception of luxury, great riches, and self-glorification. There is none of the careful attention to symbols of orderliness, the ranking of masters and servants, the relation of Savior and King that Charlemagne purposefully designed into the palace chapel and imperial buildings at Aix-la-Chapelle or that Napoléon insisted upon in every event, ceremonial or perfunctory.[4]

In seeing the extravagance of Versailles and Fontainebleau, bereft as they are of cohering symbols, it became easier for me to understand how an army of women could march out of Paris to Versailles on October 5, 1789, and overthrow every semblance of royal authority. Even though Louis XVI that very day endorsed the National Assembly's revolutionary Declaration of the Rights of Man and Citizen, it was too late. He had bumbled along far too long, playing the role of a king while all of his authority evaporated. He lacked the sense of order and authority that fueled Charlemagne to become the first Holy Emperor and that made Napoléon, despite his wretched ruthlessness, a capable successor.

The most memorable outing of this trip was a walk near the Arc de Triomphe —that great monument of self-praise initiated by Napoléon in 1806 to inaugurate his empire—to find the residence that served as the German Nazi headquarters during World War II. I found it, shuddered at all of the evil it symbolized, and imagined how I would feel if my office were among those that are in the house today. Even as I stood contemplating this symbol of order and authority gone awry, I heard sirens from a distance. Many sirens. They were not headed to a fire. They bore the distinct sound of a VIP procession, the kind one hears around the White House and in Washington every time the President goes out or a visiting head of state arrives.

As I moved from the quiet street in the direction of the Arc de Triomphe, I set aside for a moment my engagement with history. A procession of motorcycles and limousines wended their way through stopped traffic and a gathering throng. An army of police kept all of us far from the landmark many times rededicated to French military victories. As I strained to see who was in this orderly procession, I also contemplated the arch itself. I recalled photographs I had seen as a child of German troops marching through that passageway on June 14, 1940, to begin the Nazi occupation of Paris and of an almost identical shot of American troops following the same routine four years later. Originally the arch was to have had at its top a gigantic statue of Napoléon, complete with Roman toga and staff. But that bit of conceit died at Waterloo.[5]

When the caravan of cars came to an end, I watched the visiting dignitaries emerge one by one, mostly individuals whose identity eluded me. Finally there appeared the two people about whom there was all of this fuss: François Mitterrand, President of France, and Mikhail Gorbachev, then President of the Union of Soviet Socialist Republics. Directly before me was the man of our age who, more than anyone else, was trying to bring liberty, freedom, and equality to millions of people held hostage by tyrants of ideology and power most of the twentieth century. He was a man in the midst of bringing to Russia and the other fourteen republics of the Soviet Union those very rights and freedoms contested in America in 1776 and in France in 1789.

Bravo! But did he have any sense as to where he was headed? Did he know where he was taking all of those peoples who had been bundled together and held without rights and freedoms all those years? Would he be any better at orchestrating history than had been Louis XVI when faced with the same aspirations for liberty among French citizens? Would he be able to maintain order while loosing fetters? Or would he go down like the succession of French voices from Necker to Mirabeau to Marat to Danton to Robespierre—all of whom failed, even with the use of terror and mass execution, to control France's masses of liberated beings?

Thus, I was fully engaged in trying to understand revolution, change, liberty, and freedom when I left Paris for a trip that would take me to Brittany and the Normandy coast, places where those very social phenomena have driven humans for thousands of years. To Rouen, Le Havre, Honfleur, Caen, Mont St. Michel, St. Malo, Dinard, and St. Brieuc I went. And all along the way I stopped at church after church, chapel after chapel, monastery after monastery, being almost compelled to witness these charming landmarks of the French countryside. Most of them were described by travel guides and local folk as Norman in design and as deriving from that period when early Norse warriors invaded the north of France. Clean and simple, these places contrasted sharply with the bulky Gothic structures from the rest of Europe and their numerous replications in the United States.

From village to village, it became clear that those Norse conquerors not only took land and riches, they also brought simplicity and order to the land. The most magnificent example of this vast architectural manifestation is Mont St. Michel, one of the most moving visual experiences available to humankind. The sleek vaulting and wood colors in the soaring spires of that ancient monastery contrast sharply with the heavy stone and flying buttresses of Gothic structures. One of the great achievements of Norman builders, Mont St. Michel is a landmark that bears witness to a time of learning, civility, and order little noticed in our historical records.

It was while glorying in these abundant manifestations of Norman culture and still contemplating epochal struggles for liberty that I encountered in the village of Bayeux a historical document so illuminating that it transformed my notions about what it is to be a historian. The document is 231 feet long and 20 inches from top to bottom, and it consists of seventy-two scenes recounting in vivid detail the Norman conquest of England during 1066. Prepared on the orders of Odo, the bishop of Bayeux and half-brother of William the Conqueror, this extraordinary primary source, known to the world as the Bayeux tapestry, was created just after the Battle of Hastings with the affixing by hand of worsteds of eight colors to a long linen scroll.

Executed with the beauty, grace, clarity, detail—even humor—only possible to an eyewitness and gifted artisan, the tapestry depicts the siege of Dinant, the funeral of Edward the Confessor at Westminster Abbey, the coronation of his successor Harold, the dramatic appearance of Halley's Comet during the campaign, the arming and provisioning of Norman invaders, the colorful passage of Norman vessels across the English Channel, the construction of Hastings Castle, and then the bloody carnage at Hastings. Although two-dimensional in perspective, the figures and scenes are rendered in such graphic detail that the viewer is drawn directly into the epochal event. Text identifies characters, actions, and even dramatic speeches. William's rally of his men and attack on the English army seem as real as if the viewer were present at the battle.

The Bayeux tapestry tells an important story in a moving fashion, making it one of the most valuable and informative records of human history. It was exhibited on feast days and during festivals at the Bayeux cathedral to commemorate the heroic expansion of Norman order into England. Despite the fact that it tells primarily a secular story, it narrowly escaped destruction during the French Revolution when sacred objects and texts were destroyed across France. But its value as a stirring narrative of the expansion of Norman power beyond France was not lost on Napoléon Bonaparte. Always ready to establish a symbol, Napoléon transferred the tapestry to Paris during 1803 and 1804. There it remained on exhibit while the self-crowned emperor prepared for another invasion of England.[6]

It was in my encounter with the Bayeux tapestry, while filled with so many other images of revolutionary struggles, that I came to the conclusion that I should try to address an age, not just disparate events; the sweep of history, not just a few threads; and that I should do it through the experiences of dozens, perhaps hundreds of people trying to live in that age. Somehow, by looking at history through the lives of real people, I might be able to tell a story as graphic and moving as the characters of that tapestry had been to me. From that July day in Bayeux, this part of my personal pilgrimage took its focus.

Subsequently, by looking at the world both as historian and as interpreter of Benjamin Franklin, it has been possible for me to connect sources, ideas, events, and sites that I perhaps would have missed. A steady stream of new illumination followed my research and further peregrinations.

For example, while following Franklin's trail across five European nations in February 1990, I encountered other threads in the history of liberty that both startled and enlightened me. In London I visited the flat on Craven Street occupied by Franklin, his son William, and their two black slaves, Peter and King, who both fled long before the Somerset Case emancipated slaves across Britain. At Wesley Chapel, the last residence of Methodist founder John Wesley, I heard a guide describe the evangel's efforts to aid unemployed young men in getting a start in business, saw his own version of Franklin's electrical machine, and was reminded that the last thing written by both of these giants of the eighteenth century was an attack on slavery.[7]

From the window of Wesley's quarters—almost identical in size, shape, and function to those of Franklin's—I overlooked the impressive Bonhill (bone hill) Cemetery, where lay the remains not only of Wesley, but also John Bunyan, Daniel Defoe, Isaac Watts, William Blake, George Fox, and a host of Quaker martyrs who were the first in the modern world to attack the institution of slavery as a sinful practice that had to be discontinued to cleanse the heart and save the soul. Not far away I encountered the only remaining London residence of Charles Dickens, historically identified as friend of the poor and downtrodden. But it was during America's war of liberation—the Civil War—that Dickens became testy about the character and intentions of abolitionists, blacks, Northerners, and the liberator himself, Abraham Lincoln.

At the Royal Society, the Royal Society for the Encouragement of the Arts, and the Medical Society of London, I inspected Benjamin Franklin's membership papers in each organization and recognized the crucial role Franklin played in transferring knowledge, science, learning, and culture between America and Europe. Nowhere was this more evident than when I left from London and began my visits to the west of England and to Scotland. Franklin was just as busy with such organizations as the Manchester Literary and Philosophical Society ("Lit and Phil")—at the heart of Britain's burgeoning industrial revolution—and the Royal Society of Edinburgh—the engine of the Scottish Enlightenment—as he was with those other organizations in London. Eager curators delighted in showing me the evidence of Franklin's involvement.

But it was the visual and architectural record that taught me that we have perhaps not yet understood some of those basic forces that have driven American history. Manchester, although heavily bombed during World War II, spoke volumes. On departing Manchester Station an enthusiastic guide from the Lit and Phil toured me by and through a set of landmarks that left me almost reeling: the massive textile factories; the first railroad station in the world; the first train line, enabling Manchester, though inland, to operate as if it were a port city. There were the genteel clubs and libraries, such as the fabulous Portico Library, that were the products of capitalism and wealth.

But there were three specific places in Manchester that became for me symbols that I was not in a faraway place, but rather deeply enmeshed in sorting out, not just British, but American history. The first of these was the lavish hotel where the Lit and Phil put me up for the night. From my entrance through the lobby I was transported through time and space to the closing scenes of David O. Selznick's movie version of *Gone with the Wind* (1939). There before me was that haunting stairway where Rhett Butler and Scarlett O'Hara made their way and uttered their classic lines of love and reproach. Upon closer inspection and with some additional investigation through manager and staff I learned that the stairway was original, that the building had been built as a warehouse to receive cotton factors from the Old South, and that it had been designed specifically to evoke the character, proportion, and lushness of a Southern plantation mansion. On those steps merged the planters, factors, shippers, capitalists, and manufacturers who transformed the produce of slave labor into one of the greatest concentrations of wealth the world has ever known.

Moments after this jarring revelation there followed the next. In walking to my first meeting near the heart of Manchester I entered a secluded plaza. In front of me stood a life-size statue of Abraham Lincoln. Only recently installed, the statue recalled the unanticipated response of the factory workers of Manchester to Lincoln's issuance of the Emancipation Proclamation in January 1863. When the Union had closed down the flow of Confederate cotton with the imposition of a naval blockade around Southern ports in 1861, the workers of Manchester had threatened riot. After Lincoln changed the nature of the war to a crusade against slavery, he wrote a letter specifically to the workers of Manchester explaining his reasoning. Much to the surprise of everyone, a group of individuals purporting to represent the workers of Manchester wrote back their endorsement of the Emancipation Proclamation. All classes in Manchester seemed in some manner to have been attuned to the struggles for freedom, independence, or union in America—depending upon their point of view.

The third awakening occurred when I toured the Chetham Library with a guide. Known as a "public" library because it is open to the public, the Chetham is actually a privately owned collection opened during the Elizabethan Era with a vast collection of "chained" books (i.e., chained to prevent theft). Deep into this vast and dimly lit library we plunged until we came to a small appendage off one side of the building, a small reading room with many windows and bathed in sunlight. A table and two chairs were the only furnishings in the room. "And this is the table," said my guide, "where Karl Marx and Frederick Engels conceived and wrote *The Communist Manifesto* and *Das Kapital*." Though this is not entirely correct (Engels lived and worked in Manchester to write *The Condition of the Working Class in England in 1844* during 1842–43 and remained in the city from 1850 to 1869)—Engels did in fact use the library regularly, and there he wrote and revised countless essays, many of which would bear the name of Marx and some that would appear under his own name.

I was stunned. It was not merely that I felt I had entered hallowed ground. It was rather that I suddenly realized that American history, indeed Western history, converged during the 1840s in Manchester as Southern cotton factors brought their cotton, as the workers of Manchester made their fabrics and fought their employers, and as Engels, alongside many other early sociologists and political scientists, developed powerful theories about social behavior with which we still live. As Americans approached the bloodiest war of the nineteenth century (even Napoléon could not compete), the entire Western world was seething with social philosophers, capitalists, populists, and revolutionaries attempting to understand the nature of liberty, freedom, equality, and the rights of man.

By the time I left Manchester, I was limp. Franklin had been staggered by his first confrontation with the Industrial Revolution during his visit to Manchester; I was astonished by a confrontation with the wide sweep of history. And Edinburgh yielded yet another awakening. When I walked out of the proud George Hotel on my first morning to look at the Scottish capital, I was struck by the sharp differences between Old Town, perched as it is on a mound complete with castle and the Royal Mile leading up to it, and New Town, on level ground at the foot of the walled promontory. Old Town was the ancient city-fortress. New Town is the modern city.

Old Town is ancient Europe. New Town, amazingly, is revolutionary Philadelphia. Beginning in the 1760s a group of architects headed by brothers Robert and James Adam designed and built New Town. Upon visits by Benjamin Franklin, William Shippen, John Morgan, Benjamin Rush, George Logan, and many other Philadelphians, it became the model for America's first capital. What these Philadelphians witnessed in Edinburgh was the flourishing of the Scottish Enlightenment. During long walks and tours of Edinburgh with Peter Jones, director of the Institute for Advanced Studies in the Humanities·at Edinburgh, I came to understand the depth of this separate flange of the Enlightenment—practical, realist, tough—that I had passed over in previous studies. And I could readily see that it was this Enlightenment—more than that of France, of Germany, or of the Low Countries—that shaped the way Americans would deal with the problems of liberty, freedom, equality, and the rights of man. Although Franklin historically is closely linked with France, his real understanding of the Enlightenment and the Age of Reason derived from Scotland, not the French philosophes.[8]

Pondering these encounters with the past, I proceeded on Franklin's trail via Dover to Brussels, Rotterdam, Hannover, Bad Pyrmont, Göttingen, Cologne, and back to Paris. Franklin searched for truth, knowledge, and wisdom, mainly in the realms of science. I, on the other hand, measured everything I learned from past and present, from encounter and image so that I could embroider a new tapestry on the American past.

The shape for my new tapestry progressed decisively after I returned to the United States. While driving north from North Carolina to Pennsylvania in the Valley of Virginia, I stopped to look at sites I had never visited. At Lexington, Virginia, Thomas Jonathan Jackson suddenly became for me a complex, well-educated, and versatile man—and never again simply a stone wall. In addition to his military genius he was interested in art, landscape, and religion. Although educated at West Point and a professor of artillery tactics at the Virginia Military Institute, he had also traveled widely in Europe and had taught natural philosophy. He was much more the learned and universal man than our historic stereotype has let him be. While one might have assumed that he was breathing the fire of war at a hated North, he was instead enmeshing himself and his students in the culture, styles, and philosophies of Europe.

In Staunton, Virginia, I came to the birthplace of Woodrow Wilson. I had known a little about Wilson, as every American historian must. His father, Joseph

Ruggles Wilson, had been one of those proslavery clergymen I had studied for *Proslavery*. But when I saw at Staunton that his mother was Scottish-born and his father a first-generation Scottish immigrant, when I realized the strong Calvinist and Presbyterian influences from church and Princeton that pervaded his life, another light turned on. Woodrow Wilson, born in the South of parents steeped in the Scottish Enlightenment, lived through his outspoken father the rise and fall of the Confederacy. He looked at the world in moral and biblical terms—more than a little inspired to make America the great moral republic Joseph Ruggles Wilson conceived for the Confederacy. Wildly speculative though the thought might be, such epiphanies—connections between and among peoples—helped me to find ways of interpreting our history that transcend most traditional story lines.

While in Lexington and at VMI, meanwhile, I remembered the much romanticized account of the cadets joining in the battle of New Market late in the Civil War. I determined to stop at New Market on my way north to take a look at this special battlefield. One cannot contemplate the field of gore and the story of the cadets departing VMI en masse, 247 strong, without feeling directly the chill of historical drama. Bent on a mission of saving the Confederacy, they trudged in formation mile upon mile through villages and towns, rallying a beleaguered people. Arriving at New Market, where flagging Confederate troops were trying to stop a huge Federal force, they were thrown into the battle. Forty-seven fell to federal bullets and bayonets. But Confederates and the daring young cadets proved to be victors that day, the living as heroes and the dead as martyrs to a sacred cause.

At least they thought the cause was sacred, an American jihad, in which the sacrifice of one's life was fully justified. Thomas Jonathan Jackson thought so. So did Joseph Ruggles Wilson. And the VMI cadets, though tender in life, certainly believed it. They all knew the risks they were taking. But the cause was larger than any of them.

As I stood over the graves of those cadets, I conceived that we in America have missed the point, lost the lesson, and trivialized the poignancies of our past by falling into the trap of always determining that victors are right and that the vanquished are wrong. Would it not make more sense to understand the aspirations of peoples past and present and to survey the ways they went about trying to fulfill those hopes, than always to judge them as either good or evil? Is it not the function of the historian to tell the story of what happened and to propose why it happened rather than always to sit in judgment of the benevolent or wicked motives of individuals and whole peoples? I came to affirmative answers on both of these queries. And then I took this leap.

1780

| Mar 1 | US | Gradual emancipation law is adopted in Pennsylvania |

1783

| Mar–Apr | US | Continental Congress debates but fails to adopt a law to end slavery in 1800 |

1784

Jan 8	US	Connecticut's revised laws make no reference to slavery
Feb	US	Pennsylvania Abolition Society (founded 1775) is reorganized at Philadelphia
Mar 1	US	Rhode Island enacts a gradual emancipation act
Dec 25	US	At Baltimore "Christmas Conference" American Methodist Episcopal clergy declare slavery "contrary to the golden law of God" and order members to emancipate their slaves within twelve months

1785

| Mar 23 | US | New York's abolition bill is defeated |
| May | FR | Thomas Jefferson completes a limited edition printing of his *Notes on the State of Virginia,* condemning both slavery and blacks |

	US	Noah Webster calls for a new national government in his *Sketches of American Policy*
Jun	GB	Thomas Clarkson's *Essay on Slave Trade* wins a prize at Cambridge University and is published in 1786
Nov 8	US	Methodists in Virginia petition the state's General Assembly to abolish slavery

1786

Jun 19	US	Sudden death of Gen. Nathanael Greene, age forty-four, at his Mulberry Grove plantation near Savannah, Georgia
Aug–Dec	US	Daniel Shays's rebellion against taxes underway in western Massachusetts
Sept 24	US	Jupiter Hammon, Long Island slave poet, issues *An Address to the Negroes in the State of New York,* urging their contentment with slavery
Oct 12	US	Fisher Ames publishes his first essay on noisy factions under the pseudonym Lucius Junius Brutus
Oct 26	US	Twelve poems known as *The Anarchiad* written by Hartford Wits begin to appear in *New Haven Gazette*

1787

Jan	GB	Granville Sharpe sends first group of black colonists to Sierra Leone, Africa
	US	William Rotch, Sr., of Westport, Mass., returns from London, promoting colonization to Sierra Leone
Feb 4	US	Battle of Shays's Rebellion, Connecticut
Feb 22	FR	Assembly of Notables is convened by Louis XVI (continued until May 25; delegates from St. Domingue arrive too late to be seated)

Mar	GB	John Adams issues from Britain the first of three volumes titled *A Defence of the Constitutions of Government of the United States of America*
	GB	First application to Parliament to repeal the Test and Corporation Acts
Apr	US	Pennsylvania Abolition Society is reorganized by Benjamin Rush as Pennsylvania Society for the Abolition of Slavery, the Relief of Free Negroes, and for Improving the Condition of the African Race, with Benjamin Franklin as president
Apr 12	US	Free African Society is formed by Richard Allen and Absalom Jones, black clergymen, in Philadelphia, with assistance from Benjamin Rush
May	GB	Society to Abolish the Slave Trade is formed in London
May 25	US	Constitutional Convention is convened in Philadelphia (continues until Sept. 17)
Jun 2	US	Pennsylvania Abolition Society petitions Constitutional Convention to end slave trade; Society president Benjamin Franklin chooses not to present it
Jul 13	US	Northwest Ordinance enacted by Congress prohibiting slavery in Northwest Territory
Sep 17	US	Draft Constitution is approved by delegates in Philadelphia
Sep 28	US	Draft Constitution permitting slavery and slave trade is sent to the states for ratification (Rhode Island, Massachusetts, Connecticut, and New Jersey immediately abolish slave trade in their states)
Dec	US	Seventy-three black Americans from Boston migrate to Freetown, Sierra Leone, inaugurating a back-to-Africa movement

1788

| Feb | US | John Adams returns from Britain to the U.S., retiring from public service |

Feb 19	FR	Amis des Noires is formed at Paris
May	FR	"Fundamental Laws of the Kingdom" and May Edicts are issued by Louis XVI, causing a nobles' revolt
Jun	US	New Hampshire becomes ninth state to ratify the Constitution, thereby establishing United States
Jul 29	US	Death of Eliza Whitman (model for Hannah Webster Foster's best-selling *The Coquette* [1797]) is reported in *Salem Mercury* (Mass.)
Aug 2	US	North Carolina disapproves of Constitution until a "bill of rights" is added
	US	New York adopts a new slave code, retrenching slavery in the state
Nov 6	FR	Second Assembly of Notables convenes in Paris (continues until December 12)

1789

Jan 7	US	First presidential election of United States chooses George Washington
Mar 4	US	First Federal Congress begins convening in New York City (opening session is held on April 6)
Apr 30	US	Washington is inaugurated in New York City, the temporary U.S. capital
May 2	GB	Second application to Parliament to repeal the Test and Corporation Acts
May 5	FR	Estates-General convene in Paris
Jun 8	US	James Madison introduces in Congress a proposed set of constitutional amendments to become a "bill of rights" (debate continues until September 28)
Jun 17	FR	Estates-General renames itself the "National Assembly"

Jul 6	FR	National Assembly appoints a Constitutional Committee and on July 9 renames itself the "Constituent Assembly"
Jul 14	FR	Bastille Prison is mobbed in Paris, prisoners are released, and the building is dismantled
Jul 15	FR	The Paris Commune, the first of many, is formed
Jul 17	FR	Louis XVI dons a revolutionary cockade, hoping to support the rising revolution and quell mobs
Aug 26	FR	Declaration of the Rights of Man and the Citizen is issued by the Constituent Assembly
Sep 28	US	Twelve amendments approved by Congress as a "Bill of Rights" are sent to the states for ratification
Oct 5	FR	Paris mob led by women attacks Versailles, making Louis XVI and his family virtual prisoners; Lafayette and the National Guard conduct them to Tuileries Palace in Paris
Nov 2	FR	Church property is nationalized by Constituent Assembly
Nov 4	GB	Richard Price praises French Revolution before the London Revolutionary Society
Dec 16	GB	Society for Constitutional Information in London praises French Revolution
Dec 19	FR	French government begins the sale of church property

1790

Jan 14	US	Alexander Hamilton's first report on Public Credit is issued
Feb	GB	Edmund Burke's first critical comment on the French Revolution in Parliament; completes a first draft of *Reflections on the Revolution in France*
	US	John Adams, almost simultaneously, begins writing his *Discourses on Davila,* published serially in the *Gazette of the United States*

Feb 3	US	Benjamin Franklin's petition against slavery and the slave trade on behalf of the Pennsylvania Abolition Society is presented to Congress, launching a month of debate
Mar	GB	Third application to repeal the Test and Corporation Act is sent to Parliament
	US	Judith Sargent Murray publishes essay titled "On the Equality of the Sexes" in *Massachusetts Magazine*
Mar 2	FR	St. Domingue is placed with the Colonial Committee of the Constituent Assembly to prepare a constitution for the island
Apr	FR	Counterrevolutionary military uprisings begin in French provinces
Apr 17	US	Death of Benjamin Franklin at Philadelphia
May 28	SD	Colonial assembly in St. Domingue approves a constitution excluding mulattoes, free blacks, and slaves
Jun	RU	Publication in Russia of Alexander Radishchev's radical *A Journey from St. Petersburg to Moscow,* foreshadowing Paine's *Rights of Man*
Jun 19	FR	Constituent Assembly abolishes all titles of nobility
Jul	US	Congress limits naturalization to "free white persons"; the State Department forbids the issuance of passports to free black Americans
Jul 10	US	Philadelphia designated U.S. capital until a permanent capital can be built in newly created District of Columbia
Jul 14	FR	First Fete in honor of Bastille Day
	GB	London Revolution Society honors Bastille Day
Oct 29	SD	Abortive mulatto uprising is launched by Jacques Vincent Ogé and Jean-Baptiste Chavannês
Nov 1	GB	Publication of Burke's *Reflections on the Revolution in France*

Nov [15] GB Publication of Mary Wollstonecraft's *A Vindication of the Rights of Man*

Nov 27 FR Constituent Assembly orders priests to take civil oaths of office

Dec GB Publication of Catharine Macaulay's *Observations on the Reflections of the Rt. Hon. Edmund Burke, on the Revolution in France*

Dec 6 US Federal Congress convenes for the first time in Philadelphia

---

1791

Jan 1 US The Free African Society in Philadelphia holds its first independent religious service, in the form of a Quaker meeting

Mar 3 US Whiskey Tax is enacted by Congress

Mar 9 SD Ogé and Chavannês are executed, making them martyrs for the rights of mulattoes in St. Domingue

Mar 10 FR Pope Pius VI condemns the civil constitutions and confiscation of church property in France

Mar 16 GB Publication of Paine's *The Rights of Man, Part 1*

Apr US Publication of Adams's promonarchist essay in his *Discourses on Davila*

Apr 2 FR Sudden death of Honoré-Gabriel Riqueti Mirabeau, whose remains are shortly delivered in a grand ceremony to the Panthéon

Apr 18 FR Royal family of Louis XVI is prevented by force from leaving Paris

May 6 GB Burke is shouted down in Parliament by members of his Whig Party; he resigns on the spot

May 15 FR Constituent Assembly honoring martyrs Ogé and Chavannês decree full citizenship in France for mulattoes

May 21	GB	Publication of Burke's *Letter to a Member of the National Assembly*
Jun 8	US	Publication of first "Publicola" essay, written pseudonymously by John Quincy Adams, but ascribed publicly to John Adams
Jun 20	FR	Flight of Louis XVI to Varennes, where he and the royal family are arrested
Jun 25	FR	Constituent Assembly suspends powers of Louis XVI
Jul 14	FR	Second anniversary of Bastille Day is commemorated in France
	GB	Friends of Liberty celebrate Bastille Day in London
Jul 17	FR	Massacre of French citizens by the National Guard on the Champ de Mars
	GB	Birmingham riots and destruction of Joseph Priestley's house and library
Jul 29	GB	Sheffield riots expelling Joseph Gales
Aug	GB	Publication of Edmund Burke's *Appeal from the New to the Old Whigs*
	RU	Catherine II places French envoy Edmond Genet under house arrest in St. Petersburg for suspicious activities
Aug 8	US	"The Echo" series is launched by Richard Alsop in *The American Mercury* at Hartford, Connecticut
Aug 19	US	Benjamin Banneker, black astronomer, sends his first great ephemeris to Thomas Jefferson
Aug 20	GB	Publication of Paine's *Address and Declaration*
Aug 22	SD	Night of Fire I revolt of 100,000 black slaves in St. Domingue, led by Boukmann Dutty, André Rigaud, Louis Beauvais, and Pierre Pinchinat

Sep 13	FR	Louis XVI accepts the constitution adopted by the Constituent Assembly
Sep 23	FR	May 15 decree making mulattoes citizens is abrogated by the Constituent Assembly
Sep 27	FR	Slavery is abolished in France (not the colonies) by the Constituent Assembly
Sep 30	FR	Constituent Assembly adjourns and becomes on October 1 the Legislative Assembly
Nov	SD	Colonial Assembly ends white-mulatto equality
Nov 4	GB	London Revolution Society again celebrates French Revolution as Joseph Priestley assumes the pulpit of departed Richard Price at Hackney
Nov 9	FR	Legislative Assembly decrees that émigrés must return to France to retain their property
Dec	US	Publication of first edition of black astronomer Bannecker's *Almanack and Ephemeris for 1792*
Dec 15	US	Virginia's vote approving the Bill of Rights officially adds the first ten amendments to the U.S. Constitution

---

1792

Jan 1	FR	Legislative Assembly declares the period beginning with January 1, 1789, the Era of Liberty
	GB	First cheap edition of Paine's *The Rights of Man* appears at Sheffield, England
Jan 25	GB	London Corresponding Society forms to organize Friends of Liberty throughout Britain
Jan 30	GB	Publication of Wollstonecraft's *A Vindication of the Rights of Woman*
Feb 4	GB	Publication of Joel Barlow's *Advice to the Privileged Orders*

Feb 16	GB	Publication of Paine's *The Rights of Man, Part 2*
Mar 20	GB	Publication of Barlow's *The Conspiracy of Kings*
Apr 4	FR	Citizenship for mulattoes and free blacks in St. Domingue is decreed by Legislative Assembly and approved by Louis XVI
Apr 13	FR	Friends of Liberty Thomas Cooper and James Watt visit Jacobin Society in Paris
Apr 20	FR	Louis XVI declares war on Austria
Apr 27	US	President Washington signs Congressional act pursued personally by Catherine Greene to indemnify the estate of Nathanael Greene
Apr 30	GB	Burke publicly condemns Cooper and Watt's activities in Paris
May	US	Hamilton and Jefferson struggle for power in the Washington Cabinet (continued until Jefferson's resignation in July 1793)
May 8	US	Militia Act is enacted by Congress, limiting service to free white males between ages 18 and 45
May 21	GB	Parliament issues Proclamation Against Seditious Writings in Britain
Jun	RU	Catherine II expels Genet from Russia for promoting revolutionary schemes
Jun 20	FR	A mob invades Tuileries Palace and forces Louis XVI to drink a toast to the revolution
Jul 11	FR	Legislative Assembly declares emergency powers
Aug 10	FR	Legislative Assembly suspends Louis XVI from all powers and calls for a national convention with an executive council headed by Georges-Jacques Danton
Aug 12	FR	Louis XVI is arrested and placed in Temple Prison
Aug 19	FR	Lafayette becomes disenchanted with the revolution and surrenders to the enemy on the Austrian front

Sep 1	SD	Commission headed by radical revolutionary Légev-Félicité Sonthonax and an army under comte de Rochambeau arrive in St. Domingue to govern the island
Sep 2	FR	September Massacres of 1,000 prisoners in Paris (continuing for five days)
Sep 20	FR	Legislative Assembly is adjourned and National Convention convened
Sep 21	FR	National Convention abolishes the French monarchy and declares France a republic
Oct 4	GB	Publication of Barlow's *Letter to the National Convention of France*
Nov	US	Free African Society in Philadelphia secures funds for an independent black church; Allen and Jones bolt from Old St. George's Methodist Church when, in response, they are told to sit in the newly completed galleries of the church
	FR	Barlow and John Frost present revolutionary resolutions of British Friends of Liberty before the Convention
Nov 9	GB	Friends of Liberty, London Revolution Society, London Corresponding Society, and Society for Constitutional Information (with Barlow present) call for world revolution following the French example
Nov 19	FR	National Convention issues decree on Fraternity
Dec 5	US	Washington is reelected President of the United States
Dec 10	FR	Trial of Louis XVI begins in France
Dec 18	GB	Paine, in absentia, is convicted of seditious libel in Britain
Dec 27	GB	Publication of Barlow's revolutionary *Letter Addressed to the People of Piedmont*

1793

Jan 14	FR	Louis XVI is found guilty of treason and other acts against France
Jan 16	FR	Louis XVI's execution is decreed by the National Convention
Jan 21	FR	Louis XVI is beheaded in Paris
Feb 1	FR	France declares war on Britain and Holland
Feb 12	US	Fugitive Slave Act is passed by Congress, pitting slave states against free states and launching the illegal kidnapping of free blacks into slavery
Mar	FR	Barlow, Gilbert Imlay, and Genet in Paris conceive plans for "Revolutionary Legion of America"
	US	Groundbreaking ceremonies are held for the first independent African Church in Philadelphia
Mar 6	FR	France declares war on Spain
Mar 26	FR	National Convention creates the Committee on Public Safety to govern the nation
Apr	US	James Forten, black Philadelphia sailmaker, encounters Paul Cuffe, black captain of the *Mary* in Philadelphia, uniting national leaders of pro-America and back-to-Africa movements
Apr 8	US	Genet arrives in Charleston, South Carolina, to secure U.S. participation in world revolution
Apr 22	US	President Washington proclaims American neutrality in the conflicts in Europe
May 7	GB	Petition for Parliamentary Reform is defeated in Parliament
	SD	New governor Galbaud appointed to replace Sonthonax arrives in St. Domingue
May 16	US	Citizen Genet arrives to great ovations in Philadelphia, following triumphal tour from Charleston, South Carolina

May 30	US	Democratic Society of Pennsylvania is formed in Philadelphia, most important of America's democratic-republican societies
Jun 2	FR	Twenty-nine Girondonist deputies in National Convention are arrested
Jun 21	SD	Thomas François Galbaud massacres free blacks and mulattoes across St. Domingue; Sonthonax seeks revenge by urging slaves to revolt, producing Night of Fire II
Jul	SD	Toussaint L'Ouverture, fighting briefly for Spanish Santo Domingo, turns his attack toward Sonthonax
	FR	Publication of *The Emigrants,* a novel jointly written by Imlay and Wollstonecraft about the rights of men and women
Jul 13	US	Armada of ships carries 10,000 refugees from slave rebellion in St. Domingue to Baltimore, Wilmington, and Philadelphia
	FR	Jean-Paul Marat is assassinated in Paris
Jul 31	US	Jefferson submits resignation as Secretary of State
Aug 2	US	Washington's Cabinet votes to ask for the recall of Genet
Aug 12	US	Noah Webster becomes counterrevolutionary enthusiast upon meeting Genet in New York
Aug 16	US	With 2,000 or more newly arrived refugees from St. Domingue, a yellow fever epidemic begins in Philadelphia that ultimately kills one-tenth of the city's population
Aug 22	US	Combined white and black dinner celebrating roof raising of the first African Church is held in Philadelphia
Aug 29	SD	Sonthonax, facing defeat at the hands of Toussaint, declares the end of slavery in St. Domingue
Sep 5	FR	Reign of Terror begins in Paris with the creation of a Revolutionary Tribunal and the arrest of suspects against the Revolution

Sep 7	US	Free African Society members in Philadelphia offer to serve as nurses, attendants, and gravediggers during the city's yellow fever epidemic
Sep 11	US	Eli Whitney acknowledges in letter to his father that he had invented an efficient cotton gin
	US	Hamilton discredits Rush's bleeding and purging treatment for yellow fever
Sep 16	US	Dr. Edward Stevens, Hamilton friend and physician from St. Croix, attacks Rush's treatments
Sep 20	SD	British forces, intent on controlling rich St. Domingue, invade the island
Sep 26	US	Black nurses in Philadelphia begin dying at same rate as whites from yellow fever epidemic
Oct 16	FR	Marie Antoinette is executed in Paris
Oct 31	FR	Girondonists are executed in Paris
Nov 5	US	Rush resigns from Philadelphia College of Physicians, which had doubted his treatments
Nov 10	FR	Festival of Liberty is held at Notre-Dame Cathedral in Paris
Nov 14	US	Mathew Carey's *Short Account of the Malignant Fever* appears, attacking Rush and Philadelphia's black nursing corps

1794

Feb 3	US	Federal St. Theater opens in Boston, permitting the resumption of drama in Massachusetts
Feb 4	FR	National Convention abolishes slavery in all French colonies
Mar 6	US	Greene, Miller, and Whitney announce that they will gin cotton immediately throughout the South on their machines
Mar 14	US	Whitney is issued a patent on his cotton gin by the U.S. government

Mar 24	FR	Execution of the Hebertists in Paris
Apr 5	FR	Execution of the Dantonists in Paris
Apr 20	US	Noah Webster publishes *The Revolution in France,* condemning that movement and revolution in general
May 1	US	Major "civic festival" of the Democratic Society of Pennsylvania celebrating French revolution and victories
May 6	SD	Toussaint attacks former Spanish comrades at San Raphael, beginning a long campaign to free all Hispaniola of foreign governments
May 7	FR	Decree on cult of the Supreme Being is issued by the National Convention at the behest of Robespierre
May 18	SD	Toussaint declares his loyalty to France in a letter to the latest French commissioner, Laveaux
May 22	GB	Habeas corpus is suspended by Parliament in Britain until 1801
Jun 4	US	Priestley is welcomed triumphally in New York on his immigration to America
Jun 8	FR	Festival of the Supreme Being, held in Paris, is presided over by Robespierre
Jun 10	FR	The Great Terror begins in Paris (continues to July 27)
Jul	US	Rowson's play *Slaves in Algiers; or, a Struggle for Freedom* opens at Chestnut Street Theater in Philadelphia
Jul 17	US	Dedication of St. Thomas African Episcopal Church in Philadelphia, first black-controlled church in America
Jul 27	FR	Robespierre and Just are arrested and executed (July 28)
Jul 29	US	Dedication of African Methodist Episcopal Church in Philadelphia (Mother Bethel), Allen the owner and first pastor
Aug	US	William Cobbett's *Observations on the Emigration of Dr. Joseph Priestley* is published anonymously in Philadelphia

Sep	US	Whiskey Rebellion in western Pennsylvania begins (continues until November)
Oct	GB	Slavery is restored in all colonies and partial colonies conquered by British forces, particularly in St. Domingue
Nov	GB	Sensational trials of Friends of Liberty (Hardy, Tooke, Thewell) are dismissed in Great Britain
Nov 12	FR	Jacobin Club is closed down in Paris
Nov 19	US	Jay's Treaty is secretly signed in London, linking American commerce more directly with Britain
Dec 28	FR	Revolutionary Tribunal is reorganized and weakened in France

1795

Jan	US	Washington reorganizes his Cabinet following Jefferson's departure
	US	Susanna Rowson's play *The Volunteers* mimicking the Whiskey Rebellion opens in Philadelphia
Jan 29	US	Naturalization Act requiring a five-year residence is passed by Congress
Feb 21	FR	National Convention orders the separation of church and state
Mar	US	Terms of the secret Jay's Treaty are leaked in U.S., causing mass sensation
Apr 1	FR	Journée of 12 Germinal with demonstrations at the National Convention demanding adoption of the Constitution of 1793
May 20	FR	National Convention is mobbed a second time, with demands for a constitution
May 31	FR	National Convention finally suppresses the Revolutionary Tribunal

Jun 19	US	Rowson's feminist play *The Female Patriot* opens at Chestnut St. Theater in Philadelphia
Jun 24	US	Jay's Treaty is ratified by the U.S. Senate
Jul 22	SD	St. Domingue is ceded to France by Spain
Sep 8	US	Timothy Dwight succeeds Ezra Stiles (died May 12, 1795) as president of Yale College
Oct 17	GB	Wollstonecraft attempts suicide by jumping into the Thames
Oct 26	FR	Last meeting of National Convention is held
Oct 27	US	Pinckney Treaty with Spain is signed in Madrid
Nov 3	FR	Directory takes over French government
Nov 6	GB	Parliament enacts Treasonable Practices Bill, directed at Friends of Liberty
Nov 10	GB	Parliament enacts Seditious Meetings Bill, prohibiting most meetings of Friends of Liberty

1796

Mar 20	SD	André Rigaud seizes Etienne Laveaux, ending official French rule in St. Domingue
Apr 1	SD	Toussaint expels Sonthonax, ending actual French rule in St. Domingue
Aug 19	SD	Treaty of San Ildefonso is signed, paving way for Spain to declare war on Britain (October 5)
Sep 17	US	Washington delivers his farewell address, urging Americans to avoid foreign entanglements
Nov	RU	Catherine II, one month before her death, orders Russian troops to northern Italy to engage French armies and destroy the French Revolution

Dec 7	US	Presidential elections are held with Vice-President Adams eventually being declared the victor
Dec 11	FR	French Directory refuses to receive Charles Cotesworth Pinckney as American minister
Dec 17	US	Rush delivers controversial eulogium on the death of David Rittenhouse before Congress and American Philosophical Society
Dec 27	FR	French invasion of northern Ireland at Bantry Bay aborted due to foul weather

1797

Feb 22	FR	American revolutionary officer William Tate leads an abortive invasion of England at Cardigan Bay with a force of 2,000; Tate is captured, exchanged eighteen months later for British officers
Mar 29	GB	Wollstonecraft and Godwin marry when she becomes pregnant
Apr	SD	Toussaint defeats the British invading force under General Simcoe
	FR	Elections across France overturn Directorials
May 2	SD	Sonthonax is appointed governor-general of St. Domingue
May 11	US	The partnership Miller & Whitney is denied patent protection for the cotton gin in Georgia courts
May 18	GB	Parliament votes to withdraw armed forces from St. Domingue
May 31	US	President Adams appoints three commissioners to meet with the French government
Jul 9	FR	Napoléon Bonaparte declares establishment of the Cisapline Republic

Jul 14	FR	Charles-Maurice de Talleyrand-Périgard is made foreign minister of the French Republic
Aug 16	SD	Toussaint proclaims martial law under his control and again expels Sonthonax (Aug 27)
Sep 4	FR	Directorial Terror begins with the Directory taking emergency power over all French government
Sep 10	GB	Death of Wollstonecraft, resulting from birth of Mary Godwin (Shelley) on August 30
Oct	FR	Publication of Robert Fulton's *Thoughts on Free Trade*, addressed to the French government
	US	Publication of Paine's "Letter to George Washington," condemning the president for abandoning the Revolution
Oct 18	US	Ill-fated meeting of American commissioners with French agents X, Y, and Z, known as the XYZ Affair
Dec 12	FR	Fulton proposes to French government the building of a war submarine called *Nautilus*

1798

Feb 15	FR	Creation of the Roman Republic is proclaimed, providing Napoléon a new platform
	US	Congressman Roger Griswold brutally canes Matthew Lyon in the House of Representatives
Mar 5	FR	Napoléon begins invasion of Egypt
Mar 21	SD	Thomas Maitland, British envoy, arrives in St. Domingue to negotiate with Toussaint as head of state
Mar 29	SD	Théodore Hédouville arrives in St. Domingue as French governor-general
Apr 3	US	President Adams sends explosive XYZ correspondence to Congress

Apr 30	SD	Toussaint and Maitland conclude a commercial treaty between St. Domingue and Britain, recognizing Toussaint as head of government
May 8	US	National Fast Day is declared by President Adams; Jedidiah Morse at Boston announces the existence of an Illuminist conspiracy against America
May 11	FR	The Directory annuls many popular elections across France
May 12	US	George Logan addresses the Tammany Society in Philadelphia with his prorevolutionary "Natural and Social Order of the World"
Jun 7	US	Comte de Volney departs America to avoid prosecution under pending Alien Act
Jun 18	US	Congress passes Naturalization Act
Jun 25	US	Congress passes Alien Act
Jun 26	US	Benjamin Franklin Bache is arrested in Philadelphia and charged with sedition against U.S. government based on common law
Jun	US	Secretaries of War and Navy forbid the service of black Americans in the U.S. Navy or Marine Corps
Jul 4	US	Yale professor Josiah Meigs leads New Haven protest against Alien and Sedition Acts, while Dwight also in New Haven announces the existence of a world conspiracy to overthrow republics
Jul 6	US	Congress passes Alien Enemies Act
	US	John Daly Burk, editor of *NY Time Piece,* is arrested as alien enemy and charged with seditious libel
Jul 7	US	Congress repeals treaties with France
Jul 13	US	James Callender flees from Philadelphia to Virginia to avoid arrest under pending Sedition Act

Jul 14	US	Congress passes Sedition Act
Jul	US	Massive departures of French émigrés from the U.S. to avoid conviction under Alien and Sedition Laws
	SD	American envoy Stevens is sent to St. Domingue to assist American commercial interests
Aug 7	FR	George Logan arrives as private citizen in Paris to negotiate peace with the French government
	FR	French commission approves John Fulton's plan to build the *Nautilus*
Aug 23	FR	Irish revolutionary, Theobald Wolfe Tone, begins major French invasion of Ireland (continues to November)
	US	Moreau de St. Méry departs Philadelphia for France to avoid prosecution under Alien Act
Aug 29	FR	Logan departs Paris bearing decrees ending French embargo on American shipping and freeing detained American seamen
Aug 31	SD	Secret treaty is negotiated by Toussaint with Britain and the United States to cooperate commercially
Sep	SD	Hedouville enters agreement with mulatto general Rigaud to challenge Toussaint's authority over St. Domingue
Sep 2	US	A new yellow fever epidemic begins in Philadelphia
Sep 10	US	Bache, financially strapped, dies in Philadelphia of yellow fever
Sep 16	GB	Irish revolutionary James Napper Tandy leads French force in abortive invasion of northern Ireland at Rutland Island; Tandy escapes
Oct 9	US	Lyon is convicted in U.S. court of seditious libel and imprisoned for four months
Oct 10	GB	Tone leads French squadron to invade Ireland at Lough Swilly; in naval battle with English force, Tone is captured

Nov	US	Logan delivers decrees from French government to an uninterested Pickering in Trenton and to an angered Washington in Philadelphia
	US	Undeclared naval war between the U.S. and France begins
Nov 16	US	Webster publicly condemns Barlow as a traitor to America
Nov 19	GB	Tone commits suicide a day before his execution, after failing to achieve his desired Irish revolt against Britain
Dec 8	US	Adams, after a stormy meeting with George Logan, announces that war plans with France will continue
Dec 12	US	Adams asks Congress to ban individuals from communicating with foreign governments

1799

Jan	SD	Toussaint and Rigaud meet, but find no basis for cooperation
Jan 30	US	Logan Act forbidding citizens from negotiating with foreign governments becomes law
Feb	US	Fries's Rebellion in Pennsylvania, protesting taxes
Feb 9	US	Congress enacts a law permitting the reopening of trade with St. Domingue; Stevens is appointed American counsel general to the island
Feb 10	US	Riot at St. Mary's Catholic Church in Philadelphia against Alien Act and for Irish rights is led by Reynolds, Tone's brother-in-law
Mar 12	FR	France declares war on Austria
Apr 10	FR	Pope Pius VI is captured and taken to France
May 15	US	William Duane, new editor of *Aurora,* is savagely beaten by thirty militiamen in Franklin Court

May 22	SD	Toussaint, Britain, and U.S. enter into new commercial treaty to protect Toussaint's power; Toussaint opens ports of St. Dominque to British and American ships
Jun	SD	Civil war between Toussaint, representing whites and blacks, and Rigaud, representing mulattoes begins
	US	Sedition trial of Benjamin Fairbanks and David Brown for erecting a liberty pole in Dedham, Massachusetts
Jun 13	SD	Toussaint agrees not to indoctrinate slaves in British possessions or the United States with "dangerous principles"
Jun 18	FR	Directory purges councils across France
Jul 4	US	New York Abolition Act goes into effect, but with a lucrative abandonment clause compensating former slaveowners even as they keep former slaves in service
Jul 12	GB	Parliament enacts repressive Combination Act of 1799
Jul 24	US	Duane in *Aurora* charges that Secretary of State Pickering is under British influence or pay
Aug 2	US	Pickering orders Duane's arrest under the Alien Act and charges him with seditious libel
Oct	SD	Toussaint begins the bloody siege of Jacmel, stronghold of Rigaud and his mulatto army
Oct 14	FR	Napoléon arrives in Paris after renowned victories in Egypt
Nov	SD	Toussaint continues siege of Jacmel with the assistance of U.S. naval vessels bombarding the port town
Nov 9	FR	Napoléon overthrows the Directory and establishes a consulate to govern France

1800

Mar	SD	American naval vessels *Boston, Connecticut, Constitution,* and *General Greene* bombard Jacmel in support of Toussaint's armies

Mar 24	US	Duane is brought to trial before full U.S. Senate, Jefferson presiding, with A. J. Dallas and Cooper as defending attorneys
Mar 26	US	Duane goes into hiding when the Senate orders that Dallas and Cooper cannot argue his defense
Apr 9	US	President Adams orders arrest of Duane and Cooper for violations of Sedition Act
Apr 24	US	Cooper is convicted and sentenced to six months in prison for seditious libel against President Adams; Duane's trial is postponed until the Act expires
May	FR	Publication of François-Auguste-Renéde Chateaubriand's *Genius of Christianity*
Jun 13	FR	Fulton demonstrates the completed *Nautilus* to throngs in Paris along the River Seine
Jun 20	SD	Toussaint offers clemency to Rigaud to stop fighting, but the mulatto general declines
Jul 29	SD	Rigaud, in virtual defeat, flees to France
Aug 1	SD	Toussaint, marching into Les Cayes, declares Haitian control of all of St. Domingue
Oct	FR	Spain cedes Louisiana to France, paving the way for a Napoléonic venture in America
Nov 17	US	Congress meets for the first time in the District of Columbia
Dec 3	US	U.S. presidential election, the first openly contested election under the Constitution

A mericans. Grateful, joyful, almost delirious were they as a people in 1783—intoxicated with newly won independence, ecstatic that the colonial yoke of Britain had been thrown off, and delirious with hopes for the future. They set out to establish the world's first land of liberty, where men, women, and children would be governed not by the capricious decrees of governors and justices, but rather by laws. Laws, enacted by assemblies representing all the people, would enforce the principles most beautifully stated in the Declaration of Independence "that all men are created equal, that they are endowed by their Creator with certain unalienable Rights, that among these are Life, Liberty and the pursuit of Happiness." Indeed, governments "are instituted among Men, deriving their just Powers from the consent of the governed" to "secure these rights."

High purposes. Lofty aims. Welcome promises. Written into poetry and song were these great principles. Recorded in paintings and books were these sweet ideals. Drama, oratory, sermons bristled with liberty, freedom, and equality for one and all. Merchants, captains, planters, yeomen, artificers, and stevedores shared the spirit, lauded this new land of liberty.

And yet, by 1800, less than a quarter century from the time Americans declared these exalted ideals to the world, they had almost to a person rejected the very principles and ideals of their Revolution. By 1800 not only did most Americans not seek to perpetuate, expound, and practice the principles of the Revolution, they had entered into a process of attempting to supplant the values of the Revolution either with a political process that sucked all meaning out of those principles or with an alternative social and political philosophy that promised liberty—not through greater doses of freedom, but through a careful and meaningful structuring and ordering of the world. So disillusioned were they with the unfulfilled promises of liberty, they underwent a transformation that affected every segment of American society.

So thorough was this transmutation that fledgling attempts to make every American a citizen, to provide equal rights to all, to abolish slavery, and to incorporate women, African Americans, and new immigrants into American society were abandoned. Not only were these once-sacred goals deserted, the words used to describe these goals were also transformed and given new meanings. Liberty itself, once freedom from oppression, came to mean independence within a prescribed system. Freedom, once the absence of restraint, came to mean choice among defined options. Equality mutated from a philosophical description of a condition of nature to a notion of equal opportunity within one's class or social condition. The vaunted rights of man devolved from a set of natural rights provided by God to a slate of prescribed rights established by men.

And so went all of the precious symbols of the American Revolution until every word reflected a new meaning and value. Democracy came to connote a right to vote, not a fair division of property or equality of rights and treatment. Party came to describe an electoral machine, no longer a divisive faction subverting government. The republic itself stopped being a government by the people and became instead a government prescribed by a constitution devised precisely to keep the people from governing. But the most telling revision of all was the special new meaning reserved for revolution itself: chaos.

By 1798 the deed was done. By 1800 what can only be called the American Counterrevolution had reached full tide. Hardly a step had been missed in the transformation from one set of values to another, from one set of aspirations to another, and from one set of rules for human interaction to quite another. So subtle was the shift that almost no one at the time recognized or understood what had taken place. Americans only knew, if they were among the original friends of liberty, that they were no longer welcome in American society; they knew that if they continued to preach the old gospel of liberty, they might be in danger of life and limb. If they happened to be proponents of revolution, they soon met threats, taunts, and challenges to settle scores on the field of honor.

If they happened to be African Americans, they came to suffer a fate almost equal to imprisonment or death. If slaves, they saw virtually all systems of emancipation—manumission, purchase of freedom, and legislative emancipation or curtailments of enslavement—dry up. If free blacks, they saw in every state and territory of the nation a steady evaporation of rights and the erection of barriers prohibiting individual movement from state to state, as well as an aggressive expansion of inducements either to migrate back to Africa or to be colonized there. If women, they saw in every state and territory the banishment of invitations to seek independence and the issuance of commands to accept, practice, and teach domestic service as matrons of society.

The abolition of liberty in America far preceded the abolition of slavery; the eradication of freedom much predated the rise of a new individualism that gave personal sovereignty to pursue adventure and wealth with little restraint to a relatively small class of white American men; the abandonment of the idea of natural equality among humans—intellectual or spiritual—far antedated any discussions of universal male suffrage; and all the glorious notions that there was a basic set of rights that should be enjoyed by all men (and, presumably, women) were canceled except for those few Americans—again, mainly white men, who clung to those rights enumerated in the Bill of Rights.

This is the central story of *The American Counterrevolution,* a tale never before told, concerning a phenomenon previously little noticed, and surely overlooked because the reality of it fits uncomfortably with the images Americans like to have of themselves as a people and of their nation's glorious past.

In the rethinking and retelling, I have set some audacious standards. First, I have attempted—from major themes to minor details—to freshly consider the accepted wisdom concerning historical figures and events, large or small. It is not that I have capriciously attempted to overturn past theories, but rather that in the process of analyzing past verities, I have found that new insights consistently emerged.

Second, I have found that it is frequently easier to understand events in, let us say, western Pennsylvania during the Whiskey Rebellion in 1794, by looking at it from Paris or London or St. Petersburg or Port-au-Prince than from Philadelphia or even Pittsburgh. Indeed, my most compelling discovery has been that if I want to understand the warp and the woof of American history, I must move beyond the United States to determine whether an event we deem significant or unique in this context is not actually part of a larger world pattern of occurrences. By expanding my focus across oceans and nations at critical moments, I have found that the peoples of the United States mainly blinked when others did and sighed relief along with their fellow humans.

Third, I have found it instructive in attempting to understand the course of liberty and the rights of man to look at the simultaneous and shared experiences of all kinds of humans: not just men or women, not just African Americans, not just emigrants or immigrants, not just people of letters or liberators, in fact, not any singly definable group of people. My theory is that if some folk thought their rights were being expanded, probably almost everyone else did as well; and if rights were being trounced, that, too, was likely a shared experience. By looking at the world in this manner, I began to discover a rich texture among men and women of various social, political, and religious stripes that has not been so clearly discernible in the past.

Fourth, I have quite consciously pursued a method of attempting to understand the connections among particular human actors, thereby yielding an abundant harvest of fresh insights. In this volume whenever any soul visited, as an example, Benjamin Franklin, I tried to understand the circumstances and the impact of the encounter on both parties. Many a person brought from his or her meeting with Franklin a whole new fix on life—Thomas Paine, Joseph Priestley, Phillis Wheatley, Mathew Carey, Robert Fulton, Noah Webster, Tench Coxe, just to name a few. From these connections came decisions, directions, and events that vitally affected American history. In understanding the nature of those liaisons, whole new dimensions of richness sometimes emerged.

Fifth, I concluded early on that images are an important part of understanding this period and the ebb and flow of passions about liberty. During the last quarter of the eighteenth century, newspapers and periodicals began to run illustrations with portraits of political leaders and military heroes, images of colleges, towns, and buildings (such as the Bastille); and depictions of riots, executions, and exotic machines (such as the guillotine). It was also the birth of the political cartoon. Elaborate scenes—most often set forth in complicated allegories—interpreted major events affecting the course of liberty. I have used these images wherever possible to tell this story, following the rule that I would only use depictions current to the people and events here described. No romanticized image of past heroes or events has a place in these pages.

Finally, I have found a cacophony of voices, perceptions, and persuasions in my peregrinations. I concluded that dependence upon or even major reference to one of the current or fashionable theories about liberty and freedom could easily obscure my basic effort of exploring what a whole host of important people after the American Revolution thought was happening to their own liberty, freedom, equality, and rights. In letting so many people speak and describe their experiences in 1783 or 1793 or 1798, for example, it soon became obvious that those terms to which we would like to assign crisp, clear meanings were constantly being transformed to suit the purposes of the speaker. Speakers or groups who used them rarely derived their understanding of these concepts from ancient warring traditions or philosophical inquiries. Most often the meaning of these important labels came from the then current topic of debate—value-laden terms, as do living beings, war against captivation and encapsulation.

Indeed, in the following pages, we shall let many people who pursued their own liberty in America, Britain, France, the West Indies, and across the seas tell us what they meant by the words of freedom they used.

PROLOGUE

A t approximately eleven o'clock on the evening of April 17, 1790, Benjamin Franklin—perhaps the greatest friend of liberty the world had ever known—died quietly at his home in Philadelphia. Afflicted for several years with gout and kidney stones, he had come to restrict his activities principally to the commodious house he had designed and built even while living abroad in England and France. Although his body grew weak, his mind was strong and clear until sixteen days before his death. From an impostume—empyema—in his left lung, he became feverish and short of breath. Believing that death was near, he prepared himself and those around him for the end. When the impostume burst five days before his death, he lapsed into a coma. William Temple Franklin and Benjamin Franklin Bache, beloved grandsons he had nurtured almost as a father, comforted him during his last hours. His death at the age of eighty-four years and three months ended one of the most remarkable careers in human history.[1]

Word of Franklin's death flamed throughout Philadelphia, America, and the world. Primus, a black servant belonging to the Rev. Dr. William Smith, provost of the College of Philadelphia (later the University of Pennsylvania), raced with the news to the home of Gov. Thomas Mifflin at the Falls of the Schuylkill River. Mifflin was hosting a late dinner including some of Philadelphia's leading lights: Thomas McKean, chief justice of the Pennsylvania Supreme Court; Thomas Willing, president of the Bank of North America; David Rittenhouse, America's leading scientist; Henry Hill, "a private gentleman of rank" in Philadelphia; and, of course, Provost Smith. The dinner had been punctuated and briefly disrupted by a powerful spring thunderstorm.

Just as the group was about to disperse from its long repast, Primus broke into Mifflin's dining room with his unexpected message. Every member of the party was shaken with the news, coming as it did amid an eerie thunderclap. Smith, without rising from the dinner table, took pen in hand and composed a few emotional lines:

> Cease! cease, ye clouds, your elemental strife,
> Why rage ye thus, as if to threaten life?
> Seek, seek no more to shake our souls with dread,
> What busy mortal told you "Franklin's dead?"

Benjamin Frankin (1790). Hero of two continents, he was a liberator with feet of clay.

What, though he yields at Jove's imperious nod,
With Rittenhouse he left his magic rod.

Willing, touched by Smith's effusions, added his own interpretation of the incredible moment:

What means that flash, the thunder's awful roar—
The blazing sky—unseen, unheard before?
Sage Smith replies, "Our Franklin is no more."
The clouds, long subject to his magic chain,
Exulting now their liberty regain.[2]

The same man who tamed the lightning of the heavens and who charted the course of liberty for a new American nation was dead. The American Moses was no more.

Four days later, on Wednesday, April 21, twenty thousand people crowded the streets of Philadelphia to pay their respects. The funeral procession gathered first at the State House, where Franklin had served for nearly fifty years. It moved to Franklin's house and from there to Christ Church cemetery just three blocks away. First in the impressive cortege were all of the clergy of the city, including readers from the local synagogue. The corpse was carried by randomly chosen citizens of the city. The pall was born by Governor Mifflin, Chief Justice McKean, Willing, and Rittenhouse along with Samuel Powell, mayor of Philadelphia, and William Bingham, prominent citizen and vice president of Franklin's Society for Political Enquiries.

Muffled bells tolled throughout the city, and minute guns were fired as a long stream of mourners attended the procession. In order were the following groups: Franklin's family and their closest friends; the Supreme Executive Council of Pennsylvania; the General Assembly of the Commonwealth; justices of the Pennsylvania Supreme Court and officers of Pennsylvania government; members of the bar; and members of the Corporation of Philadelphia. The groups that had been closest to Franklin's heart followed: the printers of Philadelphia with their journeymen and apprentices; members of the American Philosophical Society; the College of Physicians of Philadelphia; the Society of the Cincinnati; and the faculty and students of the College of Philadelphia. Flags on ships in Philadelphia harbor hung at half-mast. As Franklin's body was lowered to its final resting place members of the Philadelphia militia company fired funeral guns. Thus concluded the largest public assembly in America's early history.[3]

In New York City, where the fledgling Congress was in session, James Madison rose in the House to pay tribute to Franklin. In a moving statement, he proposed that members of the House wear badges of mourning for a month out of respect for "a citizen whose native genius was not more an ornament to human nature, than his various exertions of it have been precious to science, to freedom, and to his country." The motion, promptly adopted and broadly reported in the American press, became the first instance whereby a branch of American government honored a private citizen.

On April 23, the American Philosophical Society voted to hold a magisterial tribute to Franklin's long career. The society ordered that a eulogy "be prepared by one of their members, to be pronounced before this Body, as soon as may be convenient."[4]

Within weeks printed tributes to Franklin's life and fame, as well as accounts of his last days, began to appear. *Massachusetts Magazine,* for May 1790, published a lengthy biography outlining Franklin's achievements, opening with the now-famous phrase:

> He snatch'd the thunderbolt from Heav'ns right hand,
> And scepter'd tyrants bow'd at his command.

The piece concluded with Franklin's self-styled, typically humorous epitaph:

> The Body of
> Benjamin Franklin, Printer,
> Like the Cover of an Old Book,
> Its Contents Torn Out, And
> Stripped of Its Lettering and
> Gilding
> Lies Here, Food for Worms:
> But the Work Shall Not Be Lost:
> For It Shall, As He Believed,

> Appear Once More,
> In a New and More Elegant Edi-
> tion, Corrected and Improved
> By the Author.[5]

The same issue of the *Magazine,* in a section titled "Seat of the Muses," carried the first of thousands of poetic outpourings that would appear throughout the world. Caloc, a pseudonymous writer, contributed an original piece called "Sacred to Heaven! and Franklin!" Eugenio, another pseudonymous author, offered an assessment of Franklin's gifts to the liberty of man:

> Heroes who fell in liberty's dear cause,
> Who dar'd resist, with him, tyrannick laws,
> Around him mov'd, and on the tempest rode,
> Sublime, midst shouting saints, to their divine abode.

By July, the *American Museum, or Universal Magazine* offered the first installment of the "Memoirs of the late Benjamin Franklin," a briefer version of what would one day be published as Franklin's *Autobiography.* Withheld from publication until his death, the "Memoirs" and, later, *Autobiography* would ensure Franklin permanent international fame.[6]

The news of Franklin's death created a sensation across the Atlantic in France. In early June Benjamin Vaughan, a longtime friend of Franklin's in London, wrote to the duc de la Rochefoucauld-Liancourt in Paris conveying notice both of Franklin's death and the action of the House of Representatives. Vaughan urged la Rochefoucauld-Liancourt to inform Franklin's closest friends in Paris, especially the marquis de Lafayette and comte de Mirabeau, so that suitable eulogies might be given in France—Franklin's beloved home from 1776 until 1785. La Rochefoucauld-Liancourt carried out his mission and passed along to Mirabeau the solemn responsibility of informing the National Assembly, which was then in session.[7]

After wrestling overnight with the story, Mirabeau rose at the end of a long morning session on June 11 and asked for the floor. Suffering from a painful case of ophthalmia and barely able to stand, Mirabeau, grand orator of the French Revolution, dramatically announced, "Franklin *est mort.*" He then delivered what many contemporaries considered the most eloquent and moving speech of his career. His theme, as it was reported in American newspapers, flowed from his grand opening, "Franklin is dead; the man who emancipated America; the sage who was the ornament of the two worlds. The Courts of Princes have often been in mourning for those who were great only in the funeral oration of their flatterers; but nations ought not to mourn but for their benefactors."[8]

Mirabeau urged the Assembly to join with Americans in paying homage before the world to both the rights of man and to the philosopher who had done more than anyone else to ensure the rule of those rights by emancipating his own nation and by framing its Constitution. Mirabeau proposed that the Assembly wear mourning for three days, making Franklin the first private citizen of another

nation to be so honored in French history. His finish, urging the Assembly to follow the example of Franklin and the United States in adopting a constitution for
France, was greeted with tumultuous ovation—especially on the left, where the
constitution was being promoted. Both la Rochefoucauld-Liancourt and Lafayette
jumped to their feet to support Mirabeau's motion, which was promptly adopted
by acclamation.[9]

Mirabeau's oration touched off an orgy of commemorations in France. On
June 13, la Rochefoucauld-Liancourt delivered his own memorable address
before the Society of 1789 of Paris, wherein he also linked Franklin's role in
promoting an American constitution—with which he did not fully concur, but
which he supported—to the pending French constitution. On June 19 sculptor
Jean-Antoine Houdon presented busts of Franklin and Washington to the
Assembly; other artists presented members with new Franklin commemorative
medals. In a debate on abolishing titles of nobility and coats of arms, vicomte de
Noailles, Lafayette's brother-in-law, asked: "Does one call Franklin marquis,
Washington count, or Fox baron? and yet these names cannot be mentioned
without admiration."

But the largest tributes were yet to come. On the evening of June 11, the
General Assembly of the Commune of Paris staged "a historical eulogy" in honor
of Franklin. The Abbé Fauchet, one of France's most popular orators, praised
Franklin at the first public function of the newly established municipality of
Paris. More than three thousand people appeared along with Lafayette, Mirabeau,
and many members of the Assembly. Fauchet's eulogy was published at once
and reprinted dozens of times through the years as one of the world's greatest
examples of oratory.

On August 10 the printers of Paris set up two special printing presses at the
Convent des Cordeliers so they could immediately print and distribute the
addresses given there. In their tributes to Franklin—the best-known printer on
earth—they celebrated their newly won freedom. Marquis de Condorcet, philosopher of the Revolution and perpetual secretary of the Academy of Sciences, organized a tribute for November 13, 1790, wherein he presented a glowing outline of
Franklin's republican ideas on national governance. On March 14, 1791, Vicq
d'Azyr of the French Academy of Medicine publicly lauded Franklin's vast contributions to science, medicine, and public health.[10]

As the lavish encomiums of Franklin spread throughout America and
Europe, assuring his everlasting fame, another story was unfolding that contradicted in a rather stark manner the seemingly endless public praise. This bizarre
sequence of events also began within hours of Franklin's death and offered an
instructive view on the nature and direction of American social and ideological
polity during the critical year of 1790.

Only two days after Franklin's funeral, evidence began to emerge in two different locales that Franklin symbolized much more than merely a renowned elder
statesman and scientist. The first hint came in the United States Senate on April 23
—the day after the House of Representatives voted to mourn Franklin's death for a
month. In the Senate, Charles Carroll of Maryland introduced a resolution to honor

Franklin almost identical to Madison's measure in the House. But before the resolution could be seconded, Oliver Ellsworth of Connecticut rose in opposition. He was quickly joined by Rufus King of New York and William Samuel Johnson of Connecticut. Before several other inveterate and longtime opponents of Franklin could speak (Pierce Butler of South Carolina; Ralph Izard of South Carolina; Richard Henry Lee of Virginia; and, not least, Vice President John Adams of Massachusetts), Ellsworth argued that the measure was certain to be lost and should therefore be withdrawn. Fearing a colossal embarrassment for Franklin, all attending members of the Senate silently concurred.[11]

While the U.S. Senate was refusing to honor Franklin, the members of Franklin's own American Philosophical Society were meeting in Philadelphia to determine how to celebrate their late president. After voting to convoke a grand tribute "as soon as may be convenient," they debated over which member of the society would present the official eulogy. The two vice presidents of the society, David Rittenhouse and Provost William Smith, received an equal number of votes. Rittenhouse, as Franklin's closest friend and scientific heir, as well as the incoming president of the American Philosophical Society, seemed the logical choice to give the eulogy. Smith, one of Franklin's bitterest enemies and political rivals for almost forty years, seemed a poor alternative. And yet, in one of those perverse twists of history, Smith was given the task of preparing the eulogy.[12]

Neither the U.S. Senate nor the American Philosophical Society might have given further thought to Franklin's death if both bodies had not been provoked by external events. Months passed, and nothing might have happened had the government of the United States not in the intervening period moved from New York City to Franklin's own neighborhood in Philadelphia.

The impulse that eventually roused both the Senate and the Philosophical Society from their slumber resulted from the original action of the National Assembly to honor Franklin on June 11, 1790. Abbé Sieyès, president of the Assembly, transmitted a letter dated June 20, 1790, to "The President of Congress" of the United States, enclosing the action of the Assembly and proposing that "the individuals of the two nations [France and the U.S.] connect themselves by a mutual affection" in the interests of liberty. When the letter arrived later in the year in the office of the President of the United States, George Washington, either in a pique over diplomatic niceties or ideological posturing, refused to open it. Shortly afterward, a similarly addressed second letter arrived from Beniere, president of the Paris Commune, enclosing copies of Abbé Fauchet's eulogy on Franklin. Washington sent the unopened letter to John Adams, president of the Senate. Adams, already aware of its contents, also declined to open it and returned it to the president. Washington, still unwilling to open the letter, sent it to Thomas Jefferson, then secretary of state. Jefferson opened it and advised Washington that Beniere's letter and Fauchet's address should be distributed to all the members of Congress.

Washington, instead of following Jefferson's advice, sent the letter and eulogies back to the Senate. Adams opened the letter before the assembled Senate and, without discussion or action, ordered that the pamphlets be redirected to the House

Benjamin Franklin (1783). Philosopher, founding father, cunning liberator.

of Representatives. When the pamphlets arrived in the House, that body voted to return half of them to the Senate and to acknowledge the gracious actions of the Paris Commune. No notice of the return was made in records of the Senate.

Public notice of the action of the House finally provoked Washington into doing something about the more important letter from the National Assembly. Though he may have been a stickler for protocol in dealing with Congress, Washington did something very peculiar with the letter from Abbé Sieyès: he sent it to Alexander Hamilton, his anti-French secretary of the treasury to draft a reply. Hamilton's clumsy response underscored the benevolence of the French king and "the indispensable principles of public order." When the draft was sent to Jefferson to be transmitted by the State Department, Jefferson kept quiet and sent the letter with Washington's signature unchanged. That happened on January 27, 1791.

On the day before, Washington finally transmitted a copy of the Assembly's letter to both houses of Congress without any recommended action and without any indication that he already had prepared a response. When the letter arrived in the Senate, it was accorded the same treatment as the previous letter from the Paris Commune. One member present in the closed hall of the Senate, William Maclay of Pennsylvania, wrote that the letter was "Received with a Coldness that was truly amazing." Indeed, Maclay captured the significance of the moment almost perfectly when he reflected how astonished the "French Patriots" will be "when they find that we, cold as Clay, care not a fig about them, Franklin, or Freedom."[13]

The provocative inaction of the Senate, whether it be interpreted as personal, political, or ideological petulance, precipitated another series of events that highlighted even further the momentousness of what was happening in Philadelphia and America. Benjamin Franklin Bache, Franklin's devoted grandson and impassioned editor of the *General Advertiser* in Philadelphia, published the full text of the letter and decree of the National Assembly on January 27. Within days, movements were afoot in a variety of directions to salvage the increasingly tarnished reputations of Franklin, of the U.S. Senate, and of the United States itself.

William Maclay, aggrieved senator of Pennsylvania, evidently persuaded his brother Samuel Maclay, a member of the Pennsylvania House of Representatives, to stir the Pennsylvania General Assembly into an action that would provoke the U.S. Senate to some movement. On February 14, Maclay offered a resolution in the House that the Pennsylvania Assembly should itself acknowledge the actions of the National Assembly of France. The Pennsylvania house adopted a resolution the following day to establish a committee to write the response. When the address was finally issued, it contained an affirmation of liberty totally contrary to attitudes expressed by either Hamilton or the U.S. Senate:

> We now view with a grateful exultation, your glorious triumph of reason over prejudice,—of liberty and law over flattery and despotic will. You have nobly broke the fetters that bound you to your former government, and have, in the view of astonished Europe, undertaken a revolution, founded on that pure and elementary principle, that the people are the source of power— that in them it is naturally inherent, and from them can alone be derived.[14]

Taken as it was in the Pennsylvania State House just a few feet from Congress Hall and reported faithfully in Bache's newspaper, this action had a telling effect.

The effrontery of the Senate also spurred Provost Smith and the American Philosophical Society back into action. At a meeting on February 4, 1791, the society appointed a committee of three to visit both Rittenhouse and Smith in order to proceed with the long-awaited eulogy. The society also decided that the event should involve dignitaries of the city, state, and nation. The committee raced ahead with plans to invite the president, the vice president, the Senate and House of Representatives, officials of the federal government, the governor and General Assembly of Pennsylvania, the diplomatic corps, judges of the federal and state courts, as well as other officials, dignitaries, and citizens.

To deliver such an audience was no small order. Certain events are suggestive of the deals made. On February 18 the committee reported that "the Business [is] . . . in forwardness." On that same date the committee delivered to Alexander Hamilton a diploma making him a member of the society. On February 22, then, without explanation, debate, or fanfare, the U.S. Senate suddenly spoke on the letter from the National Assembly by adopting the following resolution:

> That the President of the United States be requested to cause to be communicated to the National Assembly of France, the peculiar sensibility of Congress, to the tribute paid to the memory of Benjamin Franklin, by the enlightened and free Representatives of a great nation, in their decree of the eleventh of June, one thousand seven hundred and ninety.

On February 25, the society's committee met to prepare the formal invitations to the president, the Senate, and the House. The next day, the committee personally delivered the invitations to each body and received affirmative replies. It would appear that the secretary of the treasury was behind the scenes, orchestrating all of the events.[15]

The time chosen for the eulogy was early morning March 1, evidently so as not to conflict with regular sessions of the House and the Senate. In preparation for his speech Provost William Smith had implored Rittenhouse to give him a written account of Franklin's scientific endeavors and had asked Jefferson to prepare an account of Franklin's activities in France. He also had been able to get some useful items on Franklin and his character from Franklin's nephew, Jonathan Williams, a secretary of the society, and from Benjamin Rush, noted Philadelphia physician.[16]

On the morning of March 1, the American Philosophical Society held an extraordinary meeting in its halls adjacent to Independence and Congress Halls. Forty-five distinguished members attended, including Thomas Jefferson and Alexander Hamilton—the only meeting of the society Hamilton ever made. The group proceeded to the German Lutheran Church on Fourth Street, where the members were joined by the President and Mrs. Washington, the Vice President and Mrs. Adams, the Senate and the House of Representatives, Cabinet officers, and a vast assemblage of other dignitaries and citizens. At the appointed hour, Provost Smith delivered his melodramatic *Eulogium on Dr. Franklin,* which primarily contained the accounts of Rittenhouse, Jefferson, Williams, and Rush dressed in an excessive number of flowery words.

After addressing himself to "Citizens of Pennsylvania! Luminaries of Science! Assembled Fathers of America!" and announcing that he would eulogize "the venerable Sage of Pennsylvania, the Patriot and Patriarch of America," he forthrightly apologized for his role in delaying the event for almost a year. He even acknowledged that Franklin had given him an important post in Philadelphia early in his career. After recounting Franklin's many accomplishments, Smith related Franklin's latest contributions toward framing the Constitution and in organizing the Pennsylvania Society for the Abolition of Slavery. Though Smith could have described Franklin's latest antislavery writings he instead stressed Franklin's commitment to order in society:

> It was not his desire, however, to propagate Liberty by the violation of public Justice or private Rights; nor to countenance the operation of Principles or Tenets among any Class or Association of Citizens, inconsistent with, or repugnant to, the <u>Civil Compact</u> . . . ; but he looked forward to that <u>Aera</u> of civilized <u>Humanity</u>, when, in consistence with the <u>Constitution of the United States</u>, it may be hoped, there shall not be a <u>Slave</u> within their jurisdiction or territory!

Despite all of Smith's past hatred for Franklin, his *Eulogium* was generous and fair—if not particularly creative.[17]

But as if to underscore the makeshift, though ultimately spectacular nature of the public tribute to Franklin, Provost Smith engaged in a four-way squabble with the society, William Temple Franklin, and Benjamin Franklin Bache. Asked on March 4, 1791, to provide the society with a copy of his *Eulogium* for publication, he dallied for more than a year. When the work finally was published by Bache in 1792, three appended notes told the story. In one note Smith blamed Bache for printing delays and a vast number of errata. In another note Bache charged that Smith caused both the delays and an unusual number of errors by his lengthy absences from Philadelphia with the only copy of the original manuscript. A final note at the end, probably at the insistence of both Smith and Bache, explained that a catalog of Franklin's writings that was to be published with the *Eulogium* was not included because "the publication of them might interfere, in some degree, with the work which is expected from his Grandson, Temple Franklin, Esq."[18]

How can one account for all the strange behavior surrounding the death of America's best-known ambassador? What could have caused so many people in America's seat of power—in Franklin's hometown—to act as if it would be wrong to honor the genius of science, philosophy, diplomacy, and statecraft? Why was it necessary for the nation's top political leaders to come to a behind-the-scenes understanding before Franklin's ghost could be laid to rest?

Some would argue that these episodes were merely indicative of the emergence of partisan politics in the nation's capital. Others would suggest that the petty insults thrown at the memory of Franklin reflected the court jealousies prevalent in the early days of the Washington administration. Still others would hold that Washington was being overly cautious in taking any action that could establish a bad precedent. Titles, diplomatic niceties, divisions of responsibility, and other fundamentals in the organizing of a new republican government certainly needed to be carefully managed. All of these factors were indeed at play in 1790, barely a year after the inauguration of the first president of the United States and after the convening of the first Congress under the Constitution.

But there was also something of fundamental importance at work. Franklin's death occurred at a critical moment in American history, when the pendulum swing that had been impelling Americans in the direction of liberty, freedom, and equality had reached its limits. Indeed, the pendulum had begun its reverse oscillation in the direction of order, constraint, and a workable, stratified rearrangement of American republican society. And Franklin's concluding days, death, and eulogies occurred just as the opposite movement of human forces—like advancement of the enormous geological plates that make up the crust of the earth— began a reordering of American and Western history that would inaugurate collisions as awesome and destructive as earthquakes. Here were the first public and tangible inklings of a counterrevolution in the works.

PART ONE

REVOLUTION

CHAPTER 1

Friends of Liberty

1789—THE SWEET SUMMER OF LIBERTY

During the summer of 1789, the Western world—including Europe and the vast network of colonies, nations, and territories spawned by European nations—experienced the sweetest taste of liberty that would be known until the twentieth century. The Congress of the United States was engaged in formulating the Bill of Rights—a set of amendments to the Constitution, wholly unnecessary, but symbolically vital in affirming the basic rights of man. What was recognized even at the time as essentially a new American declaration of the rights of man became—unknown to participants in the drama—the high tide of American fervor for human liberty. "Though mistaken in its object," James Madison observed of the amendments, he nevertheless called upon Congress to respect the prevailing mood of the American people expressed in ratification debates. "On principles of amity and moderation," he declaimed, "let us conform to their wishes, and expressly declare the great rights of mankind secured under this constitution."[1]

As Congress debated dozens of potential provisions for the Bill of Rights, across the Atlantic in France, King Louis XVI had convened the historic Estates-General to consider taxes and other matters fundamental to the future of the French nation. In the space of barely two months, the Estates-General, an elected assembly of the nation's gifted leaders and noted thinkers, set out to reshape France in a mold inspired in part by the American Revolution and in part by a generation of liberationist philosophers. Convening initially on May 5, the body renamed itself the National Assembly by June 17. Appointing a committee to draw up a constitution for France along the American model, the group revised its name a second time on July 9 as the Constituent Assembly.

The forces of history had converged with the passions of the moment to launch the grandest revolution of modern world history. Inspired by past frustrations, a revulsive national mood, and hopes for the future encouraged by the Assembly, a Paris crowd of nine hundred folk—many pouring in from the provinces in search of food and work—attacked the ancient fortress-prison known as the Bastille on July 14. Before day's end, prisoners had emerged to freedom and the heads of their captors had been mounted on pikes. Political ideals, invigorating symbols, and bloodthirsty mobs had united to begin history's most memorable revolution.

The July 14 storming of the Bastille became the symbol of the rising revolution. The Assembly raced ahead to formulate its own declaration of rights. Only six weeks after the first Bastille day, the Assembly issued the Declaration of the Rights of Man and the Citizen. Containing seventeen articles, the document was a liberating but not a democratic pronouncement. It enunciated man's natural and imprescriptible rights, including liberty, property, security, and freedom from oppression. But it did not proclaim the equality of humans. It outlined the rights of individuals: equality before the law, freedom of expression and the press, religious toleration, and freedom from arrest. It held that property was "a sacred and inviolable right." Sovereignty lay with the people of the nation, not with the monarch; laws adopted by elected assemblies were statements of the national will. Finally, the declaration described the separation of powers necessary for national governance.

This revolutionary document drew directly upon America's own revolutionary experience, and Thomas Jefferson, minister to France in 1789, reviewed some of the early drafts. But the Assembly did not have access to the much more limited and quite specific U.S. Bill of Rights that was at the same time being formulated. Designed to complement the Constitution, the amendments were not released for public scrutiny and ratification by the states until September 28.

If the U.S. Bill of Rights was the culmination of the American Revolution, the Declaration of the Rights of Man and the Citizen touched off the French Revolution. No less a figure than the marquis de Lafayette, hero of the American War of Independence, guided the charting of human rights in France. Venerated nationally, the thirty-two-year-old Lafayette sought to control the explosive events in France during the summer and fall of 1789. As commander of the French National Guard, he fed Jefferson's advice into the National Assembly and he served as a symbol of liberation. He also hoped to maintain peace and order as France was transformed into what he believed would be a constitutional monarchy.

On September 15, however, Louis XVI made his own declaration: He refused to endorse the actions of the Assembly. His resolve quickly threw rising political factions in the Assembly and among the debating clubs of Paris into turmoil. The Assembly, nevertheless, proceeded with the establishment of a constitutional monarchy to be launched either with or without his approval. As Louis continued to demur into October, Paris again seethed with discontent. When the news circulated on October 5 that the king and queen had just held a grand banquet in the halls of Versailles Palace, the women of Paris, unable to find bread to feed their families, organized and began a twelve-mile protest march.

Sensing that a situation not unlike the storming of the Bastille was in the offing, Lafayette determined to make the march as orderly as possible. He positioned the National Guard at both the head and the rear of the throng of some sixty thousand people and sent riders ahead to warn both the king and the Assembly of the impending horde. Just before the gates of Versailles were assaulted by the angry mob, Louis announced that he would accept the Declaration without qualification. Although his action could be viewed as capitulation in the face of an unruly crowd, it set the stage and provided an excuse for Lafayette to save both the king and his kingdom. As the throng surged across the palace grounds and into the private quarters of Louis and his queen, Marie Antoinette, Lafayette rushed to their aid and escorted the royal family from Versailles to safety at the Tuileries Palace in Paris. Adding courtly gestures during the evacuation, Lafayette transformed the untidy rescue into an impromptu ceremony inaugurating the constitutional monarchy.[2]

Just a month after the ignominious transportation of Louis to the Tuileries Palace, an assembly of happy onlookers convened in London on the anniversary of the Glorious Revolution of 1688–89 to celebrate the arrival of liberty a century earlier in England and to extol the new triumphs of liberty in France. In the Meeting House at Old Jewry, Dr. Richard Price, perhaps England's most famous reformer at the time, delivered his *Discourse on the Love of Our Country,* wherein he reflected upon the auspiciousness of the times for liberty. A close friend and confidante of Benjamin Franklin and an early and firm friend of the American struggle for independence, Price headed the powerful London Revolution Society. In 1784 he had celebrated the American Revolution in a piece he titled *The Importance of the American Revolution.* On November 4, 1789, he sang the virtues of the new revolution in France.[3]

"The chief blessings of human nature," he proclaimed, "are . . . Truth—Virtue—and Liberty." This last, he said, was brought to England in the Glorious Revolution that affirmed three guiding principles:

> First; The right to liberty of conscience in religious matters.
> Secondly; The right to resist power when abused. And, Thirdly;
> The right to chuse our own governors; to cashier them for misconduct; and to frame a government for ourselves.

In 1776 these principles were then vouchsafed in a revolutionary struggle for Americans. This same liberty and enlightenment had been extended by friends of liberty to France:

> Be encouraged, all ye friends of freedom, and writers in its defence! The times are auspicious. Your labours have not been in vain. Behold kingdoms, admonished by you, starting from sleep, breaking their fetters, and claiming justice from their oppressors! Behold, the light you have struck out, after setting America free, reflected to France, and there kindled into a blaze that lays despotism in ashes, and warms and illuminates Europe!

Price happily reflected, "I have lived to see a diffusion of knowledge, which has undermined superstition and error—I have lived to see the rights of men better understood than ever; and nations panting for liberty."[4]

Lest his hearers conclude that he was welcoming the Kingdom of God on earth, Price urged them to use the propitious moment to expand the campaign for liberty both at home and abroad. The time was ripe to address a persisting inequality of representation in Parliament. Despite other revolutionary changes in Great Britain, there were still vast areas of the nation poorly or improperly represented.

The assembled members of the Revolution Society responded on the spot. During a business meeting convened in the London Tavern following Price's address, the society adopted a plan to organize revolution societies throughout Britain to bring the desired transformation of Parliament. The society also adopted a resolution, drafted and presented by Price, congratulating the National Assembly of France on its recent revolutionary activities. "Rejoicing in every triumph of liberty and justice over arbitrary power," the society offered the Assembly "their congratulations on the Revolution in that country." But the resolution also anticipated similar worldwide revolutions:

> They cannot help adding their ardent wishes of a happy settlement of so important a Revolution, and at the same time expressing the particular satisfaction, with which they reflect on the tendency of the glorious example given in France to encourage other nations to assert the unalienable rights of mankind, and thereby to introduce a general reformation in the governments of Europe, and to make the world free and happy.

The pronouncement was adopted, suitably framed, and presented by the duc de la Rochefoucauld-Liancourt to the National Assembly three weeks later on November 25.[5]

Surging interest in the formation of revolution societies also led to a reinvigoration of Britain's Society for Constitutional Information. On November 27, Price and others planned a campaign to join forces with the nation's revolution societies to secure for England the kind of representative assemblies that had emerged during 1789 in both the United States and France. When the group reconvened on December 16 to commemorate the centenary of the English Bill of Rights, the society drank twenty-six toasts to the achievements of liberty around the world and adopted a resolution celebrating

> the prospect of a complete emancipation of human society from political and intellectual servitude . . . and the concurrent disposition which, having been displayed in America, is now pervading Europe, of resisting all restraints on the Freedom of Enquiry, or exclusion from the exercise of any civil rights on account of religious opinion.

"A Birmingham Toast, July 14th, 1791, by the Revolution Society." The Birmingham Revolution Society's celebration of the second anniversary of the storming of the Bastille features Joseph Priestley calling for "The _____ [King's] Head, here!" on an empty, waiting platter.

Throughout Britain the friends of liberty began organizing their confident campaigns to reproduce American- and French-styled republicanism in the British Isles.[6]

FRIENDS OF LIBERTY IN BRITAIN, 1789–1794

The revolutionary fervor surrounding Richard Price—proclaimed by his French admirers in 1789 as "The Apostle of Liberty"—was not entirely new, nor was he alone in his liberating enterprises. As early as 1772, Price commingled with a band of ministers, philosophers, and scientists brought together by Sir William Petty, the 2nd earl of Shelburne, in London or at Bowood, his country estate. Young and ambitious, Shelburne gathered about him some of the brightest thinkers in Europe. He hired Joseph Priestley as his personal librarian and director of what became one of the world's first "think tanks." In April 1772 Shelburne hosted a five- or six-day gathering that combined Abbé André Morellet from France, Col. Isaac Barré from Ireland, David Garrick, John Hawkesworth, and, from America, Benjamin Franklin. The group discussed politics, commerce, philosophy, music, population theories, the condition of the American colonies, and some science. (Franklin is said to have made one of his famous demonstrations of the use of oil in calming turbulent waters in a nearby lake.) The close associations derived from these gatherings established lifelong collaborations.[7]

Shelburne conceived the idea for his convocation while on an extended trip through Europe in 1771. Tired of royal politics and a hapless British government, he went in search of new perspectives that might be used to bring reform to England. In Paris he gravitated toward Turgot, Malesherbes, Holbach, and the Abbé Morellet. Living in the home of Trudaine de Montigny, head of the Counsel de Commerce, he made daily contacts with a group of intellectuals who were seeking to define a national policy that would address the economic, social, and governmental needs of France. Stirred by this by-product of the French Enlightenment, he returned to England ready to unite a corps of bright innovators who could change not only his own land, but also the world.[8]

Over a period of twenty years Shelburne sustained an international contingent of closely connected thinkers who would become known as the "Bowood Circle," named for the country house where they lived for varying lengths of time—months or even years. Frequently serving as titular tutors for Shelburne's sons, they pursued their personal philosophical, scientific, or theological interests.[9]

The impact of the Bowood Circle in the half century from 1772 to 1825 can easily be seen in just a few examples. Under Shelburne's tutelage, Priestley undertook his early and most creative scientific experiments. Romilly conceived his reforms of the criminal law system of England. Here Mirabeau envisioned the framework of a constitutional republic for France. And Bentham developed the shape of his system of utilitarianism at Bowood.[10]

Indeed, in the opening phases of the French Revolution, Shelburne underwrote an extensive effort to influence the arrival and shape of liberty in France. Bentham and Étienne Dumont (tutor to Shelburne's youngest son since 1786) headed a group of collaborators that rushed to Paris in March 1789 to serve every need of Mirabeau as he sought to gain control of the National Assembly. They drafted legislation, developed political programs, researched constitutional and legal history, designed systems for judicial reform, and crafted legislative procedures. Dumont also served as Mirabeau's speechwriter and editor of his newspaper, the *Courier de Provence*. Throughout the exciting months of 1789 and the beginning of 1790, Dumont and Bentham poured out document after document buttressing Mirabeau's bold efforts to build a bridge between the ancien régime and the third estate in a constitutional monarchy. Bentham especially delighted in publishing in French his grand plans for a society that had not as yet taken root in England.[11]

Dumont and Bentham fought valiantly to uphold Mirabeau's idealistic efforts to transform France; but as Mirabeau became increasingly isolated in the National Assembly and as questions inevitably arose concerning national loyalties and adherence to the revolution, the network of English-based intellectuals became a liability. Eventually Mirabeau's constant references to England as the world's most successful constitutional monarchy proved dangerous. In a decided effort to silence Mirabeau, the Assembly adopted a measure precluding a member of the Assembly from also serving as a minister to the Crown. Mirabeau was soon made powerless. Disgusted with the increasingly nationalist direction in France, Shelburne in March 1790 recalled his troops from Paris.[12]

All the while, Shelburne was encouraging Price to promote the cause of liberty in Britain. Price tended to give the bulk of his energies to preaching and teaching at the nonconformist academy opened at Hackney in 1787, but with strong urging from Shelburne he offered his services to the London Revolution Society. By his reading of events, the world was on the verge of a revolution that would carry American and French aspirations throughout Europe and beyond. This he believed mightily, up until his rather sudden death (from a cold caught while officiating at a funeral) on April 19, 1791.[13]

Despite the loss of Price, Shelburne continued as a major sponsor of liberty and of those individuals who would promote his cause throughout the British empire and the world. And despite limited political power and periodic charges of treason, the energetic political philosopher succeeded in spreading liberationist ideas and ideals where he could not prevail politically.[14]

The record of Shelburne's best-known disciple and the successor to Price as Britain's central player in the battle for liberty, Joseph Priestley, is illuminating in this regard. Although Price was the symbolic figure most closely associated with the long-rising tide of liberty, Priestley's course illustrates the ultimate destiny of liberty in Europe and the United States after the sweet summer of 1789. It is poignant that Priestley entered onto the center stage of the battle for liberty when he presented the official oration at Price's funeral and, in due course, succeeded Price as minister at Hackney.

Born in a small village near Leeds in 1733, Priestley's father was a dyer and dresser of woolen cloth. His mother, from a farming family, died when he was seven. His education was somewhat haphazard until 1752, when he entered Daventry Academy for a three-year period. The most common element in all of his educational experiences was that he was under the instruction of nonconformist clergymen. He also read the works of dissenting clerics and taught himself a wide range of ancient and modern languages. In 1761 he became a teacher at the dissenting Warrington Academy and was surrounded by some of the most creative minds in England. That Priestley had a severe speech impediment—about which he was very self-conscious—was probably a greater factor in driving him from the pulpit than his strange theological and philosophical preachments.[15]

At Warrington Priestley found his *métier* as scientist and philosopher. Upon meeting Richard Price and Benjamin Franklin, he began discussing with them some of his ideas about electricity and air. Soon he devoted himself to the subject of "experimental philosophy," which absorbed much of his energy for the remainder of his life. With Franklin's assistance he wrote *The History and Present State of Electricity,* enabling Price and Franklin to propose him successfully for membership in the Royal Society. Ordained in the Anglican priesthood at Warrington, Priestley then served a regular parish at Leeds between 1767 and 1772. At the behest of Price and Franklin, he wrote extensively about the views of dissenters on the civil and ecclesiastical laws of England and on the rising discontent among American colonies.[16]

But it was in the employ of Shelburne between 1772 and 1780 that Priestley came fully into his own. Reluctant at first to work for someone as volatile and ambitious as Shelburne, he accepted the sinecure after Franklin's strong encouragement. There, he wrote to Price, "the whole of my time is at my own disposal, so that I can pursue what studies I please without interruption." While building his contacts with other philosophers and scientists around the world, he conducted the experiments that brought him international fame as a chemist. Between 1774 and 1786 he published six large volumes entitled *Experiments and Observations on Different Kinds of Air,* making him the father of modern chemistry.[17]

At the same time, Priestley promoted an alternative approach to established religion. He wrote dissenting essays on natural and revealed religion; he questioned tenets concerning the resurrection of Jesus and the immortality of man; and he attacked many of the leading lights of the Church of England. But his continued quibbling about religion with all comers eventually led to his separation from Shelburne. During a period of almost two years, Priestley sensed a growing dissatisfaction on the part of Shelburne with his constant attacks on others. By mutual consent in 1780 Priestley moved on to his next challenge—another pastorate in Birmingham. True to a promise made when he originally came under Shelburne's sponsorship, the generous benefactor paid Priestley an annual subsidy of £150 per year for the rest of his life.[18]

Priestley, through his essays on religion, philosophy, and the American Revolution, amply demonstrated his friendship for liberty before arriving in Birmingham. It was nevertheless in association with cadres of like-minded individuals in the industrialized cities of England that Priestley made his greatest efforts to bring the age of liberty to fruition. He soon found common ground with a group of well-educated promoters of industry, who also wanted to learn more about chemistry. Some, such as Josiah Wedgwood, porcelain manufacturer, and John Wilkinson, ironmonger, contributed directly to Priestley and his chemical investigations. Others, including James Watt, Jr., Matthew Boulton, and Erasmus Darwin, formed a philosophical discussion group with Priestley called the Lunar Society (they met during full moon evenings).[19]

Priestley and his friends devoted themselves to scientific inquiry, the application of technology to industry, Unitarian ideals, and the expansion of liberty as articulated in the American Revolution and by luminaries Price, Shelburne, and Edmund Burke. They agreed that in 1789 the moment had arrived to bring liberty fully and completely to Britain. Hence, they welcomed the call issued by Richard Price, the London Revolution Society, and the Society for Constitutional Information in December 1789, to organize forces to reform the constitution of England.

Priestley's group of eager liberators in Birmingham was replicated in many other cities and provinces of Great Britain, each with its own inspired leader. In Manchester there was Thomas Walker, a cotton merchant, aided by Thomas Cooper, a sometime dyer, chemist, or barrister and an all-the-time agitator and pamphleteer. Walker and Cooper constituted the prime movers in the Manchester Revolution Society and Constitutional Society. Among the members of the Constitutional Society was also a young hatter, one James Cheetham, who aspired, like Cooper, to a higher calling, hopefully as a journalist. In nearby Sheffield, Joseph Gales, energetic editor of the *Sheffield Register,* was the prime mover in the Sheffield Constitutional Society.

Meanwhile, in London various individuals coalesced to support a national campaign to reform British government. Benjamin Vaughan, businessman, political economist, and editor of the earl of Shelburne's radical journal *Repository,* moved around the countryside serving as a point of contact for many of the local groups in London. John Binns, a native of Dublin and a warm exponent of liberty for Ireland, moved to London in 1790 and became the executive secretary of the London Corresponding Society and one of the most energetic radicals in all of England.[20]

The provinces of Great Britain also aspired to liberty. In Wales, Morgan John Rhees, a native of Glamorganshire, oscillated between London, Paris, and Pontypool, Monmouthshire, promoting parliamentary reform, attacking slavery, and preaching the virtues of the French Revolution. A dissenting Baptist clergyman, Rhees also published a Welsh-language quarterly espousing civil and religious liberty for Wales.[21]

In Edinburgh, Scotland, another young radical, James Thomson Callender, was sharpening his pen to become a Scottish-styled Jonathan Swift. In pungent essays, poems, and a major political treatise titled *The Political Progress of Britain* (1792), Callender attempted to rekindle Scottish nationalism and independence while seeking an expansion of liberty for all Scots. A clerk in the Edinburgh Sasine Office (official records of Scotland), Callender blended reformist activities with a budding literary career.[22]

But the rise of liberating forces in Wales and Scotland was minor compared with those stirring in Ireland. The rhetoric and drama of the American Revolution helped to ignite the latest Irish yearnings for independence from the yoke of England. Among the first to come forward was Mathew Carey, who surely inspired Binns and other nascent Irish friends of liberty. While still in his teens, Carey lamented the treatment of Irish Catholics in such graphic terms that charges of libel and sedition were brought against him. To avoid imprisonment he fled to Paris, where he found safety, inspiration, and employment under the tutelage of none other than Benjamin Franklin. In Franklin's home printing shop at Passy, Carey learned printing, journalism, and liberationist philosophy from America's ambassador as he worked alongside Franklin's grandsons Benjamin Franklin Bache and William Temple Franklin. Here he befriended Lafayette, whose path he would cross at various poignant moments in the future.

Urged by Franklin and his own family to return to Dublin, Carey left France and began editing a newspaper called *Freeman's Journal.* Enthralled by the Franklin example he soon launched his own newspaper, *Volunteer's Journal,* on October 13, 1783. He consistently filled the paper with Irish nationalism, until on April 7, 1784, the House of Commons issued an order for his arrest on charges of sedition. Before being seized and confined at Newgate Prison, he vented once again his call for liberty:

> Ye men of Ireland, be firm,—ye that have arms be steady—ye
> that have not, make ready—with one voice, then, the voice of a

united nation, let us RESOLVE TO BE FREE—and if our
resolves are opposed—let the hoarse clangor of arms publish
abroad—let the thunder of our guns proclaim aloud in the ears
of an old jealous tyrant, our unalterable determination—either
TO LIVE FREEMEN, OR PERISH AS A PEOPLE.

When Parliament adjourned on May 14, he was released briefly until formal libel
proceedings could be launched through the courts. Carey quickly sold the *Journal*
to his brother and, disguised as a woman, boarded the ship *America* headed to the
United States.[23]

Carey's valiant example inspired John Daly Burk, also of Dublin and dedicated to Irish freedom. While a student at Dublin's Trinity College, he united
with other students to protect an accused Irish radical from arrest. When charges
were filed against him as an accomplice, he mimicked Carey's act and escaped by
exchanging clothes with a Miss Daly in a nearby bookseller's shop. So grateful
was he for the young woman's assistance, he adopted her surname as his own
middle name.[24]

Another rising star in the firmament of Irish heroes was Theobald Wolfe
Tone. The irrepressible young Dublin barrister was a Protestant who sought to
unite Catholics and Protestants to bring liberty to a long-embattled Ireland.
Through his efforts a United Irish Society was formed in Dublin, demonstrating
that Ireland was clearly fertile ground for the spread of liberty.[25]

William Duane, who at the time was living and working in Calcutta, India,
proved that the yearning for liberty was universal. Born near Lake Champlain,
New York, of recent immigrants from Ireland, he idealized America. When his
father died, the eleven-year-old boy returned to Ireland with his mother. At age
nineteen he married a Protestant girl and began an apprenticeship in a printing
establishment. Two years later he became a parliamentary reporter for the *General Advertiser,* a London daily newspaper. In 1786 Duane was dismissed from
his post when he inserted in the paper, without authorization, comments deemed
as libelous against the British government. He then enlisted as a private in the
military service of the East India Company and arrived at Calcutta by July 1787.
Following a series of skirmishes with the company's management, he finally
became the managing editor of the *Bengal Journal* in 1789—a position in which
he could join forces with his colleagues elsewhere in the British Empire to promote the cause of liberty.[26]

These twelve individuals—Priestley, Cooper, Cheetham, Gales, Vaughan,
Binns, Rhees, Callender, Carey, Burk, Tone, and Duane—were the gifted, outspoken, and highly visible leaders of Britain's movement to secure liberty. Each of
them affirmed the virtues of the French Revolution and urged it as a model for
reforming British government and society. Each of them witnessed the euphoria
of people devoting themselves to the great cause of freedom. They were ready to
respond to the call sent out by Richard Price, to follow the example of Benjamin
Franklin, and to join hands with Thomas Paine.

The author of *Common Sense* (1776)—a key to the American Revolution—and a man of the world, Paine observed developments keenly in both France and England. Although he was absorbed in trying to sell the model for an iron bridge he had designed while in America, he moved back and forth between Paris, London, and the English countryside, ready to foster revolutions in France, England, Ireland, and elsewhere in the world, as he had done in America in 1776.[27]

FRIENDS OF LIBERTY UNDER FIRE, 1793–1798

Despite inspired words and endless pamphleteering, Paine, Priestley, and their eager band of disciples failed to bring liberty to Britain. Each had to choose between residence in his native land and emigration to a more friendly country.

Joseph Priestley succeeded Richard Price as Britain's leading friend of liberty in the spring of 1791. Proclaiming that "the empire of reason" was ushering in a period of universal peace, he invited all humans to commemorate July 14 as a sacred holiday. "It will be remembered as such by the latest posterity of freemen. Let all tyrants read the history of both and tremble."[28]

Priestley's call came in the midst of events in both England and France that made Bastille Day, 1791, look ominous. Mirabeau's death in early April signaled the loss of a constitutional monarchy in France. Louis XVI's attempted flight from Paris on June 20 ended abruptly with his capture at Varennes on the eastern frontier of France. Five days later, an angry and vengeful National Assembly suspended his powers as king.

Meanwhile, tensions were heightening in England. Revolutionary excitement was pushed to a shrill peak when Thomas Paine published *Rights of Man: Part 1,* which validated the French Revolution. He had surpassed every other political writer of the eighteenth century by providing symbols that lodged themselves in the hearts of common citizens and could be recalled with vigor even in the lowliest tavern hall in Europe or America.

As the second anniversary of Bastille Day approached, French and English authorities prepared for potential mob violence. Despite their planning, July 14 opened a season of mayhem and destruction with a dramatic mass march to entomb the body of Voltaire in the Panthéon in Paris. On July 16, fifty thousand demonstrators favoring removal of Louis XVI coalesced on the Champ-de-Mars. Lafayette's troops soon surrounded the crowd and opened fire when the protesters began showering them with stones. Between thirteen and fifty people were killed.[29]

Meanwhile in Birmingham, a mob gathered outside the hall where the local revolution society was holding its Bastille Day dinner, breaking windows, then destroying two meeting halls, all the while chanting, "To Dr. Priestley's." Someone ran to warn Priestley of impending danger, and he and Mrs. Priestley fled to the safety of another house. They soon were discovered and had to move again in the middle of the night. Before the end of the first night of destruction, Priestley's house, laboratory, library, and his scientific papers had been completely destroyed by fire. The ordeal so frightened him that he was unable to return to Birmingham.

Priestley spent the next several years a very unhappy man. Although the National Assembly of France awarded him an honorary French citizenship and a seat in the Assembly, he found that these blessings placed him in an awkward position. The first he accepted; the second he respectfully declined. After several months, he became minister of the New Gravel Pit Chapel at Hackney, the pastorate left vacant with Price's death.

The position conferred status, but insults followed the family wherever they went. After the government issued a proclamation against political and religious dissent in May 1792, and some of his associates were arrested and brought to trial for sedition, he came to the conclusion that he could no longer reside in England. When he witnessed a petition for parliamentary reform defeated in May 1793 and new threats to liberty a year later—including the suspension of habeas corpus—he had had enough. He considered emigrating to a monastery near Toulouse, but his sons urged a move to the original land of liberty—the United States of America. His ship departed April 7, 1794.[30]

Within a little more than a year a host of Priestley's colleagues also repaired to America. Each disciple sought freedom from oppression in some corner of the British Empire and new opportunities to promote liberty's cause. Thomas Cooper, the radical mainstay of the Manchester Constitutional Society, had left in February 1794. Upon the destruction of Priestley's Birmingham home, Cooper urged the Manchester Society to adopt a tribute of respect. He then prepared a popular abridgment of Paine's sensational *Rights of Man*. In the company of James Watt, Jr., Cooper traveled to France, with plans to appear before the Jacobin Club of Paris and participate in a festival inspired by Robespierre.

Even before they could return to England, their activities were reported in Parliament. There they were described as enemies of the English nation, and their visit to Paris precipitated the sedition act issued in May 1792 that so troubled Priestley. Although Cooper defended himself, matters grew progressively worse until 1793, when he, too, began looking toward America as a possible new home. In August 1793 he made a short visit to the United States and returned to England determined to relocate to a land where his chances of success were unlimited. In February 1794, Cooper left England for America, never to return.[31]

Cooper somehow escaped the treatment some of his colleagues in the Manchester Constitutional Society received. Thomas Walker, head of the society, was arrested for sedition in June 1793. James Cheetham was arrested on July 23, along with other members of the society on the same charges. Cooper attended some of the preliminary hearings in the trials of Walker and Cheetham in December 1793 and testified against a perjurer brought forth by the government. When the trial occurred in April 1794, Cooper was already on his way to America, with Priestley following closely behind. After days of legal wrangling, the court acquitted Walker, Cheetham, and their colleagues. Although Cheetham remained in Manchester another four years, he, too, departed when a new siege of oppressive acts and riots broke forth in 1798.[32]

In Edinburgh, James Callender also suffered at the hands of the British government. Callender had become deeply involved in the reform movement in Scotland under the tutelage of Francis Garden, Lord Gardenstone, and in association with other reforming Scots living in London. In July 1792 he had participated in the organization of Associated Friends of the People, a reforming group in Edinburgh, and a small militant subgroup that met weekly to plan protest strategies. As inflammatory issues of Callender's anonymous *Political Progress of Britain* started to sound too militant, the authorities began an investigation.

A spy implicated Callender as one of the local radicals promoting Scottish independence, and an investigation into the authorship of the *Political Progress of Britain* also pointed to Callender. In January 1793 a search found evidence linking him to both local radicals and the offensive pamphlet. The government issued a warrant for his arrest. When Callender failed to appear in court on January 28, he was declared an outlaw against the king. By the time he was also suspended from his position as messenger for Lord Gardenstone, he was already en route to the United States.[33]

Morgan Rhees's Welsh-language quarterly received a similar reaction from government officials. When several of his colleagues were arrested for sedition and a warrant was issued for his arrest, he, too, chose a move to the United States. He arrived in New York on October 12, 1794.[34]

The next victims of the government's campaign to suppress Britain's revolutionary spirit were Joseph Gales and Benjamin Vaughan. In May 1795 the House of Commons established a Committee of Secrecy to expose the activities of Britain's large corps of dissenters and revolutionaries. When Parliament moved just a few days later to suspend habeas corpus (thereby permitting the arrest and detention of those suspected of treasonable conspiracy against the Crown), British revolutionaries everywhere faced either arrest or flight.

Gales and Vaughan chose to flee, while Gales's wife and printing assistants continued to publish the *Register* under his editorship for a month. On June 19, Gales published his last editorial, stating that he would move to another state to seek a livelihood "which I cannot peaceably attain in this." He fled to Germany until he could secure passage for himself and his family to the United States. In July 1795 he arrived in Philadelphia.[36]

When the Privy Council questioned Benjamin Vaughan about his conspiratorial activities, he fled to Paris, where he was promptly arrested as a suspected British spy. With Robespierre's intervention, it is said, he was released after a month and permitted to depart for Switzerland. After some months in retirement, he took passage to the United States, where he joined two of his brothers (one of them John Vaughan, secretary of the American Philosophical Society in Philadelphia).[36]

The same inquiry that spooked Gales and Vaughan eventually drove Wolfe Tone from Ireland. He had been suspected of entering into conspiracy with indicted French secret agent Rev. William Jackson while he was in Dublin. Jackson, convicted of treason, dramatically poisoned himself in the courtroom on the morning of his sentencing, frightening Tone nearly out of his mind. He quickly sold his property and arranged for passage to the United States. By August 1795 he, too, was in Philadelphia.[37]

John Daly Burk's departure from Dublin for the United States mimicked Callender's flight from Edinburgh. When a government investigation discovered that he was the author of several anonymous essays in the *Dublin Evening Post* he made his storybook flight in "Miss Daly's" clothes and arrived in the United States sometime in 1796.[38]

Perhaps the most dramatic departure of a friend of liberty from British lands to America was that of William Duane, redoubtable editor of the *Bengal Journal* in Calcutta, India. Duane had gotten himself in hot water by publishing an article offensive to the royalist French commandant still in charge of the French contingent in Calcutta. After the commandant complained bitterly to British authorities, Duane was arrested and confined to a cell in Fort William. Vociferously protesting the connivance between local British and French commanders to suppress freedom of the press in British India, Duane marveled that he was "born and bred on the bosom of America and confirmed in my love of freedom by a long residence under the British Government."

A last-minute reprieve rescued Duane from deportation to England. He continued his journalistic career as editor of a new paper he called *Indian World*. While England and France were renewing hostilities, he bravely sided with France, where the seeds "of endless glory to this great epoch and happiness to man" were being planted as opposed to England, where "the retrogradation of refined Europe to its prestine [*sic*] Gothic barbarism and brutal servitude" was being fostered. He also welcomed letters from dissident British colonists in India who disapproved of colonial rule.

On May 30, 1794, the British governor and council of Bengal ordered Duane's expulsion. In addition to his political stance, the state convicted him of two assaults on British colonists concerning women or property. On December 26, 1794, he published the last issue of *Indian World,* with a clear message:

> Englishmen, I have experienced the blessings of Liberty in
> your country and for a time I wished to be as one of you. . .
> [But now he would return to America where] I shall be
> received with esteem, . . . I left them [Americans] without dis-
> grace, I return without disgrace, I trust in God I shall find them
> free, that I may forget if possible that Slavery exists anywhere.

The British governor general invited Duane to Fort William for what Duane thought was to be a conciliatory meeting. Instead, a squad of sepoys assaulted him at the point of fixed bayonets. Deported aboard the *William Pitt,* he headed not for America, but for England.

But Duane was irrepressible. Upon his arrival in London, he took over the editorship of a daily newspaper titled *The Telegraph,* virtually the official voice of the London Corresponding Society, which often met in the newspaper's office. The president of the society was none other than John Binns, another embattled friend of liberty. Duane and Binns headed a national force of artisans and working men to clamor for parliamentary reform.

On October 26, 1795, more than a hundred thousand supporters attended a peaceful outdoor rally sponsored by the London Corresponding Society. Three days later, however, a mob attacked King George III in St. James Park. The attackers' chants echoed those from the rally: "Down with Pitt"; "No War"; "Give us Bread"; "No Famine." A stone broke through a window in the King's carriage. A mysterious man in a green coat tried to drag George from the carriage just as the Royal Horse Guard arrived to disperse the mob. A Royal proclamation four days later blamed the incident on the Corresponding Society and its "diverse inflammatory Discourses," which tended "to create groundless Jealousy and Discontent, and to endanger the Public Peace, and the Quiet and Safety of our faithful subjects." Parliament quickly introduced a treasonable and seditious practices act and a seditious meetings act.

The Corresponding Society scheduled another rally for Thursday, November 12, at Copenhagen Fields on the outskirts of London, to protest against the unfair charges of the king and the two new sedition laws. Presiding over an attendance of perhaps three hundred thousand people was Duane, who opened the meeting by urging a "free discussion on all topics which could interest or affect men." Despite the valiant efforts of the protesters to reconfirm the rule of liberty, however, the House of Lords on November 13 passed the two hated acts and by December they had become law. But before the government could try Duane for his role in the rally he escaped to the United States.[39]

John Binns was not so lucky. He refused to give up on the organizing of artisans and laborers throughout Britain. Between 1795 and 1801, William Pitt's "reign of terror" progressed, and Binns became the object of frequent arrest, trial, and imprisonment. He was twice brought before the Privy Council for questioning; investigated by the infamous Secret Committee; then imprisoned in Clerkenwell, Maidstone, and the Tower of London. Finally in 1801 he was released with a host of other political prisoners. Within weeks he had made plans to leave England, and he arrived in America in September 1801, heading to the village of Northumberland, Pennsylvania, where he would live with Joseph Priestley and Thomas Cooper.[40]

THOMAS PAINE AND FRENCH FRIENDS OF LIBERTY

Thomas Paine's path uniquely reflected the history of liberty in his native Britain and in his two adopted countries—the United States and France. *The Rights of Man* quickly became in 1791 the best-known statement in English of the theories and values of friends of liberty everywhere. And, almost everywhere it was a dangerous document. It had been Priestley's association with Paine and *The Rights of Man* that had enraged the citizens of Birmingham. Gales had published the first inexpensive edition of the book in England, making it readily available. Cooper prepared a special abbreviated edition, also for the general public. Callender and his Scottish associates distributed *The Rights of Man* in Edinburgh at the same time they came under government surveillance. Duane's publishing of

Thomas Paine (c. 1792). Marketing agent of revolution, he was a vociferous critic of the counterrevolution.

segments of Paine's writings in Calcutta had aroused the suspicions of the British colonial government.[41]

It was *The Rights of Man* that prompted in May 1791 a Royal proclamation against seditious writings to bedevil the lives of British dissidents. That the proclamation was designed especially for Paine is clear from the fact that prosecution against Paine was launched simultaneously. In December 1792 Paine was found guilty in absentia and made an outlaw in Britain. At the same time, the prosecution sensationalized *The Rights of Man* and secured for it dozens of printings in English and many other languages.[42]

Leaving England for good in September 1792, Paine accepted a seat in the French National Assembly. For a year he attempted to shape French politics as he had done in America two decades earlier. But by October 1793 he had become disgusted with the course of the French Revolution as he watched his friends and associates committing suicide or being carted off to the guillotine.

Planning to leave for America, Paine—an addictive pamphleteer—fired one last shot. On the day he completed the last of his great popular treatises, *The Age of Reason,* a warrant was issued for his arrest as an enemy of France. On the afternoon of December 28, 1793, he was placed in the Luxembourg Prison, his hopes for removing to the United States quashed by a revolutionary government that was wholly out of control.[43]

During many of the ten months that Paine endured in his isolated cell, his British colleagues—Priestley, Cooper, Gales, Vaughan, Callender, Rhees, Tone, Burk, and Duane—were making their way to America. But so were other dissenters from France and her disintegrating colony in St. Domingue. A floodtide began late in 1791 and continued until the consolidation of the Directory in 1798. Members of France's middle and upper classes, pressed out of power and hounded with threats of arrest and execution, sought refuge in the America they had tried so hard to emulate in spirit, if not always in form.[44]

Among the notable émigrés was the duc de la Rochefoucauld-Liancourt, devoted disciple of Benjamin Franklin and friend of liberty in the early stages of the French Revolution. Because he favored the establishment of a constitutional monarchy, he was removed from his army command following the suspension of Louis XVI by the National Assembly on August 10, 1792. He escaped to England until he could make his way to America.

Louis-Marie, vicomte de Noailles, associate and brother-in-law of Lafayette also escaped shortly after Louis's flight to Varennes. He, too, fled to America by way of England. Closely associated with him was Omer Antoine Talon, another veteran of the National Assembly, who fled during the Terror. Noailles was particularly fortunate in his timing, since his father and mother, his wife, and her parents were all guillotined.

Mederic-Louis-Elie Moreau de St. Mery, born in Martinique but trained in Paris, became one of the best-known refugees to America. A compiler of historical and archival treatises, Moreau wrote extensively on French society, culture, and empire. President of the Paris electors at the time of the fall of the Bastille, he also crossed swords with Robespierre. Escaping Paris the day before a warrant was issued for his arrest, he made his way to Le Havre and from there to America.

Two other scholars of international merit who left France disillusioned with the Revolution were François-Auguste-René de Chateaubriand and Constantin-François Chasseboeuf, comte de Volney. Chateaubriand, leaving France in 1791 ostensibly in search of the Northwest Passage, spent the next two years traveling in the New World, recording his experiences and reactions, and lamenting the course of the Revolution. Volney, one of the most prolific French authors on religion and cults, became identified with what were widely regarded as the atheistic tendencies of the French Revolution. He was arrested and held until after Thermidor, when he left France in search of real freedom in the United States.[45]

Victor Collot was another refugee from the Terror. While serving as French governor of the colony of Guadeloupe in 1794, he surrendered to British forces on condition that he be permitted free passage back to France. When he learned of the political executions occurring in Paris, however, he persuaded British authorities to permit him to go to the United States as a paroled prisoner of war.[46]

Other refugees who left France in search of liberty were Roman Catholic priests who had been divested of their positions in the Revolution. At least twenty-four priests fled between 1791 and 1799, among them a group of

Sulpicians who founded the first Catholic seminary in America, St. Mary's, at Baltimore, in 1791.[47]

Perhaps the most famous refugee from France was the notorious Bishop of Autun, Charles-Maurice de Talleyrand-Périgord. Hardly known for his religious convictions, Talleyrand used his bishopric to provide stature and income, enabling him to pursue a fitful career of social and political opportunism. Talleyrand, who also gained an international reputation as one of the world's most unprincipled and voyeuristic human beings, sought an appointment to a special mission in January 1792 to secure the neutrality of England in any pending skirmishes on the continent.

Talleyrand's mission was a failure. Although he had an audience with the Crown, George III was barely civil to him and the queen turned her back to his face. Prime Minister William Pitt and Secretary of State William Grenville listened unresponsively to Talleyrand's overtures. He also had to scramble through the ever-changing governments of France, but he maintained his relatively secure position in England for a short time, first as an official of the French government and later as a legal émigré. In January 1794, when Britain declared him an alien enemy for his support of the French Revolution, the penniless Talleyrand headed to America.[48]

At the same time French men and women were proceeding in great numbers from erupting St. Domingue. Uprisings among mulattoes on the rich plantation island had begun in 1790, followed by slave revolts in 1791. With the emergence of the daring black general Toussaint L'Ouverture and action by the National Assembly on April 4, 1792, giving mulattoes and free blacks the same rights as white settlers, the struggle for liberty on the island proceeded in earnest for decades, making St. Domingue, like the United States and France, a center of revolution.

When three commissioners from France and a new governor arrived in St. Domingue to implement the April 4 decree of equality, battles erupted between government forces, white dissidents, and mulatto armies. A disastrous confrontation at Le Cap in the spring of 1793 led directly to the first massive flotilla of refugees from the island to the United States. The ousted governor led a convoy of 137 vessels crammed with people fleeing the mêlée. More than ten thousand individuals—white, mulatto, and black—departed for North America.[49]

Among the refugees was Claude-Corentin Tanguy de la Boissiere, a modest coffee planter who established in 1792 the *Journal des Revolutions de la Partie Francaise de Saint-Domingue*. His radical support for equality angered the island's new commissioners, who arrested and detained him on one of their ships for nearly a month. Tanguy was taken, whether he liked it or not, along with other refugees as a prisoner to the United States. He was able to jump ship when it reached New York City, where he found his freedom once again.[50]

With the arrival of the first refugees from the island that eventually would be known as Haiti, the United States became host to the largest contingent of revolutionaries in the Western world. While many of those coming were more correctly victims rather than proponents of revolutions, others had absorbed the ideals of liberty that spread throughout Western Europe and North America during the last quarter of the eighteenth century. From wherever they came—place, condition, family, or position—they eventually encountered obstacles—laws, prejudices, mobs, or authorities—that impeded the true exercise of liberty. Ireland, Scotland, Wales, France, Geneva, India, St. Domingue had closed their doors to them. In turn, they set out for the world's only true land of liberty, the United States.

That is, all of them with one notable exception—Thomas Paine. Detained under harsh conditions in Luxembourg Prison, he made appeals to America, where he considered himself still a citizen, to secure his release. Governeur Morris, American minister to France at the time, discovered that Paine was viewed by France as a citizen of that nation because he had served as a member of the National Assembly. Morris, not one of Paine's most ardent fans, let the matter rest.

Paine nearly despaired as he watched a steady procession of France's most famous leaders pass by his view on the way to the guillotine. One morning 168 prisoners marched out to trial; only eight returned at day's end. Even Robespierre, director general of the Terror, visited Luxembourg the night before the guillotine claimed him, but the jailer refused to take him in.

Believing that Robespierre had engineered his arrest, Paine immediately applied to the National Convention and the Committee of Public Safety for his release. He also wrote to James Monroe, the new American minister to France, but heard nothing for more than a month. Finally, on October 4, Paine received Monroe's first enthusiastic overture: "By being with us through the Revolution," wrote Monroe, "you are of our country, as absolutely as if you had been born there; and you are no more of England, than every native of America is." Monroe secured Paine's release on November 4, 1794, ten months after his arrest.[51]

Paine was in no condition to travel, and within a few months of convalescing, circumstances so changed that he put off his return to the United States for another eight years. His physical condition was deplorable. An abscessed rib rendered him virtually bedridden. Minister Monroe, an admirer of Paine, invited him into his residence for a visit that ended up lasting more than a year and a half. A month after his release, the French National Convention restored the deputies who had been expelled during the Terror. Paine was also voted a pension (that he never received) for his literary contributions to the Revolution.

An inveterate meddler in the affairs of nations and governments, Paine again attempted to influence the direction of world affairs. He published *Dissertation on the First Principles of Government* (1795)—a long sermon on the basics of a free government. Not happy with the way he had left *The Age of Reason* just prior to his imprisonment, he expanded and republished it in 1795, the new edition challenging the credibility of the Old and New Testaments. Next came *The Decline and Fall of the English System of Finance* (1796). By this time he had developed an association with the ruling Directory in France and sought to demolish England and unite France and America.[52]

Paine's course during his elongated stay with the Monroes followed almost precisely the direction of those who had crossed the Atlantic. He became deeply immersed in heated discussions about the shape and future of the land of liberty. The three essays he issued following his imprisonment—especially the revised *Age of Reason*—added further fuel to the debates that were raging throughout America on the nature of the American republic and the welfare of American society.

Although Paine remained three thousand miles away, he felt a sense of responsibility for the first republic he had helped to bring into existence. For the prior nine or ten years, he had tried replicating that pristine republic in Britain and France. In the former he had clearly failed. In the latter, it remained to be seen if anything could be salvaged from the days of terror and confusion. But the American model remained true, even though he detected tendencies by 1796 that needed to be corrected. In an effusive "Letter to George Washington," published in segments by Benjamin Franklin Bache in Philadelphia beginning in October just prior to an election to choose Washington's successor, Paine outlined directions for the first American republic, the one land in the confused 1790s that remained liberty's true beacon.[53]

CHAPTER 2

Joseph Priestley and American Liberty

J oseph Priestley, probably the most renowned living scientist in the world in 1794, boarded the ship *Samson* in London on April 8. No longer welcome in his native England, he was headed to the United States, where he hoped to live in peace and to pursue his wide range of philosophical, scientific, and religious interests. The United Irishmen of Dublin sent him their best wishes as he departed, noting that "you are going to a happier world—the world of Washington and Franklin." In a florid valedictory address they continued:

> But you are going to a country where science is turned to better uses. Your change of place will give room for the matchless activity of your genius; and you will take a sublime pleasure in bestowing on Britain the benefit of your future discoveries. . . . Soon may you embrace your sons on the American shore, and Washington take you by the hand, and the shade of Franklin look down with calm delight on the first statesman of the age extending his protection to its first philosopher.[1]

Given Priestley's notoriety in Britain and that he lived under daily threats for his safety, his reception in the United States—so recently an offspring from the British monarchy—was nothing short of sensational. Gov. De Witt Clinton led a contingent of New York's most important civic, business, and religious leaders, bringing messages of welcome and self-congratulatory notes for America's newest living symbol that it was indeed the home of liberty. The *American Daily Advertiser* for that date carried an editorial that captured the essence of the event:

> It must afford the most sincere gratification to every well wisher to the rights of man, that the United States of America, the land of freedom and independence, has become the asylum of the greatest characters of the present age, who have been persecuted in Europe.[2]

The daily roll call of greeters included the Democratic Society of the City of New York, the Tammany Society of New York, the Associated Teachers of the City of New York, and the Medical Society of the State of New York.

Joseph Priestley (c. 1797). Genius of chemistry and Unitarian theology, the friend of liberty in Britain became a rejected revolutionary in America.

The Democratic Society welcomed Priestley "to these shores of Liberty and Equality" and "a land, where Reason has successfully triumphed over the artificial distinctions of European policy and bigotry."

"We rejoice," the statement continued, "that America opens her arms to receive with fraternal affection, the friend of liberty and human happiness." The Tammany Society decried the loss of Priestley's library and laboratory. But its greeting declared that in the United States, "where Providence has unfolded a scene as new as it is august, as felicitating as it is unexampled," Priestley would be restored "to every domestic and philosophical enjoyment." The Associated Teachers gave him a "hearty welcome to this land of tranquility and freedom" and eagerly anticipated the "highly valuable scientific and literary productions" that he would achieve in America.[3]

The most lavish welcome, however, was extended by The Republican Natives of Great Britain and Ireland, many of whom had come to America to experience liberty firsthand:

> We desire to be thankful to the Great Author of our being that we are in America, and that it has pleased Him, in his Wise Providence, to make the United States an asylum not only from the immediate tyranny of the British Government, but also from those impending calamities, which its increasing despotism and

> multiplied iniquities, must infallibly bring down on a deluded
> and oppressed people.

Priestley responded to each group in nearly as extravagant terms, saving his most eloquent refrain for the last, the Republican Natives. For them he attempted to characterize the differences between Britain and the United States:

> There [Britain] all liberty of speech and of the press as far as
> politics are concerned, is at an end, and a spirit of intolerance
> in matters of religion is almost as high as in the time of the
> Stuarts. Here, having no countenance from government, what-
> ever may remain of this spirit . . . may be expected soon to die
> away; and on all subjects whatever, every man enjoys invalu-
> able liberty of speaking and writing whatever he pleases.[4]

Following two weeks of festivities in New York, Priestley and his family proceeded to the American seat of government in Philadelphia, where he remained another several weeks. He met with nearly everyone through a special gathering of the American Philosophical Society convened in his honor. David Rittenhouse, Benjamin Franklin's successor as president of the society, relished the idea of having the world's foremost scientist close by in America. He also elaborated a bit upon American liberty:

> Here, we have been enabled, under the favour of Divine Provi-
> dence, to establish a government of Laws, and not of Men; a
> government, which secures to its citizens equal Rights, and
> equal Liberty, and which offers an asylum to the good, to the
> persecuted, and to the oppressed of other climes.

Priestley, by this time having exhausted every encomium available to respond to such boasts of glory, restricted his comments to his enthusiasm for being part of the society. He looked forward to participating in "a Society of Philosophers, who will have no objection to a person on account of his political or religious senti-ments." He was grateful for such a circumstance, "as it will be new to me."[5]

Priestley proceeded across Pennsylvania to the tiny village of Northumber-land. There he reunited with his sons, Joseph and William, and his former col-league, Thomas Cooper. Cooper, who would remain firmly by Priestley's side until the great chemist's death, had spent the last year collaborating with Priest-ley's sons to establish near Northumberland a vast settlement on three hundred thousand acres of land. The settlement promised a haven for all "friends of lib-erty" who might wish to join in the enterprise. In the words of Joseph, Jr., "it was set on foot to be as it were a rallying point for the English, who . . . it was thought, would be more happy in society of the kind they had been accustomed to than they would be, dispersed . . . through the whole of the United States." Although the scheme to build a mecca for English friends of liberty soon proved impractical, the Priestleys and the Coopers loved their beautiful location on the Susquehanna, and they could not be budged away.[6]

With substantial funds provided by old friends in England, Priestley designed and built a house unlike any to be found in America. Overlooking a picturesque bend in the Susquehanna River valley, the Federal-style home housed Priestley's reassembled library of twenty-five hundred books and a complete chemistry laboratory. Priestley installed a massive hood at one end of the house for exhausting gasses and fumes. The house was surrounded with safe-storage areas for chemicals and gardens for producing plants and herbs used in both laboratory and kitchen. After Mrs. Priestley's death in September 1796, the spacious living quarters became the shared home of Priestley and Cooper, where they collaborated extensively on chemistry experiments, discussed philosophical and political ideals, and held debates on religion. (Cooper cared for his mentor as colleague, friend, and nurse until his last breath in 1804. As a result, Priestley bequeathed his entire library and laboratory to Cooper.)[7]

With his house and laboratory under construction and surrounded by family and critical friends of liberty, Priestley was in 1795 America's most famous immigrant celebrity. Like Franklin before him, he personified the age and the moment. And like Franklin, he embodied the love of liberty, the pursuit of knowledge, and the application of reason to all things. But temporarily without his laboratory and his scientific apparatus, he turned his attention to religion, revelation, and moral values.[8]

Recognizing his powers and wishing to use every waking moment to advance his multiplicity of causes, Priestley proposed traveling to Philadelphia during the months of February through May each year to present public lectures. On his first trip in 1796 he arrived in Philadelphia to deliver a long series of lectures on the "Evidences of Christianity" at Elkinah Winchester's Universalist Church. His audience included Vice-President John Adams, most of the members of the U.S. Congress, and other leaders of the young nation. Priestley pleaded the case of Unitarianism and spoke constantly about insuring the free practice of religion in the United States. Afterward President George Washington invited him to "come at any time, without any ceremony." In a letter to an English friend Priestley noted, "Everything is the reverse of what it is with you." He soon published his lectures, dedicating them to none other than John Adams. His 1796 outing was a smashing success.[9]

In 1797 Priestly happily prepared a set of discourses on the subject of the "Increase of Infidelity" and "All the Evidences in Favour of Revelation." This time, however, as his son Joseph noted, "partly from the prejudices that began to be excited against him on account of his supposed political opinions . . . they [the lectures] were but thinly attended in comparison to his former set." He had become engaged in an extended debate with the French refugee Volney, but for some reason he could not explain, he did not get an audience. Moreover, his Philadelphia Unitarian Society languished. Discouraged and irritated that then President Adams attended only one of his lectures that year, Priestley retreated to Northumberland. Puzzling over Adams's coldness, he wrote, "He seemed to interest himself in my favour against M. Volney, but did not subscribe to my

"Plan of Dr. Priestley's House at Northumberland in the State of Pennsylvania"
(1800). The idyllic house, gardens, and laboratory created by Joseph Priestley
when he arrived in the U.S. in 1794.

Church History. . . . I suppose he was not pleased that I did not adopt his dislike
of the French."[10]

Priestley's rumination about Adams and the French proved prophetic. The
difference between the reception he received in 1796 and that of 1797 was symptomatic of a sharp divergence in American perceptions of Priestley, from that of

scientific hero to a potential enemy of the state. Priestley's curious experience foreshadowed the rejection of revolution in America.

William Cobbett, recently arrived from skirmishes with the English law, fumed when he witnessed the praise heaped on Priestley as a great friend of liberty. Coming from a lengthy service in the British Army and a strong allegiance to the Crown, he perceived Priestley as a troublemaker and an infidel. In August 1794 Cobbett persuaded Philadelphia publisher Thomas Bradford to issue a hateful tract titled *Observations on the Emigration of Dr. Joseph Priestley,* which created a sensation in Philadelphia, England, and France as it went through numerous editions. Cobbett's career (soon he would take the famous pen name Peter Porcupine) soared, eclipsing Priestley's, as beloved and venerated statesman of the Western world.[11]

Cobbett ridiculed each of Priestley's forays into Philadelphia. His most telling blow against Priestley was the publication of two letters from Paris, one addressed to Priestley and the other to Benjamin Vaughan in *Porcupine's Gazette.* Cobbett argued that Priestley and Vaughan were actually French agents in America. The letters written by J. H. Stone, a former parishioner of Priestley's in England, praised the course of the French in their struggles against Britain and slurred President Adams's policies. Cobbett soon followed up with a pamphlet outlining the dangerous political, social, and religious ideas of Priestley, "this Apostle of Sedition."[12]

Until Cobbett's latest attack, Priestley and his feisty companion, Thomas Cooper, eschewed any public political controversy in the United States. Both wanted to live quietly and to pursue their scientific and philosophical interests. But ambushed by a fellow Englishman Priestley decided to return fire, igniting Cooper as well.

Priestley submitted a tongue-in-cheek critique of the American government to Benjamin Franklin Bache's *Aurora* in February 1798 under the name "A Quaker." Knowledgeable readers quickly guessed the source. The first open defense of his critique of American politics came a year later in the parochial-sounding *Letters to the Inhabitants of Northumberland,* in which he criticized the Alien and Sedition Acts recently passed by Congress. He also took issue with the various policies of the Adams administration making clear that American partisan politics and violence by that time exceeded anything he had ever known in England. He asked his neighbors for understanding and for the right to live peacefully among them.[13]

At the same time, Cooper was editing the *Sunbury Gazette,* relieving the editor to print one of Priestley's works. Between April 20 and June 29, Cooper denounced American policies and Adams administration actions. He then issued his editorials in book form under the title of *Political Essays* (1799). His point of view was clear in the preface:

> I hope they [these essays] will afford some proof that I remain
> in this Country what I was in Europe, a decided opposer of
> political restrictions on the Liberty of the Press, and a sincere

> friend to those first principles of republican Government; . . .
> but I am sorry to say they [my opinions] are likely ere long to
> become as unfashionable in this Country as in the Monarchies
> of Europe.

Freedom of the press, the Sedition Acts, separation of church and state, unjust taxation, obedience to just laws, economic principles for the nation, and restrictions on foreign commerce were some of the topics he covered. But it was his last editorial in the *Gazette* and subsequently in *Political Essays* that made national news, in which he parodied the Adams administration, illustrating how the president would increase his powers at the expense of the country.[14]

By 1798 Priestley and Cooper had reemerged from quiet seclusion to play the same role they had played as friends of liberty in Britain. Received as exemplars of revolutionary fervor in 1795, just four years later they were being viewed as potential traitors. If this was to be the experience of true free thinkers, what awaited those other champions of liberty who had wrought the American Revolution and who hoped to savor the fruits of victory and independence from a repressive king?

CHAPTER 3

Friends of Liberty in the Land of Liberty

AMERICAN FRIENDS OF LIBERTY

The ill treatment received by Joseph Priestley and Thomas Cooper was not because there were no friends of liberty in America. Judging from the self-congratulatory groups greeting Priestley, it appeared that Americans believed that freedom's millennium had arrived. There were probably far more individuals and groups in the United States actively promoting the cause of freedom in June 1794 than in either France or England. After all, it was believed, America was the original land of liberty.

Just as the fall of the Bastille transformed the quiet Parisian Society of Friends of the Constitution into a national network of reformist "Jacobin" Clubs[1] (they first met in the Paris convent of the Jacobins) and spawned revolutionary societies throughout Great Britain, it also compelled Americans to create "democratic-republican societies." By the time of Priestley's arrival, thirty-five such societies ranged from Portland, Maine, to Charleston, South Carolina; from Norfolk, Virginia, to Lexington, Kentucky. Only New Hampshire and Georgia did not have active societies.[2]

The first emerged among the German population in Philadelphia in March 1793. Calling itself the German Republican Society in a prospectus issued on April 13 in the *National Gazette,* it declared, "In a republican government it is the duty incumbent on every citizen to afford his assistance . . . that its principles may remain uncorrupt; for the spirit of liberty, like every virtue of the mind, is to be kept alive only by constant action." One observer wrote to the *Gazette,* "May the example of the German Republican Society prove a spur to the friends of equality throughout the United States."

The challenge was quickly taken up in tidewater Virginia, resulting in the Norfolk and Portsmouth Republican Society. Its purpose was virtually identical to that of the Germans: "We . . . declare as our unalterable opinion, that the blessings of a just, mild, and equitable government can only be perpetuated by that pure spirit of Republican vigilance to which . . . we owe our present political ease, tranquillity and happiness."[3]

The most important soon emerged in Philadelphia, calling itself the Democratic Society of Pennsylvania. In articles drawn up and adopted on May 30, 1793,

Philip Freneau (c. 1795). Poet of the American Revolution, he was also a partisan crusader.

the new society resolved "to cultivate the just knowledge of rational Liberty, to facilitate the enjoyment and exercise of our civil Rights, and to transmit, unimpaired, to posterity, the glorious inheritance of a free Republican Government." The first president was none other than the renowned scientist David Rittenhouse. Attorney Alexander J. Dallas, Pennsylvania secretary of state, was vice president. Treasurer was Israel Israel, an ardent patriot during the American Revolution. One of two secretaries was Peter S. Du Ponceau, a French immigrant and expert in international law. Principal organizer was George Logan—physician, farmer, and U.S. senator. Head of the society's Committee of Correspondence was Benjamin Franklin Bache, editor of Philadelphia's rising star of liberty, *The Aurora*.[4]

Known by both friends and enemies as the "Mother Club" of America's democratic societies of the 1790s, this impressive assemblage established the principles, practices, and perspectives that would characterize the gatherings of future similar societies. Members went by the title "Citizen," a practice popularized in France. The society closely monitored the activities of the federal government and the Washington administration; it adopted resolutions of support for friends of liberty throughout America, France, Britain, Poland, Italy, and elsewhere. Bache publicized its resolutions to the other growing number of societies around the nation.[5]

The society also established standards for the social life of democratic societies, holding a "civic festival" on May 1, 1794, to "commemorate the successes of their Republican French Brethren." More than 800 citizens assembled "at the Country Seat of citn Israel Israel." Present were Gov. Thomas Mifflin, Jean Fauchet, French minister to the U.S., and other "Officers and Citizens" of the French Republic and "the Federal and State Governments." Flags of the "Sister Republics" (France and the U.S.) "marked and ornamented the seat of the festivity." At 2:00 P.M. the assembled throng "partook of a plain yet plentiful repast."

Fifteen long-awaited toasts ensued. "The alliance between the sister republics of the United States and France" was honored, as was the formation of the tiny, new Republic of Genoa. Then came more revolutionary perspectives: toasts to the "Mountain" (high-minded revolutionary associates of Robespierre), the armies of the French Republic, "a revolutionary tribunal in Great Britain," and "the extinction of monarchy." A partisan toast praised "the men of the people—the Minority of the Senate and the Majority of the House of Representatives of the United States." The last toast recognized the expanding number of democratic-republican societies throughout the United States.

A concluding toast offered by a "volunteer" on the spot saluted "the dispersed friends of Liberty throughout the world": "May France be the rallying point where they may collect their scattered forces, and whence they may sally forth to the <u>destruction of all the tyrants of the earth</u>." Thereupon, "the President of the democratic society gave the fraternal embrace to the Minister of the French Republic amid the acclamations of the most animated joy of all the company." The throng then marched into center-city Philadelphia, "headed by music and the colours of the French Republic and accompanied by one of the companies of volunteer infantry of this city." Leftover food was then distributed "among the prisoners confined in the Gaol of this city."[6]

Such colorful processions were replicated around the nation. Some called themselves "republican," others "democratic," and a few "democratic-republican." A few chose "constitutional" or "patriotic." Still others revived the Revolutionary era title "Committee of Correspondence." Two South Carolina societies adopted the names of heroes: The Greenville group named itself "the Madisonian Society" and the Pendleton group chose "the Franklin Society."[7]

Though rank-and-file membership was frequently identified as craftsmen, there was a balance of merchants, physicians, lawyers, printers, and teachers in all the groups. Leaders were often members of the American Philosophical Society. The only group of prominent individuals noticeably absent from the societies were clergymen.[8]

Though many of the leaders would not become the most remembered individuals in American history, they were often among the various states' most important leaders at the time. Most ordinary members would be totally lost to history—except for their names—had they not dramatically pursued the cause of liberty.

One worthy of attention would be William Tate, secretary of the Committee of Correspondence of the Republican Society of South Carolina. Known only as a reputed veteran of the Continental Army during the Revolutionary War and a sometime frontier fighter, he engaged in frontier skirmishes with the Cherokee in Georgia while looking for opportunities to fight the Spanish in Florida. Eager to enlist as a freedom fighter he organized the "Revolutionary Legion of America" in 1793. Consisting of veteran Revolutionary and Indian fighters, the ragtag Legion was prepared to fight on the borders, in Florida, in France, or wherever its services were needed.[9]

The careers of a host of individuals aptly illustrate the experience of American friends of liberty. Benjamin Rush connected the era of the American Revolution with that of the French Revolution. Studying first at the College of Philadelphia under William Shippen and John Morgan, he proceeded to the University of Edinburgh, where he received the finest medical education available at that time. There he also immersed himself in Scottish culture and the vibrant glow of what is known as the Scottish Enlightenment. Following a tour of England and France in 1768, Rush returned to Philadelphia in 1769 to practice medicine and teach chemistry at the College of Philadelphia.[10]

As the American Revolution unfolded, Rush became one of its pivotal figures. Writing and lecturing on chemistry and medicine, he assumed the role of central scientist while Benjamin Franklin was in England and France. He strongly opposed slavery, pushed for penal reform, promoted the development of hospitals, assisted in the establishment of schools, and recruited scholars, scientists, and educators—especially in Scotland—to relocate to America.[11]

Rush moved into the role of nationmaker when he was elected to the Continental Congress in 1776. Signer of the Declaration of Independence and full partner in the wranglings of Congress to establish a nation under the Articles of Confederation, Rush also served for a time as a surgeon in the Continental Army. And he played a crucial role in getting the U.S. Constitution approved at the Pennsylvania state ratifying convention. As democratic-republican societies sprang into existence in 1793, the influential Rush could be counted upon to endorse and participate in their cause.[12]

Hugh Henry Brackenridge was another friend of liberty whose career in western Pennsylvania paralleled Rush's in Philadelphia. Born in Scotland, his family migrated to Pennsylvania when he was five. While teaching grammar school, he entered the College of New Jersey as a student and rapidly befriended two talented classmates—Philip Freneau, future republican editor, and James Madison, future president of the United States. Brackenridge and Freneau coauthored a commencement poem (that the former delivered) in 1771 titled *Rising Glory of America*. Published the following year in Philadelphia, the poem expressed a growing national commitment to liberty:

> And here fair freedom shall forever reign.
> I see a train, a glorious train appear,
> Of patriots plac'd in equal fame with those
> Who nobly fell for Athens or for Rome.
> The sons of Boston, resolute and brave,
> The firm supporters of our injur'd rights,

> Shall lose their splendors in the brighter beams
> Of patriots fam'd and heroes yet unborn.

Brackenridge returned to Princeton a few years later to study divinity and soon found himself serving as chaplain in the Continental Army. Deeply committed to American independence, he wrote two popular plays, *Battle of Bunkers-Hill* and *Death of General Montgomery,* which stirred Americans to both patriotism and heroism. A series of sermons later published as *Six Political Discourses* (1788) contained the same clamoring spirit.[13]

Disenchanted, however, with creeds and churches, Brackenridge left the chaplaincy in 1778 to pursue a literary career. For a brief time as editor of the pioneering *United States Magazine* in Philadelphia, he addressed an assembly including Gen. George Washington, members of Congress, and the minister of France on July 5, 1779, with *An Eulogium of the Brave Men Who Have Fallen in the Contest with Great Britain.* When the *Magazine* faltered, Brackenridge switched careers. After studying law in Annapolis under Samuel Chase, the controversial future justice of the U.S. Supreme Court, Brackenridge moved to Pittsburgh, where his major contributions to American liberty and literature would be made during the next twenty years. There he practiced law, helped found the *Pittsburgh Gazette* (1786) and the University of Pittsburgh (1787), promoted ratification of the U.S. Constitution, and wrote his saga on American life, *Modern Chivalry.* In 1793 he founded the Democratic Society of the County of Washington, serving what he called the "western country" in the same manner as Rush did Philadelphia.[14]

Brackenridge's closest friend, Philip Freneau, had positioned himself as editor of the influential *National Gazette* to be one of the strongest voices for liberty in America. Born in New York City of a wealthy French Huguenot family that maintained close ties to France, Freneau arrived at Princeton at age fifteen and graduated three years later. He spent the next four years, 1771 to 1775, writing poetry and occasionally teaching school. He then oversaw the publication of *Rising Glory of America* during a lengthy writing sojourn in Philadelphia.

Freneau also began to explore the use of poetry to promote the concepts of liberty and American independence. As early as 1772 in poems titled "The American Village" and "Discovery," he outlined America's special destiny. By 1775 in "American Liberty" he combined hopes for freedom with war chants against British tyranny:

> For thee, blest freedom, to protect thy sway,
> We rush undaunted to the bloody fray;
> For thee, each province arms its vig'rous host,
> Content to die, ere freedom shall be lost.

Freneau turned out a host of pamphlets filled with patriotic verses that would become the lyrics of American revolutionaries. He soon became known as poet laureate of the American Revolution.[15]

Ironically, Freneau was safely outside the emerging United States for almost the duration of the war. Between 1775 and 1781 he served as secretary on a sea captain's vast estate on the island of Santa Cruz. The location stimulated some of his most successful works. He contributed to the *United States Magazine* on Santa Cruz, on Jamaica, and even on the practice of slaveholding. But Freneau was a drifter. Arriving in the United States during the latter days of the Revolution, he was briefly detained by British authorities and, despite the threat of arrest, he returned to sea. On his way to the West Indies he was again seized by British forces and imprisoned on the *Scorpion* in New York harbor. He was eventually released and described his tortured confinement in the dramatic verses of *The British Prison-Ship* (1781).[16]

Between 1781 and 1784 he worked as a postal clerk in Philadelphia and there added to his store of poems about the American Revolution. But, restless and frenetic, he was soon back at sea, sailing and shipwrecking madly for a period of five years. Although his eventual poverty led to a dependence upon a younger brother, he married in 1789 and accepted the editorship of the *New York Daily Advertiser.*[17]

There he remained until he was recruited in 1791 by Thomas Jefferson to join the Department of State in Philadelphia as a translating clerk and to serve as editor of a new anti-administration, anti-Federalist newspaper, the *National Gazette.* With Jefferson's active encouragement and support, Freneau boldly promoted worldwide liberty. He covered the activities of proliferating democratic-republican societies and reported their various testimonials in complete detail.[18]

Another friend of liberty, Matthew Lyon, came to America from Ireland at age fifteen as an indentured servant and quickly identified with American culture. By 1772 he had worked out his service to individuals in Woodbury and Litchfield, Connecticut, and had begun to acquire property. He married a niece of frontier adventurer Ethan Allen in 1773, and soon joined Allen's ventures to secure the Hampshire land grants against both Great Britain and the colony of New York, to exploit the natural resources of the rich land, and to storm Fort Ticonderoga on May 10, 1775, with the Green Mountain Boys.

After service in the Continental Army, Lyon helped organize Vermont's constitutional government. Despite the absence of a formal education, he participated in every step of government-making, from writing a revolutionary constitution (the first in America to ban slaveholding) to serving as secretary to the governor and council. He also became one of America's most successful self-made entrepreneurs. Relocating onto vast confiscated lands at Fair Haven in 1783, he began to build a small mercantile-industrial empire, first constructing a sawmill and a gristmill, then a pig iron manufacturing plant, and the first wood pulp processing operation in America. Soon his iron business included a slitting mill to make nails, a plating forge to make tools, and a blast furnace. A careful mix of confiscated lands, private capital, and ingenuity made Lyon a success by the early 1790s.[19]

Lyon's good fortune also depended upon direct support from a favorable state government. After the death of his first wife, he married the daughter of Gov. Thomas Chittenden in 1785 and became deeply ensconced in Vermont governance until 1789, when the Chittenden contingent, including Lyon, was voted out of office. Embattled against lawyers and Federalists, Lyon became one of the nation's first populist ideologues when he ran unsuccessfully for Congress in 1791 and 1793. After his second defeat in 1793, he launched a weekly newspaper in Fair Haven, titled the *Farmers' Library*, which he modeled after Benjamin Franklin Bache's *Aurora*. Lyon sought "to break down the undue influence of the Aristo-Tory faction." Stirring speeches and essays by Thomas Paine filled his first issues. Just as Bache, Brackenridge, and Freneau called for the formation of democratic-republican societies, Lyon urged their formation in Vermont and the rest of New England. By April 1794 a society existed for every county west of the Green Mountains.

Quoting the great French philosophers, Lyon established a publishing house, which he called Voltaire's Head, and began publishing popular pamphlets. In 1793 he published the first American edition of the *Works of the Late Dr. Benjamin Franklin*—lamenting their availability until that time only in French. "It is a little extraordinary that, under these circumstances . . . from the celebrity of the character of which they treat, and from the critical situation of the present times, they should so long have been with-held from the public." Touting Benjamin Franklin as his idol and Benjamin Franklin Bache as his living model, Lyon became an extraordinary self-made voice for citizenship and liberty.[20]

BENJAMIN FRANKLIN BACHE AND THE FRIENDS OF LIBERTY

Aware of the growing number of friends of liberty and of their desire for action, Benjamin Franklin Bache attempted to provide intellectual, philosophical, and ideological leadership for the movement just as his illustrious grandfather had for the American colonies. Younger than most of the other leaders in 1793, Bache had been trained almost from birth to carry on for the elder Franklin. Since Franklin's own son William had proved to be a traitor during the American Revolution and since William's illegitimate son, William Temple, proved to have little ambition in life, the great Franklin heritage descended squarely on the grandson known through his brief life as Bennie Bache.

Born of Franklin's only daughter Sarah, Bache became Franklin's substitute son. At the age of seven, he accompanied Franklin and his cousin William Temple (known as Temple) to France. For nine years Bennie Bache experienced the highest levels of French society and culture, meeting some of the most famous scientists, philosophers, and political leaders in the world. He became proficient in the French language, in the art and practice of printing, and in the habit of political discourse.[21]

Voltaire and Condorcet doted over him at Franklin's idyllic home in Passy. Bache attended boarding school for two years with both French students and a handful of American children—including John Quincy Adams. Here he learned French, Catholicism, and monarchical values. Distressed that Bache might become too French, Franklin in 1779 placed the ten-year-old boy in a year-round boarding school at Geneva. There he was exposed to classical learning, Protestantism, and a rigorously prescribed lifestyle in a small college of five hundred boys.[22]

But the young Bache experienced something else in Geneva as well. The tiny city-state was bristling with excitement over the possible formation of a constitutional republic. In 1782 an outright revolution occurred. During several months of violence, Bache's school was closed, and he had to seek refuge with the family of the schoolmaster. Bache reported in letter after letter to Franklin the extraordinary events of peoples in revolt, the clash of soldiers, and the toll of assassinations. While Americans heard the debates that led to American independence, Bache observed firsthand a revolution fought to empower a citizenry and form a revolutionary government.[23]

In 1783 Bache returned to Passy to spend two years as Franklin's companion and student. Whether watching balloon flights, conducting experiments on mesmerism, or speculating on aeronautics, Bache and Franklin were constantly in discourse. Bache worked in the Passy print shop and learned the craft of typecasting, an enterprise little known in the United States. Here Bache worked with master printers and typefounders and met such characters as Mathew Carey, political exile from Ireland who later became one of America's first national book publishers. At age sixteen, Bache organized the packing, sealing, and shipment of 128 boxes of books, equipment, furniture, and memorabilia that accompanied the Franklin entourage back to America.[24]

Bache had spent more than half of his life abroad; most of these years he had spent in isolation from the warmth of family and in protracted scholastic contemplation. His one friend, though stiff and foreboding, was his grandfather, who continued to control his life and plan his career. Back in Philadelphia Franklin first sent him to the University of Pennsylvania to complete his education. Bache then joined his grandfather in the printing and typefounding business as a full partner. Franklin then tried to match Bache with Elizabeth Hewson, a favorite who had followed him from London to Paris and finally to Philadelphia. But Bache had other ideas; he married Margaret Hartman Markoe, an intelligent, strong-willed, and ambitious daughter of a wealthy sugar planter from St. Croix. Markoe was sturdily independent and became almost as much business partner as wife during their relatively short marriage.

Despite financial backing and partnership with Franklin, Bache had difficulty building a publishing and typefounding business. He was much less successful at book publishing than Mathew Carey, and he had to jettison the typefounding business when the fonts he made for Carey proved to be faulty. Soon after Franklin's death, Bache chose to establish a newspaper to recoup his finances. On October 2, 1790, the first issue of the *Philadelphia General Advertiser* appeared, bearing the motto, "The Freedom of the Press is the Bulwark of Liberty." Though he would take the paper in many directions and publish it in a variety of formats—even changing its name in 1794 to the *Aurora*—the editing and publishing of a newspaper devoted to the cause of liberty proved to be the métier of his all-too-brief life.[25]

Vying for a place in a city that was already filled with newspapers and where three or four failed for every one that succeeded, Bache invited support from statesmen, intellectuals, politicians, and business leaders. He even courted

"A Peep into the Anti-Federal Club" (1793). A derisive view of the Democratic Society of Philadelphia where David Rittenhouse examines its revolutionary principles through a telescope (left), with a motley assortment of characters to his back, including an African (far right), saying "Fine ting . . . our turn nex."

the financial support of Thomas Jefferson, without success. Ironically, his difficulties enabled him to choose an independent course that made him one of the most remarkable journalists and friends of liberty in the early American republic. With each passing year the *Advertiser,* then the *Aurora,* improved as an expanding journal of what was happening among friends of liberty and of critical commentary on the direction of the American nation.[26]

As Bache found his place among the nation's journalists, he also made use of the Democratic Society of Pennsylvania to promote the cause of liberty. As a member of its committee on correspondence, he helped to draft the society's ringing cries for liberty. He wrote position papers fending off charges that the society encouraged radicalism, but he also used his society and the national network of friends to press forward the unfinished democratic revolution in America.[27]

What did Bache preach? Just as his grandfather had introduced Thomas Paine to America in 1775, Bache reintroduced Paine and his popular new handbook of liberty, *The Rights of Man.* Between 1791 and 1797, Bache popularized *The Rights of Man, Part 2, The Age of Reason, Dissertations on First Principles of Government, The Decline and Fall of the English System of Finance, Letter to George Washington . . . on Affairs Public and Private,* and *Agrarian Justice.*[28]

Bache was, in short, Paine's American literary agent, publisher, and advertising executive. He was selling not only the pamphlets and books; he was also peddling their ideas, concepts, and values. Bache had been thoroughly immersed in radical Enlightenment thought, and he was well prepared to promote French revolutionary ideas and Paine's political ideology without question.

Bache believed quite literally that a world revolution was in progress, that it had begun in the United States and spread to Geneva, Poland, and France, and that it was radiating into England, Ireland, Italy, Germany, and beyond. He also believed that the energy coming from France provided the moment for power in America to be extended to the people and for all of the vestiges of aristocracy to be swept away. He promoted equality, espoused universal education to provide opportunity to every citizen. He urged a more equitable division of property and wealth among citizens. And, in a time when most people who called themselves abolitionists wanted to rid the country of both slavery and its black population, Bache agitated to bring freed slaves and free blacks into the full enjoyment of American society.[29]

Bache was an idealist and a democrat of extraordinary proportions for the eighteenth century. He opposed a strong executive and thought Madison's idea of three branches of government would lead to internal warfare. He preferred the French single assembly. When France created the Directory, or multiple executive system of governance, he endorsed that as the pattern that should be copied in America.[30]

Bache was in every sense a thoroughgoing revolutionary. He viewed himself as a critical agent of revolution, an American-based counterpart of Rousseau, Condorcet, Paine, and William Godwin. He charted the course of every movement from the perspective of the advance of liberty, equality, popular sovereignty, and freedom from restraint. And he savagely attacked any current, domestic or foreign, that seemed to stem the revolutionary tide. Ultimately, he saw it as his calling and duty to publish any article, tract, pamphlet, or book that would either promote the cause or destroy the enemy. No tactic was too severe in advancing the world revolution.[31]

THE GATHERING OF FRIENDS OF LIBERTY IN AMERICA

As the rising spokesman for revolution, the youthful Bache attracted an extraordinary number of friends of liberty, partly because of his central Philadelphia base of operations. He had taken on Franklin's mantle as well as his old printing office. But mainly because of his commitment to the cause of liberty, the stream of luminaries that visited him from all parts of the globe seemed endless.

Among the first was Mathew Carey, the Irish revolutionary who had picked up where he left off in Dublin by starting a newspaper in Philadelphia. The *Pennsylvania Herald* lasted only a year, though Carey introduced the publication of the debates of the Pennsylvania Assembly. In 1787 he began *The American Museum* with Franklin's assistance. The *Museum* continued through 1792, but in 1790 Carey initiated what would become his real money machine—book publishing. In the space of two years he published an English language Bible for Roman Catholics, a history of New York, Beattie's *Morals,* and dozens of other books. With the assistance of Mason Locke "Parson" Weems, beginning in 1794, Carey built the largest publishing and distributing company in the nation.

On the road to financial success, Carey helped to organize the Society for the Lately Adopted Sons of Pennsylvania, a belligerently patriotic organization. So critical was he of an opposition editor, Col. Eleazer Oswald of the *Independent Gazetteer,* the two of them dueled with pistols on January 18, 1786. (Carey missed Oswald, but Oswald put a ball through Carey's thigh.) In March 1790 Carey aided the founding of the Hibernian Society to assist destitute Irish immigrants. A few months later he cooperated with Episcopal Bishop William White and Dr. Benjamin Rush, by then a Universalist, in forming the first national association promoting the creation of church Sunday schools. He also published pamphlets on prison reform. By 1793 Carey was deeply engaged with and supportive of the renewed efforts of Benjamin Franklin Bache.[32]

James T. Callender, the Scottish radical who barely escaped imprisonment in Edinburgh, became Carey's right-hand man. Arriving in America in May 1793 and armed with letters of introduction from friends in Scotland, Callender appealed to Carey for employment and was hired on a part-time basis to write a history of America "from the first discovery to the present time." Callender also used his shorthand skills to prepare a verbatim transcript of the proceedings of the House of Representatives for the *Philadelphia Gazette.* In January 1794 he began his American career as a columnist and occasional editor, for Bache's *Aurora* and as a paid political pamphleteer.

The *Aurora*'s news columns titled "From a Correspondent" were vintage Callender, giving the *Aurora* its special sting among America's newspapers. Here the *Aurora* unleashed attacks on liberty's enemies and explored radical democracy. Callender's pithy wit and sharp rejoinders quickly established the standard for editorial comment and investigative reporting in the nation's capital.[33]

Morgan Rhees, the Welsh friend of liberty, also found his way to America in 1794. Landing in New York, he soon explored the land to Savannah, Georgia, and then rode on to Kentucky, where he gave a remarkable July 4 oration in Greenville in 1795. He settled in Philadelphia long enough to become an associate of Benjamin Rush and to marry into society. As with the case of Carey, he busied himself with the welfare of immigrants in the Philadelphia Society for the Information and Assistance of Persons Emigrating from Foreign Countries (1796). He also speculated in western lands, especially in the development of a Welsh mining community in western Pennsylvania, named Cambria. Rhees moved to the mining town and spent most of his life preaching in Baptist churches in the surrounding communities until his death in 1804. Wherever he went, he attempted to spread the cause of liberty.[34]

Joseph Gales, exiled from Sheffield, fled to Germany, where he remained for a year until passage to Philadelphia could be arranged. With the assistance of Joel Barlow, American poet and revolutionary, Gales and his family landed in Philadelphia in 1795. Wishing to continue his journalistic career, he became a compositor for John Dunlap's *The General Daily Advertiser.* He was eventually assigned to write stories and make verbatim transcripts of the proceedings of Congress. A year later, he bought the *Independent Gazetteer* from Col. Eleazer Oswald's widow (nature succeeded where Mathew Carey had failed) and

Mathew Carey (1786). Irish rebel and fugitive, he became an American publisher and bookseller.

reissued it beginning September 16, 1796, as *Gales' Independent Gazetteer.* From the first issue of the *Gazetteer,* Gales promoted the march of freedom, the righteousness of the French Revolution, the importance of democracy and popular sovereignty. He deplored the slave trade and championed destitute immigrants in America.[35]

A month after Gales landed in Philadelphia, the Irish revolutionary Theobald Wolfe Tone and his family arrived at Wilmington, Delaware. But unlike many other friends of liberty spilling into America, Tone was torn between two different callings—to make a new home for his family or to ignite a revolution to free Ireland from British tyranny. These conflicting goals, and the fact that he was an Irish aristocrat, colored everything he saw in America.

Tone found Philadelphia a most uncongenial place to be. He considered the city incredibly expensive and the people disagreeable: "They—I mean those of Philadelphia—seem a selfish, churlish, unsocial race, totally absorbed in making money; a mongrel breed, half-English, half-Dutch, with the worst qualities of both countries." Oddly enough, this Irish revolutionary's evaluation of Irish-Americans was somewhat astonishing:

> But of all the people I have met here the Irish are incontestably
> the most offensive. If you meet a confirmed blackguard, you
> may be sure he is Irish. . . . They are as boorish and ignorant as
> the Germans, as uncivil and uncouth as the Quakers, and, as
> they have ten times more animal spirits than both, they are
> much more actively troublesome.

He considered moving to the Pennsylvania frontier, but "as I have no great talents for the tomahawk, I have therefore given up the idea of going into the woods." Finally he purchased a small 180-acre "plantation" just two miles from Princeton, New Jersey. Taken by the soil, the verdure of the area, and the little college in Princeton, Tone observed, "I fitted up my study and began to think my lot was cast to be an American farmer." [36]

Despite his adverse reaction to its people, Tone still felt that America was a blessed land of liberty: "If the manners of the Pennsylvanians be unpleasant, their Government is the best under heaven and their country thrives accordingly." One week after his arrival in America, he encountered in Philadelphia Irish revolutionary James Napper Tandy, whose adventures in escaping punishment and finding concealments equaled those of Tone.[37]

Tone met with the French minister Pierre Adet, who patiently listened to his appeal for French intervention in Ireland's cause. Tone wanted Adet to pave the way for him to go to France and lead a French army in a military invasion of Ireland. He was certain that the Irish populace would rise up and join the invaders to overthrow the British yoke. Adet asked Tone to produce letters from Irish residents who could confirm Tone's enthusiastic belief. By the end of November the conspirators succeeded in securing the letters as well as Adet's warm support.[38]

But they also acquired much more. Tone met Gov. Thomas Mifflin of Pennsylvania, who introduced him to John Beckley, longtime clerk of the House of Representatives. Beckley surreptitiously abetted Tone's cause by writing a ciphered letter to James Monroe, the American minister in Paris. The letter, clearly outside the realm of protocol, introduced Tone as "James Smith," described his aim of freeing Ireland, and asked Monroe to aid him in any way possible. The covert complicity of well-placed friends of liberty had helped foster one prong of world revolution.[39]

Only one element remained missing—from the American point of view—to set the operation afoot: Tone needed an American-based emissary who could receive and place information in the right hands. He arranged with Bache to serve that critical function. With everything in readiness, Tone dispatched his brother Arthur to Ireland. He took the first ship he could find, departing on January 1, 1796, from New York for an arrival just a month later in Le Havre de Grâce, France. The friends of liberty network there launched him on a mission for which he was confident he had been placed on earth.[40]

If America proved fertile ground for Irish revolutionaries, it was as important for French friends of liberty who were spurned or frightened by the destructive turns of the French Revolution. Moreau de St. Mery, legal scholar, historian of the West Indies, and enemy of Robespierre, became the central figure among French friends of liberty. Having escaped execution in the Reign of Terror when he fled from France in November 1793, he arrived at Norfolk, Virginia, in March 1794. In Philadelphia he opened a bookstore and printing business at the corner of Front and Walnut Streets, the center of the French exile community in the United States.

At the end of his four-month voyage to America, Moreau exclaimed upon landing: "At last I am on this hospitable soil, on this land of freedom, this land which, if the inhabitants are wise, should one day astound the rest of the universe by its power and perhaps impose upon the universe the law of being happy like itself." Introduced in the House of Representatives "as one who had been a member of the Constituent Assembly," he was invited to sit on a bench reserved for distinguished foreigners. Moved by the generous welcome, he commented, "My American heart was indeed proud and touched by this honor."

As Moreau left the session to inspect the house being built as a presidential residence, he noticed an approaching carriage containing two passengers who were waving wildly and yelling. He was astounded to discover that the carriage carried Bon Albert Briois de Beaumetz and Charles Maurice de Talleyrand-Périgord. "What joy! What happiness! What multiplied embraces!" proclaimed Moreau. These recent leaders of revolutionary France had just arrived in America from their uneasy exile in England. Soon after, he met others who had escaped the Terror. Commented Moreau: "Fresh surprise! Fresh pleasures! During our reunion there was a hailstorm and frightful thunder as though Heaven wished once again to remind us of the misfortunes we had escaped."

When word arrived that the fomenter of the Terror, Robespierre, had been guillotined, Moreau was astonished by the American reactions. Those whom he described as "Jacobins," members of the democratic-republican societies, "were profoundly grieved, as at the loss of their father, their leader, their best friend." Those who were not Jacobins, "all sincere friends of liberty," in contrast, "saw the event only as a blessing from Heaven, unfortunately conferred too late." Still others grieved the loss of Robespierre whose death would rob America of the wealth and intelligence of these many French exiles, eager to return.[41]

This French community of exiles added significantly to the cultural life of America. Moreau's bookstore became a place where one could secure the latest titles in a variety of languages. From his press came a daily French-language newspaper and a variety of works of history, law, philosophy, science, travel, and religion written by Moreau or his colleagues Rochefoucauld-Liancourt, Volney, and others. His most famous work, a two-volume history of St. Domingue, came from this press. Volney also issued his most famous and controversial book, *The Ruins, or Meditation on the Revolutions of Empires and the Law of Nature,* through Moreau. This work, contemplating the relationship between nature, religion, and civilizations, was frequently cited by theologians, clergymen, and philosophers who sought to characterize the nontheistic tendencies of French culture. Few would remember that it was written by Volney while he resided in America.[42]

Moreau and his colleagues gloried in the land of liberty. Present at the opening of Congress in 1794, Moreau commented after hearing President Washington's opening address: "This was the gathering of representatives of a nation that has won its liberty! What vast and great ideals in a group so united! How these republican forms appeal to the soul and stir the heart. What a destiny they foretell for this part of the world!" But they also yearned to salvage France. Indeed, Moreau and Talleyrand met nightly while they were both in Philadelphia: "On every night we were together, without a single exception, Talleyrand and I discussed the condition of France in the past, her present lot, and finally what would happen to her in the future." Together with other veterans of the early stirrings of liberty in France, they looked toward a day when they could redeem their homeland.[43]

While many of the immigrant friends of liberty settled in and around the capital of the United States, others arrived in a variety of ports and often witnessed the cause of liberty in those places. Benjamin Vaughan, an old associate of Benjamin Franklin, Joseph Priestley, and the Earl of Shelburne, made his way to America in 1796. Although his brother John was a mainstay of the American Philosophical Society in Philadelphia and was Priestley's most devoted Unitarian disciple in America, Vaughan chose to join another brother, Charles, on family lands at Hallowell, Maine. Vaughan contributed to liberty through quiet donations to organizations, widespread correspondence with state and national leaders, and publication of the writings of others. Quietly and deliberately he made extensive contributions to his adopted state and the New England region.[44]

John Daly Burk, escaped refugee from Ireland, landed in Boston at virtually the same time Vaughan went to Maine. He quickly launched a daily newspaper, the *Polar Star and Boston Daily Advertiser.* In one of his first issues, October 6, 1796, Burk extolled the virtues of his new nation:

> From the moment a stranger puts his foot on the soil of America, his fetters are rent in pieces, and the scales of servitude, which he had contracted under European tyrannies, fall off; he becomes a free man; and though civil regulations may refuse him the immediate exercise of his rights, he is, virtually a citizen.

Despite Burk's pleas that "the established papers [of Boston] make honorable mention of their infant brother," the *Polar Star* died within six months. Burk then next wrote a "tragedy," which he called *The Battle of Bunker Hill, or the Death of General Warren.* It was successfully staged at Boston's Haymarket Theater in 1797.[45]

Burk staged the play the following September in New York City. There it was seen by perhaps Burk's severest critic, President John Adams, who disliked the characterization of General Warren as "a bully and a blackguard." But Burk continued his pursuit of the cause of liberty in another play, *Female Patriotism, or the Death of Joan d'Arc,* opening in 1798 at the Park Theater. Almost simultaneously he took over the editorship of the *New York Time Piece* from Philip Freneau. In his first edition on June 13, 1798, he blasted the policies of his recent critic, the president.[46]

That same year saw the arrival of another English journalist fleeing rocky times in England. James Cheetham had been tried for conspiracy in 1793 for activities he had pursued with Thomas Cooper. By 1798 he was active in the revolutionary United Englishmen and was intent on overthrowing the British government. Threatened by loyalist rioters, he barely escaped physical harm, clandestinely carried on board a ship at Liverpool in a chest labeled as dry goods. On his arrival in New York, he became partner and editor of the *New York American Citizen* (an outgrowth of the *New York Argus*).[47]

This critical panoply of friends of liberty was completed with the arrival of an individual who had been a strong voice for liberty in India and London. William Duane arrived poetically on July 4, 1796, in New York City. Publisher and author John Stewart quickly hired him to write a history of the French Revolution. The history was to be attributed to a well-known American figure and was to be a popular, but authoritative, work on the subject.

Just as many thinkers were driven to understand the French Revolution, Duane happily undertook the task. What was the French Revolution intrinsically all about? How did it happen? Was it good or destructive? What lessons were to be taken from it? Which problems should be avoided? Was it about liberty, freedom, and equality? Or was it the most devastating event recorded in Western history?

Duane wrote his history. But he also traveled to Philadelphia in search of a printing or editorial position. Everywhere he was rejected because of "his wild hair, long beard and fierce expression." Arriving in Philadelphia just when President George Washington delivered his farewell address to the nation, Duane thought he heard sentiments he had recently encountered in William Pitt's statements in England.

Soon after, Duane published a "Letter to George Washington," in which he warned Americans about the aristocratic leanings of the rising government. He honed in on Washington's warnings about the formation of clubs and secret societies in America—especially the democratic-republican societies where the friends of liberty gathered. To Duane the implications of Washington's remarks were clear. Indeed, wrote Duane, Washington's views were as harsh as Pitt's on the constitutional and revolutionary societies that had sprung up throughout Britain: His "doctrines bear a most obstinate resemblance of the measures and language of the British ministry a year ago!" [48]

Duane's perception was prophetic, as was his jeremiad against Washington. A veteran of revolutionary struggles in Ireland, India, and England, he saw as most Americans could not, that the United States was part of a new struggle for liberty that had superseded the foreplay of the American Revolution. The citizens of France, England, Ireland, and Scotland knew that the struggle had begun. It was only in America—a country proud of its remarkable independence—that the reality of the revolutionary moment had not occurred.

It is poignant that William Duane—world traveler, rabble rouser, friend of liberty—should have been the prophet who told Americans that a world revolution was in progress and that they could not avoid involvement. Born in frontier America, Duane identified with American values. In Ireland, in India, and in England he preached an idealized sermon about the marvels of liberty in his native land.

Duane's adult debut onto the America scene is also poignant. Penniless, Duane submitted his adroit "Letter to George Washington" to Benjamin Franklin Bache for publication. Taken by the perceptiveness of the unknown immigrant, Bache published the essay and helped set the stage for Duane to become a preeminent voice for liberty.

The flocking of eager friends of liberty to America culminated with Duane's arrival. They had been silenced in other lands, but they were eager to join forces with the armies of friends of liberty in America to continue a worldwide revolution. With Benjamin Franklin Bache at the helm, they were sure that the era of liberty, freedom, equality, and individual rights soon would be ushered in.

CHAPTER 4

Sarah Franklin's Declaration of Independence

When he died in April 1790, Benjamin Franklin left behind a creative will, producing a sideshow that would go on at least two hundred years. A £1,000 each from his uncollected salary as president of the Commonwealth of Pennsylvania (he did not believe elected officials should be paid) he left to the cities of Boston and Philadelphia to be invested for two centuries at 5 percent interest. The cities were ordered to use the funds to make small loans to young male "artificers" (artisans) who were setting themselves up in business. At the end of the first century, two-thirds of the principal in each city was to be used for public projects. At the end of two hundred years, the program was to be concluded and the funds divided between city and state for additional public projects.[1]

In addition to this well-intentioned grandstanding, Franklin used his will to settle accounts with particular family members. For his illegitimate and estranged son, William, he left virtually nothing: a set of worthless claims for land he once wanted in Nova Scotia, whatever papers William had of Franklin's, and the cancellation of any debts due Franklin's estate (there were none). Digging in the knife once again for William's disloyalty during the American Revolution, Franklin wrote: "The part he acted against me in the late war, which is of public notoriety, will account for my leaving him no more of an estate he endeavored to deprive me of." But Franklin was much kinder to the two grandsons he had almost raised himself—William Temple Franklin and Benjamin Franklin Bache. Temple was bequeathed Franklin's library, his personal and literary papers (including title to the *Autobiography*), and, upon marriage, title to Franklin's farms in New Jersey. Bache received £1,000 worth of printing and typemaking equipment, a set of books, and a fourth of Franklin's remaining cash.

The largest portion of Franklin's estate with cash value was left to his daughter Sarah Franklin and her husband Richard Bache. They inherited Franklin's home at Franklin Court in Philadelphia, new houses built by Franklin, undeveloped lots in and around Philadelphia, and the contents of those properties, excluding the library and his papers. Franklin canceled Bache's debts of more than £2,000—with the single proviso that Bache "manumit and set free his negro man Bob." To assure that Sarah should not be wholly dependent upon her

Sarah Franklin Bache (n.d.). As the progenitor of the only Franklin descent, she rebelled against his patriarchal control.

never-successful husband, Franklin left "as her private money" one-half of the funds in his estate and income on his shares in the Bank of North America.

Franklin also singled out Sarah, known to everyone as Sally, to receive the most precious treasure in his entire estate: the miniature portrait of Louis XVI presented to Franklin by Louis himself. Studded with 408 diamonds, the miniature was of enormous value, either as a cash or commemorative asset. Franklin further stipulated that the diamonds were not to be removed for any cause, especially for the purpose of making ornaments so that neither Sarah nor her daughters would introduce the "expensive, vain, and useless fashion of wearing jewels in this country." [2]

Each Franklin child or grandchild had a different reaction to the Franklin bequest. William used the occasion to declare his independence of America: "The Revolution in America and the Shameful Injustice of my Father's Will have in a manner dissolved all my Connexions in that Part of the World of a private as well as publick Nature." Bitter, impoverished, and spiritually broken, William spent his last years in London in utter obscurity. [3]

William Temple Franklin squandered his possessions until there was almost nothing left to sell or give away. Having sold Franklin's prized library and laid waste almost all of his papers, nothing remained but the literary rights to Franklin's *Autobiography* and a few selected papers. Twenty-seven years after he was given the singular responsibility of publishing Franklin's *Autobiography* and papers, he finally produced the three-volume *Memoirs of the Life and Writings of Benjamin Franklin*—a small sample of the total works. Whatever financial rewards came from the venture sustained him for another six years in Paris, where he, like his father, died in similar anonymity.

Benjamin Franklin Bache's portion of the legacy was what he expected—the wherewithal to ply his trade as printer and typefounder. Within months he launched the *General Advertiser* and threw himself into a brilliant but short-lived career of interpreting his grandfather's principles. Although he was in financial peril at the time of his death during the yellow fever epidemic of 1798, he valiantly carried on the rich Franklin tradition.

Sarah Franklin, dutiful daughter, surprised Philadelphia and the world with her reaction to the terms of the will. Within months after receiving her inheritance, she and her husband systematically began to dismantle the core of Franklin's substantial estate. All of the Philadelphia properties were sold to extract their cash value. Household goods belonging to Franklin, irrespective of their historic or symbolic value, were sold for cash. Even Franklin's house was demolished to facilitate a financially more lucrative use of the land it occupied. Every trace of Franklin's presence in Philadelphia, save the printshop where Benjamin Franklin Bache labored on, was obliterated. Even Bache's "negro man Bob," although he was legally manumitted, was unable to support himself and was financially forced into a position of servitude for the duration of his life.[4]

Sally proceeded to defile the Louis XVI miniature. She removed a circle of the diamonds and sold them to finance a yearlong trip to Europe. In the spring of 1792 she, her husband, and daughter settled in comfortable quarters in London near her brother William. Although Franklin and William had broken ties permanently during the Revolution, Sally and he remained cordial. William, despite his poverty, served the touring Baches as guide, host, and adviser for their lengthy sojourn.[5]

Temple Franklin also joined them in the festivities, as the odd claque of descendants basked in Franklin's reflective glory on a junket fully financed by his fortune. Sally sat for a portrait by John Hoppner, a popular portraitist. Bache had his done as well.[6]

Sally's goal was to proceed to France, where she anticipated a reception appropriate for a queen. In August 1792 she wrote ahead to Franklin's friend, Louis-Guillaume Le Veillard, indicating that she hoped to spend the winter in France and asking that he send her as soon as possible the truth about what was happening in France. She could not then know that France was entering into an upheaval that would witness the arrest and beheading of nearly every member of Benjamin Franklin's circle of friends in Paris—including Le Veillard himself.[7]

Sally sadly but wisely canceled her visit to Paris. As the Terror seized France, Sally suddenly faced her own terror. Having exhausted every penny derived from the initial sale of the diamonds, there now was no money to stay longer and none to pay the passage back to Philadelphia. She quickly turned to Temple, begging for money and imploring him not to leak a word of her predicament to either Bache or William. Much to her surprise, Temple informed her that he had previously loaned money to Bache, who was already in arrears on repayment. Temple turned the table on her and demanded that she repay Bache's delinquent accounts.[8]

Fearful of Bache's reaction if she confronted him both with the fact that they were penniless and that she then knew of the outstanding loans from Temple, Sally did the only thing she could under the circumstances. She removed another circle of diamonds from the Louis XVI miniature to produce the needed cash. Worried that the less-than-trustworthy Temple might betray her to Bache, she demanded his total silence as a condition for repaying the loans.[9] Just as Louis XVI's career on earth came to an end, his priceless gift to Franklin became the sole symbol of liberty to Sarah Franklin Bache, living out a moment in time when revolution promised rights for both men and women.

Sally was born into a family that for all of its greatness was almost dysfunctional. Her ambitious father was a successful businessman and a distinguished Philadelphian when she arrived in 1743. By the time she was three, he had launched into the electrical experiments that made him a world-renowned scientist. Deborah Franklin, her mother, was doing every thing on earth to support and please her innovative husband. She helped with the printing business, serving as bookkeeper and accountant for an ever-broadening enterprise. She remained firmly grounded as Franklin floated in the clouds trying to understand lightning, electricity, and human behavior.

Somehow the two of them had a son, William, whose motherhood was never explained. Franklin did everything possible to educate his son. William had a tutor at age four, a fulltime teacher at age eight, and was enrolled in Philadelphia's best classical academy until he was thirteen. After he spent the next several years either in Franklin's printshop or on some mission as a member of the King's Army, Franklin then provided him an education in law. He first read under the tutelage of Joseph Galloway, then enrolled in Middle Temple, Inns of Court, and matriculated there when the Franklins went to England in 1757.[10]

But Franklin treated his daughter very differently. Even though Franklin as a young man had argued, "for Dispute's sake," the affirmative on the "Propriety of educating the Female Sex in Learning, and their Abilities for Study," he demonstrated little commitment to the education of Sally. She quietly begged her father for an education akin to that offered William, but she was in almost every instance denied access to anything more than the traditional home trades of spinning, knitting, embroidering, and that "dreary succession of hair-work, featherwork, wax flowers, shell-work, the crystallization with various domestic minerals and gums of dried leaves and grasses, . . . yarn and worsted monstrosities."

She once had a tutor, but it was to learn the business of making elegant buttonholes. The only frill in her development that he was willing to support was her interest in music. Franklin sent her a harpsichord from England and supplied her regularly with the most current musical scores. While she wrote to him seeking his encouragement and love, he lectured her on her spiritual development, devotion to work at home, and duty to her mother. When she was seven, Franklin arranged for her to one day marry William Strahan, Jr., at that moment the ten-year-old son of his closest friend and business partner, London publisher William Strahan. He pursued the match relentlessly when he arrived in England, imploring Deborah to bring Sally to London when she turned sixteen. Deborah would not cross the Atlantic, and Franklin, at least at the moment, thought it unwise for Sally, eager to make the trip, to sail alone.[11]

In 1763 Franklin took Sally on an extended working tour of New England, but he would not hear her pleas to accompany him when he returned to England in 1765. On this trip the two played duets, she on the harpsichord and he on his self-designed glass armonica—their only collaboration in life. He continued to lecture her about attending church and about spending too much time at social events. Back in England in 1767, he ironically showered her with social enticements—gowns, negligees, gloves, and lavender water—but he also again proposed that she cross the Atlantic to marry the wealthy Billy Strahan.

But Sally Franklin decided at age twenty-three that she wanted some of the liberty that was beginning to be discussed in America and around the world. She was tired of a life ruled by a father who acknowledged none of her wishes and respected none of her opinions. If her father would not treat her with respect, would not let her make her own decisions about religion and life, and would not in reality let her travel to England, then she would marry someone who would give her all of those things and more. Her opportunity came in the summer of 1766 when her closest friend, Peggy Ross, suddenly died, leaving behind a handsome, thirty-year-old fiancé, who just happened to be a most impressive, if not entirely successful English businessman. With his proper English background, Philadelphian society had opened its doors to Richard Bache when he arrived in 1760. From outward appearances Bache was an ideal match for Sally.

But how could she proceed with her rebellion, when both Bache and she would need, at least for a time, Franklin's financial support? When Sally, Bache on his own, and also Deborah informed Franklin of the impending marriage, he expressed little interest in the matter, leaving the decision up to Deborah. His only firm word was an order to her to not "make an expensive feasting Wedding, but conduct every thing with Frugality and Oeconomy." He concluded to Deborah that not more than £500 total should be spent for the wedding and to "fit her out handsomely in Cloaths and Furniture. . . . For the rest, they must depend as you and I did, on their own Industry and Care."

Bache's financial affairs, due to the effects of the Stamp Act and the foundering of a ship he had bought at risk, were a wreck. He owed debts of more than £3,600. William Franklin, by then ensconced as the Royal governor of New Jersey, assessed Bache's prospects and wrote to the elder Franklin of the alarming news. "If Sally marries him, they must both be entirely on you for their Subsistence." In William's estimation, Bache was "a mere fortune hunter."

The alarmed Franklin finally responded to several letters in which Bache outlined his financial difficulties and asked for assistance as well as the hand of Sally. Franklin sternly wrote:

> I love my daughter perhaps as well as ever parent did a child, but I have told you before that my estate is small, scarce a sufficiency for the support of me and my wife, who are growing old and cannot now bustle for a living as we have done; . . . I am obliged to you for the regard and preference you express for my child and wish you all prosperity; but unless you can convince her friends of the probability of your being able to maintain her properly, I hope you will not persist in a proceeding that may be attended with ruinous consequences to you both.

In a separate letter to Deborah, he insisted that she place Sally on the first ship to London; Billy Strahan was still awaiting Sally's arrival.

But it was too late. Sally's quest for liberty from her zealous patriarch was on its own trajectory. The wedding occurred on October 29, 1767:

> Last Thursday Evening Mr. Richard Bache, of this City, Merchant, was married to Miss Sally Franklin, the only Daughter of the celebrated Doctor Franklin, a young Lady of distinguished Merit. The next Day all the Shipping in the Harbour displayed their Colours on the happy Occasion.

When Franklin received the news from his sister Jane Mecom in December, he angrily responded, "She has pleas'd herself and her Mother, and I hope she will do well: but I think they should have seen some better Prospect."

For the next year Franklin refused to acknowledge the accretion of a son-in-law. But after hearing from Bache that his business prospects were improving, Franklin broke the silence with a letter accusing the young man of irresponsibility: "In this Situation of my Mind, you should not wonder that I did not answer your Letters. I could say nothing agreeable: I did not chuse to write what I thought, being unwilling to give Pain where I could not give Pleasure." He concluded his letter on a warmer note: "If you prove a good Husband and Son, you will find in me an Affectionate Father." [12]

Deborah, through her connivance, lost Franklin forever. She never saw him again. Sally Franklin never really recovered him either. She provided him with a rich progeny of eight grandchildren, the first of which was named Benjamin Franklin Bache. So delighted was Franklin with little Benny when he finally came home from England in 1775—a year after Deborah's death—that he virtually kidnapped the seven-year-old boy. He took Benny with him to France in 1776, over the violent protests of a sobbing Sally Bache. She acquiesced only when Franklin promised to provide the boy with an outstanding European education. He likewise took Temple Franklin with him without bothering to notify Temple's father, his estranged son William. [13]

Nor did Sally reclaim the affections of her father when he returned from France in 1785 to spend his final days at Franklin Court. Her role was supplanted the next year by the arrival of Polly Hewson, the daughter of his landlady.

Franklin showered on Polly the affection due his own daughter. As substitute father, he gave away the bride when Polly married in 1770. Still spurning Sally in his last days, he had Polly sit by his bedside to comfort him in his last illness. When in his dying moments Sally suggested that he would recover and live many more years, he looked her squarely in the eye and said, "I hope not." With his dying breath, he would not give his daughter credence.[14]

Sally's marriage to Bache and her sale of the diamonds surrounding Louis XVI were clear declarations of independence from a man who, though he might stand for liberty, freedom, and equality in others' eyes, was for her a tyrant. He had doted on William until political differences separated them. He had showered affection and endless forgiveness on the wayward William Temple. And Benjamin Franklin Bache, rigid and humorless, could do no wrong. But they were boys becoming men and acting out the roles acceptable for men. Sally, on the other hand, was a girl becoming a woman; dutiful service to father and husband was her role in life. However much Franklin might expound upon the rights of man—even the rights of black man—he never extended those rights to women, whatever their race. But Sally Franklin, in defying the last will and testament of her father, had declared her independence as would many other women in the late eighteenth century.

CHAPTER 5

Liberty and the Rights of Women

ROLES AND RIGHTS FOR WOMEN

Susanna Haswell Rowson, one of the world's great proponents of the rights of women, asked a question in 1797 that surely occurred to many women in the era of the American and French Revolutions: What women, past or present, provide role models for young females? Having spent the previous ten years writing novels—including *Charlotte Temple* (1791), America's all-time best-seller prior to Harriet Beecher Stowe's *Uncle Tom's Cabin* (1852)—Rowson suddenly shifted careers from that of author to teacher. In the spring of 1797 she opened what would be known as Mrs. Rowson's Young Ladies Academy of Boston. For the next twenty-five years she imparted directly to students her belief that women were equal, and in some ways, superior to men. Her advocacy for the rights of women, particularly in her play *Slaves in Algiers, or a Struggle for Freedom* (1794), helped to focus discussions of the rights of women in the land of liberty.

Rowson answered her own question about female role models in a short essay titled "Sketches of Female Biography." Biography, she thought, would be particularly instructive for her students, since it "is calculated at once to inform the mind, improve the taste, and amend the heart." Likewise, "by presenting to our view excellence actually attained, [it] excites in the bosom, a noble emulation to equal those who have gone before us." "To young females," she continued, "the memorials of exemplary women are peculiarly interesting":

> The importance of women in every civilized society is gener-
> ally acknowledged, and their ascendance in forming the char-
> acter of the other sex cannot be disputed; it is not alone to the
> nursery, or during the periods of childhood and youth, but in
> riper years, in the cabinet, in the camp, in almost every station
> in some way or other their influence is found to be unbounded.

She proposed to catalog "with generous ardour in the pursuit of what is praise-worthy" those women whose roles might be copied.[1]

Rowson's catalog was revealing. Most of the role models came from remote history: Hypatia, a fourth-century Egyptian astronomer; Chelonis, a Spartan political heroine; Eponina, a Roman martyr; Boadicea, British queen during Roman rule; Tymiche, a Lacedemonian heroine who bit off her tongue and spit it in her torturer's face rather than divulge religious secrets; and Leona, an Athenian who shielded a conspiracy through the same courage.

She also found a number of examples from the sixteenth and seventeenth centuries: Margaret De Foix, duchess D'Epernon, and Blanche, countess of Arundel, courageous defenders of their castles; Queen Elizabeth of England, "not only a great queen, but an accomplished woman"; Anne of Austria, wife of Louis XIII of France, "a woman of considerable political capacity"; Jane Grey, the tragic pawn set opposite Mary Stuart, Queen of Scots; as well as other pious, brave, Protestant women who died tragically or young.

Even when Rowson concluded that "we need not search in such remote antiquity for examples of female erudition and talents," she still surfaced with mainly seventeenth-century characters: Lucretia Cornaro of Venice, a Roman law professor; Susanna Perwich, a youthful musician; Madame Dacier, a linguist; Mary Inglis, a playwright in the era of Shakespeare; and Isabella and Catherine Clive, actresses in both Inglis's and Shakespeare's plays.[2]

Rowson, even though she was American by adoption, listed no American women in her catalog. No Martha Washington, no Abigail Adams, no Deborah Sampson—the cross-dressing heroine of the American Revolution. When all was said and done, Rowson's selection of three women who might be considered contemporaries was interesting. They were the great Catharines of the eighteenth century. First mentioned was "Mrs. Macaul[a]y, whose erudition was self attained, without the aid of preceptors." Catharine Macaulay "produced a history of England superior to many, and inferior to none." Next came Catherine I, Empress of Russia. Last was Catherine II, also Empress of Russia.[3]

Catherine I, born Marta Skowronska, fit neatly into Rowson's catalog of women of humble origins and extraordinary accomplishment. She was the "illegitimate daughter of a female peasant," orphaned at age three. She served as a domestic in various households until she became the mistress of Alexander Menshikov. Menshikov just happened to be the closest friend and adviser of Peter the Great, as well as the head of a group of Russian reformers known as "Peter's fledglings." Peter at some point put his unloved wife Eudoxia in a convent (not mentioned by Rowson) and took Skowronska as his own mistress. He eventually "privately married her," giving her the title Catherine.[4]

Catherine never left his side "whether for war or pleasure." Peter never undertook "any thing of material consequence to himself or kingdom, without her advice; by which he generally was decided." When in a savage battle with the Turks, Catherine, unknown to Peter, entered into a treaty "by which the Russians were rescued from imminent danger and enabled to make an honourable retreat," Peter acknowledged their marriage and "placed the crown upon her head with his own hands." Upon Peter's death in 1725, she ascended to the throne, aided by her former lover Menshikov. According to Rowson, Catherine reigned over the next three years "in the hearts of the emperor and his subjects, by gentleness and complacency." She "ever bore in mind the humble station from which she had been raised." In actuality, she was badly used by Menshikov, who wished to control the government of Russia.[5]

Having canonized Marta Skowronska, Rowson next examined Catherine II, whom she considered "may deservedly be classed among women excellent for talents, political discernment, and munificence." Her benefits to the Russians were legion. She "extended their territories, polished their manners, secured their liberties, and extended their commercial interest." She endowed schools, cultivated her literary abilities, drew up a new code of laws that became the Russian constitution, and superintended the education of her grandsons Alexander, Constantine, and Nicholas.

Whereas Rowson sanctified the imperfect first Catherine, she did not do the same with Catherine II. This Catherine, "so brilliant as a queen, was shaded as a woman." She provided as example the "premature death of her consort . . . together with other errors." Her life, as commendable as it was, served "to convince us, that perfection is not attainable in this mortal state." Catherine II, possessed the "mental abilities of the other sex," and "if like them she aimed at, and acquired an almost boundless power, like them also, she was capable of abusing it."[6]

For good or ill, Catherine II and Catharine Macaulay were the most frequently mentioned role models for American women during the closing years of the eighteenth century. They represented two of the three most common ways in which women in the eighteenth century pursued their liberty—through participation in government and writing history, literature, and biography. A third pursuit, especially perfected in France, was the salon. There thus follows an examination of the pursuits toward liberty of four extraordinary women of the eighteenth century, Catherine the Great of Russia, Catharine Macaulay of England, but also Suzanne Necker of France, and Mercy Otis Warren of America.[7]

Though Necker and Warren do not appear on Rowson's list, they too defined roles that would inspire generations of young women.

LIBERATED RULER: CATHERINE THE GREAT

Governance has been a principal avenue whereby women could exercise power; that is, if fate made it possible for a woman to assume a position of authority. No woman ever governed with greater direction and decisiveness than Catherine the Great. Born as Sophie Friederike Auguste von Anhalt-Zerbst, in the Pomeranian seaport of Stettin in 1729, she was the daughter of a minor prince and general of the Prussian Army. She developed by her early teens into a vigorous, beautiful, and sexually curious young woman. Physically strong, liberated, and rebellious, she surprised those around her with her loud laughter, wild dancing, and habit of riding horses astride, in the manner of a man.[8]

When she turned fourteen her mother and Empress Elizabeth of Russia arranged for her to go to St. Petersburg to marry Peter Fedorovich, the designated heir to the Russian throne. Peter, a distant cousin of Sophia, was also brought up as a Prussian Lutheran. Neither spoke Russian. But he was fascinated with Prussian military practices and did not share Sophie's interests in sexual exploration.

Sophie formally converted to Russian Orthodoxy, took on the Russian name Catherine (selected by Empress Elizabeth in honor of Catherine I, her mother), and launched into a concerted effort to learn the Russian language, habits, and customs. Peter, by contrast, ignored Catherine and all things Russian. A case of chicken pox may have left him sterile. Thus their marriage probably was not consummated following the royal wedding in July 1745.

Left to herself, Catherine devoured novels, histories, and biographies. Whereas Peter continued playing soldier and speaking only German, she grew increasingly at ease in her adopted land. Peter made fumbling attempts at passion following occasional imperial scoldings that he must produce an heir, but after five years of marriage there was neither child nor pregnancy.

Understanding the importance of producing an heir, Catherine in 1749 underwent a transformation that would change her life and the history of Russia. She began to covertly entice the first of what would be twenty-one documented lovers over the course of the next four decades. In September 1754, she produced a son. Proud Empress Elizabeth announced that he would be known as Paul and proclaimed that she would take full responsibility for his education.

With the heir to the throne produced, Catherine was, at at age twenty-six, free to do virtually anything she liked. She began a lifelong relationship with a handsome Polish count; she flourished in St. Petersburg's social life; she continued her studies. The birth of a daughter in 1757, however, led to a tricky confrontation with Peter. Knowing this time that he certainly was not the father, Peter first challenged her, but then relented months later when it became known that he, too, had begun an extramarital flirtation. By July 1758 they had agreed to pursue their separate affairs without interference from the other.

The stage was set for a dramatic royal succession story. Although Empress Elizabeth evidently considered renouncing Peter and naming young Paul her successor with Catherine as regent, she had taken no action prior to her unexpected death on December 25, 1762. At that moment, Catherine was having another affair with a dashing Russian lieutenant, Grigory Orlov. She was also six months pregnant. She considered Peter an unfortunate fool, but took no action when he declared himself Emperor Peter III without reference to the status of his wife. She, instead, entered into six months of mourning in honor of Elizabeth.[9]

During that six-month interval Peter illustrated marvelously how unsuited he was to be czar of Russia. In March 1762 he issued a manifesto on the freedom of the nobility, exempting Russia's vast number of nobles from the necessity of serving the nation except under emergency circumstances. He then announced plans for retraining the Russian military according to Prussian practice and issued an edict to secularize the lands of the Russian Orthodox Church. The only segment of Russian society left unaffected in that revolutionary six-month period was the vast army of serfs, whose status was much like that of American slaves. It would have been difficult even for William Shakespeare to have scripted the tragicomic course followed by Peter on the way to self-destruction.[10]

Catherine chose the eighteenth anniversary of her engagement to Peter to present her own drama. With the assistance of Grigory Orlov and his brother

Aleksy, Catherine called on the Royal palaces around St. Petersburg, asking disaffected Russian troops to declare their allegiance to her. Even the Russian Senate bade her warm support. To the amazement of all, she mounted astride her favorite steed Brilliant and declared to onlooking senators and troops, "I go now with the army to reinforce and to secure the throne, leaving you, as my supreme government, with complete confidence, to guard the fatherland, the people, and my son [Paul]."

As commander-in-chief of the Russian army, Catherine led a formidable force in the direction of Oranienbaum, where the pathetic Peter crumbled and gave Catherine a letter renouncing the throne and requesting permission to depart for Holstein, his native state. The astute Catherine immediately supplied him with a draft abdication document, which he signed. Eager to announce her victory publicly, Catherine marched into St. Petersburg on the morning of June 30. Six days later news arrived that Peter was dead. Although the public report stated that he died of a sudden "hemorrhoidal colic," he had been murdered by Aleksy Orlov and fourteen accomplices (probably without the knowledge or blessing of Catherine).[11]

Catherine launched into a brilliant thirty-two year reign. With foresight and deliberation, she reversed Peter's blundering policies, even though over time she embraced and implemented most of them.

In the early years of her reign she spent days and months studying the legal systems in the Western world. Her aim was to find a defining structure on which to codify chaotic Russian systems of law. She mined Montesquieu's *The Spirit of Laws,* the works of Cesare Beccaria, Jacob Bielfeld, and Johann Justi, and Diderot's *Encyclopedia* to draft a document of 22 chapters and 655 articles that she titled *The Great Instruction.* At the same moment Benjamin Franklin, John Adams, and other American patriots were beginning to discuss written constitutions and declarations of rights, Catherine was single-mindedly doing the same for Russia. When her work was published not only in Russian, but also in English, French, German, Italian, Greek, Swedish, Dutch, Polish, and Rumanian translations, she willingly assumed the mantle of "philosopher-sovereign," an idea that appealed to her tremendously. Indeed, Voltaire described *The Great Instruction* as "the finest monument of the age." Concluding that "we have never heard of any Female being a Lawgiver," he said that this special glory "was reserved for the Empress of Russia."[12]

In *The Great Instruction* Catherine described the "natural liberty" of citizens and of their rights to be treated equally before the law. Though she did not extend her theories to the institution of serfdom, she portrayed benevolence as government's goal. Rulers were to be controlled by laws, not by caprice. Unlike her counterparts in America who favored a sound education only for men, she extended the opportunity to women by opening the Society for the Training of Daughters of the Nobility (the Smolny Institute) in 1764.[13]

Although her goal of a codified legal system was never fully achieved, Catherine defended the Russian Enlightenment against all detractors. In response to a condescending travelogue depicting Russian backwardness, Catherine issued a two-volume critique titled *The Antidote.* Published at first anonymously and in French in 1770, it was republished and translated into English in 1772 by a Maria Johnson, who in the preface described Catherine as "the first and greatest woman of the present age." She also promoted the cultural development of Russia by importing French art, literature, and architecture. In opulence, her court surpassed even that of Louis XVI and Marie Antoinette.[14]

She appointed a commission to reevaluate Peter's manifesto, but eventually adopted most of its principles. She renounced his seizure of church lands, but then took them back again in 1764. She launched into a revision of Russia's legal codes with a national convocation of more than five hundred delegates in 1767. She then sent them home sixteen months later, before they reached any conclusions and before they could take on the rebellious mood of America's Continental Congress or the revolutionary spirit of France's Estates General. The longer her reign lasted, the more dictatorial and repressive her tenure became. Although she issued the Charter of the Nobility in 1785 adopting many of Peter's principles, she also greatly expanded the number of Russia's serfs and took away many of their basic rights.

With the fall of the Bastille and the harsh treatment of Louis XVI by his subjects, however, she was suddenly jolted. Hearing of his ejection from Versailles, she commented, "Yes, they are capable of hanging their King from a lamp-post, it's frightful." She could not help thinking what it might mean for Russia if it, too, followed this latest French habit.

She did not have long to wait. In July 1790 Catherine came face-to-face with a blast of liberation frenzy. Almost nine months before Thomas Paine issued his infectious *Rights of Man,* an anonymous book titled *Voyage from St. Petersburg to Moscow* appeared with ideas on liberty, freedom, and equality as radical as anything being printed anywhere else. The book was quickly traced to Alexander Radishchev, a nobleman with the kind of Enlightenment training Catherine had been advocating for thirty years.

As she painstakingly analyzed the revolutionary tract, she reached many of the same conclusions Edmund Burke would articulate in his *Reflections on the Revolution in France* a few months later: "The purpose of this book is clear on every page: its author, infected and full of the French madness, is trying in every possible way to break down respect for authority and the authorities, to stir up in the people indignation against their superiors and against the government." She concluded that "the questions brought up here are the ones over which France is now being ruined." When she ordered prosecution of the author in criminal court on July 13, she characterized the book as full of "the most harmful philosophizing, destroying the social peace, disparaging the respect due to authorities . . . [and] with insulting and rabid utterances against the dignity of sovereign authority."

Catherine directed, through written interrogatories, the full exposure of Radishchev's revolutionary mind. The court, responding to Catherine's obvious antagonism, sentenced Radishchev to beheading—a judgment moderated to exile in Siberia. Even as this more lenient sentence was being carried out, Catherine ordered all Russians traveling or living in Paris to return to their homeland. Because of her quick and decisive action, only thirty or so copies of Radishchev's tract remained in circulation.[15]

Having ordered in February 1791 close surveillance of French citizens living in Russia, Catherine discovered that Edmond Genet, French *charge d'affaires* in St. Petersburg, was sending out coded projections of revolution to every level of Russian society. She expelled him from Russia soon after. He next took his madcap revolutionary schemes to the United States, where he would play out the same script with essentially the same results.

Just as American leaders in 1798 would war with the Bavarian Illuminati and Freemasons, Catherine in the spring of 1792 began her own private campaign against them, first to ridicule and then to rid Russia of the two groups. As early as 1785 she had written and published several satirical comedies, lampooning both secret orders as among "the greatest aberrations to which the human race had succumbed." Titled *The Deceiver, The Deluded,* and *The Siberian Shaman,* the plays showed practices of the orders to be "a mixture of religious ritual and childish games." But convinced that they were screens for political conspiracies, she banned any further organizations that took on the appearance of a secret order or a Jacobin Club.[16]

Following the execution of Louis XVI in January 1793, Catherine's break with all things French and with aspirations for liberty was complete. French nationals were expelled from Russia; Russian nationals anywhere on French soil were ordered home. By the middle of 1795, Catherine had come to believe that the monster of revolution that drove France would have to be destroyed.[17]

Just a few weeks before she died in November 1796, Catherine ordered Field Marshall Alexander Suvorov to proceed with sixty thousand troops to the north of Italy. Suvorov was to launch a campaign against the French that would not be completed until Catherine's beloved grandson Alexander marched into Paris at the head of a Russian army on March 30, 1814.

Her shadow on history, through him, passed on into the nineteenth century. Despite rumor about Catherine's method of rising to power and her numerous sexual liaisons, she was a great—albeit ambiguous—role model for young women. For in looking beyond her human foibles that would have been less noted had she been a man, she had ruled a great nation across the age of revolution; she had seized the same great hope for liberty felt by Franklin, Washington, Adams, Burke, Paine, Lafayette, and Mirabeau. But she had also met, as would Adams and Burke, the destructive tendencies of revolution head-on, and she had provided, at least for Russia, an orderly transition to a new era of peace and prosperity.

SALONNIÈRES AND LIBERTY

While Catherine walked the pathway of rulers, Suzanne Curchod Necker reigned supreme in an entirely different court, the Paris salon. Born in a Protestant parsonage in the canton of Vaud, Switzerland, Suzanne received a very full and complete education, rendered unto her by a loving father. Nothing was too much for what was clearly a brilliant and beautiful daughter.[18]

By 1753 she had sufficient command of Latin, Greek, mathematics, science, and music to communicate with virtually any mind in Europe. In June 1757 she met Edward Gibbon in Lausanne, Switzerland, and entered into an enchanted but doomed romance that continued across seven years. He was deeply engaged in research for his ponderous work, *The History of the Decline and Fall of the Roman Empire,* eventually published in six volumes between 1776 and 1788.[19]

Regrettably Gibbon had a physical problem—a cancerous growth on his sexual organs—that inhibited sex and thereby a proper engagement to a lady of the realm. He repeatedly put off Curchod and her family when approached about marriage. Even intervention by Jean-Jacques Rousseau on her behalf could not dissuade Gibbon from bachelorhood. But Curchod was determined. Working as a governess to eke out a living, she saw Gibbon daily between February and April 1764. The constant intimacy did not budge the single-minded and somewhat pathetic historian. He would not divulge his impairment to anyone until his mature years, when the growth raged out of control, limiting his ability to walk and to function socially.

After seven years of pursuing the dissembling Gibbon, Suzanne Curchod moved on. She took a position as tutor for a young child in Paris in June 1764. It did not take her long to find a most suitable husband, Jacques Necker. Already a successful Genevan banker, Necker was on his way to becoming one of the wealthiest and most influential citizens of France. As both economics theoretician and as finance minister of France during the American Revolution and during the early days of the French Revolution, he was one of the most renowned statesmen of the era, a perfect foil for Suzanne Curchod.[20]

The wealthy Necker provided her with status and the freedom to establish a new salon in Paris. In 1766, the same year in which she gave birth to daughter Germaine—destined to become known as Madame de Staël—Suzanne Necker selected the only day of the week not already taken by some other salon, Friday, and began to assemble a group of distinguished participants. She scoured French society, seeking the best minds and the greatest reputations, but only among men, to be a part of her salon.[21]

Suzanne Necker was a leader in converting the salon from a leisure institution into a tool of republicanism. At a time when few careers and no public posts were available for educated women, the salon offered a backdrop where a woman who wanted to help shape policy could flourish. Suzanne Necker and other women created a setting that served as a clearinghouse for information and ideas. Ideas too outrageous for public airing could be discussed; policies too provocative for general understanding were considered.[22]

Among her first recruits were journalist Jean-Baptiste Suard, tolerant theater censor under Louis XVI; Jean-François Marmontel, poet, dramatist, political moderate, and secretary of the Académie Française; and Abbé Guillaume Raynal, radical historian and philosopher. Her goal of securing encyclopedist Denis Diderot for her salon took longer. Finally in 1769, Diderot admitted that, after "subjecting me to a regular persecution to lure me to her house," he succumbed as well.[23]

The regimen of the salon under Suzanne Necker was rigorous. She prepared detailed agendas for each meeting, listing books, topics, and literary themes to be pursued. In her journal she observed, "One is most ready for conversation when one has written and thought about things before going into society." As her own model, she selected a guide who exhibited almost perfect order—Catherine the Great. Clearly not knowing everything about her renowned contemporary, Necker dryly observed in her journal that Catherine "never had a taste for pleasure, and this characteristic was one of the causes of her greatness; it is the taste for pleasure which undermines the consideration of all women." As a result, the "maintenance of order in one's domestic interior before going into society" was an obsession that made her salon a stunning center of learning and well-considered action.[24]

By pursuing such diligence, Necker created an institution that helped shape the government of France. She once observed, "The government of a conversation very much resembles that of a State; one can scarcely doubt its influence." And on the role of women in carefully operating this engine, she was clear: "Every one in these assemblies [salons] is convinced that women fill the intervals of conversation and of life, like the padding one inserts in cases of china; they are valued at nothing, and [yet] everything breaks without them." Men fought wars, waged public debates, stood for office. Women, by contrast, hosted structured salons, fostered quiet discussion, and produced harmony and peace.[25]

Ultimately her salon had a permanent assembly of "seventeen venerable philosophers," among which she counted herself. Not included in this number, but a constant attendant was Germaine Necker, who with the rich exposure to ideas and argumentation, would become a brilliant essayist, novelist, and historian, as well as head of her own salon. Suzanne Necker deprived her daughter of love, but gave her a unique schooling, evident in the life and writings of Madame de Staël.[26]

From Suzanne Necker's salon came ideas about liberty, freedom, and equality. Abstract ideals animated citizens into action, sometimes little reflecting economic self-interest or traditional order. Some salons would become alleged centers of sensual delight, but such was not the case with hers. She was chaste, self-denying, almost puritanical.

As her husband's political fortunes rose and fell, Necker continued with her salon. When the citizens of Paris protested his dismissal by storming the Bastille, a desperate Louis XVI called him back to office and she followed him back to Paris. Throngs of people lined the streets to welcome him back as savior of the French economy. Through the drama and excitement, culminating with Necker's downfall in 1790, Suzanne Necker concentrated on death. Drawing up plans for a mausoleum to be built at Coppet, Switzerland, she spent the critical years of the French Revolution lamenting the loss of order while she was in the process of dying. In 1794 she earned the mausoleum and her long-anticipated rest.[27]

Necker's role as one of France's most renowned salonnières made her one of the most significant women of the eighteenth century. The model she established would be followed by her daughter, through whom, like Catherine the Great in grandson Alexander, she lived on for another generation. Necker's design was transferred to America, where women eagerly used the instrument to assert their ideas and put their mark on the revolution. In both France and America the salon lived on as an important institution—exclusively operated by women—for generations to come.

LIBERTY'S HISTORY

The renowned Catharine Macaulay, historian, traveler, controversialist, was herself a focus of considerable debate. Born on the River Wye, County Kent, England, Catharine was privately educated according to her father's wishes. She thrived on the study of history; early in her research she became enamored with the ideals of liberty among citizens, peoples, and nations. In 1760 she married George Macaulay, a physician fifteen years her elder with a successful London medical practice.[28]

Her husband encouraged and supported Macaulay's voracious appetite for history. Three years after her marriage, she published the first of eight volumes of her great *The History of England from the Accession of James I to that of the Brunswick Line.* Over a period of twenty years she produced a prodigious work that still influences—albeit now indirectly—how the world views England's past. Emerging as it did in 1763 and continuing over such an extended period, Catharine Macaulay's career as author and celebrity roughly coincided with that of Catherine the Great, making the two of them perhaps the most visible women in the world.[29]

Macaulay's *History* charted the march of the English people in the direction of liberty. She inspired friends of liberty in America, France, and England. With five of her eight volumes published by 1771, she urged representation in Parliament, better protection of rights, and a wider distribution of wealth and taxes. In a 1770 pamphlet reviewing Edmund Burke's own essay, *Thoughts on the Cause of the Present Discontents,* she endorsed the aspirations of Americans who were fighting for their rights. In *An Address to the People of England, Scotland and Ireland on the Present Important Crisis of Affairs,* she opposed the taxation of Americans.[30]

Macaulay traveled to England, France, and even to America, constantly preaching her message. In 1777 she met with Benjamin Franklin as he manipulated the French into ever stronger support for America. Since the writ of habeas corpus had just been suspended in Britain, however, she apologized to Franklin that she could not spend time with him or correspond with him more regularly. (She faced arrest and charges of conspiracy if she dealt with a person trying to overthrow the Crown.)

During the 1780s the leading lights of the oncoming French Revolution came to England to pay their respects and to borrow Macaulay's ideas. After she issued the final volume of her *History* in 1783, Mirabeau came to call in London in 1784 and 1785. So entranced was he with her history of liberty in England and America that he arranged for a translation of the first five volumes into French.

Catharine Macaulay (n.d.). Chronicler and champion of British liberty.

They appeared eventually in 1791 and 1792 in a two-volume format, just in time to further influence revolutionary thinking in France.[31] Also traveling to England to take counsel with Macaulay came Jacques Brissot, whose ideas about liberty and republicanism paralleled Macaulay's. Henri Bancal des Issarts, a disciple of Brissot, also made pilgrimages to Macaulay's door as he formulated his ideas about a constitutional monarchy for France.[32]

Monitoring the progress of liberty, Macaulay beamed interpretations to a broad range of correspondents. When George Washington became first president of the United States, she wrote congratulations linking his ascent to events in France and Britain: "All the friends of liberty on this side of the Atlantic are now rejoicing for an event which in all probability, had been accelerated by the American Revolution." To Thomas Brand Hollis, a founder of the Society for Constitutional Information in London, she gave thanks for the unfolding "full emancipation of all Europe from the shackles which . . . violence, ignorance and superstition had effected." As events unfolded in France in the summer of 1789, she applauded a new example in the course of liberty "unique in all the histories of human society."

All was well in the contemporary course of liberty for Macaulay until November 1790, when another student of history began to pontificate on the drift of history. Edmund Burke's *Reflections on the Revolution in France,* issued as a critique of British friends of liberty as well as of French revolutionaries, posed for Macaulay a great disturbance in the stream of liberty's progress. It assaulted her interpretation of English history and her version of the direction of events in France. The issue turned on who had the authority in 1688 in England or in 1789 in France to select government or to select or reject a monarch. Macaulay vociferously believed that both governments and kings were made and changed by a nation's people; Burke, however, stated that monarchs create states and establish succession.

Macaulay, ill and weak, forcefully responded to Burke's interruption of the world's festival of liberty. She issued a pamphlet titled *Observations on the Reflections of the Rt. Hon. Edmund Burke, on the Revolution in France,* just weeks after *Reflections* appeared. According to her, from the point of view of history, morality, necessity, and to bestow "the greatest possible happiness" on the people of France, the National Assembly had every right to supplant the powers of Louis XVI with a new constitution. Burke, she thought, had become a madman, overthrowing the natural rights of man established at such great cost. In Burke's system the rights of man would be "built on a beggarly foundation" and would depend on "the alms of our princes."[33]

Macaulay believed the French Revolution to be "an event, the most important to the dearest interests of mankind, the most singular in its nature, [and] the most astonishing in its means." And she was just as certain that it was Burke's intention "to rouse all nations and all descriptions of men against them [the French], and thus to crush in their ruin all the rights of man." Although Burke had disturbed the steady march onward, Macaulay died certain that history was on the side of liberty. Three months after her *Observations* appeared, Thomas Paine weighed in with his *Rights of Man.* Three days after her death, the National Assembly suspended Louis XVI's power. At that point, she might have begun to doubt, with Burke, where things were really going in France.

Catharine Macaulay was adjudged by men and women alike in her time as a prolific warrior for liberty and a remarkable human being. She seemed not to distinguish separate roles and rights for women, but worked in the interests of all human beings. But when the time came for women to consider their rights, she had a profound effect. She was a role model as historian and campaigner for liberty, but she also incorporated women as beings as authentic as their male counterparts. In her writings she struck resonant chords that perhaps would not have chimed as resplendently had she been a man. In November 1789, for example, Mary Wollstonecraft, author of *A Vindication of the Rights of Woman,* reviewed Macaulay's latest publication, *Letters on Education with Observations on Religious and Metaphysical Subjects.* Writing for an issue of the *Analytical Review,* Wollstonecraft praised the "masculine and fervid" style of *Letters.* Indeed, her only criticism fell on Macaulay's treatment of the education of debilitated women. "The observations of this subject," Wollstonecraft wrote, "might have been carried much further." Macaulay's words had a profound effect upon the much younger Wollstonecraft. On the verge of beginning her own campaign on behalf of liberty, she used Macaulay's analysis of the female mind in *Letters* to frame an entire section of her manifesto.[34]

Macaulay wrote that Alexander Pope was wrong when he asserted that "a perfect woman's but a softer man." To Macaulay this made as much sense as saying that "a perfect man is a woman formed after a coarser mold." Women, she argued, were debilitated and seemed lesser beings because of other forces: "These [seeming weaknesses] I firmly believe originate in situation and education only." By "situation" she meant the enslavement of women through the ages by men and the perpetual absence of either physical or mental education, which "must necessarily tend to corrupt and debilitate both the powers of mind and body." She continued that "this is so obvious a truth that the defects of female education have ever been a fruitful topic of declamation for the moralist; but not one of this class of writers have laid down any judicious rules for amendment."[35]

That last observation and Macaulay's conclusion, "Whilst we still retain the absurd notion of a sexual excellence, it will militate against the perfecting a plan of education for either sex," sent Wollstonecraft into a paroxysm of revolutionary thinking that led directly to *A Vindication of the Rights of Woman*. Launching into *Vindication* just three months after Macaulay's death, Wollstonecraft praised the woman whose role in British society she would assume for the duration of her brief life.[36]

Macaulay, like Catherine the Great, exhibited foibles that made her vulnerable to detractors after her death. She had followed a course that would be emulated in some respects by Wollstonecraft and which would similarly bedevil her reputation. It validated Wollstonecraft's comment in *Vindication* that "all heroes, as well as heroines, [are] exceptions to general rules."[37]

What plagued both of the women's lives, as it had also that of Catherine the Great, were their intimate relationships with men. No one in the era needed to know more about their private lives than, for example, the intimacies of Benjamin Franklin, Thomas Paine, or Joseph Priestley (whose personal lives were and still are mainly unknown). But when women began to emerge as independent players, they had to account for each intimacy. What was even more bothersome to them then and in histories written about them since are the frequent, none-too-subtle hints that whatever they achieved derived from the applications of their bodies and not their minds.

Macaulay's misfortune arose from the fact that the man whose surname she held died just six years after they married. Two volumes of her great *History* had been published and she was not about to quit her ambitious project. With the emergence of volume five in 1771, she entered into a decade of pursuing other interests socially and intellectually. During 1774 when she visited France, she spent as much time making social rounds as learning about France. Also that year, Dr. Thomas Wilson, nonresident rector of a church in London, persuaded her to move into his house in Bath, where she would have ready access to his offices and considerable private library.

Over the next four years Macaulay experienced the most joyful period of her life. She socialized and again toured France. She also wrote *A Modest Plea for the Property of Copyright* (1774); *Address to the People of England and Ireland* (1775); and, the most curious, *The History of England from the Revolution to the Present Time in a Series of Letters to a Friend* (1778). This last book was dedicated to none other than the Rev. Dr. Wilson. The older and widowed clergyman had not only taken Macaulay into his home, he had also taken possession of her mind and spirit. In the beginning it was a godsend for a woman whose family, except a somewhat cool brother, had died.[38]

There was no evident public complaint about their living arrangement. A reviewer of her new *History* recognized "the mutual sympathy so conspicuous between these Platonic lovers." Yet Wilson's adulation of Macaulay soon became clear to everyone. In honor of her forty-sixth birthday on September 8, 1777, Wilson placed a white marble statue of her inside the altar rail of his church, St. Stephens, Walbrook. Sculpted by John Francis Moore and titled "History," Macaulay was represented with a pen in her right hand and volumes of her great work under her left arm. Next to the statue, Wilson built a vault that would someday contain her remains.[39]

Wilson's worshipful recognition seemed a very odd act of devotion to a living figure not in any way connected with St. Stephens or with religion in general. For Macaulay it was final proof of her imprisonment by a doting lover. Wilson described Alfred House, whose title he also transferred fully to Macaulay, as "our little Tusculum which is honoured with the visits of all the Literary Persons who frequent this place; and foreigners particularly, for she is known and admired abroad more than at home." To another he referred to "the great Mrs. Macaulay—I talk of her to everybody in raptures." To a third he described her as "my great woman—the first woman in Europe for Virtues and Shining Literary Abilities."[40]

By 1777 she was caught in a snare that she would later describe as the enslavement of woman by man. After months of ever increasing control by Wilson she fled to France, spending much-needed time away from her unwanted possessor. Although she returned during 1778, her determination to restore her own liberty had been established. Her method of escape was published in *Gentleman's Magazine* on December 17, 1778, in the marriage notes: "The celebrated historian Mrs. Macaulay, to the younger brother of Dr. Graham."[41]

Macaulay declared her independence from both controller and accepted social convention. She married a man whose older brother, James Graham, was known as a "quack" doctor who used electricity, milk baths, and friction to treat his patients. William Graham brought neither fortune nor an occupation worthy of the name: a surgeon's mate. Worse, her husband was age twenty-one, she forty-seven. Questionable morals! Macaulay's act of rebellion revised the way she would be viewed by her contemporaries and in the annals of history.

Her former possessor launched a campaign of vilification that followed her for the rest of her life. Wilson bellowed, "To the great surprise of the world, Mrs. Macaulay without giving me the slightest notice at the age of 52 married a YOUNG SCOTCH LOON of 21 whom she had not seen for above a month before the fatal knot was tied." He removed her nameplate from the door and forbade her any use of Alfred House, although she legally owned it. He next sold the burial vault in his church. Finally, he removed the statue of "History" from St.

Stephens, putting it away from view until it would one day be placed outside the public library at Warrington.

But the good Dr. Wilson received plenty of help in rewriting the history of Catharine Macaulay. John Wilkes, who at the time was feuding with Macaulay over British policy toward America, amply exploited the situation. Visiting the distraught Wilson, Wilkes urged Wilson to read him Macaulay's "long letter" about her departure. Wilkes reported that the letter contained "every variety of style, it is indecent, insolent, mean, fawning, threatening, coaxing, menacing, and declamatory." "Such words," he continued, "I believe never escaped a female pen." Wilkes supported Wilson's intention to publish this and other letters he had received from Macaulay.

A storm ensued. One pamphlet titled *A Remarkable Moving Letter* purported to include the text of Macaulay's letter to Wilson. *The Female Patriot* contained another fictional letter. The first of these assumed that Macaulay left Wilson for Graham to achieve sexual fulfillment:

> Hadst thou possess'd (shame checks my falt'ring pen)
> The pow'rs that Heav'n allots to younger men,
> My frailer nature had not dar'd to rove,
> But politics had paved the road of love.

All of the scurrilous pieces, including one titled *The Bridal Ode,* assumed that her infatuation with a young husband would end her career as historian:

> Farewell the plumed Pen and Ink!
> Which made Taxation's Champion shrink;
> Here faithful Hist'ry ends.

In a play presented in July 1779, *A Widow—No Widow,* Wilson proclaimed, "She wanted to turn me out of my own house . . . she never thought of any thing but the Revolution."

Whispers about Macaulay followed her until her dying day, but she boldly maintained her devotion to liberty. In 1781 she produced two volumes of her great *History.* Despite the fact that Horace Walpole that year quipped "I believe England will be finished before her *History,*" she published the eighth and final volume in 1783. And despite widespread rumors that she and her youthful husband would not long remain married, they never left each other's side. If anyone deserved liberation from the indictment of flawed judgment, it would be Catharine Macaulay.[42]

LIBERTY'S WITNESS

Catharine Macaulay's passion for liberty and history was infectious. One of the people she inspired was Mercy Otis Warren, an American original fully of the stature of Catherine the Great, Suzanne Necker, and Catharine Macaulay. In a growing nation where there were no czarinas, little in the nature of salons, and no tradition of women historians, her enthusiastic chronicling of liberty's progress

Mercy Otis Warren (c. 1790). Chronicler of the American Revolution, she was also the first reporter of the counterrevolution.

reflected the inspiration of illustrious women contemporaries as well as her own pursuit of liberty.

For example, when John Adams, with whom Warren had a lifetime friendship and stormy literary relationship, offered a negative interpretation of Catharine Macaulay's second marriage, Warren fired back that Macaulay's "independency of spirit led her to suppose she might associate for the remainder of her life, with an inoffensive, obliging youth, with the same impunity a Gentleman of three score and ten might marry a Damsel of fifteen!" The world would benefit from Warren's candor in a career that extended two decades longer than her three renowned contemporaries.

During the summer of 1789 Mercy Warren collected a host of her poems, many previously published anonymously, and two plays never before published to form a 252-page book titled *Poems, Dramatic and Miscellaneous.* Published early in 1790, the book joined a wealth of manifestos appearing right and left. Among the first books in America published under the name of a woman, it grappled with the issues of liberty and the role of women in America.[43]

Warren dedicated her work "To George Washington, President of the United States of America." She wrote, "I only ask the illustrious Washington to permit a lady of his acquaintance, to introduce to the public, under his patronage, a small volume," mainly written during the American Revolution "when every active member of society was engaged, either in the field, or the cabinet, to resist the strong hand of foreign domination." Foregoing adulatory titles for Washington, she praised the "one who has united all hearts in the field of conquest, in the lap of peace, and at the head of the government of the United States."

She used the occasion to announce that she was engaged in preparing a detailed history of America's inspiring revolution. She had maintained "a faithful record . . . of the most material transactions, through a period that has engaged the attention, both of the philosopher and the politician"; and "if life is spared, a just trait of the most distinguished characters, either for valour, virtue, or patriotism; for perfidy, intrigue, inconsistency, or ingratitude, shall be faithfully transmitted to posterity." She did not promise when it would be delivered to the public, but she emphasized that the season of liberty that was upon the world was the best moment to reflect on America's example.[44]

Warren's bold step onto the public stage was dramatic and revolutionary indeed. It was not just that she easily found a publisher; it was rather that she spoke on equal terms with men. In *Poems, Dramatic and Miscellaneous* she revealed herself as the anonymous author of some of the most stirring poems of the Revolutionary era. While she did not include in the volume five plays she had published at critical moments between 1773 and 1779, she brought forth two new plays that daringly addressed the issues of the day.[45]

Born in Barnstable, Massachusetts, into a family that appreciated the value of learning but not of scholarship, Mercy Otis was encouraged to read, but also taught to embroider, knit, and maintain a household. Sister of James Otis, she grew up alongside the contentious patriot who brilliantly argued the demerits of the Stamp Act. What was true for James showed itself in Mercy's career and emerged yet again in the life of her embattled Federalist nephew, Harrison Gray Otis.[46]

Mercy Otis read her brother's books, sat in on his tutoring sessions with her uncle Jonathan Russell, a Harvard-trained clergyman, and took readings from James after he matriculated at Harvard. In 1754 she married merchant and farmer James Warren of Plymouth, Massachusetts. While her husband pursued his successful business career and began to serve various public capacities in Plymouth and the Massachusetts General Court, Mercy Warren pursued her intellectual interests. Not only was she stimulated by the socially and politically active Otis and Warren clans, she also befriended Abigail and John Adams. As early as 1764 John Adams was regularly visiting the Warren home and seeking the counsel of both Warrens as he grappled with history, politics, and government. From 1764 until Warren's death in 1814, she and John Adams exchanged letters, visits, and disputations in one of the richest intellectual relationships in American history.[47]

Indeed, it was about the moment John Adams and Mercy Warren met that she began her transformation from wife, mother, and closet intellectual to an open commentator. Her inspiration was none other than Catharine Macaulay, who had sent James Otis an inscribed copy of the first volume of *History of England.* "To you, Sir," Macaulay wrote, "as one of the most distinguished of the great guardians of American Liberty, I offer a copy of this book." She also wrote to John Adams and formed another literary connection, but one that would not continue beyond her marriage to William Graham. At the time, though, Adams gloried in Macaulay's historical writings, saying that she stripped off the "Gilden and false Lustre from the worthless Princes and Nobles" of England. In his judgment she was "one of the brightest ornaments not only of her Sex but of her Age."[48]

In 1773 Mercy Warren was ready to follow Macaulay's example. She wrote Macaulay, with John Adams's encouragement, to ask a revealing question: "Has the genius of Liberty," as historically charted by Macaulay, "forsaken that devoted Island [Britain]? What fatal infatuation has seized the parent state?" This poignant question opened up a warm and frequent correspondence between the two that ceased only with Macaulay's death.[49]

Behind that question lay a fundamental decision already reached by Mercy Warren. She would be to America what Macaulay was to Britain. She had already delved deeply into the subject with the publication in 1773 of a drama, *The Adulateur,* a thinly veiled story of the raging battle between colonists and the royal governor in Massachusetts. The play, written in poetic form, was filled with speeches by Brutus (representing James Otis) condemning the royal governor and Britain. *The Defeat,* another drama never totally finished, followed in July 1773. In the existing excerpts from this play, Warren has Rapatio (Gov. Thomas Hutchinson) reveal the corruption of his government in his own monologues.[50]

Her third, *The Group,* was published in 1775 in Boston, Philadelphia, and New York editions. Warren continued the device of having British officials make self-condemning speeches, revealing the viciousness of their motives and acts. The sole patriot in the play—a woman—renders a summary speech. The fourth play, *The Blockheads: or, the Affrighted Officers,* appeared in 1776 as a response to another play, *The Blockade of Boston,* written by British General John Burgoyne to satirize American rebels. A more complicated play, the same protagonists and antagonists continue their open argument about why they are fighting the war. *The Motley Assembly,* the fifth, appeared in 1779, and concentrated almost entirely on whether the women of Boston should overthrow British habits in support of a more unique American society.[51]

These dramatic offerings, never intended to be staged, enunciated revolutionary rhetoric. By publishing them anonymously, Warren was able to preach rebellion as well as introduce women to the stage of world history. She prepared the way for real women to make authentic speeches in an American setting. Her authorship was known, of course, among the privileged few who knew her, and that was all that seemed necessary at the time.[52]

Her poems, meanwhile, blended with those poured forth by Revolutionary poets such as Philip Freneau and Hugh Henry Brackenridge. Her lines were almost indistinguishable from theirs as witnessed by the following from "A Political Reverie" (1774):

> I look with rapture at the distant dawn,
> And view the glories of the opening morn,
> When justice holds his sceptre o'er the land,
> And rescues freedom from a tyrant's hand.

And these from "The Squabble of the Sea Nymphs" in honor of the Boston Tea Party:

> The virtuous daughters of the neighb'ring mead,
> In graceful smiles approv'd the glorious deed; . . .
> They saw delighted from the inland rocks,
> O'er the broad deep pour'd out Pandora's box.

Or after a battle in "To Fidelio" (1776): "May guilty traitors satiate the grave, / But let the sword forever—spare the brave."[53]

Warren was perhaps further emboldened to pursue liberty through Catharine Macaulay's yearlong sojourn in the United States. Although no longer a heroine in England due to her marriage and strong political opposition, Macaulay was a renowned virtuoso in America. Her strong endorsement of American rights during the Revolution was well remembered and opened doors for her everywhere she went. In 1785 she traveled to New Haven, visiting with Yale president Ezra Stiles, one of her life-long correspondents. Thence she proceeded to New York and Philadelphia, acclaimed in every quarter. Finally, she spent ten days with George and Martha Washington at Mount Vernon glorying over the success and promise of the American Revolution. The gratified Washington bespoke his pleasure afterward of spending days with "a Lady . . . whose principles are so much and so justly admired by the friends of liberty and mankind."[54]

Macaulay also spent long and satisfying days conversing with Warren at her home in Milton, Massachusetts. To her son Winslow, Warren proclaimed the glad tidings, "The celebrated Mrs. Macaulay-Graham is with us. She is a lady whose resources of knowledge seem to be inexhaustible." Although Warren admitted to Winslow that Macaulay's marriage was not consistent with "the superiority of her genius," she found young Graham to be "a man of understanding and virtue," and she acknowledged that "I fear the world will not readily forgive." Macaulay soon sought Warren's assistance in compiling materials for a history of the American Revolution she hoped someday to write.[55]

Macaulay's visit steeled Warren to new purpose. During 1784 and 1785 she wrote the two dramas that would be published in 1790. *The Sack of Rome,* influenced by Gibbon's *The History of the Decline and Fall of Rome,* centered on the preciousness of liberty. Just as Gibbon lay the destruction of Rome on corruption and vice in the Roman body politic, Warren used the teetering ancient republic "to throw a mite into the scale of virtue." Her purpose was to use the dramatic form to instruct citizens of the world's newest republic: "In an age of taste and refinement, lessons of morality, and the consequences of deviation, may perhaps, be as successfully enforced from the stage, as by modes of instruction, less censured by the severe." Warren's characters spoke to the destruction that derived from corruption, violence, deception. The only hope was exhibited in the demeanor of Eudoxia, virtuous widow of Emperor Valentinian, and Eudocia her daughter.[56]

The Ladies of Castile was much the same. Dedicated to son Winslow, she explained to him in a prefatory letter that she "wished" only to cultivate the sentiments of public and private virtue in whatsoever falls from her pen." She believed that the story of Charles V of Spain and the "tyranny of his successors" would "ever be interesting to an American ear, so long as they [Americans] triumph in their independence, pride themselves in the principles that instigated their patriots and glory in the characters of their heroes whose valour completed a revolution that will be the wonder of ages." Portraying the duplicity of men vying for both power and women, Warren saw the hope for freedom in the hands of an indomitable woman, Donna Maria, who withstood the taunts and threats of Castile's despotic ruler, Don Velasco. In Warren's mind, liberty's best hope in America and the world was vested in strong and wise women.[57]

Even though women played an important role in Warren's literary works, she never wavered from her main interest. To one correspondent she wrote, "I think I feel no partiality on the Female Side but what arises from a love of Justice, & freely acknowledge we too often give occasion . . . for Reflections of this Nature." Indeed, she affirmed,

> I believe it will be found that the Deficiency [between men and women] lies not so much in the Inferior Contexture of Female Intellects as in the different Education bestow'd on the Sexes, for when the Cultivation of the Mind is neglected in Either, we see Ignorance, Stupidity, & Ferocity of Manners equally Conspicuous in both.

Although some might have looked toward her for leadership in securing rights for women, she accepted as given "the Appointed Subordination" of women to men—"perhaps for the sake of Order in Families." But still, she called to all women, "let us by no Means Acknowledge such an Inferiority as would Check the Ardour of our Endeavours to equal in all Accomplishments the most masculine Heights." The distinctions between men and women she believed were temporary and artificial, and both sexes were "equally qualified to taste the full Draughts of Knowledge & Happiness prepared for the Upright of every Nation & Sex."[58]

Her focus was clearly on the rights of citizens. When the new constitution for the United States was completed, Mercy Warren castigated its drafters unmercifully because it did not include a bill of rights. In a didactic pamphlet titled

Observations on the New Constitution and on the Federal and State Constitutions (1788), she lambasted Federalist tendencies to seek "the consolidation of a strong government on any or on new principles . . . at the risk of distorting the fairest features in the political face of America." And when she learned from Catharine Macaulay that John Adams was speaking in support of an even stronger national government, she became an anti-Federalist guerrilla, bedeviling Adams's every step as diplomat, vice president, president, and elder statesman.[59]

Nor was it America alone that concerned Warren. She saw the French Revolution as a fulfillment of the bright hope of the American Revolution. This struggle for the rights of man was, she thought, "a clear revelation of the will of God." So disturbed was she with Edmund Burke's *Reflections on the Revolution in France* that she arranged for the publication of an American edition of Catharine Macaulay's rebuttal, *Observations on the Reflections of the Rt. Hon. Edmund Burke, on the Revolution in France.* Warren added her own preface to the edition, and in it affirmed her hopes for liberty:

> Whatever convulsions may yet be occasioned by the revolution in France, it will doubtless be favorable to general liberty, and Mr. Burke may undesignedly be an instrument of its promotion, by agitating questions which have for a time lain dormant in England and have been almost forgotten, or artfully disguised in America.

Bringing out Macaulay's last tract confirmed Warren's identification with the great historian of England's progress toward freedom.[60]

Inspired by the tenor of Macaulay's *History of England,* Warren's *History of the Rise, Progress, and Termination of the American Revolution (1805),* instantly became one of the world's great testaments to liberty. Its subtitle, "Interspersed with Biographical, Political and Moral Observations," hinted at the deuteronomistic quality of the work.[61]

Warren's *History of the American Revolution* was a stern assessment of the devotion of human beings to the progress of freedom. According to her, human actions were black or white. Despite the muddle of foreign diplomacy, ruined economies, starving armies, and civil strife, American right and goodness were certain. American soldiers fought with righteous spirit; British troops harassed and raped women and children. In the end America won its revolution as the first great act of a world revolution to bring liberty to all peoples.[62]

Even though Warren's *History of the American Revolution* was not published until 1805, her purpose remained little changed from her earlier poems and plays. Stirring descriptions of social and political events, the movement of armies, and the character of America's revolutionary leaders filled thirteen hundred pages. And since she was "connected by nature, friendship, and every social tie, with many of the first patriots, and most influential characters on the continent" and had maintained "epistolary intercourse with several gentlemen employed abroad in the most distinguished stations," her history was a faithful eyewitness account of the Revolution. She omitted only the descriptions of "the blood-stained field" and "of slaughtered armies." Since men were the ones who spilled and lost blood, she left the responsibility of describing those acts to them.[63]

Through her plays, poems, and history, Warren bore witness to the power of the American Revolution. At the same time, she established an American role model for women who wished to establish their independence. Alongside Catherine the Great, Suzanne Necker, and Catharine Macaulay, she inspired rising generations of women to seek the fruits of liberty promised by the American Revolution.

CHAPTER 6

Phillis Wheatley and African Liberty

On June 27, 1773, twenty-year-old Phillis Wheatley—an African-born American slave—wrote an amazing letter to Selina Hastings, the countess of Huntingdon: "It is with pleasure, I acquaint your Ladyship of my safe arrival in London after a fine passage of 5 weeks in the Ship London with my young master." She continued, "I should think myself very happy in seeing your Ladyship." Thus began what was planned to be a whirlwind visit in London where Phillis Wheatley, accompanied by Nathaniel Wheatley, son of her slave masters John and Susannah Wheatley, would be wined, dined, and honored in the best society. Although she did not meet with the countess of Huntingdon, the lord Mayor of London presented her a copy of Milton's *Paradise Lost,* and she achieved the publication of her book *Poems on Various Subjects, Religious and Moral,* dedicated to Selina Hastings.

Wheatley suddenly was becoming, amidst the swirling torrents of revolution, the most celebrated African in the English-speaking world, a symbol of the incredible potential of blacks, slave or free, if only they were given access to education and freedom to create. Eighteen prominent Bostonians, including Royal governor Thomas Hutchinson, governor-to-be James Bowdoin, and renowned John Hancock, praised her skills in *Poems.* "We, whose names are under-written," they stated, "do assure the World, that the Poems specified . . . were, (as we verily believe) written by Phillis, a young Negro Girl, who was but a few years since, brought an uncultivated barbarian, from Africa."[1]

A separate note under the name of "Mr. John Wheatley, her master," provided some background:

> Phillis was brought from Africa to America in the Year 1761, between seven and eight years of Age. Without any Assistance from School education, and by only what she was taught in the Family, she, in sixteen Months Time . . . attained the English Language, to which she was an utter stranger before, to such a degree as to read any, the most difficult Parts of the Sacred Writings, to the great astonishment of all who heard her.

Within four years of her arrival, she was writing informed letters on colonial policy and was engaged in learning Latin. After nine years in America, she was ready to proclaim the wonders of the Christian gospel in what she titled "An Elegiac Poem, on the Death of that Celebrated Divine, and Eminent Servant of Jesus Christ, the Late Reverend and Pious George Whitefield, Chaplain to the Right Honourable the Countess of Huntingdon" (1770). Published as a broadside in Boston and reprinted in Newport, Philadelphia, New York, and London, the poem was the first published by an African woman in the English language.[2]

"Hail happy Saint on thy immortal throne!" she began her paean. "We hear no more the music of thy tongue, / Thy wonted auditories cease to throng," she continued. She praised the great evangelizer for his kind gestures toward America: "He long'd to see America excell; / He charg'd its youth to let the grace divine / Arise, and in their future actions shine." She mightily approved Whitefield's appeal to Africans. "Take HIM [Jesus] ye Africans," Wheatley proclaimed, "he longs for you; / Impartial SAVIOUR, is his title due." Concluding with condolences to the countess of Huntingdon, Wheatley wrote, "Great COUNTESS! we Americans revere / Thy name, and thus condole thy grief sincere: / We mourn with thee, that TOMB obscurely plac'd, / In which thy Chaplain undisturb'd doth rest." Wheatley openly alluded to the disparity in life's treatment accorded to white and black Americans, praising Whitefield's promotion of education for blacks.[3]

Her allusions to the plight of blacks became more direct in her next poem, included in a letter of October 10, 1772, to William Legge, the second earl of Dartmouth, who had just been appointed British colonial secretary. Addressing Dartmouth College's namesake, Wheatley revealed her traumatic introduction to American slavery even as she urged Dartmouth and King George III to protect American freedoms. Describing for Dartmouth "from whence my love of Freedom sprung," she wrote

> I, young in life, by seeming cruel fate
> Was snatched from Africa's fancied happy seat:
> What pangs excruciating must molest,
> What sorrows labour in my parent's breast!
> Steeled was that soul, and by no misery moved,
> That from a father seized his babe beloved:
> Such, such my case. And can I then but pray
> Others may never feel tyrannic sway?

Dartmouth was in the inner circles of the countess of Huntingdon and was strongly attached to British Methodists, and Wheatley's almost sentimental description of the crime perpetrated upon her won religious hearts throughout the world.

It also won an invitation for the twenty-year-old African poet to visit England. Susannah Wheatley wrote ahead to the countess about the visit, "I tell Phillis to act wholly under the direction of your Ladiship." Explaining that the timing of the invitation was such that she would be unable to properly clothe

Phillis Wheatley (1773). America's celebrated colonial slave poet became a forgotten casualty of American freedom.

Phillis Wheatley, Mrs. Wheatley bade the Countess to let the poet use ample funds sent along for the purpose "to Buy what you think most proper for her." But making clear that her dress should not be lavish, she commented, "I like she should be dressed plain." The excited Wheatley used the occasion to write another poem, which she titled "A Farewell to America."

Arriving in London, Wheatley confided to her one black friend back in America that she found many friends "there among the Nobility and Gentry." She continued, "Their Benevolent conduct towards me, the unexpected and unmerited civility and Complaisance with which I was treated by all, fills me with astonishment, I can scarcely Realize it." With the publication of her *Poems* in London, Phillis Wheatley's happiness was at its peak.[4]

But even as Wheatley achieved international recognition, her struggle to achieve freedom and equality was just beginning. Until her arrival in England, she remained the slave, tool, and ornament of owners using her to flaunt their own importance, to add lucre to their own purses, and to present her as a sideshow curiosity.

It was during the course of her triumphal visit to London that the nullity of her freedom began to loom over her life. During a visit with none other than Benjamin Franklin, Phillis Wheatley's fragile connection to freedom became all too clear. In response to an appeal from his Boston cousin, Jonathan Williams, Sr., Franklin paid a visit to "the black Poetess" on July 7, 1773. According to Franklin, he "offer'd her any Services I could do her." But, as he described the situation, "Before I left the House, I understood her Master was there and had sent her to me but did not come into the Room himself, and I thought was not pleased with the Visit. I should have enquired first for him; but I had heard nothing of him. And I have heard nothing since of her." The meeting of statesman and poet was so awkward that Williams soon apologized for suggesting the encounter. "The Black Poetess master and mistress prevailed on me to mention her in my Letter," he wrote, "but as its turned out I am Sorry I Did."[5]

Except for some inquiry into the life of Franklin, this encounter would be wholly inscrutable. Although he was a slaveholder at the time and continued to own slaves until 1781, Franklin by 1773 was feeling quite conflicted on the subject of slavery. Both Franklin and his son William brought slaves with them to England in 1757. A year later, William's slave, King, ran away and was learned by Franklin to be in the "Service of a Lady that was very fond of the Merit of making him a Christian and contributing to his Education and Improvement." Of the elder Franklin's slave, Peter, Franklin complained that the slave "behaves as well as I can expect in a Country where there are many Occasions of spoiling Servants, if they are ever so good." But before Franklin's passage back to America in 1762, Peter, too, had dropped out of sight.

Until the early 1770s Franklin sounded very much like any other American, slaveholder or not. In his *Observations Concerning the Increase of Mankind,* he worried about the number of slaves in America, mainly because he believed their service tended to make whites lazy. But with the growth of a large, untutored black society in America, Franklin, in 1757, became involved with the Dr. Bray's Associates in promoting education among blacks in the colonies. With his assistance, schools were opened in Philadelphia, Williamsburg, New York, and Newport. But as late as 1770, despite the rise of Quaker opposition to slavery, Franklin was still orthodox on the subject. In his essay *Conversation on Slavery* (1770) he minimized its evils while attacking the British for overpopulating America with Africans.[6]

In 1772 Franklin and many others in America began to look askance at both the slave trade and slavery. The fervent appeals of Philadelphia Quaker Anthony Benezet in 1772 to end the slave trade sensitized Franklin to the subject. The famous Somerset Case, which brought an end to slavery in Britain, also drove Franklin to rethink his position. In response to a long struggle by British abolitionist Granville Sharp to outlaw slavery in England, High Justice Lord Mansfield freed James Somerset, a runaway slave who was on the verge of being shipped back to bondage in Jamaica.[7]

That the Somerset case attracted his attention was clear from an anonymous editorial Franklin wrote for *The London Chronicle* in June 1772. Lamenting that the decision did not extend "to the procuring liberty for those that remain in our

Colonies," Franklin urged some action "at least to obtain a law for abolishing the African commerce in Slaves, and declaring the children of present Slaves free after they become of age." He found the decision to be somewhat hollow and capricious, in that it only affected slaves who would come to England:

> Pharisaical Britain! to pride thyself in setting free a single Slave that happens to land on thy coasts, while thy Merchants in all thy ports are encouraged by thy laws to continue a commerce whereby so many hundreds of thousands are dragged into a slavery that can scarce be said to end with their lives, since it is entailed on their posterity!

Here was Franklin's new public voice on slavery, though on a personal and practical level he seemed always reluctant to ruffle feathers.[8]

Nathaniel Wheatley, the young master traveling with the slave poet, did not know this noncombative side of Franklin. Although he had been doing business with both Franklin and Williams for two years prior to the strange meeting, young Wheatley did not trust Franklin.[9]

Apprised of the Somerset Case and of Franklin's advocacy of freeing more slaves both in Britain and in America, Nathaniel Wheatley assumed that Franklin's purpose in meeting with Phillis Wheatley was to advise her of her rights. Technically all she had to do was to object to being taken back to America—and she would have become instantly free. And just as Granville Sharp was making himself the humanitarian of the century by securing the rights of Africans, Nathaniel Wheatley concluded that Franklin was on a mission to do the same for Phillis Wheatley. Despite Wheatley's worst fears, such a scenario apparently was not Franklin's purpose; or, if it was, his advice had fallen on deaf ears.[10]

Given Phillis Wheatley's grasp of current affairs in politics, law, war, and society, she could not have missed the meaning of the Somerset case and how it could have applied to her situation. Even if Benjamin Franklin did not discuss the implications of the Somerset Case with her, surely others—white and black—did. This matter assuredly would have arisen if she had remained long enough to fulfill her primary goal of meeting with the countess of Huntingdon.

But none of this was to be. Nathaniel Wheatley, fearful of losing his family's greatest treasure, scheduled a hasty departure back to America less than twenty days after their arrival in London. In a painful letter written by Phillis Wheatley to the countess of Huntingdon on July 17, 1773, she explained:

> I rec'd with mixed sensations of pleasure & disappointment your Ladiship's message . . . acquainting us with your pleasure that my Master & I should wait upon you in So. Wales . . . Am sorry to acquaint your Ladiship that the Ship is certainly to Sail next Thursday which I must return to America. I long to see my Friend there. [But I am] extremely reluctant to go without having first seen your Ladiship. . . .

Her ship sailed on July 22, ending an aborted tour that perhaps—had it continued longer—would have made Phillis Wheatley famous for much more than her poetry.[11]

As brief as was Phillis Wheatley's foray to England, the fulsome ambiguities of her existence were yet to be fully revealed. Indeed, back in America, despite the death of her mistress Susannah Wheatley in March 1774, Phillis Wheatley marched on to new triumphs. The Boston *Gazette* on January 24, 1774, announced the arrival from London of an abundant supply of her *Poems on Various Subjects—Religious and Moral.* The book sold well, and she went about promoting it. She even received another shipment of three hundred copies on May 6, 1774, just weeks before Parliament moved to close the port of Boston in retaliation for the recent Tea Party, rupturing virtually all ties between Boston and London.[12]

Phillis Wheatley bravely vied to make herself poet of the war for American liberty. She cheered on American sailors in a poem of December 1774, titled "To a Gentleman of the Navy," published in the *Royal American Magazine,* and in a sequel published in January 1775. As George Washington began assembling an army in the summer and fall of 1775, she penned one of the earliest poetic tributes "To His Excellency General Washington." Although it was not published for some months, it praised the American cause. It was "freedom's cause her [Columbia's] anxious breast alarms," she wrote. "We demand / The grace and glory of thy martial band," she wrote to Washington, as he led the charges against "whoever dares disgrace / The land of freedom's heaven-defended race!" Ending the forty-two-line poem with a military flourish, she proclaimed: "Proceed, great chief, with virtue on thy side, / Thy ev'ry action let the Goddess guide. / A crown, a mansion, and a throne that shine, / With gold unfading, WASHINGTON! be thine."[13]

Wheatley sent the poem with an equally stirring letter to Washington at his headquarters at Cambridge, Massachusetts. Writing from Providence, where the Wheatleys had repaired during the British siege of Boston, she explained:

> I have taken the freedom to address your Excellency in the enclosed poem, and entreat your acceptance. . . . Your being appointed by the Grand Continental Congress to be the Generalissimo of the Armies of North America, together with the fame of your virtues, excite sensations not easy to suppress. . . . Wishing your Excellency all possible success in the great cause you are so generously engaged in, I am,
>
> Your Excellency's most obedient and humble servant,
>
> Phillis Wheatley

Just as in the case of her poems on the death of George Whitefield and on the elevation of Lord Dartmouth, the slave poet was intimately attuned to the expanding pulse for liberty.

Her poem to George Washington landed like an arrow to the hero's passionate heart. Although he did not actually receive the poem until the middle of

December, he was overwhelmed by both it and the letter. In a private note to his secretary almost two months later, Washington wrote, "At first, with a view to doing justice to her great poetical genius, I had a great mind to publish the poem; but not knowing whether it might not be considered rather as a mark of my own vanity, than as a compliment to her, I laid it aside, till I came across it again." A few weeks later, he also wrote a letter of apology to Wheatley expressing the same sentiments and thanking her "for your polite notice of me in the elegant lines you enclosed." He testified that "the style and manner exhibit a striking proof of your poetical talents."

Washington, perhaps feeling that he had been somewhat remiss both in his tardy reply and in choosing not to publish the poem, ended his letter with a most unusual note: "If you should ever come to Cambridge, or near head-quarters, I shall be happy to see a person so favored by the Muses, and to whom nature has been so beneficent in her dispensations. I am with great respect, your obedient and humble servant." The open invitation to come to Cambridge resulted in an immediate response on Wheatley's part. She raced to Cambridge in March 1776—three months before the Declaration of Independence—to pay tribute to America's as yet unproved military hero.[14]

He, the owner of hundreds of slaves and with a title conferred making him the highest-ranking American, and she, the owner of hundreds of words and still herself owned, met as equals just as the battle for liberty was to ensue. An observer in the camp wrote, "I cannot refrain . . . from noticing the visit of one, who, though a dark child from Africa and a bondwoman, received the most polite attention of the Commander-in-Chief. . . . She passed half an hour with the Commander-in-Chief, from whom and his officers, she received marked attention." In April, Wheatley's paean to Washington appeared in Thomas Paine's *Pennsylvania Magazine,* elevating the polite warrior to his status as father of the nation.[15]

Phillis Wheatley, perverse as it would seem, achieved the pinnacle of her liberty as a wholly owned and privately subsidized artist. The war she praised totally disrupted her existence. Transformed from slave to free black, she incurred a new bondage more constraining than she had ever known before.

First came dislocation. The Wheatleys—father, daughter, and slave poet— were driven by British occupation from Boston to Providence in 1775. By the time of her visit to Washington the following spring, they had moved to Chelsea, Massachusetts. When the British returned in 1778, Phillis Wheatley fled by herself as a suddenly free woman to Wilmington, Massachusetts. On May 29, 1778, she wrote a cryptic letter to her black friend, Obour Tanner, as follows:

> The vast variety of scenes that have pass'd before us these 3 years past will to a reasonable mind serve to convince us of the uncertain duration of all things temporal, and the proper result of such a consideration is an ardent desire of, & preparation

for, a state and enjoyments which are more suitable to the immortal mind.

She had suddenly been set free. Her master, John Wheatley, died in March 1778. Soon followed the death of Mary Wheatley, the daughter she had been purchased to attend. With Nathaniel Wheatley, a declared Loyalist, permanently away in England, Phillis Wheatley became a free agent ready to enjoy all of the fruits of liberty. She would no longer have to serve a human master, no longer have to hold back her views on the real evils of slavery; she would never more be characterized as a "slave poetess."[16]

Phillis Wheatley paused not an instant in determining how she would exercise her new freedom. On April 1, 1778—days after the death of John Wheatley—she married John Peters, a free black acquaintance of at least four years' duration. Peters's great attraction was that he was one of the great impostors of the age. Posturing from time to time as grocer, baker, barber, lawyer, and even physician, the flamboyant Peters plausibly played almost any role he chose, including consort to America's most famous black woman.[17]

Peters turned out to be perhaps the worst choice freedom could bring. Obour Tanner did not approve of Peters either before or after the marriage. Within a year of the union, the celebrated poet had left Peters to his schemes in Wilmington, Massachusetts, and had returned penniless to Boston, where she found temporary shelter with a niece of her former mistress. In the interim she had given birth to a first child, who did not survive. Despite all, she signed her name no longer as Wheatley—that slave epitaph—but rather as her freely-chosen married title, Phillis Peters.

Although nearly destitute, Phillis Peters still had her nimble mind. She had the Muses in her head and a limber pen ready to translate music into words. By the fall of 1779 she was ready to publish an entirely new book of poetry that would bring her badly needed financial support. Six notices of the ambitious project appeared in the Boston *Evening Post and General Advertiser* between October 30 and December 18: "Proposals, for printing by subscription a volume of Poems & Letters on various subjects, dedicated to the Right Hon. Benjamin Franklin Esq: One of the Ambassadors of the United States at the Court of France, By Phillis Peters." Benjamin Franklin would serve the same role as had George Whitefield, Lord Dartmouth, the countess of Huntingdon, and George Washington as the venerated object and sponsor of this new project, described to be three hundred pages long with thirty-two new poems.[18]

Despite all her intense efforts, however, the needed subscribers did not come forward. For five years Peters wrote on, still addressing her poems to the renowned figures of the day—the countess of Huntingdon, Benjamin Franklin, Benjamin Rush, and popular Bostonian Dr. Samuel Cooper, but she found no publisher. Another child, a boy, was born; he, too, died in infancy. John Peters was nowhere to be found, and she resigned herself to cleaning rooms in a boarding-house for destitute free blacks.

Not until January 1784 did she again appear in print. Her elegy on the life and death of Samuel Cooper was published in a thin pamphlet, and in September that year *The Boston Magazine* published a heartfelt poem to a Boston couple whose infant son had died. Finally, in December, came *Liberty and Peace.* In it she extolled the results of victory:

> Descending <u>Peace</u> and Power of War confounds;
> From every Tongue celestial <u>Peace</u> resounds:
> As for the east th' illustrious King of Day,
> With rising Radiance drives the Shades away,
> So Freedom comes array'd with Charms divine,
> And in her Train Commerce and Plenty shine.

But this new publication came too late to save Phillis Wheatley-Peters. By the time *Liberty and Peace* appeared, there appeared another notice in the Boston *Independent Chronicle:*

> Last Lord's Day, died Mrs. Phillis Peters (formerly Phillis Wheatley), aged thirty-one, known to the world by her celebrated miscellaneous poems. Her funeral is to be this afternoon, at four o'clock, from the house lately improved by Mr. Todd . . . where her friends and acquaintances are desired to attend.

Nothing in this notice hinted at the circumstances of her death. She had died alone, too weak to keep up her chores at the boarding house, too frail to suckle her third infant child, who died soon after.

Nowhere to be found were the patrons and subscribers who had made her famous. The fact of the matter was that by becoming free and becoming just another black American struggling to survive, Phillis Wheatley had lost her exotic qualities. In slavery there was her person to sell. In freedom, she offered nothing but words, and was in competition with an abundance of white poets.

Not even her charlatan husband John Peters was on hand. While she lay dying, he languished in jail, having chosen imprisonment over assaults by his creditors. Not even in death did Peters give due respect to the legacy of this unique black woman. He took her last few belongings—her poems, her letters, her books—and scattered them to the four corners, never to be recovered.

Only her treasured copy of *Paradise Lost,* inscribed by her, "Mr. Brook Watson to Phillis Wheatley, London, July—1773," surfaced years later. A note on the flyleaf attests to her sad end:

> This Book was given by Brook Watson, formerly Lord Mayor of London, to Phillis Wheatley—after her death was sold in payment of her Husband's debts.—It is now presented to the Library of Harvard University at Cambridge, by Dudley L. Pickman of Salem, March, 1824.

Symbol of her fettered triumph, the book became, in death, an emblem of her failed freedom.[19]

One could argue that Phillis Wheatley's inability to thrive in freedom as she had in bondage was less due to her poor choices than to her being thrust into a society not yet ready to receive her as a free being. Though hundreds of Africans suddenly found themselves free from enslavement after the Revolution, the nation had yet to come to grips with the reality of having black citizens. Americans who derived from Africa—despite manumission and wholesale abolition of slavery in some states—would continue to struggle for the liberty extended to other Americans. But struggle they did, almost always holding the contradictory image of Phillis Wheatley—remembered as brilliant African poet—before their gaze.

CHAPTER 7

Liberty and the Rights of Africans

OLAUDAH EQUIANO, AFRICAN LIBERATOR

When William Wilberforce rose in Parliament on May 12, 1789, to deliver his historic diatribe against British participation in the African slave trade, he did not so much launch a war against slavery and the slave trade as he came late to join it. Even as he began his three-and-one-half hour description of the horrors of the slave trade, he held in his hands a new book describing a thirty-year history of Africans themselves attempting to cope with slavery.[1]

Every page of *The Interesting Narrative of the Life of Olaudah Equiano, or Gustavus Vassa the African,* written by Equiano, bristled with stories of how Africans had survived unscrupulous slavers and cruel masters. His was not some fugitive and forgotten tract, little known or seen by others. Equiano, as a free British citizen since 1766, publicly and privately campaigned against slavery and the slave trade. Through his international network of struggling Africans, he also knew who were the worst of a bad lot. It was he who reported to Granville Sharp the murder of 132 Africans in September 1781, when Capt. Luke Collingwood of the *Zong* threw overboard nearly a third of his cargo of 440 slaves while bound from Africa to Jamaica.[2]

It was also he who traveled throughout England and Wales during the 1780s promoting the welfare of Africans and visited Philadelphia Quakers in 1785 to see their work with slaves and free blacks. It was he who urged in the 1780s the creation of English colonies in Africa where oppressed Africans from all over the earth could return to their ancestral lands. It was he who in 1788 petitioned the Queen of England on behalf of Africans held by Englishmen:

> I supplicate your Majesty's compassion for millions of my African countrymen who groan under the lash of tyranny in the West Indies. . . . [I] implore your interposition with your royal consort, in favour of the wretched Africans, that . . . a period may be put to their misery—and that they may be raised from the condition of brutes to which they are at present degraded, to the rights and situation of freemen.

His petitions to Parliament enabled the House of Commons in 1792 to pass a bill designed to terminate the slave trade in 1796—even though its failure in the House of Lords left the battle to be rejoined over and again until 1807.[3]

Through five editions of his *Narrative,* Equiano told a tale as riveting and revealing as the *Autobiography* of Benjamin Franklin would prove to be when it appeared almost thirty years later. Born the son of a Nigerian tribal chieftain, Equiano enjoyed ten years of bliss before he was kidnapped by rival tribesmen and sold into slavery. Experiencing all of the shock, brutalities, and deprivations of passage from homeland to African coast and from there across the Atlantic, he survived in part because he could converse with others from his native region. But after most of his companions were sold in the West Indies, he was carried to Virginia, where he was sold to a Scotsman whose home was remote from any other Africans.

He was uprooted again when sold to Michael Henry Pascal, captain of a British trading ship who wanted him as cabin boy and personal servant. Pascal gave Equiano the name Gustavus Vassa and introduced him to another boy, Richard Baker, some five years older, who became Equiano's companion and teacher. By 1757, when Equiano was age twelve, he lived with Pascal during the first of many sojourns between voyages in Falmouth, England. There he befriended other men, women, and young people and continued to learn the English language. Within two years, Equiano concluded, "I now not only felt myself quite easy with these new countrymen but relished their society and manners. . . . I therefore embraced every occasion of improvement, and every new thing that I observed I treasured up in my memory." Pascal even promised Equiano his freedom. His transformation was nearly complete when he was baptized at St. Margaret's Church, Westminster, in February 1759.

A month later Equiano again accompanied Pascal, who had accepted an appointment in the British Navy. He was present for battles in the Mediterranean in 1759 against the French Navy and for an assault on Belle-Isle off the west coast of France in 1761. All the while he found on every ship and in every port willing teachers to help him with reading and to train him in the skills of cooking, shaving, and hair dressing. "This gave me new life and spirits," Equiano later remembered, "and my heart burned within me while I thought the time long till I obtained my freedom."

But just as Equiano glimpsed liberty, Pascal, otherwise a fair master, sold the seventeen-year-old back into slavery. As their ship left Portsmouth, Pascal forced him onto a waiting ship that was headed for the West Indies. Although Equiano tried every stratagem, he failed: "I was ready to curse the tide that bore us, the gale that wafted my prison, and even the ship that conducted us; and I called on death to relieve me from the horrors I felt and dreaded, that I might be in that place 'Where slaves are free, and men oppress no more.'"

Equiano had the good fortune to be sold on the island of Montserrat, among the Lesser Antilles, to a Quaker merchant named Robert King. King's home base was Philadelphia, although he was also the most prominent merchant in

Olaudah Equiano, or Gustavus Vassa (1789). World adventurer and gifted story-teller, he crusaded tirelessly for Africans' freedom.

Montserrat. Already Equiano had heard of the qualms Philadelphia Quakers had about slaveholding and of their relative kindness toward Africans. As he entered into King's service, he was mightily relieved to have a fair master. From the outset, he embraced three aspirations—that King would teach him a trade, take him to Philadelphia, and ultimately set him free.[4]

Over a period of three years Equiano's desires became realities. He quickly rose from being one of King's most trusted clerks to traveling as first mate on King's largest sloop. Before the end of his tenure as King's slave, he captained his master's ships on several occasions.

Equiano also quickly learned the trade he needed to earn the funds to buy his freedom. As he went from island to island buying goods for transport to America or across the Atlantic, he established a fairly lucrative inter-island exchange. His voyages grew longer and went beyond the islands to various American ports; he expanded the quantity and quality of his merchandise to suit the port. Although Equiano's ship captains knew of his clandestine trade, King did not learn of it until his entrepreneurial slave was ready to purchase his freedom.[5]

His most successful trading spree came in 1765 in Philadelphia. There he found the place to be "elegant" and friendly: "I soon sold my goods here pretty well, and in this charming place I found everything plentiful and cheap." His best customers were Quakers. But his most memorable experience was when he passed a meetinghouse where George Whitefield was bellowing forth one of his fiery sermons. "I thought it strange I had never seen divines exert themselves in this manner before," he wrote, "and I was no longer at a loss to account for the thin congregations they preached to." Himself stirred with Whitefield's preaching and with plenty of money in his pockets, he left Philadelphia for Montserrat, ready to confront his owner.[6]

Although Robert King was a Quaker, he was also a shrewd businessman. He still in 1766 owned many slaves, participated in the slave trade, and bought and sold slaves freely. For King, owning slaves was a way of keeping the services of his best employees. He was, therefore, most reluctant to accept Equiano's money, even though he had promised the slave his freedom as soon as he earned his price. When Equiano promised to continue working for King as a free man, he "said he would not be worse than his promise." As Equiano raced to the register office to "get my manumission drawn up," he recalled, "My feet scarcely touched the ground, for they were winged with joy, and like Elijah, as he rose to Heaven, they 'were with lightning speed as I went on.'"

Both during his enslavement and afterward as a free black, Equiano learned in the harshest of manners what it meant to be an African in America. He had witnessed the savage beatings and torture of slaves; he had seen free blacks turned upon by unscrupulous whites and sold back into slavery. Though he had never been beaten himself because he had reasonable masters and was incredibly imaginative in serving them, he quickly learned that as a free black he had to be even more creative to avoid brutality and reenslavement.

On his first foray after purchasing his freedom, he headed to Savannah, Georgia, in August 1766. While in a small craft collecting ship's cargo, he was threatened by a local slave. When the slave struck him, Equiano explained, "I lost all temper, and I fell on him and beat him soundly." Knowing that "there was little or no law for a free negro here," Equiano raced back to the protection of his captain. When the angry owner arrived, demanding that Equiano be handed over to be flogged, the captain refused, and Equiano concluded, "I was astonished and frightened . . . and thought I had better keep where I was than go ashore and be flogged round the town, without judge or jury." The slave owner, Mr. Read, soon returned with the local constable "and searched the vessel; but, not finding me there, he swore he would have me dead or alive." Equiano was placed in hiding at a local residence for five days until the captain persuaded the constable to agree to a cash settlement in return for his warrant for Equiano's arrest.[7]

That faithful captain died on the return trip to Montserrat, requiring Equiano to take over the sloop. The new captain, an old acquaintance of Equiano's, proved to be incompetent and ran the ship aground as it carried a cargo of slaves from St. Eustatia to Georgia in January 1767. After days of struggling from island to island in search of water, crew and slaves were taken by a schooner to New Providence in the Bahamas. Another ship hired there, they finally made Georgia. Just as before, Savannah proved dangerous for Equiano. While he was sitting up late with a slave friend, Mosa, a slave patrol came by and arrested

Equiano as a dangerous character even though he proclaimed he was a free man. When he was brought out of the watchhouse the next morning to be flogged, he demanded that a local physician known to him be called. Only the immediate arrival of the doctor saved him from harm.

Before he could find passage from Savannah back to Montserrat, Equiano was kidnapped by two white men. One of them claimed that the free black was his runaway slave. They would have persisted in their ruse, Equiano noted, except that his English was too perfect for their fraud to work. Finally, back in Montserrat, he wrote, "I thus took a final leave of Georgia, for the treatment I had received in it disgusted me very much against the place." He decided "to take a final farewell of the American quarter of the globe."

But before Equiano could make good his resolve to quit America, his problems compounded. His most recent captain refused to repay a loan. Equiano was without recourse and could not recover the money by law because "no black man's testimony is admitted, on any occasion, against any white person whatever." When the captain paid some of the money, Equiano stalled on the island of St. Kitts, a few short miles from Montserrat, where a ship's captain refused him passage until he had given proper legal notice of his departure from the island. Equiano described the process as a "degrading necessity which every black freeman is under, of advertising himself like a slave when he leaves an island." Luckily he found "some gentleman of Montserrat whom I knew" who vouched for his free status.

Equiano took leave of Robert King for England in January 1767. In his campaigns against slavery, he reflected on his own escape:

> I bade Montserrat farewell and never had my feet on it since;
> and with it I bade adieu to the sound of the cruel whip and all
> other dreadful instruments of torture; adieu to the offensive
> sight of the violated chastity of the sable females, which has
> too often accosted my eyes; adieu to oppressions (although to
> me less severe than most of my countrymen). . . .

Clearly the problem in America was not merely the practice of slavery. Even worse was the slave trade that preyed upon both innocent Africans and upon free blacks, leaving every human with a black skin vulnerable to be seized and sold.[8]

In some ways it was worse to be a free black in the Americas. After a year of freedom Equiano discovered that his condition had degenerated:

> Hitherto I had thought only slavery dreadful, but the state of a
> free negro appeared to me now equally so at least, and in some
> respects even worse, for they live in constant alarm for their liberty;
> and even this is but nominal, for they are universally
> insulted and plundered without the possibility of redress; . . . no
> free negro's evidence will be admitted in their courts of justice.

"In this situation," Equiano asked himself and the world, "is it surprising that slaves, when mildly treated, should prefer even the misery of slavery to such a mockery of freedom?"[9]

Equiano had isolated the problem of Africans in America. There was no safe place for blacks in America—slave or free. While Granville Sharp, William Wilberforce, Thomas Clarkson, and other white abolitionists focused their energies on the slave trade and slavery, Equiano campaigned for the rights of free blacks in the Western world. Equiano worked directly with a devoted friend of liberty, the earl of Stanhope, to secure a law "to allow the sable People of the wt Indias the Rights of taking an oath against any White Person. . . . May the Lord Bless all the friends of Humanity."[10]

Unable to make a sufficient living for himself in England, the inveterate adventurer entered another decade of travel. He everywhere confirmed that the problem for Africans was less slavery than it was a fair place in society. While in Turkey in 1769, he was amazed to be treated well. But he was shocked "to see how the Greeks are, in some measure, kept under by the Turks, as the negroes are in the West Indies by the white people." By 1771, he again began making regular trips to the West Indies, though he was careful to stay out of the local inter-island trade where his free black status made him the most vulnerable to mistreatment.[11]

But his greatest adventures came in the service of Dr. Charles Irving, surgeon and medical researcher, who valued greatly Equiano's spirit of exploration. In May 1773, Irving and Equiano joined Constantine John Phipps aboard the *Race Horse* on a dangerous search north of Greenland for the Northwest Passage. Two years later Irving took Equiano to the Mosquito Coast of present-day Nicaragua, where he hoped to establish a scientifically operated plantation. After a year of mosquitoes, snakes, and boredom, Equiano left Irving's employ—good as it was—and returned to England.[12]

Although he bore a letter from Irving testifying to his "honesty, sobriety, and fidelity," Equiano's last six months in America turned out to be his worst. On his first ship to Jamaica, he was seized by the captain to be sold as a slave. He barely escaped in a canoe. On his second ship he was forced to work as a laborer as it traveled along the Mosquito Coast looking for mahogany trees. He escaped to another vessel whereon he had precisely the same experience. For four months he was forced to work, cutting trees. When the ship arrived in Jamaica and he demanded to be paid his four months' wages, the captain refused. Only through the intervention of Dr. Irving, who happened to be in Jamaica, was Equiano able to get a penny for what amounted to four months of enslavement.[13]

It is not surprising that Equiano did not venture forth again from Britain except for his 1785 foray to Philadelphia, where a powerful free black society was emerging. Instead, he crisscrossed the British Islands preaching abolition and the rights of Africans. Given their treatment throughout the Western world, he became a powerful proponent of repatriating Africans to Sierra Leone. Although engaged as commissary of stores in organizing the first expedition to the Sierra Leone colony in 1787, he did not himself go.[14]

It was thus with a powerful voice and considerable authority that Equiano spoke when he published his *Narrative* in 1789. His special message to Parliament was that Britain would benefit much more from opening up trade with

Africans than in the trade of Africans themselves. "A commercial intercourse with Africa," he argued, "opens an inexhaustible source of wealth to the manufacturing interests of Great Britain, and to all which the slave trade is an objection." If Africans were permitted to return to Africa, he estimated they would double themselves every fifteen years. "In proportion to such increase, will be the demand for manufactures," he concluded.[15]

In addition to his plea to British economic sense, Equiano also appealed in 1789 to Parliament for justice and honor:

> May the time come . . . when the sable people shall gratefully commemorate the auspicious era of extensive freedom. Then shall those persons particularly be named with praise and honour, who generously proposed and stood forth in the cause of humanity, liberty, and good policy. . . . May Heaven make the British senators the dispensers of light, liberty, and science to the uttermost parts of the earth: then will be glory to God on the highest, on earth peace, and good-will to men.

His message was recognized in April 1792 in his wedding notice in *The Gentleman's Magazine:* "At Soham, co. Cambridge, Gustavus Vassa the African, well known as the champion and advocate for procuring the suppression of the slave trade, to Miss Cullen, daughter of Mr. C. of Ely, in the same county."[16]

Unfortunately his death came soon after the marriage. When Equiano died on April 31, 1797, Granville Sharp attended his last moments. Sharp later wrote, "He was a sober, honest man—and I went to see him when he lay upon his death bed, and had lost his voice so that he could only whisper." Nevertheless, through his *Narrative,* Equiano's voice continued to be heard as a ringing appeal for the rights of Africans. It was from reading the *Narrative*—and being so touched by it—that Granville Sharp's niece asked for and received from her uncle that warm assessment of the great African adventurer.[17]

SLAVERY, ADVENTURE, LIBERTY

The threads of Equiano's experience were replicated (both in story and fact) in the cases of thousands—perhaps hundreds of thousands—of other Africans whose lives were disrupted in Africa and who were thrown into the American sphere. Constantly on the move from one master to another, from one port to another, these Africans served as vital communication links and as champions of Africans' rights in a dangerously unfair world. They moved so silently that they were almost invisible to whites.

And it is not as if they were always crusading. They were rather trying to eke out a living, to move from slavery to freedom, and to secure better opportunities. Such was the case of Briton Hammon, known only through his tale, "A Narrative of the Uncommon Sufferings, and Surprising Deliverance of Briton Hammon, A Negro Man, Servant to General Winslow, of Marshfield, in New England." The earliest published work in America by an African American, Hammon's *Narra-*

tive contained the drama of Equiano's autobiography, albeit shorter. Covering a period of thirteen years, Hammon's story confirms the expansive movement of Africans around the Atlantic world.[18]

Hammon's origins are unknown. His owner John Winslow, scion of the distinguished Winslow family of Plymouth, may have acquired Hammon when he joined a Massachusetts expedition in 1740 to the West Indies.[19] During Winslow's long sojourn in Nova Scotia, Briton Hammon—likely left behind to fend for himself—proceeded from Marshfield to Plymouth on Christmas Day, 1747, to sign up as a sailor. With Winslow's knowledge and assent, Hammon bound himself to Capt. John Howland for what was to be a sixty-day voyage to Jamaica and back. After making Jamaica, however, Howland detoured to Florida with a load of wood. The ship there became lodged on a reef, and the entire crew abandoned the vessel. Even before their lifeboat reached solid land, Hammon and his companions "espy'd a number of canoes" being plied by local Indians. The Indians drove the crew back to the ship and picked it clean of all valuables, then they killed the captain and most of the sailors and passengers aboard.

Only Hammon survived the attack. Although he feared "they intended to roast" him alive, he was soon saved by the master of a Spanish schooner, who remembered him from a recent military engagement. Hammon next landed in Havana, Cuba, where he was bought by the island's governor. After a year of happy work, the contented Hammon one day "met with a press-gang," who tried to put him aboard a new royal ship. When he resisted he was jailed for four years and seven months. All attempts to notify the governor failed. This time, however, he was saved by a ship captain from Boston who learned of his situation from a "Mrs. Betty Howard," who inexplicably served as Hammon's advocate. The captain informed the governor, who called forth Hammon back into his service.

By this time Hammon wanted out of Cuba. He tried to steal aboard an English ship bound for Jamaica, but was ejected by the captain. After another year of confinement, he was released to the service of Cuba's Roman Catholic bishop. He, with seven or eight others, bore the bishop in his chair "thro' the country, to confirm the old people, baptize children, &c, for which he receives large sums of money." After seven months of touring Cuba in this manner, Hammon, again with the intervention of the mysterious Mrs. Howard, was taken aboard an English ship bound for Jamaica. Although Spanish troops came alongside the ship demanding his return, "the captain, who was a true Englishman, refus'd them, and said he could not answer it, to deliver up any Englishman under English Colours."

Hammon signed himself into the British naval service; he was transferred at London from the *Beaver* to the *Arcenceil,* then to the *Sandwich,* and finally to the *Hercules.* On board the last, a 74-gun ship, he and his mates met in battle an 84-gun French vessel. Seventy of the crew were killed, the captain lost his leg, and Hammon was severely wounded. "Disabled in the arm and render'd incapable of service," he was discharged from the King's service in May 1759.

Destitute in London, Hammon began searching for a ship that would take him back to Massachusetts and his long-forsaken master. Getting a slot as cook aboard a ship bound for Boston, Hammon worked on the ship for three months before hearing one day that one of the passengers coming aboard was a certain "General Winslow." Hammon later wrote, "I ask'd them what General Winslow? . . . for I never knew my good Master, by that title before." But "after enquiring more particularly I found it must be Master," and

> in a few days' time the truth was joyfully verify'd by a happy sight of his person, which so overcome me that I could not speak to him for some time—My good master was exceeding glad to see me, telling me that I was like one arose from the dead, for he thought I had been dead a great many years, having heard nothing of me for almost thirteen years.[20]

Hammon never became a free man. Yet as a slave making his way across a difficult world, he was able to secure employment, enter into agreements, receive pay, and escape confinement. He worked for a governor, a bishop, and captains. When he finally returned to service as a slave in 1760, he knew of the world, of conditions in British and Spanish islands, and of doings in the metropolis. He brought back to his comrades in slavery a knowledge and sophistication that, in turn, brought them into the broad stream of Western society.

The adventures of James Albert Ukawsaw Gronniosaw equaled those of Equiano and Hammond and revealed the extent to which evangelical dissenters of the eighteenth century helped Africans find their freedom. Child of a tribal chief, Gronniosaw was taken with the consent of his parents by an English merchant to be educated in Britain. A rival African chief, however, detained the merchant and ordered the boy to be sold as a slave. A Dutch slave trader headed for Barbados sold him to one Van Horne of New York City, who severely mistreated him.[21]

His situation attracted the attention of a Dutch Reform clergyman, Theodorus Jacobus Frelinghuysen, one of the early principals of America's first Great Awakening. The evangelical preacher soon bought Gronniosaw for a mere £50. Frelinghuysen, one of the great authoritarians in religious history, made the boy "kneel down," taught him to pray, and instructed him in the principles of religion. Gronniosaw soon learned to read the scriptures, John Bunyan, and the homiletic works of Richard Baxter. When Frelinghuysen preached repentance, young Gronniosaw "thought my master directed them [his words] to me only." Under the weight of holy appeals, Gronniosaw underwent religious conversion: "I saw (or thought I saw) light inexpressible dart down from heaven upon me, and shine around me for the space of a minute."[22]

Converted by a benevolent master, Gronniosaw in 1748 received his freedom. Frelinghuysen, at age fifty-seven, had contracted a sudden fever and died. In his will he left Gronniosaw £10 and his freedom. Despite the fact that Frelinghuysen was a colossal religious conservative, he freed the young man long before the practice of manumission became prevalent.

Having no other place to go, Gronniosaw remained with Frelinghuysen's widow Eva, her five sons, and two daughters. All of the sons became ministers and the daughters, ministers' wives. Eva Frelinghuysen died in 1750. By 1759, all five of the sons had died. Gronniosaw later commented, "I was now quite destitute, without a friend in the world."[23]

Left penniless but with his freedom, Gronniosaw first borrowed money for assistance. When he could not repay it, he was forced to go to sea on a privateer on condition that his wages would be paid to his creditor. After enduring bloody battles against the French at St. Domingue and harsh treatment at the hands of a cruel captain and crew, Gronnoisaw returned to New York. There his creditor took all his wages due, leaving him again destitute. After several years working as a servant, he was forced anew into a career of fighting. He joined the British Army headed to the West Indies under the command of Adm. George Pocock. In 1762 during an assault on Havanna, Cuba, Pocock and his forces, including Gronniosaw, were captured and shipped as prisoners of war to Spain.[24]

That maneuver, as horrifying as it must have been, brought Gronniosaw to the possibility of fulfilling his life's fondest dream, which was to live as close as possible and under the care of one of Theodore Frelinghuysen's closest friends, George Whitefield. Having met suffering and defeat everywhere else, Gronniosaw concluded, "I thought the best method that I could take now was to go to London, and find out Mr. Whitefield, who was the only living soul that I knew in England, and get him to direct me how to procure a living without being troublesome to any person." Whitefield did, indeed, take care of him until "he could think of some way to settle me in, and paid for my lodging and all my expenses."

Though Gronniosaw found safe haven with Whitefield, permanent employment eluded him. Hoping to do better among the old Dutch friends of Theodore Frelinghuysen, he made an excursion to Holland, where he was also warmly greeted. There he told his life's story before an audience of thirty-eight Calvinist ministers. He tarried there a year, as a servant to a merchant. But still dissatisfied, he returned to England, where he took up residence as servant to Andrew Gifford, a dissenting Baptist clergyman in London. Tired of constant peregrination, he married a widowed silk weaver. The two of them, with a child, lived precariously for years thereafter, unable to find a place or employment that would allow them to be independent beings.[25]

Aided by a succession of evangelical ministers and Quakers, including Benjamin Fawcett of Kidderminster, Gronniosaw late in life recounted in a published narrative his many adventures, hoping to earn a few shillings from its sale. He had been "obliged to sell all that we had to pay our debts." His wife stayed by the loom doing "everything that can be expected from her towards the maintenance of our family." The dejected Gronniosaw commented, "as poor pilgrims, we are travelling through many difficulties, waiting for the call, when the Lord shall deliver us out of the evils of this world, and bring us to the everlasting glories of the world to come." Although free of slavery, Gronniosaw never could find a real home in a white world—America, Holland, or Britain.[26]

Equiano, Hammon, and Gronniosaw were far from alone. Venture Smith paralleled their experiences in many ways. Born in Guinea in 1729, he too came from royal parentage. At age six he was captured and taken aboard a slave ship hailing from Rhode Island. Although he was one of 260 Africans stolen for shipment to Barbados, he was purchased by the ship's steward "for four gallons of rum and a piece of calico." The steward, Robertson Mumford, proud of his first effort to make an investment, promptly named the boy Venture.

Instead of landing in Barbados, Venture found himself in the happier confines of Rhode Island. Over the next fifteen years the bright African boy became Americanized and learned household and farm work. In 1751 Smith joined an Irish indentured servant and two others owned by Mumford in an attempt to escape his bonds. Stealing Mumford's boat, the four of them embarked from Rhode Island to Mississippi. The Irishman, however, took over the boat and confiscated all their belongings after a brief stop for fresh water. Smith then aided in the traitor's arrest.[27]

The Irishman was jailed. For his own deceit, Smith was sold by Mumford and thereby separated from his wife, but his new master at Stonington, Connecticut, eventually purchased Smith's wife and rejoined them. When Smith challenged his new mistress for threatening to whip his wife, he was beaten by his new owner in her stead. He took his complaint of cruelty to a local justice, but his plea for protection fell on deaf ears. Instead, his master punished him further. When he again resisted, he was chained until he could be sold.

Viewed as a rebellious slave, Venture Smith passed from hand to hand for several years. Since he would take orders from no one, he was allowed to find jobs on his own and to pay his masters. Carefully hoarding a portion of his income from chopping wood and operating a small farm, he was able in ten years' time to purchase his freedom. That was 1765. As he heard about growing hopes for liberty and freedom, he set the goal of purchasing freedom for as many slaves as he could. He moved to Long Island and began chopping wood across that land; by 1769 he was able to purchase his two sons, Solomon and Cuff. He next purchased another "negro man for no other reason than to oblige him," but the faithless man soon "run away from me, and I thereby lost all that I gave for him."

By 1773 Smith—then into his own investments—bought a farm. That same year he also bought "a sloop of about thirty tons burthen" and hired a crew to sail around New England making deliveries of wood. He also purchased his wife, who was at the time pregnant with another child he would otherwise have had to purchase later as well. As his farm prospered and his wood trade boomed, he set off on a whaling voyage. With the income from that and his other enterprises, he bought more land, another dwelling, freedom for his eldest daughter and for two additional male slaves.

Venture Smith could be proud that he had liberated eight African slaves, including himself and that he was one of the most prosperous property owners and business operatives on Long Island. He later recalled it was the property "and my industry . . . [that] alone saved me from being expelled [from] that part of the island in which I resided, as an act was passed by the selectmen of the place, that all negroes residing there should be expelled." Badgered by neighbors, he sold his property on Long Island and moved to East Haddam, Connecticut, where he purchased a farm and settled for the rest of his life. There he continued his fishing, sailing, whaling, and trading empire with another twenty sailing vessels and crews, outfitting them until his death in 1805.[28]

Coffe Slocum, also taken from Africa to Rhode Island as a young boy in 1728, was acquired in Newport, Rhode Island, by Quakers Ebenezer and Bathsheba Slocum, who provided him with their values and a limited education. Fourteen years later they sold him to their nephew John Slocum of Dartmouth, Massachusetts. A few years later—by 1745—Slocum gave Coffe Slocum his freedom. During that same year the freed man announced his intention of marrying Ruth Moses, a Wampanoag from the Dartmouth area.

Coffe and Ruth Slocum settled on the tiny, windswept island of Cuttyhunk, owned by the white Slocums, just across Buzzards Bay from Dartmouth. The pair eked out an existence combining farming, fishing, and carpentry. Coffe Slocum learned to read and write, keeping careful records of his diverse business interests. Ruth Slocum bore ten children, almost all of whom followed the productive course of their parents in farming, business, and seafaring. All were reared to follow the practices of the Quakers, but they were never admitted to the Quaker Meeting.

In the early 1760s the Slocum family moved onto Martha's Vineyard to live among the Wampanoag community at Chilmark. In 1766 they bought their own farm at Dartmouth, Massachusetts. Constantly expanding his business interests, Coffe Slocum wrote in his journal "We Heare Are . . . good Do good all Do good to All . . . Give Give Give . . . Good Do Good at all times I lern read Abcd-ABBBDDDJAATM Coffee Slocum Mister."

His life was cut short in 1772 amidst prosperity, but not before he proved what Olaudah Equiano, Britton Hammon, and Venture Smith had demonstrated before him. Africans, too, aspired to freedom and equality and would strive in every way possible to achieve those goals. This rich aspiration he planted with son Jonathan, who was on Martha's Vineyard plying trade, with son David who was on Cuttyhunk farming and trading also, and with son Paul, born in 1759, who was shipping out on whalers and merchant ships. Paul Slocum not only saw the world, he also was arrested aboard his ship and placed with other American rebels in a British war prison in New York.

By the time of his release, he was thoroughly drenched with notions of liberty for Africans as well as Americans. In a first act that would symbolize the vast career that awaited son Paul, he changed his name from Slocum to Cuffe, reaching back to his African identity and the name that his father had brought from Africa—Kofi, ("born on Friday"). So did his five brothers.

In 1780 he, brother John, and five other blacks at Dartmouth provided an even greater testimony of liberty for black Americans. Following the battle cry of the Continental Congress—"no taxation without representation"—they petitioned the General Court in Boston with a refrain of no taxation without rights: "We apprehend ourselves to be aggrieved in that while we are not allowed the Privileges of freemen of the State, having No vote or Influence in the Election with those that tax us." Poll and property taxes nevertheless were levied on them. Describing themselves as "Distressed mongrels," able to live little better than dogs, the "Poor Despised black People" found freedom "Neither by Sea nor by Land."

The court greeted their complaints with silence. In the absence of a clear statement from the General Court, the Cuffe brothers refused to pay their taxes. They were, for that bit of rebellion, indicted and arrested in early 1781, but with the assistance of Dartmouth's member of the General Court, Walter Spooner, and Gov. John Hancock, they were released and told that the state constitution implied that they had the right to vote. The Cuffes thereby petitioned their local selectmen "to know the mind of said town whether all free Negroes and molattoes shall have the same Privileges in this said town of Dartmouth as the white People . . . or, that we have Relief granted us Jointly from Taxation." The selectmen also chose the path of silence. But the Cuffes must have been satisfied in some manner, because in June, 1781, they paid £8.12 "in full for all" of their total tax bill of £154.[29]

Jean Baptiste Point Du Sable was another amazing eighteenth-century African who found success around the peripheries of America. Probably born in St. Domingue of French and African parents, he received a good education and headed across the continent. By 1779 he was operating a trading post, living with an Indian wife, and maintaining a thriving business with area Indians on the southern shore of Lake Michigan. He was arrested by invading British troops and detained for months as a probable French agent before local Indians demanded his release. At the end of hostilities he returned to his trading post, which continued to thrive. When he sold his land and business in 1800, investors in the soon thriving Eschecagou, or Chicago, made him a wealthy man.[30]

Then there was John Marrant, whose pathway was both adventure and religion. He was born free in New York, but moved with his mother to St. Augustine, Florida, then to Savannah, Georgia, and finally to Charleston, South Carolina. On his way to becoming a trade apprentice, he one day heard pleasing music and determined to pursue a career in music. By age thirteen, accomplished on both the violin and the French horn, he was beginning to make a living as a performer at weddings, dances, and other public occasions.

It was again as he was walking to a performance at a social function that Marrant encountered the voice of what he first thought was "a crazy man hallooing there." The ranting man was none other than George Whitefield, the evangel of the Great Awakening. So taken was he by Whitefield's preaching, "I was struck to the ground, and lay both speechless and senseless near half an hour." From that moment Marrant assumed the evangelical cause, had frequent religious visions, and strove often into the "wilderness" where he was once captured by Indians. Persuading his captors of the mysterious powers of his Bible, he was released to return to his family and a life of deep piety.[31]

During the American Revolution, Marrant was first "pressed" into "his Majesty's service" aboard the *Scorpion*. But his life was better than many other seamen, because on each of his sloops he served as the ship's musician. Nevertheless, this special station could not protect him against storm or battle. He was at the siege of Charleston, in various West Indian engagements, and on board the

Princess Amelia against the Dutch, where he was one of only a few survivors of a bloody fight. Following a lengthy convalescence he became a servant to "a respectable and pious merchant," John Marsden.[32]

In London he came under the influence of the countess of Huntingdon. So impressed was she by his religious powers that she persuaded him to travel to Nova Scotia as a Methodist missionary to whites, blacks, and Indians. Before departing on that five-year venture, Marrant wrote his first autobiographical piece, *A Narrative of the Lord's Wonderful Dealings with John Marrant.* Published in 1785, it described his first thirty years. Marrant's *Narrative* was an instant success and brought him fame as an impassioned religious figure throughout the English-speaking world. Over the next forty years it would appear in nineteen printed versions.[33]

Marrant, following the example of other Methodists of the period, maintained a journal of his Canadian adventures as he traveled across Nova Scotia and formed a church. For four years he compiled a journal that, when published in 1790, would extend even further his fame as a selfless itinerant.[34]

Before returning to London to publish his *Journal of the Rev. John Marrant,* he made a curious yearlong visit to the United States. During the winter of 1789 he headed from Nova Scotia to Boston; he was immediately embraced by Boston's black community. Prince Hall, venerable founder of African Masonry in America, invited him to become chaplain of the African Lodge of the Honorable Society of Free and Accepted Masons of Boston. Marrant gladly accepted and soon became an ardent proponent of the liberating powers of the secret order.

On June 24, 1789, Marrant issued before Boston's black masons a ringing, if inscrutable, declaration of the rights of man. In a *Sermon Preached on the 24th Day of June 1789, Being the Festival of St. John the Baptist,* Marrant combined biblical history and Masonic philosophy to reinterpret human history. Although Adam and Eve were driven from the Garden of Eden, God had chosen man to carry out the purposes of His creation by building cities, temples, arks, and great wonders of architecture. Infused with souls and powers of reasoning, humans would learn and perpetuate the science, mathematics, and mechanical arts of building.[35]

The faculties for building, and thus Masonry, Marrant continued, originated with Cain and were transmitted by Noah through Ham, the so-called accursed progenitor of all Africans. Ham's descendants, Africans all, were the scientists and geometricians who carried the building arts across Babylon, Canaan, Phoenicia, and Egypt, and then, with Moses, back to Israel. Although in these lands many had the status of slaves, they were both as builders and Masons free: "wherever arts flourish, a man hath a free right (having a recommendation [as a Mason]) to visit his brethren, and they are bound to accept him."

In a world that was exceedingly unfair to blacks and to many tradesmen, Marrant and Hall were attempting to construct a place in which Africans could find common ground with other men—thus following the example of white Masons. Proclaimed Marrant, "these are the laudable bonds that unite Free

Masons together in one indissoluble fraternity—thus in every nation he finds a friend, and in every climate he may find a house—this it is to be kindly affectioned one to another, with brotherly love, in honour preferring one another."

In Masonry, argued Marrant, there was an equality that existed nowhere else in society. "There is no party spirit in Masonry," he stated, to divide men into factions nor any disposition to separate out "a species below them, and as not made of the same clay with themselves." In fact, as Masons "you will there find that you stand on the level not only with them, but with the greatest kings on the earth," as "these truly great men are not ashamed of the meanest of their brethren."

By making Masonry an international common ground, Marrant found it possible, at least for the moment, to accept the existence of slavery. "If we search history," Marrant continued, "we shall not find a nation on earth but has at some period or other of their existence been in slavery, from the Jews down to the English Nation, under many Emperors, Kings and Princes." But the presence of black slavery and the fact that most blacks in Western nations were slaves "is not a just cause of our being despised," he concluded. Just as they historically had filled the ranks of Masonry and of learning—Tertullian, Cyprian, Origen, Augustine—Africans would do it again within or without the confines of slavery.[36]

But Marrant soon learned that there were other forces at work in America. "I was preaching at the west end of the town [Boston] to a large concourse of people" when a group of more than forty ruffians, complete with swords and clubs, "made an agreement to put an end to my evening preaching." Dr. Samuel Stillman, a Baptist minister and champion of religious freedom, came to Marrant's aid by providing him a safe hall in which to preach and by sending him to a Boston judge, who admonished the hooligans.

Although he went on preaching for the next six months, Marrant realized that neither religious enthusiasm nor Masonry provided a real place for blacks in the United States. On February 5, 1790, a company of black Bostonians, mainly Masons headed by Hall, "with very heavy hearts" accompanied the disillusioned Marrant to a waiting ship that would take him back to London. A year later, at age thirty-six, having given every ounce of his being to invent an engine that would extend respect and opportunity to blacks whatever their station in life, Marrant's hopeful heart stopped beating, concluding an amazing quest for freedom.[37]

John Marrant was not the only African American during this era to gain learning, adopt religion, and through religion enter into a life of high adventure. Three others, whose lives briefly interblended in the pursuit of evangelical Christianity were Andrew Bryan, David George, and George Liele. Liele, the youngest of the three, ignited the spark that drove the trio into lives of religious ardor. Born in Virginia a slave of Henry Sharp, he and Sharp moved to Burke County, Georgia, in 1773. Sometime between that move and 1778, Liele underwent religious conversion, began preaching to blacks in the area, and was manumitted by Sharp. When Sharp, a Tory officer, was killed in 1778, the surviving Sharps attempted to reenslave Liele. But as was so often the case in those dangerous years, the testimony of another British officer kept him free.[38]

Between 1779 and 1782—years of British occupation in and around Savannah, Georgia, George Liele set many hearts on fire, including those of both Andrew Bryan and David George. George, born a slave in Sussex County, Virginia, ran away to South Carolina when he was a young man. His abusive master, James Chappell, sought his return, causing George to escape again, this time among the Creek. When the Creek sold him back to Chappell, George escaped further west to the Natchez. In a three-way deal, he was purchased from the relentless Chappell by George Galphin, South Carolina planter and Indian trader, who allowed George to reside as a sales agent among the Natchez. At the start of the American Revolution, he moved to Galphin's South Carolina plantation and became a Baptist preacher until 1778, when he and many of his followers took the invitation of Lord Dunmore for slaves to cross over British lines to freedom. He rushed into Savannah and came into active collaboration with Liele so long as British occupation continued in the area.[39]

At about the same time Andrew Bryan, a slave at Goose Creek, South Carolina, heard Liele preaching and underwent his own conversion. By October 1779 he had begun preaching to both blacks and whites in and around Charleston. Until 1782, Liele, George, and Bryan held forth freely in the British occupied corridor from Charleston to Savannah. They savored the freedom offered by British policy so much that when retreat came in 1782, Liele and George decided to leave America with their friendly and assuring protectors. Liele accompanied British troops to Jamaica; George joined five hundred Georgia Loyalists to Nova Scotia. Just before he left, Liele baptized Bryan and his wife and left his parish in his apostle's good hands. Bryan, still a slave, could not take the route of liberty chosen by his colleagues and accepted, as he must instead, the land where he was owned.[40]

The directions taken and the experiences of the three colleagues in Baptist arms are instructive indeed. George Liele made his way to Jamaica as an indentured servant. Two years later, fully free, he began establishing Baptist churches there. By 1791 he had baptized four hundred new Baptists. He was then a farmer-preacher and a purveyor of goods across Jamaica. Though in the heart of the slave trade, he was given leave quite freely to build his farm and Baptist institutions.[41]

George in Nova Scotia had a small African congregation from among the three thousand free blacks who accompanied the contingent of Georgia Loyalists or who came from other former colonies. For ten years he labored among them, establishing congregations at Shelburne and in New Brunswick. He surely crossed paths with the crusading John Marrant. And he suffered the same threats of terror and opposition, describing how white settlers "came one night and stood before the pulpit and swore how they would treat me if I preached again." In 1792, discouraged with white America, he chose to migrate back to Africa and accompanied a colony of his disillusioned compatriots to Sierra Leone. There he prospered, introducing the Baptist denomination and building up a strong congregation over the next eighteen years.[42]

Bryan, who remained behind in America, surely suffered the most. Although during the British occupation he was encouraged to evangelize to free blacks and slaves, after the Revolution he was forbidden to preach altogether. He and his followers reverted to surrounding swamps for their meetings until January 1788, when a white Baptist minister ordained Bryan, baptized forty-five of his congregants, and chartered them as the Ethiopian Church of Jesus Christ at Savannah. Slave masters retaliated by prohibiting their slaves' attendance. When Bryan persisted, masters imprisoned their slaves for disobedience and had some whipped. Bryan, it was reported, "was cut and bled abundantly. . . . He held up his hand, and told his prosecutors that he rejoiced not only to be whipped, but would freely suffer death for the cause of Jesus Christ."

Bryan's master, evidently supportive of his crusading charge, provided a barn on his plantation where his slave could preach unmolested. By 1791 he had three hundred and fifty converts. By 1794, with funds from black and white Baptists alike, he was permitted to build what became the First African Baptist Church of Savannah. Upon his master's death, the family permitted him to purchase his freedom for £50. By 1800 Bryan had a congregation of seven hundred, a house near his church, and a fifty-six-acre farm four miles in the country. He, like Liele and George, had found the sainted peace he sought and deserved.[43]

Another actor in this swirling world of religious enthusiasm was an African teenage boy, at the time without a recorded name, who was taken on board the brigantine *Prospect* at St. Thomas Island in 1781. He was one of three hundred and ninety slaves who were being transferred that year from the peaceful Danish colony at St. Thomas to the harsh French colony at St. Domingue. Joseph Vesey, captain of the *Prospect,* happily unloaded his cargo to eager French planters, who were at the time making St. Domingue the richest island in the world.[44]

Captain Vesey probably did not notice the boy on the first voyage, but he could not miss him upon his next trip to Cap François months later. The angry planter who bought him thrust the boy before Vesey with a certificate from St. Domingue's royal physician declaring him "unsound and subject to epileptic fits." According to the laws of the island, Vesey had to refund the planter's money and take back his defective property. Unable to unload the boy anywhere else, Vesey made the boy his personal servant.[45]

For the next three years, the boy sailed everywhere Vesey went—across the Atlantic, to Bermuda, and among the West India islands. Everywhere he learned the ample lessons Vesey could teach him. Vesey had served as first lieutenant under John Paul Jones on the sloop *Providence* and had captained the brig *Cabot* in the Revolution, and he surely spoke of liberty and freedom for Americans. By 1778 he had become a privateer operating out of Charleston, South Carolina. It was in his guise as privateer that he had carried those three hundred and ninety slaves in 1781.[46]

By 1783, Capt. Joseph Vesey decided to take to land, bringing the sixteen-year-old African lad with him to Charleston permanently. Although he would continue to be identified as a mariner, Vesey moved from captaining ships to owning them and sending them out to return laden with slaves. Later he traded in other goods and worked as a chandler fitting out ships. Meanwhile he sent out the young slave to be trained as a master ship's carpenter during the work day.

The rest of the time the young man watched as his master moved gradually from slave importer and trader to a key player in the Charleston political scene. Vesey was there in 1793 when Edmond Genet arrived to organize world revolution and in 1794 when the Republican Society of Charleston welcomed ambassadors from the government of France. He was treasurer of the Charleston committee to assist refugees from St. Domingue, bringing black and white expatriates of the French colony into his home.

As Vesey's young African slave grew into manhood, he began to seek his own liberation. Although he developed as a marine carpenter and evidently overcame his early epileptic fits, he had not the drive to work for his freedom. He fervently believed that destiny awaited him, almost as a birthright. Hence it was a fulfillment of destiny when on November 8, 1799, Vesey's slave took title to Charleston's second great lottery.

It was on that date that one of the most classic eighteenth-century African adventurers claimed the $1,500 Charleston lottery prize. With that cash he bought his freedom from Vesey for $600. Partaking of the religious enthusiasm released by George Liele and stoked by Andrew Bryan, he conceived how in another quick stroke all of Charleston's Africans could achieve their release from bondage. From the date of the lottery prize, at least, and into all of history thereafter he would be known as Denmark Vesey. He took his name from his Danish origins on St. Thomas and from the benevolent captain who brought him to America. He would become synonymous with the overthrow of enslavement by black Americans themselves, with bloody revolution and lightning reward. In Denmark Vesey culminated all the conflicting forces of an almost universal willingness to see Africans thrown into slavery against an equally irrepressible desire on the part of Africans to pursue liberty.[47]

AFRICAN-AMERICAN REVOLUTIONARIES

Since the Continental Congress declared to all the world on July 4, 1776, that America was entering on a course of independence, black Americans had every reason to believe that there was something in this action for them as well. After years of resolutions, of tracts and broadsides, and of fiery speeches declaring liberty, black Americans answered in abundance the call to arms.

But almost from the outset black Americans were placed in a confused situation. Continental Congress did not free a single slave. And when black Americans stepped forth to secure the rights of white Americans enunciated in the Declaration of Independence, they were restrained from exercising those rights—including the right to serve in the American Continental forces and many state militias. Although a number of blacks thronged to New England units, General George Washington on July 10, 1775, forbade the recruitment of further black volunteers, and on November 12, 1775, issued orders prohibiting further service by any blacks.

Matters became more complicated when John Murray, earl of Dunmore and Royal governor of Virginia, issued a proclamation the following week guaranteeing freedom to any slaves or indentured servants escaping their masters and joining the King's forces. Although Washington quickly removed his ban on blacks serving in the Continental Army and various states lifted their bar against militia service, the status of black Americans remained clouded throughout the Revolution.[48]

More than five thousand African Americans stepped forth to fight in America's land and naval forces. Their contributions to the American cause were truly inspiring, especially given the ambivalence of most white Americans toward their black fellow citizens. There was, of course, Crispus Attucks, frequently cited as the first casualty of the American Revolution. On the night of March 5, 1770, after scuffles between British troops and teenage taunters in Boston, British officers and soldiers decided they would take no more jeers. When another group arrived, led by a tall, robust black man, the British troops decided to send a message. They had planned to fire only a warning shot, but when the crowd pressed upon them, the British soldiers instinctively fired into the oncoming throng. Five Americans fell dead. The first among them to die was a "stout man named Attucks, who was born in Framingham [Massachusetts], but was lately belonging to New-Providence [Bahamas], and was here in order to go for North-Carolina, killed on the Spot, two Balls entering his Breast."

Attucks's heroism in defying the British troops marked him as the first martyr of the Revolution and the star victim of what would become known as the Boston Massacre, even though immediately after the event, it became widely known that Attucks had been for twenty years a runaway slave. His size and frame were well described in a 1750 notice of his flight from slavery:

> Ran away from his Master <u>William Brown of Framingham</u>, on the 30th of <u>Sept</u>. last, a Molatto Fellow, about 27 Years of Age, named <u>Crispas</u>, 6 Feet two inches high, short curl'd Hair, his Knees nearer together than common; had on a light colour'd Bearskin Coat, plain brown Fustian Jacket, or brown all-Wool one, new Buckskin Breeches, blue Yarn Stockings, and check'd woolen Shirt.

Offering a £10 reward, Brown warned, "all Masters of Vessels and others, are hereby caution'd against concealing or carrying off said Servant on Penalty of the Law." That is precisely what Attucks did; he disappeared into the throng of men who could survive for years on the sea, freed from a more exacting identity than if they had lived on land. Nevertheless, the circumstances of his death made him a hero of liberty.[49]

Just as Attucks was the hero of the Boston Massacre, two other Massachusetts blacks—one slave and the other free—became among the earliest heroes when the war commenced. Peter Salem, a slave from Framingham, and Salem Poor, a free black from Andover, were credited with firing the shots that killed two principal British officers at the Battle of Bunker Hill on June 17, 1775. Salem killed Maj. John Pitcairn. Poor, in turn, shot Lt. Col. James Abercrombie. The first published chronicle of the event reported: "Among the foremost of the [British] leaders was the gallant Maj. Pitcairn, who exultingly cried "the day is ours," when Salem, a black soldier, and a number of others shot him through and he fell." Salem received a contribution from his fellow soldiers and "was presented to Washington as having slain Pitcairn." As for Poor, fourteen officers petitioned the Massachusetts General Court recommending a reward for his bravery, testifying that he "behaved like an Experienced Officer, as Well as an Excellent Soldier" and that "in the Person of this sd. Negro Centers a Brave & gallant Soldier." [50]

Although Washington's ban on the further service of black soldiers temporarily affected Salem and Poor, both heroes reenlisted on January 16, 1776, and both served gallantly to the end of the war. Salem saw further carnage at Saratoga and Stony Point; Poor at Valley Forge and White Plains. Salem later was immortalized by John Trumbull in his painting of the Battle of Bunker Hill. Trumbull witnessed the battle from Roxbury across the harbor and later painted Salem at the center of his heroic battle scene. [51]

As General Washington and Lord Dunmore, Congress and Parliament battled a cold war over how to utilize or neutralize the vast African population in America, other blacks stepped forward to battle for the American cause. In the area where Dunmore was organizing his "Ethiopian Regiment," free black William Flora suddenly emerged during the Battle of the Great Bridge, near Norfolk, Virginia, in late 1775 to win the day for the American forces. As Dunmore's troops, black and white, sallied forth from their island fortress on the attack, the 2nd Virginia Regiment was waiting in breastworks. Capt. Thomas Nash later wrote that at the moment the British forces were about to prevail over the Virginians,

> Flora, a colored man, was the last sentinel that came into the breast work . . . he did not leave his post until he had fired several times. Billy [Flora] had to cross a plank to get to the breast work, and had fairly passed over it when he was seen to turn back, and deliberately take up the plank after him, amidst a shower of musket balls. He . . . fired eight times.

In one of the first battles of the Revolution in the southern colonies, a black soldier fought for American liberty—against other black soldiers also desperately trying to secure their freedom. [52]

When Washington made his famous crossing of the Delaware on December 25, 1776, he was accompanied by two notable black soldiers, Oliver Cromwell, a free black from Burlington County, New Jersey, and Prince Whipple, a slave belonging to Gen. William Whipple of Portsmouth, New Hampshire. Cromwell, a farmer, enlisted in the 2nd New Jersey Regiment at the beginning of the war and fought in the battles at Trenton, Princeton, Brandywine, Monmouth, and Yorktown, where he witnessed the last casualty of the Revolution. For his devoted service throughout, Washington personally presented Cromwell his honorable discharge on June 5, 1783.[53]

Prince Whipple's service to the American cause was another matter altogether. His prominent African family had sent him at age ten along with a cousin to colonial America to be educated. A brother had returned from such a venture four years earlier. As with so many other Africans, however, the ship's captain sold him into slavery at Baltimore. Prince was purchased by William Whipple, who dabbled in the transatlantic slave trade. Whipple in about 1760 gave up seafaring for a mercantile business in Portsmouth. He must have trained young Prince in his business. He then took the bright African along with him to the Continental Congress of 1776 in Philadelphia.

Whatever the actual circumstances were, Whipple and his slave joined Washington's forces as they crossed the Delaware River to attack Trenton. His presence at memorable battles later inspired him to lead a group of nineteen "natives of Africa" in 1779 to petition the New Hampshire Assembly for the restoration of the freedom they knew at birth.

Arguing that having been born free in Africa, they had every right to have that freedom restored:

> [T]he God of nature gave them life and freedom, upon the terms of the most perfect equality with other men; That freedom is an inherent right of the human species, not to be surrendered but by consent, for the sake of social life; That private tyranny and slavery are alike detestable to minds conscious of the equal dignity of human nature.

Whether by his master's act or public action, Prince Whipple was freed during the Revolution. His freedom, however, was short-lived; he died at age thirty-two, leaving behind a widow and children.[54]

Agrippa Hull, by contrast, was born free at Northampton, Massachusetts, and willingly joined the Continental Army in May 1777. Inspired by the daring example of Gen. John Paterson of Lenox, Massachusetts, Hull served Paterson faithfully for two years. In return, Paterson commended him to his friend Gen. Tadeusz Kościuszko, Polish hero of the American Revolution. Hull then served Kościuszko as an orderly and aide for the next four years, moving battle by battle from Saratoga to Eutaw Springs in South Carolina until his discharge at West Point in July 1783. The grateful Kościuszko, when awarded a grant of land by Congress in 1797, ordered that it be sold and the funds used to establish a school for blacks in America.

Just as Agrippa Hull saw heavy fighting everywhere he went during the Revolution, so did Jack Sisson of Rhode Island, who volunteered as one of forty men to participate in the capture of British general Richard Prescott in July 1777. Sisson's role in the venture was so memorable that it was remembered for generations in a ballad celebrating the "tawny son of Afric's race." By legend, Sisson broke down the door of Prescott's chamber with his head and found the general in bed. When Prescott demanded his pants, Sisson in the ballad said, "Your breeches, massa, I will take, / For dress we cannot stay." Such brave service was also rendered by Moses Sash of Massachusetts, who enlisted as a private in the Massachusetts regiment in August 1777 and served until the end of the war.[55]

Even in Georgia, where slaves were forbidden from serving in American forces, Austin Dabney was pressed into service by a master who himself resisted enlistment. Swearing that Dabney was a free black and could thereby take his place, master Richard Aycock introduced Dabney to the Battle of Kettle Creek in February 1779, fighting alongside patriots against a force of Loyalists. Although injured there with a bullet through his thigh that crippled him for life, Dabney was treated as one of the brave survivors of Kettle Creek.[56]

Other African Americans who aided the American cause in the southern states included the Virginian Joseph Ranger, who served on four separate American warships during the Revolution and who was captured with the entire crew on the last, the *Patriot,* and Caesar Tarrant of Hampton, Virginia, who piloted the same *Patriot* during an earlier voyage on which the crew captured the British brig *Fanny* while it was taking supplies to Boston.[57]

Probably the most renowned of the Virginia black patriots was James Armistead, who, as a slave, initially serviced the marquis de Lafayette. Lafayette quickly learned that Armistead could write clearly and concisely. And he could act. In early July, Lafayette dispatched Armistead to the headquarters of British general Charles Cornwallis as a spy. Armistead took to the role and began providing Lafayette with information that enabled Lafayette and Washington to trap Cornwallis's forces at Yorktown. Lafayette later wrote:

> This is to certify that . . . James [Armistead] has done essential services to me while I had the honour to command in this State. His intelligences from the enemy's camp were industriously collected and more faithfully delivered. He properly acquitted himself with some important communications I gave him and appears to be entitled to every reward his situation can admit of.

Armistead's reports had enabled American ground forces and a menacing French fleet to thwart Cornwallis so decisively.[58]

Armistead's vital contributions to the astonishing defeat of British forces in America, when joined with those of so many other black Americans, made the achievement of American independence a prize shared jointly by whites and blacks. The black Americans who joined in the war and the families for whom they fought had every reason to believe that the rights of man sooner or later would be extended also to them. Not a soul in those heady days of revolution insisted that liberty was just for whites or just for men. Although all of the claims were much in the abstract and had yet to be made specific, no person residing in America was informed as they chose sides to support or throw off British rule that, when the conflict was done, the highly vaunted rights of man would not be for him or her. Glorious days they were, for everyone.

HAITIANS TO THE RESCUE OF AMERICAN LIBERTY

On September 23, 1779, Capt. John Paul Jones, in command of the *Bonhomme Richard* (named by French authorities in honor of Benjamin Franklin's nom de plume) and operating under the direction of that same Benjamin Franklin, pulled off one of the most famous naval victories in American history. After more than a year of raids into English and Irish ports, Jones departed Brest, France, on August 14 to take prize ships in waters between Scotland and Ireland. Sailing under American colors but on orders developed jointly by Franklin and Lafayette, Jones seized seventeen ships before encountering the dreaded British ship *Serapis* on September 23.

Outsized, outmanned, and outgunned, Jones did the only thing he could under the circumstances. He pulled alongside the much larger vessel, neutralizing its great guns, and, over a three-hour period of hand-to-hand fighting, subdued the British ship. Although the *Bonhomme Richard* was damaged beyond repair and sank two days later, Jones hobbled victoriously into Texel, Holland, on October 3 aboard the *Serapis*. Lionized in Paris, he became, alongside Franklin, one of the most popular American idols of the Revolutionary era.[59]

While Franklin conspired with Lafayette to use American privateers in the seizure of British ships and in attacks on British and Irish towns, he also planned the use of French forces in bolstering the American cause. In fact, even as John Paul Jones was raiding British ports, his French counterparts were descending on American ports, seeking to evict the British and Loyalist forces that occupied them. Franklin had already received funds from Louis XVI for the enterprise, and chief among the targeted ports was Savannah, Georgia, occupied by British troops in December 1778.[60]

One detail in the Franklin and Lafayette plan for French involvement at Savannah forever changed the history of liberty in the Western world. That particular dealt with the source and nature of those troops French commanders would bring into the fray. Although the combined naval and land operation was under the command of Admiral-General comte Charles-Hector d'Estaing, unpredictable veteran of numerous campaigns in Europe and the West Indies, his troops were to be drawn from every corner of the French empire.[61]

An article in the *Paris Gazette* published a few months after the campaign's conclusion revealed the diversity of d'Estaing's army:

FRENCH TROOPS
1. Europeans: draughted from the regiments of Armagnac, Champagne, Auxerrois, Agenois, Gatinois, Cambresis, Haynault, Foix, Dillon, Walsh, le Cap, la Guadeloupe, la Martinique, and Port au Prince, a Detachment of the Royal Corps of Infantry of the Marine, the Volunteers of Vallelle, the Dragoons, and 156 Volunteer Grenadiers, lately raised at Cape François

2,979

   2. <u>Colored</u>: Volunteer Chasseurs, Mulattoes, and Negroes,
      newly raised at Saint Domingo

		545
AMERICAN TROOPS		<u>2,000</u>
	Total	5,524

It was not the uniting of soldiers from all parts of France that made d'Estaing's force unusual or even that so many troops were called forth from French colonies. It was rather that for the first time in history a detachment of warriors was formed from volunteer "Chasseurs, Mulattoes, and Negroes" from St. Domingue, a land where the worst cruelties toward Africans were practiced.[62]

At the base of the French army was a new force of fighters whose names were not even recorded at the time. Among them were such proud names as Jean-Baptiste Chavannes, Louis Jacques Beauvais, Martial Besse, Jean-Baptiste Mars Belley, André Rigaud, and Henri Christophe. They had been mustered up when d'Estaing landed his fleet of ships in late July 1779 in Cap François, principal city of St. Domingue, and shortly thereafter in Port-au-Prince. In two weeks, he recruited what one naval officer described as "eight hundred free mulattoes" from St. Domingue.[63]

These volunteers, promised pay and adventure, were packed on six frigates that joined a larger fleet of ships. Only two weeks after recruitment, with no training for war, the convoy of twenty-five ships arrived off the coast of Georgia. The element of surprise, however, was lost when the French armada was noticed near Tybee Island. As provisions diminished and the weather grew worse, d'Estaing kept his force cooped up for almost a week. Because he dallied so long offshore, d'Estaing's objective of attacking Savannah soon became universal knowledge and was even published in a Charleston newspaper.[64]

After cruising around the various approaches into Savannah, d'Estaing's troops began landing—still miles from the city. Meanwhile, the small British force in Savannah was augmented with eight hundred Loyalist troops arriving from Beaufort, South Carolina, under the command of Col. John Maitland. Maitland and his men slipped past the French armada, with the deft assistance of "some negro fishermen who were well acquainted with all the creeks through the marsh, and who informed him [Maitland] of a passage . . . by which small boats could pass at high water."[65]

By September 16 when d'Estaing finally asked Gen. Augustin Prevost, the British commander in Savannah, to surrender, the number of British and Loyalist defenders had increased from a skeletal force to 2,360. Included in this number were "200 Negroes armed" and ready to defend British rights. Another four to five hundred slaves dug trenches and bolstered defenses around Savannah. Given the chasseurs from St. Domingue and armed blacks and slaves serving the British, well over a thousand blacks and mulattoes were engaged in the impending battle for Savannah.[66]

40   *SIEGE OF SAVANNAH.*

1779.   RECAPITULATION.

FRENCH TROOPS, ... 4456
AMERICAN " 2127

TOTAL STRENGTH OF THE ALLIED ARMY, ... 6,583

Anthony Stokes,* Chief Justice of the Colony of Georgia, who was in Savannah during
the siege, estimates the besieging force at about 4500 French and 2500 Americans.
In the Paris Gazette of January 7, 1780, the besieging forces are enumerated as
follows.

FRENCH TROOPS,

    1. *Europeans:* draughted from the regiments of Ar-
       magnac, Champagne, Auxerrois, Agenois, Gatinois,
       Cambresis, Haynault, Foix, Dillon, Walsh, le Cap, la
       Guadeloupe, la Martinique, and Port au Prince, a De-   2.979
       tachment of the Royal Corps of Infantry of the Marine,
       the Volunteers of Vallelle, the Dragoons, and 156
       Volunteer Grenadiers, lately raised at Cape François.
    2. *Colored:* Volunteer Chasseurs, Mulattoes, and Ne-
       groes, newly raised at Saint Domingo, . . .   545

AMERICAN TROOPS, ... 2,000

Total, ... 5,524

"The Siege of Savannah" (1779). The Paris Gazette's report of
January 1780 on the battle at Savannah.

Under what conditions did they serve? The British slaves, of course, had little hope that service at Savannah would end their drudgery. The armed blacks in
British service, on the other hand, would have their freedom at the termination of
war. The blacks and mulattoes from St. Domingue had a completely different
experience. According to d'Estaing's printed orders, the "people of color" in his
army were to "be treated at all times like the whites." "They aspire," he continued, "to the same honor, they will exhibit the same bravery." Even though there
was a tendency to assign the blacks and mulattoes of St. Domingue the most
menial and backbreaking work, d'Estaing repeatedly insisted that they be treated
as *des mousquetaires*.[67]

When General Prevost refused to surrender, more delays occurred as
d'Estaing landed more of his troops, bringing the French force to three thousand
five hundred. With an additional two thousand American troops under the command of Gen. Benjamin Lincoln, the Franco-American force far outnumbered
the defenders. But every step in the siege seemed as ill-advised as the preparations leading up to battle. On September 27 some entrenched French troops mis-
took an arriving group of men just after midnight as the enemy and killed or
wounded fifteen of their own men, most of them black laborers who had been out
digging trenches. The same thing happened again the next morning, with the the
loss of two more friendly soldiers.

Five days later, as d'Estaing bombarded Savannah from both land and sea, a
similar disaster occurred. A ship's steward supplied one ship's bombardiers with
a keg of rum instead of the usual keg of beer during battle alert. The cannoneers
thus "being still under the influence of rum, their excitement did not allow them

to direct their pieces with proper care." Their bombs fell directly into French trenches, causing general alarm.[68]

But some French shells did fall on British and Loyalist targets in Savannah. When the bombardment began, black and white Savannah residents alike lost their lives. One of the first bombs fell on the home of Lt. Gov. John Graham, where "a Mullato Man and three Negroes" were killed in his cellar. In the same bombing, "the House of the Late Mrs. Lloyd, near the Church," one record reported, "was burnt by a shell, and seven Negroes lost their Lives in it." The report continued: "Another burst in the Cellar, under the Office of the Commissioner of Claims, killed one Negro, and wounded another." British major T. W. Moore described his losses as "my fine Negro Carpenter and a beautiful Mare that cost me 20 Guineas" and "my Store of Wine." At the home of Chief Justice Anthony Stokes four slaves were killed instantly and four others were "so much scorched, that they died in a few days." Another "forty women or children of various colors" lost their lives in the intense bombardment.[69]

Both before and during the shelling, many women, children, and slaves fled to Hutchinson Island across the river from Savannah to the plantation of James Graham. Thousands made their way there and were living off the ample but finite provisions of Graham's large harvest. Without soldiers to protect these refugees, General Prevost undertook a most unusual and controversial action. He created an armed garrison consisting of Cherokees and two hundred slaves. Although Prevost claimed that his action was prompted by the French arming of black West Indians and that the plan worked well, there was a storm of protest among Americans—Patriot and Tory—that such action surely endangered white populations.[70]

At the end of four days of shelling, only one British soldier had been hit. Getting desperately short on provisions, d'Estaing decided on October 8 to launch a frontal assault on the city. The attack got underway at midnight and continued throughout the early morning of October 9—despite horrible weather conditions and the depletion by disease and starvation of support crews on French ships. A select force of sixty volunteers led the way, using sadly incorrect logistic information from American engineers. As d'Estaing later recalled, "disorder beg[an] to prevail."[71]

The sixty volunteers were cut down to a man, and their commander, Baron de Steding, was wounded. "Three times d[id] our troops advance en masse up to the entrenchments which [could not] be carried," wrote d'Estaing. "More than half of those who enter[ed were] either killed or remain[ed] stuck fast in the mud." D'Estaing was himself twice wounded, once in the right arm and then in the calf of his right leg. Count Casimir Pulaski—a hero forever to Polish patriots—while leading a brave and continuous charge of his veteran cavalry unit was mortally wounded in the battle. Although d'Estaing himself was barely able to withstand the debilitation of his wounds, he remained in command throughout the carnage. In his notes on the battle, writing in the third person, d'Estaing recalled, "the General, with perfect self-possession, survey[ed] this slaughter, demand[ed] constant renewals of the assault and, although sure of the bravery of his troops, determine[d] upon a retreat only when he [saw] that success [was] impossible."[72]

"View of the Village of Savannah," (October 1779). "Colored Chasseurs, Mulattoes, and Negroes newly raised at Saint Domingo [Domingue]" were positioned for battle just beyond a supply tent and lone tree in the left forefront of this panorama of the battle.

Much of the slaughter of French and American troops was accomplished by two companies of black volunteers who operated on the fringes of the battlefield and by a large armed force of blacks placed directly in front of parapets at the center of attack. By eight o'clock in the morning 61 French officers and 760 French soldiers had fallen. With them 312 Americans, including Pulaski, had been stopped. The rout was so complete that Loyalist colonel John Maitland ordered his troops out of their trenches in pursuit of the badly routed Franco-American army. They chased across the marshes as proud French troops raced away. The marquis de Noailles, whose forces had been shelled by his own navy, saw the British squadrons coming and decided to meet the enemy squarely.[73]

Having lost most of his troops, Noailles called forth his reserve of Volunteer Chassiers from St. Domingue. According to d'Estaing's account, "when the Viscount de Noailles perceiv[ed] the disorder reigning in the columns, he [brought] his reserve corps up to charge the enemy: and . . . afford[ed] an opportunity to the repulsed troops to reform themselves in his rear." Indeed, he made "a demonstration to penetrate within the entrenchments in case the enemy should leave them, and prepare[d] to cut them off in that event." It was d'Estaing's conclusion that "the enemy did not make this apprehended sortie [due] . . . to this excellent disposition of his [d'Estaing's] forces, and this prompt maneuver on the part of the Viscount de Noailles." Noailles and his black corps formed a bold "rear guard" and permitted the French survivors to "retire slowly and in perfect order."

What the British troops came face-to-face with for the first time in their history was a formidable army of black soldiers. These strangely recruited black forces from St. Domingue had been held in reserve to dig trenches, to drive horses, to serve officers. But when they were finally engaged in the battle, their role was decisive. The French and American force was so terribly decimated that the survivors could easily have been slaughtered. But the war-ready St. Domingans stopped the slaughter.[74]

The volunteer chasseurs stopped the counterattack and made it possible for the foolhardy d'Estaing to withdraw his vanquished army and navy. They saw for the first time what it was to face European armies that fought predictable battles. The five hundred or so of them watched eagerly as d'Estaing moved ships, men, armaments, and supplies across waters, marshes, and inhospitable terrain. They saw and used European armaments, observed troop formations and battle plans. And they witnessed the French and British arrogance about the ability of Europeans to extinguish untrained, native, and black enemies. Although armed blacks on both sides had played decisive roles in the outcome of the siege of Savannah, nothing in the rout diminished either d'Estaing, General Prevost, or Colonel Maitland's confidence in the innate superiority of Europeans to wage war.

Even as those five hundred St. Domingans stared down approaching British troops and saved d'Estaing's army from extinction, they also learned much to complement their introduction to European military ways. Henri Christophe, a twelve-year-old boy when he was purchased by a French commander and taken along as a body servant on the venture, fondly recalled his discovery at Savannah of the concept of liberty. (He had never before heard the term.) But Jean-Baptiste Chavannes had excited the young Christophe with stories about liberty, freedom, and equality. That was the meaning of the siege of Savannah, the inspired Chavannes explained. And those goals should have a home, he argued, just as much in St. Domingue as in America.[75]

In just a few short years, Chavannes would launch the campaign for independence from colonial rule in St. Domingue. Christophe concluded that process in 1806 when he installed himself as the first king of an independent Haiti. During the intervening years of bloody revolution, the lessons of Savannah animated the most sustained campaign for liberty and independence in the modern world. Just as black Americans could not know from the outcome of the American Revolution their ultimate fate in the independent United States, neither could those black and mulatto St. Domingans who transported hopes for liberty back to their island in 1779. But it was clear that all peoples of African descent in the process of the American Revolution took on consuming aspirations ever thereafter for liberty.

PART II

WORLD REVOLUTION

CHAPTER 8

Yale College and World Revolution

D uring those sensational years of the American Revolution, there came together on the campus of Yale College in New Haven, Connecticut, a group of individuals who would over the next generation determine the course of liberty in America. Some of them would direct the energies of the abundant corps of philosophers, revolutionaries, soldiers of fortune, and would-be emperors who stalked the earth during the turbulent era of world revolution. Others would establish themselves in positions of power where they could serve as the arbiters of American social, political, and ideological culture. How this cohesive and remarkable group dealt with the challenges and opportunities of American independence and world revolution revealed much about the fate of liberty in America and the Western world between 1776 and the end of the century.

The Yale group consisted of two concentric circles of associates, almost all of whom were at Yale sometime between the years 1771 and 1778. The smaller circle included several ambitious members of the Yale class of 1778. The larger circle encompassed a close-knit group of aspiring poets who came to be denominated as the Hartford Wits. Whatever their literary pursuits, they were more important for the parts they played in defining the role of liberty in American culture.

In the class of 1778 were Richard Alsop, financier of universal interests; Joel Barlow, poet and citizen ambassador abroad; Josiah Meigs, scholar and college president; Zephaniah Swift, congressman and Connecticut jurist; Oliver Wolcott, U.S. secretary of the treasury and longtime Connecticut governor; and, probably the most universally known of all, Noah Webster, journalist and lexicographer. Linking them to the Hartford Wits were their two tutors at Yale, Timothy Dwight, future long-tenured president of Yale, and John Trumbull, future Hartford attorney and leader of the Connecticut litterateurs. Rounding out the eventual group of Wits were Lemuel Hopkins, Hartford physician, and David Humpheys, a career army officer and diplomat who became a successful wool manufacturer at Derby, Connecticut. Younger than all of these, but central in bringing the work of the Hartford Wits to world attention, was Elihu Hubbard Smith, a physician at Wethersfield, Connecticut, who studied medicine under Benjamin Rush in Philadelphia.[1]

Except for Smith, who arrived at Yale in the 1780s, the other ten shared a number of things in common. They derived from deep Connecticut roots (although Swift was born in Massachusetts) and from families accustomed to status and education. They were steeped in New England culture and religion, impelling them by tradition to think first about careers in the clergy before veering off into other less highly called professions. Whatever their chosen direction in life, however, they were determined to be of service to their communities in particular and to society in general.

They also shared an unusual experience at Yale. Most of them were at Yale during the tempestuous days of the American Revolution and saw some strange twists in the tradition of collegiate education. English had just supplanted Latin as the official classroom language. Theology had been downplayed, as greater emphasis came to be placed on science and mathematics. Classroom seating became alphabetical rather than by family social status. Literary and debating societies emerged, tackling the major questions of the age. Enlightenment philosophy was at its height, informing every aspect of instruction, study, and discourse. The efficacy of science and the use of reason infused all branches of learning.

All of the formal learning was bracketed by the onset of revolution. As tensions between Britain and the colonies grew in 1774 and 1775, the fever of impending war impinged on campus life. In February 1775 Yale students began preparing for war. With the assistance of army regulars, a militia company was formed and breastworks were constructed. When word arrived on April 21 that fire had been exchanged between colonists and British troops in Massachusetts, Capt. Benedict Arnold assembled the Yale militia unit and marched it off toward Boston, armed and ready for battle. After a six-week suspension, classes resumed, only to be disrupted again when Loyalist students were driven off campus and when various army dignitaries such as George Washington showed up for inspections and visits.

During 1776 things grew more chaotic at Yale. Classes had to be suspended twice due to disease and lack of food. The student body, led by Noah Webster and Joel Barlow, rose in protest against Yale's tottering president, Naphtali Daggett. Although both Webster and Barlow left school multiple times to participate in military encounters, when they and other students were drafted to serve in the Continental Army in August 1776, their class hired an attorney to secure a deferment. The next year, the New Haven campus closed down, and each class with its tutor dispersed to a different town. In April 1777 the library was removed for safe keeping. Finally, in January 1778 students were sent home to continue studies on their own. Members of the class of 1778 who completed study assignments on their own returned one by one to pick up their degrees.[2]

Amid the direst moments for the student body—just after the declaration of America's independence—Timothy Dwight spoke at graduation ceremonies held on July 25, 1776. He used the occasion to characterize the emerging United States as a new Eden and a latter-day Zion, "the favorite land of heaven" and "the greatest empire the hand of time ever raised up to view." Noting that the historic "progress of liberty, of science, and of empire has been with that of the sun, from east to west, since the beginning of time," he prophesied that in America "the progress of temporal things towards perfection will undoubtedly be finished." Along the way the United States would become, by example and perhaps even by force, the liberator of the world's enslaved peoples from tyranny and superstition.[3]

Dwight's admonitions about America's special destiny combined with the excitement of the moment proved infectious among students and tutors alike. John Trumbull, fellow tutor with Dwight and already a widely published poet, picked up the spirit in *M'Fingal* (published in part in 1776, in full in 1782), the most popular poem of the revolutionary era. A burlesque narrative on the misfortunes of a Scottish Tory, the initial canto reviewed in comic detail the blunders of British leaders. More than thirty pirated editions made it second only to Paine's *Common Sense* in the number of editions and copies distributed as the Revolution progressed.[4]

The rest of the Yale crowd responded by joining the American forces or by versifying about the cosmic struggle being played out in America. David Humphreys heard Dwight's call and joined the armed forces in 1776, writing, "Adieu, thou Yale, where youthful poets dwell." By 1780 he was a lieutenant colonel and aide-de-camp for Gen. George Washington. He would use his writing skills to immortalize American war efforts, especially the martyrdom of Israel Putnam. Lemuel Hopkins served as a medical officer in the Continental Army. Webster marched to Canada in 1776 to fight alongside his brother. The next year he joined his father's company in battle against Burgoyne. Dwight was appointed chaplain of a Connecticut brigade and was soon writing songs for the troops, among them "Columbia, Columbia, to glory arise."[5]

But Joel Barlow and Noah Webster were the two who pondered most seriously the meaning of liberty and the future of America even as the Revolutionary War unfolded. Barlow remained at Yale from 1778 until 1780 writing poetry and laying the groundwork for *The Vision of Columbus,* an epic poem that he continued to revise and expand until it became the monumental *The Columbiad* (1807). The vision of Columbus was Barlow's grand hope for a newly formed American republic. Commissioned an army chaplain in 1780, he served for the duration of the Revolution and he continued to refine *The Vision* until 1782, when he began searching for an appropriate publisher. The full poem, issued in 1787, became an instant bestseller.[6]

Webster, meanwhile, tried to come to grips with the meanings of liberty and revolution for America. In a variety of essays that appeared in the early 1780s in the *New York Packet,* the *Freeman's Chronicle,* and his 1785 book, *Sketches of American Policy,* Webster set forth his own vision for America. He viewed the revolution as a radical break from the past, in which patriarchal systems of governance (monarchy) were replaced with social contracts (constitutions). The rule of reason and the pursuit of virtue replaced the constraints of tradition. In America a utopia was finally possible, in which there would be a more equitable distribution of property among citizens, the end of aristocracy and landed estates, the separation of church and state, the abolition of slavery, and the beginnings of universal education. Webster believed that when "the sovereign power resides in the whole body of the people, it cannot be tyrannical," since "the same power which frames a law, suffers all the consequences, and no individual or collection of individuals will knowingly frame a law injurious to itself."[7]

Timothy Dwight also embraced revolution ideology as he spun out America's first epic poem in 1785, *The Conquest of Canaan*. Written like Barlow's *Vision of Columbus* over a period of years, Dwight attempted to provide the new-born nation with an epic comparable to the *Iliad* or the *Aeneid*. Just as Joshua's victories permitted Israel to enter the promised land, Washington's defeat of British imperialism inaugurated a new Israel in America; God had selected a new chosen people to serve as a light to the world.[8]

The same sentiments appeared in the collaborative works of the Hartford Wits throughout the 1780s. Poems and essays by Alsop, Barlow, Hopkins, Humpheys, and Trumbull appeared in the *American Mercury,* edited by Barlow during 1784 and 1785. The same principles bristled throughout the collaborative "The Anarchiad, a Poem, on the Restoration of Chaos and Substantial Night," appearing over the course of a year in *New Haven Gazette* (1786–87). Editor of the *Gazette* during this period was Yale classmate Josiah Meigs, who was at the time also practicing law and serving as elected city clerk of New Haven. Meigs stirred his fellow Yale graduates to write extensively about liberty and the role of America. At a July Fourth celebration in New Haven in 1789, Meigs gave an address "calculated not only to preserve and feed the sacred flame of liberty, but [also] to recommend industry, manufactures and the liberal arts, and conciliate all parties to a cheerful acquiescence in the new Federal Government."[9]

Although Connecticut was associated with conservative social and political thought, the Yale literati displayed through most of the 1780s a devotion to liberty and a belief in governance by the people. They were working constantly to improve government, society, and education—and they clung to the notion that the United States was indeed the long-awaited land of liberty. Whether they remained at their various posts in Connecticut or ventured across the world, they believed that the millennium of liberty had arrived and that America would forever be its home.

CHAPTER 9

American Liberators
and World Revolution

AMERICAN LIBERATORS ABROAD

While most of the Yale litterateurs settled into careers that would keep them in Connecticut, a number of them traveled elsewhere in America and abroad. Noah Webster oscillated between Hartford, Philadelphia, and New York in the 1780s teaching school, preparing grammar books, and commenting on every issue facing America. In Philadelphia he collaborated with Benjamin Franklin on the study of language and phonetics. Oliver Wolcott also went to New York and then Philadelphia, where he worked in the U.S. Treasury and succeeded Alexander Hamilton as secretary in 1795. Elihu Smith moved to New York, where he was instrumental in publishing *American Poems,* an anthology of the work of the Hartford Wits.[1]

Three of the Yale group went abroad to seek fortune and fame. David Humphreys entered the diplomatic corps. In May 1784 he was appointed secretary of the American Commission for Negotiating Treaties of Commerce with Foreign Powers, and he soon journeyed to Paris for a diplomatic orientation from Benjamin Franklin himself. In 1790 he gathered intelligence for the American government in London, Lisbon, and Madrid. In 1796 he began a five-year term as minister plenipotentiary to Spain. It was in this last position that he collaborated with fellow Hartford Wit, Joel Barlow, in concluding a treaty with the Barbary states to free American prisoners.[2]

Josiah Meigs sought out the Bermuda Court of Vice-Admiralty, where he represented Connecticut clients. As the only American attorney on the island, his business grew exponentially as British privateers seized American ships, cargoes, and crews. By 1794 he had obtained favorable rulings for Americans against so many British privateers that some of the angry losers sought revenge, bringing trumped-up charges against him. He was arrested for treason and held in custody awaiting trial, but was acquitted and released with the assistance of Bermuda governor Henry Hamilton. Narrowly escaping further threats of violence, Meigs and his family headed back to New York, where his considerable pursuit of scientific interests while in Bermuda was rewarded by his election as professor of mathematics and natural philosophy at Yale College.[3]

The foreign adventures of David Humphreys and Josiah Meigs were surpassed by their close associate Joel Barlow. After pursuing four careers—army chaplain, professional poet, newspaper editor, and lawyer—Barlow sailed from New York for France in May 1788. Over a period of seventeen years in Europe, he made a vast fortune.[4]

But he also fell into a life of adventure that would make him for a time perhaps the most important private American citizen residing outside the United States. His willingness to take breathtaking risks placed him among the ranks of Franklin, Jefferson, and Paine. Indeed, by 1790, when he was joined by his equally fascinating and influential wife, the former Ruth Baldwin, Barlow had taken upon himself the mantle of Benjamin Franklin. Though the activities of the Barlows in Europe are little known among historians (there are reasons!), for the next decade and a half Barlow was to France what Franklin had been during his own sojourn there a decade earlier.

Like Franklin, Barlow was deeply interested in science, engineering, printing, pamphleteering, controversy, intrigue, partnerships, quick investments, socializing with the rich and famous, politicking, and frequenting the salons of Paris. From his initial departure when he set out to deliver George Washington Greene, son of Revolutionary hero Nathanael Greene and godson of the President, to Lafayette until he returned in 1805 to the United States, Barlow was at the center of world action.

Barlow's ostensible reason for being in Europe was that he represented the Scioto Company, a development enterprise disposing of lands in Ohio. Just as Franklin had spent a considerable portion of his time in London trying to get Europeans to emigrate to his available tracts, Barlow tried to unload lands of questionable title in Ohio. When the company collapsed in 1790, Barlow came under investigation. While he was found not guilty of fraud or any other crime, his business career was badly derailed for several years until he was able to sell these same lands to people fleeing the violence of revolution.

Whatever was his business, Barlow could view firsthand the players and the scenes of the revolution that were turning Europe upside down. When he first arrived in Paris in 1788 he immediately met both Lafayette and American minister Thomas Jefferson. He shortly traveled to London, where he met Thomas Paine, Joseph Priestley, and Richard Price. He was in Paris on the occasion of the storming of the Bastille, which to him seemed to be the dawning of liberty for France and Europe. In July 1791 Joel and Ruth Barlow moved to London just in time to observe the Birmingham and Sheffield riots that destroyed the homes of Joseph Priestley and Joseph Gales in reaction to the appearance of Thomas Paine's *Rights of Man.*

In the process of finding a publisher for two relatively minor projects, the Barlows became deeply enmeshed with England's most renowned friends of liberty. Bearing his own translation of Brissot de Warville's *Nouveau Voyage,* an account of Brissot's visit to the United States in 1788, and a copy of John Trumbull's *M'Fingal,* Joel Barlow encountered Joseph Johnson, publisher of *Rights of Man, Part 1,* and J. S. Jordan, soon to be the publisher of *Rights of Man, Part 2.*[5]

Also among the lights encountered by the Barlows was Mary Wollstonecraft, the editor for Joseph Johnson's *The Analytical Review.* Even before Thomas Paine could draft the first part of *Rights of Man* in response to Edmund Burke's *Reflections on the Revolution in France,* Wollstonecraft had written and published the first recorded rebuttal, *A Vindication of the Rights of Man.* Burke's *Reflections* had appeared on November 1, 1790, the anniversary of Richard Price's famous sermon. Wollstonecraft, eager to avenge Price, her old pastor and friend, and to demolish Burke's savage attack, issued her *Vindication* just weeks later. Her anonymous essay was so well received that a revised edition bearing her name was issued by Joseph Johnson in December 1790—still just weeks after Burke's initial publication.

Written in the first person and exhibiting flurries and rage at Burke's snickering treatment of the venerable Price, Wollstonecraft set an enviable model that would be followed by hundreds of others within a few short years.

> I perceive, from the whole tenor of your Reflections that you
> have a moral antipathy to reason. . . . The birthright of a man,
> to give you, Sir, a short definition of this disputed right, is to
> such a degree of liberty, civil and religious, as is compatible
> with the liberty of every other individual with whom he is
> united in a social compact.

It was the first of a distinguished string of publications that would follow over the remaining seven years of her brief but productive life.[6]

Just after the publication of *A Vindication of the Rights of Man,* Wollstonecraft met the Barlows. It was a momentous time for her and for them. After years of desperate struggle to provide financial support for her father, a brother, and two sisters, Wollstonecraft at the age of thirty-one was suddenly coming into her own professionally. The Barlows, also struggling financially, were badly in need of finding their own identities in the world. When the three of them came together in London in the summer of 1791, little did they know that they were about to transform themselves and the world.

Wollstonecraft and the Barlows became fast friends as they daily encountered Thomas Paine breathing fire into what would become his *Rights of Man, Part 2.* William Godwin, the radical reformer who would later marry Wollstonecraft, William Blake, and dozens of other radical thinkers gathered around their convivial publishers, Johnson and Jordan. That summer was so inflammatory, in fact, that Johnson decided to turn over the handling of *Rights of Man, Part 1* and the publication of the second part in early 1792 to the more daring Jordan.[7]

In this atmosphere Mary Wollstonecraft chose the Barlows as both role models and her confidants. The Barlows were, according to Wollstonecraft's estimation, passionate lovers when they were together and effusive love letter writers when apart. Wollstonecraft delivered Joel Barlow's letters to Ruth, jealously wishing that she could be the recipient of such intimacies. Inspired by what she saw as a most sensuous union and having led a life devoid of sex, Wollstonecraft suddenly decided to change the course of her life. She sent away her perennially dependent family and moved into a spacious apartment that could accommodate male visitors. She changed her wardrobe, getting herself deeply in debt. And she began making a yearlong effort to win the affections of artist Henry Fuseli, a handsome, adventurous romantic originally from Zurich and eighteen years her senior. He also was married.[8]

As she pursued Fuseli, she entered into one of the happiest and most productive seasons of her life. Noting that Talleyrand had just submitted a plan for national education to the National Assembly, Wollstonecraft reacted vehemently when she discovered that the plan provided a guaranteed education only for males. Talleyrand's unfortunate oversight provided the perfect pretext to publish one of the most important manifestos in the history of liberty, *A Vindication of the Rights of Woman*. Wollstonecraft began writing furiously in the first weeks of October 1791.[9]

Just a few blocks away, Joel Barlow took to his own desk to parallel Wollstonecraft's heroic effort. Picking up some of the inspiration that had caused him to write his *Vision of Columbus* years earlier, he, too, would now take on the world. While Wollstonecraft planned to instruct the public on the proper role and education of women, Barlow wrote what he eventually titled *Advice to the Privileged Orders, in the Several States of Europe, Resulting from the Necessity and Propriety of a General Revolution in the Principle of Government*. By privileged orders he meant anyone in any position of power. Just as Wollstonecraft thought the privileged orders had a moral obligation to correct the treatment of women, Barlow thought they had the same calling to revolutionize all of the outmoded governments of Europe.[10]

Moreover, Thomas Paine stalked the same neighborhood, feverishly working on a new treatise on "kingship." Paine came from France to London virtually the same week as the Barlows. Just before leaving, however, he attended the American contingent's July Fourth celebration at the home of American envoy William Short. There Gouverneur Morris, the American minister and never a great fan of Paine's, thought the radical Paine was "inflated to the eyes and big with a litter of revolutions." In London Paine's enthusiasm for revolution mushroomed as he heard of the incredible popularity of *Rights of Man, Part 1*. *Rights of Man, Part 2* would very closely complement the efforts of both Wollstonecraft and Barlow.[11]

The atmosphere in this London neighborhood must have been electric in the fall of 1791. Joseph Johnson, the eagerly awaiting publisher of both Wollstonecraft and Barlow's treatises, held dinners regularly where the three reformers met and exchanged ideas (it is clear from their resulting texts that they shared much common territory). On November 13, when they would have been deeply absorbed in their respective projects, William Godwin visited specifically to meet Thomas Paine. Though Paine was present, Godwin reported that Wollstonecraft was so animated that she dominated the evening's conversation. She talked so much, Godwin wrote, "I, of consequence, heard her, very frequently when I wished to hear Paine." She criticized everything and everyone that evening, including Godwin. Although they would eventually marry, he said about the evening, "Mary and myself parted, mutually displeased with each other."[12]

Although Godwin did not mention whether or not the Barlows were at the November 13 affair, Joel Barlow described to his brother-in-law his state of mind at the same moment. He said he was working on an assault he intended to call "The Renovation of Society, or An Essay on the Necessity & Propriety of a Revolution in the Governments of Europe." He then revealed,

> I have such a flood of indignation & such a store of argument accumulated in my guts on this subject, that I can hold in no longer; & I think the nurslings of abuses may be stung more to the quick than they have yet been by all the discussions to which the French Revolution has given occasion. Taking it for granted that a similar change through all Europe is inevitable, I propose to examine how far it is desirable, and what will be its consequences.[13]

If Wollstonecraft was in a revolutionary mood and was conscious of it, so was Barlow. Just as she was providing a blueprint for the education of women, he was drawing up a plan for transforming all of the governments of Europe into representative republics.

Paine, on the other hand, seemed to be headed beyond revolution into anarchy. Although Jordan's name appeared on the title page as publisher of *Rights of Man, Part 2,* the latter stages of its publishing were frantic indeed. Thomas Chapman, an admirer of Paine, wanted to publish the book and offered Paine one hundred guineas for the copyright after he had seen its early pages. When Paine declined, Chapman upped his offer to five hundred guineas and then to a thousand. Paine still balked, complaining that if he gave up the copyright he would also lose control of the contents.

Chapman's compositors nevertheless went to work on the first 112 pages of the book. Chapman was pleased. But when he received page proofs for pages 113 to 128, he discovered a dramatic change in focus and tone.

Paine had suddenly shifted from the rights of man to scorn of the British king and government. Sensing that these were potentially seditious statements, Chapman sent a note to Paine cancelling the project. Four hours later an intoxicated Paine appeared at Chapman's office. The discussion—more properly, argument—deteriorated over another four-hour period into a shouting match. At ten in the evening, Chapman's wife offended Paine so badly that he rose in a huff, shouting that he "had not been so personally affronted in the whole course of his life before." Thereupon he summarily fired his publisher.[14]

While Paine was battling with his publisher, Wollstonecraft and Barlow were handing over to Joseph Johnson the final manuscript pages of their works. Just as Chapman had been doing with Paine, Johnson sent a clerk almost daily to pick up newly written pages of *Rights of Woman.* Just as she turned over the last lines and before the book appeared, Wollstonecraft lamented that the system of rapid composition and simultaneous typesetting foreclosed the revisions the work needed. She swore that her next book would be completed before typesetting "for it is not pleasant to have the Devil coming for the conclusion of a sheet before it is written." But on the book's faithfulness to her own outlook and values, she was more certain. She described the book in terms of a portrait that was simultaneously being done of her: "I will send you a more faithful sketch—a book that I am now writing, in which I myself, for I cannot yet attain to Homer's dignity, shall certainly appear, head and heart."[15]

Wollstonecraft gave Johnson her last pages on January 3, 1792. Barlow turned over his last sheets a week later. On January 16 Paine's fissure with Thomas Chapman occurred. Within another week he had entered into a three-way agreement with Johnson and Jordan. Johnson agreed to underwrite part of the costs of publication for the right to sell much of the first printing. Jordan agreed to have his name appear on the title page as publisher for the same right extended to Johnson. In addition to retaining the copyright, Paine stipulated that he alone was the "author and the publisher of that work."[16]

By the third week in January 1792, Johnson had struck a publishing bonanza. Before the end of January, he released Wollstonecraft's *A Vindication of the Rights of Woman;* on February 4 he issued Barlow's *Advice to Privileged Orders;* on February 16 he offered for sale both parts of Paine's *Rights of Man*. Before the end of 1792, Wollstonecraft's book was issued in a second edition and translated into other languages. In under six months Barlow's book saw a second edition and various translations. Within two weeks of publication, Paine's *Rights of Man* exhausted an initial print run of five thousand copies and was in its fourth printing. The all-time bestseller in the English language had just been launched.[17]

JOEL BARLOW, REVOLUTIONARY

The simultaneous publication of three revolutionary works by Mary Wollstonecraft, Joel Barlow, and Thomas Paine further inflamed revolutionary forces throughout Europe. Even as these calls for reform and revolution excited hopes among previously unheard populaces, they alerted those in power to the implications of the revolution at hand. They also put in the minds and on the lips of people the rhetoric of revolution.

Authoring such earth-shattering texts also impacted heavily on each of the writers. The alcoholic Paine, of course, continued to rebel against authority, law, and tradition. Before the end of 1792 he would be forever outlawed in Britain. Within a year, he would find himself imprisoned in France for his revolutionary activities. He never tamed his rebellious temperament.

Wollstonecraft followed a different course. She became a keen and cautious observer of the revolution she had helped to foment. Whatever her own instincts, she was able to stand outside the revolution and dispassionately evaluate its tendencies.

Barlow, unlike either Paine or Wollstonecraft, was one of the most dangerous types to have around during a revolution. He loved revolutionary intrigue. He loved secret deals. He thoroughly enjoyed all of the pageantry that came with organized politics, parades, and military clashes. He was one of the original schemers, willing to help launch invasions, deliver weapons and shoes to armies,

Joel Barlow (1793). Poet, entrepreneur, and instigator of worldwide revolution.

and assist engineers develop new weapons of war. Given his widespread business interests in the exchange of property, commodities, and business partners, he pursued games of war all over Europe from February 1792 until his return to the United States in 1805.

Advice to the Privileged Orders launched Barlow, and during 1792 and 1793 he played the role of revolutionary to the hilt. Although the first two editions of *Advice to the Privileged Orders* amounted to a total of only one thousand copies, coming as it did as part of a triple barrel shot of revolutionary works, the names Barlow and Paine were almost always conjoined. The shared publicity made Barlow, for a few years, an international figure. Emulating Paine's frenzied dash from one publication to another, Barlow kept his name in circulation.[18]

A month after the publication of *Advice,* Joseph Johnson issued *The Conspiracy of Kings, a Poem: Addressed to the Inhabitants of Europe, from another Quarter of the World.* In October Barlow's third revolutionary piece of the year, *A Letter to the National Convention of France, on the Defects in the Constitution of 1791, and the Extent of the Amendments which Ought to Be Applied* appeared. Barlow also finished part two of *Advice* and turned the text over to Johnson. By that time, however, Barlow had become almost as odious to British authorities as Paine. Johnson, already under indictment for his involvement with

Rights of Man, thereby withheld publication. When the second part finally appeared in print in September 1793, it came from the English Press of Paris. Not until July 4, 1795, would it appear in London under the imprint of a new publisher, Daniel Isaac Eaton.[19]

By 1792 Barlow had made himself persona non grata to the British government. In December 1792 Edmund Burke rose on the floor of the House of Commons and derided him as "Prophet Joel" and as one "who threatened to lay our capital and constitution in ruin." Ruth Barlow wrote to him on January 1, 1793, "Here you cannot return at present; everything evil is said of you." Nine days later, she sounded the same theme: "You cannot think how much you are abused here. . . . You are very obnoxious here and it is thought you cannot return with safety; the Alien Bill would prevent you, if nothing more."[20]

He had said plenty, in print and in public, that proved his mettle as a revolutionary. In *Advice to the Privileged Orders* he had not only heartily approved the French Revolution, he also had urged that it be expanded throughout the world. "The change of government in France is," he wrote, "properly speaking, a renovation of society." It "comes recommended to us under one aspect which renders it at first view extremely inviting," he continued, "it is the work of argument and rational conviction, and not of the sword." He exhorted those in power to embrace the revolution:

> To induce the men who now govern the world to adopt these ideas, is the duty of those who now possess them. I confess the talk at first view appears more than Herculean; it will be thought an object from which the eloquence of the close[s]t must shrink in despair, and which prudence would leave to the more powerful argument of events.

When the question of what to do about Louis XVI arose for Barlow, he considered "royalty is preserved in France for reasons which are fugitive." Rather, "a majority of the people will learn to be disgusted with so unnatural and ponderous a deformity in their new edifice, and will soon hew it off." There was no alternative because "a general revolution is at hand, whose progress is irresistible."[21]

Like most Americans, Barlow frequently cited instructive American models. Urging the extension of liberty to all peoples, Barlow wrote:

> In the United States of America, the science of liberty is universally understood, felt and practised, as much by the simple as the wise, the weak as the strong. Their deep-rooted and inveterate habit of thinking is, that <u>all men are equal in their rights</u>, that <u>it is impossible to make them otherwise</u>; and . . . they have no conception how any man in his senses can entertain any other.

Idealizing America's electoral system, Barlow wrote, "The President of the United States, who has more power while in office than some of the kings of Europe, is chosen with as little commotion as a churchwarden."[22]

In the poem *The Conspiracy of Kings* Barlow continued his call for world revolution, especially against the existing powers in Europe:

> Of these no more. From Orders, Slaves and Kings,
> To thee, O Man, my heart rebounding springs.
> Behold th' ascending bliss that waits your call,
> Heav'n's own bequest, the heritage of all.
> Awake to wisdom, seize the proffer'd prize;
> From shade to light, from grief to glory rise.
> Freedom at last, with Reason in her train,
> Extends o'er earth her ever-lasting reign. . . .
> Shake tyrants from their thrones, and cheer the waking world
> In northern climes where feudal shades of late
> Chill'd every heart and palsied every State.

The model for the "wide world . . . skirts the western sky" in the United States where "that rare union, Liberty and Laws, / Speaks to the reas'ning race 'to freedom rise, / Like them be equal, and like them be wise.'"[23]

The most direct of Barlow's 1792 publications was his *Letter to the National Convention of France,* wherein he offered a list of radical correctives to the draft constitution. Arguing that the people of France get rid of the king and follow the example of the United States, Barlow playfully compared the process with other realms:

> A republic of beavers or of monkeys, I believe, could not be benefited by receiving their laws from men, any more than men could be in being governed by them. If the Algerines or the Hindoos were to shake off the yoke of despotism, and adopt ideas of equal liberty, they would that moment be in a condition to frame a better government for themselves, than could be framed for them by the most learned statesman in the world.

Barlow concluded by stating, "On considering the subject of government, when the mind is once set loose from the shackles of royalty, it finds itself in a new world." Despite his call to eliminate the monarchy, Barlow's advice indicates that he drew heavily upon provisions of the U.S. Constitution in recommending revisions to France's document. Whether the National Assembly listened or not, most of Barlow's suggestions were eventually incorporated in the French constitution.[24]

Barlow's central message goaded the French to follow the example of Americans and rid themselves of monarchy, aristocracy, and privileged orders. His deeds during 1792 were consistent with his written words. Just a month after the appearance of *Advice to the Privileged Orders* he helped rejuvenate London's Society for Constitutional Information. He and Thomas Paine persuaded the organization to adopt resolutions calling for a reformation of Parliament by abolishing the representation there of "privileged orders":

> Resolved, That a fair and impartial representation can never
> take place until partial privileges are abolished; and the strong
> temptations held out to electors affords a presumptive proof,
> that the representatives of this country seldom procure a seat in
> parliament, from the unbought suffrages of a free people.

Barlow then left London on a strange mission to the eastern frontier of France
where Lafayette was poised to attack the Austrian Army at the end of April. After
conferring with Lafayette, he proceeded to Paris where on June 20 he watched an
angry mob attack the Tuileries and humiliate Louis XVI. In his letter to Ruth
Barlow about the attack he wrote, "This visit to the king by armed citizens was
undoubtedly contrary to law, but the existence of a king is contrary to another law
of a higher origin."[25]

By the time he returned to London in July, *Advice to the Privileged Orders*
had gone into a second edition and he was being proposed for French citizenship.
Brissot de Warville's newspaper praised Barlow's work and described his book as
"almost equal in merit to the work on the Rights of Man by Mr. Paine." Even
before his *Letter to the National Convention* could be delivered, he was elected to
citizenship, joining the select company of Washington, Hamilton, Jefferson,
Madison, and Paine.[26]

Before sending his *Letter* to France, Barlow presented it to both the Constitution Society and the London Corresponding Society. In his letter of transmission,
Barlow observed that "the present disposition in Europe towards a general revolution in the principles of government is founded in the current of opinion, too powerful to be resisted, as well as too sacred to be treated with neglect." The Constitution Society happily endorsed Barlow and the *Letter,* stating that the members
"trust, that your excellent writings in general, and the letter to the Convention of
France in particular, will be eminently conducive to the success of final triumph of
that cause, which you justly style 'the most glorious that ever engaged the attention of mankind.'" Barlow forwarded his published *Letter* to Thomas Paine, who
presented it formally to the National Convention on November 7.

By that time Paine had become not only a citizen of France, but also a member of the National Convention. Barlow evidently decided that what was good
enough for Paine would also be right for him. In preparation for Barlow's move
to France, the Constitution Society appointed him to prepare an address congratulating the National Convention on its suspension of Louis XVI and its declaration
of the French republic. On November 9 the society adopted Barlow's report and
deputized him along with another member of the society, John Frost, to deliver
the document to the National Convention. The address bristled with Barlow's
revolutionary rhetoric:

> Servants of a Sovereign people, and Benefactors of mankind!
> We rejoice that your revolution has arrived at that point of per-
> fection which will permit us to address you by this title . . .
> Every successive epoch in your affairs has added something to

> the triumphs of liberty . . . The lustre of the American republic
> . . . arose with increasing vigour . . . till the splendour of the
> French revolution burst forth upon the nations in the full fer-
> vour of a meridian sun. . . . In this career of improvement your
> example will be soon followed: for nations, rising from their
> lethargy, will reclaim the Rights of Man with a voice which
> man cannot resist.

For a brief moment Barlow was the principal voice of the friends of liberty in the
English-speaking world.

A week later Barlow and Frost headed to Paris. Just two weeks before Louis
XVI would be put on trial, they appeared before the National Convention with
their message from the Society for Constitutional Information. After presenting
"their congratulations on the triumphs of liberty," Barlow added: "After the
example which France has given, the science of revolutions will be rendered
easy, and the progress of reason will be rapid. It would not be strange if, in a
period far short of what we should venture to predict, addresses of felicitation
should cross the seas to a national convention in England." Barlow and Frost
boasted to the Constitutional Society that they were "received with universal
applause." The president of the Convention gave them "the kiss of fraternity in
behalf of the French nation, which we returned on behalf of our society." The
event "drew tears from a crowded assembly" of friends of liberty representing
England, Ireland, Scotland, France, and, with Barlow's presence, America.
Observed Barlow, "The wounds which had bled for ages were closed and forgot,
while the voice of nature declared they should never more be opened."[27]

Barlow moved to Paris to observe firsthand the revolution. He embraced his
French citizenship and announced that he would stand for election to the National
Convention. He reported to the Convention that the Constitutional Society of
London had "sent to the soldiers of liberty [Lafayette's troops] a patriotic dona-
tion of 1000 pairs of shoes" and that the society would send an additional thou-
sand pairs weekly for at least six weeks.[28]

The depth of Barlow's commitment to world revolution, however, was best
revealed by another letter he wrote on December 27, 1792, to the citizens of Italy.
Written in French and published simultaneously in both French and Italian, Barlow's *A Letter Addressed to the People of Piedmont, on the Advantages of the
French Revolution, and the Necessity of Adopting Its Principles in Italy* was one
of the most militant documents ever written by an American openly promoting
the overthrow of a foreign government. Acknowledging that he had never been to
Italy, Barlow opined that a revolution would be a good thing for Italians: "You
are my fellow-creatures; as such I love you, and cherish the ties which ought to
be mutual between us. You are in a condition which appears to me to call upon
you to burst the bands of slavery; in this view, I am ready to hail you as brothers,
and wish to aid you in your work." He argued that Italians would be better off
under the French government than the King of Sardinia, since France "when

engaged, as she now is, in the defence of liberty" was "a match for all the other powers of Europe, when united in defence of tyranny." He boldly declaimed, "France is now your natural friend, the friend of all people and the enemy of all tyrants."[29]

As 1793, the Year of Terror, opened, Barlow was thoroughly committed to promoting revolution throughout the world.

LIBERTY AND LOVE

As Joel Barlow chased revolution all over France and beyond, fellow revolutionary Mary Wollstonecraft played out her own revolutions publicly and privately. She was also making herself one of the most acute observers of the extraordinary events driving Europe. Her maturing powers made the years of terror into seasons of both bliss and bitter disappointment. Her extreme experiences were provoked in part by the direction of world revolution, but even more by the course of Barlow and one of his fellow American revolutionaries.

The publication of *A Vindication of the Rights of Woman* in January 1792 wrought a transformation of the history of women and of Wollstonecraft. The text of the manifesto and subtle changes between the first and the second edition hint at the change. Both editions began with an open letter to Talleyrand in which Wollstonecraft declared that "I plead for my sex—not for myself." Her hope was "to see woman placed in a station in which she would advance, instead of retarding, the progress of those glorious principles that give a substance to morality." She continued: "My main argument is built on the simple principle, that if she be not prepared by education to become the companion of man, she will stop the progress of knowledge and virtue; for truth must be common to all, or it will be inefficacious with respect to its influence on general practice." Outlining "the pernicious effects which arise from the unnatural distinctions established in society," she called not only for a full and enlightened education for women but also for all men, in place of the conventional education in warfare they received.[30]

However bold her theories, her first edition contained an interesting bit of timidity. Her printed letter to Talleyrand displayed a clear note of deference: "But, Sir, I carry my respect for your understanding still farther; so far, that I am confident you will not throw my work aside, and hastily conclude that I am in the wrong, because you did not view the subject in the same light yourself."

In the second edition, this pleading note had disappeared. She knew by then that Talleyrand took her work seriously. In removing to London on his fugitive diplomatic mission, Talleyrand paid a long visit to Wollstonecraft to discuss the book.[31]

While Talleyrand was in flight, Wollstonecraft yearned desperately to get close to the fray in Paris. She proposed that she and her publisher, Joseph Johnson, accompany the Fuselis on a tour of France in the summer of 1792. They set out on the adventure in early August. But before they could cross the channel at

Dover, word arrived that the Assembly had deposed Louis XVI and that he had been imprisoned. Turned back toward London, Wollstonecraft missed a six-week taste of revolution as well as the opportunity of being constantly with Henri Fuseli, the object of her infatuation.

Frustrated that she could not consummate her relationship with Fuseli, Wollstonecraft conceived the notion of moving in with his family. In response, Fuseli's wife forbade her from ever seeing the artist again. Even more downcast at that point, Wollstonecraft decided to join the Barlows in Paris. On her departure she wrote, "At Paris, indeed, I might take a husband for the time being and get divorced when my truant heart longed again to nestle with its old friends." She departed England just as Louis XVI went on trial for his life. Little did she know that she would soon have her own faith in revolution put severely to test.

Wollstonecraft very quickly came face-to-face with the realities of a nation in the midst of revolutionary upheaval. Even as she found happy company with the Barlows, Thomas Paine, and the band of émigrés there to promote the arrival of liberty, she witnessed the growing rage of the French citizenry. Louis XVI, on his way to his death sentence passed by her window, "moving silently along (excepting now and then a few strokes on the drum . . .) through empty streets." She wrote, "The inhabitants flocked to their windows, but the casements were all shut, not a voice was heard."

That scene and the trail of blood that followed pierced Wollstonecraft to the core. Her reaction to seeing the king was telling: "I can scarcely tell you why, but an association of ideas made the tears flow insensibly from my eyes, when I saw Louis sitting, with more dignity than I expected from his character, in a hackney-coach, going to meet death." As executions piled up, she began to wonder what had happened to the great cause of liberty. "Out of the chaos of vices, follies, prejudices and virtues, rudely jumbled together," she attempted to discern "the fair form of Liberty slowly rising." But she could not find it. "Before I came to France," she lamented, "I . . . anticipated the epoch, when, in the course of improvement, men would labour to become virtuous." But she had to admit that "the perspective of the golden age . . . almost eludes my sight." [32]

As revolution devolved into chaos, Wollstonecraft carried out her personal revolution. In response to her pleas for help in finding a husband, the Barlows introduced her to a fellow American adventurer, Gilbert Imlay. An officer in the American Revolution, Imlay was handsome, ambitious, and well-educated. Like Barlow he was a speculator in lands and business and became a competent author. After the Revolution he worked in Kentucky as surveyor and speculator on the American frontier, but soon became entangled in a web of financial difficulties. When his liabilities became unbearable, he fled America and ended up a few years later in England. [33]

Through his frontier experience, Imlay found new careers in writing and international intrigue. Thomas Cooper introduced him to friends of liberty throughout England. These contacts then enabled him to publish in 1792 *A*

Topographical Description of the Western Territory of North America, a tantalizing depiction of the American frontier combining history, natural science, and the folkways of American pioneers. He glorified America's revolutionary trajectory as a model for the world, hoping that Europe's "governments will arrive at perfection, and FREEDOM, in golden plumes, and in her triumphal car, must now resume her long lost empire."[34]

Imlay joined Barlow as both business partner and schemer. Barlow negotiated deals to supply France with raw materials from Scandinavia and America; Imlay scheduled, coordinated, and oversaw shipments and deliveries. Barlow planned and joined with French officials to export revolution to Italy, Austria, and Louisiana; Imlay planned to captain the French forces that would liberate Louisiana from Spain. It was Imlay and Barlow's scheme for a "Revolutionary Legion of America" that Edmond Genet tried to implement as he paraded across America in 1793. What came to be viewed as French political intrigue and which led to Genet's downfall was actually a plan conceived by Americans abroad.[35]

It was at the very moment Barlow and Imlay were conspiring with Genet in Paris that Wollstonecraft met Imlay. She described him as tall, handsome, warmhearted, and "perfectly in unison with [her] mode of thinking." By April 19, Joel Barlow wrote to Ruth, saying, "I believe she has got a sweetheart—and that she will finish by going with him to A[meric]a a wife." The union, seemingly made in heaven, would bring together a daring English proponent of liberty and an American adventurer who not only believed in revolution, but who was making it his business to organize it. There began one of the most famous love affairs in modern history.

As the Reign of Terror began, they blended their revolutionary ideas. Imlay was writing a novel that he titled *The Emigrants.* It became a joint project that, when published in July 1793, was an expansion upon Wollstonecraft's *Rights of Woman.* The pair probed the meaning of liberty, the laws of nature, free love, mutual responsibility, marriage, and divorce. Moreover, it revealed Wollstonecraft's desire to emigrate with Imlay to America.

The fall of the Girondist government at the end of May made it suddenly unsafe for English and American foreigners to remain in Paris. Wollstonecraft and Imlay found a house in the village of Neuilly, and only the Barlows knew of their happy union there. Wollstonecraft's private revolution became complete as she began, happy and inspired, to write her history of the French Revolution. By the end of the summer her fulfillment was complete when she realized she would bear a child.[36]

Imlay shrewdly worked with Barlow to import essential goods through the English naval blockade. This vital service protected Imlay and Barlow in a country that had turned on nearly every foreigner. It also enabled Imlay to get a certificate declaring Wollstonecraft as the wife of an American citizen—despite the fact that neither of them planned to be married. But it also took him away to Le Havre, where he oversaw his part of the partnership with Barlow. When he departed Paris in September 1793, leaving Wollstonecraft to face her pregnancy and the French Revolution alone, Imlay launched fully into the role of a mercenary of revolution.[37]

While he aided the French military machine he abandoned Wollstonecraft. For four months she begged him to return to Paris. When he did not, she borrowed money from Ruth Barlow and headed to Le Havre five months into her pregnancy. Although Imlay remained civil and helpful to Wollstonecraft, their brief flirtation was over. The child, a girl, was born in May 1794. In September Imlay announced a trip to London from which he would never return. Following six months of increasingly agitated letters, Wollstonecraft headed to London. Finding him living with another woman, Wollstonecraft wrote Imlay a farewell letter and swallowed a large dose of poison.[38]

Though he was duplicitous, Imlay was not heartless. When Wollstonecraft's letter arrived more quickly than anticipated, he raced to her rescue. To get her out of her suicidal mood, he urged her to take a trip to Scandinavia, where she could represent him in concluding a variety of business deals. The ploy worked quite well since, on that trip, Wollstonecraft composed her peaceful and elegant *Letters Written During a Short Residence in Sweden, Norway, and Denmark*. She also wrote a spate of powerful love letters to Imlay. But nothing worked. Though he responded with an equal number of caring letters, he was no longer hers.[39]

Returning to London in October 1795 to find that Imlay had once again "formed some new attachment," Wollstonecraft became despondent. After unsuccessfully imploring Imlay to return to her, she again chose death. She gave Imlay instructions on the disposition of her daughter, her clothes, and her funds, then wrote, "Let my wrongs sleep with me! Soon, very soon, I shall be at peace. . . . I shall plunge into the Thames where there is the least chance of my being snatched from the death I seek." She took a small boat upriver to the Putney bridge where water currents were strong and the area dark. After a half-hour soaking up a driving rain to make herself heavier, she plunged into the river. When her body floated by a riverboat two hundred yards downstream, boatmen pulled her out and rushed her to a tavern, where a physician was able to revive her.[40]

Although she wrote a few more painful letters to Imlay, the spell was broken. A month later, Imlay left for Paris with his new mistress. In his wake, he left a sordid financial mess that was suddenly transferred to Wollstonecraft. To rid herself of debts, she published her letters from Scandinavia. She also returned to her career with the assistance of her faithful publisher, Joseph Johnson. Within months she tumbled into a new affair with William Godwin, her former irritant. Theoretically opposed to marriage, they nevertheless took marriage vows in March 1797, and soon after she revealed she was pregnant. On August 30, Mary Godwin, later renowned as Mary Shelley, was born. But the birth was fatal to Mary Wollstonecraft. On September 10, she was freed from her short life.[41]

As for Gilbert Imlay, without Mary Wollstonecraft or Joel Barlow, he was an American adventurer afloat in Europe without portfolio. There are no clues to his further life. His principal contribution to the cause of liberty, it turned out, was to stoke the fires of Mary Wollstonecraft's troubled but unbounded creativity.[42]

LIBERTY AND INTRIGUE

Gilbert Imlay was not the only American adventurer skulking around Europe in the name of liberty. Nor was Mary Wollstonecraft the only woman daring to challenge convention. Europe in the 1790s, and especially France, was filled with an extraordinary assortment of characters, participating in the world's longest-lived season of revolution. So many appeared that vast catalogs of names and of largely forgotten events are required to track the galleries of illustrious players.

There was, for example, Marie-Olympe de Gouges, a beautiful actress and woman of letters, who anticipated Mary Wollstonecraft's appeals for the rights of women. Her pleas before the National Assembly in 1791 and publication that year of *Declaration of the Rights of Women and Citizenesses* set the stage for Wollstonecraft's more monumental and memorable *A Vindication of the Rights of Woman.* She also sympathized with the plight of Louis XVI to the point of offering to defend him during his lengthy trial. For this defiant act she was arrested in July 1793 and guillotined during the mass execution of the Girondonists on November 4.[43]

There was also the more widely recognized Germaine Necker de Staël, who influenced politicians, generals, ambassadors, and kings throughout the entire generation of revolutions from 1789 until the fall of Napoléon. From the moment of her internationally negotiated marriage in 1786 until she and liberal theorist Benjamin Constant, the last of her long list of acknowledged lovers, helped inspire the overthrow of Napoléon, she was constantly at work pulling strings and levers.[44]

She, like so many others, was driven by her search for personal liberty. When she married she took over her mother's salon, a gathering that had brought her face-to-face with Voltaire, Rousseau, Diderot, and D'Alembert. Her male audience helped inspire her toward a distinguished literary career in fiction, critical essays, and political treatises culminating in a posthumously published history, *Considerations on the Principal Events of the French Revolution* (1818) that informed virtually all future histories of the Revolution.[45] Although she started her career with two autobiographical novels, *Sophie* (1786) and *Jane Grey* (1787), her first philosophical work, *Letters on Jean-Jacques Rousseau* (1788) stoked the enlightenment fires that launched the French Revolution.[46]

Through her salon, de Staël established a stable of lovers. Her practice of taking multiple lovers, of conducting business in bedroom and bath, and of dressing or undressing before guests made her name synonymous with a revolutionary mode of decorum. While such behavior might have shocked John Adams, it seemed not to bother Benjamin Franklin, Gouverneur Morris, or Joel Barlow. Indeed, the lifestyle adopted by the Barlows for the remainder of their lives—whether they were in Paris or in Washington, D.C.—suggests that they and other Americans embraced the sexual revolution that accompanied the French Revolution.[47]

But it was due to her father's role in the latter days of the ancien régime that de Staël managed always to be on the scene as the French Revolution unfolded. She accompanied him from their Swiss home to his triumphal reentry into Paris after the storming of the Bastille in 1789. She was with him at Versailles in October 1789, when French mobs brought Louis and Marie Antoinette to Paris. She also witnessed the attack of twenty thousand Parisians on the Tuileries in June 1792.[48]

The onset of terror drove de Staël to reflect on human suffering. When her friend and compatriot Marie Antoinette came to trial in the summer of 1793, she wrote *Reflections on the Trial of the Queen, by a Woman,* urging understanding and forgiveness for the foreign-born queen. As the terror deepened she labored over analyses of perverse human behavior including *Reflections on Peace, Addressed to Mr. Pitt and the French* (1794), *Reflections on Internal Peace* (1795), and *On the Influence of Passions on the Happiness of Individuals and of Nations* (1796). In these de Staël outlined the framework for an orderly liberal republic that would become classic works for generations of leaders across the world seeking to build and preserve republics.[49]

Wherever de Staël went, she busied herself with the affairs of government and nations. During the height of the Terror, she exiled herself to Juniper Hall, a mansion at Surrey, England, that she maintained for herself and other friends away from the killings. There she interacted daily with Louis XVI's minister of war, with Talleyrand, and with other fugitives who conspired desperately to end the French excesses.[50]

While biding her time back in Switzerland, de Staël encountered her other best remembered conspirator, Benjamin Constant. Although from a wealthy family, Constant passed from matron to tutor, temporary home to boarding school, mistress to jail until he joined forces with de Staël in late 1794. Having attended private academies, Oxford, and Edinburgh, he had just enough background in languages, philosophy, history, and economics to become a dangerous ideologue. Like de Staël, he began to doubt the direction of the French Revolution while still espousing liberty and republicanism.[51]

This odd pair of activist intellectuals descended on Paris in 1796. They immediately established a new salon, the Constitutional Circle, or Club de Salm, as a place to assemble co-conspirators. They published a new liberal manifesto under Constant's name, *On Political Reactions* (1797). Most importantly, de Staël arranged for the appointment of her first and most persistent lover, Talleyrand, as minister of foreign affairs under the Directory. By mid-1797 de Staël and her retinue of male admirers had pervaded the governance of France.[52]

LIBERATING ENGLAND AND IRELAND

As the French Revolution lost its direction, Europe and America entered into a season punctuated by sensational covert insurgencies. The new wave of revolution consisted in the exercise of military force. Wherever those forces were being poised for war, impassioned Americans and other exiles joined the field of battle.

The political culture that brought forth de Staël, Constant, Talleyrand, and even Napoléon was the perfect place for adventurers, ideologues, and visionaries to act out their missions. At the same time Talleyrand returned to France, two strange figures arrived from America: Theobald Wolfe Tone, hoping for support to liberate his homeland, and the shadowy William Tate, seeking an army to invade England. Each man believed with every fiber of his being that the peoples of Ireland and England would rally to the support of a military force whose purpose was the overthrow of the tyrannical British monarchy.[53]

After spending much of 1794 organizing a Revolutionary Legion in America, only to see the French government cancel its use, Tate crossed the Atlantic in June 1795 to reside in Paris at the Maison Boston on Rue Vivienne. While awaiting confirmation of his appointment in the French army, Tate began spinning plans to capture Jamaica for France with his Revolutionary Legion. Theobald Wolfe Tone arrived in Paris in February 1796 and lodged in the Hôtel des Étrangers, also on Rue Vivienne just a few doors from Tate's residence. Within weeks the two adventurers, Tate in his early seventies and Tone in his early thirties, became an odd pair of co-conspirators.[54]

Tone had made some impressive connections while he was in America. He came to France bearing a coded message from John Beckley intended for American minister James Monroe and another coded message for the French Directory from Pierre Adet, French minister to the United States. Monroe, himself a friend of liberty and an avid supporter of the French Revolution, warmly received Tone. Indeed, it was through Monroe's connections in the Directory that Tone received a hearing for his plans to use French support to liberate Ireland.[55]

By April the Directory had embraced the notion of sending a French force to invade Ireland. Authorization was given in June to assemble three corps of troops, twenty-seven thousand strong, complete with a fleet of ships for support and artillery to take whole cities. Tone proceeded to Dunkirk in September, where the army would be organized and trained with his assistance as adjutant general. There, however, he was shocked to find that the promised forces consisted of deserters, convicts released on condition of military service, troublemakers transferred from other army units, and inexperienced Irish political refugees. Tone viewed the growing Légion Noire as a pack of "desperadoes" who might create havoc wherever they went, but who probably could not be made into an effective fighting force.[56]

Tone almost despaired in November when the French generals decided to attack England rather than Ireland. At that point Tate was suddenly placed in command of the ragtag force and plans were redrawn to make two English landings, one near Newcastle and the other at Bristol. The object of the exercise would be to cause panic in the English countryside, level Bristol, and then threaten the same fate for Liverpool. If all went as planned, great sums of money would be extorted from the British government to spare Liverpool. Tone watched helplessly as his hopes to liberate Ireland spiraled into an ambitious raid on England. He had to swallow his pride doubly when he was asked to translate French orders to Tate into English.[57]

Tone eventually developed a relish for the attack on England and an attachment for the old, but "dashing" Tate. As he pondered the objectives of burning whole cities, Tone reflected,

> But such a thing is war! The British burned without mercy in America; they endeavoured to starve 25,000,000 of souls in France, and, above all, they are keeping, at the moment, my country in slavery, my friends in prison, myself in exile. It is these considerations which steel me against horrors which I should otherwise shudder to think of.

But just when Tate and Tone had become an effective working force, Tone was removed to serve as a special aide to the French general Louis-Lazare Hoche. Tate was left to undertake the invasion of England without Tone's inspiration.

With elaborate campaign instructions, William Tate as Chef de Brigade was ready to undertake the plan in February 1797. Two of the largest frigates in the French Navy, the *Vengeance* and the *Resistance,* were assigned to carry Tate and his men across the Channel. Encountering ill winds, they could not land at Bristol as planned. After some angry words between Tate and the French commodore about shoddy seamanship, the force headed to their secondary objective, Cardigan Bay.

By this time the presence of the squadron had been noted. A British ship captain reported seeing "three Ships of War which appeared to be Frigates of about 40 guns each." Four days later a retired sailor on the Cardiganshire coast reported a sighting of "four ships of war flying the British colours, their decks crammed with troops." When one of the ships approached Fishguard Bay, an alert bombardier in the fort fired a 9-pound blank saluting the arrival of the British colors. The French commander, believing his ship was instead being fired upon, lowered the British flag and hoisted the French tricolor. Entirely by mistake, the battle was joined.

Before February 22 was over, word of the invasion had reached the British Admiralty. The invading force also disembarked that day—17 crowded boats, 2,000 arms, 47 barrels of gunpowder, and food stores. By late afternoon of the next day, Tate, tall and in blue officer's uniform, stood on the rocks below firing pistols from each hand, bidding the squadron farewell. Local residents, perched on cliffs above, sent excited messages in all directions that England had been invaded by a hostile force. Scrambling to learn anything it could about French intentions, Admiralty officers began interrogating recently arrested prisoners of war and learned that a second force of ten thousand men would shortly join Tate's lead party of two thousand. Shocked at the potential proportions of the invasion, British officials scrambled to counter what seemed to be the beginning of a bloody flood tide.

Tate sent an advance party under the command of a young Irish rebel, Lt. Barry St. Leger, to establish a headquarters in a nearby farmhouse. Over St. Leger's orders the place was ransacked, but it served its purpose during the first phase of the invasion. On the following morning Tate divided his force into two groups, sending them eastward in parallel lines to nearby villages. His purpose was rally local residents to his cause and to organize them into his army. As they advanced, his troops hoisted the French tricolor. But provisioned for only four days, they soon had to begin foraging for their own food and supplies.[58]

The search for food, horses, and drink clarified the true nature of Tate's force. As they divided into ever smaller foraging parties, they raced from house to house taking every live animal and morsel of food they could find. Their exploration for drink was greatly enhanced by the fact that every cottage contained at least one cask of wine recovered just days before from a nearby shipwreck. Foraging quickly devolved into gluttony and drunkenness. When the parties returned to Tate's encampment, they brought not only food and drink, but also guns, swords, tools, candleholders, furniture, and anything else of value. Others became so drunk that they did not bother to return. One group attacked a local farmer and took his silver watch, shoe buckles, and money. When Tate ordered the execution of the leader of this band, his troops refused to carry out the order.

By the end of the first day the great invasion of England had degenerated into farce. Even before Tate could begin his first military action, British militia were advancing to repel the invaders. Seeing that he had lost entire control of his army and alienated everyone in the area of Fishguard Bay, Tate decided to surrender. Meanwhile his officers, mainly Irish rebels, were incensed that they were attacking England, not Ireland. Tate, sensing a disaster in the making, rushed to find a bloodless solution.

Early on the morning of February 24, Tate sent word to Lord Cawdor, commander of the British defense, that he would surrender on any terms. Thousands of citizens gathered, meanwhile, to see the anticipated battle from the cliffs above. Lord Cawdor, however, received both Tate's unconditional surrender and his sword. The remaining troops marched off under guard, singing, shouting, and laughing, happier as prisoners of war than they had been as invaders. Tate and his officers were taken across Wales and to London, hounded by angry mobs wherever they went. Tate, embarrassed by the failure of his long-planned invasion, wrote, "I have . . . no other care than to avoid becoming a subject of derision to my enemies in the United States of America who are no other than the British (and Spanish) partisans." He desperately did not want to be deported to the United States under the circumstances of his dismal defeat.[59]

On March 4 Tate and his fellow officers arrived in London to face their fate. Under questioning, the men stated that they rebelled when they learned that they were in Wales and not in the West Indies, where Tate had once promised they would be going. They tried to distance themselves from Tate and the invasion, since, at least the Irish officers, could be treated as traitors rather than as prisoners of war. Charges of treason were not preferred. They were confined as prisoners of war for eighteen months, then paroled to France. St. Leger escaped captivity. Tate was exchanged for British prisoners of war in France on November 24, 1798. Tate had no little difficulty getting himself reestablished in the French Army. Eventually restored to half pay, he resumed his role of dreaming up ways to attack the British, remaining in French uniform until he was almost eighty years old.[60]

Theobold Wolfe Tone (1798). Quixotic Irish revolutionary; sentenced to die, he committed suicide and thus became a martyr.

Tone, meanwhile, was not discouraged by the ill-fated invasion of England. After a failed landing at Bantry Bay in December 1796 and Tate's debacle in February 1797, lesser men might have given up hope. But the irrepressible Tone bided his time in Paris hobnobbing with James Monroe and his difficult guest, Thomas Paine. Even nonproductive sessions with the inscrutable Napoléon Bonaparte, whom Tone considered "the greatest man of Europe," did not destroy his ardor. It was not until the arrival of James Napper Tandy, after a three-year residence in America along with Tone's family and fellow Irish revolutionary, Archibald Hamilton Rowan, that the campaign to liberate Ireland seriously resumed.

Renowned but penniless, Tandy attracted considerable attention when he arrived in Paris in February 1798. Based almost entirely on his own self-promotion, the French Directory gave him the title of general and made him commander of the *Anacreon,* a swift-sailing corvette. Tone, by comparison, was made adjutant general of the Armée d'Angleterre. The Directory finally gave approval in the summer of 1798 for an invasion of Ireland. Tandy departed Dunkirk on September 4 and headed toward Rutland Island off the coast of Donegal, where he intended to organize Irish peasants to pursue the revolution. Tone left Brest on September 20 in the company of a force of three thousand men on ten vessels to land on the northern tip of Ireland.[61]

Tandy's mission was the first to play itself out. When he went ashore on September 16 on Rutland Island, he hoisted an Irish flag and issued a proclamation calling for Irish citizens to "strike from the blood-cemented thrones the murderers of their friends," that is, their fellow Irishmen. The peasants fled in fear. After eight hours into the venture, Tandy had to be carried back to the *Anacreon* in what was described as a "disgusting state of intoxication." Spotted by two English merchants in pursuit of the *Anacreon,* Tandy is said to have directed a successful escape in the direction of France while sitting on deck with a pint of brandy.[62]

Tone soon learned that Ireland would not be as easy to liberate as America. His force was encountered at the entrance to Lough Swilly on October 10 by a large English squadron. Tone and his troops could have escaped, but they decided to make a stand against the much stronger naval force. For four brutal hours Tone commanded a battery on the *Hoche,* the largest of the ten vessels in his convoy. When the resistance failed, Tone and the other survivors were captured.[63]

Tone was immediately recognized as the infamous, disaffected Irish rebel that he surely was. Although he tried to plead his rights as a French officer, he was charged with treason. When he came to trial, he was silenced by the court-martial from making inflammatory statements and denied his fervent request to be spared the ignominy of the gallows. Presenting his papers as chef de brigade in the French Army, he begged to be awarded a soldier's death by firing squad. His request was refused by Charles Cornwallis, viceroy and commander-in-chief of Ireland and the defeated commander-in-chief of British forces in the American Revolution.

Although efforts were undertaken to transfer his case from military to civil courts, Cornwallis ordered that Tone be executed within forty-eight hours of his conviction. A writ of habeas corpus for the transfer was produced, but Tone's military captors refused to acknowledge its validity. The chief justice of Ireland, in turn, ordered them into custody. All of the wrangling over Tone's fate, while admirable and honorable, was in vain. Determined that he would not die ignobly, Tone attempted to take his own life on the evening prior to his scheduled execution. Making use of a pen-knife hidden in his clothing, he slit his own throat. The wound proved fatal: After suffering in excruciating pain for longer than a week, he died on November 19.[64]

Tone, Tandy, and Tate stand as examples of the heroic albeit misguided efforts of individuals to build credible republics. Although one might question the reasonableness of their methods, it is difficult to disregard their zeal for liberating revolution. But it is also instructive to note their fates in the annals of history. Tone remains a martyr in the pantheon of Irish heroes. Tandy, while also on the list, continues to be a comic hero of somewhat lesser proportions. By contrast, the American Tate, however great his ideals and intentions, has been universally ignored by history.

LIBERATORS AND ARMAMENTS

A parade of American officials—Thomas Jefferson, Gouverneur Morris, James Monroe, Charles Cotesworth Pinckney, John Marshall, Elbridge Gerry, William Vans Murray, Oliver Ellsworth, and William R. Davie moved in and out of Paris with regularity between 1790 and 1800. Ruth and Joel Barlow also watched a train of private citizens pursuing dreams of liberty or wealth. They shared that gleam of ambition, that cloak of idealism, that large dose of passion that impelled the Tones and the Tates of this world. But they also understood how to make use of government preferments and opportunities.

Surely the most interesting American to come into the Barlows' presence during this time was Robert Fulton, a widely known but little understood figure. When Fulton arrived in Paris in the summer of 1797 at the age of thirty-one, he would soon revolutionize not only world systems of transportation, but also the technology of conducting warfare. Seven years after Fulton's birth, his family moved to Lancaster, Pennsylvania, where he spent his entire childhood. Although his father died in 1774 and left a wife and five children almost penniless, Fulton was in an environment where he could pursue an extraordinary range of interests in drawing, dreaming, and tinkering. Surrounded by artisans and craftsmen and near a good library operated by scientist-mechanic William Henry, Fulton discovered an inventiveness that allowed him to fashion a Roman candle, an air gun, a lead pencil, and a fishing boat with mechanical paddles while yet in his teens. He also worked with watercolors to fashion portraits and landscapes.[65]

Fulton even encountered the meaning of liberty while living in Lancaster. When the British occupation of Philadelphia forced Congress to meet elsewhere, Fulton delighted in meeting signers of the Declaration of Independence and other such stars as Thomas Paine as they trooped to and from a temporary capital at nearby York. At age fifteen, Fulton was apprenticed to a Philadelphia silversmith and relocated to the vibrant seat of American liberty. Making and decorating silver objects, observing the artwork of Charles Wilson Peale, and conducting his own experiments in painting, Fulton was already an accomplished artist by 1785 when he joined the Philadelphia throng that welcomed Benjamin Franklin on his triumphal return from France.

Franklin's arrival in Philadelphia transformed Fulton's life. As was the case with others, Fulton fell under the benevolent sway of Franklin. At Franklin's house, a mecca for friends of liberty and of invention, Fulton saw Thomas Paine's model of his cast-iron bridge and heard John Fitch's ideas for a stern-paddle steamboat. Franklin soon encouraged Fulton to go to England to work under the tutelage of Benjamin West, famous American painter for King George III and

Robert Fulton (c. 1795). Genius of both art and engineering, he became the fabled fabricator of engines of war.

former friend of Fulton's family in Lancaster. Bearing a glowing letter of introduction from Benjamin Franklin, Fulton arrived in London to begin a twenty-year career of mingling art and engineering with liberty and warfare.[66]

Although he did not become one of West's select group of students immediately, West provided him a tutor and advised him on how to qualify for entry into the Royal Academy of Arts then headed by Sir Joshua Reynolds. Over the next four years Fulton received the finest artistic training available in the English-speaking world. He spent his last year under the direct eye of West, who in 1792 succeeded Reynolds as president of the Royal Academy. West's career as a historical painter surely influenced three of the four Fulton paintings hung in the Royal Academy in 1793. The three were finely executed prison scenes interpreting the pathetic last days of three monarchs: *Louis XVI in Prison Taking Leave of His Family*, *Mary Queen of Scots under Confinement*, and *Lady Jane Grey the Night before Her Execution*. His depiction of Louis XVI just months after his execution revealed Fulton's growing interest in the subject of revolution.[67]

Fulton developed even more dramatically as a civil and mechanical engineer. In November 1793 Fulton began a complicated correspondence with Charles, the third Earl of Stanhope, on the subjects of ship design, canal construction, and heavy equipment for use in digging canals. Stanhope, perhaps England's most notable engineer, found it somewhat amusing that Fulton offered to enter into partnership with him. He perhaps was less amused when Fulton published their exchange of correspondence and the artist's rapidly emerging schemes in a finely illustrated masterpiece titled *A Treatise on the Improvement of Canal Navigation* (1796). Combining artistic skills and engineering genius, Fulton demonstrated his ideas for small canals, inclined planes, digging and lifting machinery, and locks and aqueducts in a novel format that was as much art as design.

Fulton's *A Treatise on the Improvement of Canal Navigation* was well ahead of its time. Despite his hopes that his ideas would be rapidly embraced in England, France, and America, the slow-to-change world of transport would wait nearly a full generation before it would adopt his plans. The *Treatise,* nevertheless, made Fulton famous throughout Europe and America and served as a platform from which he could persuasively sell patent rights, enter into partnerships to build canals around the world, and propose more innovative devices for transportation and for war. Basking in his new renown but disgusted with repressive political conditions in England, Fulton decided in June 1797 to offer his unique engineering services to the republic of France.[68]

Fulton idolized the Earl of Stanhope, who supported parliamentary and electoral reform, Irish home rule, abolition of the slave trade, and the French Revolution. He wore plain clothes, refused to powder his hair, and removed his coat of arms from house, carriage, and silverware. He gave up sugar in 1791 to protest the exploitation of African slaves in the West Indies and boldly criticized the ill treatment of English friends of liberty. Between 1788 and 1790, he chaired the historic meetings of the London Revolution Society and the Friends of Liberty. His record was one that surely appealed to Fulton.[69]

When Fulton arrived in France in 1797 he was bent on a general mission to spread liberty in the world and specifically to provide the French republic with the armament to do it. When he arrived in Paris that summer, he took up residence at a convivial boarding house, Madame Hillaire's, where Ruth Barlow lived temporarily awaiting the return of her husband from his lengthy mission to Algiers. Fulton threw himself headlong into French culture, science, and politics. Embracing the Parisian art institutions and outlining patent applications for a string of inventions, Fulton shared with the French his views on liberty and republicanism.[70]

In a letter titled "To the Friends of Mankind" and in a pamphlet titled *Thoughts on Free Trade,* published in October 1797, Fulton described his ideas for the expansion of liberty throughout the globe. These two documents outlined what Fulton called "The Republican Creed," which argued that France should hasten to end all wars and promote worldwide free trade. War subverted the free exchange of produce and of genius, undermined education, and foreclosed human improvements; free trade, on the other hand, allowed these social needs to flourish. Fulton also called for educational efforts to overthrow inherited prejudices. He espoused freedom of religion, freedom of movement from one nation to another, and freedom to enjoy property and industry. He demanded efforts to "harmonize Men and nations" and the application of industry "to useful works [as] the source of all the conveniences of society." Finally, he believed that "the whole Interior arrangements of Governments should be to promote education and Industry."[71]

On December 13, 1797, Fulton offered the French government an eighteenth-century version of a "star wars" plan that would, if implemented, end all wars. In a letter to the Directory he proposed to design, build, and personally navigate—without government capital investment—"a Mechanical Nautulus" [*sic*] or a submarine that could easily destroy the British Navy! Recompense was a flat fee of four thousand livres per gun for the destruction of British warships bearing forty guns or more and two thousand livres per gun for smaller vessels. Among the special provisions of his plan were two notable items addressing his political status and loyalties. First,

> As a citizen of the American States I hope it may be stipulated
> that this Invention, or Any Similar Invention, shall not be used
> by the Government of France Against the American States,
> Unless the Government of America First apply the Invention
> Against France.

Second, to protect himself in case he might be captured in battle, he specified that the French government must issue "Commissions Specifying that all persons taken in the Nautulus [*sic*] or Submarine expedition Shall be treated as Prisoners of War."

One month later Georges René Pléville-le-Pelly, French marine minister, informed Fulton that the ministry approved his plan at half the proposed bounties and without the guarantee of prisoner of war status in case of capture. Despite the quick endorsement by Pléville-le-Pelly, the proposal then became mired in the political bureaucracy of the Directory. Six months later, with a new marine minister in place, Eustace Bruix, Fulton resubmitted his plan revealing that he had built a "beautiful model of the Nautilus five feet long complete in all its parts." An evaluating commission, which included former French minister to the United States, Pierre Auguste Adet, a distinguished chemist, became euphoric when it saw the model at Fulton's residence on August 7, 1798. It recommended not only that the plan be implemented, but that Fulton should be reimbursed for all of the funds he had invested to date "in so novel a weapon."[72]

Despite the advice of the commission, Fulton's plan would have continued in limbo without Joel Barlow's crafty assistance. Having returned from Algiers in September 1797 and meeting Ruth Barlow's new and handsome young friend for the first time, Barlow soon adopted Fulton in every sense of the term except legally. Childless, the Barlows were as captivated by Fulton as they had been by Mary Wollstonecraft. Fulton soon moved in with them for the remainder of his life. There is also a strong likelihood that Fulton and the Barlows entered into a *ménage à trois*. Indeed, the content and tone of letters among the three, with ample references to their mutual sexual interests, suggest that they probably shared a fulfilling sex life together.[73]

With Joel Barlow's political assistance and frequent financial backing, Fulton's career flourished. While awaiting action on the *Nautilus* project, Barlow helped Fulton make a major public statement in Paris. In early 1799 Fulton constructed a building to house a massive bird's-eye view painting of Paris. The Panorama, as he called the place, was a popular and financial success. Its great appeal led to the addition of a second panoramic painting depicting "The Evacuation of Toulouse by the British in 1793."

Barlow also advised Fulton and helped arrange financing for his next effort to implement the *Nautilus* project. The concept of the *Nautilus,* in the minds of some, posed a moral as well as a technological problem. Fulton addressed the quandary in July 1799 in an essay he titled "Observations on the Moral Effects of the Nautilus Should It Be Employed with Success." He firmly believed it was so revolutionary and would be so effective against conventional ships that it would make naval warfare impossible. France therefore had a duty to build the weapon, not only to protect itself, but also to promote peace among nations. He concluded the essay with a warning that if France would not act he would have "to seek in Holland or America the encouragement that I would hope to find in France and which Liberty and Philosophy demand."[74]

Acceptance from the French government came quickly in early 1800 when Pierre Forfait, one of the enthusiastic members of the 1798 *Nautilus* commission became marine minister of France. Forfait authorized Fulton to build the visionary vessel and to stage a public demonstration of its use. With childlike enthusiasm, Fulton refined his design and oversaw the construction of the world's first submersible fighting machine. By May 1800 he was ready to show it to the world.[75]

June 13, 1800, surely compared with that day in August 1783 when Benjamin Franklin and fifty thousand Parisians observed the first manned balloon flight in history. Sending personal invitations to hundreds of scientists, government officials, and military leaders, Fulton also publicly advertised his promised display. It would be held on the River Seine in the middle of Paris and could be observed from the Cours de la Reine to the Pont de la Révolution.

At the appointed hour Fulton and his chief assistant, another American, Nathaniel Sargent, lit a candle and disappeared into the conning tower of the *Nautilus.* With neither oars nor sails, the odd-looking machine moved mysteriously to the center of the river. Quickly it plunged below the river's surface. After twenty minutes, just when the onlooking crowd thought that the craft had gone to the bottom, it suddenly emerged hundreds of yards from where it first dived. Just as surprisingly, it plunged again and reappeared at the point of its origin. Then, despite unfavorable winds, Fulton raised a mast on the vessel and showed that he could sail it back and forth across the river.

In one amazing presentation of scientific and engineering creativity, Fulton had blended dozens of principles and instruments in a wholly new machine. He devised a two-bladed propeller that moved the *Nautilus* twice as fast under water as two men could row on the surface. A horizontal propeller controlled depth. His compass worked just as well underwater as above. A lead anchor, weighing 360 pounds, that could be tethered from inside the submarine kept the craft in a stationary underwater position. With a revolving periscope he devised, he could observe activities in every direction while submerged. Compressed air released into the submarine permitted the submariners to remain submerged for hours.

Fulton's achievement was as remarkable as the Jacques-Alexandre-César Charles hydrogen or the Joseph Montgolfier heated air ascensions in 1783. Fulton proceeded immediately to Rouen, where he conducted further tests of the craft and began to prove various torpedoes that would be delivered by the *Nautilus* to sink unsuspecting British ships. Though he obtained gunpowder from the French Navy for use in the torpedoes, he still did not have the promised commissions that would protect him and his crew in the event of capture. After Barlow's further intervention, however, Fulton in early September was titled an admiral, Sargent a captain, and a third French crew member a lieutenant. On September 12, he drove the *Nautilus* from Rouen to the Normandy coast and prepared to attack British vessels. Despite heroic attempts to overtake two British brigs, gale-force winds precluded any effective contact.[76]

Putting the *Nautilus* in winter storage, Fulton, in the full flush of success, demanded direct meetings with Forfait to discuss further elaborations of his submarine, torpedoes, and other armaments spinning out of his fertile imagination. He soon received new funds to make improvements on the craft and to build a line of experimental torpedoes. Although the Peace of Amiens concluded Fulton's efforts to destroy the British, he still hoped to sell new armaments, ships, and canals to France, the nation that had taken up the mantle of universal liberation.

Fulton, in the process, had changed from a crusading liberator to a man who would sell his soul to play out a dream of building a greater weapon than had been seen before. Receiving little notice at home, despite the fact that he spent ten years trading with America's greatest enemies, Fulton was gaining a reputation as one of the world's leading engineers, creating an image in Europe as an American entrepreneur, and moving further and further afield from his early devotion to liberty. Estranged from ideological concerns after a decade of revolution, he was in 1800 hard at work building the implements of transportation, earth-moving or war, that a transforming world would buy.[77]

By 1800 the world revolution as witnessed by operators such as Barlow and de Staël, naive liberators such as Tate and Tone, and entrepreneurs such as Fulton had fizzled out. Politics, business, and war had returned to their usual patterns—they became all about national interests and not very much about liberty.

CHAPTER 10

Citizenesses in the
Land of Liberty

THE RIGHTS OF CITIZENESSES

On May 15, 1793, Priscilla Mason rose to give the salutatory oration before her schoolmates and "a numerous audience" at the Young Ladies Academy of Philadelphia. After greeting the "venerable trustees of this Seminary," the "worthy Principal," her classmates, and her "respected and very respectable audience," she launched into an oration "in vindication of female eloquence."[1]

Without apology, Mason proclaimed the right, the responsibility, and the necessity for women to become orators. The "free exercise of this natural talent," she continued, "is a part of the rights of woman, and must be allowed by the courtesy of Europe and America too."

> Leaving my sex in full possession of this prerogative, I claim for them the further right of being heard on more public occasions—of addressing the reason as well as the fears of the other sex. . . . Our right to instruct and persuade cannot be disputed, if it shall appear, that we possess the talents of the orator. . . . The talent of the orator is confessedly ours. In all these respects the female orator stands on equal,—nay, on <u>superior</u> ground. . . . Our high and mighty Lords (thanks to their arbitrary constitutions) have denied us the means of knowledge, and then reproached us for the want of it.

The field of battle was not level. "They doom'd the sex to servile or frivolous employments on purpose to degrade their minds, that they themselves might hold unrivall'd, the power and pre-eminence they had usurped."

Mason was certain that, given the chance, women could equal or excel male counterparts. This was proved, she argued, by such women as Catharine Macaulay, Elizabeth Carter, Jane Elizabeth Moore, and Elizabeth Singer Rowe. Except for Macaulay, the women on Mason's list were principally writers of religious tracts. These and "other illustrious female characters have shown of what the sex are capable, under the cultivating hand of science." But supposing that women were given all of the advantages of an education, where would they use their talents?

Norris House, Philadelphia (c. 1798), from whence Deborah Norris observed the birth of the American nation and issuance of the Constitution.

> The Church, the Bar, and the Senate are shut against us. Who shut them? <u>Man</u>; despotic man, first made us incapable of the duty, and then forbid us the exercise. Let us by suitable education, qualify ourselves for those high departments—they will open before us.

In the case of the bar she concluded, "I am assured that there is nothing in our laws or constitution, to prohibit the licensure of female Attornies; and sure our judges have too much gallantry, to urge <u>prescription</u> in bar of their claim."

With regard to service in the Senate, Mason offered a proposal drawn from the example of Roman Emperor Heliogabalus, who made his grandmother a member of the Roman Senate. He also established a separate senate consisting entirely of women and "committed to them the important business of regulating dress and fashions." Observing that "the dress of our own country, at this day, would admit of some regulation," Mason proposed that "it would be worthy the wisdom of Congress, to consider whether a similar institution, established at the seat of our Federal Government, would not be a public benefit." Mason explained the critical importance of fashion:

> We cannot be independent, while we receive our fashions from other countries; nor act properly, while we imitate the manners

of governments not congenial to our own. Such a Senate, composed of women most noted for wisdom, learning and taste,
delegated from every part of the Union, would give dignity,
and independence to our manners; uniformity, and even authority to our fashions.

The involvement of women would "call forth all that is human—all that is <u>divine</u>
in the soul of woman; and having proved them equally capable with the other
sex, would lead to their equal participation of honor and office."

At a school that opened June 4, 1787, "for the instruction of Young Ladies in
Reading, Writing, Arithmetic, English Grammar, Composition, Rhetoric, and
Geography," Priscilla Mason thus uttered an American declaration of rights for
women. Following the Declaration of the Rights of Woman and Citizenesses presented to the French Assembly in 1791 by the revolutionary Marie-Olympe de
Gouges and the famous *A Vindication of the Rights of Woman* published by Mary
Wollstonecraft in January 1792, Mason's plea for the rights of women grew out
of the American yearning to authenticate the rights of all human beings. Not
inspired directly by either de Gouges or Wollstonecraft, Mason bespoke a revolutionary spirit that was alive in all parts of the Western world. And she reflected
innocently, but concretely, an active campaign that was at that moment underway
in America to secure the rights of women.

WOMEN AND THE AMERICAN REVOLUTION

In America a strong contingent of female voices was emerging, intent on establishing the rights and prerogatives of women either by precept or example. Some
of them had been working at it almost as long as Mercy Otis Warren, who had
been writing poems and dramas about the subject of liberty since the early 1770s,
while others absorbed the excitement surrounding the revolution in France. All
were inspired by such heroines as Catherine the Great, Suzanne Necker, and
Catharine Macaulay. And every one of them fought valiantly in the 1790s to
affirm the rights of women.

Eight women in particular illustrate the strange career liberty took in the case
of women during the revolutionary era. These eight—all with a record of publications setting forth their views on aspects of liberty and life—showed how
women could play a prominent role in American society. Two of them were
closer in age to Mercy Otis Warren: Elizabeth Sandwith Drinker and Elizabeth
Graeme Ferguson, both of Philadelphia and both affected as mature adults by the
American Revolution and its aftermath. The other six women were members of
the next generation, born between 1751 and 1762. All of them experienced the
American Revolution as young women. Judith Sargent Murray, Hannah Adams
(no relation to Samuel or John Adams), and Hannah Webster Foster came from
Massachusetts and witnessed revolutionary Boston. Though Susanna Haswell
Rowson was born in Portsmouth, England, she spent her childhood in Massa-
chusetts living next door to James Otis, who embraced her as "my little scholar."
Rounding out the group of eight were Catharine Littlefield Greene, who was born

in Rhode Island, and Deborah Norris Logan, who came from one of the great families of Philadelphia.[2]

The eight women came from vastly different backgrounds, some from prominent families (Ferguson and Logan), some from impoverished circumstances (Greene and Adams), some from merchant families (Drinker, Murray, and Foster). A number of them had lost their mothers at a relatively young age, but they all received solid educations. Drinker and Logan attended the Quaker school in Philadelphia operated by the reformer Anthony Benezet. Ferguson, Adams, and Rowson were educated principally by their fathers. Foster is said to have attended a boarding school. Greene was adopted by a prominent aunt, Catharine Ray, who provided tutors and schooling. Murray, thanks to the presence of a brother preparing to attend Harvard, was able to join his tutoring lessons, read his books, and converse with him on any and every subject. These women proved the thesis that, given access to an education, women could do as well as men.

These women handled books well, but they also were exposed to provocative individuals, situations, and events that helped shape their characters. A fourteen-month residence following the death of both her parents with renowned Philadelphia Quaker, Thomas Say, helped send Elizabeth Drinker on a career of studying, reading, conversing, and writing a detailed diary covering almost forty years. Elizabeth Graeme Ferguson, due to the prominence of her father, and Catherine Littlefield Greene, living in the adoptive home of a Rhode Island political leader, met some brilliant minds and took part in ample political discussions. Both of them also fell under the influence and, in some ways, the dark shadow of Benjamin Franklin.

Young Elizabeth Graeme in 1757 fell madly in love with William Franklin, Benjamin Franklin's illegitimate but openly embraced son. The two fathers, however, were bitter political enemies, and as the elder Franklin set off to England to battle the proprietors of Pennsylvania, some kind of disaster seemed inevitable. Whether to enable William to see the world or perhaps to keep him from marrying Elizabeth, Franklin whisked his infatuated son away to New York as spring blossomed that year. The depth of affection between the young pair was evident in William's letters to her before his sudden departure, and he wrote of his dire loss of her as he sat in New York awaiting passage to England. In one letter, he observed that the only possible good use of a parson would be to unite the two of them so that she would have "a WILL of your own." From New York he wrote of "having bound my Soul to you by indissolveable Ties." When he and Franklin, delayed in their departure, took a tour of northern New Jersey, he wrote, "I a Thousand Times wish'd you present, and fancied to myself the Raptures you would be in."[3]

Before the Franklins' departure, the couple had entered into an engagement to be married upon the young man's return from England. When a year and a half later, William Franklin had not returned and no longer wrote letters to her, Graeme asked for some explanation. He replied finally that her letter was "fill'd with harsh and cruel Reflections." His own letter, in turn, was a disorganized harangue of excuses for his behavior. Six months later, Elizabeth Graeme declared the engagement null and void. The relationship ended so badly that she began to oscillate between depression and extraordinary literary pursuits.[4]

Catharine Greene's brush with Benjamin Franklin was indirect. She was brought up by her aunt, Catharine Ray, who in the early 1750s had herself fallen in love with Franklin. Catharine Ray met Franklin in Boston at the home of her sister at the moment he was gaining world renown for his electrical experiments. Although half the age of the married Franklin, the two of them became absorbed with each other and Catharine accompanied him to Rhode Island on his way back to Philadelphia. Little concerned with direction or speed, they lingered several days at Newport.

Although they eventually parted, both remained deeply smitten with each other, as revealed in their letters over the years and in Franklin's further visits before and after Catharine's marriage to prominent Rhode Islander William Greene. Catharine Littlefield, as she grew up, was well aware of Franklin's letters, visits, and his strong affection for her aunt. She would in 1774 marry Nathanael Greene in the room where Franklin had sat in courtly admiration of Catharine Ray.[5]

As girls, Judith Sargent, Hannah Webster, and Deborah Norris constantly were exposed to brilliant minds and state and national leaders. The Norris house in Philadelphia was two doors from the State House, where on July 8, 1776, Deborah heard the first reading of the Declaration of Independence from her perch on a garden fence. Hannah Adams was inspired by her father, who collected and sold books and by divinity students boarding in her home in Medfield, Massachusetts. Susanna Haswell, living next door to James Otis from age five until thirteen, met the stream of prominent men and women coursing through the Otis estate.

Seven of the women married, four of them before the onset of the American Revolution. Elizabeth Sandwith married a widowed Quaker merchant, Henry Drinker, in 1761. The marriage lasted forty-six years and resulted in nine children.[6] Judith Sargent married Capt. John Stevens, a seafarer and ten years her elder, in 1769 with great hopes for a life of luxury and writing. By the time Stevens, debt-ridden and under indictment, disappeared in the West Indies in 1786, Judith Stevens was already infatuated with John Murray, founder of the Universalist Church in America. After residing together for some years, they married in 1788, brought forth two children, and, together, powerfully promoted Universalism.[7]

Elizabeth Graeme, following a dozen years of trying to recover from the end of her relationship with William Franklin, secretly married Henry Hugh Ferguson, a native Scot and kinsman of philosopher and historian Adam Ferguson. Ten years younger than she, Ferguson proved a poor choice. Their bond was not revealed for six months until after her father's death. Ferguson was away in Scotland and England on business, where he principally remained during the five or six years of their marriage.[8] Catharine Littlefield's marriage to Nathanael Greene in 1774 formed a passionate union that resulted in five children within the years of the American Revolution—despite the fact that she saw him only when she traveled across battle lines to his encampments at such places as Valley Forge and Charleston, South Carolina.[9]

Deborah Norris and pacifist George Logan married in September 1781, when he returned from receiving his medical education in Edinburgh and London. In a forty-year marriage from which issued three sons, Deborah thrived, despite the sometimes quixotic antics of her husband. In 1785 Hannah Webster married the Reverend John Foster, pastor of the First Church (Unitarian) of Brighton, Massachusetts. Foster provided a stable environment over the next forty-five years, enabling Hannah Foster to raise six children and to pursue her interests as a writer. Susanna Haswell's marriage in England in 1787 to William Rowson, merchant, trumpeter, and actor, was less fortunate. The unsuccessful Rowson became a lifelong tagalong as she pursued her meteoric career in writing, acting, and teaching school. Of the eight women, only Hannah Adams never married, and it is not clear if she had any interest in doing so.[10]

The lives of these eight creative women were disrupted by their personal experience of the American Revolution. Elizabeth Drinker and Deborah Norris lived in occupied Philadelphia and were enmeshed in the struggle between revolutionaries and loyalists and between Quaker pacifists and warriors. Both Elizabeth and husband Henry opposed war, but they also sided with Britain against the revolutionaries. For expressing himself on these two subjects, Henry Drinker spent much of 1777 and 1778 as a prisoner of the American forces.[11] George Logan, given his actions in the 1790s, surely would have suffered a similar fate had he not been across the Atlantic during the conflict.

Although Judith Stevens and John Murray did not unite until after the war, she was already religiously and emotionally involved with him in 1778 when he was accused of being a British spy. For defending Murray, the Stevens family was suspended from the First Parish Church of Gloucester. John Stevens's and Hannah Adams's fathers were both financially broken by the war, leaving Judith dependent upon the Sargent family and Hannah with no financial support. Hannah had to learn to weave bobbin lace, "which was then saleable, and much more profitable to me than spinning, sewing or knitting, which had previously been my employment." While Judith was able to pursue her literary interests during and after the war, Hannah "found but little time for literary pursuits."[12]

The considerable sufferings of these four women were nothing compared to those of Susanna Haswell, Catharine Littlefield Greene, and Elizabeth Graeme Ferguson. Brought by her father, William Haswell, a British tax collector, to Massachusetts in 1768, Susanna over the next seven years heard the growing crescendo of hatred shouted by Americans against the taxing system. Despite friendship with the Otis clan, as Haswell applied to depart for Britain, his property was confiscated; he and Susanna were imprisoned as loyalists. After three years of internment during which Haswell's health was ruined, he was paroled and permitted to take his family to Nova Scotia. Somehow they made their way to London, where they lived in poverty awaiting a government pension. Susanna, at age sixteen, had no choice but to begin working as a governess.

The structure of Catherine Greene's happy life collapsed in late April 1775 when her warrior husband, once a Quaker pacificist, left on a tour of duty that kept him away for the next eight years. She had no choice, if she wanted to see him, but to travel to his winter encampments. She journeyed, with amazing regularity, to Cambridge, Long Island, New Jersey, Valley Forge, Newport, and South Carolina.

From each of the visits she came home pregnant with another child to be cared for by her alone. By the end of the war she was physically and emotionally drained. Nathanael Greene, despite his valor and devotion to America, returned to Rhode Island in 1783 physically worn and financially ruined. He was heavily indebted to South Carolina merchants from whom he bought uniforms and food for his army, which had been guaranteed by his own credit. The Greenes moved in 1785 to a Georgia plantation given to Nathanael Greene for his wartime services.[13]

The American Revolution left Elizabeth Graeme Ferguson in an even more devastated condition. She and her husband maintained an on-again, off-again relationship at beautiful Graeme Park, the estate inherited from her parents. In 1775 Henry Ferguson departed for England, ostensibly on business. He returned two years later in the company of Gen. William Howe and his occupation army of Philadelphia. George Washington, who admired Elizabeth Ferguson for her literary accomplishments, would not allow the Tory Ferguson to return to Graeme Park.

Serving as Howe's commissary of prisoners, Ferguson also dabbled in negotiations between British and American forces. In October 1777 Ferguson handed Elizabeth a letter written by her eccentric pastor Jacob Duche to be delivered to Washington. Although Duche had served as chaplain to the Continental Congress, his allegiance changed after Howe occupied Philadelphia. In the letter Elizabeth carried, Duche urged Washington to surrender. The angry Washington reproached her and sent the letter to Congress. Still an innocent acting in her husband's behest, a year later she transmitted to Joseph Reed, a member of Congress and aide to Washington, an offer of ten thousand guineas and a political appointment if he would urge Washington to lay down arms.[14]

Neither Reed, Washington, nor Congress were amused at this second putative collaboration with the enemy. The Pennsylvania General Assembly, without bringing charges against Elizabeth, proscribed Henry Ferguson as a loyalist and seized Graeme Park as loyalist property. Abandoned by her unscrupulous husband, Elizabeth Graeme Ferguson (she retained her married name until death), with the assistance of many influential friends and admirers, petitioned the Pennsylvania Assembly in March 1781, to restore Graeme Park to her.

Endorsed by Benjamin Rush, Elias Boudinot, Jonathan Dickinson, George Clymer, Philip Muhlenburg, Robert Morris, Thomas McKean, Thomas Mifflin, and William Smith, provost of the University of Pennsylvania, the petition claimed that, while legally married to Ferguson, Elizabeth had inherited Graeme Park from her father, and at the time of the seizure Ferguson was not a resident at the place, nor even an American citizen. Fortunately, the Assembly heard her plea and restored the property to her for the duration of her natural life. But destitute and alone, ten years later she found it necessary to transfer the property to Smith to provide herself with a meager living.[15]

Based on the harsh experiences of Elizabeth Graeme Ferguson and her peers,[16] it would be difficult to conclude that the American Revolution had done much for women. They remained dependent upon men, be it fathers, brothers, or husbands. A few women secured basic educations, but most did not. And while the war provided thrilling, even exhilarating moments for some, it was for most women an ordeal of fear, loneliness, deprivation, and, in some instances, the sequestration of property and basic rights.

WOMEN'S DECLARATIONS OF INDEPENDENCE

There was, nevertheless, so much talk of liberty between the period of the American Revolution and the French Revolution that it was inevitable that American women would begin to seek ways of declaring their own independence. Some composed poetry; others wrote novels or plays. Still others became historians. At least one or two attempted to establish salons. And a few chose to battle it out in the political arena, not as elected officials, but as individuals lobbying elected and appointed personages for their rights.

Among the first to establish her independence was Elizabeth Graeme. Upon the end of her engagement with William Franklin in 1759, she began work on a poetic translation of Fénelon's *Télémaque,* which, though completed, was never published. Hoping to help her out of a lengthy depression that threatened her health, her parents arranged in 1764 for her to travel to England in company with Richard Peters, rector of Philadelphia's Christ Church. Although Peters left her in London and spent much of his time with his nephew in Liverpool, he worried about her tendency to stay home in the evenings. "Will not confinement hurt you?" he wrote. "It has always appeared to me that it does. You get into thinking about Philadelphia or upon some warm scene in a well wrote Book—and forget that you are too apt to let these things enter deeper into your heart than they should do."

In the company of the Penn family, Laurence Sterne (author of *The Life and Opinions of Tristam Shandy*) and members of the Royal family, and under the doting care of the famous Dr. John Fothergill, Graeme slowly improved her outlook on life. She also met Nathaniel Evans, a young clergyman and poet from Philadelphia, who was in England to be ordained by the bishop of London. Evans returned to America on the same ship with Peters and Graeme. When Peters sent Evans to meet her, he wrote that Evans "will please you vastly with a sprightly conversation."[17]

Elizabeth Graeme came back to America with a new idea that would make use of her many talents and permit her to take on an important role in Pennsylvania and American society. The idea undoubtedly came from the humorist Sterne, who, when she met him, had just returned from two and a half years of living in Paris and the south of France. With six of the eight volumes of *Tristam Shandy* already in print, he became one of the most demanded guests at the Paris salons. He was there, in fact, just at the moment that Suzanne Curchod Necker launched her popular Friday night salon. The stories he undoubtedly shared with Graeme of his Paris salon conquests had a deep effect.[18]

Since she had almost unlimited financial support from her physician-farmer-statesman father, Graeme decided to start her own Saturday night salon,

Elizabeth Graeme Ferguson (n.d.). American poet and inspired salonniere.

complete with dinner and agenda. Her distinguished attendees included William Smith, provost of the College of Philadelphia; physician and statesman Benjamin Rush; lawyer and Revolutionary general Joseph Reed; composer and poet Francis Hopkinson; the flirtatious poet Nathaniel Evans; and the learned Dr. Graeme himself. In 1765 she entered into the most creative and fruitful period of her life.[19]

Graeme Park became America's most authentic salon of the pre-Revolutionary era, one in which Elizabeth Graeme intertwined literary, political, and philosophical discussions among some of the nation's most energetic minds. The attendees at her salon also debated religion, science, education, medicine, music, and law. Among the things all of the participants in her salon held in common was that each of them had lived and studied for a time in Britain—roughly about the time Graeme was there—and had been stimulated by currents of the Enlightenment. Fueled by the literary and philosophical ferment there, they joined Graeme in stimulating discussions in Philadelphia, rivaling their French counterparts in Paris.[20]

Elizabeth Graeme's salon gave her the kind of power in American governance and society exhibited by her contemporaries in France. She conspired with Smith and Rush on dozens of projects and collaborated with Hopkinson and Evans in their literary and musical productions. It was due to the dynamics of her salon that she could, like Suzanne Necker and Madame de Staël, engage in the business of intrigue and politics. Her continuing engagement with Smith, Rush, and Reed made her a logical choice to carry messages between loyalists and revolutionaries. That, after all, was the role of the *salonniere*—to foster and facilitate discussion and to search for common understanding.[21]

It is not strange that Elizabeth Graeme should have developed warm, even intimate relationships, with a number of her male participants. Although five years older than Nathaniel Evans, she delighted in their word games and poetic exchanges after their return from England. She was emotionally shattered a second time in life when he died of tuberculosis at age twenty-five as he launched his missionary career in Gloucester County, New Jersey. Just before he died he entrusted his poems and literary papers to Graeme and Smith, who collaborated in transcribing and editing them. They secured 759 subscribers for their publication, and in 1772 they published Evans's work in a volume titled *Poems on Several Occasions, with Some Other Compositions.*[22]

Elizabeth Graeme Ferguson unquestionably made a mark among these men. When Graeme Park was torn from her for supposed acts of disloyalty, they came to her defense, saving her family home. When she could no longer care for it and needed funds to support herself in 1791, Smith and another powerful friend, Elias Boudinot, came to her assistance in securing the legal right to sell the property even though its title was technically in dispute as long as her husband still lived. Their devotion was revealed in a note made by Benjamin Rush upon her death ten years later in Philadelphia:

> This morning died at the Billet near Philadelphia Mrs. Eliz. Ferguson, a woman of uncommon talents and virtues, admired, esteemed, and beloved by a numerous circle of friends and acquaintances. Her life was marked with distress from all its numerous causes, guilt excepted. An early disappointment in love, the loss of all her near Relations, bad health, an unfortunate marriage connection, poverty, and finally a slow and painful death composed the ingredients that filled up her cup of suffering. . . . I owe to her many obligations. She introduced me into her circle of Friends.

Without a doubt Elizabeth had declared her independence, although the price was high and the blessings of liberty were tainted with grief.[23]

Elizabeth Graeme Ferguson's declaration of independence set the stage for many other women to do likewise, particularly in the literary realm. Although not a line of her own writings would be published during her lifetime, Elizabeth Drinker in her extensive diary, begun in 1758 and continued until her death in 1807, chronicled a life of reading, discovery, and interaction with others. She intended to create an accurate and complete historical record of her time that presumably would someday be published. In 1799 she explained:

> I intended the book for memorandums, nor is it any thing else . . . as what I write answers no other purpose than to help the memory—I have seen Diarys of different complections, some were amusing, others instructive, and others repleat with what might better be totally let alone—my simple Diary comes under none of these descriptions. . . . I was never prone to

> speak my mind, much less to write or record any thing that
> might in a future day give pain to any one.

Except on the rarest of occasions, Drinker revealed in her almost fifty-year record little personal whim or emotion. She rather reflected upon the world represented in fiction and nonfiction as compared to the banal realities around her.

But her *Diary* was also a view on the world from the perspective of a knowledgeable woman. As a wife, mother, and caretaker of a household, her views on the nature of revolutions, battles, elections, epidemics, and deaths differed from those of the men who chronicled the period. As an unannounced Loyalist during the American Revolution, she recorded the unbecoming behavior of revolutionaries in as much detail as their heroics. As a Quaker slaveholder, she agonized over both the institution and how to control sometimes lazy and rebellious servants. Although a pacifist, she battled both the government of Pennsylvania to secure the release of her imprisoned husband and British officials to deter the lodging of army officers in her home. Combining intellectual and political independence in virtually all aspects of her life, Drinker established a course of pursuing liberty that surely was followed by many women, albeit without leaving the same rich historical record.[24]

Other women also were establishing their independence as published authors. Catharine Macaulay's grand tour of America in 1784 seemed to sanction the rush of women authors into print. Impoverished Hannah Adams, at Medfield, Massachusetts, printed the first of a series of books that would make her America's first professional woman writer. *Alphabetical Compendium of the Various Sects Which Have Appeared from the Beginning of the Christian Era to the Present Day* (1784) grew directly out of Adams's boundless curiosity about religion in a world with an endless number of religious denominations and persuasions. This was but the first of a popular series of useful publications that entitled her at her death to be honored with burial and a monument in Boston's cemetery for the affluent, Mount Auburn.

Conscious of her status as one of the earliest professional women writers, she penned a memoir late in life that bore marks of Benjamin Franklin's famous *Autobiography.* She had Franklin's tongue-in-cheek model in mind as she began outlining her rich life, "notwithstanding I am sensible that a retrospect of past errors [Franklin called them errata], faults and misfortunes, will be exceedingly painful." The *Autobiography* recently had been published in 1818 by Temple Franklin as *Memoirs of the Life and Writings of Benjamin Franklin.* As Franklin began his story when he was sixty-five, thinking that most of his life was over, so did she. Just as Franklin wrote to his son William and then left the *Autobiography* as a legacy to benefit his grandson William Temple, Adams wrote for "a highly esteemed friend" and left her *Memoir* as a legacy to benefit her sister. Just as Franklin was born into an impoverished family, she had been deprived by similar circumstances. Both Franklin and she were primarily self-educated, although both grew up in atmospheres filled with words, books, and writing.[25]

By age ten Franklin was working for his father; as an apprentice to his brother James at twelve he began to learn the printing trade. Adams, due to lack of money, poor health, and "timidity," received little formal education prior to her mother's death when she was twelve. Franklin said that "From a Child I was fond of Reading, and all the little Money that came into my Hands was ever laid out in Books." Adams similarly wrote: "From my predominant taste I was induced to apply to reading, and as my father had a considerable library, I was enabled to gratify my inclination." Just as Franklin was by seventeen on his own, Adams, due to the impecuniousness of her father, was left with a dependent sister to care for. And just as Franklin and Adams shared "bookishness," they both turned early in life to the written word to find paying careers—he as printer and editor and she as compiler and author.[26]

Although Franklin and Adams differed markedly on religion (he was arm's length, she devotional), they both made religion the subject of their literary debuts. Franklin refuted William Wollaston in *A Dissertation on Liberty and Necessity, Pleasure and Pain,* self-published in London in 1725 and his first literary effort other than newspaper essays. Adams launched her career by clarifying religious differences in her *Alphabetical Compendium of the Various Sects,* printed with the financing of four hundred subscribers. Franklin's *Dissertation* sold not at all and angered his printer employer; he thus commented in the *Autobiography,* "My printing this Pamphlet was another Erratum." Adams's *Alphabetical Compendium,* by contrast, sold extremely well, but the printer kept all monies paid for the book (her only compensation was fifty copies). The deal was so awful, in fact, that in her *Memoir* she did not mention the printer "whose name, out of respect to his descendants, I omit to mention."[27]

The central theme of both autobiographies was to show how the authors established their independence in life through hard work. Nevertheless, both Franklin and Adams required sponsors and friends. If Franklin invited the help of governors, politicians, and the wealthy, so did Adams. Fisher Ames in 1790 responded to Adams's petition to seek passage of a general copyright law to protect herself against her printer. Episcopal clergyman James Freeman of Boston, learning of her first misfortune with printers, volunteered to be her literary agent. Freeman's arrangement for a second edition of the *Alphabetical Compendium* protected with a copyright brought success: "the emolument I derived from it not only placed me in a comfortable situation, but enabled me to pay the debts I had contracted . . . and to put out a small sum upon interest."[28]

The publication of this second edition allowed Hannah Adams her independence. The sale of the book was so phenomenal that she was able to turn herself fully to the business of research and writing. Although still characterizing herself as timid, by 1793 she had plunged into state archives to research what would become the first comprehensive history of New England. She wrote to David Ramsay, author of *The History of the American Revolution* (1789), seeking permission to make extensive use of his work in her New England story. Martha Ramsay replied with an adoring letter, giving permission as well as sending funds for a subscription to Adams's new book. A third edition of her *Alphabetical Compendium* cemented her financial security and guaranteed her independent writing career.[29]

As Hannah Adams was publishing her *Alphabetical Compendium,* Judith Sargent Stevens (not yet Murray) began publishing essays and poems on a variety of subjects in *Gentleman and Lady's Town and Country Magazine.* Her first essay, titled "Encouraging a Degree of Self-Complacency, Especially in Female Bosoms," introduced both a subject on which she would write extensively, i.e., women, and the pen name by which she would forever be known, "Constantia." With the demise of that sheet shortly thereafter, however, she did not resume the publication of her works until the auspicious year of 1789 and her marriage to her supportive and encouraging pastor and live-in guest, John Murray.

Her most productive career coincided with her second marriage, wherein she was associated with a man who crusaded to transform religion in America. Poems poured forth with the arrival of her first child in 1789. Although the boy died in a few days, her writing continued in contributions to the new *Massachusetts Magazine,* the first being the lament "Death of an Infant." Feeling the spirit of liberty in the air, she prepared for the March and April 1790 issues her most famous essay, "On the Equality of the Sexes."[30]

Although not a declaration of the rights of woman in the same sense as those issued by Marie-Olympe de Gouges and Mary Wollstonecraft in later years, the essay foreshadowed the same kind of thinking. What it resembled most was Catharine Macaulay's *Letters on Education with Observations on Religious and Metaphysical Subjects,* which was being almost simultaneously issued in London. Arguing that women were by nature provided with imagination, reason, memory, and judgment equal to that of men, she maintained that "from the commencement of time to the present day, there have been as many females, as males, who, by the mere force of natural powers, have merited the crown of applause; who, thus unassisted, have seized the wreath of fame." In her opinion women should be educated rather than "be allowed no other ideas, than those which are suggested by the mechanism of a pudding, or the sewing the seams of a garment." She was marching toward a declaration whose time was ripe and surely would come.[31]

A visit in 1790 to Philadelphia, where her husband Murray was organizing a national Universalist convention, further spurred her efforts. She arrived just after the death of Benjamin Franklin, but she met his clan, including Sally. She also met Benjamin Rush, already an advocate for the education of women. At New York, where Congress was in session, she crossed paths with George and Martha Washington, John and Abigail Adams, and with "some of the best speakers" of the day—James Madison, Theodore Sedgwick, Jonathan Jackson, and John Vining.

Her meeting with Martha Washington reflected the direction of her thinking about the role of women in American society. The spouse of the first American president was, like her husband, establishing precedents in demeanor and habits. She actually operated a salon, although it was limited exclusively to women. Surprised to be accepted as a visitor into this exclusive circle, Murray was pleased when Washington in "her matron-like appearance" took her by the hand and "seated me by her side, and addressing herself particularly to me, as the only stranger present . . . engaged me in the most familiar and agreeable conversation."

"The unmeaning fopperies of ceremony," she continued, "seem to make no part of her character." But the pedestal on which Murray placed Washington was evident in her final assessment: "Thus benignly good, and thus adorned with social virtues is our Lady Presidentess." In this first year of the American presidency, Murray and, surely other women, had high expectations of the chief official's wife.[32]

With the arrival of a daughter in 1791, Judith Murray threw herself fully into mothering and literary work. In February 1792 Murray launched a series of essays in the *Massachusetts Magazine* that established her intellectual independence. In a sometimes complex series of literary forms, she discussed virtually every policy, issue, or value affecting American society. Written as letters from a man described as "the Gleaner," her essays appeared as regular installments for two and a half years until September 1794. Carefully crafted, although at times verbose, the spate of essays placed her among America's most fervent friends of liberty.[33]

In her first essay, Murray introduced herself as "rather a plain man, who, after spending the day in making provision for my little family, sit myself comfortably down by a clean hearth" to enjoy "an amusing tale, a well written book, or a social friend." She continued, "I have been seized with a violent desire to become a writer, ever since the commencement of your Magazine." Announcing her intentions to submit "scribblings" regularly to the magazine, she also declared "I do hereby adopt, the name, character, and avocation of a GLEANER." She promised to "ransack the fields, the meadows, and the groves; each secret haunt, however sequestered, with avidity . . . to crop with impunity a hint from one, an idea from another, and to aim at improvement upon a sentence from a third."[34]

Her strategy of presenting herself to the public as a man was carefully calculated. As she would later explain, she wrote as a man because she wanted to discuss some issues solemnly and directly with both men and women. She also could avoid "the indifference, not to say contempt, with which female productions are regarded." Moreover, as a male voice she could disclose frankly the normally hidden opinions of women: "It afforded me [the opportunity] of making myself mistress of the unbiased sentiments of my associates." But, finally—and revealingly—"I was ambitious of being considered independent as a writer." Since she was a married woman with an articulate husband, she wanted to avoid the assumption that her work was ghost-written or heavily edited by her husband. Indeed, she concealed her project from John Murray until he guessed that one of the published stories sounded familiar.[35]

Whereas other women were beginning to publish under their own names (Macaulay, de Gouges, Wollstonecraft, de Staël), Murray concluded that she could achieve more in the guise of an anonymous male voice. She sent what eventually turned out to be a hundred sequentially numbered installments. More than a quarter of the offerings constituted a carefully contrived autobiographical, didactic novel titled *Margaretta,* the life story of a young child adopted by Mr.

Vigillius (the Gleaner) and his wife Mary and how she was to be brought up, educated, and made into a full participating member of American society. Through teachings, examples, letters, and written lessons in history, biography, religion, manners, and morals, Margaretta developed into an ideal American citizen. A powerful story, it was told by a mother capable of instructing the world.[36]

The use of biography as an instructional tool was particularly evident in Margaretta's story. Murray began her own catalog of heroes with a series of classical Greek and Roman characters. In her view, "The heroes of antiquity, grouped together, may be considered as a splendid constellation, illumining those tremendous periods, which, fraught with blood and murder, unveiled scenes that seemed to threaten the universal wreck of nature!" Lycurgus, Solon, Numa Pompilius, Valerius, Camillus, Cincinnatus, Cimon, and Philopoemen were a few of the ancient heroes honored. Alfred the Great, Mary, Queen of Scots, Henry IV of France, Charles I of England, Peter the Great, and William Penn provided more contemporary models.[37]

Murray built up to a finale that defined her work as an early testament to women's rights. In four essays titled "Observations on Female Abilities," she returned to a theme that had absorbed her attention for many years—a revision of her 1790 essay "The Equality of the Sexes," this time expanded with new insights from Wollstonecraft, de Gonges, and many others. With the appearance of female academies and a general belief that a young woman was "now permitted to appropriate a moiety of her time to studies of a more elevated and elevating nature," she thought that "in this younger world, 'the Rights of Women' begin to be understood."

As she launched into a declaration that should have been issued as a separately published vindication in the nature of Wollstonecraft's tome, she began, "such is my confidence in the SEX, that I expect to see our young women forming a new era in female history." Women henceforth would avoid "every trivial and unworthy monopolizer of time" and mere "adorning their persons," In fact,

> Thinking justly will not only enlarge their minds, and refine their ideas; but it will correct their dispositions, humanize their feelings, and present them the <u>friends of their species</u>. . . . A sensible and informed woman—companionable and serious—possessing also a facility of temper, and united to a congenial mind. . . . Surely, the wide globe cannot produce a scene more truly interesting.

The conclusion of her gaze at the moment of liberty was this: "<u>The idea of the incapability</u> of women, is, we conceive, in this <u>enlightened age</u>, totally <u>inadmissible</u>; and we have concluded, that establishing the <u>expediency</u> of admitting them to share the blessings of equality, will remove every obstacle to their advancement."

Having established the principles of the new era, Murray then demonstrated the classic struggles of women and identified some memorable heroines. From ancient Sparta to modern Hungary, from biblical Judah and Egypt to classical Rome, wherever women were venerated, they exhibited firmness, courage, and perspicacity. Wherever they were treated cruelly and oppressed by men, the opposite was the case, as would also be the result if men were similarly crushed. For in Murray's mind, men and women were mentally equal: "the minds of women are <u>naturally</u> as susceptible of every improvement, as those of men." This, she thought, could be proved by both historic and contemporaneous example, which she set out in a series of ten mini-essays to demonstrate.

<u>First</u>, Alike capable of enduring hardships.

<u>Secondly</u>, Equally ingenious, and fruitful in resources.

<u>Thirdly</u>, Their fortitude and heroism cannot be surpassed.

<u>Fourthly</u>, They are equally brave.

<u>Fifthly</u>, They are as patriotic.

<u>Sixthly</u>, As influential.

<u>Seventhly</u>, As energetic, and as eloquent.

<u>Eighthly</u>, As faithful, and as persevering in their attachments.

<u>Ninthly</u>, As capable of supporting, with honour, the toils of government. And

<u>Tenthly</u>, and <u>Lastly</u>, They are equally susceptible of every literary acquirement.

Greek, Roman, British, and American history yielded examples aplenty to illustrate her points, as heroic figures paraded across her vibrant pages.

In the last of her essays on female abilities, she came to her most fundamental point. "THE SEX," she proclaimed, "should be taught to depend on their own efforts, for the procurement of an establishment in life. . . . With proper attention to their education, and subsequent habits, they might easily attain that independence, for which a Wollstonecraft hath so energetically contended." With such independence "the term, <u>helpless widow</u>, might be rendered as unfrequent and inapplicable as that of <u>helpless widower</u>." Given "the <u>capability</u> of the female mind to become possessed of any attainment within the reach of <u>masculine exertion</u>" there was no reason that women should not be able to establish their independence.

Already in France there was Madame de Genlis and Madame Roland. In Britain Anna Barbauld, Anna Seward, Hannah Cowley, Elizabeth Inchbald, Fanny Burney, Charlotte Smith, Ann Radcliffe, and, yes, Mary Wollstonecraft. "Nor is America destitute of females, whose abilities and improvements give them an indisputable claim to immortality," she argued. America itself was made possible by "the penetration and magnanimity of Isabella of Spain." While she found present-day "female genius," she had to glory in its representatives mainly through their pseudonyms: "when we contemplate a [Mercy] Warren, a Philenia, an Antonia, a Euphelia, &c. &c. we gratefully acknowledge, that genius and application, even in the female line, already gild, with effulgent radiance, our blest Aurora." Citing two other examples, a gifted husbandwoman in Massachusetts and a businesswoman in the Spanish port of St. Sebastian, Murray concluded her plea for the independence of women. It was not that she wanted women to take over "the counting-house"; it was rather that she wanted every woman to make herself "so far acquainted with some particular branch of business, as that it may, if occasion requires, assist in establishing you above that kind of dependence, against which the freeborn mind so naturally revolts."[38]

Independence. That was what Judith Sargent Murray wanted for every woman and for herself. Through her essays in the pages of the *Massachusetts Magazine,* albeit under a pseudonym, she had placed herself in a position to posit her views on matters ranging from "the present times" to "the American Constitution" to "the acrimony of party spirit." Although the consistent publication of her essays in the *Magazine* was discontinued after August 1794, she kept on writing them just the same. And she explored other forums for expressing her views, continuing to express a strong, single-minded voice.

The crowning achievement of Murray's literary career came with the publication of *The Gleaner* in three large volumes in early 1798. Containing the essays and fictional accounts that had appeared in *Massachusetts Magazine,* plus an additional sixty essays, dramas, and other writings—all produced in the period from 1792 until 1797—*The Gleaner* recorded a brilliant mind. Produced to provide income as well as fame for the author, it found 759 subscribers who purchased 824 sets of the books at a dollar per set.[39]

The list of subscribers read like a who's who of the early republic: George and Martha Washington (who subscribed separately), John Adams (two copies), Fisher Ames, Nicholas Brown of Providence, Christoph Ebeling of Hamburg, Germany, Rev. James Freeman of Boston (sponsor of Hannah Adams), Elbridge Gerry, John Hancock, Capt. W. H. Harrison and Mrs. Harrison (separate subscription), Israel Israel of Philadelphia, Gen. Henry Jackson, Gen. Henry Knox, Jedidiah Morse, Harrison Gray Otis, Josiah Quincy, and Increase Sumner. A good third of the subscribers were women, who purchased separate subscriptions from spouses. Her dedication of the work to President John Adams added dignity to her efforts. Praising President Washington in the dedication as America's "DELIVERER," she "exult[ed] in an Adams, whose transcendent talents, and whose vigilance, are fully adequate to the emergencies and the dangers of a FREE GOVERNMENT."

Nor did Murray shrink from the heights of liberation that she had achieved. "My desires are, I am free to own, aspiring—perhaps presumptuously so," she wrote in the preface:

> I would be distinguished and respected by my contemporaries;
> I would be continued in grateful remembrance when I make
> my exit; and I would descend with celebrity to posterity.

To achieve that fame, in *The Gleaner*'s last chapter, titled "The Gleaner Unmasked," she acknowledged that "the Gleaner" was none other than Constantia. Although the name Judith Sargent Murray nowhere appears in the entire work—the title pages bearing only the name Constantia—everybody in America of a literary bent recognized the author. They also knew that Murray had achieved her long-sought independence.[40]

DRAMATIS PERSONAE

Among the list of women subscribers for *The Gleaner* were two notable American playwrights—"Mrs. Rowson," and Mrs. Mercy [incorrectly spelled "Mary"] Warren, Plymouth." Murray, combined with the older Mercy Otis Warren and the younger Susanna Haswell Rowson, wrote most of the American plays penned by women prior to 1800. Separately, and then as influences on each other, they discovered, as Murray articulated in *The Gleaner,* "The stage is undoubtedly a very powerful engine in forming the opinions and manners of a people." Each had definite notions—especially on the subject of liberty and the rights of women.[41]

Noticeably absent from Murray's list of subscribers was a woman whose assistance she had sought fewer than two years earlier—Sarah Franklin Bache. Writing from fashionable "Franklin Place" in Boston on June 19, 1795, Murray had made a heartrending plea for help. Her husband's finances and health were beginning to fail, and Murray suddenly found herself responsible for an aging husband and a four-year-old daughter in need of the education that Murray had described in such passionate detail in *The Gleaner.*

Addressing Bache as "Madam," she began her entreaty by reference to a visit she had made to the Bache home some time past:

> Often since the afternoon upon which you did me the honor to
> number me among your guests at your house in Philadelphia,
> have I reflected with sensations of the utmost complacency,
> upon the rational moments, which I then past [passed]; and I
> have not failed to breathe a fervid wish for their reiteration.

From the obeisant tenor of her opening, one would think that she was addressing not an equal, but royalty. Certain that Bache would "be at a loss to recollect the person who now addresses you," she identified herself as Mr. Murray's "companion in the voyage of life."

Continuing her deferential tone, Murray explained her uncharacteristic language:

> Madam, I am <u>principally</u> emboldened by a knowledge that you
> are the <u>daughter of Doctor Franklin</u> and the daughter of Doctor
> Franklin must be the <u>patroness</u> of <u>industry and application</u>
> although it may be apparent that Nature hath not been remark-
> ably liberal to the Claimant who may need her leave.

Susanna Rowson (c. 1798). Renowned novelist and acclaimed actress, she was also a vehement feminist.

"I have, Madam," she continued, "long been a <u>Scribbler</u>." But throughout her writing days she had "spurned the idea of accepting pecuniary emolument for those little attempts." Then she came to her point: "Having now an infant daughter for whose education it becomes me to be solicitous . . . I have conceived it my duty to lend my family what assistance may be within my grasp."

Next came Murray's description of her most recent efforts:

> I was last winter encouraged to draw my pen in a new line, and I was assured that a new Comedy written in Boston would be very productive. This assurance originated the play, which I take the liberty to inclose to you. It was introduced to Mr. Powell, the Manager of the Boston Theatre—whose reception of it was sufficiently flattering. He immediately put it into rehearsal, and it was speedily brought forward. The first act was marked by uncommon applause—but early in the second, the female who performed Dovinda Learnwell [?] entirely forgot her part and bursting into tears quit the stage. This circumstance threw a cloud over the piece and although the remaining scenes were hobbled over, yet the good humour of the players and audience was but imperfectly restored. The piece, it is true, was <u>not</u> in the theatrical phrase <u>dàmned</u>—but it appeared that it did not give that pleasure which was expected. . . .
>
> Having said thus much—I conceive that my reasons for pressing upon the <u>known indulgence</u> of your character, will be obvious. If you, Madam, will condescend to become the Protectress of the Medium [her play] I shall be sure of its success.

> My wish is that it may be brought upon the Philadelphia stage
> and that the Author may be concealed from every person
> except yourself—unless the production should be favorably
> received by the public. My first object, as a Writer, I am free to
> own, is <u>fame</u> and I feelingly regret that my circumstances has
> given me a secondary motive. . . . I will <u>abide by any agree-
> ment</u> which <u>you Madam may condescend to make in my
> behalf</u>. . . . If it is thought proper, the play may be printed in
> your City, in which case I shall request a few copies, and I
> repeat my entreaties that my name may, for the present, be kept
> a profound secret.

Having stated her case and outlined the terms she thought appropriate, Murray
returned to her adulation of Bache's father. "I repeat, Madam, that viewing you as
the Descendant of the illustrious Franklin, and conceiving that his virtues are the
heritage of his daughter, I am induced to imagine, that an apology for this freedom would be superfluous if not impertinent."[42]

On the same day that Murray wrote this appeal, a daring new play titled *The
Female Patriot* opened at the Chestnut Street Theater in Philadelphia. On that
same day Susanna Rowson witnessed the production of the third in her series of
plays dealing with the universal rights of men and of women. Barely a year earlier, her first play, *Slaves in Algiers; or, A Struggle for Freedom* had opened on
the same stage. Focusing entirely on slavery and women's rights, Rowson used
American fascination with the Algerian pirates to explore the evils of both slavery and the exploitation of women. Three women characters—two concubines
and a daughter fettered by a tyrannical father—discuss at length the nature of
their enslavement. As one of the concubines states,

> I wish for liberty. Why do you talk of my being a favourite; is
> the poor bird that is confined in a cage (because a favourite of
> its enslaver) consoled for the loss of freedom. No! Tho its
> prison is of golden wire, its food delicious, and it is over-
> whelm'd with caresses, its little heart still pants for liberty;
> gladly would it seek the fields of air . . . nor once regret the
> splendid house of bondage.

All three of the characters rebel in the end and find liberty, though in one case
through suicide. Liberty rang loud in Philadelphia when the three women
repeated in unison the last lines of the play: "May Freedom spread her benign
influence thro' every nation, till the bright Eagle, united with the dove and olive
branch, wave high, the acknowledged standard of the world."[43]

The reception to the *Slaves in Algiers* was so overwhelming that Rowson
excitedly continued her stage exhibitions. Moving from the setting of Algiers to the
mountains of western Pennsylvania, she next wrote *The Volunteers,* which opened
in Philadelphia in January 1795. Although presented as a musical farce, the play's
concentration on the activities of participants in the recent Whiskey Rebellion

brought home the fact that even in the land of liberty, freedom's fate had to be protected. The success of *The Volunteers* then opened the door for Rowson to focus squarely on the rights of women in *The Female Patriot,* and in a follow-up series of verse recitals she read directly her declaration, "The Standard of Liberty."[44]

This outpouring in favor of liberty in America took on amazing proportions, considering that Rowson's life was totally disrupted by the internment of her family and the confiscation of their property by American rebels in 1775. Forced to work as a governess for an aristocratic family in Britain, she traveled, met engaging people, and exercised some of her tendency toward audacity. These experiences formed the basis for a novel, *Victoria,* published in 1786 with the assistance of her employer, the Duchess of Devonshire. Although Rowson married the following year, it soon became clear that she would have to be the mainstay of the family.

While she wrote, she and her husband took to the stage in Edinburgh during the 1792–93 acting season. It was there that Thomas Wignell, recruiting for the new Chestnut Street Theater in Philadelphia, booked them to come to America. In Philadelphia Susanna Rowson was able to pursue her penchant both for writing drama and for playing the parts she created. She danced, sang, played the harpsichord and guitar, wrote lyrics, and composed librettos. During the first five years following her arrival in America she acted in 129 different roles and played in 126 different productions—at the same time finagling employment for her undermotivated husband.[45]

Given Rowson's performances in Philadelphia and elsewhere, the year 1795 became the moment when women discovered in drama a critical medium in which they could explore the meanings of liberty and the rights of man. The outpouring occurred in an era when women on stage could speak women's thoughts, and women authors could draft their speeches. Some, such as Rowson, played the parts they wrote the way they wanted them to appear. In addition to Warren, Murray, and Rowson, other women put out plays dissecting current turmoils and events, and a first wave of popular actresses emerged to enact them, including Anne Julia Kemble Hatton, Anne Brunson Merry, Mary Palmer Tyler, and Polly Wayne.[46]

Mercy Otis Warren, by adding *The Ladies of Castile* and *The Sack of Rome* to her list of published works in 1790, set the example for this floodtide. By focusing on liberty and introducing women as thoughtful and opinionated characters, she established a new voice for women in America. Judith Murray acknowledged this contribution in an essay in *The Gleaner,* writing in the guise of a drama critic, "We conceive that Mrs. Warren, while delineating Donna Maria [*Ladies of Castile*] traced in her own strong and luminous intellect the animated original which she presented." Calling for someone to stage Warren's two great tragedies ("If compositions of this description find no place on the American stage, what can the more humble adventurer expect?"), Murray pronounced "our celebrated countrywoman the *Roland* of America."[47]

Murray then made her own contribution. When the ban on dramatic performances was lifted in Massachusetts in 1793, she became one of the strongest proponents in Boston for good theater. Declaring the continued partial ban outside of Boston a "flimsy subterfuge" and "the domination of prejudice," she deemed it "as a tyrant, that if once brought to the guillotine, would . . . leave an opening for the introduction of an era far more friendly to the progress of <u>genuine</u> and <u>corrected</u> liberty."

In *The Gleaner* she refuted the public arguments against theater. Against cries that it was a waste of time and money, an encouragement of idleness, and an inducement for immorality, she argued the opposite:

> Young persons will acquire a refinement of taste and manners;
> they will learn to think, speak, and act, with propriety; a thirst
> for knowledge will be originated; and from attentions, at first,
> perhaps, constituting only the amusement of the hour, they will
> gradually proceed to more important inquiries.

She also described the features of the new Federal Street Theater—"the elegant and superb theatre . . . erected for the reception of Drama in the State of Massachusetts"—opened on February 3, 1794.[48]

Beyond proclaiming theater as an exercise essential to a land of liberty, Murray also responded to the call of Boston's first theater managers for American-written plays by drafting her own. *The Medium,* the drama described by Murray in her letter to Sarah Franklin Bache, opened at the Federal Street Theater on March 2, 1795, for its only Boston performance. The first American play to be produced and presented in Boston, neither the production nor the reaction to it was at all what Murray hoped for or expected. Although the play was announced in the *Federal Orrery,* Boston's semiofficial drama newspaper, on February 26 as a comedy "written by a Citizen of the United States," on the day of its opening the *Orrery* in an anonymous communication told that it "is said to be the joint production of Mr. and Mrs. Murray." Given John Murray's controversial views on religion, that bit of misinformation deeply colored every potential viewer's perception of the play.

John Murray angrily wrote to Robert Treat Paine, editor of the *Federal Orrery,* "I declare, in the most solemn manner, that I never saw a single sentence, line, or even word of the comedy . . . until I saw it, precisely in the state, in which it was . . . presented to the public." Nine days after the performance a letter from "Candour" published in the *Columbian Centinel* of Boston called for another performance, saying, "the imperfection of the performance certainly did not admit of its having a fair trial. . . . Does the Manager think to keep it back, because it hath not the English stamp upon it? Or what is his reason for not allowing it a second representation?" In the opinion of Candour, at least, "the plot appears to be well laid, and interesting."[49]

The truth was that Judith Murray found herself caught in one of those situations she had long detested. The suspicion of John Murray's involvement robbed her of a fair hearing for her work on its merits. And even the connection of her name with the work risked besmirchment, since the public tended to believe that there was a man involved in every woman's literary work. As Judith Murray later acknowledged in *The Gleaner,* she herself "declined the second presentation, which the justice of the Manager honourably tendered her." So depressed was she "by remarks . . . officiously handed her both by friends and enemies," she simply could not face another embarrassing performance.[50]

Moreover, Murray feared that her whole objective in writing *The Medium* would be lost. Despite the universal judgment that it was a shaky comedy and lacking in plot, its purpose was to argue the equality of men and women. Through all of its tedious lines, Murray was attempting to practice what she had preached—that the stage could and should be used for instruction and enlightenment. Because the play had to have a fair hearing for its message to be grasped, she called out for Sarah Franklin Bache's assistance. Two years later, when she published the text of the play in *The Gleaner,* she wrote, "the author of *The Medium,* disgusted with an appellation which has been sufficiently productive of vexation, now entitles her Comedy '*Virtue Triumphant.*'"[51]

Still desperately looking for a source of income, Murray soon produced another play, *The Traveller Returned,* which opened on March 9, 1796, at the Federal Street Theater and played for two nights before it was withdrawn. Here Murray turned to the Revolution and the theme of liberty in her second dramatic effort. Despite eulogies to General Washington, the introduction of spies, and heroic adventures, the play exhibited the same weaknesses as *The Medium*: too many long-winded speeches, shallow characters, and an absence of plot. Robert Treat Paine, the leading Boston critic, suggested in his review, "Should the comedy be again represented, for the author's benefit, a prudent use of the pruning knife would be of service to some of the soliloquies and many of the national ebullitions."[52]

Murray, enraged by Paine's searing comments, fired off a review of his review. Paine sarcastically published her critique. This piece was then answered by a letter defending the play and its production. Paine, sure that the defense came from none other than John Murray, whom he dubbed "Parson Flummery," sniped some more at the play's greatest weakness: "From beginning to end of her comedy we continually meet with turgid phrases, stale Hibernianisms, filched ribaldry, and forced conceits, without one single solitary spark of wit, to cheer, with a momentary TWINKLE, the immense vacuum of Dulness." Although he did not mention John Murray by name, a few days later Paine published a letter addressed to the minister accusing him of being the true author of *The Traveller Returned.* Paine gloated that the play was by then "deceased," having died a "natural death"; and, given the absence of "Christian faith" in Murray's religion, there was no hope for a "resurrection!"

John Murray sent a futile letter to a rival newspaper, stating, "I do most solemnly declare that I never wrote 'The Traveller Returned,' or a single line in that or any other play." He again affirmed the excellence of the play, proved "not only from the general bursts of applause it met with on its representation, but from the judgement of some of the best judges of dramatic excellence in this town." As for nasty claims registered about him by Paine, Murray denied that he was ever "a player of the strolling or stationary kind, in Ireland or elsewhere."

Once again Judith Murray's efforts to exercise a voice for liberty were frustrated by her attachment to a husband whose reputation beclouded anything associated with her name. Whatever the merits of her dramatic contributions, her work could not be measured objectively; she was not given an opportunity essential to every playwright—that of testing, revising, testing again, and refining. The helpful criticisms provided even by Paine were quickly contorted into issues of religion, politics, and passion. What was worst was that Judith Murray was deprived of an income at a time when she desperately needed it. With her husband failing professionally and physically, his continued presence closed all doors to her.

Murray's desperate circumstances lend poignancy to the absence of Sarah Bache's name from the list of 759 subscribers to Murray's 1798 edition of *The Gleaner.* It was John Murray who had urged his wife to undertake the compiled work. Reflecting, in a letter to an English friend, on his poverty, his age, his health, and his mortality, Murray, on December 29, 1795, wrote, "considering she has a little daughter, who, with herself may be thrown on an unfeeling world without the means of making friends by the mammon of unrighteousness, I have, as well as some others of her friends, ventured to persuade her to make this trial." The venture was, of course, successful. The publication provided her with funds for living, for caring for her ailing husband, and for educating little Julia Maria. She was able, for a time at least, to maintain her hard-won independence.[53]

But no thanks were due to any Franklin or Bache. Murray, in appealing to Sarah Franklin Bache for help in presenting her drama and in publishing *The Gleaner,* probably touched a chord that Benjamin Franklin's daughter could not abide. By characterizing Sarah Bache over and over as "the <u>daughter of Doctor Franklin</u>"; by supposing that "the daughter of Doctor Franklin must be the patroness of <u>industry and application</u>"; and by "viewing you as the Descendant of the illustrious Franklin, and conceiving that his virtues are the heritage of his daughter," Murray characterized her proposed benefactor precisely as she did not want to be known. Murray could not know that Franklin had never granted Sarah Bache even a modicum of freedom. Murray unwittingly did unto Bache precisely what she had wanted people to stop doing unto her: She linked Sarah Bache's identity with that of a man—a man with whom she was perpetually identified.

Whether Bache's sponsorship would have helped to salvage Murray's career as a dramatist is unknown. But the struggles of Murray, Rowson, and Bache to secure their independence reflected the complicated social, intellectual, and psychological forces they had to face. Nevertheless, their fiction, drama, and prose revealed the fact that a world revolution was at work struggling to establish the rights of man and woman.

NOVELISTS

The makings of what could have been a great American novel began with the birth of Elizabeth Whitman in Connecticut in 1752. Her father and Jonathan Edwards were cousins, and she was a cousin of poet John Trumbull. Well educated and bright, she courted and was courted by two other Connecticut poets, Joseph Buckminster and Joseph Howe. But her greatest love affair was with poet and revolutionary Joel Barlow, who in 1779 simultaneously pursued Eliza Whitman and Ruth Baldwin, daughter of Connecticut ironmaster Michael Baldwin and sister of longtime congressman from Georgia Abraham Baldwin.

While boarding at the Baldwin home as a schoolteacher, Barlow evidently fell in love with the charming daughter. His letters to Whitman abated as Barlow took a greater interest in Baldwin. Although Whitman was in love with Barlow and gloried in calling him her "husband," no consummation took place. By June 1779, at least from Barlow's point of view, the affair with Whitman was at an end. Whitman continued to live with her mother in Hartford. Joel Barlow continued to work there as poet, lawyer, and editor, and he secretly married Ruth Baldwin in January 1781.[54]

The next concrete bit of information about the fortunes of Eliza Whitman appeared in the *Salem Mercury* (Massachusetts) on July 29, 1788, about two months after Barlow had sailed from New York for his long adventure in France. Written by Captain Goodhue, the landlord of Bell Tavern in Danvers (now Peabody), Massachusetts, the story related a melancholy tale:

> Last Friday, a female stranger died at the Bell Tavern, in Danvers; and on Sunday her remains were decently interred. The circumstances relative to this woman are such as excite curiosity, and interest our feelings. She was brought to the Bell in a chaise . . . by a young man whom she had engaged for that purpose. . . . She remained at this inn till her death, in expectation of the arrival of her husband, whom she expected to come for her, and appeared anxious at his delay. She was averse to being interrogated concerning herself or connexions; and kept much retired to her chamber, employed in needlework, writing, etc. . . . Her conversation, her writings and her manners, bespoke the advantage of a respectable family and good education. Her person was agreeable; her deportment, amiable and engaging; and, though in a state of anxiety and suspense, she preserved a cheerfulness which seemed to be not the effect of insensibility, but of a firm and patient temper.

In actuality, Whitman had checked into the tavern in late May or early June as "Mrs. Walker" and was large with child. Late in July she delivered a stillborn child. From the ordeal she contracted puerperal fever and died a week later.[74]

Within days the story was repeated in dozens of newspapers throughout New England. Each embellished the story over its predecessor, especially when it

"Congress Hall & the New Theatre on Chestnut Street, Philadelphia" (1798). While political drama played out in one half (left), American dramatists and players depicted or derided what was at stake in the other.

became known that before she died, Eliza Whitman burned all of her letters except one left for her lover. Addressing him only as "Fidelio," she wrote: "Must I die alone? . . . Why did you leave me in such distress? . . . May God forgive in both what was amiss."[55]

From the moment the story became known, with its tantalizing missing elements—Who was the father? Was there really a husband? How did she come to this pitiable situation alone?—speculation abounded about Whitman, and morals were drawn. Like a great murder mystery in a prominent family that can captivate public attention from first notice to sentencing of the culprit, the Whitman story entered into the New England oral tradition as a moral lesson in the training of young women. Ministers, mothers, and authors of morality books highlighted the story in an effort to provide sound guidance for young women.

Just a year after the incident, William Hill Brown in the first American novel, *The Power of Sympathy, Or, The Triumph of Nature. Founded in Truth* (1789), used the Whitman story to steer young women away from the practice of novel reading. Whitman, he proclaimed, "was a great reader of novels and romances and having imbibed her ideas of the characters of men, from those fallacious sources, became vain and coquettish, and rejected several offers of marriage, in expectation of receiving one more agreeable to her fanciful idea." This verdict came straight from one of the newspaper articles following the revelation.[56]

While moralists used the story to forewarn young women, speculations followed a host of men suspected of leaving Whitman in her lamentable condition.

The revolutionary Joel Barlow, given his wide-ranging sexual appetite, was a leading suspect. Among the other leading candidates was Pierrepont Edwards, lawyer, politician, and son of Jonathan Edwards. Edwards, a distant cousin of Whitman, was savagely attacked for his morals, his politics, and his campaign to disestablish the Congregational Church in Connecticut; he had all of the best villainous qualities. Also frequently suspected was Aaron Burr, another Whitman cousin whose credentials for iniquity also were impeccable. A more likely candidate for these dark honors, however, was Jeremiah Wadsworth, Connecticut businessman, financier, and congressman. Though the others became the most popular choices because of their later notoriety in history, Wadsworth's proximity, mind-set, and questionable values point to him.[57]

The story of Eliza Whitman would have remained one of regional lore and titillating speculation had not Hannah Webster Foster, also a distant Whitman cousin, decided to convert it into a fascinating tale titled *The Coquette; or, the History of Eliza Wharton; A Novel; Founded on Fact,* published in Boston in 1797. Incorporating her considerable writing skills and her inside knowledge of the details of the Whitman case, Foster wove a story advocating independence for women. She changed Whitman to Wharton in the book, then spoke directly to women on the matters of women's education, employment, legal and political rights, and the double standard. Eschewing the stereotypical interpretations of the Whitman story, Foster lifted it to the highest level of social and moral criticism.

In *The Coquette* Foster developed the novel as another voice for women to use in declaring their rights and desires. That she did it well was demonstrated by the success of the book, which had remarkable sales in its massive first edition and another issued in 1803. A critical tool of female self-examination well into the nineteenth century, the book remained one of America's best-sellers. (Between 1824 and 1828 alone, it was reprinted eight times.) It also provided a classic model for other novelists, especially women, to produce new examinations of the role of women in so-called free societies.[58]

Foster was not the first nor the top-selling author of such works, however. Susanna Rowson wrote a multiplicity of novels in England and after her arrival in America in 1793. She actually nudged American men and women into writing novels, when her *Victoria* was published in 1786 and her popular *Charlotte Temple* was published in 1791. By age thirty, she had published *Inquisitor, or Invisible Rambler* (1788), *Poems on Various Subjects* (1788), and *Mary, or the Test of Honour* (1789), *Mentoria, or the Young Lady's Friend* (1791), and the autobiographical *Rebecca, or the Fille de Chambre* (1792).

As she rose to the height of her fame as dramatist and actress with her play *Slaves in Algiers,* her novel *Charlotte, a Tale of Truth* (better known as *Charlotte Temple*) was reprinted in Philadelphia with great success. The novel became America's best-selling book and remained so consistently until the publication in 1852 of Harriet Beecher Stowe's *Uncle Tom's Cabin.* Classed as a "sentimental seduction story," *Charlotte* spun the tale of an English schoolgirl seduced by a British army officer who took her to New York and there abandoned her. Filled with allusions to sex and the power of seduction, the book provided a ready-made model for Hannah Foster's *The Coquette,* published three years later. The subtitle's hint that *Charlotte* was based on a true story may or may not be true, although some parallels existed with the escapades of Rowson's cousin, Col. John Montresor. The subtle emphasis on a true story was, of course, perfect for the popular case of Eliza Whitman.[59]

In both plays and other novels the prolific Rowson explored the role of women, particularly young maturing women, in free societies. The four-volume *Trials of the Human Heart,* published in Philadelphia in 1795, continued the pattern, as did the play *Americans in England, or Lessons for Daughters,* acted in Boston in 1797, and another historical novel, *Reuben and Rachel,* published in 1798.[60]

While other authors would in future years exploit the model of charting the life of young women facing sexual maturity, Rowson, Murray, and Foster established the form and exploited it well. The writing of such novels provided a voice with which articulate women could publicly discuss matters theretofore hushed into closed chambers. And the readings of them gave every young woman stories of the experience of others and served as powerful moral lessons. Produced by women who struggled mightily to achieve their own independence, these novels were heart-to-heart talks among women about how to deal with a world dangling revolutionary promises of freedom.

EXERCISING POWER

However close to the seats of power they came, Mercy Otis Warren, Elizabeth Graeme Ferguson, Hannah Adams, Judith Sargent Murray, Susanna Haswell Rowson, Elizabeth Drinker, and Hannah Webster Foster exercised their influence through the written word and through the world of literature and drama. A few other women played for power in the worlds of commerce, politics, and the law. For Catherine Littlefield Greene, a different set of experiences in those realms occurred. She found herself caught up in entanglements that threatened her liberty, but she also discovered ways not only to survive, but also to thrive. On the morning of June 19, 1786, Catherine Littlefield Greene's entire world caved in upon her. In the bedroom of her unfinished Mulberry Grove mansion near Savannah, Georgia, lay the body of forty-four-year-old husband, Revolutionary War hero Nathanael Greene. His attending physician declared death due to sunstroke—probably just a stroke.[61]

Greene died leaving an estate woefully in debt to contractors and vendors from whom he had purchased food, supplies, and clothing for America's Revolutionary War army in the South. As George Washington's most faithful general, he had jeopardized his extensive business enterprises and property holdings in the state of Rhode Island.

To escape total impoverishment he expanded his line of credit with trusting business partners. His only hopes for repayment of his debts were twofold: first, he had to take his large family to Georgia and live on one of the plantations presented to him for his Revolutionary War service; and, second, he had to persuade

Nathanael Greene (c. 1780). Revolutionary hero and war creditor.

Congress to repay bills he had personally assumed on behalf of the American government. Given the economic conditions in post-Revolutionary America and given the inability of Congress to make binding financial decisions, his task was difficult at best. Worse, positions of governance on local, state, and national levels were being assumed by men whom Greene perhaps ruffled, stymied, or angered during eight long years of war, rendering the recovery of his debts virtually impossible.

If the task of financial recovery would have been almost insurmountable for a war hero, how much more difficult it would be for his widow. As she and Greene often were separated throughout the war, she had little knowledge of his transactions. Moreover, many records had been destroyed or lost with the untimely death of John Banks, an agent and speculator who handled many of Greene's purchases. Banks evidently had lost a considerable portion of Greene's funds in side speculations. Greene himself had almost given up hope when he traveled to Richmond, Virginia, in search of Banks, only to find his grave.

In the summer of 1786, Catharine Greene was barely six months into living for the first time on a vast plantation with dozens of slaves, hundreds of miles away from Rhode Island. She had not been able to learn about the operations—financial or otherwise—of the plantation, since during these six months she had been pregnant for the eighth time in ten years. In April 1786, in fact, she had injured her ankle and a hip in a fall, inducing premature labor. The baby did not survive. Although she had committed with Nathanael Greene to make Mulberry Grove a profitable enterprise to support themselves and five living children, she was barely emerging from the physical and psychological effects of her last pregnancy when he died.

These were the immediately obvious liabilities facing Catharine Greene when she became the head of a household, the administrator of a large plantation, and the principal beneficiary or loser in the settlement of the Greene estate. Despite the gloomy outlook before her, she possessed some strong intangible assets. She had a will to succeed and was able to delegate responsibilities to individuals with the training, ability, and cunning to do them well. She also showed an aptitude for grasping the most difficult problems and finding simple solutions. And she was, finally, a risk taker, willing to stake her estate, her person, and her future on something she believed in.

Her most powerful asset was her ability to charm men. She entranced a string of men into feeling that each was the most beloved person in her life. Each of them strove to win and maintain her confidence. There were Generals Henry Knox and Anthony Wayne, both of whom provided her counsel, Wayne from his own plantation adjoining Mulberry Grove. There were Lafayette and Alexander Hamilton. Lafayette would take George Washington Greene, Greene's oldest son, to France and pay for his education. Hamilton advised her on dealings with Congress and the new federal government. There were Nathaniel Pendleton of Savannah and Edward Rutledge of Charleston, both lawyers, who advised her professionally and personally on the Greene estate and other matters large and small.

In addition to these advisors, there were three men in 1786 with whom Greene had intimate relationships, each on different planes and in distinct ways from all the others. The first was Phineas Miller, Jr., a Connecticut native, Yale graduate, and recommended in 1785 by Yale president Ezra Stiles to become a tutor for the Greene children. He traveled with the Greene family from Rhode Island to Savannah in October 1785, bound for his in-residence position at Mulberry Grove.

Catharine Greene, confined below decks by the early stages of her pregnancy and by her fear of the sea, spent most of the time conversing with Miller, gaining trust in his learning, humor, and judgment. Eight months later, he being the only adult, white man at Mulberry Grove, became full-time manager of the plantation. Sometime in roughly that same period, the two of them, despite a ten-year age difference, became lovers. They would remain so, despite her long string of flirtations, for the next eighteen years.

The second man who was critical to Greene in the years immediately following her husband's death was George Washington. Catharine had charmed both George and Martha Washington during the cold winter encampments of the Revolution and by naming her first two children after the couple. As soon as she learned of the tangled condition of the Greene estate, she rushed to Mount Vernon for advice and assistance. George Washington gave her wise counsel on how to prepare a claim of indemnity against the Confederation government and on how to present it in Congress. Both Washingtons advised her on the education of her five children; George Washington offered to bear the full expense of educating his namesake, George Washington Greene.

From Mt. Vernon, Greene raced back to Georgia to prepare the claim of indemnity. Even though she was almost penniless, she got ready to wage war in Congress. Confident that she would be victorious, she sailed with her five children to spend the summer of 1787 in fashionable Newport, Rhode Island. She spent money for the plantation, for clothes, and for travel as if the anticipated Congressional windfall was already in hand.

That she was able to do so was due to the influence of the third of the special men in her life after Nathanael Greene's death. Her travels, her special pleasures, and most things beyond the confines of Mulberry Grove were quietly being paid for by Jeremiah Wadsworth, another flame from Revolutionary War days. Wadsworth, from Hartford, Connecticut, had been a longtime business partner with Nathanael Greene. It was Greene who made him commissary general after Washington persuaded the wealthy Rhode Islander to serve in the thankless capacity of quartermaster general of the Continental Army in the Valley Forge winter of 1778. It was there that Catharine Greene and Wadsworth met. For him it was fascination at first sight, despite his married status. The fact that Wadsworth himself was handsome, convivial with women, and becoming one of the wealthiest men in America made it easy for Catharine Greene to count him among her special group of men.

But Greene was always wary of the flirtatious Wadsworth. In her husband's letters during the war, Wadsworth insisted that playful notes be added from him. In a letter giving Catherine Greene instructions on traveling from Rhode Island to Washington's headquarters at Newburgh, New York, Greene wrote, "You will make a stop in Hartford if possible or Wadsworth will not forgive you." In another, Greene announced that Wadsworth would be making regular deliveries of food and provisions to their home in Westerly, Rhode Island. The visits of Wadsworth and other male admirers while Nathanael Greene was battling British forces in the South soon churned the rumor mill about Catharine Greene's activities.

On one occasion when Wadsworth traveled to Philadelphia where he thought he would find Catharine Greene, he sent a jealous message to her while she was at Mount Vernon on her way south to join Nathanael. Receiving the note during a party, she left her company briefly to send a response: "I am trembling for fear I shall not have the pleasure of seeing you before I go to the South. . . . Be assured if I can not see you I shall go Mourning all the way. The Company is in a high Romp which I hope will excuse me to my Dear Friend." This message, perhaps reflecting some ambivalence about Wadsworth's motives, is somewhat inscrutable in that she then remained at Mount Vernon for more than a month.

The fact of the matter was that Wadsworth was manipulating financial affairs in a direction that would make Nathanael Greene, and thereby Catharine Greene, dependent upon his good graces. Nathanael Greene borrowed heavily from

Wadsworth, as well as from Robert Morris of Philadelphia and from Lafayette. Various partnerships with Wadsworth had lost thousands of pounds, making Greene further indebted to his wily partner. As a result, Greene was compelled to make his former commissary general coexecutor of his estate. The other coexecutor—to whom he was not similarly indebted was the supportive Edward Rutledge of South Carolina.

Catharine Greene was at first pleased with the prospects of assistance from one of her most devoted paramours and the ever-constant Rutledge. But she was in for several rude awakenings. On her first trip to Newport following Greene's death in 1786, where she met with Wadsworth and Rutledge to get estate proceedings underway, she was shocked to learn that a major portion of the estate's indebtedness was to none other than Wadsworth. She also learned that most of the estate's real property holdings in Georgia and South Carolina had been used by Greene to secure his debts. There was no cash to be had. Until the American government reimbursed the Greene estate, she and her children were almost wholly dependent upon Wadsworth for funds.

In that vulnerable circumstance Catharine Greene gradually discovered Wadsworth's true character. Yes, he paid for her trip to Newport in 1787, ostensibly to talk over estate matters, but on condition that she make a lengthy visit to Hartford. Although the visit was primarily in the Wadsworth home in the presence of Wadsworth's older wife and youngest daughter, his pursuit of the youthful widow was remembered by them as a dark moment in the family's history. Wadsworth ratcheted Greene's hopes up several notches when he announced his candidacy to Congress. If elected, he promised to present her indemnity claim in Congress.

Wadsworth was duly elected to Congress, beginning his service in 1788. During the summer of 1788 Greene returned again to New England, this time with Phineas Miller. By then impoverished, Greene took a cottage at Wethersfield, near Hartford. From there she informed Wadsworth, who was detained by Congressional meetings in New York, that she had lost nearly everything of value that was movable, either surrendered to creditors or sold to produce some ready cash. "The furniture is gone, some people would say to the dogs [creditors]—but I would say to the Devil," she wrote. She begged him for two or three hundred dollars: "I wish to have that money to get me a little furniture." Never in her life was she more dependent on another human being for her very existence.

Wadsworth oddly continued in New York while she waited for him in Wethersfield. She grew desperate for news on the indemnity claim in Congress. "I cannot help running out to the Stage every time it passes in hopes of seeing you," she wrote. That was in August. When on September 19, he still remained in New York, she announced that she was going to present her case before Congress herself. She would argue that Nathanael Greene had risked his fortune and the future of his family to save his soldiers from winter storm and starvation. "Can Congress hear and know this," she sighed, "and be deaf to the Miseries of the widow and fatherless—No—I will not yet believe mankind so ungrateful, so unjust."

In one of her most eloquent letters she underscored her bold determination:

> It shall never be told me, that I set myself down quietly and waited for my Ruin—No—I am a woman—unaccustomed to any thing but the trifling business of a family. Yet my exertions may effect something—if they do not—and if I sacrifice my life to the cause of my children, I shall but do my Duty—and follow the example of my illustrious husband.

When she arrived ready for battle, Wadsworth told her that the two of them should not be seen together in public. With little alternative left to her, she agreed to meet him in his living quarters. He then discouraged her from appearing before Congress. When she pressed him for information on what he might be doing to promote her case, he dissembled with various excuses. He, in turn, berated her for bringing Phineas Miller to Connecticut and accused her of having an affair with her plantation manager, intimating that she and Miller had been sleeping together before Nathanael Greene's demise.[62]

As she desperately tried to defend herself and not lose her one slim hope of financial support, she finally gave in to Wadsworth's persistent demands for sex and for domination over her. Greene, who loved to dominate the men about her, succumbed to his power in order to secure his financial support. Wadsworth, who maneuvered constantly to dominate the women he fancied, won over Greene in this brief moment.

Before the encounter was over, Wadsworth lost her forever. He was forced to admit that the reason for his inaction in her behalf, for not returning to Hartford, and for not wishing to be seen with her in public was that he was suspected of being the unfaithful lover who left Eliza Whitman, the Hartford socialite, to die in Bell's Tavern. The week of Greene's visit was the moment that Eliza Whitman's story spread throughout the nation, thus he was terrified that any action on Greene's behalf would serve to increase suspicion. Though he may have averted a modicum of public scrutiny, his dominion over Greene surely caused her to believe that he was indeed the missing "Fidelio" in Whitman's pathetic letter.[63]

Their behavior after this moment soon confirmed the distorted nature of their relationship. He provided her with money to keep going and to educate her children in the manner she wanted. George Washington Greene was, of course, in France with Lafayette. Nathanael Ray Greene ("Nat") was left with Wadsworth, who promised to oversee his education. Martha Washington Greene ("Patty") and Cornelia Greene were enrolled in the Moravian female academy in Bethlehem, Pennsylvania, with some of the money Wadsworth advanced. As she headed to Charleston, to spend weeks with the coexecutor, Edward Rutledge, she wrote Wadsworth, "I begin to be in better humor with mankind."

Her improved mood was short-lived as Wadsworth renewed his doubts about her relationship with Phineas Miller and revealed that his wife had made accusations about the nature of his correspondence with Greene. These were matters of the heart that she could handle, but just three months after he had advanced money for Greene and her children, he demanded repayment of his cash advances and the balance he was due from the Nathanael Greene estate. She quickly assured Wadsworth not to worry about Miller: "You do not have the reasons you suppose. I . . . send you a kiss to convince you of it." On the matter of his "cerious misfortune" with his wife, she wrote, "I thought my letters were burnt long since," when Wadsworth reported that he had just then burned them.

On the matter of repaying both new and old debts to Wadsworth, she was devastated. In a letter of January 31, 1789, Greene expressed a sternness never before evident in letters to him:

> I am grieved to find you are so distressed in your circum-
> stances, . . . I have sent you the very first of the crop as you
> desired. I hope you have nothing to fear from the advances
> made for the children—for while I live you can not possibly
> suffer. I will take care that you are paid every farthing due you.
> I have property, and <u>power</u>, sufficient to secure—and you know
> my pride (if I had no better motive) would not permit me to
> suffer you or your children to be wronged for mine.

She, nevertheless, again acknowledged the nature of the power struggle between them in response to another Wadsworth jab that he would never see her again. She wrote that given the nature of their relationship that was entirely up to him: "I consider myself as a kind of ambassador—liable to be recalled by my sovereign."

But Wadsworth was without principle in dealing with Greene. He next wrote a letter to Phineas Miller in the latter's capacity as manager of Mulberry Grove, accusing him of withholding repayments owed him by Greene. She described to Wadsworth Miller's reaction as "very much hirt" and said, "I confess I think he had some reason for it." When, shortly thereafter, a former army captain and Savannah politician returned from a trip to New York with graphic tales of Greene's visits to Wadsworth's room, Miller's mood shifted from hurt to rage. After the man began proclaiming on the streets of Savannah that Greene "had Mr. Miller and Mr. Wadsworth in keeping," Phineas Miller sought him out and "cained him without mercy." He also challenged the man to a duel, which never occurred. Instead, the man rushed from Savannah back to New York, where he promised to expose Greene, Miller, and Wadsworth.

On April 19, 1789, Greene announced to Wadsworth that she was returning to New York to present her claims before Congress. Wanting something from him this time, she wrote, "Nothing will prevent me from declaring in person how much affection I feel for you." But Wadsworth could not be moved. Still feeling the heat of his wife's rage and of the persisting rumors connecting him to both Whitman and Greene, he told Greene that it would be better for her simply to send a letter to Congress. Edward Rutledge disagreed violently and insisted that Greene go personally to Congress: "The effects of personal application, with justice, humanity, and gratitude on your side are wonderful. They ought to be irresistible."

Shoving Wadsworth's qualms aside, Greene sailed in midsummer 1789 to New York. Although Wadsworth brought her son Nathanael to meet her, his reception at the wharf and over the next weeks and months could not have been cooler.

As she visited newly installed President Washington and newly appointed cabinet officers she had known in Revolutionary military camps, Greene made herself one of the first and most proficient lobbyists in the new federal government. Henry Knox, secretary of war, and Alexander Hamilton, secretary of treasury, at the beckoning of the charming widow, helped her frame her legal appeal. Wadsworth, still fearful for his reputation, did not attend the sessions of Congress.

Bitterly disappointed by what she considered to be Wadsworth's betrayal of her interests—not to mention his own—Greene cried out her chagrin when she arrived back at Mulberry Grove in December: "It is not all fair play between you and myself, or you are not the man I have taken you for." Not only had he not helped her get a reimbursement from Congress, he had forwarded to her a whole new set of bills demanding immediate repayment. "To describe to you the continued torments I feel on account of my debts is impossible," she lamented again.

Recognizing finally that Wadsworth would do nothing to help her, she devised an entirely new tack. Depending upon Washington, Knox, and Hamilton for guidance, she began formulating her strategy in early 1791. In March that year Hamilton wrote with advice for overcoming one major flaw in her claim. In May, Washington visited her at Mulberry Grove while on his fabled tour of the South. The two were able to talk privately beyond the sensitive ears of Martha Washington. By December, as Greene embarked for Philadelphia, the new national capital, she was ready to present her appeal.

In Philadelphia she took her well-documented file directly to Alexander Hamilton, who approved it and added his own official endorsement. He forwarded the petition to the House of Representatives, where Greene had turned her hopes for congressional action to her next-door neighbor and another old flame, Gen. Anthony Wayne. Having also been presented a plantation by the state of Georgia for his Revolutionary War service, Wayne tired of raising rice and in early 1791 stood for election against incumbent James Jackson, a veteran politician who did not favor Greene's indemnity claim. Wayne won the election and headed off to Philadelphia to demand justice for Greene.

Unfortunately, Wayne's election had been rigged, and Jackson brought legal action to unseat him. A race ensued as Wayne tried to forward the Greene claim before Jackson could succeed in taking away his seat. Just as her appeal was ready to come before Congress in March 1792, Wayne lost his case before the House of Representatives. The House then took up a resolution to award Jackson the vacant seat. After days of argument as to whether the House could seat someone not certified as elected, a vote was taken that ended in a deadlock. Speaker of the House Jonathan Trumbull from Connecticut broke the tie, thereby forcing Georgia to hold a new election.

Greene's case now could be considered on its merits. When it came to a vote a few weeks after Wayne's banishment, it passed by a margin of nine votes. Greene sat in the gallery of the House on April 27, 1792, when a message came back from President Washington that he had "this day approved and signed an act for indemnifying the estate of the late Nathanael Greene." She was to be paid

$47,000 immediately and to receive three additional installments over a period of three years. Victory was hers!

As she reflected in the coming weeks over the meaning of her victory, she wrote sternly to an old friend who had promoted Wayne's removal, "Thank God W[ayne] kept his seat long enough to do me the most essential services, . . . it is to his exertions . . . that I principally owe my independence." In the same letter, she also acknowledged:

> I am in good health and spirits and feel as saucy as you please—not only because I am independent, but because I have gained a compleet tryumph over some of my friends who did not wish me success—and others who doubted my judgement in managing the business—and constantly tormented me to death to give up my obstinacy as it was called—they are now as mute as mice—Not a word dare they utter, . . .

She had every right to savor her new role in the world as she concluded the foregoing song of victory with the words, "O how sweet is revenge!"[64]

FOSTERING INVENTION

The proof of Catharine Littlefield Greene's independence lay not merely in winning a widow's victory against mistreatment, but it was to be found in the way she pursued her life after independence was hers. During the twelve months after Congress settled her indemnity claim, she inspired men around her to change the world. As a shrewd power broker, she demonstrated that she was willing to risk every penny she had to achieve her goals.

The next episode in this extraordinary woman's life began a few short months after Alexander Hamilton happily handed her a first indemnity check for $47,000. As a favor to a neighbor near Mulberry Grove, a Major Dupont, Greene consulted Yale president Ezra Stiles about a tutor for Dupont's children who could both teach and bring some industry and culture to his plantation. Stiles, one of the better college placement officers of his era, supplied Greene with a suitably qualified recent Yale graduate. His name was Eli Whitney.[65]

Whitney was twenty-seven years old at the moment, a year younger than Phineas Miller. In almost every respect an odd duck, he little fit the typical image of Yale alumni. Born on a farm in Worcester County, Massachusetts, Whitney took little interest in things educational in his early years. He learned to read, but did little of it; he learned to farm, but cared not much for it. He did demonstrate an early interest in the various tools in his father's wood- and metalworking shop. He spent his teenage years in his father's forge, first making nails and then hatpins to supply home needs when imports were no longer available.

At age eighteen, Whitney decided to find a career that did not involve working with his hands. He spent a few months at nearby Leicester Academy preparing to teach, then three years conducting a school at Hopkinton, Massachusetts, before entering Yale. April 30, 1789, the day George Washington was inaugurated America's first president, Ezra Stiles noted in his diary, "I gave a phil. Lect. Examd & admitted a Freshman." That freshman was twenty-four-year-old Whitney.

Seven or eight years older than most of the entering freshmen, he nevertheless applied himself and graduated from Yale in September 1792. With few prospects, he was happy to have an invitation to take a tutoring job in Georgia in November 1792, even though he knew nothing about the family or the place he was going. Suspicious that "the climate of the Southern States is something unhealthy," he hoped "by temperance and Prudence to withstand it." He wrote his father, "If I should find my health declining, I shall return, if possible before it is too late."

Whitney was encouraged, however, by Phineas Miller's successful example on the Greene plantation. About Catharine Greene, he knew nothing worth mentioning in his detailed letter to his father.

Most men would have turned back home if they had experienced the same introduction Whitney did to his new assignment. He sailed from Boston to New York in early October 1792, only to have his packet ship run aground miles from his destination. Dripping wet, he and four other passengers made their way by wagon into the city, where he happened across another Yale graduate. To his utter amazement, the fellow whose hand he shook so gladly was infected with small-pox. Fearful that he would die from this great peril, he decided to be "enoculated" and suffer through the disease. By October 17 he reported to a friend that he was recovering from a light case of the malady and was that day boarding a packet ship headed to Savannah. As he was "committing" himself "to the boisterous ocian," he bade his friend to pray that "God Almighty bless you and Land me safe in Georgia."

Whitney's misadventures continued when he arrived in Savannah. There he learned that the wages he had been promised were twice what he actually would be paid. He refused the position. When he relaycd this information back home after five months of stark silence, he concluded, "You know I always considered this a dam'd kind of world, and to say the truth, I have no great reason to change my opinion since I saw you." But he was enigmatic in his letters, not hinting at why he had been silent nearly half a year and not accounting for how he was supporting himself during the intervening period of joblessness.[66]

Whitney was, in fact, trying to keep secret a story he was not yet ready to tell. When, finally, on September 11, 1793, he decided to unburden himself to his father, he had two remarkable stories to tell. First, he was in love with Catharine Littlefield Greene. He had met her in New York as they were boarding the packet ship and had been in her company all the way from New York to Savannah. From their first moment together, he remained almost constantly in her presence, delighting for the first time in his twenty-eight years in the charms of a woman. Although she was eleven years older, the captivated Whitney happily resided at Mulberry Grove, where he catered to Greene's every desire.[67]

Whitney's second account was in some ways just as revolutionary as the concurrent proceedings in Paris. Whereas hc had expected to travel with Greene's contingent to Savannah and then proceed immediately to the plantation of Major Dupont, he instead went directly to Mulberry Grove to pursue a quixotic project promoted by Greene herself. "There were a number of very respectable Gentlemen at Mrs. Greene's," Whitney confided to his father, "who all agreed that if a machine could be invented which would clean the cotton with expedition, it would be a great thing both to the Country and to the inventor." He wrote, "I involuntarily happened to be thinking on the subject [of ginning cotton] and struck out a plan of a Machine in my mind." Encouraged by both Miller and Greene to pursue his idea, Miller "said if I would pursue it and try an experiment to see if it would answer, he would be at the whole expense, I should lose nothing but my time, and if I succeeded we would share the profits."

In ten days he had built a model so revolutionary that he was offered "a Hundred Guineas" on the spot for the title to it. Pleased with his invention, "I concluded to relinquish my school [Dupont's] and turn my attention to perfecting the Machine." He soon had produced a device "which required the labor of one man to turn it and with which one man will clean ten times as much cotton as he can in any other way before known and also cleanse it much better than in the usual mode." Several years later he described the creative moment. His "original Idea was to make a whole row of teeth of one piece of metal . . . out of sheet Iron," but there being no such material available in Georgia that spring of 1793, he had to turn to something else. With the help of "one of the Miss Greens [who] had broug[ht] out a coile of iron wire to make a bird cage and being embarrassed for want of sheet iron and seeing this wire hang in the parlour[,] it struck me that I could make teeth with that."[68]

One other problem remained as Whitney one evening demonstrated his machine to the Greenes, Miller, and their lawyer, Nathaniel Pendleton. As Whitney cranked the machine, putting raw cotton in the top and dropping liberated seeds through thin slots at the bottom, cotton fibers clinging to the teeth, eventually clogged the slots. Catharine Greene found the solution by holding up a hearth brush to suggest that a stiff brush be added to the machine. Whitney, in turn, acknowledged this important hint as he added another ingredient to his improved device. While the machine was clearly Whitney's invention, Greene provided an incubator in which his genius could thrive and gave him the necessary warm approval to exercise that wonderful gift.

But Greene did much more. She encouraged the two young men in her life, Phineas Miller and Eli Whitney, to form a partnership to secure a patent for their new machine and to manufacture it. It was Greene who paid Whitney a salary in 1793, and it was Greene who gave Miller the $1,000 he needed to buy from Whitney half interest in the invention and to set up the firm of Miller & Whitney. She also used her monies received from Congress to underwrite an enterprise of manufacturing gins and of setting them up across Georgia and the South.[69]

She even paid for the first public advertisement about the revolutionary gin on March 6, 1794. An article in Savannah's *Gazette of the State of Georgia* bespoke the revolutionary intentions of Greene, Miller, and Whitney:

> The subscriber will engage to gin, in a manner equal to picking
> by hand, any quantity of the green seed cotton, on the follow-

ing terms: viz. for every five pounds delivered him in the seed he will return one pound of clean cotton for the market. For the encouragement of cotton planters he will also mention that ginning machines to clean the green seed cotton on the above terms will actually be erected in different parts of the country before the harvest of the ensuing crop.

They were not planning to sell the gin—their goal was to have a monopoly on ginning all of the cotton of the South, and of the world. In a year's time—with Catharine Greene's financial backing—they hoped to be in a position to gin the world's cotton and, in the process, to gain title to four fifths of the earth's cotton production![70]

All thoughts of teaching disappeared from Whitney's mind. During the spring of 1793, on a salary of two guineas per day with a promise of advancing to five per day in a matter of months, Whitney was engrossed in Greene and the ginning of cotton. As he was about to return to his shop in Connecticut, he told a friend, "I hear of wars and rumors of wars; but very little of the news of the Day. I have not seen a News Paper these three months." With memorable kisses from Greene, he headed to Philadelphia in June 1793 to secure a patent under the recently enacted patent law.

So new was the law, in fact, that Whitney procured the personal counsel of Thomas Jefferson, secretary of state, on what procedures to follow. For more than two weeks Whitney studied the process and prepared his patent application, asking the United States to "cause Letters Patent to be made out . . . granting to him your sd. Petitioner, his heirs, Administrators & assigns, for the term of fourteen years . . . the full and exclusive right & liberty of making, constructing, using and vending to others to be used, the sd. Invention." With Jefferson's resignation at the end of July and the onset of the yellow fever epidemic in August, Whitney's application was set aside, and his patent was not issued until March 14, 1794.[71]

With funds advanced by Greene, Whitney nevertheless began manufacturing cotton gins at his shop near New Haven with tools bought in Philadelphia and New York to facilitate the process. By February 1794, when he was ready to take one of his perfected gins to Philadelphia, he stopped by Yale to show the thing to Ezra Stiles. Calling it "a curious & very ingenious piece of mechanism," Stiles watched as Whitney cleaned twelve pounds of cotton in twenty minutes. From Philadelphia a month later, Whitney reported, "I accomplished everything agreeable to my wishes. I had the satisfaction to hear it declared by a number of the first men in America that my machine is the most perfect & the most valuable invention that has ever appeared in this Country."

With his patent in hand, Whitney announced that he was ready to deliver his machines to Georgia and "thence I expect to go to England, where I shall probably continue two or three years." He continued in his jubilation,

How advantageous this business will eventually prove to me, I cannot say. It is generally said by those who know anything

> about it, that I shall make a Fortune by it. . . . I am now so sure
> of success that ten thousand dollars, if I saw the money counted
> out to me, would not tempt me to give up my right and relin-
> quish the object.

Just as the world was flying apart in revolutionary France, Whitney was sure that
he, with the critical assistance of Catharine Greene, had gained control of it.[72]

Whitney's euphoria was punctured early in 1795 when a fire swept through
his workshop, destroying his tools and all the gins he had made. He quickly
bounced back and delivered twenty-six machines by the end of October, with
Greene financing the replacement of the workshop. He then learned that British
manufacturers did not like and would not buy the short-grained knots coming
from his machine. But that proved to be nothing compared to the reactions of
Georgia planters to the attempts of the firm of Miller & Whitney to monopolize
cotton ginning. Rival gins, copying Whitney's design, soon began to appear in
Georgia and South Carolina. Miller, Whitney, and Greene watched helplessly as
other ginners flaunted Whitney's patent rights with impunity.

By the end of 1795 the trio's hopefulness was gone. Phineas Miller wrote
Whitney in desperation, urging him to go to England and meet with reluctant manufacturers: "The utmost stretch of my capital will not be equal to meet the
expenses of another year unless this Difficulty is removed—and we have even
now trespassed very largely on the funds of the estate of Genl. Greene." To make
matters worse Greene and Miller had invested heavily in the Yazoo Land Company scam to purchase 35 million acres of undeveloped land in Georgia. On the
advice of her new son-in-law, John Nightingale, a principal in the Yazoo Company, Greene signed notes secured with the assets of the Greene estate. In 1796,
when it became clear that Nightingale and others had bribed Georgia legislators to
get the sweetheart sale approved, Georgia planters and citizens canceled the deal.[73]

The Yazoo collapse placed Greene and the firm of Miller & Whitney in a
precarious condition. Cash reserves from the Greene estate had evaporated and
title to Mulberry Grove itself was thrown into question. As rival gins grew across
the South, Miller & Whitney began focusing more directly on the status of the
patent itself. If they could not gin all of the world's cotton, they could at least collect royalty payments from people making use of their patented gin design. The
world of cotton ginning was transforming so dramatically from 1794 to 1796 that
they had no other choice. But protecting the patent would require legal fees to
bring suits against individuals infringing their rights.

In May 1797, Miller & Whitney brought their first patent suit against a rival
Georgia gin manufacturer. Miller attended to the court appearance, Greene
financed the fight, and Whitney supplied the documents. When Miller reported
the outcome of the trial to Whitney on May 11, his news was heartbreaking. The
Georgia jury that heard the arguments was swayed by old military foes of
Nathanael Greene, by planters who resented the Miller & Whitney attempt to
create a ginning monopoly, and by a judge who instructed them that Miller &
Whitney had not a case.

"The event of the first Patent suit," Miller wrote, ". . . has gone against us." The rival gin manufacturer was upheld. "In a private conversation had with the Judge afterwards," he explained, "he told me that we could have no hope of protecting our Patent rights without an alteration of the law." Then came the effects of this all:

> Thus after four years of assiduous labour fatigue and difficulty are we again set afloat by a new and most unexpected obstacle. . . . The actual crisis has now arrived which I have long mentioned as possible, and sometimes almost or indeed quite apprehended as probable. The crisis is our insolvency as a Partnership.

The real problem was not just the "insolvency" of the partnership; it was rather that Miller & Whitney had run through the assets of the Greene estate. The partnership actually owed the estate for its considerable advances.[74]

Greene had placed her hopes in the dreams of two young men and, though her estate was drained, she continued to support their efforts. She was as much the creator of the cotton gin as the tinkerer that gave it teeth. And she was as much convinced of its value as other inventors and their backers have been through history. Every great invention required time, patent battles, and technical argument. Robert Fulton's steamboat would need protection, as would Samuel F. B. Morse's telegraph, John Ericsson's screw propeller for the *U.S.S. Monitor,* and the wing warping and ruddering of the Wright Brothers' first flyer.[75]

Because Miller & Whitney could not pay its debts, the Greene estate could not pay its creditors. In the fall of 1798, Mulberry Grove had to be sold. First, twelve slaves were pawned to produce cash; then the entire estate itself had to be unloaded when property values dramatically declined. A mere $15,000 was all Greene received for the palatial mansion and the thousands of acres surrounding it. Greene, Miller, and her entourage of children, slaves, and cotton gins moved to Cumberland Island, Georgia, an undeveloped property bought by Nathanael Greene on speculation at the end of the Revolution.[76]

But Catharine Greene never gave up on the patent rights for the cotton gin. Although the pursuit of lawsuits on the patent reduced her to near poverty, she unstintingly supported Phineas Miller and Eli Whitney. And they remained devoted to her. Even though she broke Whitney's heart in May 1796 by marrying Miller in a private ceremony in Philadelphia, witnessed only by George and Martha Washington, he never lost interest in her. He battled on, trying to recover the fortune he had hoped to gain from the cotton gin—not merely to enrich himself, but also to repay Catharine Greene. Although perpetually on the edge of poverty and again married, Catharine Greene remained in 1798 one of the most truly independent women in America. She and a few other women had discovered how to operate freely in a world where liberty was preached, however little it might in reality be practiced.

VENERATE THE PLOUGH

CHAPTER 11

Africans in the Land of Liberty

LABORING FOR LIBERTY

The eighteenth century witnessed Africans' pursuit of freedom through adventure, through movement, and, in the case of some, through learning. But the most inspiring stories were those of the thousands of black men and women who simply labored their way to independence, paving the way for others. Frequently their naive understanding of liberty—their acceptance of the rhetoric of the American Revolution at face value—made it possible to hurdle obstacles blocking their rights as humans.

Few careers were more remarkable than those of Amos and Violate Baldwin Fortune. Born in Africa and brought to America by 1725 as a slave, Amos Fortune was sold in 1740 at the age of thirty to Ichabod Richardson, a tanner in Woburn, Massachusetts. Between 1740 and 1768, when Richardson, an unmarried man, died, Fortune learned every facet of the tanning business. As he became a master tanner and was able to carry the business on his own shoulders, he desperately wanted to become a free man. Richardson had at least once along the way voiced the possibility of manumitting the hardworking Fortune. In 1763 Richardson actually drew up a document in which he did "Covenant, promise grant and agree to, and with my Negroe man Amos That at the end of four years next . . . the Said Amos Shall then be Discharged, Freed, and Set at liberty from my Service."

The manumission agreement, although preserved by Fortune, regrettably remained forever unsigned. When Richardson on his deathbed in May 1768 drew up his last will and testament, he made no provision for Fortune's manumission. He did not even mention the slave, leaving it to his executors to divide his estate equally among three heirs. By happy circumstance, Fortune was allocated with the division of all the other property (houses, land, barns, oxen, the tannery, a blanket, and a Bible) to Richardson's sister, Hannah, and her children. He had already lived in Hannah Richardson's home for twelve years, and she evidently wanted him to be free. She arranged for him to be bound to her son-in-law, Simon Carter, to continue working as a tanner, but also provided through the agreement that he would be able to purchase his freedom.[1]

This arrangement was a godsend for Fortune. In eighteen months, he was able to buy his freedom. At age sixty, on November 11, 1770, he became a free man and continued the tanning business for the Richardsons on a rental basis. By July 20, 1774, he had the funds to buy a lot and build his own home. Although war raged around him, on June 23, 1778, he bought a slave, Lydia Somerset, and two weeks later made her his wife. When she died just three months later, he began setting aside money to purchase another slave woman to become his wife. Twelve months later in October 1779, he bought Violate (Vilot in the deed) Baldwin, and two weeks later they married. As a tax-paying property owner and prosperous business-man, Fortune also contributed to his Congregational church at Woburn.[2]

In 1781 Amos and Violate moved to the frontier area of Jaffrey, New Hampshire, where they hoped to establish their own businesses on their own property, he as tanner and she as weaver. The town had no tannery, and Amos intended to capture the market for leather in the surrounding countryside. To get started, he proposed to Jaffrey selectmen that he establish the tannery on land rented from the town until he could buy his own property. Ten years later both Fortunes had developed their businesses; they had secured a twenty-five-acre farm; Amos had taken on both black and white apprentices; and they had adopted two orphan girls as their own children.[3]

The Fortunes received various insults in their first years in Jaffrey. For example, they were forced to sit in a segregated balcony of the village church. The lot where they started out became forever known as "the Nigger piece." Nevertheless, by 1790 they were among the most solid citizens of the Jaffrey area. Amos Fortune regularly loaned money to needy individuals. He was one of twenty-two charter members of the town library and served as the leather bookbinder for the library's most valuable books. When he sat down to write his will in his ninety-first year, he specified that, after provision had been made for Violate and adopted daughter Celyndia and other bills paid, "a handsome present" was to be made to his church. He also directed that the residue of his estate be put into a perpetual endowment for the town school in Jaffrey. His generous bequests were accomplished following his death in 1801 and Violate's in 1802.[4]

Far away from Jaffrey in the Moravian settlement called Wachovia in pied-mont North Carolina, another African also used the tanning trade to establish himself. Abraham Neger (for Negro) was born in or near Guinea in 1730. He served among Mandingo chiefs until approximately 1760, when he was captured in warfare, his ears were severely mutilated, and he was sold into slavery. Like so many other Africans he was taken to St. Domingue to work on a sugar plantation. There he remained long enough to learn French and to take on a spirit of rebelliousness that has marked the people of that island from the eighteenth century forward. Ten years later he was bought again and taken to Virginia from whence in 1771 he was taken with another slave, Jupiter, to be sold to the Moravian Church in North Carolina.

Moravians, although famed for their abundant missions to American Indians and to African slaves in the West Indies, had no qualms about slavery. But they did discourage individual ownership of slaves: Slaves belonged instead to the

Church itself. By the 1770s the Moravian community of several thousand owned twenty-five slaves. All decisions relating to the slaves' lives and work were made directly by the Church, either by a conference of elders (on spiritual matters) or by a board of laymen (on material concerns).

When Abraham arrived in Wachovia, he had no given name and was merely called Sambo; he was lame; and he was suffering from severe infection in his feet. The Moravians thus took him at a discounted price, in part as a charity case. But the rebellious "Sambo," clearly mistreated everywhere he had been, resisted Church authority. Although he was assigned to work as an assistant in the community tannery, he and other slaves set fires to property, shunned work, and occasionally ran away. When the American Revolution erupted in 1775, "Sambo" tried to make his way to Virginia to join the British Army. Three weeks later he was found wandering aimlessly in the wrong direction. For his escape he was severely flogged. In April and May 1776, he threatened individual Moravians and once more attempted to flee. Twice again he was flogged so harshly that he was "in a very poor state and unable to work because of the beating he has received."

By 1779 "Sambo" evidently decided that resistance was getting him nowhere. That December he asked to be baptized and to be accepted as a Single Brother in the Moravian Church. Single Brothers lived democratically in monastic dormitories and were assigned various jobs in the community. Over the next year church elders drew lots monthly to determine his acceptability. Although "Sambo" was "extremely perplexed about his long-delayed baptism," in December 1780, the elders finally "drew an affirmative lot and the rite was performed." During the ceremony, he was given the Christian name Abraham and was officially installed as a Single Brother. Despite the fact that he legally remained a slave and property of the Moravian Church, his status instantly changed. As one Moravian bishop described the status of slaves received into the brotherhood, "there is no difference between them and other brothers and sisters." He continued, "They dress as we do, they eat what we eat, they work when we work, they rest when we rest, and they enjoy quite naturally what other brothers and sisters enjoy."

From the moment of his baptism, Abraham's life was completely transformed. He was allowed to marry—his wife, of course, to be selected by the elders. He was permitted to sponsor the baptism of other African Americans into the brotherhood—including Jupiter, with whom he had arrived in 1771. He was educated along with others in the community. He was taught German and music. He participated in discussions of Moravian missions to black slaves in the West Indies, a subject he "enjoyed . . . very much, thought of it daily in his prayers, and also contributed his part."

In the tannery where he became a master tanner under the tutelage of Heinrich Herbst, the most gifted tanner in North Carolina, he was treated with equality. During April 1789, as liberty coursed across the Western world, a white apprentice in Herbst's tannery, Jacob Spach, complained that he did "not care to learn this trade and does not want to work with the Negro." Church elders agreed with Herbst's decision to dismiss Spach for his unbrotherly demeanor.

Abraham thrived as a tanner. When he became a Single Brother, he was paid wages for his work, and he accumulated over the years a substantial estate. For twenty-six years he labored away, making fine leather. When he died in 1797, he left a "testament concerning his own estate, in which he makes his widow Sarah heir of his cash money, with the condition that one Brother should keep it and give it to her from time to time as she needs it." Most tellingly was the remainder of his testament: "The rest of his belongings he has given to Brothers and boys in the tannery." Abraham's devotion to labor among a religious sect where slavery was embraced had brought him an amazing degree of freedom in the era of revolution.[5]

Hard work and tenacity also paid off for Abijah Prince and his young wife Lucy Terry, one of America's earliest black poets. Abijah Prince won his freedom and a parcel of land near Deerfield, Massachusetts, as a result of military service to the Crown. Lucy Terry was kidnapped and sold into slavery in Africa at age five. At Bristol, Rhode Island, she was purchased by Ebenezer Wells of Deerfield. Wells had her baptized and provided her with an education sufficient enough to write a stirring ballad describing the frightful Indian attack on frontier Deerfield in 1746. Among the victims listed in her rough-hewn poem titled "The Bar's Fight," was one woman:

> Eunice Allen sees the Indians coming,
> And hopes to save herself by running,
> And had not her petticoats stopped her,
> The awful creatures had not catched her,
> Nor tommy hawked her on her head,
> And left her on the ground for dead.

Although the poem was not published until 1855, everyone in Deerfield knew the ballad and its sprightly author.[6]

Prince purchased Terry in 1756 and, although twice her age, made her his wife. The two became a devoted hardworking couple. When Abijah inherited a hundred-acre farm from a former employer at Guilford, Vermont, in the early 1760s, the Princes repaired there to become a family complete with six children. Abijah was also one of fifty-five original grantees to receive one-hundred-acre plots in Sunderland, Vermont. In the process of rearing her family and caring for two farms, Lucy Terry Prince undertook three public appeals during the 1780s that made her an almost mythic figure in Vermont and American history. All of them came at that critical moment in the wake of the American Revolution when African Americans were working desperately to take their place in society.

Her first appeal derived from persistent attacks on the Prince farm by white neighbors at Guilford. Local authorities refused to take action against the Noyes family, who openly tore down Prince fences and burned their haystacks. Lucy Prince appealed in person to Governor Thomas Chittenden for assistance, and on June 7, 1785, Chittenden and his council ordered town selectmen to protect the Princes. Then a neighbor to their Sunderland farm, Col. Eli Bronson, contested the validity of Abijah Prince's grant. When local and state authorities could not settle the dispute, the case was appealed successfully by the Princes to the U.S. Supreme Court.

Lucy Prince next appealed to the trustees of Williams College to admit her youngest son, Abijah, Jr., to the school. Although she laid out her case directly to the college trustees, citing her family's military contributions, their good citizenship, and her personal friendship with Col. Ephraim Williams—namesake and donor of the land where the college stood—the Williams board denied her request. Despite failure in this third attempt to secure her family's rights, Abijah and Lucy Prince brought forth two Revolutionary War soldiers, a fighter with the Green Mountain Boys, a gifted musician, and a daughter who became a respected regional poet.[7]

And then there was Elizabeth Freeman, whose audacious pursuit of liberty, even as she spent her entire life in the service of others, compared favorably with the efforts of Lucy Terry Prince. The daughter of African parents and born into slavery, Mum Bett (as she was known in her early years and to closest associates through life) and her sister were purchased by Col. John Ashley of Sheffield, Massachusetts, early in life. Although subject to the Massachusetts slave code, Freeman departed from the Ashley household when Mrs. Ashley attempted to strike her sister. When Colonel Ashley attempted to force her return, Freeman turned to the young attorney Theodore Sedgwick for assistance.

According to Sedgwick and his daughter Catherine Sedgwick—both of whom left loving accounts of the industry and power of Elizabeth Freeman—it was her idea to resist Ashley's legal efforts to force her return with the argument that under the Massachusetts constitution all citizens were "born free and equal." She conceived the idea while waiting tables and listening to politicians talk about the bill of rights contained in the state constitution. Sedgwick argued this line before the county court at Great Barrington, Massachusetts, in 1781. When the jury rendered its verdict, Elizabeth Freeman was set free and Ashley was ordered to pay damages of thirty shillings. Although Ashley offered her work for wages, she refused him, instead joining the Sedgwick household as housekeeper for many years. Her hard work, determination, and dignity inspired the Sedgwicks to oppose slavery and to promote the rights of African Americans. Her court case, joined with similar verdicts across Massachusetts, established the principle that the state had, in effect, abolished slavery in adopting its revolutionary constitution.[8]

While most African Americans struggled to make a basic living and to preserve some limited rights, some others were able to convert their labors into profit and power, enabling them to influence the rights of Africans across America and the Western world. Preeminent among them was Capt. Paul Cuffe, the extraordinarily successful son of Coffe Slocum, who after the American Revolution built a growing business in shipping, trade, and manufacturing. It was Cuffe and his brother John who had in February 1780 joined company with five other Massachusetts blacks to demand that they be relieved of taxes if they were not to be given the full rights of citizens. Following protracted litigation and indictments to collect unpaid taxes, they, in the end, won their right to vote.

Paul Cuffe (n.d.). American seafaring merchant and African colonizationist.

The seventh of ten children, Paul Cuffe had watched his father and Native American mother become free and independent people, successful at farming, business, and fishing off the Massachusetts coast. When Coffe Slocum died in 1772, Paul began a seafaring career that had few equals. After ten years at sea, in 1783 he married Alice Pequit, a Pequot from Martha's Vineyard and rented a shoemaker's shop, where he worked for only a short time. Before the end of the year he was off on a whaling trip; he then left for a trading trip to North Carolina. Six children—four daughters and two sons—were later born to the Cuffes, all of whom would work directly or with their spouses in Paul Cuffe's shipping empire.

In 1787 Cuffe launched the first of at least ten ships he owned himself or in partnership with others. The first was a twenty-five-ton schooner, *Sunfish,* built at Westport, Massachusetts, where Cuffe made his headquarters. The *Sunfish* harvested seven whales during its first outing that year. The forty-two-ton *Mary* followed, also from Westport, in 1792. And the sixty-two-ton *Ranger* was duly launched in 1796. Each christening signified a new plateau in the expansion of a business that by 1796 had Cuffe and his all-black crews sailing everywhere in the Atlantic. The arrival of the *Ranger* in Newport, New Bedford, and Philadelphia that year inspired countless African stevedores and sailors.

The same effect spread among blacks in southern ports as Cuffe sailed into Norfolk, Virginia, where each of his sailors could have been seized under America's harsh Fugitive Slave Act of 1793. From Norfolk the *Ranger* proceeded deeper into plantation country as Cuffe made for Vienna, Maryland, on the Nanticoke

River. On this route, he and his crew passed countless plantations, where slaves tilled fields and hailed the crews of every passing ship. When the ship moored at Vienna, a crowd gathered to witness the unusual sight. One eyewitness, noting that "the people were filled with astonishment and alarm," wrote:

> A vessel owned and commanded by a person of color, and manned with a crew of the same complexion, was unprecedented and surprising. The white inhabitants were struck with apprehension of the injurious effects which such circumstances would have in the minds of their slaves, but perhaps they were still more fearful that, under the veil of commerce, he had arrived among them with hostile intentions.

Fearful that Cuffe's visit might incite rebellion among local slaves, some in the crowd demanded that James Frazier, customs agent at Vienna, seize the ship and crew. They were shocked when Frazier reported that Cuffe's credentials were flawless and that the *Ranger* could unload its cargo.

Cuffe had already warned his crew that their behavior had to be exemplary. The same observer who reported the locals' fear when the *Ranger* arrived also stated that Captain Cuffe from beginning to end over a period of several days exhibited "candour, modesty and firmness, and all his crew behaved not only inoffensively, but with a conciliating propriety." Cuffe, moreover, invited prominent citizens to tour his prized ship; his hospitality was returned with various dinner invitations. As the *Ranger* sailed from Vienna filled with a cargo of Indian corn, Cuffe had risen above every possible suspicion.

When international trade for American ships became treacherous in the late 1790s, Cuffe restricted his trade to a lucrative triangle between Nova Scotia, Wilmington or Philadelphia, and New Bedford, Newport, or Nantucket. By 1799 he expanded his shipping compound and homestead by 140 acres at a cost of $3,500. To provide education for his children and grandchildren he built a schoolhouse on his land and invited others in the area to send their children as well. By 1800 he had added a gristmill, a windmill, and partners to operate a full-scale milling operation. His business assets of more than $10,000 made him one of the wealthiest African Americans in the United States.

Cuffe's race, his business success, his routes of travel, and his religious persuasion—he was a Quaker by upbringing and choice—anointed him a leader of African Americans. And so it was, as Cuffe traveled from his own Quaker community at Westport to the larger Quaker centers in Philadelphia, Wilmington, and Newport, he became engaged in discussions of African-American destiny. When William Rotch, Sr., the wealthiest Quaker in Newport returned from Europe in 1787, he excitedly told Cuffe about the work of Granville Sharp and British Quakers to abolish the Atlantic slave trade and of the departure of three shiploads of former American slaves living in London to establish a new colony in West Africa. In December 1787 Cuffe received news of another seventy-three blacks in Boston who were headed to join the settlement being called Province of Freedom in Sierra Leone.[9]

Cuffe was immediately taken by the idea of establishing a new homeland for Africans. Although he was not personally interested in migrating to Africa, he increasingly came to the conclusion that a free African nation could be an ideal solution for many Africans who did not feel at home in the Western world. And although his active leadership of a movement to repatriate Africans to Sierra Leone did not emerge in its fullest until after 1800, he was formulating his plans, discussing the merits of African colonization with Quakers and other black leaders, and establishing an international network of cooperative individuals.

One of those individuals, whose judgment Cuffe came to value most, first encountered the black captain in just the same manner as those black stevedores in Norfolk and Vienna in 1796. James Forten, who had recently been appointed foreman of the largest sailmaking shop in Philadelphia, was on an errand to the Delaware River waterfront in the spring of 1793 when he noticed a ship anchored at the public landing at Pine Street in Philadelphia. Forten, himself a promising black American sailmaker, stared at the schooner *Mary* out of Westport, Massachusetts. He could not believe his eyes. Onboard the vessel were the captain and entire crew—and all were black. So taken was he by this unique scene that he determined to meet the captain before nightfall. That historic meeting did occur, and the two of them soon became lifelong friends and associates.

James Forten, seven years younger than Cuffe, would become equally prosperous in the business world. Born the son of a sailmaker in the shop of Robert Bridges, James was a second-generation free black and thereby received opportunities in Philadelphia available to very few other black Americans. He was also able to attend school under the tutelage of Anthony Benezet, a renowned white champion of black rights. Only the death of Forten's father when the boy was seven stood in the way of a most promising life.[10]

James Forten (n.d.). Black sailmaker and entrepreneur, he became the voice of Americanized Africans.

Forten, at age ten, watched every movement around Pennsylvania's State House as Congress issued the Declaration of Independence and as George Washington, accompanied by the youthful Lafayette, marched his troops through the city. Among the brigades were black soldiers marching alongside white comrades. Forten clearly absorbed all the talk about liberty, freedom, and equality. He also suffered the privations of other Philadelphians during a long British occupation and the economic downturn that followed.

By 1781 with the war still raging, Forten yearned to become a part of the action. At fifteen he signed on the *Royal Louis* as a powder boy. He became one of five thousand or so African Americans who fought for liberty in the American armies. When the *Royal Louis,* a 22-gun privateer with a crew of two hundred, weighed anchor in July 1781, Forten was one of twenty blacks on board. Sooner than anyone there wished, the *Royal Louis* entered into a bloody engagement with the British ship *Lawrence.* Forten was the only survivor at his gun station. On the next voyage his ship was captured following a fierce battle. He was made a prisoner of war and consigned to the *Old Jersey,* a death trap of a prison moored in the New York harbor. Although hundreds of American prisoners died there, Forten survived to be released seven months later as the war subsided.[11]

Back in Philadelphia, Forten worked on docks and around ships until February 1784, when he signed to sail for England onboard the *Commerce.* Upon arrival in Liverpool, he worked for a time as a stevedore, observing daily the disturbing arrival and departure of slave ships. Deeply troubled by this commerce in humans, a practice schoolmaster Benezet had condemned many years before, Forten, encouraged by a Quaker encountered in Liverpool, decided that he wanted to meet Benezet's British counterpart, Granville Sharp.

Forten headed to London, where he easily found work along the Thames. He soon met another Quaker, who told him of a meeting on the subject of the slave trade, where Sharp was scheduled to speak. It was Sharp, originally inspired by the writings of Benezet, who had waged an almost singlehanded battle to abolish slavery from Britain and who was then battling the slave trade. Forten's luck was considerable, for not only did he meet Sharp, he also met Thomas Clarkson, who announced at that meeting his plans to devote his life to the abolition of the slave trade. Over the next few months Forten attended many such meetings as he considered what he might be able to do to advance the rights of Africans living in the Western world.

By the fall of 1786 Forten was back in Philadelphia, where he had signed apprentice papers to work in the sailmaking loft of the same Robert Bridges who had employed his father. By 1791 he had become foreman of the loft. In that capacity he supervised the work of forty employees, white and black, apprentices and master sailmakers. He also invented a device for managing cumbersome large sails. When Bridges became too old to manage the business, he offered to sell it to Forten. Shipping magnate Thomas Willing, who had observed Forten's creativity and hard work, loaned him the money to make the purchase in 1798. Since Bridges had over the years left more and more of the business operations to Forten, the transition from making sails to running the business was an easy one for him. He, in fact, thrived, becoming alongside Paul Cuffe one of the wealthiest blacks in America.[12]

Even as he worked out his personal fortunes, however, James Forten continued to be concerned about the status and treatment of African Americans—slave or free. He closely followed activities affecting blacks across Philadelphia, at home and abroad. He supported local efforts to organize a benevolent brotherhood called the Free African Society, and he supported the work of Philadelphia black clergymen to form schools and churches for African Americans. He joined and became a pillar of the first African church in America, St. Thomas African Episcopal Church in 1794. And he was engaged in every important meeting, every petition, and every organization where the future of blacks in America was discussed. Through correspondence and Cuffe's regular visits, he engaged with the future of Africans around the world. He, Cuffe, and a few others around the English-speaking world closely monitored the rise and fall of the rights of blacks in the age of revolutions.[13]

AFRICAN-AMERICAN ENLIGHTENMENT

On August 19, 1791, Benjamin Banneker sat down at his home near Baltimore, Maryland, to write a heartfelt letter to Thomas Jefferson, then secretary of state. A free black farmer, a self-trained mathematician and astronomer, and an observant student of human affairs, Banneker wished to present "a copy of an Almanack which I have calculated for the Succeeding year [1792]."

He then went on to explain the origin of his complex arithmetical exercise:

> This calculation, Sir, is the production of my arduous study, in this my advanced Stage of life [age 60]; for having long had unbounded desires to become Acquainted with the Secrets of nature, I have had to gratify my curiosity herein thro my own assiduous application to Astronomical Study, in which I need not recount to you the many difficulties and disadvantages which I have had to encounter.

Among those were the absence of sufficient books and instruments to do his calculations and the want of time during the preceding six months—especially due to his three-month tenure assisting the surveyor of the Federal Territory, Washington, D.C. Jefferson, on behalf of President Washington, oversaw the charting of the capital's boundaries and streets, and Jefferson knew that Banneker worked on the project, recording astronomical data.

But Jefferson also knew that Banneker was black, a first-generation son of an imported African and of a black mother. Hence, in his reply, Jefferson alluded strongly to the almanac maker's race and origins: "No body wishes more than I do to see such proofs as you exhibit, that nature has given to our black brethren, talents equal to those of the other colors of men, and that the appearance of a want of them is owing merely to the degraded condition of their existence, both in Africa & America." Regarding Banneker's endeavor as proof that blacks could make worthy contributions to society, Jefferson informed his correspondent that "I have taken the liberty of sending your Almanac to Monsieur de Condorcet, Secretary of the Academy of Sciences at Paris . . . because I considered it as a document to which your whole colour had a right for their justification against the doubts which have been entertained of them."

True to his word, on August 30, 1791, Jefferson rushed off a letter to Condorcet, stating, "I am happy to be able to inform you that we have now in the United States a negro, the son of a black man born in Africa, and a black woman born in the United States, who is a very respectable mathematician." Recounting how "I procured for him to be employed . . . in laying out the new federal city," Jefferson testified, "I have seen very elegant solutions of Geometrical problems by him. Add to this that he is a very worthy & respectable member of society. He is a free man." Jefferson concluded on a scientific note, "I shall be delighted to see these instances of moral eminence so multiplied as to prove that the want of talents observed in them [blacks] is merely the effect of their degraded condition, and not proceeding from any difference in the structure of the parts on which intellect depends."[14]

By viewing Banneker's achievement merely in terms of race, Jefferson missed the fundamental importance of the amateur mathematician's work. Here was evidence that black Americans, despite all the constraints placed upon them, were participating in the Enlightenment. Benjamin Banneker, much as his white counterpart, Benjamin Franklin, was born and grew up in very limited circumstances. Both were self-taught. Both loved mathematical puzzles. Both were fascinated by nature, patterns of weather, and astronomy and fabricated instruments to record their observations. Both enjoyed making almanacs, those handy guides to phases of the moon, tides, and hours of daylight and to wise advice and curious information. Both of them continued researches and cogitations into elder years, quite apart from the drift of the world, prime products of the Age of Enlightenment.[15]

Although Benjamin Banneker could and did interest himself in the condition of other black Americans and in the condition of the world at large, his life pursuits were more defined by an enchantment with mathematics and astronomy than with human affairs. The grandparents on his mother's side were an African named Bannaka (thus Banneker) and white Molly Welsh. His parents were freed slaves, and Benjamin Banneker was taught by his strong-willed grandmother from childhood to seek knowledge. Born onto a small tobacco farm next to the Patapsco River near Baltimore, his formal schooling was limited to a few short sessions in a neighboring country school. More interested in his daily and nightly self-study than in pursuing property or wealth, Banneker remained on the same farm tract from birth to death.

When he was twenty-one he made a wooden clock after examining a pocket watch and calculating mathematically the wheel, gear, and movement ratios. When he was twenty-eight his father died, making him owner and operator of a hundred-acre tobacco farm. But the seasonal demands of tobacco cultivation left days and weeks of time to read, to pursue a serious interest in music, and from 1771 forward to study the construction and operation of the plants at Ellicott's Lower Mills—flouring, sawing, and iron-making operations. The five Ellicott brothers, Quakers all, descended on the region just before the American Revolution and revolutionized Banneker's life. Principally through George Ellicott, son of one of the brothers, Banneker gained access to books on science, mathematics, and astronomy. He was taught to handle precision viewing and recording devices, and he won a friend who shared his interests.

George Ellicott was astonished when Banneker in 1789 presented him with a projection of the next solar eclipse. Ellicott found the mathematics to be perfect, although the final result was slightly off target. Banneker, ever precise in his intricate calculations, traced the error to the two source books he was using. Ellicott was even more shocked in the same letter to read Banneker's proud claim, "Now Sir if I can overcome this difficulty I doubt not being able to Calculate a Common Almanack." At age fifty-eight, with the aid of Ellicott's books, Banneker had discovered his true mathematical genius and had happily succumbed to a life of round-the-clock theorizing, postulating, and calculating. From that moment forward his farming career virtually ceased.[16]

Benjamin Banneker (1794).
The prodigious mathematician.

Banneker was preparing a complete ephemeris for 1791—a day-by-day calculation of solar and lunar eclipses, the times of rising and setting of sun and moon, identification of remarkable days, weather forecasts, and tidal ebbs and flows. The hours required were endless; the work excruciating, exacting, and, to Banneker, intoxicating. His hope was to become America's premier almanac maker, but he so loved the work of calculating his ephemeris for, say, Philadelphia or Richmond or, later, London, that he would have done it even without remuneration or publication.[17]

His principal obstacles to publication, at least initially, were twofold. First, his chief rival in the production of ephemerides was none other than his old friend Andrew Ellicott, chief surveyor of the federal district boundary. Second, when he identified himself as black, potential publishers immediately doubted both authorship and accuracy. Two publishers turned down his 1791 ephemeris without examination, and the third, principal publisher of Ellicott's system, sent Banneker's work to Ellicott himself for review! Although Banneker appealed directly to Ellicott for quick approval, time elapsed until it was too late for the mathematician to find another publisher for 1791.

Distribution and publication of Banneker's 1792 ephemeris was a different matter. Ellicott, busy in 1791 surveying New York's western border, had actually forwarded Banneker's work to James Pemberton, the reigning president of the formidable Pennsylvania Society for Promoting the Abolition of Slavery, the Relief of Free Negroes Unlawfully Held in Bondage and for Improving the Condition of the African Race. Pemberton leaped into action. To confirm Banneker's identity, he turned to members of the newly organized Maryland Abolition Society. He then turned to David Rittenhouse, America's foremost scientist at the time, and to William Waring, Philadelphia mathematician and another ephemerides calculator, to verify the accuracy of the work.

Two quick responses from the Maryland Abolition Society proudly extolled both Banneker and his independent work. Elias Ellicott, another member of the vast Maryland Ellicott clan, wrote of Banneker:

> He is a man of strong Natural parts and by his own Study hath
> made himself well Acquainted with the Mathematics. About
> three Years Ago he began to study Astronomy by the Assis-
> tance of some Authors which he with much difficulty procured
> soon became so far proficient as to Calculate an Almanac. . . .

Ellicott, aware that Banneker "hath a Copy now ready for the Press for the Year
1792," urged Pemberton to see to its publication in Philadelphia if at all possible.

The reviews from Rittenhouse and Waring were just as positive. Rittenhouse,
aging rapidly, ill, and overworked, wrote Pemberton that Banneker's ephemeris
was "a very extraordinary performance, considering the Colour of the Author."
Having "no doubt that the Calculations are sufficiently accurate for the purposes
of a common Almanac," he also urged publication with the further comment,
"Every Instance of Genius amongst the Negroes is worthy of attention, because
their oppressors seem to lay great stress on their supposed inferior mental abilities." Mathematician Waring was equally generous to a rival almanac maker: "I
have examined Benjamin Banneker's Almanac for the Year 1792, and am of the
Opinion that it well deserves the Acceptance and Encouragement of the Public."

A tug-of-war soon ensued among three publishers for the right to publish the
first Banneker almanac. In June 1791, Banneker sent a copy to Georgetown
printer Charles Fierer. He personally delivered a second copy to Baltimore printer
William Goddard shortly thereafter. A third copy was hand-delivered by an associate of Elias Ellicott to James Pemberton on July 21. Within days Pemberton
wrote back that Philadelphia publisher, Joseph Crukshank, first American publisher of the poems of Phillis Wheatley's poems, would bring out Banneker's first
almanac. When Goddard got wind of Crukshank's plans, however, he claimed
exclusive rights to Banneker's work and withheld an introduction by Maryland
senator James McHenry written specifically for Banneker's almanac. Although
Banneker swore that no exclusive right had been given to Goddard, the Philadelphia publisher chosen by Pemberton decided not to bring out a separate edition.
He and others instead bought and distributed Goddard's edition.

*Benjamin Banneker's Pennsylvania, Delaware, Maryland, and Virginia
Almanac and Ephemeris for the Year of our Lord, 1792,* when released by Goddard in December 1791, was an immediate success. Distributed by four separate
publishers, the first edition was immediately exhausted, and Goddard published a
second edition. So impressive and popular was it that another Philadelphia publisher, William Young, quickly published his own separate edition.[18]

Nearly everyone, it seemed, wanted to see the proof of Goddard's advertised
claim that this new "COMPLETE and ACCURATE EPHEMERIS for the year
1792" had been

> calculated by a Sable Descendant of Africa, who, by this Spec-
> imen of Ingenuity, evinces, to Demonstration, that mental Pow-
> ers and Endowments are not the exclusive Excellence of white
> People, but that the Rays of Science may alike illumine the

Minds of Men of every Clime, (however they may differ in the
Colour of the Skin) particularly those whom Tyrant-Custom
hath too long taught us to depreciate as a Race inferior in intellectual Capacity.

This, along with McHenry's account of Banneker's life, made the mathematical
virtuoso an instant celebrity. Already Banneker was touted with Phillis Wheatley
and a few others as the black geniuses of the age and as one of America's master
astronomers.

The 1792 *Banneker's Almanac* met with such success that both Goddard in
Baltimore and Crukshank in Philadelphia brought forth glowing 1793 editions.
Goddard introduced his edition with the claim that Banneker's first almanac had

engaged the Approbation of Characters highly distinguished
for their profound abilities, and alike exalted by their Philan-
thropy, both in EUROPE and AMERICA—among whom may be
mentioned those eminent Orators, Statesmen, and Patriots—
PITT, FOX, and WILBERFORCE—who produced the Work, in the
British House of Commons, with much Applause, as an Argument in favour of the Cause of Humanity they had espoused
and with a View of putting a Period to the diabolical Traffic in
human Flesh on the Coast of AFRICA.

Success bred further triumph for 1794 with even more simultaneous editions.
The 1795 edition saw three separate versions published in Baltimore alone; a
Wilmington publisher produced five editions for various distributors; and three
Philadelphia printers offered editions, as did another in Trenton, New Jersey.

At least nine separate editions of Banneker's 1795 almanac appeared in print.
Most of them for the first time bore a woodcut portrait of Banneker, revealing a
serious, mentally engaged man of indeterminate age. From total obscurity just
four years earlier, Banneker had been transformed to one of the mythic heroes of
the age, whose name, like that of Phillis Wheatley, would be brought forth to
dismiss racial slurs. Banneker, unlike Wheatley, discovered his genius wholly as
a free man, not a slave. Although he was assisted by various individuals fighting
against slavery, he was not similarly paraded across the world as a rare specimen,
as a freak of nature. A child of the Enlightenment, he gloried in his learning and
spent the rest of his days engaged in his studies, calculating his annual
ephemerides, and, occasionally, receiving guests who wanted to meet this free
black man who stood as a genius of the age of liberation.[19]

CHAPTER 12

Liberty in America's Other Land of Liberty

NIGHT OF FIRE I: LIBERTY INSPIRED

On July 17, 1791, mobs in Birmingham, England, burned the home of Joseph Priestley, while crowds teemed onto the Champ-de-Mars in Paris, only to be slaughtered. Ten days later riots across Sheffield, England, underscored the fact that the world was in a mood for revolution. The same impulse on the night of August 22, 1791, sent as many as fifty thousand slaves off West Indian sugar plantations in the north of St. Domingue into the plush quarters of Cap François, a principal city of the sugar island. Urged on by African priests, they killed their white masters, destroying the lavish homes and opulent hostels of whites, and laid low the houses, mills, and barns of the plantations where they labored. With painted faces and bodies smeared with ritual ashes and blood, they streamed across fields, streets, and alleys, slaughtering every white person met along the way or torn from any building.

White planters and their families were massacred and maimed in every conceivable way, their bodies made objects of torment and destruction. Limbs were severed from bodies; spent bodies became gruesome exhibits; heads became trophies to be carried on spears or perched at street corners. Two thousand white residents of the island died.

One white observer of the scene, a young man of sixteen who had the previous day arrived from years of schooling in France, wrote about how white families fled to the coast to escape by boat from the mêlée:

> The frightened families among our neighbors met together at our plantation. The men armed to face the storm; the mothers, wives, sisters were lamenting and gathering in all haste a few precious effects. Desolation and fear were painted on all faces. The sky seemed on fire. Guns could be heard from afar and the bells of the plantations were sounding the alarm. The danger increased. The flames at each moment were approaching and enclosing about us. There was no time to lose; we fled. The victims who escaped at sword's point came to swell the num-

ber of fugitives, and recounted to us the horrors which they had witnessed. They had seen unbelievable tortures to which they testified. Many women, young, beautiful, and virtuous, perished beneath the infamous caresses of the brigands, amongst the cadavers of their fathers and husbands. Bodies, still palpitating, were dragged through the roads with atrocious acclamations. Young children transfixed upon the points of bayonets were the bleeding flags which followed the troop of cannibals.

Miraculously, he and his entire family, the de Puechs, escaped death that night.[1]

But not so the de Puech's huge sugar plantation situated midway between Cap François and Fort Dauphin on the ocean. Of sugar plantations, 180 were destroyed; of coffee plantations, 900 fell. Every building was put to the torch. Everything that could be ignited was burned: cane and tobacco fields, sugar mills, tools, storage bins, slave quarters, every manifestation of plantation and slave life. The event has been remembered ever after in St. Domingue and across the world as the "night of fire," the opening salvo in one people's search for liberty that would never again be suppressed. Despite invading armies, dictators, and endless bloody wars, colonial St. Domingue—soon to become the independent republic of Haiti—began on that night of gore its march to become the Western world's second, or other true land of liberty.[2]

The night of fire was but the opening scene in a drama where the peoples of this strangely contorted but rich island began their journey toward freedom, equality, and the rights of man. Although much of the slaughter was touched off by mysterious African priests and voodoo rituals, the cataclysmic event was part and parcel of the world's dance with liberty. The same winds that stirred American farmers, English workers, Irish tinkerers, and French peasants to seek revolution had roused the twenty thousand white planters and their families of St. Domingue who chaffed under the inequities of French colonial rule; the twenty thousand or so mulattoes of French parentage who sought the same rights extended to whites; and, finally, the half million black slaves who had lived under one of the world's harshest systems of slavery.

Moreover, the struggle for freedom in St. Domingue was complicated by the fact that mulattoes on the island rarely sided with blacks—slave or free. Most often they identified with white colonists when it was to their advantage, against both whites and blacks when they were legally or militarily able to do so. The three-pronged racial rivalry, engendered by the unique development of this island, promised that the battle to extend the rights of man to all residents of St. Domingue would be messy and that foreign powers who attempted to deal with the island's racial factions would be constantly foiled in their efforts to control it.

Despite the appearance of spontaneous combustion, then, the night of fire had cause. Indeed, ever since the days when 545 "Volunteer Chasseurs" from St. Domingue held forth at the siege of Savannah in 1779, aspirations for liberty on the island had been rising. One of those veterans of Savannah, Jean-Baptiste

Chavannes, had in 1790 joined with the wealthy, militant mulatto planter, Jacques Vincent Ogé, to campaign for mulattoes' rights in St. Domingue. Ogé, and perhaps also Chavannes, were in Paris during 1789 and early 1790 observing the swath of revolution across the nation. With each passing month and with each colossal event—the convening of the Estates-General, the creation of a National Assembly, the fall of the Bastille, the Declaration of the Rights of Man, the imprisonment of Louis XVI—the effect on French colonials became increasingly problematic.[3]

Every act of the French government affected the delicate balance in St. Domingue between whites, mulattoes, free blacks, and black slaves. For years mulattoes—often well-educated, wealthy, and plantation owners themselves—had demanded the same rights as white colonists. From the first calling of the Assembly of Notables in 1787 until March 1790, when the governance of French colonies was placed under a newly constituted Colonial Committee of the National Assembly, mulattoes both in Paris and in St. Domingue vied strenuously for representation. And with the creation in Paris on February 19, 1788, of the *Amis des Noirs* by such luminaries as Brissot de Warville, Mirabeau, and Condorcet, to battle for the rights of all blacks, their expectations only increased. While the mulattoes always wanted to be lumped with whites and free men, the activities of the *Amis des Noirs* consistently associated them with whatever fate awaited the majority of blacks.[4]

Ogé and Chavannes were among the chief promoters of rights for mulattoes. They argued the case in St. Domingue and then pushed the question in Paris. When it became clear that neither the king nor the National Assembly sympathized with their argument, Ogé and Chavannes threatened to raise up aggrieved mulattoes in rebellion against an unjust government. After complaining to Thomas Clarkson in Paris, Ogé traveled to London in August 1790 to collaborate with the famous abolitionist. From London he progressed to Charleston, South Carolina, to converse with the French consul there and to purchase arms for shipment to St. Domingue.[5]

By October 21 Ogé and Chavannes were back in St. Domingue, planning a revolt against white planters of the island. Ogé headed to his plantation at Dondon just a few miles from Cap François and there made Chavannes and his brother Jacques his principal lieutenants. With a force of more than two hundred mulattoes, he and Chavannes marched on the town of Grande Rivière, taking it with little opposition. Another five hundred mulattoes then joined him and supported his demand on October 29 that the provincial assembly recognize their rights. When no reply came to his letter, he marched toward Cap François, only to be routed by a larger army sent by the white-controlled assembly. Ogé and Chavannes, the first heroes of what would eventually be known as the Haitian Revolution, lost the battle and fled across the mountains to Santo Domingo and to detainment at the hands of that province's Spanish government.[6]

The time had not yet arrived for a reckoning on mulatto rights. The white-controlled provincial assembly demanded extradition of Ogé and Chavannes from Governor General Joaquin Garcia y Moreno, and they got it. Ogé and Chavannes were held for trial until February 1791. When the proceedings began, they were tried along with other suspects for the crime of inciting rebellion among slaves against the white colonial government. Twenty-one, among them Ogé and Chavannes, were sentenced to death; another thirteen were sentenced to life service as galley slaves. Ogé and Chavannes were sentenced on February 25 as follows:

> They are to be taken to the place d'Armies, and to the opposite side to that appointed for the execution of white criminals, and have their arms, legs and ribs broken, while alive, upon a scaffold erected for that purpose, and placed by the executioner upon wheels, with their faces turned towards heaven, there to remain as long as it shall please God to preserve life; after this, their heads to be severed from their bodies and exposed upon stakes.

This cruel sentence was faithfully carried out on March 9, 1791. Ogé's head was placed on a stake by the road leading to Dondon from whence the rebels came. Chavannes's head was displayed by the road to Grand Rivière, where the rebellion had ended. For the next three years, they remained as grim reminders of the first efforts to extend the rights of man beyond white colonists in St. Domingue.[7]

For Henri Christophe, who probably saw service in the militia force that routed Ogé and Chavannes, the savage execution of Chavannes, his mentor at Savannah, was an incredibly moving event. At age twenty-four he had spent the intervening twelve years since Savannah as a white-shirted waiter in one of Le Cap's finer hotels. While serving drinks and food to the hotel's wealthy white clientele, he absorbed every debate then current in the Western world about liberty and the rights of man. Although he ruefully watched the death of his beloved teacher, he waited another few years before throwing his energies into the rising revolution.[8]

There were no trepidations, however, on the part of two other veterans of Savannah, Louis-Jacques Beauvais and André Rigaud. Both mulattoes, both educated in France, both experienced soldiers, Beauvais and Rigaud recruited and trained strong armies of mulattoes that would control vast areas of southern and southwestern St. Domingue throughout the stormy years of the Haitian Revolution. Although Beauvais had a career as a schoolteacher and Rigaud that of a goldsmith, they became full-time military chieftains. Beauvais and Rigaud treated the fallen revolutionaries as martyrs to the cause of mulattoes, not blacks, and they preached martyrdom on the island and in France. Reaction in France to the grisly executions caused the National Assembly to enact at once the May Decree, providing full citizenship in the colonies for property-owning mulattoes.[9]

Spurred by the sympathetic decree of the National Assembly, Beauvais and Rigaud moved rapidly to secure mulatto rights on the island. In early August 1791 they formed a council of forty mulattoes to articulate their aims to the island's local government. But their requests were firmly denied. Out of sheer frustration on the night of August 20—two days before the night of fire—Beauvais, Rigaud, and other mulatto leaders met in the woods near Port-au-Prince to organize an armed rebellion of mulattoes against the white population of St. Domingue. They were ready to march on Port-au-Prince when word arrived that black slaves in the north had demolished Cap François and the surrounding plantation countryside.

As might have been expected, the panic among white colonists following the night of fire worked momentarily to unite white and mulatto leaders. Although the combined white and mulatto population amounted to only forty-five thousand against five hundred thousand slaves, the mulattoes were among some of the island's most experienced soldiers. Indeed, two concordats between white and mulatto leaders to implement the May Decree were signed on September 7 and 11. These were reaffirmed at a provincial assembly on October 17 and were fully adopted in elections held at Port-au-Prince on November 21. White-mulatto solidarity was finally forged on the island. There would be just two classes of citizens, free men and slaves. For the moment at least that seemed to be the result of the first night of fire on August 22, 1791.[10]

NIGHT OF FIRE II: REVOLUTION AND LIBERTY

At the very moment mulattoes were about to achieve the rights of full citizenship, chaos ensued—again inspired by forces and actions external to the island itself. The reaction in France to the night of fire was abrupt and set the National Assembly on a wildly truncated course concerning St. Domingue. On September 23—just thirty-one days after the conflagration—the Assembly repealed the May Decree, thereby returning Haitian mulattoes to the same status as slaves. In the same act the Assembly initiated a policy that would bedevil St. Domingue over the next twelve years. Certain that the residents of the island could not govern themselves, the Assembly appointed a commission of three—the first of many externally designated governors, governors-general, and military governors over that time—to take over affairs on the island.

The effect of this act was to declare that a different set of rules would apply to French colonies than to France itself. The act momentarily cheered white colonists, but it quickly alienated colonial mulattoes. Just four days later the Assembly muddied the waters of race relations even more by abolishing slavery throughout France, but not in the colonies. The National Assembly, careening toward the world's most famous Reign of Terror, zagged once again in March, following with an act to bring in St. Domingue "the reunion of the men of color and the colonial whites." Contradicting their act of just six months before, the Assembly awarded full citizenship for all mulattoes *and* free blacks and appointed a new governor and commission to carry the news of liberty to the island.[11]

Appointed to deliver the act placed into law with the signature of Louis XVI on April 4, 1792, were Leger Félicité Sonthonax, Étienne Polverel, and Jean-Antoine Ailhaud. All three were ideological paragons of the French Revolution. Sonthonax, a devoted admirer of Rousseau, a well-trained lawyer, and a prolific author of revolutionary articles and pamphlets, had written in 1790 on the matter of liberty for Africans: "We confidently predict that the day will come—and it is no longer very far off—when we will see kinky-haired Africans, who will then be judged only on their virtues and talents, participate in all our political processes and address our national assemblies." Confident that French liberty would work

*"Attack and Combat at Leogane, St. Domingue" (1791). French troops under
the command of civil commissioner Saint-Leger attempt to retake Leogane
from the control of armed mulattoes and freemen at the beginning of the
Haitian Revolution.*

as well in the colonies as in the mother country, the three devout revolutionaries
arrived at their destination in late September 1792.[12]

When Sonthonax and the other commissioners arrived, bringing with them
the newly appointed governor-general, Desparbes, it appeared that liberty and
history had just been joined on the troubled island. Sonthonax made it clear from
the first moment: "As far as we are concerned there are two clearly defined
classes of people on Haiti at the moment. The one consists of free individuals
against whom there is no discrimination, no matter what the color of the skin.
The other is made up of the slaves." Moreover, the future of that second group
had been placed entirely in the hands of the island's duly elected assembly. No
longer would there be French interference: "We declare that only the Assembly
that was created on this island in accordance with the Constitution has the right to
decide the fate of the slaves."[13]

The new commissioners and governor-general arrived with an army of six
thousand French troops under the command of Generals Étienne Laveaux and
Donatien-Marie de Rochambeau. From the perspective of liberty the appointments of Laveaux and Rochambeau seemed propitious indeed. Count Laveaux
was both an experienced soldier and a devotee of liberty. He had fought heroically against Prussians and Austrians in service of the king and had supported

the abolition of slavery. Count Rochambeau, son of comte J. B. Donatien Rochambeau, commander of French troops in the American Revolution, brought to St. Domingue a love of liberty from his own vivid experiences in the American Revolution and service to France.[14]

St. Domingue could not have received a more committed band of liberators. At Cap François in the north, Commissioner Sonthonax established a Jacobin club; at Port-au-Prince in the west, Polverel proclaimed the rights of man; at Jacmel in the south, Ailhaud announced the new day of freedom. The French generals and troops scattered about the island as a peacekeeping force to stop civil skirmishes among whites, mulattoes, free blacks, and slaves. Sonthonax— the most committed of the revolutionaries—abolished churches, prohibited religious orders, and proscribed royalist conspirators against the Revolution. His decrees soon brought forth outspoken enemies of the Revolution (almost all among the white planters of the island), but he quickly had them imprisoned, deported to France, or guillotined on the scaffold.[15]

Each well-intentioned act taken by Sonthonax to bring liberty to all except slaves reaped yet another whirlwind. As he committed or exiled white colonists for treason against the Revolution, he lost the support of the white planters he needed to unite. As he sent Laveaux and Rochambeau out to skirmish with warring bands of mulattoes who were still not satisfied that their rights were being respected, his support among them eroded. And with news of the abolition of slavery in France and the elevation of free blacks and mulattoes to citizenship on the lips of every slave across the island, the days of continued subservience to forked-tongued liberators were numbered.

The course of the French Revolution in St. Domingue was checkered. Within a month after the arrival of Sonthonax and his colleagues, Ailhaud confronted the power and tenacity of mulatto liberators against his governance in the south. He immediately abandoned his post and scurried back to France. Within two months after the arrival of the smart force of six thousand French troops, more than half of them were dead—most from tropical diseases. This loss of men without the firing of a single shot quickly sapped the revolutionary idealism of Generals Laveaux and Rochambeau. The former put down every slave who rebelled against French authority; Rochambeau, on the other hand, moved from liberator to executioner. Rather than take rebellious blacks prisoner, he ordered the immediate execution and decapitation of every black or mulatto seized.[16]

With the collapse of white support and the loss of mulatto confidence, Sonthonax suddenly found himself in a tenuous position. Just as miracles for liberty were reaching their climax in France with the onset of the Terror, in Britain with the quashing of the reform movement in Parliament, and in America with the contorted arrival of Citizen Genet in Philadelphia, the revolution in St. Domingue was undergoing a dramatic transformation. On the same day Parliament voted down reform, May 7, there arrived in Cap François a new governor-general, handpicked by Robespierre's ill-famed Committee of Public Safety to take control of the chaotic island. Thomas François Galbaud on that day, with a small force of a few hundred soldiers aboard four frigates, entered the provincial capital to announce his ascendancy.[17]

His arrival was greeted by Sonthonax with the same distrust American Federalists had for Citizen Genet and British ministers for Thomas Paine. On the pretext that Galbaud was not qualified to serve his post because he owned a plantation on the island, Sonthonax ordered the would-be governor back to his ships. The increasingly desperate Sonthonax then demanded that Galbaud deliver another load of white political prisoners on his return to France. Galbaud, aware that he had somehow been set up for this ignominious fall, packed his ships and retreated.

Sometime between the middle of May and the middle of June, Galbaud underwent a change of heart. Instead of returning sheepishly to France, he decided to take up the cause of his unhappy but articulate cargo. By simply freeing his prisoners and letting them recruit relatives and friends, he in short order raised an army. The freed prisoners made an instant force of two thousand; days later, with new recruits on the island, the number swelled to five thousand.

By June 20 Galbaud was ready to reckon with Sonthonax and with rebellious mulattoes and blacks on the island. His force of angry white colonists and sailors made an armed landing that day and headed for the center of Cap François. They captured the government arsenal and overran the capital's offices, forcing Sonthonax and Polverel to flee the city. There followed on the night of June 21 the Haitian Revolution's second night of fire, as Galbaud and his men pillaged the city and ruthlessly murdered its black and mulatto population. They burned out black homes, killed their inhabitants, and looted every home, store, and warehouse. When the killing was done, they celebrated their bloody victory by dousing thirsty gullets from the stash of wine and spirits they had seized.

The young Commander de Puech, whose family plantation had been destroyed in the first night of fire, joined in Galbaud's attack. Although he was still weak from wounds suffered in earlier expeditions, he took up his weapons "to join the brave volunteers." So confusing was the expedition, he wrote, "we did not yet well know for whom, or against whom, we must fight." But the appearance of "a column of Mulattoes soon ended our uncertainty." What followed was combat "the cruelest" he saw in several years of fighting. "You cannot form an idea of the excesses, the wrongs, the crimes, of that deplorable day," he later recalled:

> I saw artillerymen, against every remonstrance, aim a thirty-six pound cannon against a single man, fire, miss their target, but blow up a house. . . . I saw a general, frightened by a false alarm, throw himself into the sea to rejoin his barque. . . . I saw dragoons proudly leading us and haranguing us into excitement, who, when they had accompanied us as far as the batteries of the enemy, turned upon us a murderous fire and retired amidst the ranks of our adversaries, laughing at our credulity.

Despite the confusion, they soon emptied the town of its last black inhabitants and settled into the business of drinking.

While Galbaud's warriors became a drunken mob, Sonthonax was in the countryside preparing to take a measure of mad desperation, the only card for him then left unplayed. Sonthonax decided to unleash one of the largest untapped, but ready-to-fight armies in the world—the black slaves of St. Domingue. On the afternoon of June 21, Sonthonax and Polverel issued a proclamation guaranteeing freedom from slavery and the full rights of French citizenship to all slaves who would fight to defend France against her enemies, foreign or domestic. Before the day was over, bands of slaves appeared before the commissioners to swear allegiance to France and to avenge the slaughtered blacks of Cap François.

Out of the hills poured thousands of former slaves, seizing their first breaths of freedom and vanquishing a drunken army unprepared for the avalanche that descended upon them. The marauding blacks raked the city, burning its remains and killing every white or mulatto in sight. As young de Puech described it,

> All at once, horrible shrieks resounded in our ears; a great brightness lit the black skies. From the summit of the mountains down the roads to the plain, came immense hoards of Africans. . . . From all sides flames were lifted as in a whirlwind and spread everywhere. . . . I can still hear the whistling of bullets, the explosions of powder, the crumbling of houses; I can still see my brave comrades contending vainly against steel and fire.

Evidently forgetting the ravages he and his colleagues had rendered the night before, he concluded, "These heinous Africans, all stained with blood, were replacing murder with excesses, amidst a population without refuge, without clothes, and without food." [18]

Ten thousand people died in the slaughter. Another ten thousand whites and mulattoes raced to the port and swam to Galbaud's expanded armada of seventeen vessels. When they were filled to their limits with people, clothes, books, and a few other portable possessions, this flotilla of refugees aimed for Norfolk, Baltimore, Wilmington, and Philadelphia, places where life might begin again. [19]

Having struggled aboard the *Rosalie,* "exhausted with fatigue and in need of food" and his clothes "covered with blood, sweat, and dirt, and almost entirely in tatters," the young Commander de Puech reflected ironically on the disaster by versifying a speech that might have been given on the occasion by the "cowardly Solons" Sonthonax and Polverel:

> Perish the treasures of this wicked isle,
> Perish Whites and Blacks, perish the country,
> Perish the whole human race

Rather than betray
The Sacred Rights of Man and our precious Maxims!

"Completely ruined, without home, without money, without clothes," he and his fellow refugees longed for a landing in the Chesapeake.[20]

And what were the results of this second great night of carnage? The white population of colonial St. Domingue was forever removed and, although there would be invitations for them to return, they would never again have a significant presence in Haitian society or government. Second, virtually all efforts by the French government to pursue the policies of the Revolution came to an end. Although Sonthonax still held on by a thin reed following the second night of fire, his power to shape events now depended entirely upon capricious and rival leaders of mulatto and black factions. And sadly, as St. Domingue became an island wholly populated by people principally of African descent, it became the focus for wave after wave of invasions by European and American powers seeking to exploit the island's natural wealth.

But as the departure of Galbaud's white armada forever transformed St. Domingue from a European-controlled colony to a land of self-determination, one other legacy of revolutionary attempts to govern the island was left behind. When Sonthonax and Polverel returned to Cap François on June 27 to enjoy their victory, they found the mere shrouds of a city. They also found a new population of black faces eager to enter into the new day of freedom promised earlier by Sonthonax. Faced with the necessity of trying to bring order, of restarting the plantations, and of pacifying still unhappy mulattoes, Sonthonax suddenly blinked in recognition that he had lost all control.

On July 11, under great pressure from those blacks who had dismantled Cap François, he extended freedom to the wives and children of those men enrolled in the army of the French republic. On July 25 he proclaimed both soldiers and their families free. But this was not enough for the black captains of scattered military units whose service had to be negotiated. By the end of July, everyone on the island knew that war had broken out in Europe between France and practically everyone else. Spain, partly to protect its lands in Santo Domingo, and England, concerned that its rich plantations in nearby Jamaica might be endangered by spreading slave rebellions radiating from St. Domingue, had formed an alliance to overthrow French rule there and to partition the colony between themselves. Spain took the north, Britain the south.[21]

As Spanish troops crossed the mountains in July and took the lush sugar plantations of the north, and as news came that British forces would imminently land in the south, Sonthonax found himself again against the wall. With the remaining whites siding with Spanish and British invaders, with mulatto warriors still hoping to gain control of the island, and with black commanders demanding freedom for more and more black slaves, Sonthonax on August 29, 1793, took a unilateral step without authority from France, without consultation with any legislative bodies at home or on the island, and with the vote of no one. Even without consultation with his faithful fellow commissioner Polverel, he decreed the abolition of slavery throughout the French colony.[22]

Once done, it could never be undone. St. Domingue, by tactical military necessity, suddenly became, at least potentially, the most advanced land of liberty in the Western world. It did not yet have political independence, but it had rid itself of slavery. And try as many would over the years, the institution of slavery could never be reestablished. It was gone forever.

FOUNDING FATHERS OF THE BLACK REPUBLIC

Just as Chrispus Attucks and Nathan Hale died as martyrs of the American Revolution, the deaths of Vincent Ogé and Jean-Baptiste Chavannes annointed the Haitian Revolution. Just as Francis Marion—the Swamp Fox—and John Paul Jones fought for America at land and sea, so did Georges Biassou and General Jean-François, intrepid fighters who acted variously as patriots, pirates, and rebel Maroons. And just as Nathanael Greene fought with an inspired level of military precision unexpected outside of Europe, the mulatto generals Louis Jacques Beauvais and André Rigaud controlled the southern, western, and central portions of Haiti against every major army of the Western world—French, Spanish, and British.

And just as Americans in their revolution had a George Washington to command and to inspire, an Alexander Hamilton to manipulate and conspire, and a Thomas Jefferson to declaim and consolidate—Haitians in their revolution found in Toussaint L'Ouverture their Washington, in Jean-Jacques Dessalines their self-destructive Hamilton, and in Henri Christophe, their inscrutable and sadly torn Jefferson. And just as the American Revolution focused on the majority population of the land, white Europeans, the Haitian Revolution relied on the majority population of that island—black Africans. As white Europeans in America ultimately prevailed over the imperial power that held them, the black Africans in Haiti ultimately overthrew not only the power that held them, but also all of the other jealous powers that wished to possess them.

All of these founding fathers of Haiti—most of them inspired veterans from the 1779 siege of Savannah—played critical roles in extracting liberty from French colonial governors and commissioners. But none surpassed the ingenuity of the person who became the central figure of the Revolution—Toussaint L'Ouverture—one of the few Haitian revolutionary leaders who did not see service at Savannah. He rose up, almost Lincoln- or Napoleon-like, from the depths of society and shaped affairs in St. Domingue.

Born in Haiti on May 20, 1743, the celebration of All Saints Day, he was named François-Dominique Toussaint. Although of African parentage and born into slavery on the Breda plantation near Cap François, his godfather was the priest Simon Baptiste. The priest taught the slender boy to read and write and provided him with a grounding in Latin that he would use throughout life. The manager of the huge Breda plantation, Bayon de Libertad, moreover, loaned Toussaint books from the estate's well-stocked library.

The gifted Toussaint evidently showed so much promise that he came to be treated almost as a free man on the plantation. He had his own farm and coffee planting; he supervised the Breda household personnel and served as principal coachman, and, at age thirty, he was permitted to take a wife in marriage. Two sons, Isaac and Saint-Jean, were born. Known as a man of piety, Toussaint also learned enough about medicine to provide first aid to injured slaves and herbal remedies for their various ailments.[23]

Toussaint was forty-eight when the first night of fire occurred on August 22, 1791, making him considerably older than most of the rising leaders in the Haitian Revolution. But his age, his education, his plantation experience, his horsemanship, his management and medical skills, and his black (not mulatto) heritage made Toussaint a superb candidate for leadership. He also was a man of sound judgment. For example, on the first night of fire, he arranged for his wife and children to be delivered across the border to safety in Santo Domingo and he then delivered his mentor, Bayon de Libertad, and his wife to the coast, where they boarded a vessel to America. Only then in September 1791 did Toussaint join one of the many armed camps of former slaves.[24]

From the moment he arrived, his medical practice, his abilities to organize men, and his ability to devise tactical strategy thrust him to the forefront of leadership. Through letters and written speeches Toussaint soon became a stirring spokesman for his fellow slaves. He may have helped write a letter under the date of September 4, 1791, to the governor stating the wishes of the slaves: "Until our last drop of blood, we want only one thing: our freedom. We have also taken up arms to defend the King, who has been taken prisoner by the whites in Paris because he had decided to free the blacks, his faithful subjects." This letter—with its odd view of events, but clear message—bore no signature. The next one a few weeks later—with more logic and fewer demands—actually bore Toussaint's name as one of the signatories. Even as he demonstrated military skills, he also began to show a proficiency for diplomacy.

But it was his military style that won for him the name by which he would be known, L'Ouverture (opening). His patented approach to warfare was carefully planned, lightning attacks, followed by quick withdrawals and preparations for a succession of certain but unpredictable blows. While other military leaders of the period drilled their troops in march formation, Toussaint drilled his troops on rapid methods of attack from unexpected angles and directions. Using this system of guerrilla warfare against every kind of army, Toussaint found openings for both attack and sudden escape. For this practice, he was given his adopted name by the French Count Laveaux.[25]

Toussaint also led and controlled some of the most savage commanders in military history. Jean-Jacques Dessalines, Moyse Breda, and Henri Christophe were the generals most persistently under his sturdy command. Though Toussaint developed alliances with black generals Jean-François and Biassou and with mulatto generals Beauvais and Rigaud, he depended most consistently on these faithful lieutenants to vanquish their foes, deliver secret messages, or to destroy

Battle of Serpents' Ravine, St. Domingue (1803). Toussaint's guerrilla warfare withstands encirclement by the invading army of Gen. Donatien Rochambeau, ironically a hero of American liberty at Yorktown in 1781.

entire villages. Across ten years of endless fighting, Toussaint and his officers formed the most formidable army on the island.[26]

During 1792 Toussaint proved his abilities against French forces time and again. To forward the effort of overthrowing French colonial rule in St. Domingue, Toussaint took his officers and troops under the wing of Santo Domingo in May or June 1793. Breaking oppressive French rule and securing the universal abolition of slavery were his principal goals in life, and he set his sights on achieving them both. When he joined in the Spanish efforts to capture Fort Dauphin in the north, he and his troops were able to accomplish in nine days what Spaniards had not been able to do in almost a year. His victory diminished the French base in St. Domingue to only Cap François and a small surrounding area.[27]

During the time Toussaint turned his allegiance to the Spanish rulers of Santo Domingo, he also was positioning himself where he could usher in the end of slavery in St. Domingue and perhaps on all the island. When Commissioner Sonthonax decreed the end of slavery in French St. Domingue on August 29, 1793, Toussaint seized the occasion to address blacks all over the island:

> Brothers and friends:
>
> I am Toussaint L'Ouverture.

> Maybe my name is already known to you. I have taken on the task of revenging you. I demand that freedom and equality reign on this entire island. It is the only goal that I want to attain. Come and join me, brothers, and fight on our side for the same cause.
>
> Toussaint L'Ouverture
> general of the armies of the King for the public good

Instead of using the occasion of Sonthonax's proclamation to rejoin the French, Toussaint remained aloof, training his army and attacking the few remaining French enclaves. After all, Sonthonax was a weak reed, with almost no authority to deliver on his promise of ending slavery.[28]

Just days after Toussaint's victory as a Spanish commander over the French at Fort Dauphin on January 28, 1794, there occurred in Paris in the National Convention the event long awaited by black (though not mulatto) revolutionaries throughout St. Domingue. On February 3 six delegates from St. Domingue arrived at the National Convention and asked to be admitted. They had been sent by Commissioners Sonthonax and Poverel to represent the colony at the Convention and to argue for the national recognition of the abolition of slavery on the troubled island. Two of the delegates were white, Dufay and Ganot; two mulattoes, Laforet and Jean Baptiste Mills; and two blacks, Mars Belley and Boisson.

Of the six, all are shrouded in history—except Mars Belley—the former slave who had purchased his freedom and who had served with distinction at Savannah during the American Revolution. The other veterans—Chavannes, Beauvais, and Rigaud—had made their contributions to Haitian liberty. Henri Christophe was making ready to join in the campaign. But at the moment Belley was in the spotlight.[29]

Perhaps with guilt over the bloodshed in the colony and clearly with a sense that the black slaves of St. Domingue had been deprived of the rights of man despite the Revolution, the Convention voted immediately to seat the delegates. The Chairman of the Committee on Decrees spoke for the body:

> Since 1789 the aristocracy of birth and the aristocracy of religion have been destroyed; but the aristocracy of the skin still remains. That too is now at its last gasp, and equality has been consecrated. A black man, a yellow man, are about to join this Convention in the name of the free citizens of Saint-Domingue.

Upon their introduction into the body of the Convention, one delegate arose to "demand that their introduction be marked by the President's fraternal embrace." At which point the delegates advanced to the podium of the president to receive the fraternal kiss of the Revolution to the applause of the delegates.

On February 4, Mars Belley addressed the Convention and argued for the wholesale abolition of slavery. He held forth on a long and feverish oration.

There were no rebuttals; there were no seconds. Instead, Deputy Arnaud Levasseur arose to make a point of order:

> When drawing up the constitution of the French people we paid
> no attention to the unhappy Negroes. Posterity will bear us a
> great reproach for that. Let us repair the wrong—let us pro-
> claim the liberty of the Negroes. Mr. President, do not suffer
> the Convention to dishonour itself by a discussion.

By acclamation the Convention agreed to curtail any discussion. Deputy Lacroix, who the day before had called for fraternal kisses, demanded another round to the applause of the joyful deputies.

Deputy Lacroix, obviously caught up in the moment, next called for the Minister of Marine to "despatch at once advices to the Colonies to give them the happy news of their freedom." He also proposed that the official decree read as follows:

> The National Convention declares slavery abolished in all the
> colonies. In consequence it declares that all men, without dis-
> tinction of colour, domiciled in the colonies, are French citi-
> zens, and enjoy all the rights assured under the Constitution.

Without objection, but with momentous jubilation, the act passed and was broadcast across the world. To seal the day of glory in Paris, members of the Convention proceeded to the Cathedral of Notre-Dame for another ceremony in honor of the Supreme Being in that place rededicated just three months earlier as the Temple of Reason.[30]

Toussaint, meanwhile, still in the service of Spain and occupying village after village in central and northern St. Domingue, received a copy of the decree in late April or early May. The time of his notice is clear, for he took critical action before announcing his shift in loyalty. On May 6, 1794, he and a hundred of his troops attended mass at the cathedral in San Raphael, Santo Domingo—the same place where a year earlier he had been decorated heroically with the Order of Queen Isabella. At the end of the service as he mounted his horse, he blew his whistle calling forth Dessalines and Moyse with their commands to kill every Spaniard in the town. From there he proceeded to expel Spanish forces not committed to him from every village in St. Domingue.

Only then did Toussaint explain his strange behavior. On May 18, 1794, he wrote a long letter to Count Laveaux, then the commanding French general in St. Domingue. Reminding Laveaux that he had previously approached him "fervently hoping that we would be able to unite our forces and fight the enemies of France together," Toussaint observed that collaboration had been impossible for one major reason: "Unfortunately for both parties, the ultimate condition that I proposed, i.e., official recognition of freedom for the Negroes, was always rejected." He evidently meant "official recognition" by the national government in France. For that reason he had accepted "the Spanish offer for protection and freedom."

But suddenly everything had changed and he was willing to rejoin forces with "my true brothers, the French." The reason was very simple:

> Now I have seen the National Convention's decree, dated February 4, 1794, with my own eyes. Slavery has been abolished; it is the most wonderful news for all friends of the human race. Therefore, let us now unite and remain united forever, while forgetting the past. Let us obtain our revenge on these false and perfidious Spanish neighbors.

This was truly Toussaint's version of "Mine Eyes Have Seen the Glory of the Coming of the Lord." He finally had seen with his own eyes the "official recognition." This was something for which he and all of the five hundred thousand slaves of St. Dominguc had been praying since they heard the first refrains about liberty and equality wafting over from the British colonies in North America two decades earlier.

It did not matter that at the moment Toussaint wrote his epochal letter, the colony of St. Domingue had been invaded not only by Spain, but also by Britain. It did not matter that much of the island was in control of inimical black and mulatto warlords. It did not matter that what French government there was, was still in the hands of the deceitful Sonthonax. Every plantation, every institution, every city, every road, and practically every building was a shambles. For Toussaint the only thing in the world that mattered was that slavery had been abolished.

Even though British and Spanish invaders cooperating with former white colonists were intent on restoring slavery and even though in the future France itself would seek to restore slavery on the island, Toussaint had in this abolition act a weapon that could and would be used to unite Haiti's majority population. Just as North Americans united themselves over and again to resist political "enslavement" at the hands of George III and an evil parliament, Toussaint and every one of his successors could from 1794 forward use that same cry to throw off their enemies.

Although in the summer of 1794 the colony of St. Domingue was far from independent, it was on its way to becoming in a way the greatest land of liberty in the Western world. Absent of slavery, ripe for a constitution, and yearning for a government of laws, the black majority in St. Domingue in 1794 were looking for the same fulfillment of liberating revolution that had been achieved by their fellow colonists in North America.

As if to mark the revolution that had been wrought in St. Domingue in that spring of 1794, Toussaint began at once to pay homage to the founding fathers of America's first slave-free nation and what would be the world's first black republic. Upon establishing his concordat with Count Laveaux and seeing Sonthonax and Poverel recalled to France in June 1794, Toussaint solemnly marched out from Cap François to the crossroads where one could head either in the direction of Dondon or to Grande Rivière. From beside the road to Dondon he took down the rotted head of Vincent Ogé. From beside the road to Grande Rivière he removed the head of Jean-Baptiste Chavannes. For three years they had stood as grim sentinels of the Haitian struggle for freedom. And by giving proper burial to these founding fathers of the Revolution, Toussaint, like Washington in America, made himself chief among them for the rising Haitian nation.[31]

PART III

THE LIMITS OF LIBERTY

CHAPTER 13

Annus Mirabilis I,
1793

T he year 1793 opened as one of the most hopeful years in American history. George Washington had just been elected to a second term as the first president of the United States. During his first term the country had undergone a transformation from a loose confederation to a united federation under a central government. While detractors of the single government would argue for most of the next century as to whether membership in the union was fixed, at the beginning of 1793 all of the eligible states were firmly and enthusiastically on board. And while Americans would argue forever about the proper roles of presidents, cabinet officers, Congress, and the courts, all of these officers in the world's first modern republic were seated and were functioning confidently.

A written, ratified constitution—the first of its kind—was in place, describing the reciprocal relations of states and the central government, of territories and Congress, of government agencies and private corporations, and of the United States and foreign powers. Federal agencies had moved swiftly and persuasively to organize western territories, to assume the national debt, to choose a permanent national capital, and to provide for the common welfare. Moreover, Congress had proposed and the states had ratified a model bill of rights guaranteeing to Americans a basic set of inviolable freedoms that could not be abridged by any citizen or government agency.

America was the marvel of the world. How flattering it was in those early years of constitutional government to be praised by the government of France—that ancient world power that had done so much to help bring the United States into existence! How appropriate it was that the people of France should challenge their own monarch, establish a National Assembly, write their own constitution, and issue a declaration of the rights of man! How sanguine it was that the National Assembly should declare an era of liberty retroactive to January 1, 1789! How fitting it was that the National Convention should establish a republic!

These all seemed part and parcel of the American experience and inspiration. They all seemed to be logical steps, since they copied American historical patterns and precedent. There was even evidence that revolutionary and constitutional societies in England also were in the process of transforming Britain's monarchical governance. It seemed that the daughter of Britain was in the process of helping to transmute the motherland into the image of the child.

But with the promise of the future came mixed signals that did not wholly fit the exuberant hopefulness of the moment. Early in 1793, just when Americans were cheering the creation of the French republic, they learned that King Louis XVI had been found guilty of high crimes and misdemeanors. In just seven days after the rendering of that verdict, before a proper appeal could be filed (but to whom?), King Louis XVI—savior of America, friend of Franklin, and bumbling father figure of France—was guillotined.

And for what? For attempting to govern France, and for trying to cooperate with those who wanted change within the ancien régime. Americans had overthrown (but they had not killed!) George III. They nevertheless embraced the new French republic. Many were ready to join in the cause, and most thought that was what they were doing when they joined one of the many democratic-republican societies sprouting up in the spring and summer of 1793. The frenzy of organizing the new revolution in the United States followed chronologically the appearance of Jacobin clubs in France and constitutional societies in England. But that hopeful organizing also coincided with the arrival in the United States of one of the most renowned liberators to walk the earth in those heady days of the early 1790s.

Edmond Charles Genet was the first minister of the French Republic to the United States. He had spent thirty years preparing for a sensational five-month entry on the world's stage, and he would then spend another forty years justifying, explaining, and reflecting upon that extraordinary but brief performance.[1] Born in Versailles of a father high in the French foreign service, Genet had all the advantages of access to king and queen. His sisters worked for Marie Antoinette. He prepared many translations of French documents into other languages. At age fourteen he was put to work translating documents of the American Revolution into French. Here and in later assignments following the death of his father in 1781, it was his job to explain the American experience to the French government and the French people.

In 1783 he went to England and, due to his literary and scientific interests, fell in with that enlightened and revolutionary circle of intellectuals surrounding Lord Shelburne. He met with Joseph Priestley and listened to his ideas about liberty, society, and chemistry. He watched Priestley conduct chemical experiments, which he later described in great detail to the French chemistry genius Lavoisier. Back in France he developed an intellectual kinship with Benjamin Franklin and his disciples La Rochefoucald and Condorcet. His

Edmond Genet (1793). French missionary of world revolution.

knowledge of the European world was completed when he was sent to St. Petersburg as French chargé d'affaires in 1789. With the French Revolution in high gear, he soon was viewed by Catherine the Great, who objected to the antimonarchist and antiauthoritarian strains of the movement, as a dangerous agent of subversion. When news arrived about the invasion of the Tuileries on June 20, 1792, by a Paris crowd—at which time Louis XVI was forced to toast the Revolution—Catherine expelled Genet from Russia.

Upon his return to Paris during the summer of 1792, the still youthful Genet was swept up by the spirit and tune of the revolution. So important had he become to France and the Revolution, he was appointed minister plenipotentiary to the United States on November 19, 1792, by then one of the most coveted positions in the French government. Although he was chafing to export the French Revolution, he was detained in Paris until the final verdict was rendered on the fate of Louis XVI. At one point it was hoped by many that Genet might take the hapless king into an American exile. After that matter was settled with such grisly decisiveness, Genet departed on his mission to America.[2]

He arrived in Charleston, South Carolina, on April 8, 1793, at perhaps the apogee of world revolution. There he was feted by Governor Moultrie and a vast number of friends of liberty. So warm was the welcome that he set himself headlong into organizing the American theater of the world revolution. He outfitted four privateering ships to operate out of the port of Charleston, where he met with William Tate, American soldier of fortune, whom he appointed commander of the Revolutionary Legion of America and whom he authorized to recruit an army of two thousand men. It was Genet's intent to use the ships and Tate's legions to overthrow the Spanish at St. Augustine and to liberate other areas of the Western Hemisphere.[3]

Genet then left Charleston for Philadelphia. Everywhere he went he was greeted with honor and excitement, as if he had just liberated America herself. The *Embuscade,* his ship, went to Philadelphia by sea; he by land. The frigate blared forth Genet's message with great banners, bearing revolutionary phrases such as "Enemies of equality, reform or tremble!" and "We are armed for the defense of the rights of man!" Genet arrived in Philadelphia by public stagecoach on May 16, underscoring that he was "citizen," not count or lord. Church bells nevertheless rang out, and crowds descended upon him as he approached Philadelphia's City Tavern. The following morning, members of the Democratic Society of Pennsylvania marched three abreast from Independence Hall to City Tavern to hear from the world's sudden superstar of liberty. Finally, on May 18 he presented his credentials, first to Secretary of State Thomas Jefferson and then to President George Washington, America's symbol of liberating revolution.[4]

Even as Genet made his glorious entrance into Philadelphia, other curious events began to unfold. News of the French declaration of war against England, Holland, and Spain arrived, while Thomas Jefferson and Alexander Hamilton waged internecine war in the shadow of George Washington. Hundreds of unhappy French refugees arriving in Philadelphia stirred the political pot against Genet, whom they viewed as the upstart emissary of a soured revolution. Then suddenly, in July Philadelphia was invaded by two thousand refugees from yet

*Philosophical Library and Surgeon's Hall, Philadelphia (1798). Where physi-
cians, philosophers, and politicians debated the best treatment for yellow fever
in 1793, 1797, and 1798.*

another revolution in St. Domingue. Finally, in August—amid the most intense
heat ever known in the city—the worst happened: A yellow fever epidemic swept
across Philadelphia. It would eventually kill a tenth of the city's population.

The emotional vagaries of life in Philadelphia that summer is difficult to
imagine. With a population of fifty-five thousand, a shortage of housing, and a
massive influx of black and white French-speaking refugees, conditions in the
city became unbearable. On August 5 and 7, Dr. Benjamin Rush, America's foremost medical practitioner, was called out to treat patients with what was
described as "bilious fever." Two weeks later he and two other doctors examined
the dying wife of a West Indian merchant, Peter Le Maigre. As they left the house
on Water Street between Arch and Race Streets, Rush noticed a heap of putrefy-
ing coffee, dumped from one of the ships bearing the St. Domingan refugees,
that was contaminating the entire neighborhood with noxious fumes. Rush and
his colleagues quickly concluded that rotting wastes from St. Domingue and the
West Indian refugees were the source of the scourge menacing Philadelphia.

Four days later, August 24, Rush counted 150 people who had died from
"bilious remitting yellow fever." But he also determined that the cause of fever
was of domestic origin—from local rotting wastes—and that, contrary to his earlier view, it was not from St. Domingue. As panic spread across Philadelphia,

every possible tonic against the fever was tried: burning great fires, firing gunpowder, blasting cannons. The Philadelphia College of Physicians advised that afflicted people should be quarantined, their houses marked. Vinegar and camphor were to be used for the ill; fatigue was to be avoided. Bells were not to be tolled in the case of deaths. Burials were to be undertaken in private, not public ceremonies. The implication of the warnings of the College of Physicians was that the West Indian refugees *had* brought in the deadly scourge.

Rush countered publicly on August 29, arguing that the disease arose from local conditions and that it was stoked by fatigue, heat, intemperance, fear, and grief. Twenty-four people died that day. Neither Rush nor anyone else connected the disease with the widely observed proliferation of mosquitoes. The presence of the annoying insects was oddly mentioned on that same day in an article adjacent to Rush's notice. The piece suggested to citizens wishing to control "those poisonous insects" by pouring a few drops of oil into "rain-water tubs" where they bred.[5]

The yellow fever epidemic of 1793 took 4,044 lives in the nation's capital. The American government had to be shut down. Many fled Philadelphia until the scourge had run its course. Public health policies on the treatment of the infected, the quarantining of the sick, and the burial of the dead inflamed professional jealousies, stirred political factionalism, and ignited racial hatreds that forever transformed the city and indirectly the nation.

While the fever was local to Philadelphia in 1793, it occurred at a moment when the nation's euphoria with liberty was just beginning to tarnish. As news of arrests, assassinations, and guillotinings in France began to strip the patina off that revolution, the yellow fever epidemic in Philadelphia underscored just how little control Americans had over nature and destiny.

As the epidemic took brother, parent, child, friend, master, and servant, the entire undergirding of confidence and hope in the future began to sap away. By the time the epidemic subsided, the Terror in France had reached its worst proportions: Marie Antoinette had been guillotined and the revolutionary leaders of France who had been cultivated by the likes of Lord Shelburne, Richard Price, Joseph Priestley, and Benjamin Franklin had been executed. Eruptions in St. Domingue had spewed forth refugees, tremors, and fears that no life was safe from enemies lurking in the shadows. As Philadelphians solemnly counted the dead, surviving radicals in Paris gathered at the Cathedral of Notre-Dame in Paris to celebrate the triumph of liberty in France.

France had, in the space of a few months during 1793, converted from an exuberant rising republic to a scene of terror and death. And so had St. Domingue, a bellwether in the New World's vast archipelago of human enslavement. Although America had as yet only seen the terror in the form of an epidemic in its capital, evidence of the fragility of life and liberty in France, Britain, St. Domingue, and the rest of the world began to take its toll also in the United States. A year that opened with exuberance and confidence ended for Americans in lassitude and fear.

Indeed, the revolutionary year 1793 was for France, for America, and for all of the Western world an annus mirabilis—a year of wonder, a year of change.

CHAPTER 14

Liberty and Revolution in America

FRIENDS OF LIBERTY AND WORLD REVOLUTION

As the noxious August of 1793 turned into deadly September in Philadelphia and as the lamentations of death in October gave way to November thanksgivings for survival and relief from the scourge of yellow fever, a storm of reaction to liberating revolution began to afflict friends of liberty throughout America. Between 1793 and 1798 every friend of liberty in America would be sorely tested and attacked, challenged and sometimes indicted, imprisoned, exiled, or—in some cases—converted to a new and rising order. Each friend of liberty had to establish peace with a world where revolution came to an end. Or be extinguished.

Thomas Jefferson—known friend of liberty and proponent of revolutionary France—picked up the dissembling spirit early. As early as July 31, 1793, he gave up on the Washington administration and resigned as secretary of state. He would henceforth devote his life to partisan politics, not to ideological causes or to bureaucracies. He stayed on after announcing his resignation long enough to stop Edmond's Genet's plans to outfit a world revolution from Philadelphia—the presumed capital of worldwide liberating activities. He registered a request that Genet be checked by his own nation and recalled from his revolutionary mission to America.[1]

Jefferson's seeming betrayal of the revolutionary movement he had so recently espoused left Genet in limbo as he awaited word from a French government that was mutating almost monthly. But Jefferson's retreat began to affect many other friends of liberty as well. Philip Freneau, poet of the American revolution and promoter of more liberty in America, as a result of Jefferson's departure found himself ejected from his comfortable position as translating clerk at the Department of State. Freneau's ouster was not merely a case of changing administrations. He had been brought by Jefferson from New York to Philadelphia in August 1791, not so much for his translating or poetic abilities as for his talents as a newspaper editor. With Jefferson's encouragement and financial support, Freneau issued on October 31, 1791, the first number of the *National Gazette*—a strenuous Jeffersonian antidote to the Hamiltonian *Gazette of the United States,* edited by John Fenno.

The deal for Freneau was sweet. Jefferson gave him full reign of his office at the Department of State and as much of his work time as might be needed to produce the *National Gazette*. For two years Freneau lambasted Hamiltonian policies and aristocratic tendencies in American government and society. He rhapsodized the rights of man, Thomas Paine, and leaders of the French Revolution. He covered the activities of the democratic-republican societies in glowing detail. The arrival of Genet in Philadelphia seemed to him a messenger from heaven opening the millennium of liberty.

So sure was Freneau of Genet's mission, he found himself in the summer of 1793 at odds with his benefactor. While Jefferson joined Washington and Hamilton in demanding Genet's banishment from America, Freneau urged the French minister onward, underscoring his pleas for the support of the American people against an unwise government policy. When yellow fever hit Philadelphia, Freneau's prospects for the future went from bright to exceedingly dim.

The disease took away, first, his readers and, then, many of his subscribers. Jefferson soon withdrew his personal support for the *National Gazette* since the paper no longer reflected his point of view. Freneau suspended the paper for good on October 26, 1793. And when Jefferson relinquished the office of Secretary of State two months later, Freneau was on the streets again, a jobless poet.[2]

Hugh Henry Brackenridge, Freneau's college chum and fellow poet, meanwhile, was having the experience of a lifetime across the Allegheny Mountains in Pittsburgh, far removed from the fevers and partisan wrangling in the national capital. Just as enamored with liberty as Freneau, Brackenridge gave his assessment of the rising revolution in a speech at Pittsburgh's official Fourth of July celebration in 1793. Though aware of political killings in France, of Genet's activities, and of a growing debate about America's alignment with foreign powers, Brackenridge recounted the birth of liberty in America and followed its happy progress across the world: "The light kindled here has been reflected to Britain, and a reform in the representation of the commons is expected. The light kindled here has

Hugh Henry Brackenridge (c. 1800). Innocent friend of liberty, but a crafty queller of rebellion.

[also] been reflected to France, and a new order of things has [there] arisen." He found it sad that there had been incidents of dissension and violence in both nations. Nevertheless, "thy principles, O! Liberty, are not violent or cruel; but in the desperation of thy efforts against tyranny, it is not always possible to keep within the limit of the vengeance necessary to defense."

Brackenridge paused briefly to address what course America should take in the struggle between France and Britain. To him, the answer was clear. First, "we are bound by a higher principle . . . the great law of humanity." Hence, "it is the cause of republicanism which would induce our efforts." And, if we are devoted to liberty and republicanism, "is not our fate interlaced" with that of France? "For, O! France," he declaimed, "if thy Republic perish, where is the honor due to ours?" Having cleared the matter of American loyalties, Brackenridge blessed the festivities over which he presided: "The anniversary of the independence of America will be a great epoch of liberty throughout the world. Proceed we then to celebrate the day; advance to the festive board; pour out libations to sentiments of liberty; and let the loud-mouthed artillery be heard on the hill." With the impending tug and pull of liberty and revolution not wholly in evidence, Brackenridge and his fellows still basked in freedom's joy.[3]

The throng addressed by Brackenridge accepted an invitation from the Democratic Society of Pennsylvania in Philadelphia to organize a local branch of that organization at Washington, Pennsylvania. They called it the Democratic Society. Other hearers formed the Society of United Freemen at nearby Mingo Creek, Pennsylvania. Still others organized the Republican Society at the Mouth of the Yough "to form a speedy communication between ourselves and the citizens of Westmoreland, Washington, Fayette, and Allegheny counties, and a more perfect union to ourselves and our posterity."[4]

Just as the Paris Jacobin Club spawned like-minded affiliates in Bordeaux and Marseilles and as the London Revolution Society inspired partner organizations in Manchester and Edinburgh, the Philadelphia Democratic Society had sparked people in the mountain areas around Pittsburgh into action. No one person or group was directing affairs or commanding a subversive force in any of the three nations or in their outbacks. Liberty and revolution seemed manifestly in the air. A contagion had been set loose that animated hopes, speech, and actions. There was a belief that well-meaning peoples could by common agreement obliterate economic and social barriers.

The friends of liberty around Pittsburgh had specific goals. One of them was "the free enjoyment of the navigation of the river Mississippi" all the way from Pittsburgh to the Gulf of Mexico. In a "remonstrance" adopted by the Democratic Society of Washington on March 24, 1794, such free transport was described as "a right inseparable from their [the petitioners'] prosperity." Hugh Henry Brackenridge called a meeting in Pittsburgh on April 12 to discuss this and other matters concerning people of the "western country." He wrote, "I have charged myself with the making an arrangement to procure the sentiments of the people of this county." The meeting of delegates from various election districts resulted in the production of a resolution joining hands with the Democratic Society of Kentucky, also concerned with a free Mississippi.

By the latter days of June, however, attitudes had begun to change. In the intervening period President Washington issued his Proclamation of Neutrality (April 22), leaving westerners in limbo against a menacing British presence on the western frontier. The same hopeful members of the Democratic Society of Washington came together on June 23, saying, "we are under the painful necessity of censuring in sundry particulars" the "conduct of the executive of the United States." The president, they thought, should have consulted Congress, and he should not have sent a Supreme Court justice (John Jay) to deal with another government. Arguing that someone who understood the needs and desires of plain Americans should have been sent instead, they wrote,

> The revolution in France has sufficiently proved that generals may be taken from the ranks, and ministers of state from the obscurity of the most remote village. Is our president, like the grand sultan of Constantinople, shut up in his apartment and unacquainted with all the talents or capacities but those of the seraskier and or mufti that happens to be about him?

Whatever the intended purpose or audience of this curiously worded slap at the first president of the United States, it landed like a bombshell when it appeared in Benjamin Franklin Bache's *Daily Advertiser* on July 29, 1794.[5]

The condemnation of Washington coincided with a violent explosion of opposition to the national excise tax on whiskey, the second obstacle friends of liberty in the western country sought to overcome. Even as they promoted free passage upon the Mississippi, they also groused ever more loudly against a tax enacted in 1791 that they thought fell too heavily on home brewers and distillers living in the backcountry of America. By July 1794, when they learned that the U.S. Treasury Department (under the direction of Alexander Hamilton) was about to punish sixty distillers in western Pennsylvania who had failed to secure a tax registration for their distilleries, sentiments of discontent—a not unreasonable state of mind under any government—erupted into postures of rebellion, another matter entirely.[6]

The stage was set in Pittsburgh and the surrounding countryside to play out a drama every bit as sensational as the storming of the Bastille, the *journée* to Versailles, or the invasion of the Tuileries in revolutionary France. The story was beautifully chronicled by Hugh Henry Brackenridge in *Incidents of the Insurrection in Western Pennsylvania in the Year 1794* (1794), one of the most remarkable eyewitness accounts in American history. Written in daily segments and shipped off to Philadelphia for immediate publication in Bache's recently renamed *Aurora,* Brackenridge's account told in graphic narrative exactly what was happening in a real-life backwoods theater. The story's plot was to describe the motives and behavior of everyone involved in the drama, but it also revealed a massive transformation of character among its participants and, almost as certainly, signaled to contemporary readers that liberty in America had come face-to-face with revolution.[7]

Just as he had done in the matter of free navigation on the Mississippi, Brackenridge attempted to control the dangerous balance between striving for liberty and pursuing rebellion. Given his visible position as attorney, publisher, author, and community leader in Pittsburgh, it was a logical role for him. Much the same could be said of Albert Gallatin, another voice for liberty recently removed from Philadelphia to the frontier to build a dream home, a trading business, and a real-estate empire at Friendship Hill in southwestern Pennsylvania. Brackenridge and Gallatin sat patiently amid the seething mobs of armed men. But struggle as they might to define what was right or wrong, proper or improper in this revolutionary setting, the mobs, Brackenridge, and Gallatin came away from a season of discontent transformed.[8]

The drama began when David Lenox, U.S. Marshal of the Treasury Department and special agent of Alexander Hamilton, arrived in western Pennsylvania to serve documents on unregistered distillers. In Fayette County alone he delivered writs to thirty delinquents. Shortly after Lenox arrived in Pittsburgh in the middle of July, an armed mob attacked the home of John Neville, a local treasury inspector. During the altercation that ensued, Neville's "Negroes[,] from some adjoining small building[,] fired upon the flank of the assailants and they were repulsed with six wounded, one mortally." Brackenridge quickly threw himself into the situation:

> I easily conceived that, as the disaster of the first attack had brought a second, the repulse of a second would bring a third; and the numbers and the rage would increase. I am not a fighting man; and it was most natural for me to think of policy and the giving the rioters the piece of paper which they had their mind upon and let the justices of the peace, the constables, the sheriffs, and the grand juries of the courts, settle it with them afterwards.

Through summer and fall Brackenridge risked life and limb to steer a middle course between the orders of law and rebellion.

Cautioning local authorities and militia leaders that they did not have the authority to send a force against a growing band of discontents, Brackenridge volunteered to "ride out without arms and address the people." Before he arrived at Couche's fort, the insurgents departed again for Neville's house, where they pillaged the building and burned it to the ground. Retreating toward Pittsburgh, from a nearby hill Brackenridge "saw the failing flame of the burning and heard the firing and the shouts of the parties on their way home from it." Four days later, July 21, the leaders of the attacking band wrote to Brackenridge, inviting him to join them at the Mingo Creek Meeting House to discuss their grievances. Despite the fact that he was "greatly alarmed at the idea of having correspondence with [individuals] involved in the guilt of treason," he agreed to meet a "committee" of the insurgents.

When he arrived at Mingo Creek, he was shocked to find that instead of a committee there was "a large convention." The marauders had lured hundreds of others into their campaign, including prominent leaders from the surrounding counties, who also happened to be officers of the three local democratic-republican societies. David Bradford, rising attorney and friend of liberty from

Washington, Pennsylvania, spoke first: "His declamation was of considerable length and extremely violent." He urged the arming of everyone in the country-side and a show of strength against government authorities. A "dead silence" fol-lowing Bradford's diatribe put Brackenridge in a dangerous position: "My situa-tion was delicate. There was but a moment between treason on the one hand and popular odium on the other, popular odium which might produce personal injury before I left the ground. To withdraw would be the same as to oppose." Bracken-ridge courageously advised the group that both what had been done and what was being proposed "might be morally right, but it was legally wrong. In con-struction of law it was high treason." While the group deliberated, Brackenridge returned to Pittsburgh, not knowing what would happen next.

He soon found out. Part of the Mingo Creek group decided to intercept the U.S. Mail near Greensburg to look for official documents and to examine the opinions of local citizens writing to the outside world. That was on July 26. Brad-ford and his fellows then issued a circular on July 28 inviting all able-bodied men to rendezvous at Braddock's Field on August 1. The evident purpose was to march on Pittsburgh and there punish excise officers and other offending parties. Not knowing where he stood at this point, Brackenridge nevertheless had the pre-science to assess the circumstances quite correctly:

> I saw my situation perfectly and canvassed in my mind the practicability of lying by and remaining a spectator or the necessity of abandoning the country. I thought also of taking part, but the cause was not good; at the same time [it was] hazardous and nothing [was] to be got by it. A revolution did not suit me nor any man else. . . . A secession of the country from the government presented nothing that could be an object with me. The repealing [of] the law by an exhibition of force might be the only thing in view, . . . but I knew they would not stop there. The opposing one law would lead [them] to oppose another; they would finally oppose all and demand a new modeling of the constitution; and there would be a revolution, or they would be suppressed. For my part, I had seen and heard enough of revolutions to have any wish to bear a part in one.

There it was for Brackenridge—the critical moment. Prior to that time he was one of America's greatest friends of liberty. Now, he became something else.

After some time spent deeply delving into his soul, Brackenridge chose to throw his energy into quelling what he believed to be open rebellion. If he could move quickly and wisely, perhaps he could avert "revolution." Just a year prior to this moment he was preaching world revolution to protect liberty. Now he would do anything to avert it. Revolution in his mind suddenly shifted from symbolizing "liberation" to meaning "chaos." Very directly and personally he could see chaos at hand.

Brackenridge headed to Braddock's Field. There he found battalions of men "dressed in what we call hunting shirts, many of them with handkerchiefs upon their heads." Every man was armed; most were shooting randomly into the air, demonstrating how they would vanquish the enemy. Brackenridge sensed mob hysteria, in which no opinion would be brooked contrary to the notion that the excise tax was a crime against humanity:

> Every man was afraid of the opinion of another. . . . The great bulk of the people were certainly in earnest, and the revolutionary language and the ideas of the French people had become familiar. It was not tarring and feathering, as at the commencement of the revolution from Great Britain, but guillotining, that is, putting to death by any way that offered. I am persuaded that if even Bradford himself, that day, had ventured to check the violence of the people in any way that was not agreeable to them . . . they would have hung him on the first tree.

Chaos almost ensued when the Pittsburgh contingent, without provisions to join the encampment, began to leave for the night. Fearful that the unannounced departure might ignite the powder keg, Brackenridge "rode after them with great haste and [re]turned them to the field with orders not to leave it, let their want of food be what it might."

As the men boasted about punishing enemies or attacking targets, Brackenridge rode through the camp lobbying anyone who would listen for the formation of a committee to determine what should be done. Enough others agreed for a committee to be elected the next morning, consisting of three delegates from each regiment present. Brackenridge was one of the delegates from the Pittsburgh militia. When the group convened, David Bradford opened with a tirade that they were there for one purpose only: "to chastise certain persons who had discovered sentiments friendly to the excise law [whose] . . . sentiments had come to light through the vigilance of some persons who had intercepted the mail and found their letters . . . [that] speak for themselves." As the committee deliberated, fresh battalions arrived, electing their own delegates. Whenever the committee seemed to reach some resolution, a new group of bellicose delegates arrived and had to be dealt with.

The process of deliberation was so democratic that no resolution could be achieved. Brackenridge had to use the ploys of a court jester to reorient the mob mentality ruling the camp. At every rest break delegates would be recharged by frustrated members of their regiments. Bradford, eager for action, proposed that the entire throng march on Pittsburgh. Before anyone could counter, the committee disbanded to begin the march. Fearful that all had been lost, Brackenridge shrewdly yelled after the members, "Yes, by all means . . . to give proof that the strictest order can be preserved and no damage done. We will just march through and, taking a turn, come out . . . and taking a little whiskey with the inhabitants of the town, the troops will embark and cross the river."

Although the committee did not take up Brackenridge's parting comments, he acted as if everyone had agreed to his plan, dashing from group to group to enunciate how the march would be accomplished and emphasizing the whiskey that awaited the throng of fifty-four hundred men when they had finished an orderly march. Just as Lafayette organized the French National Guard to escort the mob that descended on Versailles to bring Louis XVI back to Paris in 1789, Brackenridge organized the Pittsburgh militia to escort the throng of malcontents in what he tried to portray as a triumphal march. And just as Lafayette had done, Brackenridge positioned one group of his militia at the head of the march and another detachment at the rear. He then recruited all the members of the deliberating committee and assigned them the task of personally carrying, in view of their own regiments, the whiskey that would be consumed at the end of the march. Somewhat tongue-in-cheek, he described the strategy: "Members of the committee set the example by carrying water and whiskey to these whiskey-boys, as they have since been called." Taking no chances on the failure of the plan, Brackenridge closed all taverns along the way and invited the tavern keepers to be servers at the end of the march.

Brackenridge then removed all of his books and papers from Pittsburgh and spent every moment of the march troubleshooting potential disruptions. Despite his efforts a group of two hundred men dallied in Pittsburgh and descended on the houses of two of the tax inspectors. Brackenridge stopped one group from torching a house by dramatically leaping in front of them and promising that "the people of Pittsburgh will pull it down and throw it in the river" themselves. Another outside of Pittsburgh was, however, set ablaze by a separate group. Nevertheless, contrary to rumors and near clashes, Pittsburgh survived the danger of being burned. That it was saved was amazing, since mob action over the range of five adjacent counties succeeded in destroying the offices and dwellings of every tax agent. The turmoil, moreover, led to the expulsion of every tax officer from the western territory.[9]

The crisis did not end there. Alexander Hamilton dispatched commissioners to investigate the violent activities in western Pennsylvania. Incensed over the behavior and attitudes of people whom he considered rebels against national law, Hamilton persuaded President Washington to call up fifteen thousand militia from Virginia, Maryland, New Jersey, and Pennsylvania to deal with the insurgents. After a month of fruitless negotiations between commissioners and leaders of the movement, Washington issued a second proclamation on September 24 ordering the suppression of the self-styled army of malcontents. Goaded on by Hamilton, he felt by then, as was expressed by a Virginia editor, that revolutionary chaos had been transferred from France to the American frontier: "The malignant vapours of a discordant nation have been borne across the Atlantic, to taint the clear atmosphere of Liberty." Washington called upon citizen militias "to turn out and suppress an insurrection, which, as a black hydra rising in the west, would wrap you in its poisonous web."

Just as yellow fever believed by many to have been imported by French West Indians a year before—enveloped the nation's capital, another disease—

just as insidious, equally demonic, and virtually intractable—had invaded America's frontier populace. Call it whatever you like—rebellion, mutiny, revolt, yes, even revolution—it was a disorder that had to be eradicated or the nation would end up like France, in total chaos. Whether one looked at it from the inside, as in the case of Brackenridge, or from the outside, as in the case of Hamilton, Washington, and countless other Americans, a new and menacing malady was loose upon the land. Washington took the situation so seriously, in fact, that, for the first and subsequently only time in American history, the president took to the field as actual commander-in-chief of the hastily assembled military force. From October 4, when he arrived in Carlisle, until October 20, when he completed his westernmost advance at Bedford, Pennsylvania, Washington commanded the nation's militia army just as Lafayette had led the French National Guard in the early stages of the French Revolution.[10]

As Washington's mighty force approached western Pennsylvania to quell the distemper that afflicted thousands of Americans, Brackenridge put on paper precisely what was happening:

> I saw before me the anarchy of a period, a shock to the government and possibly a revolution—a revolution impregnated with the Jacobin principles of France, and which might become equally bloody to the principal actors. It would be bloody unavoidably to them, and to the people, destructive. Let no man suppose that I coveted revolution. I had seen the evils of one already, the American; and I had read the evils of another, the French. My imagination presented the evils of the last strongly to my view and brought them so close to probable experience at home that, during the whole period of the insurrection, I could scarcely bear to cast my eye upon a paragraph of French news.

Brackenridge's defense of his actions also acknowledged that during the summer and fall of 1794 Americans had transformed the meaning of the term *revolution* from liberation to chaos.

When he grasped the significance of what was happening, Brackenridge worked just as feverishly to cure the malady of spirit as Benjamin Rush did to control the yellow fever epidemic. In a sense, his approach was no less radical. He and Albert Gallatin organized a committee of sixty delegates representing the disaffected groups. This "scrub congress" wrangled endlessly from August 28 into September. Opinions often were so diverse and so vehement that Brackenridge feared the group might adopt some of the practices of the French National Convention, such as "arresting me or others that were obnoxious; and between an arrest and putting to death, as there so here, there would be but little interval." Secession from the union was debated; David Bradford wanted war. Tempers were so heated that votes could be taken only by secret ballot wherein members received a scrap of paper bearing yea or nay. To avoid any possibility of having one's views revealed, the paper was to be torn in half, with the yea-or-nay vote placed in a hat and the other half, by common agreement, eaten. When the votes were counted, a majority had opted for peace, not war.[11]

Meanwhile, the American army, accompanied personally by Alexander Hamilton, proceeded westward from Bedford, arresting dissidents along the way. Brackenridge feared that he would be assassinated by some of those who thought he had betrayed the cause. As he read reports of his behavior in the Philadelphia press, he also began to fear that he might be arrested and tried for treason: "I looked forward to a trial before a jury in Philadelphia which heated with prejudice against me, would differ little from a revolutionary tribunal in Paris." But the actual tribunal he faced was none other than Alexander Hamilton, before whom he appeared on November 16. There, Brackenridge gave a full and detailed narrative of his activities, fears, and purposes over the last half year. Hamilton had come to the hearing certain that Brackenridge had been one of the leaders of the rebellion, but he evidently was persuaded otherwise when he heard the amazing story. On the second day of the hearing, Hamilton dismissed him from any further proceedings.[12]

Despite the fact that the immediate threat had passed, Brackenridge was a changed man. Neither he nor any of his fellow residents of the western country would ever again view America as a pristine land of liberty from which proceeded world revolution. From that time forward they saw it as a land bent on avoiding revolution at all cost. The famous authors of *Rising Glory of America,* Philip Freneau and Hugh Henry Brackenridge, to that moment hopeful revolutionaries, had to rethink what America was and what they wanted it to be.

REVOLUTIONARY CHARACTER AND SEDITION

As Americans looked out across a world of revolution during the 1790s, it became increasingly difficult for them to understand the ideas and actions of devoted friends of liberty. As the zeal for liberation subsided, many had trouble determining whether a particular friend of liberty was a friend or an enemy of the nation. Indeed, some friends of liberty began to appear to many as supporters of chaos and traitors to the nation's governors, if not the nation itself.

No one puzzled American observers more than Matthew Lyon. Just as Brackenridge organized democratic societies in western Pennsylvania, Lyon did so in Vermont. The societies proliferated across virtually every county in Vermont during the spring of 1794. And not only did they promote liberty for citizens in America, they also used the movement to explore the possibilities of Vermont's independence from America. Although Lyon and his colleagues promoted American alliance with France and condemned monarchical and aristocratic Britain, they also envisioned campaigns using French force to conquer Canada or British force to win independence. Lyon was particularly intrigued, as were many other frontier Americans, by the overtures of Citizen Genet to organize world revolution. Even after Genet had been denounced by the American government, Lyon in an open letter praised Genet for his "zeal and activity in the cause of the Republic you represent . . . and the cause of Mankind."

During 1794 Lyon responded to Genet's call. According to the secretary of the Rutland Democratic Society, Lyon accepted blank commissions from Genet to recruit a force that would overthrow British rule in Canada. Although Genet's fall from power aborted the plan, Lyon explored the possibilities of this and another separatist movement to unite Vermont with segments of lower Canada in an independent nation. Throughout all of these activities, later viewed as traitorous to America, Lyon was driven by his desire to achieve liberty for citizens and the dominance of local government over any national or foreign government. Just as Brackenridge's fellows wanted to control the Mississippi, Lyon and his colleagues wanted to make Vermont an independent empire.

Lyon dreamed of Vermont independence even as he campaigned every two years for a seat in Congress. Twice he was defeated by lawyers and propertied interests who he thought had conspired against him. Finally in 1796, in a hotly contested election, complete with political intrigue and mandatory runoff elections, Lyon was elected to his first term in Congress. Believing that he had received a mandate from the people of Vermont, he exhibited a brand of fervor from the moment he arrived in Philadelphia that brought the cause of revolution to the heart of the American government. First, he declared the various ceremonial trappings of Congress to be un-American; next he fought with southern Congressmen on the subject of petitions protesting slavery and the slave trade. He then clashed with Harrison Gray Otis, who sought to limit immigration by imposing a hefty tax on naturalization certificates. When Otis announced that he wanted to discourage "hordes of wild Irishmen" and "the turbulent and disorderly of all parts of the world" from coming to the United States, Lyon rose in protest: "We had told the world, that there was in this country a good spring of liberty, and invited all to come and drink of it. We had told them that the country was rich and fertile, and invited them to come and taste of our fruits." How can we suddenly close down the land of liberty? he asked.

Lyon's adamant preachments, his rustic manner, and his use of his franking privileges weekly to distribute two hundred copies of Benjamin Franklin Bache's *Aurora* soon drew fire from rival Congressmen—especially New Englanders wary of his radical influence back home. Lyon, who lacked respect for most of his New England colleagues, even dared to boast on January 30, 1798, that "if he should go into Connecticut, and manage a press there six months, although the people of that State were not fond of revolutionary principles, he could effect a revolution." And in that revolution he would turn out the state's congressmen. Roger Griswold, Connecticut arch-conservative, overhearing Lyon's braggadocio and considering him "as a meer beast and the fool of the play," shot back with a slur on Lyon's revolutionary war record: "If you go into Connecticut, you had better wear your wooden sword." When Griswold repeated the slur moments later, Lyon spat directly into his face.

Although Lyon quickly rendered a written apology to the Speaker of the House, a motion was introduced to expel him from Congress. Two weeks of debate followed as newspapers made Lyon overnight into one of America's best-known friends of liberty. Caricatures and poems dubbed him as "Spitting Matt," "The Lyon of Vermont," "Matt, the Democrat," and "The Spitting Hero." But despite a vote of 52 to 44 in favor of expelling him, the two-thirds vote necessary to remove him from Congress could not be achieved.[13]

But the failure to expel Lyon did not end the matter. Griswold, seething over Lyon's impudence, made a visit to McCallister's store on Chestnut Street in Philadelphia and purchased a handy weapon—a sturdy hickory walking stick. Feeling that the House of Representatives "by their decision had sanctioned violence within those walls," Griswold chose the chamber of the House as the proper place to settle his score with Lyon. On the morning of February 15, before the House came into session, Griswold took his revenge:

> As soon as I saw him [Lyon] in his seat I took my cane and walked across the floor in front of the speakers chair. . . . He saw me before I struck him, and was endeavoring to draw a sword cane when I gave him the first blow. I call'd him a scoundrel & struck him with my cane, and pursued him with more than twenty blows on his head and back until he got possession of a pair of tongues [tongs], when I threw him down and after giving him several blows with my fist, I was taken off by his friends.[14]

Despite the severity of the violence, a House committee established to investigate the incident concluded that neither Griswold nor Lyon should be expelled for their actions! The full House concurred in a vote of 73–21.

Although both Griswold and Lyon had been preserved for the moment, Lyon's character soon came under stauncher scrutiny.

If Matthew Lyon's revolutionary antics could be explained by the rudeness of his life on the Vermont frontier, how then could one account for those of a well-educated revolutionary who published the widest circulating newspaper in the nation's capital? One who was the grandson of the nation's most internationally celebrated founding father?

Benjamin Franklin Bache was utterly daring in 1798 when he revealed the inner workings and failures of the John Adams administration as it seemed to be bumbling America into war with her sister republic France. Bache was certain that America could negotiate with France, especially since French foreign affairs had been taken over by Maurice de Talleyrand less than a year after he left Philadelphia. After all, Moreau, Volney, and La Rochefoucauld had remained in the city and were all on confidential terms with Talleyrand. Their services certainly could be called upon to encourage favorable treatment for America.[15]

Bache insisted upon the centrality of an alliance with France for America's future. For this he began to encounter stiff criticism and even threats. His loudest rival editor, William Cobbett, described Bache as "the most infamous of the Jacobins" and gave as his vita the following: "Editor of the *Aurora,* Printer to the French Directory, Distributor General of the principles of Insurrection, Anarchy and Confusion, the greatest of fools, and the most stubborn sans-culottes in the United States." Cobbett eventually urged Americans to treat Bache "as we should a TURK, A JEW, A JACOBIN, OR A DOG." [16]

Some heeded Cobbett's call. When twelve hundred militant young men paraded through Philadelphia on May 7, 1798, in support of the administration's anti-French policy, they stopped at the President's residence and listened to Adams, in full military regalia, issue a ringing call to arms. Later in the evening, after many drinks, a group of them attacked Bache's house. Although neighbors and friends drove them away, they or others returned two nights later and smashed the windows of his home. On another occasion, while inspecting the frigate *United States* in the Philadelphia shipyard, Bache was savagely attacked by dockworker Clement Humphries. Severely bruised in the beating, Bache brought charges against Humphries, who was later convicted and fined. [17]

But the threats of physical violence did not silence Bache. Indeed, there is sufficient evidence to suggest that his devotion to principle along with his precarious financial situation in the spring of 1798 caused him to speak out ever more daringly in hopes of selling papers. On June 16, 1798, he published a confidential letter dated March 18 from Talleyrand, two days before it was officially received by members of Congress. The letter questioned President Adams's motives in dealing with France. Clearly written for public consumption, the letter seemed to have conspiracy written all over it, and Bache appeared to be the nation's number one conspirator. The seemingly magical emergence of the letter on the pages of the *Aurora,* William Cobbett gloated, proved that "the infamous Lightning-rod, jun. was a hireling of, and in correspondence with the despots of France." [18]

Ten days after publishing the Talleyrand letter, despite his efforts to prove that he was not in direct communication with the French government, Bache was arrested and hauled into court on charges of "libelling the President & the Executive Government, in a manner to excite sedition, and opposition to the laws, by sundry publications and re-publications." Three days later, represented by Alexander J. Dallas, he appeared before U.S. District Judge Samuel Peters and was released on bail and sureties amounting to $8,000 pending trial scheduled for October 1798. With authorization from President Adams, whose wife Abigail clamored for the editor to be "seazed," Bache was charged with sedition on the basis of common law. Although Adams and his friends in Congress were at the very moment enacting a spate of new federal laws to banish enemies of the national administration, Bache's crime was viewed as being so heinous that no delay could be allowed in bringing him to punishment. [19]

That federal authorities should move so precipitately against Bache suggests the siege mentality that had taken over American government by the spring of

1798. On the day of Bache's arrest, the last of four laws to silence discordant voices in America, the Sedition Act, was introduced in the U.S. Senate. By July 14 it was passed and signed into law, giving President Adams and his administration powers never before known in colonial America or the United States. It forbade citizens or resident aliens from entering into unlawful combinations to oppose the execution of national laws, to obstruct the work of a federal officer, or to aid "any insurrection, riot, unlawful assembly, or combination." This vague, but menacing police power, added to the Naturalization Act (June 18), the Alien Act (June 25), and the Alien Enemies Act (July 6), authorized Adams to obliterate rights and privileges thought to have been secured forever by the Bill of Rights. Dismayed by Congress's speed in annulling some of the basic rights of man secured by the American Revolution and the U.S. Constitution, Bache asked, "whether there is more safety and liberty to be enjoyed at Constantinople or Philadelphia?"[20]

AMERICAN REIGN OF TERROR

Everywhere he looked, Bache saw the onset of an American reign of terror that, except for an absence of bloodletting, equated that of revolutionary France. It did, in fact, replicate the lines, the acts, and the oppressive effects of William Pitt's reign of terror in Britain, where the Alien Act of 1792 and the Treasonable Practices and the Seditious Meetings Acts, both enacted in 1795, established ready-made precedents for Americans. The British laws had been and were being used to quell editors, to halt public and private gatherings, and to banish organizations that disagreed with government policy. British prisons were jammed with individuals under indictment for treason and sedition, and the courts were blanketed with trials, eventually martyring dozens of the heroes and villains of British and Irish history.[21]

Bache had only to look within his own newspaper office to see the effects of the American terror. James Callender, the clever Scottish political author with a penchant for strong invective, continued to serve as writer and editorialist for the *Aurora*. With support from House clerk John Beckley and a coterie of Jeffersonian enthusiasts, Callender wrote social, political, and economic propaganda against the policies of the Washington and Adams administrations. But he also wrote serious analyses of American and international economic practices. After assisting Tench Coxe in the production of the influential *A View of the United States* (1794), Callender contributed his own *A Short History of the Nature and Consequences of Excise Laws* (1795), demonstrating the anti-equalitarian effects of such taxes. Reflecting on the recent Whiskey Rebellion, he argued that excise taxes "may fairly be classed with that noted trio, famine, pestilence, and the sword . . . [and] like the worm that never dies, they are constantly acting . . . not only to destroy industry, but likewise to subvert the morals of those who are subject to them."

He also believed that the only real revolution the world had seen was the French Revolution—at least in its early stages. The American Revolution, by contrast, was a partial one that had failed to bring equality for all Americans. From Callender's point of view, the principal cause and course of the American Revolution could be little defended. His outline of the Revolution differed from most:

> A gang of banditti from the town of Boston began the American revolution, by unfurling the standard of villainy. They wantonly destroyed 342 chests of tea, in presence, and with the approbation of an immense crowd of spectators. The act of parliament for shutting up the port of Boston, was the natural and suitable consequence of that shameful transaction. . . . The whole continent was dragged prematurely into war, to save the factious townsmen of Boston from a chastisement that some of them highly deserved. . . . If the people of New England had behaved with equal moderation and dignity as those of Virginia, it is likely enough that we might still have been British colonies, and in a happy situation, without any revolution at all.

While this revision of the actions of Boston patriots arose from a political caprice Callender attempted to address, it is clear that his view of revolution was the search for liberty, not the onset of chaos.

However brilliant Callender's analyses may have been, the meager sustenance he eked out came from his more crass political editorials and writings. He dared to tarnish the image and character of the nation's most revered icons. It was he who first scored George Washington for abandoning the American Revolution by entering into a treaty with England. "If ever a nation was debauched by a man," Callender wrote, "the American nation has been debauched by Washington." Deploring Washington's deceit, he intoned:

> Let his conduct . . . be an example to future ages. Let it serve to be a warning that no man may be an idol, and that a people may confide in themselves rather than an individual. . . . [It is clear] that the marque of patriotism may be worn to conceal the foulest designs against the liberties of the people.

And it was Callender who, almost from inaugural day, lambasted John Adams as a pathetic old man, a petulant enemy of liberty, and no friend of the rights of man.

And it was also Callender who published revelations about Alexander Hamilton's sex life. At a moment when Hamilton was eyeing the presidency and when there were open speculations about Benjamin Franklin's flirtations, Bache and Beckley provided Callender with documents substantiating a long-rumored affair between Hamilton and Maria Reynolds, wife of a speculator with whom he had questionable dealings. The documents were published in Callender's political chronicle, *History of 1796*, the second in a series of annual registers he compiled to show the progress of politics in the United States.

Between his savage editorials in Bache's *Aurora* and his character assassinations in the *History of 1796* (published 1797), Callender was a prime target for reprisal. Impoverished and forced to reach for the sensational to sell his writings, Callender knew that the Alien and Sedition Acts were designed especially for him. Certain that he would be expelled under the Alien Act, he became on June 4, 1798, a naturalized American citizen. Equally sure that he would be indicted under the Sedition Act, he wrote his last editorial for the *Aurora* on June 22. To avoid arrest, he fled from Philadelphia on July 13—the day before Adams signed the Sedition Act—to backwater Virginia, abandoning his wife and children. He never returned to the city.[22]

Joseph Gales, former publisher of the Sheffield *Register* and for two years publisher of *Gales' Independent Gazetteer* in Philadelphia, came to much the same end. After struggling to reestablish the paper against criticism of his foreign views, he sold it to Samuel Harrison Smith, a young journalist, in November 1797. He also reacquainted himself with Joseph Priestley and became the first lay reader in Priestley's Philadelphia Unitarian church. As the rage against foreigners and immigrant editors increased, Gales began searching for a way to get out of Philadelphia. He stayed on, doing printing work for members of Congress through the spring and summer of 1798. With the onset of another epidemic of yellow fever that August, Gales responded to an invitation from North Carolina congressman Nathaniel Macon to relocate to that state's capital in Raleigh. After he was wined and dined by state and local officials friendly to Thomas Jefferson and was promised a lucrative state printing contract, he decided to depart Philadelphia during the summer of 1799. He launched the *Raleigh Register* on October 22.[23]

That Philadelphia and much of America was turning into a hellhole for both foreign and domestic friends of liberty became evident when the Adams administration took measures to deport the capital's contingent of French exiles. Even before the passage of the Alien Act in the spring of 1798, Adams and his henchmen were threatening outspoken French intellectuals, who were increasingly viewed as dangerous aliens in the land of liberty. Despite the fact that many of them had become esteemed members of the American Philosophical Society (Moreau, Talleyrand, La Rochefoucauld-Liancourt, E. I. DuPont, Volney, and Louis-Philippe), their loyalties were held in doubt. Chief suspect was Comte de Volney, scientist and theorist, who pursued his writing career while living in Philadelphia. Singled out especially for his deistic views and theoretical ideas about revolutions and governments, Volney came to symbolize for some Americans all that was wrong with the French Revolution.[24]

That Volney could be depicted as a dangerous presence was underscored when Priestley, himself a bit tarnished, blasted the French philosopher. In *Observations on the Increase of Infidelity, with Animadversions upon the Writings of Several Modern Unbelievers, and Especially THE RUINS of Mr. Volney* (published in three ever-expanding editions in 1795, 1796, and 1797), Priestley argued a relatively minor point of theology in his typical overheated style. But by including such red-hot words as "infidelity" and "unbelieving" in an otherwise stiff intellectual exercise, his pamphlet became more a political statement than an intramural religious discussion. Priestley's condemnation was even more subversive, and it surely ruined Volney's reputation. Moreover, as Priestley supervised the publication of the third edition of the attack in Philadelphia in the spring of 1797, he repeated the same message from his Philadelphia Unitarian pulpit.[25]

Volney was stunned that a former collegial associate could publish not one, but three diatribes. When the third edition was issued, Priestley sent Volney a copy inviting his comments and demanding that Volney point out any errors of fact or attribution. After the critique was published, Volney encountered Priestley on Spruce Street in Philadelphia, whereupon Priestley took "me [Volney] by the hand as a friend, and [spoke] of me in a large company under that denomination," Volney reported. "Now I ask the public," he continued, "what kind of a man is Dr. Priestly [*sic*]?" Having asked the question, Volney answered it under the date of March 10, 1797, in "A Letter to Dr. Priestley." He quickly arrived at the main point:

> Such is your artful purpose, that, in attacking me as doubting the existence of Jesus, you might secure to yourself, by surprise, the favor of every Christian sect, although your own incredulity in his divine nature is not less subversive of Christianity than the profane opinion, which does not find in history the proof required by English law to establish a fact.[26]

By condemning infidelity and deism, Priestley was working to bolster Unitarianism.

But Volney further analyzed the unreality of Priestley's attacks. Reaffirming his belief that the book of nature was a more reliable source of truth "than leaves of paper blackened over with Greek or Hebrew," he thought that Priestley's "design is less to attack my book than my personal and moral character." Chiding Priestley a bit for mixing up his purposes, he noted

> I am come to America neither to agitate the conscience of men, nor to form a sect, nor to establish a colony, in which, under the pretext of religion, I might erect a little empire to myself. I have never been seen evangelizing my ideas, either in temples or in public meetings. . . . I am every day less tempted to take on me the management of the minds or bodies of men.

In fact, all of Priestley's theorizing on the fine points of theology was sound and fury without meaning, since "the course of the seasons, the path of the sun, the return of rain and drought, are the same for the inhabitants of each country, whether Christians, Mussulmans, Idolators, Catholics, Protestants, etc."[27]

Despite his pleadings, Volney became persona non grata in America. Thousands of other French refugees came to the same conclusion either before or soon after the passage of the Alien Act. During July and August fifteen ships left from Philadelphia loaded with French refugees who hoped to find freedom either back in France or in St. Domingue. It is well that they did, since President John

Adams, working through his secretary of state, Timothy Pickering, was intent on removing what he considered a menacing French presence from America.

Immediately after the passage of the Alien Act, Adams authorized Pickering to begin proceedings against Victor Collot, former French general and governor of Guadeloupe. Suspected of masterminding a French attempt to seize Louisiana and described by Adams as "a pernicious and malicious intriguer," Pickering followed Collot's every move, but could not get sufficient evidence to arrest him. Collot avoided Pickering's snares until 1800 but voluntarily left for France in August of that year.[28]

Tanguy de la Boissiere, one of the leaders of the St. Domingan revolution who escaped his French captors in New York harbor, became so disgusted with America in 1798 that he also left for France. After publishing a newspaper in Philadelphia calling for the restoration of the French colony in St. Domingue and writing a thorough history of its revolution, Tanguy requested a passport to France, hoping to do more there for his native island.[29]

Whereas Collot never came under arrest as an undesirable alien, Moreau de St. Mery, the heart and soul of the French refugee community in Philadelphia, was placed on a list of Frenchmen approved by President Adams for prosecution and deportation. Moreau inquired about his listing through Senator John Langdon of New Hampshire. Adams is said to have told Langdon only that "he's too French." In his diary Moreau documented the Adams administration's attitudes toward the French and of Americans' fear of a French invasion. He wrote, "Everybody was suspicious of everybody else: everywhere one saw murderous glances." As the antagonism increased, he became the only person in Philadelphia who continued to wear the red French cockade. His American associates (Bache and Beckley) fearing that he might be attacked, provided him with keys to two shelters where he could escape.[30]

Volney began the exodus of French refugees from America and Moreau concluded it. He and his family sailed for France on August 23, 1798. Before the end of June, a fellow French refugee told him, "All those who have no love for Robespierrism had better get out and get out quick!" Moreau and those who did not take Volney's swift exit soon experienced the same kind of terror known throughout human history when a nation, a state, or a society decides to ostracize, persecute, or eradicate a class of people because of their racial, ethnic, or gender identity. When he was finally able to arrange passage, he and his family were taken to the safety and freedom of France aboard the ship *Adrastes*—the Nemesis. What is even more poignant is that Volney—true offspring of the Enlightenment, proponent of reason and rationality—left ten weeks earlier aboard the *Benjamin Franklin*.[31] It had been Franklin, a symbolic Moses to French friends of liberty, who had lured French citizens to America. When America failed to live up to its billing, it was appropriate that a ship perpetuating his memory should deliver the first wave of disparaged souls back to France.

Others also grew disheartened with the direction of America. In New York City, John Daly Burk, the Irish playwright, resumed full-time newspaper work

"Congressional Pugilists" (1798). The attack of Roger Griswold of Connecticut on Matthew "Spitting" Lyon in the House of Representatives.

when he took over editorship of the *New York Time Piece* from Philip Freneau on June 13, 1798. As a recent immigrant, as a proponent of Irish revolution, and as an incurable critic of government authorities, Burk assumed his visible post at a most unpropitious time. Launching his editorship athwart the passage of the Alien and Sedition Acts, he was a sure target for the American reign of terror. Within two weeks Burk was being savagely attacked by Noah Webster, rival editor of *The Commercial Advertiser.* Webster directly condemned Burk for "his turbulent, revolutionary Jacobin sentiments." He also published reported rumors that Burk had rejoiced over the French invasion of Ireland and had hoped that France would attack America so that "every scoundrel in favor of this government [the Adams administration] would be put to the guillotine."[32]

Although Burk responded to the charges in the *Time Piece* and in a letter to the *Advertiser* and publicly swore allegiance to the Constitution at a Fourth of July rally of United Irishmen, he was powerless against the poisoned climate in America. Whatever he wrote, however innocent and well-intended, was turned against him. In two editorials in the *Time Piece* on July 2 and 4 he questioned President Adams's handling of negotiations with Talleyrand and asked rhetorically if it might be seditious "to say the President is incorrect in a part of History." In the second piece he discussed the fragile condition of freedom of speech in America and the tendency of the Adams administration to charge every critic with Jacobinism. Nothing more was needed. Burk was arrested on July 6 and charged with seditious and libelous statements against President Adams.

Although Burk was soon out on bail and never came to trial, the arrest destroyed his New York editorial career. Within days Burk was feuding with the co-owner of the *Time Piece* about whether the paper should carry further editorials on President Adams. Their disagreement led to a violent type-throwing contest and fisticuffs. Just two weeks after the arrest, Burk's partner in effect fired him, when a notice appeared disclaiming responsibility for any debts contracted by Burk as editor. The *Time Piece*'s days were numbered as well; the last issue appeared on or about August 30, barely six weeks after Burk first appeared in its pages. Certain that he would be found guilty of sedition and that, as a resident alien, he would be deported, Burk begged for clemency. After six months of waiting he was told "the President thinks it may be expedient to let him off, on condition . . . that he Burke [*sic*] forthwith quit the United States." Although he notified Secretary Pickering that he was leaving America in May 1799, he actually repaired into hiding in Virginia, where he took an assumed name and served as "principal of a college." [33]

While Callender, Gales, and Burk escaped the terror by finding new refuges in a less disturbed South, Matthew Lyon—member of Congress, political crusader, and devout friend of liberty—could not as easily elude ensnarement. Following his spitting and cudgeling altercations with Roger Griswold, Lyon was a marked man. Detested by Adams and by most of the New England delegation in Congress, Lyon's every move was monitored by a band of enemies. And, of course, Lyon—forever opinionated—provided plenty of fodder for watchful eyes.

On June 20, 1798, Lyon responded to a sniping letter in *Spooner's Vermont Journal* that attacked his criticisms of the Adams administration. He claimed in his letter to the *Journal* that he could not support Adams "when I see every consideration of the public welfare swallowed up in a continual grasp for power, in an unbounded thirst for ridiculous pomp, foolish adulation, or selfish avarice." So noisy was Lyon in his opposition to the Alien and Sedition Acts that when he left Philadelphia in July to return to Vermont, he was hounded along the way. On July 21 in New York City—at the height of the terror—bands of organized young men marched the streets to the home of Edward Livingston and to the homes where Albert Gallatin and Lyon were staying. Singing "God Save the King," they derided the opposition congressmen with the terms "Jacobin," "Frenchman," and "Democrat."

When Lyon reached Vermont to begin his reelection campaign, he continued to print his opinions about liberty, sedition, and the direction of Adams and the Congress. The *Farmers' Library,* his campaign newspaper edited by his son James, contained Lyon's populist point of view. But to underscore his ideological commitment to liberty and his hatred of the vestiges of nobility in America, he launched in October 1798 a paper titled *The Scourge of Aristocracy.* In the *Scourge* he lampooned the Sedition Act as a betrayal of the American Revolution. And in his campaign visits across Vermont, he read openly from a sensational letter sent by poet Joel Barlow from Paris to Abraham Baldwin, a Georgia congressman, accusing Adams of deliberately seeking war with France. Barlow considered Adams's duplicity with the French so obvious that he "wondered that the answer of both Houses [of Congress to Adams's official message] had not been an order to send him [Adams] to a madhouse."

For all of these sundry affronts against the character of President Adams, Lyon learned on October 5, 1798, that he was about to be arrested for violating the Sedition Act. Although advised by some to flee Vermont, he did not. He appeared before a carefully assembled grand jury consisting almost entirely of people who had opposed his election on October 7 and was summarily indicted. When the trial opened two days later, Lyon had selected his opponent in the pending election, Israel Smith, as his reluctant attorney. The effervescent Lyon went on to represent himself for the duration of the trial, ending it with a two and a half hour address to the jury. Despite a brilliant lay performance and a strong defense of freedom of speech by Lyon, the jury could not be persuaded. After only one hour of deliberation, the jury returned a guilty verdict. Presiding Judge William Paterson, Associate Justice of the Supreme Court, ordered that Lyon be imprisoned for four months, pay the costs of prosecution and a fine of $1,000, and remain committed in prison until the payments were made.

Although Lyon was thunderstruck by the verdict and the harsh sentence, he was soon championed in both Vermont and across America. If his reelection to Congress was originally in doubt, it was suddenly assured. From his prison cell he waged a campaign through *The Scourge of Aristocracy.* The purpose of the magazine was "to oppose truth to falsehood[,] . . . to elucidate the real situation of this country . . . at this agitated and awful crisis[, and to] prepare the American mind for a state of abject slavery . . . to a set of assuming High Mightinesses in our own country, and a close connection with a corrupt, tottering monarchy in Europe." With the assistance of Senator Stevens T. Mason of Virginia, Lyon raised funds to pay his fines. And when the election was held in December 1798 the imprisoned Lyon received 4,576 votes, compared with 2,444 for his closest rival. He had won the election despite efforts to discredit him.

A movement was launched immediately to seek a pardon for Lyon and to have his fine remanded. John Cosens Ogden, an itinerant Episcopalian rector from New Hampshire, gathered up a petition of several thousand Vermonters and headed to Philadelphia to deliver the plea personally to Adams. Ogden got his hearing, but Adams would not budge, declaring that "penitence must precede pardon." Ogden was then followed back to New England by agents of Secretary of the Treasury Oliver Wolcott. When Odgen stopped for the night in Litchfield, Connecticut, he was arrested to recover a $200 debt, probably reported by his political and religious enemies.

When he was released in February 1799, Lyon paraded across Vermont and then to Philadelphia amid the applause and approval of many Americans. Anthony Haswell welcomed Lyon to Bennington, Vermont, with a poem titled "Patriotic Exultation on Lyon's Release from the Federal Bastille in Vergennes":

Come take the glass and drink his health,

Who is a friend of Lyon,

First martyr under federal law

The junto dared to try on.

Although he arrived in Philadelphia as a martyr of the American reign of terror, his fame did not deter a movement in Congress to have him expelled for his criminal conviction and imprisonment as "a notorious and Seditious person."

The ensuing debate constituted the careful analysis of the relationship between sedition and free speech that should have preceded the adoption of the Sedition Act. When the votes were cast in the House of Representatives, Lyon's expulsion was favored 49 to 45. Again, the vote had failed to achieve the two-thirds majority required for expulsion. Lyon remained until the end of his term, long enough to play a decisive role in assuring the succession of Thomas Jefferson rather than Aaron Burr to the presidency in 1800. Wherever he went for the remainder of his life, Lyon's martyrdom during the American reign of terror was never forgotten.[34]

TERROR, MADNESS, TRAGEDY

The effects of the terror, already noted among some friends of liberty, can best be understood through the lives of two notable revolutionaries—Benjamin Franklin Bache and Benjamin Rush. Both of them, under savage attack during the summer of 1798, became incapable of exercising sound judgment. As a consequence, both were driven toward courses that could only be described as self-destruction.

Bache, already under indictment for seditious statements, was awaiting his final trial set for October. Nearly bankrupt, he was spending off his modest inheritance from his grandfather attempting to keep the *Aurora* alive. He had personally subsidized the paper to the tune of at least $14,700, but it was still a losing proposition. His efforts to manufacture type and to publish books had not been successful. In addition, he was constantly angering this group or that, who would then cancel subscriptions. His circle of supporters and friends seemed to be dwindling, and his coterie of French intellectuals from whom he derived so much pleasure were fleeing America. Even his wife, Margaret Markoe, thought he was on the verge of collapse. To protect herself and their three children against certain bankruptcy, she urged Bache to sign over his property to her so that it could not be taken by creditors.[35]

Bache nevertheless held on to the ideal of liberty and the image of his embattled grandfather. How well he knew the battles Franklin had fought against political enemies throughout his career, against Provost William Smith, against the Penn family, and against the British empire itself. So Bache continued to be filled with revolutionary fervor in a world that was becoming disillusioned with the idea of revolution. He would fight on, even if not a soul agreed with him.[36]

First, he hired William Duane to take the place of the fleeing James T. Callender. Second, he announced that he would publish a three-day-a-week newspaper

"Pennsylvania Hospital in Pine Street, Philadelphia" (1798). America's first hospital, founded by Benjamin Franklin, was overwhelmed by waves of yellow fever epidemics.

for subscribers outside the Philadelphia area, hoping to capture an elusive national market. Third, even as reports of new cases of yellow fever arrived, indicating that Philadelphia was in for another season of epidemic, Bache announced bravely that he would not observe the normal cessation of publication during the months of September and October. With a fourth child on the way, he simply could not afford to lose two months of income. On September 7, he declared that the *Aurora* would be published until the "cruel malady" struck the last person in the office.[37]

As for the matter of liberty and revolution in America, Bache exhibited the symptoms of both personal and social paranoia. By early August he was advising friends of liberty to arm themselves to be able "to defend their persons and property." When he heard that an "armed association" was being formed in New York City to counteract attacks on individuals speaking out against the government, he endorsed the idea. If the friends of liberty armed themselves, he believed, all of the foolishness about inhibiting individual rights and overthrowing the Constitution would end. Three weeks later as the terror deepened, he again advised "every republican . . . to provide himself with arms and to habituate himself to the constant use of them." These unwise counsels in moment of crisis reveal the depth of Bache's despair and fear. He had descended to the point where he advised his democratic friends to recklessly pursue exactly what the Alien and Sedition Acts forbade.[38]

Benjamin Rush, meanwhile, was facing his own trials. During both yellow fever epidemics of 1793 and 1797 his approach to the practice of medicine—abundant purging or bloodletting—had come into question. Among the ringleaders was Alexander Hamilton, who, along with his wife, had suffered cases of yellow fever during 1793. Bolstered by Dr. Edward Stevens, his personal physician, who advocated cold baths, quinine water, and Madeira as the best fix for the affliction, Hamilton took it upon himself to discredit Rush both as a misguided friend of liberty and as a wrongheaded, even dangerous physician. In communications to Rush's College of Physicians and to the Philadelphia press, Hamilton drew lurid pictures of Rush's deadly bloodlettings.[39]

Hamilton was joined by William Cobbett of *Porcupine's Gazette*. Cobbett, a master at dismantling icons of liberty in this early phase of his long career, took especial delight in destroying Rush. Among his victims had already been Joseph Priestley, James Madison, Lafayette, Thomas Jefferson, Thomas Paine, and even Benjamin Franklin. But Cobbett developed an obsession with Rush, who responded in kind. As a signer of the Declaration of Independence, a leader in the Continental Congress, a founder of Pennsylvania educational institutions, a correspondent with the intelligentsia of the Western world, and America's most respected physician, Rush was just the kind of pedestal Cobbett liked to topple. And in that Rush harbored a most colossal ego, he made himself a magnetic target—not only for Cobbett, but also for other enemies of liberty in America.

Rush's problems began with his lavish bloodletting during the epidemic of 1793. But he survived due to the self-promotion of his radical cure in an internationally reprinted essay titled *An Account of the Bilious Remitting Yellow Fever, as it Appeared in the City of Philadelphia, in the Year 1793* (1794) and through Mathew Carey's even more widely published and translated *Short Account of the Malignant Fever Lately Prevalent in Philadelphia* (1793). As these pamphlets were translated and reprinted throughout the world in cheap popular editions, Philadelphia developed a most unenviable reputation. Rush became something of a menacing celebrity.[40]

He might have salvaged his reputation had he not chosen to speak out on the subject of liberty at a most inauspicious occasion and time. On December 17, 1796, at the American Philosophical Society's eulogium to honor its late president David Rittenhouse, Rush made a surprise announcement. At First Presbyterian Church in Philadelphia in front of an audience consisting of President George Washington, Thomas Jefferson, members of the Senate and House of Representatives, Supreme Court justices, Pennsylvania officers, Philadelphia elected officials, the College of Physicians, the faculty of the University of Pennsylvania, and the membership of the society, Rush declaimed for an hour on Rittenhouse's genius, virtues, wisdom, and piety. But as he referred approvingly to Rittenhouse's love of liberty, he continued to declare himself a lifelong devotee of liberty and republicanism. In one particularly florid display he said: "Be just, and loose the bands of the African slave. Be wise, and render war odious to our country. Be free, by assuming a national character and name, and be greatly happy, by erecting a barrier against the corruptions in morals, government, and religion, which now pervade all the nations of Europe." Like a lightning rod in a thunderstorm, Rush drew upon himself all of the growing opposition to the forces of liberty. According to Cobbett's view Rush was grandstanding his own ideas, since Rittenhouse had never done anything worthwhile for anyone: "The remorseless Dr. Rush shall bleed me till I am white as this paper before I'll allow that this [hyperbolic eulogium] was doing good to mankind."[41]

From that moment forward Rush fell under an avalanche of attack from every quarter. When Rush applied his purges and bloodlettings during the yellow fever epidemic of 1797 with a fervor equal to 1793, John Fenno of the *Gazette of the United States* called his treatments a "lunatic system of medicine." Cobbett, of course, went further to criticize Rush's mercury purges that accompanied bloodletting:

> Dr. Rush in that emphatical style which is peculiar to himself, calls mercury "the Samson of medicine." In his hands and in those of his partisans, it may, indeed, be justly compared to Samson; for I verily believe they have slain more Americans with it, than ever Samson slew of the Philistines. The Israelite slew his thousands, but the Rushites have slain their tens of thousands.

Insult followed insult throughout the fever season of September and October: "The times are ominous indeed, / When quack to quack cries, purge and bleed."[42]

The anti-Rush campaign devastated his reputation and career. By the end of the 1797 epidemic his medical practice in Philadelphia was destroyed. Nearly destitute, Rush cast about for a means of livelihood. First he hoped to practice medicine elsewhere and even received a tentative offer to become Chair of the Practice of Medicine at Columbia College in New York City. Before the appointment could be made, however, Alexander Hamilton learned of the plan and quashed it. When word of the scheme was initially leaked in Philadelphia with not a little praise for Rush's great value to American society, Cobbett found ways to compare the physician's usefulness to the world: "And so is a mosquito, a horse-leach, a ferret, a pole-cat, a weazel: for these are all bleeders, and understand their business full as well as Dr. Rush does his."[43]

Rush was convinced that his career as a physician had just been torn from him, not because of medical reasons, but due only to his adherence to liberty: "My remedies for yellow fever would have met no opposition this year had I not signed the Declaration of Independence and latterly declared myself a Republican in the *Eulogium* upon Mr. Rittenhouse." But it was in an odd way due to Rittenhouse's death that he finally found a salvation. Rittenhouse had been at the time of his death director of the United States Mint. For services in defense of Hamilton's treasury program, Elias Boudinot, a powerful New Jersey congressman, was appointed to the post. Boudinot also just happened to be the uncle of Rush's wife. When treasurer of the Mint, Dr. Nicholas Way, died in office in 1797, Boudinot proposed Rush for the position. Although Rush had outspokenly promoted Thomas Jefferson over John Adams in 1796 and even though Abigail Adams distrusted the radical doctor, Adams approved Rush's appointment. To Abigail Adams he wrote, "We must put up with the vagaries of our flighty friend."[44]

Rush would remain treasurer of the United States Mint until his death in 1813. The position from the beginning was primarily a retirement sinecure that permitted him to attempt to vindicate his record both as a physician and as a friend of liberty. Before the end of 1797 he had filed a libel suit against William Cobbett for damages to his medical reputation and career. When the suit finally came to court in 1799 Cobbett fled to the safety of New York City. Having abused and defamed nearly every living being in Philadelphia and Pennsylvania, it was not surprising that the jury should find the absent editor guilty and recommend an award of $5,000 in damages.

Despite the verdict, Cobbett continued his single-minded mission to destroy Rush. Between February and May 1800, when he returned to England, Cobbett issued repeated salvos in a new publication titled *Rush-Light,* devoted soley to the discrediting of Benjamin Rush. Not only did he not pay Rush the $5,000 ordered by the Pennsylvania courts, he had his New York admirers raise the funds to pay a negotiated settlement and arrange a deal to transfer Cobbett's property and interests to John Ward Fenno at a profit of $10,000.[45]

When the American reign of terror in 1798 was followed by yet another season of yellow fever, Benjamin Rush was already a broken man. From his lowly post at the U. S. Mint he could only look on weakly and sadly as he witnessed the destruction of so many careers and reputations: Joseph Priestley, Thomas Cooper, James Callender, John Daly Burk, Philip Freneau, Hugh Henry Brackenridge, Matthew Lyon, as well as French and St. Domingan refugees. As one who favored the oppressed throughout his long life, Rush could only lament the state of the nation in 1798.

Given his lifelong association with Benjamin Franklin and with Franklin's grandson, Benjamin Franklin Bache, Rush was surely saddened in the summer of 1798 to see the grandson's pathetic circumstances. Under indictment, almost bankrupt, his friends and associates under fire, and his principles under attack, Bache suffered a malady that Rush would eventually classify in his famous psychiatric treatise *Medical Inquiries and Observations on the Diseases of the Mind* (1812). Having virtually no place to turn, Bache became almost suicidal.

As the yellow fever epidemic spread across Philadelphia, a sorely depressed Bache wrote to his father on September 2 that he would have to continue the *Aurora* through the deadly fever season because his finances were so bad. In the throes of financial ruin he wrote, "Is it not heartrending that the laboring poor should almost exclusively be the victims of the disease." They could not flee the city. To make matters worse, Margaret Bache went into labor on that same day and was delivered of a baby boy on the morning of September 3.

"The Times: A Political Portrait," shows Benjamin Franklin Bache being trampled by American soldiers commanded by George Washington as a dog expresses counterrevolutionary opinion on Bache's paper, The Aurora.

Even before the boy could be named, Bache became ill with yellow fever. The first symptoms occurred on September 5. Despite his long friendship with Rush, Bache called for a French doctor and followed the West Indian prescription for treating the malady—cool baths, quinine, and mineral waters. Only Margaret was there to care for him. She wrestled him in and out of a tub that leaked and soaked the surrounding floors.

On September 7 Bache oversaw the publication of another issue of the *Aurora* and wrote a will leaving his property entirely to Margaret, confident that "she will bestow on our dear Children a suitable and enlightened Education, such as shall be worthy of us, and advantageous to themselves and render them virtuous, generous, and attached to the immutable principles of Civil Liberty." Three days of fever-induced madness followed. In his last moments of consciousness, Bache valiantly continued his mission to the world. Spared the radical bleeding and purging Rush would have applied, he was able to dictate a "confidential memorandum." Having revealed his financial predicament to Tench Coxe,

Philadelphia businessman and contributor to the *Aurora,* Bache used his last bit of energy to implore Coxe to do whatever might be necessary to preserve the *Aurora* for the benefit of his "family, his country and mankind." Victim of the horrible fever and his own pride, he was also, like so many of those who fell before the guillotine in that other terror, a martyr for liberty.[46]

CHAPTER 15

American Liberators As Outcasts

LIBERTY AND PEACE

If Joel Barlow assisted Robert Fulton in giving the world new engines of war—ostensibly in the name of liberty—he also participated in efforts to find a lasting peace wherein liberty would be secure. Unlike Fulton, who lost sight of ideological principles, Barlow, energized by Thomas Paine, Joseph Priestley, and Mary Wollstonecraft, chased after a platonic conception of liberty until his death in 1812. The wealthy and cultured Barlow never wavered from his goal of having liberty reign over the earth.

He undertook endless initiatives to match up American diplomats and private citizens with the right bureaucrat or officer to negotiate deals that might promote his hopes for liberty. Outside the political mainstream, he operated with a naïveté derived almost wholly from idealism. His *Advice to the Privileged Orders* (1792), his *Conspiracy of Kings* (1792), and his major literary work, *The Columbiad* (1805) emerged from such a wellspring. His principles drove him to be a lifelong defender of Thomas Paine, an admirer of discredited American minister James Monroe, and a champion of Robert Fulton's many schemes. The desire to be of service to America led him to respond to the plea of Yale classmate David Humphreys in 1795 to travel to Algiers as American consul and secure freedom for American prisoners held by the "Barbary" states of Africa.

Barlow's ideals also made him one of the most misunderstood and little appreciated figures in American history. After he returned from almost a year's residence in Algeria in September 1797, Barlow saw a changed world in France. Moving immediately to pursue his liberating ideals in the world of the French Directory, he little knew nor understood the new clashes of ideology and politics that were occurring in his idealized America during the administration of President John Adams. James Monroe had been recalled and Charles Pinckney, new minister to France, had arrived, to be followed by John Marshall and Elbridge Gerry, the other two members of the American delegation to negotiate peace with France.

When the American delegation was spurned by Foreign Minister Talleyrand, Barlow wrote a detailed analysis of America's welfare abroad. He set his observations in a confidential letter addressed to his brother-in-law, Abraham Baldwin, a powerful congressman from Georgia, but also a fellow native of Connecticut and graduate of Yale. In the letter Barlow outlined a history of America's dealings with France from the onset of the French Revolution. Although he marked the letter confidential, he also sent a copy through William Lee, a trusted friend, to be delivered personally to Vice President Thomas Jefferson.

From the opening moments of the French Revolution, Barlow wrote, the French people and government venerated the republican model established by the United States. George Washington's image and Thomas Jefferson's diplomacy had united the two great republics. Gouverneur Morris, Jefferson's successor as American minister to France, undermined the Franco-American alliance with his every action. While James Monroe mended some of the fences, his sudden recall combined with Jay's Treaty between England and the United States sent a signal that the republican alliance was threatened or perhaps broken. And John Adams's actions since he became president served only to make matters worse. Openly critical of the French and ridiculing their Revolution as the work of "pirates and plunderers," Adams made rapprochement impossible. Barlow urged Baldwin and Jefferson to work for the appointment of a Monroe or a Madison to treat with France and wondered why Congress had not repudiated Adams, given his suicidal words on the subject of France, with "an order to send him to the Mad-house."[1]

Then, in the absence of an official American delegation to France following the recall of Pinckney, Marshall, and Gerry, Barlow assisted as a private citizen in negotiating peace. During the lull in which there was no official American presence in France, Joel Barlow and Robert Fulton worked with other Americans abroad to achieve one of the greatest diplomatic feats of American history. George Logan, Quaker physician and descendant of James Logan, William Penn's secretary, arrived in Paris in August 1798 prepared to resolve the disagreements between France and the United States. Wealthy master of Stenton, one of colonial America's grandest private homes, Logan was bent on a course equal in daring to those of Barlow, Paine, Wollstonecraft, de Staël, Tate, Tone, and Fulton.

Brought up at Stenton on the edge of Germantown, Logan had many advantages in his upbringing. At age fourteen his early training in a Philadelphia Friends school was advanced when he was sent to England to enter the Friends school at Worcester. Three years later he returned to Philadelphia and was apprenticed to a Quaker merchant from Jamaica. After five years of work, he happily headed back across the Atlantic to Edinburgh, where he studied medicine under the world's most renowned physicians, scientists, and philosophers—the same folk who trained Benjamin Rush and many other talented Philadelphia physicians.

Logan spent three years at Edinburgh at the feet of Joseph Black and William Cullen. He became the first American to be elected president of the university's Medical Society in 1779. His cosmopolitan education was completed when he traveled in the summer of 1779 to Paris to spend time with Benjamin Franklin and to evaluate medical sciences in France. By the time he left Franklin in April 1780, he had carefully stowed away much of his Quaker pacifism and had become a fairly strident American patriot. He not only favored American independence, but

"Liberty . . . Giving Support to the Bald Eagle" (1796). Liberty treads over tyranny and sustains America (the eagle) even as the nation is under fire (lightning striking Boston in the right background).

also was slowly developing into one of America's most ardent friends of liberty and world revolution.[2]

At the conclusion of the American Revolution, Logan was back in America, where he forswore the practice of medicine for the life of a farmer at Stenton. In 1781 his economic and social success was assured when he married Deborah Norris, daughter of one of the wealthiest families in Philadelphia. Deborah's own considerable schooling under the tutelage of Anthony Benezet prepared her to become a strong partner and one of Philadelphia's most productive early historians. While Logan marched off across the world, Deborah turned Stenton into a salon for America's foremost friends of liberty.[3]

During the 1780s the Logans' interest in politics and public service grew, especially under Benjamin Franklin's influence. Franklin, it seems, encouraged them to read the great French philosophers and economists. Logan also served in the Pennsylvania Assembly, where Franklin presided as president and bespoke principles of liberty in government and society. Through his own reading and reflection, Logan discovered the idea of benevolence as the proper guiding rule for human society. He concluded that true benevolence was "a practicable principle" for the foundation of real and lasting happiness among individuals and in states."[4]

Following the ratification of the U.S. Constitution and the placement of the nation's capital in Philadelphia, Logan became a sharp critic of the encroaching federal government, Hamiltonian fiscal policies, and what he considered Washington's regal style. Deborah Logan expanded the use of Stenton as a salon for thoughtful friends of liberty; David Rittenhouse, Alexander James Dallas, Benjamin Franklin Bache, Thomas Jefferson, and many others found the place a comfortable setting for the discussion of philosophy and politics. From these discussions Logan penned increasingly radical essays and pamphlets on the importance of liberty. He presciently feared that some of the most fundamental principles of the American Revolution were being compromised:

> Americans have submitted to a second revolution, by which they have bartered their domestic rights, liberty, and equality for the energy of government and the etiquette of a court. After having wrested the sceptre from the hand of the British tyrant, they have suffered it to be assumed by a monied aristocracy, where it will be found more oppressive and injurious to the people.[5]

Like a Jeremiah witnessing a people turning against their basic religion, Logan cried for reformation and a return to the principles of liberty.

It was only a logical extension of his drift toward republicanism that Logan should become a supporter of the French Revolution. He was quick to support Edmond Genet in 1793, and he became one of the few American members of Genet's Philadelphia-based *Société francaise des amis de la liberté et de l'égalité*. Deborah Logan also found the fiery Frenchman quite compelling as he sat discoursing for hours on the grounds at Stenton. During the yellow fever epidemic of that year, George Logan was one of the first American physicians to side with French and West Indian doctors in condemning Benjamin Rush's drastic treatments for afflicted individuals. When democratic societies formed in Philadelphia, Logan helped draft an approving letter to the National Convention in France, but demurred when the Philadelphia society denounced whiskey rebels in western Pennsylvania. His close correspondence with James Monroe on matters in France showed in one of Monroe's letters to Logan, providing ammunition for the minister's sudden recall by Washington.[6]

While the Washington administration treated the deposed Monroe as an outcast, Logan organized a great testimonial dinner at Oeller's Hotel in Philadelphia —in the shadow of Congress Hall. During Monroe's extended visit to Stenton, Logan brought him together with American friends of liberty and with refugees from France, Ireland, England, and Russia to discuss the fate of liberty in France and elsewhere around the world. Increasingly fired up by Jefferson, Monroe, and figures such as as Justus Erich Bollman (Lafayette's liberator from an Austrian prison), Irish radical James Napper Tandy, and Polish liberator Tadeusz Kósciuszko, Logan began to envision world revolution. Frustrated further by the bumbling diplomacy of John Adams, Logan by the spring of 1798 was ready to pursue what the American government seemed incapable of achieving—a treaty of peace with France, the world's other land of liberty.

On May 12, 1798, in the Columbian Wigwam of the Philadelphia Tammany Society, Logan pronounced his views in a speech titled "The Natural and Social Order of the World." In an atmosphere where the Adams administration was preparing for war against France, Logan decried all wars as the follies of national magistrates—whether kings or presidents. Wars encroached on liberties and freedom; indeed, those who emigrated to America from Europe came to be free of debilitating wars. The American Revolution was fought to free the American colonies from European wars and to secure peace and liberty for all Americans. Without saying so directly, Logan condemned the course Adams was taking, and his audience certainly understood. They boisterously cheered his words and toasted Logan, the glorious French Revolution, and the ultimate triumph of liberty in America.

Elated with his popularity and sure of his views, Logan made final preparations to undertake a one-person mission to France. Thomas Jefferson provided him with a letter of introduction, certifying that he derived from "one of the most ancient and respectable families of the said commonwealth [of Pennsylvania], of independent fortune, good morals, irreproachable conduct, and true civism." Gov. Thomas McKean provided him a certificate of citizenship. Philippe-André Joseph de Letombe, French minister in Philadelphia, gave him two critical letters of introduction, one addressed to Philippe-Antoine Merlin, head of the French Directory, and the other to Talleyrand. Armed with these impressive credentials, Logan on June 12 boarded the *Iris* in Philadelphia headed for France—just one week prior to the passage of the first of the alien and sedition acts. Fearful that ill-fortune might prevent his return, he turned over all of his property and affairs to his trusted partner Deborah.

Logan's activities became known almost from the moment the *Iris* landed in Hamburg. It so happened that Lafayette, recently released from his Austrian imprisonment, was in Hamburg. Logan directly visited the hero of the American Revolution to ask his assistance in securing a passport to travel into France, and Lafayette undoubtedly let it be known that Logan was there and that he carried official letters to the Directory, since this information quickly filtered to William Vans Murray, American minister in Holland. Conspiring with John Quincy Adams, American minister to Germany, Murray sent a secret agent after Logan. Somehow the agent found Logan and ascertained both the contents and authorship of the secret documents. Shocked that one of them was from the vice president of the United States, Murray ordered Dutch authorities at Rotterdam to arrest Logan. John Quincy Adams heartily endorsed the stern measures, describing Logan's mission as "the gauntlet of civil war" in the United States.

When Logan arrived in Paris on August 7, unaware that he was under American surveillance, he headed for Joel Barlow's residence. There he encountered Robert Fulton, Fulwar Skipwith, the American consul general, and Nathaniel Cutting, American consul at Le Havre. There was Tadeusz Kościuszko, who recently had been Logan's guest at Stenton and who was traveling under the name of Thomas Kannberg. Kościuszko also was playing the role of world peacemaker. With the blessings of this tiny colony of American-inspired friends of liberty, Logan set off for a fateful meeting with Foreign Minister Talleyrand.

Talleyrand at first parried with Logan and revealed little about his intentions with respect to the Quaker visitor, who he undoubtedly had met in Philadelphia. He tried to dissuade Logan from meeting Merlin de Douai, the head of the French Directory. But recognizing the Philadelphian's insistence and perhaps not wishing to nudge America any further in the direction of alliance with Britain, Talleyrand acceded to Logan's demands.

Those were threefold: (1) that the French embargo against American shipping be ended; (2) that the hundreds of American seamen imprisoned in France be released; and (3) that an American minister be received to restore the Franco-American alliance. Although Talleyrand revealed nothing in this first meeting, he sent his chief aide, Antoine La Foret, to Logan two days later with the incredible word "that everything will be done according to our wishes."

The astonished Logan immediately summoned Fulwar Skipwith to make sure that everything was put in writing. Knowing of Talleyrand's reputation for deceit, Logan continued his brash course of meeting directly with every crucial official in the French government. He met with Merlin, who listened cordially to his descriptions of conditions in America and the desire of Americans to restore unity with the world's other great republic. Merlin then held a dinner in Logan's honor and invited the principal heads of the French government. A round of toasts honored "The Republic of France," "The Batavian Republic," and "The Cisalpine Republic." Logan, filled with emotion, leaped to his feet and toasted "The United States of America, and a speedy restoration of amity between them and France." Merlin demanded that this last toast should instead be his. And as

George Logan (c. 1798). Citizen ambassador for world peace; discredited victim of partisan politics.

Logan left from this triumphal fete, he carried with him official copies of the decrees ending the embargo and freeing American seamen. When Paris newspapers reported the dinner the following day, they proclaimed Logan a new American hero. *"Le brave Logan,"* they announced. Like Benjamin Franklin twenty years earlier, Logan became an instant national icon. His plain dress and antiwar testimonials fit perfectly one of the American stereotypes beloved by the French public. Over a period of three weeks Barlow and Fulton presented him at every conceivable gathering as the hero of the hour—at the Louvre, the Jardin des Plantes, the National Institute, the Council of Five Hundred, the Council of Ancients, and one of Helen Maria Williams's renowned dinner parties. Logan's quiet, modest manner fit him perfectly for the role of peacemaker. When he left Paris on August 29 for Bordeaux and passage back to the United States he was one of the best-known Americans in Europe.[7]

LIBERTY AND POLITICAL ORDER

As George Logan was making his way back to the United States to announce peace between the two republics, events in the United States were threatening to undermine his achievements. At the apex of Logan's success, Benjamin Franklin Bache was entering his final pathetic days. Benjamin Rush had lost his credibility as a medical practitioner and reformer. Naysayers against the Adams administration had come under indictment. And the Alien and Sedition Acts had driven out an entire generation of immigrants who had come to America to find freedom.

While Logan awaited his ship at Bordeaux writing letters to Merlin, Talleyrand, Barlow, and Fulton, extolling the rediscovered virtues of the American and French Revolutions, Deborah Logan, back at Stenton, was facing a test by fire. Though she had anticipated difficult times during Logan's absence, she had not imagined the intensity that actually occurred. "I could not help being appalled with . . . the clamour which would be raised upon his departure," she noted. "As soon as his committee of surveillance [Adams officials] missed their charge [Logan], there was a prodigious stir in the city; they looked upon each other with blank faces, as having suffered an adroit enemy to escape their vigilance." Among the members of the "committee" was none other than Benjamin Rush himself, who years later acknowledged his involvement to Logan. Deborah Logan recalled, "with some circumstances that I suppress because they might look as if I remembered what is best forgotten."

Within a few days after Logan's departure on the *Iris,* Deborah Logan read in Andrew Brown's *Philadelphia Gazette,*

> There cannot be the least questions but the Doctor, from his inordinate love of French liberty, and hatred to the sacred constitution of the United States, has gone to the French directory, fraught with intelligence of the most dangerous tendency to this country. . . . For can any sensible man hesitate to suspect that his infernal design can be anything less, than the introduction of a French army, to teach us the genuine value of true & essential liberty by reorganizing our government, through the brutal operation of the bayonet and guillotine. Let every American now gird on his sword. The times are not only critical, but the secret of the Junto is out.

These sentiments combined with the passage of the Alien and Sedition Acts stirred Deborah Logan's fears of retaliation against Logan upon his return.[8]

Throughout Logan's absence, Stenton was under constant surveillance. Deborah Logan recalled years later, "I experienced what it was to lay under the ban of political excommunication myself; for it was said that those would be marked who should be seen to enter our gates." Friends of liberty nevertheless continued to call: Benjamin Franklin Bache, John Vaughan, and even Vice President Thomas Jefferson. Jefferson, indeed, urged her "to evince my thorough consciousness of his [Logan's] innocence and honour by showing myself in Philadelphia as one not afraid nor ashamed to meet the public eye." But even Jefferson sought to "elude the curiosity of his spies" by coming to Stenton late in the day and by taking "a circuitous route by the Falls of Schuylkill" and entering a back gate on York Road. When Jefferson's visits became known, both he and Deborah Logan were slandered by hostile press. William Cobbett charged that Jefferson remained for three days and then asked, "*Quere:* What did he do there? Was it to arrange the Doctor's valuable manuscripts?"[9]

One curious comfort for Deborah Logan during the months of her husband's absence was a side effect of the yellow fever epidemic in Philadelphia. In that the epidemic was largely confined to the city itself, hundreds of people fled to the villages of Roxborough, Germantown, and beyond to avoid the plague. That August and September, she had more than twenty people living at Stenton, all to be cared for.

Entertaining and nursing sick relatives did not relieve the political pressure on Deborah Logan concerning her husband's activities in France, however. Benjamin Franklin Bache during his last days defended Logan's mission, even as William Cobbett described it as treasonous. In an effort to relieve some of the tensions, Deborah supplied friendly editors with an early letter from Logan revealing the success of his efforts. Written from Bordeaux on September 9—a day prior to Bache's death—Logan wrote,

> I have the pleasure to inform you that I embark this day . . . for Philadelphia, and shall bring with me dispatches for our

government, calculated to restore that harmony, the loss of which has been so sensibly felt by both countries. All American vessels in the harbours of France have been released, all American prisoners have been set at liberty; and the most positive assurances have been made that France is ready to enter on a treaty for the amicable accommodation of all matters in dispute.

Not only were these matters resolved, Logan concluded, but also "the appearance of a reconciliation between the two republics affords the highest satisfaction to all classes of citizens in this country." [10]

But what appeared to friends of liberty as the greatest conceivable news looked to others like treason. The remorseless William Cobbett led the charges against Logan. Cobbett thought Logan's letter was clear evidence that some so-called "patriots" were "willing to sacrifice the liberty of their country, to the insidious designs of an unprincipled foreign foe." And when Logan's ship, the *Perseverance,* arrived in Philadelphia, Cobbett continued his sarcastic attack: "He is come! He is come!! He is come!!! ENVOY LOGAN, THE PEACEMAKER, is come. . . . It is reported that he is to make his public entry this afternoon, bearing in his hand an <u>Olive Branch</u>, and accompanied by his secretary of Legation." [11]

When Logan arrived in early November, he made his way quickly and quietly to Germantown for a happy reunion with Deborah and his family. Pausing only for the night, he rushed the next morning toward Trenton, New Jersey, where government offices had been temporarily moved during the yellow fever epidemic. At Bristol he ran into Charles Cotesworth Pinckney, one of the victims of the abortive XYZ mission. Recently named major general in the army being formed to battle France, Pinckney was on his way to Trenton for a council of war when his carriage broke down. Pinckney treated Logan courteously, but when Logan offered the veteran of the Revolution a ride to Trenton, Pinckney diplomatically declined. [12]

Arriving at Trenton alone, Logan searched at once for the sometimes cantankerous Secretary of State Timothy Pickering, who was deeply involved at that moment with Alexander Hamilton in planning an attack on Spanish fortifications in Louisiana and Florida. Pickering was chagrined to see Logan. Although they had long worked together to improve American agriculture, Pickering tossed aside the dispatches presented by Logan after months of work at his own expense. Pickering's only comment was that he had already seen another set brought by messenger on a faster ship. As Logan produced another dispatch Pickering had not seen, the secretary began to deride Logan's foolish idealism at a moment when war was imminent. Showing Logan to the door, Pickering sternly said, "Sir, it is my duty to inform you that the government does not thank you for what you have done." [13]

Angered by the shabby treatment accorded him, Logan went to Philadelphia, where George Washington had just arrived on November 13 to take charge of America's armed forces. Lodged at Rosanna White's boarding house, Washington, too, was planning American military strategies when Logan arrived. Somehow he and Rev. Robert Blackwell, rector of St. Peter's in Philadelphia, received a private hearing with the heroic general. From the moment Washington entered the room, however, it was clear that he had little time or patience in dealing with Logan. Refusing to shake what was later described as Logan's "polluted hand" and addressing his conversation solely toward Blackwell, Washington persisted in avoiding Logan (even to the point of not mentioning him by name in a memorandum summarizing the meeting).

Refusing to be shunted aside by the former president who also in the past had spent time at Stenton, Logan invited Washington to move his quarters to Stenton. The persistent Quaker also began extending greetings from Lafayette, from Merlin, and from others in France who still idolized the living American icon. Washington seemed unmoved until Logan began to recount the glorious results of his visits in France. The French government and people, Logan reported, wanted peace and unity between the world's two great republics. At this point, Washington's face reddened and, with a loud and angry voice, he growled that if France wanted peace, she would have to repeal her obnoxious decrees against America. Despite Logan's strenuous protests that such was the effect of the dispatches he brought from the Directory, Washington persisted in his argument that "the spirit of this country would never suffer itself to be injured with impunity by any nation under the sun." Virtually declaring war on France, he also suddenly ordered an end to the uncomfortable interview.

Devastated that all ears seemed closed to him, Logan next placed his hopes in persuading President Adams that France was ready to resolve misunderstandings with America. Two weeks after meeting with Washington, Adams arrived in Philadelphia from Massachusetts and held a long, somewhat odd meeting with Logan. Adams was, at that moment, in trouble on nearly every front—foreign, domestic, and even within the confines of his own cabinet, a group of rebellious officers he had inherited directly from George Washington. Tending to distrust everyone, he frequently recoiled from those who actively attempted to sway his opinions. And what was true generally was borne out in the case of Logan. Adams listened carefully to Logan's argument that France was ready to receive an American minister. At that point Adams rose and blurted out, "Yes, I suppose if I were to send Mr. Madison or Mr. Giles or Dr. Logan, they would receive either of *them*. But I'll do no such thing; I'll send whom I please." Logan responded confidently, "And whoever you do please to send will be received." [14]

Clearly Adams neither believed nor trusted Logan. Despite other direct assurances from William Vans Murray, Elbridge Gerry, Paris merchant Richard Codman, and even his own son John Quincy that the Logan report was accurate, Adams persisted in a belief that Logan had made a secret deal or had been duped by Talleyrand. On December 8 Adams stood before Congress flanked by uniformed Generals Washington, Hamilton, and Pinckney on one side and by the British and Portuguese ministers on the other. He read a speech drafted by Pickering and Oliver Wolcott, Hamilton's faithful followers, arguing that France had given no indication of acceding to American demands. Preparations for war would continue until France agreed to negotiate on honorable terms. [15]

Not only did Adams not believe Logan's advice or that of his ministers abroad, he also believed that the Quaker peacemaker had committed an offense proscribed by the Alien and Sedition Acts. On December 12 in his message to the U.S. Senate, he wrote:

> Although the officious interference of individuals without public character or authority is not entitled to any credit, yet it deserves to be considered whether that temerity and impertinence of individuals affecting to interfere in public affairs between France and the United States, whether by their secret correspondence or otherwise, and intended to impose upon the people and separate them from their government, ought not to be inquired into and corrected.[16]

By urging Congressional consideration of Logan's mission to France, Adams now provoked another public debate about liberty and political order.

What resulted in the space of just six weeks was the enactment of one of the most curious laws in the annals of American history: a law providing for the imprisonment of any citizen who without the permission of the United States government should "directly or indirectly, commence or carry on any verbal or written correspondence or intercourse with any foreign government, or any officer or agent thereof, relating to any dispute or controversy between any foreign government and the United States, with an intent to influence the measures or conduct of the government having disputes or controversies with the United States." Introduced by Roger Griswold on December 26 in the House of Representatives, the bill became law on January 30, 1799, with the signature of President Adams. "The Logan Act" oddly and capriciously condemned forever goodwill efforts on the part of private citizens. Rarely in human history had a nation turned itself so persistently and blindly against the possibilities of honest hope.

CHAPTER 16

Liberty Abolished in America

ANTI-LIBERATING MANIA

By January 30, 1799, it had become clear that the pursuit of liberty, as it had been defined from the time of the American Revolution until the convulsions of the 1790s, was systematically being abolished in the United States. Everywhere one might look, friends of liberty were being challenged, arrested, expelled from seats of government and from America itself. No one who had associated him- or herself with the cause of liberty escaped the national upheaval that suddenly labeled friends of liberty as enemies of America.

Nowhere was the trend more evident than in the halls of Congress where the Logan Act was bitterly debated. From the day Roger Griswold introduced the bill until its passage by the U.S. Senate, it was clear that some form of madness had seized the Congress and the American body politic. Griswold had already silenced Matthew "Spitting" Lyon, who at the time was confined in federal prison for expressing his views on President Adams's foreign policy. In the process of deliberating the Logan Act other political careers became launched or forever marred. Roger Griswold, Harrison Gray Otis, and Robert Goodloe Harper exhibited forms of behavior for which they never would be forgiven. Albert Gallatin, Nathaniel Macon, and Abraham Baldwin valiantly attempted to protect the nation's fragile seedling of liberty, but during the course of a month of debate, reputations were established or trashed with abandon.[1]

Immediate victims of the massacre included, of course, George Logan. Despite his publication of a candid letter addressed "To the Citizens of the United States" on January 12, 1799, seeking "to vindicate myself with a short statement of facts," his symbolic trial and judgment by Congress consigned his creative pursuit of liberty to a dark column in American history. "Convinced that, upon the strictest examination, my conduct whilst in Europe will be found neither dishonourable to myself nor injurious to my country," he was stunned by the verdict of Congress. Neither defanged nor destroyed, however, Logan lived to test the Logan Act himself again. But he would not see it repealed.[2]

Another victim was Joel Barlow. His works in promoting the glories of the American Revolution, the cause of liberty throughout Europe, and the interests of

American business and government in Europe and even Africa, he thought, gave him a special place as an honored statesman. As a consequence, he shared his views liberally in letters to his vast network of fellow Yale graduates. His 1798 letter to brother-in-law Abraham Baldwin and its copy to Thomas Jefferson had been the ammunition used by Matthew Lyon to discredit John Adams and to test the recently passed Alien and Sedition Acts.

All of the controversy surrounding the publication of that letter and the subsequent conviction of Lyon began to transform Barlow from heroic American ambassador to a potentially dangerous villain. The political press skewered Barlow: A Boston paper charged that the letter was written in Talleyrand's office while the "arch apostate, sat at the elbow of the duped American and dictated every word." Barlow's act was treasonable "compared with which that of Judas Iscariot is but a foible." A New York paper tapped into the growing American feeling that "the Gallic revolution destroyed the character of Barlow's mind, and his residence in, or near, the French republic has rendered him a traitor to his country, and a blasphemer of his God."

That Barlow had somehow pierced the very essence of what America was about is evidenced by the fact that some of his closest and dearest allies—even his confidants among the Hartford Wits—turned on him as well. Richard Alsop, Yale classmate, constant friend, and Barlow's collaborator on *The Anarchiad,* used their shared love of poetry to satirize Barlow's revolutionary activities:

> His wandering wits, and cunning call'd in,
> Writes o're "his book" to Parson Baldwin . . .
> What eye can trace this Wisdom's son,—
> This "Jack-at-all-trades, good at none,"
> This ever-changing, Proteus mind,—
> In all his turns, thro' every wind;
> From telling sinners where they go to,
> To speculations in Scioto, . . .
> From morals pure, and manners plain,
> To herding with Monroe and Paine,
> From feeding on his country's bread,
> To aping X, and Y, and Z[ed],
> From preaching Christ, to Age of Reason,
> From writing psalms, to writing treason.

Such public charges were replicated more harshly in private among the Yale alumni. Classmate and friend James Watson, U.S. Senator from New York, responded to one of Barlow's letters that he should mind his own business. Sending a copy of the letter to another classmate, Oliver Wolcott, Watson wrote, "Although there are few men I have loved so much, there are few whose present conduct I detest more."[3]

Something had happened to separate individuals whose lives had once been so closely intertwined intellectually, philosophically, and even spiritually. What it was, was best described by another of Barlow's Yale classmates and close friends, Noah Webster. Their careers had in many ways been remarkably similar. But by November 16, 1798, when Webster sat to write a letter to Barlow about the contents of the famous letter to Abraham Baldwin, the budding lexicographer told all. Webster found the letter shocking not only to Americans, "but especially among your particular friends who have been intimately acquainted with you from your youth." Webster wrote that "as I know your character better than many of my countrymen, I am better entitled to comment freely on your opinions."

In a letter sent both privately and published widely, Webster came immediately to the point:

> You are so fundamentally wrong in all the principles which regard the French Revolution and the connection of the United States with France that to discuss your whole theory would be to discuss all the important questions in religion and government. . . . Indeed, fanaticism alone can have blinded you, for had not your intellectual powers been warped by some strong passions, your own natural sense would have kept your opinions more correct.

Not only was Barlow wrong in his opinions, he had, according to Webster, been seized by some demon that caused him not to see correctly. Barlow, Webster thought, had become a captive of the revolutionary distemper that held France in thraldom.

Having dismissed Barlow as mentally disordered, Webster proceeded to rewrite the story of American and French relations and of their revolutions. France, instead of helping America win its revolution, actually had retarded independence by increasing British resolve. But to make matters worse, since 1778, when Benjamin Franklin negotiated the Franco-American alliance, France's attitude toward America and the rest of the world had undergone an alarming, fundamental change. Wrote Webster, "We observe the French government professes to be pursuing liberty while it is extending its territories." France, in Webster's view, was using the bible of liberty, not to free the peoples of the earth, but rather to invite "insurrection in all countries by promising to assist the people against the government." That France was "making no discrimination between despotic and free governments" was evidenced by the fact that "they labored as zealously to effect a revolution in the United States and to overthrow the government of the people's choice as to subvert any monarchy or aristocracy in Europe."

According to Webster, French efforts to overthrow America's government began with the arrival of Citizen Genet in 1793 and continued without cessation for six years. Webster had a special characterization for the new and insidious French form of subversion:

"Preparation for War to Defend Commerce" (1798). A Philadelphia scene in which warmongers and shipbuilders prepare for war with France.

> It is this principle, Mr. Barlow, of secretly and silently under-
> mining the government of a foreign nation, now pushed with
> unwearied zeal by the French, against which we set our faces
> like a flint. It is a principle more dangerous to society than war,
> famine, and pestilence.

The French, Webster believed, "have devised a new mode of extending this practice, a mode for unhinging moral and religious principles and for arming subjects
against government, which despotic princes never invented." As a republic, without the courtesies of nobility, "the French policy creeps in the darkness of midnight into the heart of a country, secretly undermines all political confidence, and
arms neighbour against neighbor [*sic*]."

"It is the Pandora's box of evils," Webster continued in his tirade, "which are
let loose upon the world to curse mankind." Then he threatened: "If the French
will not suffer us to enjoy our government, our good old institutions, and even
our religion, Sir, which you so much despise, we will be their enemies. We are
able to defend ourselves, and we will defend ourselves." Webster also lectured
Barlow on the matters of religion and good manners: "You went from America
with a good character for talents and for good breeding." But Barlow's depiction

of Adams as "stupid" in his letter to Baldwin revealed his loss of moral fiber:
"No, Mr. Barlow, in divesting yourself of religion, you have lost your good manners, and like the French by the same process you have commenced a rude, insulting, dogmatical egotist."

Webster's opprobrium was not restricted merely to the Yale revolutionary. Thomas Paine, still in France throughout this period, became restive when America seemed to begin losing its appetite for revolution. Believing that he had been betrayed by George Washington, whose inaction left him in prison in France for nearly a year, Paine bitterly revealed his feelings in an angry jingle:

> Take from the mine the hardest, roughest stone,
>
> It needs no fashion, it is WASHINGTON.
>
> But if you chisel, let your strokes be rude,
>
> And on his breast engrave ingratitude.

Paine's hatred for his former comrade in arms spilled out in a public "Letter to George Washington" written in the summer of 1796. Questioning Washington's adherence to the principles of the American Revolution, Paine wrote, "the world will be puzzled to decide whether you are an apostate or an impostor; whether you have abandoned good principles or whether you ever had any."

Published in October 1797 by Benjamin Franklin Bache, the letter had the effect of drawing American attention to the activities of Paine, Barlow, Fulton, and other Americans living in France and working with the French Directory. Paine—along with Barlow, Fulton, William Tate, Wolfe Tone, and other American revolutionaries abroad—had been deeply involved in developing plans for the invasion of England and Ireland. He had served as public relations man for Tone and John Napper Tandy in promoting Irish independence. Like Fulton, he also designed gunboats that could be used in a novel form of attack.

But unlike Fulton, who simply hoped that his inventions would not be used against America, Paine became so angry with Washington and then John Adams that in the summer of 1798 he proposed to Talleyrand a plan for using his gunboats to conquer the United States. His obsessive hatred for America's aristocratic and British-leaning government persuaded even Talleyrand to break ranks with this noisy and troublesome friend of liberty. Obviously guilty of sedition as an American citizen, Paine fortunately was too far away to suffer the vengeance practiced by Adams and his cabinet against those close at hand in the United States.[5]

Comte Constantin de Volney (c. 1796). Fugitive French philosopher in America, later deported as a dangerous alien.

If Barlow and Paine had been in America instead of Paris during 1798 and 1799, they surely would have suffered more than verbal condemnations. If Thomas Cooper and Matthew Lyon ended up in prison, if James T. Callender and John Daly Burk went scurrying from Philadelphia for the safety of Virginia and Joseph Gales to a haven in North Carolina, and if nearly the entire refugee French and Irish populations were intimidated to recross the Atlantic, Barlow and Paine little knew the security they enjoyed by living beyond the seas. Had they spent those years in Philadelphia, they certainly would have been on John Adams and Timothy Pickering's list of seditious Americans. Like George Logan they would have been publicly smeared. Or, like Benjamin Franklin Bache, they might have risked their lives in the face of a yellow fever epidemic to carry on their witness in favor of liberty.

THE ORDEALS OF WILLIAM DUANE AND THOMAS COOPER

Those who persevered, suffered. There was, for example, William Duane, successor editor of Benjamin Franklin Bache's *Aurora* and eventual spouse to his widow Margaret, who carried on the outspoken editorial tradition of Franklin and Bache. When Duane had arrived in Philadelphia in October 1796, Bache gave him various editorial and writing tasks at the *Aurora* once he recognized Duane's considerable talents. As there was insufficient work for Duane at the *Aurora,* Bache helped him find other editorial work during the next two years. For a time he edited Thomas Bradford's *Merchants' Daily Advertiser,* which closely reflected Bache's social and political outlook. Next Duane edited the *Philadelphia Gazette* for Andrew Brown, Jr., although the two of them differed on many issues.

By the spring of 1798, Duane was again penniless, his wife Catherine was bedridden suffering from cholera, and his family was housed in a single room of a frame house on a smoke-filled alley. He tried unsuccessfully to collect money due for writing a new history of the French Revolution. Then on June 7 his landlady seized his few belongings in partial payment for his overdue rent. Five weeks later on July 13, Catherine Duane died.

Destitute and in despair, Duane turned again to Benjamin Franklin Bache. In early July he went to work for Bache at the *Aurora,* taking the place of the fleeing James Callender. After Bache succumbed to yellow fever, Duane helped Margaret Markoe Bache resume publication on November 1, 1798, just as the killer epidemic subsided. Despite his American birth and childhood in New York and Philadelphia, Duane was quickly declared a dangerous Irish revolutionary. And when he set out to organize Irish Catholics in support of an Irish revolution and to oppose the despised Alien and Sedition Acts, he confirmed the worst fears of Adams, Pickering, and others in American government.[6]

On Sunday, February 10, 1799, just days after John Adams signed the Logan Act, Duane, in the company of three Irish militants, visited St. Mary's Catholic Church in Philadelphia to secure signatures denouncing the Alien Act. Dr. James

William Duane (1802). Rebel editor and liberator in Britain, India, and America.

Reynolds, a distinguished physician and close friend of the late Bache, led the group as the chief American spokesman for Irish independence. That he was brother-in-law of the recently martyred Irish revolutionary, Theobald Wolfe Tone, merely added to his stature.

The four revolutionaries posted notices on the church door and gates that Sunday, inviting worshipers to sign their petition after the church service. As communicants left the service, Reynolds was perched on a tombstone, where he was "haranguing" some twenty or thirty people, many of whom had already signed the petition. Some of the church's trustees, not wishing to have a political rally in the church yard, asked Reynolds to leave the premises. Just as they spoke to Reynolds, a fifteen-year-old boy shouted a taunt at him. Then, according to one account, "Reynolds instantly pulled from his pocket a loaded pistol, and . . . presented it to the breast of the boy." Someone knocked the gun away and upended Reynolds. At this point angry church members became a mob and "with one accord . . . seized upon Reynolds and his gang, and dragged them forcibly to the Mayor's office," collecting a crowd of spectators as they wrestled their captives through the streets.

Despite mighty protests, all four were indicted and tried on charges of riot and assault, with Reynolds also accused of intent to murder the boy. After a thorny and tempestuous trial, the four were acquitted of the official charges, but not cleared of the obloquy of mounting the first "United Irish riot" in America. Indeed, Duane instantly became the target of both anti-Irish ruffians and Adams administration officials. Just two months later, when he editorialized against the conduct of a Pennsylvania militia unit while putting down the Fries rebellion, officers of the regiment led their fellows in a day raid on Duane's *Aurora* offices.

Thirty members of the regiment gathered at Hardy's Tavern before noon on May 15 and marched to Franklin Court and into the second-floor press room, where Duane, his son William John, and other pressmen were at work. Capt. Joseph McKean, son of Pennsylvania Chief Justice Thomas McKean, first addressed the senior Duane, asking him which company or companies of the regiment Duane had in mind when he leveled his charges of misconduct. When Duane refused to answer, McKean called him "a damned liar" and slapped him in the mouth with the back of his hand. Duane struck back in kind, setting off a mad rush from the "whole gang." Dragging Duane down the stairs and into the courtyard, the mob "formed a ring about [Duane] as if it had been a cock fight."

At that point, Peter Meircken, described by Duane as "their leviathan" and the principal instigator of the raid, supervised the rest of the beating. Meircken delivered savage blows leveling Duane, at which time the other "young cubs" would kick and strike him as well. Each time Duane went down, he would again struggle to his feet, "but, as I know nothing of boxing, and Meircken had studied under Mendoza, it was not surprising that I could not stand long before him." Duane later wrote, "I recollect perfectly that having hit him severely, he collected himself, and was about to give me one of his scientific strokes, when I received a blow from behind, under my right ear, which brought me to the ground." When he was finally beaten senseless and could not rise again, the mob whipped him savagely with a cowskin as a final measure of discipline. The group then headed back to Hardy's Tavern for a season of rejoicing at their symbolic victory over the forces of evil.

The offending culprits were neither indicted nor condemned for the savage beating of a newspaper editor. John Ward Fenno, editor of the *Gazette of the United States* and principal rival of the *Aurora,* actually defended the militia force, since Duane had described them unfairly as "thieves, ruffians and caitiffs." Fenno rationalized that Duane "was not an American but a foreigner, and not merely a foreigner, but a United Irishman, and not merely a United Irishman, but a public convict and fugitive from justice."[7]

Duane's antics not only attracted the attention of opposing editors and ruffians; he also piqued the interest of John Adams and Secretary of State Timothy Pickering. Throughout the spring and summer of 1799 Adams and Pickering snipped what they considered seditious articles from Duane's *Aurora.* Finally, on July 24 an article by Duane outlining the distressing degree of British intrigue at the highest level of American government pushed Pickering over the edge. In the article Duane charged Pickering directly as being under British influence and perhaps even pay. Pickering immediately told Adams that Duane should be charged with sedition and be banished as a dangerous alien. Thinking him a British subject, Pickering told Adams that Duane "came to this country to stir up sedition and other mischief."

Even before Adams could respond, the aggrieved secretary arrested Duane for seditious libel. By the time Duane was bound over on August 2 for trial in October, Adams wrote that "the matchless effrontery of this Duane merits the execution of the alien law." Even George Washington concurred, observing that "there seems to be no bounds to his attempts to destroy all confidence that the People might and . . . ought, to have in their government; thereby dissolving it, and producing a disunion of the States." To buttress their case even further, Pickering and government attorneys kept on clipping Duane's editorials to bring additional charges of sedition.

When Duane's case came to trial, Alexander James Dallas, Duane's attorney, in a bit of astute legal maneuvering, received a postponement until June 1800. Galled at the court system's failure to silence Duane, Pickering next persuaded Federalist senators to establish a standing committee on privileges and to bring Duane to trial for publishing a controversial election bill then pending secretly in the U.S. Senate. Arguing that the Senate's privileges to operate in secrecy superseded in some instances freedom of speech, Sen. Uriah Tracy from Connecticut led the charges in bringing Duane to punishment.

The choice of Tracy to lead this strange witch-hunt began to make the American war against liberty look like a Yale intramural activity. A native of Connecticut and a graduate of Litchfield Law School, Tracy also happened to be a member of Joel Barlow's Yale class of 1778. Tracy succeeded in establishing a committee on privileges and persuading it to find Duane guilty of sedition without ever interviewing him. On March 20, 1800, Duane was ordered to appear four days later to defend his offensive conduct and to receive his sentence. The Senate would then deliberate his fate.

In one of the oddest moments in American congressional history, Duane appeared before the full U.S. Senate sitting as a court under the gavel of Vice President Thomas Jefferson. Duane's legal counsel consisted of Alexander James Dallas, secretary of the Commonwealth of Pennsylvania, and Thomas Cooper, embattled friend of liberty and associate of Joseph Priestley. Duane and his rarified counselors planned to challenge the jurisdiction of the Senate under the Constitution to conduct such a trial. But when the Senate refused to allow the attorneys to undertake motions or to speak except on Duane's alleged seditious past writings, Dallas and Cooper resigned their posts in fury. Duane, in turn, used the absence of legal counsel as a pretext for not appearing again before the Senate.

When he failed to appear on March 26, 1800, the chagrined Senate declared Duane guilty of contempt and issued a warrant for his arrest by the sergeant at arms. The warrant, smelling suspiciously like contemporary Parliamentary sanctions, was issued by Jefferson and required that all marshals, deputy marshals, and civil officers of the government "and every other person" assist in seizing Duane. Following the precedents of Thomas Cooper, Joseph Gales, Mathew Carey, James T. Callender, James Cheetham, William Rhees, John Daly Burk, and many other authors and editors who lived through Pitt's reign of terror in Britain, Duane went into hiding. There he remained until Congress adjourned and the warrant thereby expired.

Throughout that spring session of Congress, however, the picture was becoming ever clearer that friends of liberty were enemies of America. In a conjoining of many of the players and symbols of the moment of madness, John Ward Fenno in the *Gazette of the United States,* wrote:

> From the Senate D[uan]e flying,
> As advised by Mr. D[allas],
> Out to St[e]nt[o]n snugly lying,
> Bids defiance to the gallows.
> There with L[ogan], hatching treason,
> Sowing seed on his plantation,
> Brooding o'er Paine's Age of Reason,
> D[uan]e seeks for consolation.

The broad assumption that Duane was hiding out with the already notorious Logan embittered the Senate and the Adams administration even further. As a consequence, when the Senate adjourned, it requested Adams to indict Duane under the Sedition Act.[8]

Not only did Adams happily comply with the Senate's request, he expanded the list to include Thomas Cooper, who had helped Duane defy the Senate's orders. While Duane, through his various astute maneuvers, was able to avoid final trial until the Sedition Act expired, Cooper was not so lucky.[9]

The circumstances of Cooper's ordeal were similar to those that brought Duane under fire. After living quietly with Joseph Priestley for several years at Northumberland, Pennsylvania, he emerged in 1799 to relieve the editor of the *Sunbury Gazette* for a few months. Cooper used this temporary podium between April 20 and June 29 to pen a long stream of criticism of American policies and Adams administration actions. All was fine until his last editorial on June 29, wherein he issued a parody on how, if he were the chief executive, he would increase his powers at the expense of the rest of the country, i.e., just as John Adams had!

When this essay appeared a few days later in the *Aurora,* both Cooper and Priestley came under savage attack at the hands of Federalist newspapers and politicians. One such attack in the *Reading Weekly Advertiser* on October 26 infuriated Cooper so badly that he directly criticized Adams for divulging confidential letters Priestley and Cooper had sent to him in 1797 concerning a government post for Cooper. Pickering, whose responsibility it was to enforce the Alien and Sedition Acts, sent a copy of the *Aurora* version to Adams. Pickering proposed that charges of sedition be brought against Cooper and that Priestley should be expelled from America. Adams immediately declared Cooper's writings seditious, but thought that Priestley must have been duped into ill-advised statements by the fiery Cooper. The president vetoed any action against Priestley, but urged Pickering to apply the Sedition Act against Cooper.[10]

On April 9, 1800, Cooper was arrested for seditious libel. Though a variety of his actions precipitated the charges, his handbill of November 2, 1799, was explicitly cited in the indictment. The trial began seven days later in Philadelphia and was presided over by Justice Samuel Chase and District Judge Richard Peters. Although Cooper attempted to subpoena President Adams and other federal officials, his motion was denied. He also failed to secure various necessary public documents when Adams would not cooperate in producing them. The trial took on the air of a circus as it was attended by three cabinet officials and Adams's own private secretary. Pickering sat with the judges; members of Congress also attended. Philadelphia's political press followed the proceedings daily in great detail. When the trial concluded, Justice Chase charged the jury in such manner that they had little choice in their findings. Cooper was found guilty as charged. On April 24 Justice Chase sentenced Cooper to six months in prison and assessed a fine of $400. He was also to post a $2,000 surety bond upon his release guaranteeing his good behavior.[11]

What Cooper had successfully avoided in England—despite lengthy visits in revolutionary France and caustic critiques of Parliament and the king—he could not escape in the land of liberty. He spent the next six months in federal prison, seething at the treatment he had suffered, lamenting the death of his wife—who died while he was behind bars—and steeling himself to seek vengeance against John Adams upon his release.

Priestley, too, quickly became disillusioned with America, as editorial indictments of Cooper rarely appeared without reference also to Priestley. The aging genius of chemistry decided to defend his actions and his association with Cooper, publishing a second and expanded edition of his *Letters to the Inhabitants of Northumberland* in both Northumberland and Philadelphia in 1801.[12]

Thomas Cooper (1819). Rebel Briton, seditious American.

When he arrived in Philadelphia to arrange the Philadelphia edition of *Letters,* his first visit since the failure of 1797, he was shocked to find that his Unitarian society was nearly dead and that he had come under renewed attack in the press. To add insult to injury, he fell victim there to pleurisy, from which he never fully recovered. Treated by Dr. Benjamin Rush with his favored treatment for many dire ailments—profuse bleeding—Priestley survived to thank Rush: "I believe that I owe my life to your judicious direction of it." But with continued attacks upon his personality, his views of religion and politics, and his association with the likes of Thomas Cooper, Priestley retreated to Northumberland, where he lived quietly for the remainder of his days.[13]

Priestley's sad assessment of America was poignantly underscored by his last years and the events surrounding his death. With the help of Thomas Cooper, he continued to be productive in science, philosophy, and religion until the very day of his death. But when he died on February 6, 1804, he was discredited by most Americans. It is true that the American Philosophical Society decided to eulogize Priestley, but it took almost a year after his death, along the same lines previously accorded to Benjamin Franklin and David Rittenhouse. Dr. Benjamin Smith Barton, a vice president of the society (no relation to Provost William Smith who declaimed at Franklin's eulogium), was selected to give the eulogy.

On January 3, 1805, in Philadelphia's First Presbyterian Church, members of the society proceeded to the church en masse as they had at Franklin's eulogy. Invitations were issued to a vast array of Philadelphia luminaries: "the Revd. Clergy of the city; the college of Physicians; the Medical Society; the gentlemen of the Bar, with the students at Law; the trustees and faculty of the University of

Pennsylvania, with their students in the Arts and in Medicine; the judges and officers of the federal and state Courts; the foreign ministers and other public characters then in the city; the mayor; aldermen and city councils: the trustees and session of the First Presbyterian Church; the directors of the City Library; the directors and Physicians of the Pennsylvania Hospital, of the Alms House, and of the Dispensary; the proprietor and Director of the Philadelphia Museum; and the contributors towards the Cabinet and Library of the Society."

While the event was reported in William Duane's *Aurora,* the one paper friendly to Priestley to the end, it was not reported who actually attended. Dr. Smith, by vote of the society, however, was asked to submit a copy of his remarks for publication. Regrettably, this was never done. Seven years later, November 6, 1812, the society registered its last plea to Smith to complete his assignment. Priestley's eulogium was never submitted and never appeared in print. Priestley was lost in obscurity outside the American pantheon of heroes in the cause of freedom, left to be exhumed from time to time by historians of science, philosophy, or religion.[14] While Thomas Cooper battled on another three decades attempting to rescue liberty in America and defending his role in bashing every national administration, Joseph Priestley's presence and sad demise in America would be virtually forgotten.[15]

ENDINGS OF FRIENDS OF LIBERTY IN AMERICA

Benjamin Franklin Bache (1769–1798). Arrested and charged with common-law libel on June 26, 1798, for publishing Talleyrand's letter to the American commissioners to France. While awaiting trial, he contracted and died of yellow fever on September 10, 1798.

Joel Barlow (1754–1812). Deeply ensconced in Paris pursuing commercial, diplomatic, literary, and artistic interests, while assisting Robert Fulton in securing contracts from the French government to develop the submarine *Nautilus* for use against the British Navy. He remained somewhat oblivious to counterrevolutionary changes in America and the widespread condemnation of his views on liberty and revolution, not only by politicians, but also by his fellow Hartford Wits, including Noah Webster.

Hugh Henry Brackenridge (1748–1816). Frightened by the near insurrection of the Whiskey Rebellion, he retired in 1795 from public politics to write about the event and expand his satire on American life, *Modern Chivalry.* In 1798 he entered conventional politics as a leading Jeffersonian in Western Pennsylvania. His support was rewarded in 1799 with an appointment for life as a justice of the Pennsylvania Supreme Court.

John Daly Burk (1775–1808). After the failure of newspapers in Boston and New York, he moved to Petersburg, Virginia, to write histories of Ireland and of Virginia. At Powell's Tavern on April 9, 1808, he insulted a French tobacco agent named Coquebert, who challenged him to a duel. They met the next morning and Burk "was shot through the heart at the second fire" and killed instantly.

James Thomson Callender (1758–1803). Fled from Philadelphia to Richmond, Virginia, in 1798 to avoid the Sedition Law. With support from Jefferson he published *The Prospect Before Us* (1800), sharply critical of President Adams. Indicted and convicted for seditious statements in the book, he was fined $200 and sentenced to nine months in prison. Pardoned by Jefferson in 1801, he soon turned on his benefactor and published accounts of the scandals that have surrounded the third president from that time to the present. On July 17, 1803, his body was found in three feet of water in the James River, dead from intoxication.

Mathew Carey (1760–1839). Moved from newspaper to magazine to book publishing. He capitalized on both books and the events of American life, including the widely disputed yellow fever epidemic of 1793 and the rechartering of the Bank of the United States.

James Cheetham (1772–1810). Turned to the darker side of partisan politics, publishing exposés on the political and moral failures of Aaron Burr and Thomas Paine. Just after publishing an account of the sordid last years of Paine in 1809, he died of probably a stroke after spending hours walking in a hot September sun.

Thomas Cooper (1759–1839). Campaigned against John Adams and sedition laws while he spent six months in prison in 1800. Although identified with Jefferson thereafter, he drifted toward counterrevolutionary principles, which he espoused with venom and vigor in Pennsylvania and South Carolina until his death four decades later.

Paul Cuffe (1759–1817). Expanded his shipping business throughout the 1790s and became convinced that African Americans might best find their permanent home in Africa. While he found opposition to his plan in Philadelphia, he pursued the idea and carried shiploads of free blacks back to Africa until his untimely death.

William Duane (1760–1835). Indicted for sedition in 1799, his trial was twice postponed until the newly inaugurated Jefferson ordered the charges be dropped. Although constantly under attack for his radical perspectives, he found success as editor of Bache's *Aurora*.

Timothy Dwight (1752–1817). An early defector from the friends of liberty, Dwight became a counterrevolutionary at least by 1788 with the publication of *The Triumph of Infidelity* and made himself one of the leaders of what became the American Counterrevolution.

Olaudah Equiano (1745–1797). Became one of the most famous black opponents of slavery and the slave trade with the publication of *The Interesting Narrative of the Life of Olaudah Equiano, or Gustavus Vassa, the African* in 1789. He oversaw nine editions of the autobiography before his death and saw it reviewed by some of the most important exponents of liberty of the age, including Mary Wollstonecraft in *The Analytical Review*. His efforts on behalf of Granville Sharp's colonization of Sierra Leone were rebuffed when his position as commissary for the stores in the colony was terminated in 1787. Although he died in relative obscurity, he was noted in the "Obituary of remarkable Persons" in *The Gentleman's Magazine* and he left an estate valued at £950 in 1816.

Elizabeth Graeme Ferguson (1737–1801). Although given a life estate in Graeme Park by Pennsylvania following the Revolution, she had to give it up in 1791. Unsuccessful in getting her poems published in 1794, she lived in obscurity and poverty, with occasional gifts from Benjamin Rush and Provost William Smith, until her death.

Philip Freneau (1752–1832). With the resignation of Jefferson from his position of secretary of state in 1793, Freneau lost his post as translating clerk and as editor of the *National Gazette*. He lived in poverty and retirement thereafter until his death.

Joseph Gales (1761–1841). Departed sedition-law Philadelphia under fear of indictment in 1798 for North Carolina, where he established the *Raleigh Register* on October 22, 1799, reminiscent of his *Sheffield Register.* In Raleigh, he and his gifted wife Winifred became among of the most important citizens of their adopted state.

Edmond Charles Genet (1763–1834). From his arrival in Philadelphia as an agent of the French Revolution in August 1793, he was at the center of a storm about liberty and revolution. Rejected by Jefferson and the American government, he retired from public life, married a daughter of Gov. George Clinton of New York in 1794 and lived there in obscurity until his death.

David Humphreys (1752–1818). One of the Hartford Wits, was in American foreign service from 1790 forward and minister to Spain 1796–1801. Although he broke ranks with Joel Barlow on matters of liberty and revolution, the two of them cooperated in negotiating with Barbary warlords.

Gilbert Imlay (c. 1754–1828). Following his last unhappy encounter with Mary Wollstonecraft in 1796, the American adventurer disappeared from the pages of history other than the record of his death in a church register on the Island of Jersey.

Deborah Norris Logan (1761–1839). Organized the records housed at Stenton for posterity and wrote the *Memoir of Dr. George Logan of Stenton.*

George Logan (1753–1821). Rebuffed by Adams and Washington following his successful trip to Paris in 1798, he suffered further humiliation with the enactment by Congress of the Logan Act in 1799. Despite the public repudiation he was appointed to the U.S. Senate in 1801 and in 1810 defied the law named for him by traveling to London, where he attempted, unsuccessfully, to avert the War of 1812.

Matthew Lyon (1750–1822). Convicted of seditious libel in October 1798 while member of Congress and spent four months in prison. He returned triumphantly to Congress to cast a deciding vote in favor of Jefferson for President. In 1801 he migrated to Kentucky from which he was again elected to Congress, serving from 1803 until 1811. There he promoted the expansion of slavery to industrialize the South.

Catharine Macaulay (1731–1791). Promoted liberty and education for women in her last work, *Observations on the Reflections of the R. Hon. Edmund Burke, on the Revolution in France* (1790), in which she praised both the American and French Revolutions.

John Marrant (1755–1791). After preaching to black and white Loyalists in Nova Scotia for the Countess of Huntingdon between 1785 and 1788, he moved to Boston and served briefly as chaplain to Prince Hall's first lodge of black Masons. Disgusted with the mission in Nova Scotia and with conditions for blacks in Boston, Marrant returned to England in March 1790. A year later he died of undisclosed causes.

Josiah Meigs (1757–1822). Hounded from his faculty position at Yale by the counterrevolutionary tactics of President Timothy Dwight, he moved with the assistance of Joel Barlow and his brother-in-law Abraham Baldwin to Georgia, becoming the first full-time president of the University of Georgia. After a ten-year battle with Georgia citizens and politicians, he resigned and moved to Washington, D.C., where he held a variety of government posts until his death.

Judith Sargent Murray (1751–1820). Following the failure of her plays, but with the successful publication of *The Gleaner* volumes in 1798, she spent the next decade living in poverty in Boston and caring for her ill and failing husband.

Thomas Paine (1737–1809). After the recall of James Monroe from his ministerial post in Paris, Paine lived off the charity of his loyal followers in France. He returned to the United States in 1802 to find that he had become persona non grata throughout the land. Increasingly ridiculed for his radical philosophies, he lived in isolation and poverty in New Jersey and New York until his death.

Joseph Priestley (1733–1804). Ostracized religiously and politically and associated with the seditious behavior of his companion, Thomas Cooper, he lived in obscurity in Northumberland, Pennsylvania, conducting chemical experiments and writing on religious subjects until the last hour of his life.

Morgan John Rhees (1760–1804). Met great criticism and opposition to his speeches and publications (*The Altar of Peace,* 1798) on the state of liberty in America. After entering into Pennsylvania land speculations with Benjamin Rush, he moved to Somerset, where he held petty public offices until his death.

Susanna Rowson (1762–1824). Badgered by William Cobbett during 1795 and 1796, she retired from the stage and public life in the spring of 1797 to spend the rest of her life conducting a school near Boston for young ladies. Although she published more stories and novels, most of her later writing was confined to tracts and textbooks for young women.

Benjamin Rush (1745–1813). His medical practice destroyed in the yellow fever epidemics of 1793 and 1797 and his devotion to liberty ridiculed by William Cobbett, he took a bureaucratic sinecure provided by his father-in-law Elias Boudinot as treasurer of the U.S. Mint in 1797. There he remained until his death, limiting his medical activities to writing *Medical Inquiries and Observations upon the Diseases of the Mind* (1812), the foundation of modern psychiatry.

Moreau de St. Mery (1750–1819). Aware of his pending deportation as a dangerous resident alien, he left for France in August 1798, where he was given a variety of government posts until 1806, when he was summarily dismissed by Napoléon without benefit of pension. He lived in poverty in Paris until his death.

William Tate (unknown). Following the ignominious defeat of his French-clad, but mainly Irish-born invasion force into Wales in February 1797, he was taken with his immediate officers to London for trial. There he was granted prisoner-of-war status and transferred to a prison ship at Portsmouth. He was sent to Paris for a prisoner-of-war exchange on November 24, 1798. His rank and pay in the French army was restored and continued until 1809, when he was granted indefinite leave to return to the United States. At the age of eighty he was still hoping to fight British troops in an American army.

Theobald Wolfe Tone (1763–1798). Captured two days after leading a French invasion of Ireland, the Irish revolutionary was court-martialed on November 10, 1798, and found guilty of treason. When his request to be shot by a firing squad was denied, he slit his own throat with a penknife, and died seven days later.

Benjamin Vaughan (1751–1835). After facing charges of treason in Britain and arrest in revolutionary France, he fled in 1796 to America, where he lived quietly at Hallowell, Maine, as a nominal Federalist for the rest of his life.

Constantin Volney (1757–1820). Increasingly under attack in the United States for his atheistic views, he returned to France in 1798 and became a strong supporter of Napoléon. He was of considerable assistance to Robert Fulton in acquiring French government funds to build the experimental *Nautilus*.

Mercy Otis Warren (1728–1814). Continued to criticize the antiliberating tendencies of the U.S. Constitution and the new federal government, both of which she documented in her massive *History of the Rise, Progress, and Termination of the American Revolution* (1805).

Noah Webster (1758–1843). Swung in the 1790s from revolution to counterrevolution, condemning the French Revolution, Joseph Priestley, and even his confidant Joel Barlow. In 1798 he retired from public life to become the foremost lexicographer of the American English language.

Mary Wollstonecraft (1759–1797). Died at the height of her career from complications at childbirth of daughter Mary Wollstonecraft (m.n. Shelly). While her treatise, *Vindication of the Rights of Woman* (1792), eventually became a touchstone for women's rights, her reputation—like that of her compatriot Thomas Paine—was besmirched and critically impaired by the end of the century.

PART IV

COUNTER-REVOLUTION

CHAPTER 17

Edmund Burke, Friend of Order

As he lay dying in Bath in the spring and early summer of 1797, Edmund Burke, renowned British philosopher and politician, felt more threatened than at any other moment of his life. His fear was not of impending mortality. Indeed, shortly before his death, he wrote to one of his faithful followers, "If God has anything to do for me here—here he will keep me. If not, I am tolerably resigned to the Divine pleasure." His dread was instead of living enemies who, if given a chance, would physically attack him and his family. Not political enemies, even though he had plenty of those. Not thugs, although Britain abounded with those, too. Rather it was a band of bloodthirsty murderers denominated by Burke as "French revolutionists." So deep was his anxiety, Burke, three days before his death, ordered that he be buried "unknown, the spot unmarked and separate from his son, wife and Brother on <u>account of the French Revolutionists.</u> "[1]

Far from being the rantings of a deranged man, Burke was dealing with a bundle of realities of the moment. He had, over the period of the previous eight years, waged a mighty war against both the French Revolution and everything French. In letters, essays, books, and parliamentary oratory, he had undertaken every measure possible to destroy the idea that anything of value could be born from the revolutionary fires burning in France. He had portrayed all apostles of the French Revolution as enemies of mankind. His widely distributed sentiments about France influenced anyone who had opinions about political realities of the day.

But Burke's fears were more immediate than potential backlash from the political battles he had fought. Indeed, during the six months prior to the issuance of his burial dictum, Burke witnessed alarming political unrest throughout England and Ireland, as well as menacing indications that France intended to invade England. Mutinies and threatened upheavals attracted a powerful French fleet and an invading army of fourteen thousand men to Bantry Bay in the north of Ireland in December 1796. Although the expedition failed after eleven days of impossible weather, the force remained four days unchallenged in Bantry Bay, causing Burke to charge that "these harbors of the British dominions are the ports of France." Incensed that the ruling party still wished to negotiate with republican France, Burke charged that the traitorous French "meditated the very

Edmund Burke (c. 1785). Prophet of counter-revolution, he was the foremost friend of order.

same invasion, and for the very same purposes, upon this kingdom, and, had the coast been as opportune, would have effected it."[2]

Hardly had he penned those words in his attack on revolutionary France in *Letters on a Regicide Peace* when a second invasion force, under the command of American William Tate, drove a corps of thousands into Bristol Bay. Following the same plan that would have been used at Bantry Bay had weather permitted, Tate's invasion had commenced on February 22 at a secondary site on Cardigan Bay—just a few short miles from where Burke lay ill and dying.[3] The scale and timing of the albeit unsuccessful strike served only to reinforce the accuracy of Burke's prophetic interpretations of the nature of the French Revolution.

That prophetic voice set Burke apart from almost everyone else in the Western world who—at least in the sweet summer of liberty in 1789—wanted to see liberty come to the land of Louis XVI. Indeed, less than a month after the storming of the Bastille on July 14, 1789, Burke wrote that "this whole affair is one of the most curious matters of Speculation that ever was exhibited." Certain that it was no accident, Burke boldly argued "that people [the French] are not fit for Liberty." In one of his prescient conclusions he noted: "Men must have a certain fund of natural moderation to qualify them for Freedom, else it become noxious to themselves and a perfect Nuisance to everybody else."[4]

Just a month later, as everyone else in England was praising the deliberations of the National Assembly, Burke had concluded that the French nation no longer had a central authority capable of governing. Weeks before a Parisian mob of thirty thousand forced Louis XVI back to Paris from Versailles, Burke considered Louis already powerless, and "it does not appear to me, that the National assembly have one jot more power than the King." Even worse, the Assembly lacked "any real deliberate capacity, or the exercise of free Judgement in any point whatsoever" because "there is a Mob of their constituents ready to Hang them if They should deviate into moderation, or in the least depart from the Spirit of those they represent."[5]

When he learned on October 10 that Louis had become a prisoner in the Tuileries as a result of the *journées* of October 5 and 6, Burke brought his prophetic utterances full circle. The newspapers confirmed, he thought, "the portentous State of France—where the Elements which compose Human Society seem all to be dissolved and a world of Monsters to be produced in the place of it—where Mirabeau presides as the Great Anarch; and the late Grand Monarch makes a figure as ridiculous as pitiable." In Burke's view, then, by October 1789, France was ungoverned and had all of the appearances of being ungovernable.[6]

Burke, then, was shocked to read the words of his old colleague, Richard Price, before the venerable London Revolution Society on November 4. When Price declared that "the times are auspicious," that kingdoms were "breaking their fetters," and that in France, in particular, there had been "kindled . . . a blaze that lays despotism in ashes, and warms and illuminates Europe," Burke thought the clergyman had lost his sanity. And as Burke read the resolutions adopted by the Revolution Society lauding the National Assembly and commending the French example, he flew into a fit of rage that would drive him furiously for the remaining eight years of his life.[7]

The wide disparity between Burke and Price on matters in France on November 4, 1789, was nowhere better exhibited than in a surprisingly dispassionate letter written by Burke to a young friend in Paris, Charles-Jean-François Depont. Depont asked for Burke's assessment of French efforts to secure liberty, since it was Burke who first excited the young man about the virtues of that beloved ideal. Burke responded happily by first describing what is this thing liberty "to which I think all men intitled":

> It is not solitary, unconnected, individual, selfish Liberty. As if every Man was to regulate the whole of his Conduct by his own will. The Liberty I mean is social freedom. It is that state of things in which Liberty is secured by the equality of Restraint; A Constitution of things in which the liberty of no one Man and no body of Men and no Number of men can find Means to trespass on the liberty of any Person or any description of Persons in the Society. This kind of Liberty is indeed but another name for Justice, ascertained by wise Laws, and secured by well constructed institutions.

Burke then asked Depont to determine for himself whether these circumstances prevailed in the revolutionary France of 1789. Somehow he hesitated in rendering the firm judgment to his idealistic young friend that he routinely provided to his other correspondents and friends.

Instead Burke supplied Depont with measures that could be used to come to his own conclusions:

> When therefore I shall learn, that in France, the Citizen, by whatever description he is qualified, is in a perfect state of legal security, with regard to his life, to his property, to the uncontrolled disposal of his Person, to the free use of his Industry and his faculties; . . . When I am assured that a simple Citizen may decently express his sentiments upon Publick Affairs without hazard to his life or safety, even tho' against a predominant and fashionable opinion; When I know all of this of France, I shall be well pleased as every one must be.

Burke then issued a helpful warning: "You have theories enough concerning the Rights of Men. It may not be amiss to add a small degree of attention to their Nature and disposition. It is with Man in the concrete, it is with common human life and human Actions you are to be concerned."

Written without the venom that permeated nearly all of his public statements on the French Revolution, Burke's letter to Depont contained the vital seed of a social and political philosophy that would emerge in its total fullness as the aging savant pondered the aspirations, passions, and dreams that cut across all of Europe and America in the 1790s. It obviously was written before Burke received a printed version of Price's November 4 oration, complete with the rhapsodic resolutions of the London Revolutionary Society. For, from the moment that publication came into his hand during the third week in January 1790, Burke made a conscious decision to take on the wild-eyed friends of liberty not only in London, but throughout the world.

Given that he had already spent a good deal of energy advising his friend Depont on the subjects of liberty and France, it was entirely logical that he should use his letter, vastly refined and expanded, as the first of many vehicles for expressing his views. What he said in his landmark book, *Reflections on the Revolution in France and on the Proceedings in Certain Societies in London Relative to that Event in a Letter Intended to Have Been Sent to a Gentleman in Paris* (1790)—one of the most debated books in the English language—was foreshadowed in an angry outburst in Parliament in early February:

> The French had shown themselves the ablest architects of ruin that had hitherto existed in the world. In that very short space of time [seven months following the fall of the Bastille] they had completely pulled down to the ground, their monarchy, their church, their nobility, their law, their revenue, their army, their navy, their commerce, their arts and their manufactures. Our

> friendship and our intercourse with that nation had once been,
> and might again become more dangerous to us than their worst
> hostility.

And with this public volley, Burke added two elements not present in his original letter to Depont: (1) a penchant to bash everything French in often the crudest of terms and (2) the introduction of his views to the partisan political struggles in which he was daily engaged. In this first public outburst, and in every statement he would make thereafter, Burke mixed and matched philosophy, politics, and French-baiting to such a degree that one is at great pains to comprehend the boundaries between the three pursuits.[8]

From the onset of this angry behavior, some of his closest friends and advisors cautioned him against the high-strung tenor of his views. Indeed, in that same February, when he completed a first draft of *Reflections*, he sent the manuscript to Philip Francis, longtime political associate and friend, for comment. Francis quickly responded with sage advice: "Have you thoroughly considered whether it be worthy of Mr Burke, of a Privy Councillor, of a man so high and considerable in the House of Commons as you are, and holding the station you have obtained in the opinion of the world to enter into a war of Pamphlets with Dr. Price?" Worse, though, was the effrontery of Burke's mission: "You now undertake to correct and instruct another Nation, and your appeal in effect is to all Europe. Allowing you the liberty to do so in an extreme case, you cannot deny that it ought to be done with special deliberation in the choice of the topics, and with no less care and circumspection in the use you make of them."

Francis objected particularly to Burke's portrayal of Marie Antoinette as a vile adulteress and evil corrupter of the French monarchy and society. He found Burke's words, images, and overheated emotions so offensive and the manuscript so "loosely put together" that the whole project should be abandoned:

> Look back, I beseech you and deliberate a little, before you
> determine that this is an office that perfectly becomes you. . . .
> The mischief you are going to do yourself is, to my apprehen-
> sion, palpable. It is visible. It will be audible. I sniff it in the
> wind. I taste it already. I feel it in every sense and so will you
> hereafter when I vow to God (a most elegant phrase) it will be
> no sort of consolation to me to reflect that I did every thing in
> my power to prevent it.

Despite the power of Francis's appeal, Burke was profoundly offended and responded that he "intended no controversy with Dr Price or Lord Shelburne or any other of their set." His purpose was much loftier: "I mean to set in full View the danger from their wicked principles and their black hearts; I intend to state the true principles of our constitution in Church and state—upon Grounds opposite to theirs."[9]

Undaunted by the judgment of others, Burke determined to bring the project to a quick conclusion. When *Reflections on the Revolution in France* was released on November 1, 1790, it touched every corner of the Western world. At a time when philosophers, scientists, clergy, and politicians were applauding the French Revolution, Burke predicted that the real revolution was yet to come. In his view, what had been accomplished up until November 1790 was a demolition of national governance in France. The stage was set for the onset of chaos. Throughout the tract Burke hinted at what would be forthcoming. Mobs, the overthrow of religion, economic turmoil, absence of civil justice, savage executions, elimination of the monarchy and of elected heads of government, and even the rise of "some popular general, who understands the art of conciliating the soldiery"—all of the well-remembered and famous events of the French Revolution, but which were yet to come—were outlined in unnerving clarity.[10]

Even though *Reflections* merits comparison with the memorable utterances of Jeremiah and Isaiah, Burke badly mixed and blurred his most immediate political petulance with his provocative analysis of conditions in France and his penchant for argumentativeness with his astonishing command of history.

More confounding yet is that Burke also chose this multifaceted vessel to burrow in a philosophy of history, governance, and society that would be timeless in its impact on Western history. And it is precisely because Burke pursued this blending of purposes that his contemporaries, as well as subsequent devotees and critics, have had so much difficulty evaluating his true meaning.

Reflections is an expanded letter to Burke's Paris correspondent, Depont. It is a critical review of Richard Price and the London Revolution Society. It is an analysis of British constitutional history and a critique of French history and constitutional development. It is a denouncement of the influences of the Enlightenment, portraying the essential role of the Church in civil polity. It is a legal brief on the ownership of property and responsibility for debt. It is an examination of the nature of monarchies, aristocracies, and clergies in societies. Finally, it is an investigation into the character of constitutions—how they are formed, and how and why they function or fail to function.[11]

Burke's perceptive study of these and many other topics made *Reflections* an absorbing and useful book for contemporaries and a trove of insights and scintillating quotations for historians, philosophers, and political scientists. But in addition to all of his imaginative analysis, Burke's annihilation of the French Revolution as a enterprise devoted to liberty and his articulation of a counterrevolutionary philosophy of history, governance, and society made the book a work for the centuries. With regard to the French Revolution, Burke viewed it as a disastrous reversal of natural, historical, and political order. Whereas the National Assembly in the name of liberty, equality, and freedom appeared to have achieved these ideals, it had actually destroyed all possibilities of achieving them. It had obliterated the monarchy, dismantled the aristocracy, deposed the clergy, undermined the national economy, rendered the monetary system unworkable, subverted the judicial system, politicized the military, and destroyed the taxing system. In fact, the National Assembly had left France with no executive authority, no judicial rule,

"Mr. Burke's Pair of Spectacles for Short-Sighted Politicians" (1791). Edmund Burke holds forth a pair of counterrevolutionary eyeglasses to aid politicians in understanding the revolutionary struggle over the rights of man.

and, despite a piece of paper called a constitution, no government other than the most current majority of the Assembly itself:

> The power . . . of the House of Commons, when least diminished, is as a drop of water in the ocean, compared to that residing in a settled majority of your National Assembly. That assembly, since the destruction of the orders, has no fundamental law, no strict convention, no respected usage to restrain it. Instead of finding themselves obliged to conform to a fixed constitution, they have a power to make a constitution which shall conform to their designs.

As a consequence, the ancient nation of France was in 1790 under what Burke described as mob rule. Whoever can survive a steady diet of "outrageous insults and murderous threats" constitutes the ruling mob: "There a majority, sometimes real, sometimes pretended, captive itself, compels a captive king to issue as royal edicts, at third hand, the polluted nonsense of their most licentious and giddy coffeehouses." Their behavior was almost laughable: "They act like the comedians of a fair before a riotous audience."[12]

The French republic, in short, was the antithesis of liberty, that beloved prize of the age. But in the process of revealing what was wrong with France, Burke formulated a set of ideas that could, he thought, be used to organize life in the Western world to achieve real liberty. A partial catalogue of his philosophical principles as outlined in *Reflections* and expanded in other writings follows:

1. *Rights of Man.* The French Declaration of the Rights of Man and Citizen was a philosophical chimera deriving from theories of the philosophes. According to Burke the "real rights of men" derived from the creation of a civil constitution. Once a constitution is formulated and a body of law defined, men have a right to live by that constitution. And a proper constitution would provide for and protect men's rights, including these:

> They have a right to the fruits of their industry and to the means of making their industry fruitful. They have a right to the acquisitions of their parents, to the nourishment and improvement of their offspring, to instruction in life, and to consolation in death. Whatever each man can separately do, without trespassing upon others, he has a right to do for himself; and he has a right to a fair portion of all which society, with all its combinations of skill and force, can do in his favor. In this partnership all men have equal rights, but not to equal things.

When it came to "the share of power, authority, and direction which each individual ought to have in the management of the state," Burke believed that this had to be defined by the civil constitution of each separate state.

2. *Government.* If the rights of man ultimately derive from a civil constitution, then men's government "is a contrivance of human wisdom to provide for human wants," including protection of those rights deemed appropriate in a particular society. Sometimes rights will change, depending upon that society's needs and wants. Therefore, "the rights of men are in a sort of middle, incapable of definition, but not impossible to be discerned." Government, then, must assure those human rights while also providing "a sufficient restraint upon their passions":

> Society requires not only that the passions of individuals should be subjected, but that even in the mass and body, as well as in the individuals, the inclinations of men should frequently be thwarted, their will controlled, and their passions brought into subjection. . . . In this sense the restraints on men, as well as their liberties, are to be reckoned among their rights.

As a consequence, governments will constantly change within certain limits "as the liberties and the restrictions vary with times and circumstances and admit to infinite modifications." [13]

3. *Equality.* By the very nature of man, according to Burke, there can be no such thing as equality. "Believe me, Sir, those who attempt to level, never equalize." He wrote:

> In all societies, consisting of various descriptions of citizens,
> some description must be uppermost. The levelers, therefore,
> only change and pervert the natural order of things; they load
> the edifice of society by setting up in the air what the solidity of
> the structure requires to be on the ground. . . . In this you think
> you are combating prejudice, but you are at war with nature.

Indeed, disparities in abilities, in ownership of property, and in inheritance make human beings unequal. To believe otherwise was to subvert the "natural" order of things. On the contrary, inequalities should be cherished and encouraged since "ability is a vigorous and active principle," property holders are "the ballast in the vessel of the commonwealth," and "some preference . . . given to birth is neither unnatural, nor unjust, nor impolitic."

4. *Class Distinctions.* To secure the permanence of any form of government and to enable any type of society to operate, there must be, according to Burke, class distinctions. While they need not be legislated or inherited, "every such classification, if properly ordered, is good in all forms of government, and composes a strong barrier against the excesses of despotism." A diversity of interests was to be encouraged, since diversity enriched society, enabled it to function, and ultimately protected the freedom of everyone in it to pursue the highest goals. Laws and efforts seeking to level all distinctions among humans, on the other hand, almost certainly would bring chaos.[14]

5. *Leadership.* Class distinctions, however, had no explicit connection to leadership in a republic. Burke saw no reason to "confine power, authority, and distinction to blood and names and titles." On the contrary, he argued, "there is no qualification for government but virtue and wisdom, actual or presumptive." Wherever people are found with these qualities, "they have, in whatever state, condition, profession, or trade, the passport of Heaven to human place and honor." On this subject, Burke waxed eloquent to extreme:

> Woe to the country which would madly and impiously reject
> the service of the talents and virtues, civil, military, or reli-
> gious, that are given to grace and to serve it. . . . Woe to that
> country, too, that passing into the opposite extreme, considers a
> low education, a mean contracted view of things, a sordid, mer-
> cenary occupation as a preferable title to command!

Leadership should be open and available to every human. "No rotation; no appointment by lot; no mode of election operating in the spirit of sortation or rotation" should be permitted. But not everyone could or should lead. The "road to eminence and power, from obscure condition, ought not to be made too easy." Every leader should "pass through some sort of probation" on the road to office: "The temple of honor ought to be seated on an eminence."

6. *Democracy.* While leadership should be open to the qualified and the virtuous, there was no need for selection or governance through purely democratic

procedures. Echoing Aristotle, he believed that "a democracy has many striking points of resemblance with a tyranny." In fact,

> Of this I am certain, that in a democracy the majority of the citizens is capable of exercising the most cruel oppressions upon the minority whenever strong divisions prevail in that kind of polity, as they often must; and that oppression of the minority will extend to far greater numbers and will be carried on with much greater fury than can almost ever be apprehended from the dominion of a single scepter.

A democracy, for a minority, could be "a much more deplorable condition than in any other" form of government, since "those who are subjected to wrong under multitudes are deprived of all external consolation." In fact, they "seem deserted by mankind, overpowered by a conspiracy of their whole species."

7. *Order.* The basis of all things is order in society and government, worked toward endlessly and assiduously:

> To be enabled to acquire, the people, without being servile, must be tractable and obedient. The magistrate must have his reverence, the laws their authority. The body of the people must not find the principles of natural subordination by art rooted out of their minds. They must respect that property of which they cannot partake. They must labor to obtain what by labor can be obtained; and when they find, as they commonly do, the success disproportioned to the endeavor, they must be taught their consolation in the final proportions of eternal justice.

Order in the universe, society, and government was the most fundamental principle of all of Burke's ruminations. There was, he believed, a transcendent order established by God that commanded the reverence of all beings. Reverence included duty to one's station and respect for all other stations in the universe. Whether one happened to be king, lord, farmer, or peasant, he was part of a divinely ordained and observable order of things.[15]

8. *Tradition.* The divine order of the universe and of society was to be maintained. A fundament in preserving order was the maintenance of institutions and laws that provide justice, peace, and liberty for everyone in society. Indeed, one of the great difficulties of both Enlightenment philosophers and of French revolutionaries was their inability to understand the power of tradition:

> With them it is a sufficient motive to destroy an old scheme of things because it is an old one. . . . They conceive, very systematically, that all things which give perpetuity are mischievous, and therefore they are at inexpiable war with all establishments. They think that government may vary like modes of dress, and with little ill effect.

On the contrary, it was better to build within established orders that provide infinite flexibility to deal with any problem and meet any crisis.

9. *Education.* According to Burke, society is a perpetual contract among people, orders, and institutions. Critical in maintaining these was proper education. Education itself is best rooted in tradition, "adhering in this particular, as in all things wise, to our old settled maxim, never entirely nor at once to depart from antiquity." Proper instruction in philosophy, politics, law, and religion not only produced good and dutiful leaders; it also carried forward a happy and productive populace. Education should be universal and commensurate with one's station and aspirations in life.[16]

10. *Religion.* Hand in hand with education was religion: "We know, and what is better, we feel inwardly, that religion is the basis of civil society and the source of all good and of all comfort." Indeed, as Burke saw revolutionary France destroying its religious institutions and demolishing its churches and cathedrals, he argued that church and state were inseparable. The British people, in contrast to the French, "consider it [the Church] as the foundation of their whole constitution, with which, and with every part of which, it holds an indissoluble union." By this he clearly meant not that church and state had to be legally interblended, but rather that one was fundamental to the proper operation of the other. After all, it was the Church that provided universal education. It was the Church that trained people to play their proper roles in an orderly society.

11. *Atheism and Fanaticism.* The absence of religion and, furthermore, warring on religion were the sources of chaos and the collapse of society. Any attempts to undermine religion were efforts to overturn the natural order of the universe: "We know, and it is our pride to know, that man is by his constitution a religious animal; that atheism is against, not only our reason, but our instincts; and that it cannot prevail long." Since religion was "one great source of civilization amongst us and amongst many other nations," to remove it created a void "that some uncouth, pernicious, and degrading superstition might take place of it." And the superstition most likely to creep in was that of "atheistical fanaticism" of the type emerging among the theorists and leaders of the French Revolution:

> These writings and sermons have filled the populace with a black and savage atrocity of mind, which supersedes in them the common feelings of nature as well as all sentiments of morality and religion, insomuch that these wretches are induced to bear with a sullen patience the intolerable distresses brought upon them by the violent convulsions and permutations that have been made.

This kind of fanaticism was destroying France and was being exported across Europe and the Western world. Atheism had to be eschewed to maintain order and peace.[17]

12. *Reform and Revolution.* "The ceremony of cashiering [dismissing] kings . . . can rarely, if ever, be performed without force" nor be justified, according to

Burke. In fact, "a revolution will be the very last resource of the thinking and the good." Because revolutions were destructive exercises, whether one looked at the problems of France or of any other nation, Burke considered it always better to reform than to overturn. France had, in Burke's estimation, all of the necessary foundations to fix its problems: "You possessed in some parts the walls and, in all, the foundations of a noble and venerable castle. You might have repaired those walls; you might have built on those old foundations." Had France pursued reform rather than revolution, "You would have rendered the cause of liberty venerable in the eyes of every worthy mind in every nation." Instead, by pursuing an "unnatural" course,

> They have found their punishment in their success: laws overturned; tribunals subverted; industry without vigor; commerce expiring; the revenue unpaid, yet the people impoverished; a church pillaged, and a state not relieved; civil and military anarchy made the constitution of the kingdom. . . . The fresh ruins of France . . . are not the devastation of civil war; they are the sad but instructive monuments of rash and ignorant counsel in time of profound peace.

By following the "false lights" of revolution rather than reform, Burke concluded, France "bought undisguised calamities at a higher price than any nation has purchased the most unequivocal blessings."[18]

Burke's *Reflections* not only threw doubts on the French Revolution, it also questioned the nature and direction of the Enlightenment. But the work's most remarkable quality was that it also was a manifesto for a new future in the Western world. It provided a new lens for examining traditional problems of governance, social structure, human values, liberty, freedom, equality, and order. Between the immediate political purpose it served and the overarching principles Burke enunciated, there was a blueprint to inspire a counterrevolutionary movement across the Western world—equal to, if not greater, than the revolutionary fires that had ignited France.

The story of how Edmund Burke came to be the world's preeminent friend of order is intriguing. One part of the story involves his own career, the other, the quite separate career of *Reflections on the Revolution in France,* his manifesto of order. Irish-born, Burke was profoundly conscious of his Irishness until his dying day. Born in Dublin just across from Trinity College on January 12, 1729, Burke was bookish in the extreme from his earliest days. He attended a country school, then a very good Quaker school that prepared him to enter Trinity College in 1744 at age fifteen. Omnivorous in intellectual appetite, Burke ransacked every field of study—languages, the classics, philosophy, mathematics. He read English and classical authors until he could quote with ease from Virgil, Cicero, Sallust, and Xenophon, as well as Shakespeare, Spenser, and Milton.[19]

Before departing Trinity in 1748, Burke completed a first draft of his *Philosophical Inquiry into the Origins of our Ideas on the Sublime and Beautiful,* eventually published in 1757. He then decided to relocate to London and there pursue whatever might become the focus of his career. First he studied law at Middle Temple to satisfy his father. But by 1756 it became clear that he was more inclined toward a literary career. In that year he published a *Vindication of Natural Society,* a parody on Bolingbroke. Already in this volume can be seen the outlines of Burke's assault on Rousseau and French proponents of a "natural society," as opposed to one made up of historical, political, and ecclesiastical traditions and institutions. Next came a revised *On The Sublime and Beautiful,* also an attack on French philosophes and their abstract approach to understanding perception.

With his marriage to Jane Nugent of Bath in 1757, Burke had to become as serious about his income as he had been theretofore about his writing career. In 1759, he contracted with a London bookseller to establish, compile, and edit the *Annual Register,* a landmark British publication that has been published from that time to the present. In compiling the *Annual Register,* Burke became a familiar name around the world. American authors and historians used the publication extensively in the absence of libraries and the ability to do on-site research.

But the *Annual Register* was not enough to support a family, to entertain friends, and to lead the life of a gentleman. In 1761 Burke found a patron in William Gerard Hamilton, who paid Burke handsomely and made it possible for him to return to Dublin periodically. From 1761 until his retirement from Parliament in 1794, Burke was under the pay or patronage of one or another ambitious politician. Except for two brief periods, 1765 and 1782, Burke's patrons were of the loyal opposition, which meant that during most of his lengthy political career he was at war with King George III and His Majesty's long string of ministers.

Burke, nevertheless, made a place for himself in the world of British public affairs. Beginning with early rumblings leading to the American Revolution and continuing with the rise of revolutionary sentiment in Ireland, Burke made himself an expert on colonial affairs. During the American Revolution, he proved, along with Richard Price, to be a great friend of the American colonies. So outspoken was he on the rights of Americans that he became a beloved favorite in the rebellious colonies. Perfecting a public style that included carefully timed, masterly drawn orations in Parliament and the issuance of sharply honed essays at politically critical junctures, Burke exerted decisive influence on British policy concerning America, Ireland, India, and, finally, France.[20]

Given the dividing line in Burke's life where he sought to expound great principles when he was deeply involved in the battles of partisan politics, reactions to his speeches and essays widely varied and were even greatly delayed as the meaning of his words became manifest. For all of Burke's insights, he tended to muddle them in documents large and small. Joined with these considerations was Burke's fierce partisanship, injecting political elements into every word uttered and sentence written. It was easy for contemporaries, as it has been for historians, to misunderstand Burke's words and actions.

Hence it was with *Reflections on the Revolution in France.* Just days after the tract appeared on November 1, 1790, Philip Francis—who had urged Burke not to go through with the publication—gave Burke his opinions on the final product. As he had previously noted, Francis thought the work ill-advised and sure to cause Burke political difficulties. He also thought that Burke had misinterpreted the role of religion in contemporary life. Europe was much more enlightened on this score than when popes, cardinals, and monks everywhere reigned supreme. Despite his negative view of *Reflections,* Francis promised to defend Burke's views, if called upon: "You may be perfectly sure that I shall never say another word, unless it be to support and defend you to the utmost of my power. That is my Office now." Nonetheless, Burke was incensed at the letter and immediately responded with a searing note that concluded their long friendship: "Your paper has much more the character of a piece, in an adverse controversy, carried on before the tribunal of the Nation at large, than of the animadversion of a friend on his friend's performance."[21]

As it happened, Burke found few defenders of the character and contents of *Reflections.* Within a few months, a number of significant responses had been published, charging Burke with abandoning the cause of liberty and of turning his back on his long-standing battle to protect the rights of man. Mary Wollstonecraft denounced Burke in her initially anonymous *A Vindication of the Rights of Man* in November 1790. So powerful was her response that it was reissued over her name in December. Thomas Paine followed in March 1791 with *The Rights of Man,* an instantly popular attack on Burke, but also an articulation of a different view of happenings in France. James Mackintosh followed with *Vindiciae Gallicae* (1791), wherein he praised Burke's ability to present ignominious ideas with unequaled literary flourishes.[22]

The reaction to *Reflections* was so entirely negative in nearly every quarter that Burke became an embattled man. As he sought to vindicate his unpopular views, his presentation of the principles of order became increasingly obscured. In April and May of 1791, members of his own Whig party shouted him down unceremoniously when he attempted to present his views on the French Revolution in Parliament. At least twenty members of the House of Commons walked out rather than listen to his harangue. When he finished, Charles James Fox, party head, rose and condemned both Burke and *Reflections* in such a manner that Burke felt compelled to resign from the Whig Party on the spot.[23]

Fox and the other critics held that Burke had departed longstanding Whig principles in his condemnation of the French Revolution. The champion of the rights of Americans, of the Irish, and of Indians seemed suddenly opposed to the rights of French citizens or of British subjects who were clamoring for Parliamentary reform. Upset with the tidal wave of criticism, Burke launched into a series of responses that would continue until his death. A significant expansion on his ideas in *Reflections,* written in much the same tenor, was Burke's *A Letter to a Member of the National Assembly.* Penned in January 1791 but not published until May, it appeared just in time to put another nail in Burke's political coffin.

Addressed to François-Louis-Thibaut de Menonville in response to another letter, Burke used the piece to expand on his notion that Jean-Jacques Rousseau had an evil influence on France.

Burke's *Letter to a Member of the National Assembly* criticized specific French leaders, including Mirabeau and Talleyrand. Mirabeau was "a fine speaker—and a fine writer—and a fine—a very fine man," but Burke could not fathom how he could be qualified to be the "supreme head" of "ecclesiastical affairs" in France. Or how "persons not to be suspected of any sort of Christian superstition," such as Talleyrand, could be made a bishop. But the fiction that France had a king and a queen tore most madly at Burke, as he surveyed the absurd pretension that Louis XVI and Marie Antoinette ruled the nation: "Assuredly I do not wish ill to your king; but better for him not to live (he does not reign) than to live the passive instrument of tyranny and usurpation." In fact, Burke accused the leaders of the National Assembly of toying with the whole concept of monarchy:

> In spite of their solemn declarations, their soothing addresses, and the multiplied oaths which they have taken, and forced others to take, they will assassinate the king when his name will no longer be necessary to their designs; but not a moment sooner. They will probably first assassinate the queen . . . At present, the advantage which they derive from the daily threats against her life, is her only security for preserving it. They keep their sovereign alive for the purpose of exhibiting him, like some wild beast at a fair; as if they had a Bajazet [Racine's slain fictional hero] in a cage.[24]

Even before the attempted escape of Louis and Marie Antoinette to Varennes on June 20, 1791, Burke thus prophesied to a dismayed and disbelieving public.

When Burke's *Letter* appeared on May 21, Charles James Fox described it in Parliament as "mere madness," sending Burke into the most elongated defense of his recent opinions. *An Appeal from the New to the Old Whigs,* written in the third person and published anonymously in August 1791, was Burke's greatest effort to refute charges of his political and philosophical inconsistencies—especially in relation to his support of the American Revolution and his opposition to the French Revolution. As in the case of most of his publications, he buried the core of his argument amid a plethora of detail including ancient and more recent parliamentary history, a recounting of the Revolution of 1688, and British constitutional history.[25]

At the heart of his *Appeal,* however, was a meeting between Burke and Benjamin Franklin, just as Franklin was leaving England in 1775 to lead the American colonies in their struggle for independence. Burke and Franklin had frequently corresponded on political and philosophical topics. Whenever Franklin had found himself at cross-purposes with King George III and his ministers, Burke usually sided with Franklin.[26] At the moment when the spirit of Franklin was being invoked in France to justify revolution, Burke called upon the vast

Franklin legacy to demonstrate that there were at least two kinds of liberty and two kinds of revolutions.

"It was, I think, the very day before he set out for America," Burke's third-person voice stated, "that a very long conversation passed between them, and with a greater air of openness on the Doctor's side, than Mr. Burke had observed in him before." Franklin was usually quite "locked up" and reticent about expressing his true feelings. But on this occasion he "opened" his ideas fully to Burke:

> In this discourse Dr. Franklin lamented, and with apparent sincerity, the separation which he feared was inevitable between Great Britain and her colonies. . . . America, he said, would never again see such happy days as she had passed under the protection of England. He observed, that ours was the only instance of a great empire, in which the most distant parts and members had been as well governed as the metropolis and its vicinage: But that Americans were going to lose the means which secured to them this rare and precious advantage. The question with them was not whether they were to remain as they had been before the troubles, for better, he allowed they could not hope to be; but whether they were to give up so happy a situation without a struggle?

Burke had other conversations with Franklin about the same time, but in none of them, "soured and exasperated as his mind certainly was, did he discover any other wish in favour of America than for a security to its ancient condition."[27]

Through the dead and sanctified Franklin—who in 1774 had been defended in Parliament by Burke, Richard Price, and Joseph Priestley—Burke tried to make clear that he had always been in favor of liberty, but "not French liberty": "That liberty is nothing but the rein given to vice and confusion." The liberty he favored "is a liberty connected with order." This, as he argued in 1774 when he defended the rights of Americans, "not only exists with order and virtue, but cannot exist at all without them." Indeed, "it inheres in good and steady government, as in its substance and vital principle." Burke's position on liberty in 1774 had remained unchanged in 1791, despite the derision of his critics.

There was Burke's central and unforgettable message: Human beings gathered in societies cannot have liberty without order, cannot achieve just treatment without structure in society, cannot enjoy freedom without the observance of traditions. By the same token, revolutions to establish or restore order, structure, and tradition—such as the American Revolution—were just revolutions and were likely to bring liberty. Those based upon theories that liberty can be dished out like food rations by acts of a national legislature—such as the French Revolution—brought only chaos and doomed liberty.

By defining an alternative route to liberty and freedom, Burke gave birth to a counterrevolutionary spirit that would forever wage war on the libertarian promises of democratic movements and revolutions. By dint of history, logic, and example, he demonstrated that liberty and freedom are among the most perishable of quantities and that hordes of people with the power of the ballot are least able to deliver, preserve, and protect them. Liberty could be attained only with true constitutions—those that evolve naturally and are not merely written—and with well-bred institutions such as the courts, the Church, an established executive, fixed laws, and responsible public officials.

Burke spent his final years reiterating this message. It became easier with the passage of time, as the imprisonment of King Louis XVI led step-by-step to a reign of terror and the chaos Burke had predicted. In *Thoughts on French Affairs* (December 1791), written for British leaders only, Burke cried out for a counter-revolution against what he described as "a Revolution of doctrine and theoretick dogma." Its effect was "to introduce other interests into all countries than those which arose from their locality and natural circumstances." In that respect it was more like the Reformation in that it knew no borders and as "on that occasion . . . the spirit of proselytism expanded itself with great elasticity upon all sides; and great divisions were every where the result."[28]

When Prime Minister Charles James Fox introduced in the House of Commons in December 1792 a motion "for sending a Minister to Paris to Treat with the Provisional Government of France," Burke became crazed. With the public trial of Louis XVI daily proceeding, Burke thought his own government was abetting the onset of revolutionary chaos. In one of the most dramatic speeches of his life, he decried the fact that a British manufacturer had made three thousand daggers for export to France. To the horror of the staid Commons, Burke drew a concealed dagger from his vest "and with much vehemence of action threw it to the floor." Then pointing to the dagger, he proclaimed, "This . . . is what you are to gain by an alliance with France: wherever their principles are introduced, their practice must follow."

Even as he attacked the revolution in France, he became deeply involved in efforts to bring liberty to his native Ireland. In the early 1790s he was one of the most influential individuals in London when it came to the development of policies regarding Ireland. He cheered as Theobald Wolfe Tone formed the Society of United Irishmen in Belfast. He encouraged his beloved son Richard to become agent of the Catholic Committee in Ireland. Together Richard Burke and Tone sought to redress the ancient grievances of Irish Catholics and attempted to secure their enfranchisement.

Although Burke and Tone met only once, through Richard Burke, they achieved a special bond. As Burke surveyed conditions in Ireland and observed, under Tone's tutelage, the rise of a militant "Jacobinism" rivaling that of France, he refined his ideas about liberty and revolutions even further. So badly did he wish to loosen the fetters on Irish Catholics that he found it necessary to distinguish between Jacobinism "which is Speculative in its Origin" (French) and that "which arises from Penury and irritation, from scorned loyalty, and rejected Allegiance" (Irish). Revolution could not be justified in the first instance, but it could be in the second. The first brought only chaos; the second might be necessary to bring liberty to an oppressed people. Indeed, in his latest writings on Ireland, Burke thought that it would be justifiable for the Irish to pursue rebellion to secure liberties withheld by a Protestant-controlled British government.[29]

Burke's aspirations to bring a permanent solution to his native land were dashed in August 1794, when his son Richard succumbed to an acute attack of tuberculosis. Ten days after the younger Burke was first elected to a seat in Parliament, his lungs and trachea faltered. Four days later he was dead, taking with him Burke's hopes for the future. Theobald Wolfe Tone grieved with Edmund Burke and attempted to fill the large role the young Burke had come to play in Irish affairs until in June 1795, under suspicion of treason, he fled to the United States.[30]

Theobald Wolfe Tone's revolutionary spirit fascinated Edmund Burke. Even when he learned of Tone's suspicious "Connexions" with French agents, Burke found that he could not condemn the intractable rebel. Although Tone ballyhooed Thomas Paine's *The Rights of Man* and condemned Burke's *Reflections on the Revolution in France,* Burke could not dislike the leading fomenter of Irish revolution. Nor could Tone dismiss Burke's constant efforts on behalf of Ireland. But in Tone's opinion, Thomas Paine and the French provided the public "political creed" needed in Ireland, even though Burke worked behind the scenes to aid liberty for Irish Catholics.

The mutual admiration between this pair ran so deep that each found himself in the oddest of circumstances rationalizing the behavior of the other. When Tone arrived in France in 1796 in search of a French army to invade Ireland, his path quickly crossed with Thomas Paine. Paine gloated over the shattered state of Edmund Burke—retired, broken, but still ranting about the French Revolution. To Tone he expressed a grim glee that *The Rights of Man* had brought discredit and shame to the once proud Burke. *The Rights of Man,* Paine stated, "had broken his heart." Tone quickly set Paine right: "I am sure the Rights of Man have tormented Burke exceedingly, but I have seen myself the workings of a father's grief upon his spirit, and I could not be deceived."[31]

Just as Tone knew the mind of Burke, the friend of order could see into the spirit and heart of the Irish rebel. As Burke sought to stanch what he believed to be the tyranny of French Jacobinism over life, liberty, and property through *Letters on a Regicide Peace,* he also confronted the reality that perhaps only a revolution could salvage a deteriorating Ireland. Confined to his bed and no longer able to wield a pen, Burke dictated angry judgments against the French Directory:

> The Regicides . . . have renounced the creed of the Rights of Man, and declared equality a chimera. . . . They have apostatized from their apostasy. They are renegades from that impious faith for which they subverted the ancient government, murdered their king, and imprisoned, butchered, confiscated, and banished their fellow-subjects, and to which they forced every man to swear at the peril of his life.

But from that same bed, in a "reduced state of body and in the dejected state of mind in which I find myself at this very advanced period of my life," Burke also composed a final *Letter on the Affairs of Ireland* in which he wistfully hoped for a break in the intractable war of Protestants on Catholics.[32]

It was amid these final works that Burke learned of French assaults onto Bantry Bay in Ireland and Cardigan Bay in England. He then also learned that the mastermind behind these attacks was none other than Theobald Wolfe Tone, the beloved friend of his son Richard. Indeed, Tone headed the expedition into Bantry Bay. As he brooded over this startling revelation, Burke finally realized that interpreting revolutions required the heart as well as the head. He was driven to differentiate between the tyranny of revolutionaries in France and that of British authorities over Catholics in the north of Ireland. Assessing the meaning of Tone's efforts to foment a revolution in Ireland while wearing the uniform and leading the charges of an enemy Burke detested, he dictated his last words on revolutions "by snatches, as a relief from pain gives me the means of expressing my sentiments. . . . I do not wish to have it concealed that I am of the same opinion, to my last breath, which I entertained when my faculties were at the best," he whispered faintly. But on "this melancholy subject" of Ireland, he concluded, a resort to rebellion could well be justified. And as for Tone's efforts to foment that revolution in a French uniform, Burke could not, would not, and did not utter a word of condemnation.[33]

It was during these same days that he became fearful that French revolutionists might seek him out dead or alive in retribution for his denunciations of what he then deemed "the atheistical fanatics of France." Burke observed: "I am their neighbor; I may become their subject. . . . I certainly should dread more from a wild-cat in my bed-chamber than from all the lions that roar in the deserts behind Algiers."

Iterating his desire to be buried "unknown, the spot unmarked," Burke drew his last breath shortly after midnight on July 9, 1797. A funeral service held at Beaconsfield, Burke's home from 1768 until his death, on July 15, brought together a cast of political leaders representing each of Britain's ruling factions and the great causes to which Burke devoted his energies, less one. No one from the United States or with whom he had defended the rights of American colonials attended his last rites. Although no Americans appeared to honor this friend of the American Revolution, Philip Francis, who had urged Burke not to publish the *Reflections on the Revolution in France,* was in attendance lamenting the silence between them that had extended over seven years.[34]

CHAPTER 18

Friends of Order

MALESHERBES, TOCQUEVILLE, AND CHATEAUBRIAND

On the morning of April 22, 1794, Chrétien-Guillaume de Lamoignon de Malesherbes watched sadly as his daughter Marguerite and his granddaughter Aline-Therese and her husband Jean-Baptiste Chateaubriand submitted to the guillotine at Port-Libre prison on the outskirts of Paris. On the prior day Marguerite's husband, Lepeletier de Rosanbo, former president of the Parlement of Paris, had been beheaded for "conspiring against the liberty and sovereignty of the French People." In coming days Malesherbes's seventy-six-year-old sister, Comtesse de Senozan, also would be executed along with his two secretaries. He must have sighed a bit of relief that his wife, a victim of suicide in 1771, was not there to share his agony and fate. Other grandchildren, including Louise and her husband Hervé Clerel de Tocqueville remained in the prison awaiting their doom. Stricken to his core by the mad course taken by France, but strong and bold to his last breath, the seventy-two-year-old Malesherbes quietly placed his head beneath the tool of death that, in place of liberty, became the symbol of the French Revolution.[1]

On the day prior to his execution Malesherbes had confronted the system of justice then at work in liberated France. The charges brought against him derived from a comment he had made to his elder sister. When she told him that grapevines on her estate had frozen, he replied, so it was reported, that the disaster was a good thing since it was wine-drunk peasants who had brought on the revolution. Based on this flimsy evidence of conspiracy against the people of France, the tribunal declared that "Lamoignon-Malesherbes presents all the characteristics of a counter-revolutionary." Further, the court found that Malesherbes's writings, which were considerable, dwelled constantly on the abolished order and that he was at the center of a group of conspirators intent on overthrowing the government and restoring monarchy to France.[2]

In spite of the kangaroo-court proceedings against Malesherbes, the finding that he was a counterrevolutionary could not have been more accurate. But it was not that he was engaged in any activity to overthrow the government or to restore monarchy. Although he had served as attorney for Louis XVI in his trial before the National Convention, he was not involved in any of the counterrevolutionary movements in and outside of France. It was rather that he wanted to restore order to France.

Throughout his long career of service to France he had always taken the side of order against every authority, including Louis XV and Louis XVI. But it was order to provide liberty. For example, when he served Louis XV as director of the Royal Library, he had the power to annul the publication of any book. But believing in a fundamental freedom of press, he presided over the publication of volumes by Rousseau, Diderot, and others that would later be judged radical and atheistical. As president of the Cour des Aides, Malesherbes attacked an edict of Louis XV that abolished local courts and replaced them with appointed magistrates loyal to the Crown. With the coronation of Louis XVI, he hoped the drift of French kings toward absolutism, bureaucracy, and arbitrary government could be replaced with a different kind of monarchy—one that could be decentralized, with elected officials, and based on a strong body of law. He joined in Louis XVI's first ministry to achieve these goals but soon discovered that the young king lacked both the understanding and the will to pursue a reformed monarchy. By 1775 Malesherbes was back at his chateau, where he pursued farming, exploring, writing, and providing legal advice to the nation.

When in 1788 Louis XVI finally considered reforming the French government, Malesherbes had come into contact with Lord Shelburne's Bowood circle and, with that group, had proposed a constitutional monarchy with a constituent assembly. But when Malesherbes learned that Louis was considering a convocation of the Estates-General, he penned a strenuous objection to the king. Whereas some monarchists might conceive the Estates-General a constituent assembly, it was actually "a vestige of ancient barbarism, a battlefield where three factions of the same people come to fight each other; . . . a collision of all interests with the general interest . . . a means of subversion, not a means of renovation." Calling the Estates-General a "ruin," Malesherbes pleaded, "Let a King at the end of the eighteenth century not convoke the three orders of the fourteenth century; let him instead call together the proprietors of a great nation renewed by its civilization." Almost prophetic in his advice, he concluded, "A King who submits to a constitution feels degraded; a King who proposes a constitution obtains instead the highest glory among men and their liveliest and most enduring gratitude."

Nevertheless, Louis XVI did not heed his advice, and the worst of Malesherbes's fears became a reality in the fall of 1792, when Louis, under arrest, had achieved history's most memorable degradation. Malesherbes stepped forth and volunteered to serve as Louis's defense attorney. From December 11, when "Louis Capet" was brought from the Temple to hear the indictment against him, until the trial ended on January 4, 1793, Malesherbes was the king's constant companion. Fearing almost certain defeat, Louis dictated a will to Malesherbes on Christmas day. Although they disagreed on legal strategies for the trial (Malesherbes thought the National Convention could not legally serve as judge and jury, Louis XVI thought the monarchy constitutionally immune to such a proceeding), Malesherbes and two colleagues did their best to defend their king.

Eleven days after the trial ended, the Convention took three votes. On the subject of the King's guilt or innocence all of the deputies who voted—693 of a membership of 749—found Louis guilty. As to whether this decision should be appealed to a national referendum, 424 voted nay, while 283 favored an appeal. In a session lasting until dawn on January 16, the last ballot involved the sentence. In a sharply divided vote among 721 deputies present, 361 voted unconditionally for immediate execution, 319 for imprisonment and banishment after the current war, 23 for a death sentence with a possible reprieve, 8 for death coupled with banishment of the Bourbons from France, 2 for execution following the war, and 2 only for the option of life imprisonment. Malesherbes, forced to stand for the duration of the voting—more than thirteen hours—pleaded that the moment called for compassion and common decency, not for blood. Breaking into tears, he stumbled through his words, "Citizens, excuse my difficulties. . . . I have observations to make to you . . . will I have the misfortune of losing them if you do not allow me to present them . . . tomorrow?" Unfortunately for Malesherbes and his heartfelt sensibilities, the deed was done. Despite a last minute appeal by Thomas Paine to banish the condemned king to the United States, Louis XVI was guillotined on the morning of January 21, still proclaiming his innocence.

In addition to the profound effect the trial and execution of Louis XVI had on France, Europe, and the Western world, the impact on Malesherbes was even greater. The last defender of the hated king faced certain doom as the French Revolution devolved into a reign of terror. And given the insidious nature of the Terror, it was clear that his family stood in equal danger of dying with him. He could have fled, but he did not. He could have advised his family to emigrate, he but did not. Instead, they gathered at his chateau near Pithiviers, except daughter Françoise-Pauline, who had previously fled to London. While they awaited their fate the youngest daughter, Louise, married Hervé de Tocqueville on March 12, 1793, in a wedding held at the chateau.[3]

When the last of the Malesherbes heads fell into the guillotine's basket in April 1794, there miraculously remained three survivors who, because of their love for Malesherbes, spent the remainder of their lives defining a counter-revolutionary movement that would change France and much of the Western world. They would inspire a campaign to explain to rising generations, much in the style of Edmund Burke, all that was wrong with the French Revolution, while also propounding a philosophy that overturned eighteenth-century notions of liberty, freedom, and equality.

Who were these survivors who carried on the mighty torch? First were Louise and Hervé de Tocqueville who, perhaps due to their youth or recent union at the Malesherbes chateau, seemed less threatening than other members of the family. After several months of imprisonment, they were released with the emancipation that accompanied the Thermidorian reaction. While neither Louise nor Hervé achieved great fame in their lifetimes, they taught their son Alexis, born in 1805, to become one of the world's most influential thinkers on matters of liberty, revolution, and democracy.

Indeed, in the middle decades of the nineteenth century, Hervé and Alexis together composed a powerful force in trying to explain to another generation—again in the grips of destructive revolutions—why no one wanted to see a repeat of the French Revolution. Between Alexis's perennially powerful *Democracy in America* (2 vols., 1835, 1840), *Recollections* (written 1850, published 1893), and *The Old Regime and the Revolution in France* (1856), and Hervé's *Philosophical History of the Reign of Louis XV* (2 vols., 1847), and *Survey of the Reign of Louis XVI* (1850), one has several thousand pages of influential narrative and analysis lapped up at the time by emotionally racked populations. Alexis's *Democracy in America* and his *Old Regime* became classics that have spoken to every generation to the present. Had he not died tragically of tuberculosis in 1859 at the age of fifty-four, he most likely would have provided another classic in his partially completed book on the advent of the French Revolution.[4]

While there were many differences in style, emphasis, and approach between the works of father and son, they shared a philosophy that much resembled that of Malesherbes. Though Hervé remained a royalist throughout his life and Alexis promoted republicanism, both of them were ultraconservative in their views of society. Both believed that every society had to have some form of aristocracy, whether hereditary or appointed. Both believed that the only road to freedom and equality was through the creation of institutions and traditions that would enforce order on society. Hervé dwelt on the noble ideas of Malesherbes to make these points, while Alexis drew upon his conservative temper and sociological analyses.[5]

The third person mercifully absent from the execution of the Malesherbes family was the younger brother of Jean-Baptiste Chateaubriand. Almost constantly under the somewhat tyrannical eye of his eldest brother, François René Chateaubriand was wounded at the siege of Thionville as he fought in the French Army. With a gangrenous injury to his hip that seemed impervious to treatment and a lung infection that rendered him unable to walk, the young Chateaubriand escaped to London in May 1793, where he hoped to safely recuperate. His timing was perfect in every respect, as he regained health and avoided the guillotine.[6]

Living on the edges of poverty as a freelance author, editor, and translator, Chateaubriand was shattered when he received word that his brother and Malesherbes died on the same scaffold. If anything, the loss of Malesherbes overshadowed that of his none-too-kind brother. Being the youngest by far of seven children, Jean-Baptiste came to remind him of his tyrannical and unloving father. Malesherbes, on the other hand, was a wise and gentle spirit—just the kind of individual every boy needed in a father. Shunted aside by both parents, Chateaubriand wandered from one school to another, from his mother's home in St. Malo on the coast of Brittany to the family's chateau Combourg. Intent on restoring the family to the landed nobility of France, his father, Réne August de Chateaubriand, ruthlessly followed every rule and tradition of the ancien regime, including devising two thirds of his estate to Jean-Baptist, the eldest son.

No one took the brooding and aimless Chateaubriand seriously until late in 1787, when he first came into contact with Malesherbes. Jean-Baptiste, as eager as their late father to cement the noble rank of the Chateaubriands, brought the nineteen-year-old to Paris that year to introduce him in polite society and to have a mandatory audience with Louis XVI and Marie Antoinette. Chateaubriand awkwardly went through the motions of meeting king and queen in their levies, dining with them, and participating in a royal hunt. But the only thing of lasting value to him came from his acquaintance and friendship with the elderly Malesherbes. Taking a deep interest in the future of the young man, Malesherbes urged him to expand his reading from the classics to Rousseau, from literature to the sciences, and from poetry into useful fields such as botany and geography. As they pored over some of Malesherbes's books and maps, they together conceived a grand ambition sometime to leave France and go in search of the as-yet-undiscovered Northwest Passage over North America.

Chateaubriand encountered Malesherbes just in time to share with the statesman the oncoming French Revolution. He experienced firsthand the bloody riot that grew out of the first meeting of the Estates-General of Brittany province. He watched the riots surrounding the storming of the Bastille from his hotel window in Paris. While others shuttered their windows as mobs raced by with decapitated heads waving on top of pikes, Chateaubriand held his place, believing that he was witnessing the arrival of liberty in France. Despite his newly won rank among the nobility, he uttered his revolutionary sentiments during those stirring days to Malesherbes. The wise man retorted, "I ought to advise you to moderate your enthusiasm lest it do you as much harm as it has some of your friends." But he also admitted, "I used to be like you; injustice revolted me; I have done what I could without expecting much gratitude for it."

By the fall of 1790, Chateaubriand saw Malesherbes's prophecies come true. Still eager for reform but grasping the rapid slide toward chaos, Chateaubriand decided that he must leave France at once and pursue a meaningful life elsewhere. He decided that his best option was to go in search of the Northwest Passage, then raced to Malesherbes's study with the news. Unwilling or unable to discourage Chateaubriand's ardor, Malesherbes said, "If I were younger, I'd go with you, and spare myself the sight of all this crime and cowardice and madness." As the youthful adventurer headed off, the fatherly adviser called out, "Don't forget to write to me by every ship, to let me know how your travels and your discoveries get on."

With letters of introduction Chateaubriand sailed in April 1791 from St. Malo to Baltimore, arriving in late July. Eager to get on his way toward the Northwest, he headed to Philadelphia, where he hoped to meet and solicit the support of President Washington. As he explained his mission to discover the Northwest Passage, he sensed that the president did not wish to comment on the plan. The young Chateaubriand saved the day by saying, "But it is less hard to discover the North-West Passage than to make a nation as you have done!"

Despite negative judgments at every turn, he took a packet boat to Albany, New York, and there engaged a Dutch guide to blaze a trail with him across uncharted wilderness by way of the Great Lakes to the Pacific Ocean. Once at the Pacific his plan was to turn right and follow the coastline until he returned to the Atlantic Ocean. Certain of his logic, they headed in the direction of Niagara Falls and Lake Erie. But, much to his surprise, he found well-traveled trails and scattered settlements. Even the Native Americans, whom he expected would be living as savages, spoke broken French and English and possessed goods and implements imported from Europe. And, when he thought he had finally broken into wilderness, he was astonished to come upon a village where a Frenchman, complete with powdered wig, played a violin for a rapt native audience.

By the time he arrived at Niagara Falls, he had discovered the madness of his scheme. He had not found in America the great land of liberty he had expected. Indeed, he considered it poignant that the first person to greet him in America was a female slave. Nor did he find in the wilderness the noble savage projected by Rousseau and Malesherbes. Just as he was contemplating what he would do next, he saw an English-language newspaper with a headline titled "Flight of the King." As he read the story of the abortive escape of Louis XVI and Marie Antoinette by way of Varennes, he suddenly converted from a sympathizer with the Revolution to an enemy of the Revolutionary government. Although far in the backcountry of North America pursuing a chimera, he decided to join a counterrevolutionary movement to restore both monarchy and order to his beloved France. By December 10 he had departed the port of Philadelphia en route to Le Havre.

Back in St. Malo by February, having squandered his small inheritance on his American adventure, Chateaubriand was unable to proceed with his first objective of traveling to Koblenz to join the Army of the Princes. Unable to extract funds from Jean-Baptiste and his mother, he married a young woman he barely knew to get what he hoped would be a considerable dowry. But in typical Chateaubriand fashion, he had leaped before he looked. Celeste Buisson de la Vigne's dowry was more than modest, but it was in the hands of a group of trustees. With a wife he would not see for eight years (but who would be with him for a lifetime), he finally cajoled two of his sisters to sign a note guaranteeing a loan of ten thousand francs. After losing most of the money in an all-night gambling match, he and Jean-Baptiste left Paris in July for Koblenz. Their departure was made all the sweeter by a last meeting with Malesherbes, in which Chateaubriand not only shared notes and descriptions of America, he also received Malesherbes's blessing for his new venture.

Fighting with the Army of the Princes turned out to be just as foolhardy as his search for the Northwest Passage. The army lived in pleasant quarters and ate well, but it had no ranks, no training, no discipline, no equipment, and no support. The siege of Thionville, as a consequence, turned out to be a disaster for both the army and for Chateaubriand. After several days of continuous storming of the town and hand-to-hand battle, Chateaubriand collapsed from exhaustion at the outer wall. When he awoke the following morning, he found that he had been injured in the thigh by an exploding shell. His wound, and another infection that turned out to be smallpox, resulted in his discharge from the madcap army. Over the next four months he hovered between life and death, cared for by strangers, by gypsies, and finally by Jean-Baptiste, who found him prostrate in Brussels. Although not yet fully recovered but cognizant of the treatment being accorded counterrevolutionaries throughout France, in May 1793 Chateaubriand made his way to England.

Within months, as he brooded over the death of Malesherbes and doubtless read the new works of Edmund Burke, he established a new voice for order that would become to France what Burke was to Britain.[7]

Malesherbes, Tocqueville, and Chateaubriand were a new breed of friends of liberty who believed that liberty could be achieved only by first assuring in government and society a strong measure of order. While they, along with Edmund Burke, might in their own time have been classed as social and political oddities, they were actually in the process of defining an alternative approach to governance and civil polity that conformed neither to ancient tradition nor to the abstractions of the Enlightenment. Distraught by the chaotic world they saw before them, they focused their attention on the means of achieving and preserving an order that would provide liberty to every human being in the largest possible measure. Their enviable example and their golden words would be replicated throughout the Western world.

CONTOURS OF COUNTERREVOLUTION

Whereas counterrevolutions are often discounted by historians as feeble and improvident efforts to restore a previous government or order, they may actually be enlightened programs to achieve the goals of revolution. If one focuses upon the commitment spawned by the French Revolution toward liberating human beings, rather than upon the endless bickerings characteristic of the period, the reblending of life and culture it wrought in the Western world can be appreciated. From an era in which the rights and liberties of human beings were little discussed and less appreciated, the liberating revolutions of the eighteenth century introduced an age in which those topics could never again be ignored. The counterrevolution's great achievement that emerged all across the Western world was not in denying the goals of revolutions, but rather in proposing alternative, perhaps more effective ways of achieving those ends.

Though Edmund Burke has often been credited with fomenting what counterrevolution there was, he was merely the most effective spokesperson. Throughout France and elsewhere in Europe there were others who experimented with many of the same doctrines and who came to similar conclusions. Far from being a lone reactionary, as he is often pictured, Burke had aplenty friends of order helping to shape what they believed would be a world in which both liberty and order could reign.

In France, a host of voices emerged with every step of the Revolution. In early 1789, comte Emmanuel-Henry-Alexandre de Lunai d'Antraigues, with a background and career very similar to that of Chateaubriand, published a pamphlet titled *Memoires sur les Etats generaux,* setting forth a doctrine of social and political order drawn heavily from Fénelon, Boulainvilliers, Saint-Simon, and, especially, Montesquieu. Instead of arguing for the powers of the monarch, he stressed the importance of a constitution and a legislature to counteract the powers of a monarch. His brief but influential work reflected that the philosophes of the Enlightenment were thinking in terms of an enlightened monarchy, rather than a republic or a democracy, as the proper model for France.

Indeed, it may be said that Louis XVI participated fully, if not enthusiastically, in the French Revolution's essential aims. The goal of a constitutional monarchy was actually acceded to and propounded in the opening addresses of the Estates-General and in the Royal Declaration of June 23, 1789.

Meanwhile, comte Dominique de Reynaud de Montlosier, a late arriving delegate to the Estates-General, published in 1791 two clarion calls for counterrevolution titled *De la necessite d'operer une countre-revolution en France* and *Des moyens d'operer la countre-revolution.* In these and in another tract published in 1790, *Essai sur l'art de constituer les peuples,* he argued for reforms in government and society that would alter the monarchy of France and protect the rights of citizens. But he believed that those rights could best be preserved by maintaining the historic orders in French society, by elevating the Third Estate, and by focusing on the status of families rather than that of individuals.

There were a host of other counterrevolutionary theorists, some of whom may have informed the writings of Edmund Burke. Antoine de Rivarol, in pamphlets and in articles in his *Journal politique national,* hoped for reforms in France but attacked every step of the Revolution. The comte Ferrand in his *Essai d'un citoyen* (1789) and in later works favored a constitutional monarchy for France to secure liberty for all citizens. Viewing liberty as "a natural right, the key to both individual and social happiness," he thought it consisted in property, personal security, and freedom of thought.

Senac de Meilhan, in a book titled *Des principes et des causes de la Revolution française* (1790) published in London, saw the Revolution as an essential cleansing mechanism, but also as an aberration deriving from the Enlightenment. Like Burke, he thought the Revolution's excesses came from "the fermentation of minds" by false ideals. Abbé Barruel, in essays and books beginning in 1789, argued that the Revolution was divine punishment for the moral and intellectual decline of French society. Barruel focused on the role of religion and the family in restoring the nation's stability. And as time passed, he contributed additional, even alarming, opinions about the origins of the Revolution.

Although he acknowledged an awareness of the works of Burke, Jaques Mallet du Pan, having lived through the Geneva Revolution in 1782, proved to be a watchful critic of the Revolution in the pages of the Parisian *Le Mercure de France.* Expressing strong support for liberty, Mallet also feared anarchy, which he detected at virtually every step of the revolution—from the convening of the Estates-General to the Declaration of the Rights of Man and the flight of Louis XVI in 1791. In *Considérations sur la nature de la Revolution de France* (1793), a work modeled upon Burke's *Reflections on the Revolution,* Mallet explored the incompetence of the Third Estate in managing French affairs. The Revolution was eventually seized by the "sans-culottes," who lacked an appreciation of philosophy, laws, or institutions. Written from the safety of Bern, Switzerland, *Considérations* made Mallet an international star, whose advice was sought by the various courts of Europe. In 1798 he moved to London to edit *Le Mercure britannique* and to head the British spy network that operated in Napoleonic France.

Joseph de Maistre, both a Freemason and a Catholic, deplored in his *Considérations sur la France* (1796) the passing of the old regime. Along with Burke he believed that a new aristocracy would have to be created to govern and maintain standards and traditions in the new republic. Humans were not, he argued, made for freedom. Institutions had to be established to provide and protect freedom. Like Burke, de Maistre took terms of the Enlightenment such as "nature" and "reason" and gave them wholly new and opposite meanings. Nature transmuted from innocence to irrationality; reason from rationality to prejudice. The Revolution, in his mind, became a war between Christianity and philosophy, between religion and irreligion, between order and anarchy. Hitting many of the same chords chimed out by Burke, de Maistre provided a solid base for an evolving philosophical counterrevolution that would touch most of the Western world.

He was joined in this enterprise by vicomte Gabriel-Ambroise Louis de Bonald, of noble family and mayor of Millau during the Revolution, who published in 1796 *Theorie du pouvoir politique et religieux dans la société civile, demontree par le raisonnement et par l'historie*. De Bonald also considered religion to be the core institution of society. He believed that constitutions naturally evolved and could not be imposed on society as was attempted in the French Revolution. But he also developed the idea, central to America's counterrevolution, that citizens did not so much have rights as they had duties. Citizens deserved opportunities to live, to work, and to procreate, but they were obligated to serve society, government, and God faithfully.

Counterrevolutionary thinking was not confined to Burke and to France; Germany also had counterrevolutionary theorists, either independent of Burke or influenced by his passionate pleadings. Johann Gottfried von Herder and Justus Möser strenuously opposed rationalism both before and during the French Revolution. At the outset of the Revolution they characterized the work of the French National Assembly as the height of irrationality, based in theory and far from the realities of history and experience.

With the appearance of Burke's *Reflections on the Revolution in France*, German theorists—especially in Hannover whose dynasty ruled both there and in England—began replicating and expanding upon his philosophy of order. At the University of Göttingen, the principal center of learning in Hannover, the faculty welcomed Richard Burke in 1791, during whose visit his father's ideas were broadly discussed. Ernst Brandes and August Wilhelm Rehberg published in 1791 and 1792 works critical of the French Revolution, strongly tinged with Burkean philosophy.

Burke's influence was even more evident in the case of Friedrich von Gentz, a Prussian official who translated Burke's *Reflections on the French Revolution* into German beginning with his first reading of it in 1791. In April of that year, he wrote, "As prejudiced as I am against its principles and conclusions, I am reading this book with infinitely more pleasure than one hundred insipid panegyrics of the Revolution." Always a proponent of constitutional liberty, von Gentz viewed the French Revolution favorably until he read Burke. He quickly became absorbed in revealing the Revolution's destructive tendencies. Publishing Burke's book in 1793, he next translated and published in 1794 Mallet du Pan's book, *Considérations sur la Revolution de France.* In 1795 he translated Jean-Joseph Mounier's *Les Recherches sur les causes qui ont empeche les Français de devinir libres* and published critical articles on the radical views of Robespierre and Saint-Just.[8]

Von Gentz's understanding of the relationship between revolution and order was revealed in one of his most significant essays, titled *The French and American Revolutions Compared,* published in 1799 in his *Historisches Journal* and republished in English in the United States in 1800. Although the American Revolution "had, in the course of events, been the nearest neighbor to that of France," the two movements were fundamentally different, he argued. They only seemed to be related because some of the same individuals had been involved in both, many of the same principles had been discussed, and because Europe had seemed ready for change after the happy conclusion of the recent American war. But "the melancholy experience of ten disastrous years," he continued, "has indeed considerably cooled down this belief.[9]

Von Gentz developed a perspective that upon its American publication helped shape both historical and ideological understanding. He charted the historical, commercial, and legal records that made sense of the American Revolution. It "was grounded partly upon principles, of which the right was evident," whereas the French Revolution "was an uninterrupted series of steps, the wrong of which could not, upon rigorous principles, for a moment be doubted." The "lawfulness" of what the Americans did was never in doubt; that of what leaders in France did was never discussed. Their actions were disguised in a vague cloak always called the "rights of man."

The American Revolution was a "defensive revolution"; France's was "an offensive revolution." The American Revolution had a "fixed and definite object"; France ran "in a thousand various directions . . . [and] through the unbounded space of a fantastic arbitrary will, and of a bottomless anarchy." The American Revolution, finally, had a massive internal resistance to combat; France "challenged almost every human feeling . . . to the most vehement resistance, and could therefore only force its way by violence and crimes."[10]

Von Gentz went to considerable lengths to demonstrate that while Thomas Paine had been present at and had issued popular tracts for both revolutions, only one of them had a salutary effect. *Common Sense* appeared in 1776 after the course of the American Revolution had been decided, while *The Rights of Man* (1791) emerged just in time to throw the French Revolution into chaos. Von Gentz concluded: "France was drenched in blood, to decide the great question, whether Brissot, or Marat, the federalists, or the unitists, the Girondists, or the mountaineers, the Dantonians, or the Hebertists, should prescribe a republican constitution." No such misguided chaos had occurred in the case of the American Revolution, because its object was always clear.[11]

As was the case with so many of the great minds that tried to come to grips with the meaning of the French Revolution, von Gentz was no mere theoretician. Through his studies of the French Revolution he prepared himself for a career as "Secretary of Europe." As author, as adviser to Klemens von Metternich, and as secretary of the Congress of Vienna, von Gentz helped establish order in Europe for more than thirty years.

As a student of Immanuel Kant and with intellectual contacts in France, Germany, Austria, and America—including such figures as Benjamin Constant de Rebecque, Madame de Staël, duc d'Orléans, Goethe, and John Quincy Adams—von Gentz became a great proponent of Burkean principles of social and political order. Convinced that liberty and individual rights could be achieved only by providing a limited, lawful, orderly government, he petitioned the king of Prussia in 1797 to introduce a "revolution from above" with a constitutional government. When his petition was denied, he left government service until after the Napoleonic wars. But through his vast writings, von Gentz proved himself to be one of Europe's most influential friends of order.[12]

THE BAVARIAN ILLUMINATI

While in Hannover and in Prussia philosophers promulgated Burkean principles, a separate phenomenon radiating from Bavaria complicated the way Europeans and Americans discussed revolution, liberty, and order in the closing years of the eighteenth century. It began in the fertile mind of Adam Weishaupt, professor of law at the University of Ingolstadt. Orphaned at seven, his education was provided for by his godfather, Baron Ickstatt, who afforded the boy a vast library and who placed him under the care of Jesuits. Weishaupt, studious and full of curiosity, devoured everything he could find on the subjects of law, economics, politics, history, and philosophy. With the support of Ickstatt he graduated from Ingolstadt in 1768 and rapidly advanced to dean of the faculty of law in 1775.

His appointment in canon law, a realm dominated by Jesuits for nearly a century at Ingolstadt, placed the young Weishaupt at odds with the Society of Jesus in Bavaria. But professional jealousies merely shrouded his desire to bring reason, enlightenment, and liberty to reign in a world dominated by clerical orders and religion. On May 1, 1776, he founded with five others an organization called the Order of the Illuminati. Taking a cue from the structure and procedures of Freemasons, Weishaupt designed his order to have three grades of membership: Novice, Minerval, and Illuminated Minerval. The Illuminati would recruit its membership from throughout the world, teach the recruits the principles of reason and enlightenment, and through them seek the goals of human progress and perfection. Monthly meetings, constant instruction, and advancement through the elevated grades would assure the desired progress.

The truths of human equality and fraternity were pursued in assemblies of the Illuminati. Members strove for a civilization of reason and enlightenment not pos-

Adam Weishaupt (c. 1788). German progenitor of world illuminism, a phantom enemy of order in America.

sible under existing religious and civil institutions. From Weishaupt's own negative experience with the Jesuits the order was infused with a heavy measure of anticlericalism. Though the order affirmed the centrality of Christianity in securing a new world and recognized Jesus of Nazareth as the grand master of the Illuminati, it was highly opposed to the form of ecclesiastical domination extant throughout Europe.

The organization began to take off in 1780 with the recruitment of Baron Adolf Franz Friedrich Knigge, another student of law trained at Göttingen with a wide practice in the courts of Hesse-Cassel and Weimar. He had retired early in life, with a considerable fortune, to pursue an interest in secret societies—Masonic, Rosicrucian, as well as the Illuminati. Knigge brought to the Illuminati his knowledge of the inner operations of secret societies and a direct link with Freemasonry. He added lofty grades to the order and sharpened its focus to work against superstition, despotism, and tyranny throughout the world. The teaching functions imagined by Weishaupt were reduced in importance.

Through its affiliation with Masonic lodges, the Order of Illuminati spread rapidly through Bavaria and Germany and into Austria and Switzerland after 1780. As numbers increased, so did the quality of membership, including dukes, barons, princes, philosophers, and poets. By 1784 the membership approached three thousand. But as the order grew so did obstacles against it. Weishaupt and Knigge began to rival each other for control of the organization. Externally, Carl Theodore, Elector of Palatine, on June 22, 1784, issued an edict banning societies and brotherhoods that had not been sanctioned by the Elector. The Illuminati believed themselves exempt from this decree, but Carl Theodore, fearful of a growing spirit of revolution in Bavaria, issued a second edict on March 2, 1785, specifically banning the Illuminati from his realm.

Counterrevolutionary repression of the Illuminati in Bavaria continued as officials undertook a campaign to stamp out all traces of the order, confiscating masses of papers and compiling names of members. Military officers, public officials, clergy, college professors, and students were required to confess their connections with the order under penalty of arrest and imprisonment. Weishaupt fled Bavaria to Regensburg two weeks prior to the second edict. Over the space of a few months he issued nine books and pamphlets defending the order against the Bavarian government, with the effect only of making matters worse for members who remained behind. The campaign of repression came to a head when police in

October 1786 entered the house of Xavier Zwack, a state councilor deposed for his Illuminati connections, and seized a new stash of papers revealing the continued operations of the order.

Among Zwack's papers authorities found evidence to destroy the Illuminati. The documents revealed that the organization was devoted to the overthrow of governmental and religious institutions and that every method of achieving those ends was under consideration. A brief by Zwack held that the order could exercise the right of life or death over its members. Others by him defended suicide, abortion, and atheism. A description for fabricating a machine to safeguard secret papers, to counterfeit official seals, and to print receipts for procuring abortions was found. Documents relating to abortions confirmed a well-founded story concerning Weishaupt's efforts in 1780 to deal with the pregnancy, for which he was responsible, of his dead wife's sister.

With this further evidence a renewed reign of terror was carried out against members—former and suspected—of the Illuminati. Carl Theodore issued a third edict on August 16, 1787, to facilitate the annihilation of the order, which provided for death by the sword for any person, without respect to title or rank who was found to be involved in recruiting members for the organization. Recruits themselves had their property seized and were banished from Bavaria. Members again were banned from meeting or associating with each other. The edict and concerted efforts to enforce it both within and outside Bavaria succeeded in destroying the order. Broken in fortune and spirit, Weishaupt issued a few additional pamphlets in his defense, but he lived in obscurity under the protection of Duke Ernst of Gotha until his death forty years later.

Although Carl Theodore had stamped out and dispersed the leadership of an organization that ostensibly wanted to overthrow the ecclesiastical and civil government of Bavaria, he did not succeed in destroying the spirit or the lore of Illuminism. And even though the Bavarian government published in 1787 every document taken in its raids exposing operations and memberships, the secret nature of the organization and its hidden purposes elicited an aura of fear that Illuminism could never be stopped.

Every effort of authorities to penetrate the order only led the devoted Illuminati to become more clandestine in their operations. Illuminism, despite its founder's incompetence, remained in the Western world as a persistent, sinister threat to religion, government, and society itself—just as awesome in myth and rumor as if Weishaupt continued to reign over a world order of devoted Illuminati.

Church and government leaders in Bavaria had been so spooked by the strange phenomenon that, despite the absence of any evidence of members or organization, Carl Theodore continued to issue ever stronger orders against Illuminism. In 1791 ninety-one suspected members of the order were banished. Meanwhile in Prussia, Frederick William II, convinced that the Illuminati had invaded his kingdom, urged investigations of suspicious meetings rumored to be secret conclaves of leaders of the order.

Knigge, Weishaupt's most effective lieutenant, continued to stir fears that he was manipulating minds and governments until his death in 1796. Proponents of a German union were suspected throughout the era of the French Revolution of being clandestine Illuminati. Not until the death of Carl Theodore in 1799 did the reign of threats and banishments come to an uneasy close. By that time, his paranoia about the continued existence of the Illuminati was shared throughout the Western world.

The power of the Illuminati legend became clear during the course of the French Revolution. As France grew ever bloodier, observers sought explanations for the descent of a proud nation into chaos. Abbé Augustin Barruel, a member of the Society of Jesus in France, thought he had found the origins of the French Revolution when he published his *Memoires pour servir a l'histoire du Jacobinisme* in four large volumes during 1797 and 1798. Written while he was exiled in England, his *Memoires* were quickly translated into English, German, Polish, Dutch, Portuguese, Spanish, and Italian editions. Dozens of abridgements and variations were published during the next century.

According to Barruel, a Jesuit from 1756 until the Society of Jesus was banned in France during 1773, three groups conspired to produce in France a revolution more horrible than anything ever seen before. First were the "philosophers" or "sophisters of impiety" who "conspired against the God of the Gospel, against Christianity, without distinction of worship, whether Protestant or Catholic, Anglican or Presbyterian." Next came the "sophisters of rebellion" who were neatly huddled among the "occult lodges of Free-Masonry." Finally, there were "sophisters of anarchy" who "conspire not only against Christ and his altars, but against every religion natural or revealed." This last group, Barruel said, were "known by the name of Illumines." Together with the others they formed "the club of the Jacobins" who were responsible for launching a revolution against order, government, authority, and religion.

Barruel's four volumes detailed in breathtaking language the greatest conspiracy in the history of the human race. It began with the publication of the *Encyclopédie,* the bible of the enlightened philosophers. The suppression of the Society of Jesus, the banning of Christianity, and the destruction of houses of worship followed. Finally came the capture of the Académie des Sciences by Voltaire, Montesquieu, and Rousseau. In the lodges of Freemasonry, members were secretly indoctrinated in the philosophy of liberty, equality, and fraternity. But to transform philosophy into revolution there was the secret Order of Illuminati.

The Illuminati, "a band of Conspirators," had coalesced with the Encyclopedists and the Masons to pull off the revolution:

> They more silently prepared the explosions of the Revolutionary volcano, not merely swearing hatred to the Altar of Christ and the Throne of Kings, but swearing at once hatred to every God, to every Law, to every Government, to all society and social compact; and in order to destroy every plea and every

foundation of social contract, they proscribed the terms MINE
and THINE, acknowledging neither Equality nor Liberty but in
the entire, absolute and universal overthrow of all PROPERTY
whatever.

Through clandestine meetings, concealed messages, and cryptic symbols this
force set July 14, 1789, as the day of general insurrection. As soon as the
Bastille fell, the secret lodges were dissolved and the Jacobins—the entire band
of conspirators—openly proceeded with the dismantling of government, church,
and society.

    With the force of Jeremiah, of Isaiah, and of Ezekiel combined, Barruel
unleashed a contorted form of Burke's thundering thesis that the French Revolution was a conspiracy worked by the philosophes and forced onto France. By fun-
neling the conspiracy through the secret operations of Freemasonry and the Illuminati, Barruel concretized a frightening, entirely believable view of the mechanical
operations of the Revolution. Plumbing the human fear of the hidden and
unknown, Barruel gave a new life to Illuminism that no amount of logic, argument,
or documentation could kill. Even though skeptics dismissed his fantastic scheme,
many others found Barruel's explanation of conspiracy mysteriously appealing.

    To make matters worse, Barruel did not rest his case with France alone. As
he looked across the world in 1797, he saw that the Illuminist conspiracy had
already spread to Belgium, Holland, Italy, Malta, Switzerland, Sweden, Austria,
Prussia, Poland, and even Russia. Bonaparte was presently taking it to Egypt.
But in a passage that threatened to play an ominous trick on American minds,
Barruel observed that the same forces were beginning to show up in the Western
hemisphere:

> As the plague flies on the wings of the wind, so do their tri-
> umphant legions infect America. There apostles have infused
> their principles into the submissive and laborious negroes; and
> St. Domingo and Guadaloupe have been converted into vast
> charnel houses for their inhabitants. So numerous were the
> brethren in North America, that Philadelphia and Boston trem-
> bled, lest their rising constitution should be obliged to make
> way for that of the great club.

He ruefully concluded with a note that would shudder the minds and hearts of
countless Americans: "God grant that the United States may not learn to their cost,
that Republics are equally menaced with Monarchies; and that the immensity of
the ocean is but a feeble barrier against the universal conspiracy of the Sect." [13]

    In countless editions over the next twenty years Barruel continued to hone
his story of evil subversion until it became part of the Western view of history. It
would emerge in every moment of crisis when human beings felt their churches,
their governments, and their societies threatened. While Bavarian authorities may
have stamped out the Order of Illuminati, Barruel's Illuminism continued, with a
vigorous life of its own.

SCOTTISH ENLIGHTENMENT

While German kings and dukes were stamping out all vestiges of Illuminism, a different kind of revolution was playing itself out in the tiny realm of Scotland and wherever Scottish folk happened to migrate. At the end of the Enlightenment, there occurred an extraordinary Golden Age in Scotland, whose influence in Europe and America was almost unfathomable. Indeed, the culture that flourished in Scotland roughly between 1760 and 1790 was so thoroughly embraced in the English-speaking world that historians did not recognize until recent years that these ideas had distinctive origins in a land little noticed in world history. But it happened among a people who had been warring for independence against enemies from the south at least from Roman times until 1707, when a union between England and Scotland was formed.

While the rest of the world focused on French learning, on endless wars, and on religious rivalries or revivals, a profound and fertile peace settled in Scotland, allowing ideas to thrive. Scots defined almost every realm of learning in ways that would be understood down into the twentieth century. David Hume recast philosophy. Adam Smith invented the science of economics and outlined the world of capitalism. Adam Ferguson fashioned what would become sociology. William Robertson formulated historiography. James Hutton founded modern geology. Joseph Black restructured chemistry. William Cullen originated clinical medicine. John Millar related the studies of law, philosophy, social structure, and history. Hugh Blair designed the tools for analyzing rhetoric and literature. Henry Home, Lord Kames, combined legal, philosophical, and literary studies with experiments in agriculture. James Burnett devised studies in cultural anthropology. Dugald Stewart combined philosophy and economics. Thomas Reid originated a "common sense" philosophy that would enter the matrix of English and American societies. James Watt wrought a technological revolution with his steam engine. And the brothers Robert and James Adam systematized architecture, town planning, road construction, and bridge building for an expanding world.[14]

All of these brilliant minds conspired individually and jointly to improve man's understanding of himself and the natural world and to use this knowledge to enhance man's culture, society, and physical environment. Their curiosity about everything they encountered spurred their efforts to systematize knowledge. They were optimists, as were so many Enlightenment minds, but they also had a realistic assessment of the nature and limitations of man that eluded many French philosophes. Threatened with absorption into a British nation, they were driven to historical and anthropological studies more than any other group of thinkers in eighteenth-century Europe.

Other characteristics of this Enlightenment made Scotland a rare place in a world otherwise focused on revolutionary France. The Scots rediscovered the classics just as the French were throwing them overboard. The Scots emphasized benevolence and morality while the French discovered capitalism. The Scots valued religion and an enlightened clergy while the French tried to abolish religious institutions and banish their clergy. The Scots held a belief in order and social hierarchy at a time when everyone in France clamored for classless citizenship.

The Scots unapologetically exuded confidence in social, political, and religious conservativism in a world that rewarded radicalism and revolution. So confident were the Scots of their direction that while revolutionary fires were threatening to tear apart France, the town fathers of Edinburgh—the historic center of past Scottish royal glories—laid out a New Town that brought together in design and plan all the principles of classicism, order, and rationality that infused the Scottish Enlightenment.

Yet, at the center of this order was liberty itself. When James Craig earned a gold medal in 1767 for his plan for New Town, he selected lines from a poem by his uncle titled "Liberty" to express his pleasure:

> August, around, what Public Works I see!
>
> Lo! stately Street, lo! Squares that court the breeze!
>
> See long Canals and deepened Rivers join
>
> Each part with each, and with the circling Main
>
> The whole enlivened Isle.

Human progress, orderliness, ingenuity, communication, and creativity when fully exercised brought liberty and social happiness.

Within the Scottish Enlightenment were insights, institutions, a literature, and a spirit that paralleled the French Enlightenment and Revolution. David Hume's *Philosophical Essays Concerning Human Understanding* (1748) and *Enquiry Concerning the Principles of Morals* (1751), Adam Smith's *Inquiry into the Nature and Causes of the Wealth of Nations* (1776), Hugh Blair's *The Philosophy of Rhetoric* (1776), Lord Kames's *The Gentleman Farmer* (1776), Adam Ferguson's *Essay on the History of Civil Society* (1767), James Hutton's *Theory of the Earth* (1795), and many other texts became the standard literature of the English-speaking world. *The Encyclopaedia Britannica* written and compiled "by a Society of Gentlemen in Scotland," published initially in 1771 and soon expanded sixfold, rivaled the work of the Encyclopedists in France of the same period. The movement included the entire body of knowledge and culture—poetry, music, belles lettres, the sciences, and medicine.[15]

When Benjamin Franklin arrived in England in 1757, he quickly made his way to Scotland, where he made important contacts with David Hume, Adam Smith, Lord Kames and other savants. There he honed in on Scotland's universities at Edinburgh, Glasgow, Aberdeen, and St. Andrews as centers of study for Americans and as models for rising colleges and universities in America. After spending six weeks in Scotland in the fall of 1759 Franklin wrote Lord Kames,

> I must say I think the time we spent there was six weeks of the
> densest happiness I have met with in any part of my life; and
> the agreeable and instructive society we found there in such
> plenty has left so pleasing an impression on my memory that,
> did not strong connexions draw me elsewhere, I believe Scot-

land would be the country I should choose to spend the remainder of my days in.[16]

With Franklin's encouragement hundreds of American students rushed to Scottish universities before the end of the century and hundreds of learned Scots migrated to America to head colleges, to teach, to preach, and to serve as factors. They also helped the American colonies declare their independence, frame a constitutional government, and fend off the chaotic influences of the French Revolution.

The enormous power of the Scottish Enlightenment is best seen in the lives of those who experienced it. John Robison, professor of natural philosophy at Edinburgh, and one of his students, James Mackintosh, were both exemplary products of this special environment. Born at Boghall, Scotland, and educated in grammar school and at the university in Glasgow, Robison studied under Adam Smith (economics), Robert Simson (geometry), and Robert Dick (natural philosophy). Shortly after his graduation he was selected to travel with and instruct Edward, the Duke of York, in mathematics and navigation. Between 1759 and 1761, he sailed to America and briefly served a military command in Canada. He also traveled to Jamaica and the West Indies to help establish official longitude and latitude tables. Returning to Glasgow in 1761 to study theology, he fell under the sway of Joseph Black, one of the greatest chemists of the age, and of fellow student, James Watt, who was on the verge of building his revolutionary steam engine. Robison became intimately involved with the researches of both of these geniuses.

Although recommended by Black to become his successor at Glasgow when the chemist moved to Edinburgh in 1766, the adventurous Robison soon departed for St. Petersburg, Russia, where he was engaged to improve the methods of building, rigging, and navigating Russian ships of war and to reform its naval operations. Although he also accepted the mathematical chair at the Imperial Sea Cadet Corps of Nobles in 1772, Robison jumped at the professorship of natural philosophy at Edinburgh upon the death of James Russell in 1773. From 1774 until his own death thirty-one years later, Robison embodied the Scottish Enlightenment. He lectured in mechanics, hydrodynamics, astronomy, optics, electricity, and magnetism—his mind rapid, but logical.

Robison made enormous contributions to the heritage of the Scottish Enlightenment. From 1783 until his death, he served as General Secretary of the Royal Society of Edinburgh—the preeminent learned body of Scotland, then and now. Although attacked by a debility in December 1785 that kept him in constant and excruciating pain for the rest of his life, he remained an extraordinarily productive scientist and science writer. To the *Encyclopaedia Britannica,* when it expanded from three to eighteen volumes, he contributed most of the articles relating to science. His entries covered more than a thousand printed pages. While he was engaged in this decade-long project, he also edited and published the lectures of his mentor, Joseph Black. He then began publishing his own lectures on mechanical philosophy. While several volumes were published before his death, his entire *System of Mechanical Philosophy* was published in four volumes in 1822.[17]

James Mackintosh, a quarter century younger than Robison, derived from a titled and once wealthy family from the fabled Loch Ness near Inverness. His father was a soldier who traveled the world; his mother died when he was fifteen. But the boy was a prodigy, whose reading, writing, and oratory by his early teens suggested he would rival a Priestley, a Price, or a Burke. At fifteen he began attending lectures at King's College, Aberdeen. In 1784 he repaired to Edinburgh, where he studied the sciences under John Robison and medicine under the tutelage of William Cullen. Among his fellow students was Benjamin Constant, whose rough-and-tumble life eventually evolved along lines similar to those of Mackintosh. The two soon became deeply involved in Edinburgh's Medical and Speculative Societies, where they debated issues medical, philosophical, and political.

Despite his medical training, Mackintosh never pursued a medical practice. Upon getting his degree in 1787 and with the death of his father shortly thereafter, he moved to London, where, like Chateaubriand, he toyed between a career as a writer and as a public servant. He wrote articles for various papers and did some short-term editing. He also wrote a couple of heated pamphlets while studying law. As he searched for a firm direction, he fell under the influence of the radical John Horne Tooke, whose ideas about freedom mightily appealed to him during the sweet summer of liberty in 1789.[18]

Under Tooke's patronage and among the friends of liberty in and around London, including Price, Priestley, Paine, and Joel Barlow, Mackintosh was inspired in early 1791 to write a short rebuttal to Burke's *Reflections on the French Revolution,* which ended up as a lengthy book, *Vindiciae Gallicae: Defence of the French Revolution and Its English Admirers Against the Accusations of the Right Hon. Edmund Burke.* And it was perhaps the most formidable of the forty or fifty responses to Burke that appeared during 1791 and 1792.[19]

Responding also to the absence of learning and literature in Thomas Paine's *The Rights of Man* that appeared two months earlier, Mackintosh upheld the French Revolution as an honorable and necessary process. Whereas Paine appealed to the emotions and Burke invoked ancient traditions, Mackintosh strolled through classical and philosophical literature to justify the concept of revolution. Whereas Paine venerated pure democracy and Burke deplored democracy as unworkable, Mackintosh upheld the notion of a "mixed democracy" with checks and balances against the tyranny of majorities. And whereas Paine preached equal rights for all and Burke found humans fundamentally unequal, Mackintosh recognized the reality of two kinds of inequality,

> the one personal, that of talent and virtue, the source of whatever is excellent and admirable in society; the other that of fortune, which must exist, because property alone can stimulate to labour, and labour, if it were not necessary to the existence, would be indispensable to the happiness of man.

Mackintosh "met Burke perfectly his equal in the tactics of moral science, and in beauty of style and illustration." Although Paine appealed to the working classes and Burke to the aristocracy, Mackintosh aimed at the literati, "a class—perhaps too influential in society—to whom the manner of Paine was repulsive."[20]

The *Vindiciae* went through three quick editions in England. The duc d'Orléans translated parts of it into French. The National Assembly offered Mackintosh French citizenship and a seat, along with Paine and Barlow, in that body. Madame de Staël and Benjamin Constant revered the work. The book appeared in America in 1792. Mackintosh, only twenty-five years of age, became an instant hero throughout England, France, and America. He presided over dinners in London and at coffeehouse meetings of new groups including the Friends to the Liberty of the Press and the Association of the Friends of the People. He attacked the antireformist policies of British leadership in *A Letter to the Right Honourable William Pitt* under the moniker of "An Honest Man." And he traveled in August 1792 to Paris, where he was feted as a hero of liberty.

Mackintosh made his way to Paris at one of the most inopportune moments in the history of liberty. He arrived in early August 1792 and, over the period of a few short weeks, witnessed the suspension of royal authority by the National Assembly, the confinement of King Louis XVI in Temple prison, the surrender of Lafayette to French enemies, and the massacre of more than a thousand inmates in French prisons. So revulsive was Mackintosh's holiday that he promptly rejected not only the proffered seat in the National Assembly, but also the direction of the French Revolution. Indeed, during the days of executions and terror that enveloped France, Mackintosh underwent a transformation that moved him from any further identification as a friend of liberty to the ranks of the friends of order.[21]

By the time Burke issued his remarkable *Letters on a Regicide Peace,* Mackintosh had come to agree with the renowned critic. First, he wrote an anonymous review of Burke's pamphlet in *The Monthly Review* in which he praised the author effusively: "No idea appears hackneyed in his hands; no topic seems common place when he treats it." When Burke confessed that he enjoyed the review, Mackintosh seized the moment to speak directly to the dying political giant. In a letter to Burke describing his change of mind and heart, Mackintosh wrote:

> I cannot say (and you would despise me if I dissembled) that I
> can even now assent to all your opinions on the present politics
> of Europe. But I can with truth affirm that I subscribe to your
> general principles, and I am prepared to shed my blood in
> defence of the laws and constitution of my country.

Admitting that "for a time [I was] indeed seduced by the love of what I thought liberty," he declared that he would never again refute Burke's opinions.[22]

In discovering that his principles were those of the Scottish Enlightenment, Mackintosh also expressed a wish to visit with Burke at Beaconsfield. Though assenting to the visit, Burke doubted the depth of Mackintosh's "supposed conversion," confiding to a friend, "I suspect, by his letter, that it does not extend beyond the interior politics of this island." With regard to France, Burke was certain the new disciple "remains as frank a Jacobin as ever." But when the pilgrim visited Beaconsfield near Christmas in 1796, Burke recognized the unity of their views. One account of the visit noted that Mackintosh "renounced his early errors, and received absolution." He went away declaring that Burke, his idol, "was without any parallel, in any age or country, except, perhaps, Lord Bacon and Cicero."[23]

Mackintosh soon assumed the mantle of the master in word and deed. In November 1798 he requested the use of a hall at Lincoln's Inn "to deliver a series of lectures on the 'Law of Nature and Nations'" for the benefit of judges, lawyers, and students. When the proposal was rejected due to the radical views he had set forth in *Vindiciae Gallicae,* Mackintosh published a brief essay titled *A Discourse on the Law of Nature and Nations* outlining his projected thirty-nine lectures and giving the substance of the first. With the intervention of some influential friends, his request was approved, and the stir about his use of the hall actually helped him to attract 150 registrants for the course.[24]

From February to June 1799, Mackintosh proclaimed his doctrines before students, peers, interested onlookers, and members of Parliament. Cicero was his Old Testament and Burke his New. William Godwin, an old friend with whom he had dined happily along with Mary Wollstonecraft, became the object of his attacks. Boldly he shouted,

> I profess publicly and unequivocally, that I abhor, abjure, and for ever renounce the French revolution, with all its sanguinary history, its abominable principles, and for ever execrable leaders. I hope I shall be able to wipe off the disgrace of having been once betrayed into an approbation of that conspiracy against God and man, the greatest scourge of the world, and the chief stain upon human annals.[25]

Godwin himself, Samuel T. Coleridge, William Wordsworth, Robert Southey, Viscount Castlereagh, and William Hazlitt—all of whom once venerated the French Revolution—attended at least some of the lectures and heard directly Mackintosh's born-again adherence to Burkean principles of order. As Hazlitt observed,

> Those of us who attended day after day, and were accustomed to have all our previous notions confounded and struck out of our hands by some metaphysical legerdemain, were at last at some loss to know two and two made four, till we heard the lecturer's opinion on that head.

Some, such as Godwin and Hazlitt, felt betrayed by their former associate's conversion; others soon underwent the same kind of transformation. Coleridge lamented with Mackintosh his own former opinions: "I have snapped my squeaking baby-trumpet of sedition, and the fragments lie scattered in the lumber-room of penitence. I wish to be a good man and a Christian, but I am no Whig, no Reformist, no Republican."

Mackintosh's transformation soon allowed his once rejected application to be a distinguished guest at highbrow Holland House to be accepted. Elizabeth Vassall, Lady Holland, protector of the institution's gilded reputation, wrote on May 26, 1799, about the once "furious Jacobin":

> Nay, two years ago he wished to come here, and I refused seeing him on account of his principles, as I have always dreaded this house becoming a foyer of Jacobinism, and have invariably set my face against receiving all who are suspected of being revolutionists etc etc. However, since M. has regained his character . . . I admit him.

On the day prior, Mackintosh had been honored at the house along with a considerable crowd of confirmed friends of order. One success led to others. A few months later the Duchess of Gordon, protector of Pall Mall House—Tory heaven—invited him there as well. There he conversed with William Windham, Burke's closest political heir. Said Mackintosh of the discussion, "We talked with equal enthusiasm of Burke and with equal abhorrence of Democrats and Philosophers."[26]

Mackintosh, infused with the principles of the Scottish Enlightenment, when faced with talk of liberty, freedom, and the rights of man, could not resist the attraction of these fond hopes. As a Scot whose ancestors had fought for their freedom, he could not but wish to see their rights accorded to every human being. But faced with a revolution that had brought chaos, Mackintosh found it easy to resist the trance of feigned liberty. He, like Burke, fomented a counterrevolutionary ideology that would last.

WORLD CONSPIRACY

While Mackintosh propounded the principles of ordered societies, his mentor at Edinburgh, John Robison, was headed down another path. Indeed, given the inflammatory rhetoric of the essays and discourses given by Burke and Mackintosh, it is not surprising that even at the epicenter of the Scottish Enlightenment— the strongest force for order in revolutionary Europe—one of the deans of learning embraced the notion that the Bavarian Illuminati had infiltrated every nation in Europe.

Abbé Barruel from his London exile was spewing forth volume after volume documenting the world's vastest conspiracy. As he detailed the operations of the philosophes, the Illuminati, and the Masons, he filled the air with the same sentiments that made the Book of Revelation one of the most controversial documents in Western history. Throughout the Western world during 1797, unbelievable stories suddenly became life-threatening realities. No one could avoid the intoxicating tales of some unidentified enemy at the gate, ready to subvert social harmony.

Professor Robison, paragon of the Scottish Enlightenment, read such stories in various publications emanating from Germany and France. Himself a Mason and exposed to Masonic lodges during his travels in Brussels, Aix-la-Chapelle, Berlin, and St. Petersburg, Robison began to see in 1797 the outlines of a scheme among masons "for venting and propagating sentiments in religion and politics, that could not have circulated in public without exposing the author to great danger." He "observed these doctrines gradually diffusing and mixing with all the different systems of Free Masonry" until

> at last, AN ASSOCIATION HAS BEEN FORMED for the express purpose of ROOTING OUT ALL THE RELIGIOUS ESTABLISHMENTS, AND OVERTURNING ALL THE EXISTING GOVERNMENTS OF EUROPE. I have seen this Association exerting itself zealously and systematically, till it has become almost irresistible.

The "Association" of which he spoke was, of course, "the order of ILLUMINATI, founded in 1775 [1776] by Dr. Adam Weishaupt . . . and abolished in 1786 [1785] by the Elector of Bavaria." It had been secretly revived and "still subsists without being detected, and has spread into all the countries of Europe."

So disturbed was he by the looming forces that he threw together a book exposing the worldwide plot and titled it *Proofs of a Conspiracy against All the Religions and Governments of Europe, Carried on in the Secret Meetings of the Free Masons, Iluminati, and Reading Societies.* Published initially in 1797 in Edinburgh, a second edition appeared in London before the end of the year. Two more English editions appeared in London before the end of 1798, along with a French edition published there. German and Dutch translations followed from Königslutter, Hamburg, and Dordrecht. An instant sensation throughout Europe, the book absorbed rumors by political hacks, popular writers, and disaffected clergy, then rebroadcast them as "proofs" by one of the foremost scientific minds of Europe. All that went before was clangor. Robison's hefty tome not only could not be dismissed; it was itself captivating.

Robison covered the same grounds as Barruel but in an even more sensational manner. He discovered the Illuminati while he was researching the

"The Illuminati and English Freemasonry" (1787). A graphic illustration of the origins of Illuminism as later depicted by John Robison—from a root and not the main trunk of English Freemasonry.

history of Freemasonry. Indeed, "when the Illuminati came in my way, I regretted the time I had thrown away on Free Masonry." But after the find was made, "the whole appeared to be one great and wicked project, fermenting and working over all Europe." The Illuminati's secret schemes were introduced into the Masonic lodges of Paris in 1789 by Mirabeau and Talleyrand. These, in turn, illuminated the minds of conspirators against the government of France, including the duc d'Orléans and even the women of France.

On the contamination of women, Robison far surpassed Barruel. The "present humiliating condition of [French] women" was one of "the accursed fruits of Illumination." The ill effects were obvious when he saw "Madame Tallien come into the public theatre, accompanied by other beautiful women, (I was about to have misnamed them Ladies), laying aside all modesty, and presenting themselves to the public view, with bared limbs, a la Sauvage, as the alluring objects of desire." Robison's linkage of the conspiracy to female immodesty introduced a chord little played in France, but wildly resonant in the English-speaking world.

So savage was Robison's treatment of the Illuminati conspiracy that Abbé Barruel, getting a copy as the third volume of his *Memoirs of Jacobinism* was going to press, sought to distinguish his course slightly from *Proofs of a Conspiracy.* But only scarcely, for after listing the differences between their works, he admitted "Without knowing it, we have fought for the same cause with the same arms, and pursued the same course." Although they were in a sense competitors covering the same grounds, they actually reinforced each other in the public eye. Their alarming thesis could not be easily dismissed.[27]

Introduced into a world where England, France, Austria, Germany, Italy, Spain, and Russia were poised for war, Robison's *Proofs of a Conspiracy* along with Barruel's *Memoirs of Jacobinism* explained to expectant millions what was happening to their lives. The rhetoric of Robison and Barruel resonated in human psyches hungry for nourishment, but ill-equipped to distinguish between various nutrients. Following almost a decade of unrelenting revolutionary fires, Robison and Barruel had found an enemy that lurked in the shadows and provided to millions the reasons they needed to stomp out the revolution.

Even as Burke lay dying and William Tate, Theobald Wolfe Tone, and Robert Fulton were setting out on military adventures in the name of liberty, the elements for an international counterrevolution had been defined and were in place. The French Revolution had been dismissed philosophically, politically, and even emotionally. Once it was transformed by Robison and Barruel into a vast conspiracy against all governments, all societies, and all religions, nothing statesmen, historians, philosophers, or theologians could say to defend the Revolution or its principles would salvage it. However tantalizing might be the notion of achieving liberty through revolution, the nature of the beast *revolution* could not be tamed. And, counterrevolutionary ideologues argued, societies must never again unleash that menacing fiend.

CHAPTER 19

Annus Mirabilis II, 1798

COUNTERREVOLUTION AT YALE COLLEGE

If 1793 was a year of miracles, 1798 was a time of even more fundamental change. The year 1798 marked the end of chaos and indecision. During this second watershed year, the Western world recovered from the intoxicating miasma of revolution and began to experience a counterrevolution that gave form to a new world of politics, philosophy, and social values. Although the counterrevolution worked itself out in slightly different ways within the context of individual nations, nearly everyone in the Western world operated henceforth in the same kind of arena and, oftentimes, with corresponding results.

Although some nations remained monarchies and some became republics, while others oscillated from one to the other, the days of self-evident national governance were gone. So were the days of obvious economic, commercial, and industrial policies. As Western nations entered the postrevolutionary era, it became evident that the world flux could not be fixed by either monarchs or virtuous republicans. Governments were of little use in repairing the damage done to hearts, minds, and spirits; other tools were needed—religion, symbolic social structuring, town planning, informal organizations, and benevolent instincts—to help arrange a new world of safe havens from the storms of change.

Nowhere were the transforming powers of the counterrevolution more evident than on the campus of Yale College, where old and sacred friendships were no insulation against ideological warfare. Josiah Meigs and Timothy Dwight—both of them Hartford Wits—found themselves in charge of Yale in 1795 and responsible for interpreting current events to a new crop of Yale undergraduates.

Upon his return in 1794 from a sojourn as an admiralty lawyer on Bermuda, Meigs was appointed by Yale president Ezra Stiles to the post of professor of mathematics and natural philosophy. A member of Joel Barlow's many-faceted class of 1778, Meigs had maintained an interest in science and natural history even as he practiced law. He read his inaugural lecture on November 20, 1794, and was formally inducted into his chair on December 4. Within a few months, however, Meigs's benefactor, Stiles, president since 1778, was dead. The long-tenured president soon was succeeded by one of Meigs's favorite college tutors,

Timothy Dwight, on September 8, 1795. As both president and professor, Dwight and Meigs constituted the entire faculty.[1]

Just weeks before Dwight's arrival in New Haven, Meigs was in the process of exercising his opinions about the state of affairs in France, England, and America. An ardent proponent of the aims of the French Revolution and a firm supporter of Joel Barlow, Meigs, on July 23, 1795, told his brother that he was "displeased" with the policies of the Washington administration toward France. "They appear to me," he proclaimed, "to have lost sight of the great leading traits of freedom." Even in France, things seemed muddled: "I am not pleased with the moderation prevailing in France. Moderation does not do in the midst of gold, treason, and perfidity." So strongly did Meigs support the causes of liberty that he had at least once previously became embroiled in a New Haven mob scene where he tussled with others inimical to French and American radicalism.

Even though Timothy Dwight had been deeply involved with the tightly knit band of Hartford Wits and had gloried in the American Revolution, he quickly determined that Meigs's love of liberty was too extravagant. At first Dwight abided Meigs's convictions, especially as enunciated at Ezra Stiles's funeral and in lectures and colloquies with students. But when Meigs joined in a demonstration expressing opposition to the Alien and Sedition Acts on July 4, 1798, Dwight urged Yale trustees not to renew Meigs's annual faculty contract.[2]

Meigs, however, pleaded his case in a letter to "the honored and reverend Corporation of Yale College," dated September 11, 1798. "I have been, by the public, charged with being an enemy to the constitution and liberties of my country," he wrote. He then reviewed his career in support of liberty: his days as a New Haven newspaper editor, when he published the Hartford Wits and supported the adoption of the Constitution; his efforts in Bermuda to protect American ship masters and owners; his public statements on national policy. "My expressions respecting the Government of the United States have indeed been too free," he admitted, and "I freely own that they have been rash, highly imprudent and unjustifiable." He continued, however, that "my opinions have had an extensive circulation, and an importance has been given them which I never thought they would deserve to obtain." Yes, he attested, "I was indeed a warm friend of the French Revolution . . . I flattered myself that it would be productive of human happiness."

He nevertheless begged for the renewal of his contract and in the process prostrated himself before the board of the corporation. "To acknowledge an error to the proper authority is perhaps all that can be reasonably requested or demanded from a person who has any reason to respect his own opinions." Noting that he had not expressed his opinions publicly since he returned from Bermuda in 1794, he argued that his participation in the Fourth of July event had been blown out of proportion. Indeed, he supported sentiments there proclaimed in the song "Hail Columbia": "Immortal Patriots, rise once more, / Defend your rights, defend your shore." Promising to write an explanatory piece for "the principal papers of this state . . . to remove the unfavourable impressions respecting me," Meigs concluded his plea for the board not to separate him from a place

Timothy Dwight (1817). Pope Timothy of New England Congre-gationalists, he was the spiritual leader of the American Counterrevolution.

where he had "passed twelve of the first and best years of my life, as a pupil—as a tutor & as a Professor."[3]

Unfortunately, Meigs registered his plea for liberty at a moment when freedom was being compromised across America. It came one day after Benjamin Franklin Bache's pathetic death in Philadelphia and amid a social and political squeeze that sent thousands of French and St. Domingans fleeing America for France. It occurred at a moment when the American president and his cabinet were searching the land for troublesome aliens and seditious Americans. The American Counterrevolution was under way, and not to be stopped. The situation was becoming so intolerable—especially in Connecticut—that Joel Barlow, far away in France, wrote to one of his 1778 classmates, "you and Meigs are the only friends that remain to me in Connecticut . . . the only two republicans existing in that state among my acquaintance."[4]

Although Yale College allowed Meigs to cling to his post for another two years, his career at Yale was finished. He proclaimed that "I am determined to support the Executive of the United States in the defence of their Constitutions, their liberties and independence." He promised never again to speak on social and political issues. When in 1800, however, he could no longer hold his peace amid renewed assaults on friends of liberty, Dwight, Yale, and Connecticut decided that they had had enough of Meigs. Under attack publicly at the hands of stern politician Theodore Dwight, Timothy's brother, and privately by a transformed Timothy Dwight—no longer a friend of Meigs, Barlow, or of liberty—Meigs was summarily dismissed. He had come to be viewed as a foreigner and enemy of harmony at Yale College, and there no longer was room for him at Yale, in New Haven, or in Connecticut. Feeling betrayed, Meigs followed the trail of others burned by the antilibertarian heat rising in many parts of America and retreated to Georgia in 1801. With the assistance of fellow Yale alumni Joel Barlow and his brother-in-law Abraham Baldwin—both of them still firm friends of liberty— Meigs became the first full-time president of the University of Georgia.[5]

AMERICAN ILLUMINATI EXPOSED

What could have happened to convert two friends and colleagues into such bitter enemies? Unfortunately for Meigs, he had chosen the worst day in American history, that July 4, 1798, to oppose the recently passed Alien and Sedition Acts. For on that very day, Timothy Dwight had decided to reveal the worldwide conspiracy that had animated the French Revolution and that was about to threaten the existence of America's government, society, and religion. In a powerful sermon before the citizens of New Haven titled *The Duty of Americans at the Present Crisis,* Dwight turned to the Book of Revelation to chart the millennial history of governments, Satan, beasts, antichrists, and God. He found two alarming developments that were ready to consume the world of his hearers: "the preparation for the overthrow of the Antichristian empire; and the embarkation of men in a professed and unusual opposition to God, and to his kingdom, accomplished by means of false doctrines, and impious teachers."

The Antichristian empire, for Dwight, was the Pope and the Roman Catholic Church. During the most recent months the world had witnessed the demise of the Pope: "His person has been seized, his secular government overturned, a republic formed out of his dominions, and an apparent and at least temporary end put to his dominion." So much for the Antichrist.

But then there was the hidden force of "impious teachers." Using both Abbé Barruel's *Memoirs of the History of Jacobinism* and John Robison's *Proofs of a Conspiracy,* Dwight charted the mysterious story of the Bavarian Illuminati from 1728, when Voltaire "formed a systematical design to destroy christianity," to the formation of the Order of Illuminati by Adam Weishaupt to "strike at the root of all human happiness and virtue." He then explicated the current moment in America when the Illuminati, having infiltrated the governments of Europe and America, were seeking "the overthrow of religion, government, and human society civil and domestic."

Outstripping both Barruel and Robison in his depiction of the evil intents of Illuminists, he described their basic principles as follows:

> The being of God was denied and ridiculed.
>
> GOVERNMENT was asserted to be a curse, and authority a mere usurpation.

CIVIL society was declared to be the only apostasy of man.

CHASTITY and natural affection were declared to be nothing more than groundless prejudices.

ADULTERY, assassination, poisoning, and other crimes of the like infernal nature, were taught as lawful, and even as virtuous actions.

To crown such a system of falsehood and horror all means were declared to be lawful, provided the end was good.

The Illuminati had succeeded in implementing all of these principles in France and they were marching on. "Nor have England and Scotland escaped the contagion," he proclaimed, and "several such societies are recorded as having been erected in America, before the year 1786."

And in the habit of every Jeremiah from the great prophet himself through the authors of Daniel and the Book of Revelation, Bernard of Clairvaux, Meister Eckhart, John Huss, and Cotton Mather, Dwight exhorted his hearers to "be eminently watchful, to perform our duty faithfully, in the trying period, in which our lot is cast." In fact, true watchfulness required every American to adhere to certain duties; among them, he shouted in his shrill voice, "none holds a higher place than the observation of the Sabbath." Indeed, "religion and Liberty are the two great objects of defensive war." He continued, "Conjoined, they unite all the feelings, and call forth all the energies, of man." Through the proper practice of religion, liberty could be achieved: "Where religion prevails, Illuminatism cannot make disciples, a French directory cannot govern, a nation cannot be made slaves, nor villains, nor atheists, nor beasts."[6]

Beside the duty to practice religion faithfully against all forms of evil, Dwight's other duties paled in significance. A second duty was "an entire separation from our enemies," namely disbelievers, Jacobins, and foreign emissaries. His third duty was "union among ourselves" in support of "our existing rulers [who] must be the directors of our public affairs, and the only directors." And, last," Dwight prescribed "unshaken firmness in our opposition. . . . If we are united, firm, and faithful to our selves, neither France, nor all Europe, can subdue these States." Though the Illuminists had succeeded in toppling governments all over Europe in the guise of the French Revolution, adherence to the worship of God would save America from the same fate.[7]

These were not the words of some misguided preacher seizing upon a moment to advance his brand of religion. This was not a practiced evangel emptying bombastic phrases and lurid images upon a meek flock. This was a circumstance in which the basest fears of Americans had been touched by a train of events that seemed to threaten the very existence of America. As the governments of Europe collapsed, as the Pope was given a thorough drubbing and churches everywhere dismantled, and as America moved to drive out aliens and domestic enemies of the freely elected government of John Adams, there was a need for prophets. Timothy Dwight, as evidenced in his epic poems, essays, and sermons, was ready to be that prophet in 1798, calling his people, like Moses in the wilderness, back to the practice of true religion.

Dwight was not the only prophet who called on Americans to unite against the worldwide conspiracy. On the day he rendered his address, a host of other voices proclaimed the same message. He, in fact, shared his podium with the redoubtable Noah Webster, who also "exposed to their [the listeners'] view, in a feeling manner, those principles of modern philosophy which desolate Europe, and threaten the universe with mighty evils." Those present were described as "an enlightened audience, composed of the citizens of New-Haven, the members of our university, and many clergymen, civilians, and other respectable inhabitants from the adjacent towns." Dwight's brother Theodore addressed a rapt audience in Hartford, where he claimed that the government of France had been controlled for six years by the Illuminati."[8]

Across the border in Massachusetts, Dwight's closest friend, Jedidiah Morse, was in the process of converting the Illuminist conspiracy into a momentous crusade. A native of Woodstock, Connecticut, and a 1783 graduate of Yale College, Morse, like Dwight, was no intellectual lightweight. Morse had studied theology, taught school, and tutored for a time at Yale before being ordained as a Congregational clergyman in 1786. Following a short stint as pastor of Midway Congregational Church in Liberty County, Georgia—an odd but significant outpost of New England culture—he settled as pastor of the First Congregational Church of Charlestown, Massachusetts, in 1789. From that pulpit over the next thirty years, Morse made himself known not only as one of the nation's leading clergymen, but also as America's best-known geographer and most formidable opponent of liberal ideas—whether they be found across the street at Harvard College, among Unitarian theologians, or in growing throngs of politicians. As author of the most commonly used geography textbook and of the section on "America" in the *Encyclopaedia Britannica,* Morse was one of the few Americans outside of politics known to nearly every citizen.[9]

It was probably through his work on the first American edition of the *Encyclopaedia Britannica* that Morse came to know John Robison. It was Morse, at any rate, who persuaded Thomas Dobson, Scottish-born Philadelphia publisher of the *Britannica,* to print an American edition of Robison's *Proofs of a Conspiracy* in 1798. Morse found the book to be so compelling that he staked his entire reputation and career on the veracity of Robison's evidence, beginning on the national fast day declared by President Adams for May 8, 1798. He believed in the factuality of the Illuminati conspiracy so deeply that he fell into something of a booby trap, threatening his otherwise extraordinary career.[10]

On May 8 Morse astounded Boston with his revelations of the Illuminist conspiracy as described by Robison. Within weeks other clergy joined with Morse in sending an address to President Adams that decried the creeping revolutionary currents radiating from France. Throughout the summer of 1798 and into the fall, Morse expanded the argument to suggest that America's democratic societies formed in 1793 were themselves offspring of the Illuminati. In his

Thanksgiving Day sermon, Morse inched further on this course, arguing that the United States was rife with Illuminati agents. By April 1799, in another fast day sermon, Morse claimed to have a letter that revealed the existence of fourteen lodges introduced mainly by immigrants from France and St. Domingue. With this last revelation he concluded, "You will perceive, my brethren, . . . that we have in truth secret enemies, not a few scattered through our country; . . . enemies whose professed design is to subvert and overturn our holy religion and our free and excellent government." [11]

Although Morse spoke in generalities when he delivered his sermon, the printed version contained excerpts from his highly vaunted documents. His principal source was a French-language list of members of the Wisdom Masonic Lodge of Portsmouth, Virginia. Morse's interpretation of the coded manuscript was that it was the 2,660th branch of the Grand Orient of France, the mother society from which sprang the contagion. The Virginia lodge, in league with seventeen other lodges with at least seventeen hundred members throughout the nation, clearly was on a mission to overthrow the government of the United States.

Morse sent copies of his printed sermon throughout America. He raced to Philadelphia to discuss counteracting the threat with Adams, Oliver Wolcott, Timothy Pickering, and anyone else who would listen. There he obtained a copy of an English edition of Abbé Barruel's *Memoirs on the History of Jacobinism*, which further inflamed his already overheated mind and spirit. He and others prepared abridgements of Barruel's work for publication in New England newspapers. Morse and Dwight, who also was not shrinking from the fray, now saw that the battle lines had been drawn between good and evil, religion and infidelity, government and chaos. By the summer of 1799 they were marshalling every clergyman, every politician, every student or graduate of Yale, every friend of order they could find to battle a hidden enemy, but one that was becoming increasingly evident. They were sure that they were on the verge of finding lists of Illuminati among the various lodges that had clothed themselves lightly among the vast network of the Masonic order. The year of miracles—1798—had given way to a war that would rage openly across New England over the next two decades and covertly, in cycles, through much of American history. [12]

COUNTERREVOLUTION AND TRUTH

So certain was Morse of his quarry that he consulted with one of his longtime German correspondents on the status of the Illuminati in its home origins. Early in 1799 he wrote to Cristoph D. Ebeling, well-known Hamburg geographer who eventually authored a seven-volume history and geography of America. Morse had consulted Ebeling extensively on matters geographic and trusted his judgment. When the reply dated March 13, 1799, arrived, Morse was chagrined to find that his colleague described the Illuminati as a dead phenomenon in Germany and that, even when it was alive, the order had sought only to liberalize matters in church and state, not to destroy them. Ebeling also characterized Robison's and

Barruel's books as frauds. Robison's book, in particular, had to be government-inspired propaganda, written to bolster British foreign policy.[13]

Ebeling's response did nothing to restrain Morse's ardor for stamping out Illuminism. The fear of Illuminism had clouded his judgment, making it possible for him—and many others—to see evil in every corner. A mantle of fear-fed emotion attached itself to the body politic, and truth, no matter how clearly demonstrated and documented, became irrelevant.

Morse and Dwight continued to associate Illuminism and Masonry ever more closely until respected Masons could no longer bear the false vilification. One of the first to complain was fellow clergyman William Bentley, pastor of East Church in Salem, Massachusetts. A Boston native, Harvard graduate, and follower of Joseph Priestley's brand of Unitarianism, Bentley was also a lifelong Mason who knew there was no truth to the charges of Morse and Dwight. Bentley charted daily his growing distaste for Morse and Dwight's penchant for finding conspirators throughout the world, and he became the first and most effective of the countervailing speakers who tried to bring some sense to the overheated counterrevolutionary atmosphere that flared up in 1798 and continued unabated into 1799.[14]

Because of Morse's constant bashing of Harvard, Unitarian theology, and every other American geographer—including the Salem pastor—Bentley early on developed an antipathy for Morse that verged on contempt, relishing any critical reviews of Morse's geographies. As early as 1793, Bentley gloated over an article by James Freeman, another clergyman geographer, who "expose[d] that Geographer [Morse] so fully to the world, as to lay his geographizing abilities under suspicion, & perhaps they in the future will be in little demand." Bentley also had doubts about Dwight's "liberality," from the moment it was announced in 1795 that he would succeed to the presidency of Yale College. Bentley suspected that the only revolution that interested Dwight was the promotion of Calvinism, and the only liberty he sought was the freedom for Congregational churches to remain the established religion of New England.[15]

Bentley's disdain for Morse and Dwight grew dramatically during 1798, when Morse first revealed his theory, presenting it as fact. Bentley commented in his diary that "Dr. Morse has . . . quite run himself down below notice." But, he continued, "I have come to a present resolution to make no reply as my friends say he is in the mud." But then, Morse overstepped the boundary, Bentley wrote, when he, "at last, to create hatred rather than refute, has insinuated that I might be one of the Illuminati." When Bentley publicly refuted the charge, Morse only dug deeper with another angry outcry:

> His only fort was in recourse to vulgar prejudice. He did not dare to meet an argument fairly. He ranted upon the zeal of Masons his old Copy of Robison, then condemned all Secret Societies, & after saying that 3/4s of what had been said was nothing to the point, he ended by saying that nothing was understood.

Jedediah Morse (c. 1800). A counterrevolutionary clergy-
man and popular geographer.

Bentley's revulsion increased in 1799 when Morse began to point out specific groups as branches of the Illuminati: "Dr. Morse is as lucky as Jude for he has found out illuminatism in everything, & has promised to expose a Lodge of Emigrants." [16]

In his struggles with Morse and Dwight, Bentley possessed a secret weapon unknown to either of his arch enemies. Morse was not the only American correspondent with Christoph Ebeling. From the time Joel and Ruth Barlow spent in Hamburg during 1794 and 1795, Ebeling had associated with American thinkers and doers. Barlow had, in fact, prepared a long list of Americans interested in geography who could be helpful to the German scholar. Morse was only one of them. Ezra Stiles, Dwight's predecessor at Yale, was another. Also on the list were Thomas Jefferson in Virginia, Jeremy Belknap in Massachusetts, and William Bentley. While Morse was trying to suck from Ebeling information that would enhance his popular geography, Bentley was supplying Ebeling with lists of documents, books, and draft town plans of such places as Marblehead, Massachusetts. [17]

Ebeling—far from being an obscure geographer hidden away in Germany—became a significant figure in the history of early America. Over a career of forty years, he made himself the most knowledgeable geographer of the United States and collected the largest library in the world of American state and local history and literature. When the Barlows brought him into the Yale circle during

1795, he pored through Morse's geographical works, Dwight's poetic effusions, and Noah Webster's political and linguistic essays. Soon he was receiving books, pamphlets, and newspapers from the who's who of American society—Mathew Carey, John Ormrod, and Dr. Benjamin Smith Barton of Philadelphia; James Iredell of North Carolina; and David Ramsay of South Carolina. His voice in support of America and liberty was strong throughout Germany. His authority with American men of letters was by then surpassed by few others in Europe.[18]

From his first review of Morse's geographical works, Ebeling was suspicious of the methods of the entrepreneurial clergyman. When he obtained the third edition of Morse's American geography during the summer of 1797, he wrote that Morse's description of Europe was, "I confess rather too defective and erroneous." He resolved to "send Dr. Morse annotations if I shall not offend him by my liberty." Although he devoured everything from Morse's pen, he concluded that he "could not make much use of his Geography, as he is not particular enough."

When it came to history and religion, the German master concluded that Morse was near maniacal. When Ebeling received requests from his American geographical correspondents to comment on the accuracy of Robison's *Proofs of a Conspiracy* and saw how Morse was using the Scot's rambling work, Ebeling went on the warpath. He sent to both Bentley and Morse a page-by-page and line-by-line refutation of nearly every argument and shred of evidence adduced by Robison. Declaring to be "neither Mason nor Illuminati, nor in any order whatsoever but a Cosmopolite," he thought himself well suited to critique Robison: "I am well acquainted and think myself impartial, for I wish the happiness of mankind which only can be promoted by religioun [*sic*], virtue, liberty and good government."[19]

Ebeling, however, was a decided friend of liberty. Long before Morse inquired about Ebeling's views on the Bavarian Illuminati, the German geographer had been sending his opinions to Bentley. As early as December 1798, Bentley had a letter from Ebeling that would have refuted Morse, Robison, and Barruel on the history and present dangers of the Bavarian Illuminati. Bentley offered an extract of the letter at that time to an editor who refused to publish it unless he could have the entire letter and could explain its origins. To this Bentley would not agree. But when Ebeling sent Bentley a confidential copy of his response to Morse, Bentley confidently waited for the impetuous enemy of Illuminism to hang himself.

Morse did just that with the publication of his secret documents on American lodges of Illuminati and with his insinuations that Bentley had to be one of the American conspirators. Bentley sought revenge in an anonymous article in the *American Mercury* on September 26, 1799, in which he described Morse as "a celebrated calumniator of Masonry" and "an eagle-eyed detector of Illuminatism." But the piece ended with an arrow sure to pierce Morse's heart:

> Many people wonder why the Rev. Granny, who has officiated
> at the birth of so many mice (when Mountains have travailed),

had not published the letter he has lately received from Professor Ebeling: many others suppose he will publish it as an
Appendix to his next Fast-Day Sermon.

The arrow fired, Bentley awaited the frantic dance of his wounded prey. [20]

Morse played the part of a foolish child caught with his hand in the cookie
jar. First, he demanded the name of the article's author. Then he demanded that
the editor condemn the article as "a tissue of the most vile and calumnious falsehoods." But then he admitted that there was a letter, entirely "private" in nature.
He produced affidavits prepared by Harvard Professors David Tappan and
Eliphalet Pearson declaring that they had reviewed the said letter and that it was
not the letter described in the article in *American Mercury*. Finally, Morse admitted that Ebeling did discuss the subject of the Illuminati in the letter, but that
Ebeling "is evidently of the *New divinity modern Socinianism*—which is very
little different from Illuminism & in politics a modern French Republican." As a
consequence, he concluded that Ebeling's views "so far from discrediting it
[Robison's book]—confirms its general authenticity, & importance." [21]

When Bentley handed over his copy of Ebeling's epistle for publication in
the *Massachusetts Spy* in October 1799, Morse's credibility was surely in doubt.
The letter revealed a scathing critique of *Proofs of a Conspiracy* and the whole
theory of the Illuminati. In Ebeling's view, Robison's book "certainly is a party
writing, not without design." He also concluded that Robison "knows a little of
all and nothing exact." He did not understand Masonry, German history, or the ill-
fated career of the Bavarian Illuminati. In case after case, Robison misidentified
German individuals, events, and attitudes. Because he did not know the German
language and relied on second- and thirdhand sources, his history of the Illuminati did "as much mischief as the French propaganda may have done." By dredg-
ing up a false conspiracy, Robison had done a grave disservice to the cause of liberty: "As on one side liberty and its glorious sake has been shamefully betrayed,
on the other despotism, intolerance, the feudalism of nobility and the superstition
of popish or its like Hierarchy find their abettors." [22]

Although appearing somewhat buffoonish, Morse continued in his crusade
against a worldwide conspiracy. Nothing Ebeling or any one else could say would
sway Morse, Dwight, or any of their fellow believers from this certainty. They
embraced Abbé Barruel's volumes, not as welcome replacements for Robison's
discredited work, but as additional irrefutable proof. Ebeling chiseled away at
Barruel's research, too, noting that it was "forbidden even at Vienna lately . . .
because it contains great many base slanders . . . and is taken from pamphlets
already forbidden because they contain the same invectives and lies." When both
of these works had been translated and published in Germany, Ebeling gloated
that they "met with universal derision."

Ebeling was not alone in this judgment. He was pleased to find in July 1801
that a book proclaiming his point of view had just been issued from the sharp pen
of Jean-Joseph Mounier. Mounier's French edition of *On the Influence Attributed
to Philosophers, Free Masons and to The Illuminati, on the Revolution of France*

(1801) had just been published at Tübingen and was given a rave review in *Gottingische Anzeigen,* one of Ebeling's favorite journals. Ebeling instantly translated the review into English and sent it along with an unbound copy of Mounier's book to Bentley for publication in America. He also sent a copy of the book directly to Morse, commenting to Bentley, "If the latter [Morse] is in any way open to conviction and not incorrigible, he must yield." In a separate letter to John Eliot, another of his American correspondents, Ebeling declared that Mounier's book "in a great measure confirms my letter"—the one that exposed Morse.[23]

In his excitement Ebeling praised Mounier's work exuberantly as the most correct assessment yet to appear on the debate about the Illuminati and revolution. To Eliot and Morse he sent letters and reviews of Barruel's and Mounier's works "written by very impartial Men and no friends of innovations, nor of any Orders, who highly disapprove of the Jesuit's book, and praise Mounier's." He loved that Mounier had settled in Germany as a favored guest and friend of German historian von Gentz and the Duke of Saxe-Weimar after a stormy career in the early days of the French Revolution. He identified with Mounier's movement in 1795 to open a school to train young men for careers in public service, emphasizing history and philosophy in their curricula. As a solid friend of liberty, he approved of Mounier's view that the French Revolution resulted from the apostasy of the ancien régime and not from any conspiracy.[24]

But Mounier did not need Ebeling to give him authentication. Mounier was a giant of the French Revolution who pressed both monarchists and revolutionaries to the limit, but who mercifully was spared the terror visited upon most of his associates. Derived from a wealthy family and trained for the practice of law, Mounier was among those who promoted the establishment of a constitutional monarchy in 1789. With Lafayette and Mirabeau he did everything possible to persuade Louis XVI and the National Assembly to agree on a constitution. He proposed the "tennis court oath" holding the National Assembly together against the king. He then rushed to Versailles ahead of the women of Paris to get Louis XVI to accept the Declaration of the Rights of Man and Citizen on behalf of the people of France.

But Mounier also advocated a constitutional monarchy that would give the king an absolute veto. Moreover, he thought France ought to have a bicameral national assembly like the British Parliament with an aristocratic upper house. Clearly a conservative, he also opposed the type of parliamentary reform pursued by the friends of liberty throughout Britain. Despite his antidemocratic positions he was elected president of the National Assembly in September 1789. But as bloody clashes replaced the rule of reason, Mounier disgustedly left Paris for his native Dauphiné. In 1790 he went into exile, principally to his antirevolutionary haunt in Germany, until his family urged his return in 1801.[25]

Given his career, Mounier was an excellent candidate to set the record right about the Illuminati. At a distance of ten years he reflected that the French Revolution was seen only "through the mist of prejudice," which meant that "causes are assigned for its rise, its spirit, effects, progress, and tendency, numerous as the persons who have presumed to assign them." Some of the interpretations were worse than others, however, since they were used for political purposes to control whole nations and peoples. This was obviously the case with the work of Abbé Barruel, Mounier thought, in that it indirectly justified a warlike foreign policy by Britain against France and Germany and a policy of antirevolutionary repression in Germany itself. Although Mounier also refuted Robison's work, he acknowledged in a separate note that the Scot's book "bears throughout the marks of purity of intention" and contains "the most useful truths." By comparison with Barruel, Robison was clearly "the enemy of Despotism and of Superstition" despite the defects of his scholarship.

Addressing the three principal theories for the origins of the French Revolution, Mounier began with the thesis that the great conflagration was a conspiracy of philosophers. Though it was possible to fault Voltaire and Rousseau for some of their false beliefs, Mounier concluded that "we find a Revolution rendered necessary by causes which have not the slightest connexion with philosophers." The odium heaped upon "the good, the respectable Malesherbes" could not be sustained, since that "generous champion of justice" could not possibly "partake of that terror with which truth inspires tyrants." Nor did it make sense to blame philosophers for dreaming up sophistic ideas like that of equality. After all, "[t]he love of equality is not, any more than liberty, an invention of modern times: it is a natural inclination of the human heart, which must be regulated and conciliated with public order."

Mounier also argued that it was inappropriate to associate the term "jacobinism" with philosophers. That term should be reserved for those anarchists who during the Revolution and afterward "wish for the ruin or death of those who have not the same opinions."[26]

In his refutation of the theory that the Revolution was brought on by Masons, Mounier took especial aim at Robison, since in three editions of *Proofs of a Conspiracy* Mounier was himself held to be a Mason. In the most strenuous of terms, Mounier proclaimed, "I declare solemnly that I have never been either Free-Mason or Martinist. . . . I hope my readers will excuse this declaration . . . [since] one party may consider this quality an honour, others as a subject of blame; but it does not belong to me, and it is my duty to say so." And to condemn Masons for the Revolution made no sense at all, because "men of all professions have appeared on the scene in this bloody tragedy."

Mounier saved his heaviest artillery to refute the role of the Illuminati in the French Revolution. Indeed, he attempted to shame anyone who used the term, since "all the mystic quacks of the present century have been denominated Illuminati; and all those who employ themselves about alchemy, magic, cabalistic ceremonies, ghosts, and connexions with intermediate spirits." The term, like that of Jacobin, had been separated from its historical association and was by 1801 used as a title of infamy and hatred. In reviewing the history of the order, Mounier found it ludicrous that anyone could believe that such a discredited and outlawed group could have the power to overthrow monarchies.

Mounier was personally offended that a revolution he himself had helped to inaugurate had been attributed to some secret group:

> I lived in the first period of the Revolution among the friends
> of true liberty; and I hope that I shall have the honour of
> being reckoned in this number. I am ready to declare on oath,
> that I never had the slightest reason to suspect any influence
> of the Societies of Illuminati, or of Free-Masons, or their
> principles.

He concluded that Barruel, Robison, and the others around the world who perpetuated the stories of conspiracies among philosophers, Masons, Jacobins, or Illuminati had some other agenda—political, religious, or ideological. The facts of history were otherwise.[27]

Between the detective work of Christoph Ebeling and the grand testimony of Mounier, the world had plenty of evidence in 1801 that there was no conspiracy that had thrust the French Revolution on a hapless Europe. But even with Jedidiah Morse and Timothy Dwight's claims of a conspiracy refuted, those who hoped for peace would not soon find it. Whereas Ebeling hoped Mounier's book would silence this bugbear, the noise only grew louder and more defiant.

As Mounier's book circulated around America disclosing the truth about the alleged Illuminati conspiracy, Morse angrily lashed out at his doubters. Again charged with concealing the contents of his correspondence with Ebeling, he judged his critics to be part of the machinations. No matter how many errors were pointed out in either Robison's work or Barruel's, Morse continued to defend the existence of a threatening plot:

> That there have been & still exist extraordinary efforts, & for-
> midable combinations, to subvert established principles in gov-
> ernment, religion & even morals, there can, I think, be no
> doubt. . . . It is operating like a cancer on the stamina of our
> civil & religious Institutions—& many good people seem
> determined not to believe the danger, till the destruction of the
> foundations of all that is dear to us, is accomplished.

Morse and Dwight, indeed, attacked again, and established the *New England Palladium* in January 1801 in part, "to expose Jacobinism in every form both of principle & practice, both of philosophism & Licentiousness." They also encouraged Seth Payson, a fellow Congregational minister in New Hampshire, to respond to Mounier's critique of Robison and Barruel.[28]

Titled *Proofs of the Real Existence, and Dangerous Tendency of Illuminism* (1802), Payson's effort attracted little attention as the debate came to be confined to an ever smaller group of squabblers. Although Morse wrote Ebeling in 1801 asking for corrections to Robison's and Barruel's volumes, both he and Dwight continued to contend publicly and privately that the conspiracy existed and continued.[29] For them the counterrevolutionary campaign could never rest because the enemies of government, society, and religion were waiting to seize power and overwhelm unwary hearts and minds. It did not matter that they never had proof for their accusations; conviction was stronger than truth.[30]

ILLUMINATI AND REALITY

Christoph Ebeling spent a career trying to figure out what drove Jedidiah Morse to tilt with imagined hordes of Jacobins and Illuminati. He never understood that Morse was leading a counterrevolution against a world of revolutionary forces that he believed would bring not liberty, but chaos. The closest Ebeling came to realizing the power that drove people like Morse was in late 1801, when he received from John Robison, the original popularizer of the Illuminati frenzy, a personal letter of bitter complaint. More than a year after the fact, Robison had procured a copy of the original American newspaper article (September 26, 1799) revealing the contents of Ebeling's disputed private letter to Morse. In that letter Ebeling had made various charges about Robison's character, accused him of forgery, and noted that the Scottish professor had been forced into exile in France, recently expelled from the Masonic Lodge in Edinburgh. Based on this depiction of Robison by a respected German authority and its worldwide dissemination, Robison faced the fate of being forever portrayed as at best a marginal, probably crazed character.

Sensing that he was already being consigned to history's trash heap, Robison in a letter dated October 21, 1801, challenged Ebeling to explain his false characterization of a man who stood firmly on his reputation as among Scotland's most eminent scientists. Robison explained to Ebeling that he did not, at first, take the article very seriously, thinking it "not likely to make any serious impression on the public Mind." But after reading other assassinations of his character for an entire year, he came to see that "its assertions meet with credit even among sensible Men." Reiterating the charges attributed to Ebeling, Robison demanded to know "the names of those Scoundrels who have so much abused your confidence and villified [sic] my character." And if Ebeling denied making those accusations, Robison demanded a letter stating his denial within three weeks.

Distressed to learn the true character and reputation of an individual he had maligned hundreds of times, Ebeling wrote back to Robison and to his American colleagues, "Such criminal slander never came into my head and never could be written by me." Even though he had in hand a copy of the original article, he denied that it came from his pen: "It will certainly be disavowed by all my friends and I hope they will think me incapable of such mean behaviour." Moreover, he prepared a paper to be given to newspaper editors in England, Scotland, and America setting forth his corrected estimate of Robison, the man.

To one of his American correspondents, Ebeling wrote, "I seriously believed he the author of the proof was an english Clergyman of the high Church, not even supposing the Author of a great Part of the New british Encyclopedia was the same with the Author of the Proofs." But he also checked on Robison's character: "Friends of mine who are Masons know Mr. Robison personally and give him the best moral Character tho' he is strangely prejudiced in all matters relating to his Proofs." Try as he might, Ebeling never overcame the sense that no matter how good and accomplished a person Robison might be, the

Scottish scientist still suffered a strange distemper that caused him—like Morse—to fabricate enemies.[31]

Neither could Robison's student and official biographer John Playfair. Successor to Robison on the Edinburgh faculty, Playfair orally presented a brief biography of Robison in early 1815 before the membership of the Royal Society of Edinburgh, where Robison had served as General Secretary for twenty years. Playfair portrayed his mentor as a paragon of the Scottish Enlightenment until he came to the subject of Robison's *Proofs of a Conspiracy.* Then in what he described as a "digression" from the story of the rising achievement that filled the rest of Robison's life, Playfair struggled to explain the birth and career of this strange work.

Choosing his words carefully, Playfair found that he could do little better than Ebeling. According to Playfair, through the French Revolution "a body was put in motion sufficient to crush whole nations under its weight." No one "had the power or the skill to direct its course." As a consequence, "a year was magnified into an age; and . . . in a few months one might behold more old institutions destroyed, and more new ones projected or begun, than in all the ten centuries which had elapsed between Charlemagne and the last of his successors."

He continued, "when danger is all around, every thing is of course suspected: and when the ordinary connection between causes and effects cannot be traced, men have no means of distinguishing between the probable and the improbable; so that their opinions are dictated by their prejudices, their impressions, and their fears." It was in just such a moment—a time of disorder among humans and their societies—that Robison "undertook to explain the causes of that revolution."

There also were all of "the crimes which the name of Liberty had been employed to sanction." The destruction of religious institutions "wounded those sentiments of piety which he had uniformly cherished from his early youth." Under these circumstances Robison wrote his book with all the fury of a religious zealot. Playfair did not know how Robison settled on the Illuminati and Freemasonry as the objects of his search, but he noted that "the style of the works from which Mr. Robison composed his narrative, is not such as to inspire confidence; for, wherever it is quoted, it is that of an angry and inflated invective."

Playfair ruefully concluded, "From the perusal of the whole [of *Proofs*] it is impossible not to conclude, that the alarm excited by the French Revolution, had produced in Mr. Robison a degree of credulity which was not natural to him."

In the end Playfair not only digressed to acknowledge the remarkable departure from sane judgment on Robison's part; he also found it necessary to sit in judgment. There was no truth in any of Robison's so-called proofs:

> Truth and justice require this acknowledgment; and in making it,
> I think that I am discharging a duty both to Mr. Robison and
> myself: —It is a duty to Mr. Robison, in as much as a concession

made by a friend, is better than one extorted by an adversary; it
is a duty to myself, because I should feel that I was doing wrong,
were I even by silence to acquiesce in a representation which I
believed to be so ill-founded and unjust.

Just like Ebeling, Playfair ended his "digression" on *Proofs of a Conspiracy* on
this sad, mystified note.[32]

Though critics, biographers, and historians, almost without exception, treat
the story of the Illuminati and the fear of conspiracies as a momentary divergence, it was actually at the epicenter of the European and American counterrevolutions. Though the story of specific conspiracies—of the Bavarian Illuminati, of Freemasonry, and other occult movements—might be quickly discredited,
the underlying theme has repeatedly been dredged up time and again throughout
American history.

As recently as 1935, for example, historian Bernard Faÿ, a prolific student of
Benjamin Franklin, published *Revolution and Freemasonry, 1680–1800,* in which
he charted in more than three hundred detailed pages the methods whereby Benjamin Franklin, working through the machinations of a world controlled by
Masons, engineered not only the American Revolution, but also the French Revolution. Faÿ argued that Franklin used Masonic secrets to mount a revolution in
France to destroy the world's nobility. Faÿ had introduced this theme in his earlier
Franklin, the Apostle of Modern Times, published in 1929 and, at the time, the
fullest Franklin biography. Faÿ had uncovered a cache of new Franklin manuscripts in which he claimed to have found the details of the conspiracy.[33]

The gusto of Faÿ's argument easily rivaled Robison's and Barruel's. In 1935,
in a world on the brink of confronting Nazi Germany, he wrote: "Freemasonry
had bewitched nobility and utilized it to spread propaganda aimed to destroy this
same nobility. Backed by the aristocracy, Masonry preached the equality which
was to be imposed so brutally on the nation by the coming French Revolution."
By Faÿ's calculation it was the aspirations of Franklin, Voltaire, Washington,
Lafayette, Mirabeau, the duc d'Orléans, and other like minds that imposed
Freemasonry on the world and that controlled governments and societies from the
eighteenth century until the twentieth.[34]

Faÿ came to believe that the conspiracy lived on in the 1930s. While serving as a history professor at the Collège de France in 1937, he declared before
the Academy for the Rights of Nations meeting in Hitler's Berlin that the
ancient conspiracy had recently found its place in the plots of world commu-
nism and that Methodists and Baptists across the world were being seduced by
the thousands.[35]

When Hitler's forces overthrew the French government early in the Second
World War, Faÿ emerged in August 1940 as general director of the French
National Library. In this capacity he waged war on those Freemasons who he
thought were still conspiring to overthrow governments. With access to the
records of the Grand Orient Lodge of Paris in the French National Archives con-

taining lists of Freemasons throughout France, he turned over sixty thousand names to German authorities, published thirty-three pamphlets against Masonry, and produced an anti-Masonic film titled "Occult Forces." Thousands of Masons, it was determined in investigations at the war's end, were arrested, deported, and executed as a part of the Holocaust. Arrested in August 1944 and charged with collaborating with the enemy and other war crimes, Faÿ in December 1946 was sentenced to life imprisonment at hard labor for his bloody campaign to destroy Masonry.[36]

As Faÿ's grim record attests, there frequently come along characters who fear that the world will be absorbed by a conspiratorial superpower. Timothy Dwight and Jedidiah Morse splashed this fear across America in reaction to what they perceived as the chaos of revolution. But their actions were crucial as a part of the great American counterrevolution, for in the Illuminati experience of 1798 they introduced a new terminology into the American parlance that would linger for the next two centuries—revolutionary, brigand, Jacobin, infidel, illuminati, enthusiast, anarchist, liberal, conservative, and much else. This was an ideological nomenclature that would be used to control or intimidate peoples by force of suasion, not by arms, throughout the nineteenth and twentieth centuries.

After 1798 it did not matter whether or not the Order of Illuminati existed anywhere in the world. The specter of the Illuminati existed in powerful and threatening images, transcending human form. Infidels, illuminati, and conspirators in revolutionary intrigue could be invoked at will by people like Morse and Dwight and thousands of crusading American leaders who followed in their footsteps. The year 1798 was indeed another year of miracles. Events of that year fueled a counterrevolution from which there would be no turning back.

CHAPTER 20

The Course of Counterrevolution: Webster, Cobbett, Chateaubriand

NOAH WEBSTER, COUNTERREVOLUTIONARY

On that fateful July 4, 1798, when Timothy Dwight began his campaign against the Illuminati in New Haven, he shared the podium with his friend Noah Webster, editor of the famous Federalist paper, *The Minerva,* published in New York City. Webster had just relocated his family to New Haven. Although Webster did not reveal any great conspiracies, he joined Dwight in condemning revolutionary movements in Europe and America and revealed in his speech, published as *Oration, Pronounced before the Citizens of New Haven,* that he, too, was ready to welcome—yea, to lead—a counterrevolution in America.[1]

Destined to become the American Samuel Johnson and to be enshrined in dictionaries bearing his name, Webster came out of that same class at Yale in 1778 that had spawned the nation's first band of brash poets. He overlapped with Alsop, Barlow, Meigs, Dwight, Trumbull, Humphreys, and the rest of the Yale crowd that employed words and a new wellspring of American exuberance to form a literature and to establish an American voice. Whereas his fellows used language to express themselves, Webster was more interested in the origin, meaning, pronunciation, and spelling of those words that made up language. And, like Jedidiah Morse (also overlapping Webster at Yale), who provided America with a popular school geography, Webster fashioned the nation's first spelling book, originally titled *Grammatical Institute of the English Language* (1783). With the addition of a grammar in 1784 and a reader in 1785, Webster at the age of twenty- seven became a household name—forty years before the publication in 1828 of his great *An American Dictionary of the English Language.*[2]

Just as entrepreneurial as Morse, Webster commanded the bulk of the market share for school spelling books (100 million copies sold). But he was also deeply in love with America and reveled in the wonder of the American Revolution and the promise of the new nation. Whereas his colleagues wrote epic poems, Webster infused his speller and grammar with a celebration of America's revolutionary doctrines. In instructions, stories, and examples Webster touted the glories of American rebellion against tyranny, the virtues of reason and enlightenment, the perfectibility of human beings in the new nation, the absence of corruption in America, and the promises of liberty for every citizen. He firmly believed that "America must be as independent in literature as she is in politics, as famous for arts as for arms." And he believed that he was the person who could show the way.[3]

Exceedingly proud of his work, Webster sent Benjamin Franklin, just returned from France in 1786, a copy of the unpublished revision and expansion of the *Grammatical Institute* for the personal review and endorsement of the famous American revolutionary. "It is designed," Webster wrote, "to collect some American pieces [stories] upon the discovery, history, war, geography, economy, commerce, government, &c. of this country . . . in order to call the minds of our youth from ancient fables and modern foreign events, and fix them upon objects immediately interesting in this country." He also told Franklin that he would do himself "the honor to call in a few days and take the advice of his Excellency, whose library may also be of service."[4]

Whether this note was written before or after Webster met Franklin for the first time on February 17, 1786, is not clear. On that date he visited Franklin in the latter's capacity as president of the trustees of the University of Pennsylvania to secure a room at the school where he would give public lectures. Either this initial meeting or Webster's revised *Grammatical Institute* inaugurated an intellectual exchange between the two—reminiscent of the way Franklin mentored dozens of other men and women. The encounter and Webster's sense of mission launched him into a phenomenal career as America's lexicographer. Impressed with Webster's grasp of orthography and language, Franklin viewed the youthful author as a potential collaborator in reforming the English language into a simpler, more consistent American language. Franklin had already in 1768 devised *A Scheme for a New Alphabet and Reformed Mode of Spelling,* which he used to exchange a few awkward letters with another of his favorite pupils, Polly Stevenson.[5]

Over the course of the following year and a half Webster met with Franklin at least a dozen times to discuss this and other matters of mutual interest.[6] In a "memoir" written years later, Webster recalled his interchanges with Franklin wherein the elder statesman tried to persuade him to adopt his odd new alphabet. Webster found the attention to be somewhat "embarrassing" and the plan for a new alphabet "impracticable." He politely declined the collaboration, "alledging that he could not risk the expense of the undertaking, especially during the troubles of the times." Yet, he made extensive use of Franklin's well-stocked library. And while there, he met the greatest legends of the age—Thomas Paine, Benjamin Rush, David Rittenhouse, and David Ramsay.[7]

It was while Webster was living in Philadelphia during 1786 and 1787, together with Joel Barlow and Jedidiah Morse and under the gaze of America's revolutionary leaders and constitution makers, that he became committed to charting the nation's future. As an entrepreneurial author having to travel from state to state to secure copyrights for his textbooks, he had become frustrated with the unwieldy Articles of Confederation. Already he observed firsthand the difficulties of commerce among the states and abroad as he traveled to Baltimore, Norfolk, Charleston, Philadelphia, and New York. Worried about the comparative availability of education,

NOAH WEBSTER, JUN. ESQ.

Noah Webster (1789). America's master lexicographer was also its first counter-revolutionary.

books, teachers, and libraries across the various states, he and Yale friends—Barlow, Morse, Dwight, Meigs, Humphreys—discussed these matters constantly as if it was their duty to fashion the new republic.[8]

Indeed, so acutely did Webster feel called into nation-making that in 1785 he poured out his heart in a pamphlet titled *Sketches of American Policy,* a publication that—even though it lacked polish—landed at precisely the right moment to swing the nation's civil and political leaders into action. Webster carried copies of the pamphlet with him as he traveled up and down the coast securing his copyrights. He handed out copies everywhere he went, urging thoughtful Americans to come to the aid of the ailing, loosely organized republic. The pamphlet pingponged among the nation's leaders. The copy he personally presented to George Washington, for example, ended up in the hands of James Madison. Everywhere the case was the same.

The young Webster screwed up his courage, called upon his knowledge of history and government, and announced a plan for revising American polity and government. Inspired by Richard Price's influential sermon of 1784 titled *The Importance of the American Revolution,* Webster outlined how America might further secure the blessings of the Revolution. He first rehearsed the prevailing theory of government in America, the Rousseauian social contract placing "sovereign power" in "the whole body of the people collectively." Then, in preparation for rendering his prescription for American polity, he surveyed the glaring defects of all the "governments on the eastern continent," i.e., Europe. Every single European government, past and present, was flawed because "the basis of every constitution of civil government on the eastern continent, was laid by barbarians, in whom the military spirit was predominant." The force of arms, of titles, and of established religion was used there to compel civil obedience.

American states, by contrast, were governed by "constitutions of civil government . . . framed in the most enlightened period of the world." Each state worked unto itself due to "an equal distribution of landed property" among free citizens. The holding of title to property by individuals without title or preferments was in Webster's mind "the foundation of republican governments and the security of freedom." Indeed, Webster refuted as nonsense Montesquieu's claim that public spirit was the driving force behind republics. Except in Southern states where, due to the presence of slavery, some Americans lived in an aristocratic fashion, citizens of the United States enjoyed the fruits of republicanism. With a broader distribution of property, the annihilation of hereditary titles, and the abolition of established churches, liberty increasingly reigned. Noting that with absolute freedom of movement, access to books and newspapers, and freedom to speak and worship ("every man in New-England is a theologian"), Americans savored a degree of freedom never before known on earth.

That being said, nevertheless, it in no sense provided certainty that the American nation would work as a union. As Webster reviewed the absence of unity among the states within the Confederation, he questioned what glue might hold them together: "The American constitutions are founded on principles different from those of all nations, and we must find new bonds of union to perpetuate the confederation." According to Webster, "there must be a supreme power at the head of the union, vested with authority to make laws that respect the states in general and to compel obedience to those laws." He then described "a system of continental government" providing for a powerful Congress with a president or "supreme magistrate, cloathed with authority to execute the laws of Congress."

As Webster outlined a national government that would be established under the U.S. Constitution four years later, he also began to sketch in this early reforming treatise a social philosophy that he and others would make the core of the American counterrevolution. After depicting a new national government, he moved on to several other matters "that may serve, in a more remote manner, to confirm the union of these states." First was education, essential in erasing prejudices, evil passions, and local jealousies: "Education will gradually eradicate them, and a growing intercourse will harmonize the feelings and views of all the citizens." A second ingredient in building America was religion, which had to be disestablished, but at the same time allowed to flourish, since it was "calculated at least to promote the peace and happiness of society."

A third element in making a great republic was the pursuit of industry on the part of all citizens. The chief obstacle to this, Webster observed, was the presence of slavery in America. Slaves, he wrote, "support luxury, vice and indolence more than all other causes." Expressing no moral or religious judgment on slavery's impact upon the enslaved, his only concern was the institution's effects on the productivity of white Americans: "Nor are slaves so profitable as white people; for one man, who lives by his industry, and eats hearty food, will do as much labour as five negroes." Slavery's main fault was that it engendered "a haughty, unsocial, aristocratic temper, inconsistent with that equality which is the basis of our governments and the happiness of human society."

Webster's final prescription for making America "an independent empire" was for it "to assume a national character." In his mind "nothing can betray a more despicable disposition in Americans than to be the apes of Europeans." He called for manners, fashions, language, and habits reflecting American values and attitudes, for if Americans did not establish their own, they would be perpetual vassals: "In politics, our weakness will render us the dupes of their power and artifice; in manners, we shall be the slaves of their barbers and their coxcombs."

Webster demonstrated in matters of language, grammar, lexicography, and much else what he meant by American independence.[9]

Although in *Sketches of American Policy,* Webster called for a new national government to carry forward the American Revolution, he also delineated those principles that would cascade across America during the 1790s and beyond as the ideology of a powerful counterrevolution. Central to the counterrevolution would be emphasis on education and religion and tools for bringing social and civil order, for teaching citizens how to act in the American republic, and for training leaders schooled in history, philosophy, and religion. Critical to the counter-revolution would be a spirit of enterprise and the freedom of the individual to pursue his or her calling within a carefully defined social structure. In this counterrevolution, too, slavery would forever be evil only in that the enslaved were Africans and that American counterrevolutionaries could not countenance a role for blacks in America. Finally, Webster personified the pursuit of a unique American form of republicanism, one that conformed to the geography, demography, and experience of Americans seizing a vast continent.

Though Webster flirted with liberty of the kind romanticized by American poets, friends of liberty in Britain, and early revolutionaries in France, he was from the outset on a clear course toward an epiphany in 1794 that would turn him against revolution and make him one of America's prototypical counter-revolutionaries. He gloried in America's constitution-making enterprise, conversing daily with the delegates in Philadelphia. He met regularly with Washington, Franklin, Madison, Sherman, Ellsworth, Livingston, and many others during the Convention. Thomas Fitzsimmons, Pennsylvania delegate, even leaked to Webster a copy of the near final draft for his reading and comment. When the end came, he noted in his diary, "The Great Convention finish their business & offer to the public the New Federal System." He stood watching on September 18 as "Dr. Franklin presents the Speaker of the House of Assembly in Pennva with the Federal System . . . Bells ring. All America waits anxiously for the Plan of Government."[10]

By the end of 1787 Webster was sounding like a great reformer as he edited in New York a venture titled *The American Magazine.* In this short-lived periodical and in separate pamphlets, Webster promoted universal education, even expounding extensively on education for women because of the need to "enable them to implant in the tender mind, such sentiments of virtue, propriety and dignity, as are suited to the freedom of our governments." Educated women were needed, he wrote, due to "their influence in control[l]ing the manners of a nation." He excoriated slavery in articles and pamphlets for being a drag on American industriousness, harping on statistics to prove "that the labour of slaves is less productive than that of freemen." In 1789 he published his seminal *Dissertations on the English Language,* his long-awaited response to Franklin's challenge. Although he eschewed Franklin's phonetic alphabet, Webster dedicated the volume to his Philadelphia mentor, as he urged Americans: "Let us seize the present moment and establish a national language, as well as a national government."[11]

When the French Revolution got underway, he greeted it as an extension of America's courtship with liberty:

> Fair Liberty, whose gentle sway
> First blest these shores, had cross'd the sea,
> To visit Gallia, and inflame
> Her sons their ancient rights to claim.

While practicing law between 1789 and 1793 in Hartford, Webster continued his love affair with what he considered to be the American utopia. As late as the summer of 1793, just prior to returning to New York to edit *The Minerva,* he reflected optimism about the ultimate triumph of "true republicanism" both in America and in France. In a little piece he published in the *Connecticut Courant* on August 12, 1793, Webster wrote what would be his last affirming note on the course of liberty and revolution. Although he no longer talked about equal ownership of property within republics, he still espoused equal rights among humans according to their "talents and virtues."[12]

On the same day, August 12, when Webster arrived in New York to begin his tenure with *The Minerva,* he experienced an epiphany that sent him from the ranks of cautious revolutionary to counterrevolutionary enthusiast. Making his way to his temporary residence at Bradley's Tavern on Maiden Lane, he encountered a mob feting Edmond Genet, the fiery revolutionary French minister to America. Over the previous four days, Genet's triumphal arrival in New York had been marked by processions, songs, cockades, speeches, and slogans. Genet happily greeted his admirers by day, as he met at night with French admirals and generals to lay plans for a world revolution. Within two hours of Webster's arrival, the two met each other. At nearly the same hour, word arrived from Philadelphia that Genet had privately threatened to bypass the unfriendly policies of President Washington and to appeal for support to the American people.[13]

Webster was shocked to see the ebullient crowds under the spell of the revolutionary Frenchman. He was further disturbed when he heard the swaggering threats of the French minister. In a carefully worded "Affidavit" written a month afterward and sent to President Washington, Webster recounted the fateful words Genet uttered over the dinner table at Bradley's Tavern. The company included Timothy Phelps from New Haven, a Mr. Haxhall from Virginia, Genet, a Captain Bompard, and Genet's secretaries. Webster retold the French delegation's reaction to the news that the governor of Massachusetts had ordered the seizure of a French ship. One of Genet's secretaries, Webster wrote, "immediately replied in French 'Mon. Washington fait la guerre a la nation Française,' or in words to that effect; to which Mr. Genet & Capt Bompard both assented saying Yes."[14]

Webster, having just spent four years in law practice continued in his ponderous legalese to nail Genet:

> Mr Genet proceeded & said that the Executive of the United
> States was under the influence of British Gold—the deponent

asked him if he meant the President of the United States; he replied No—Mr Genet declared he had very good letters which gave him this information. The deponent represented to Mr Genet that it would be impossible to subject the independent freemen of America to British or any other foreign power, and that the Executive Officers, the President, Mr Jefferson, Mr Hamilton, & Gen. Knox to be fools; to which Mr Genet replied, Mr Jefferson is no fool.[15]

This document, sworn before a magistrate and mailed off to Philadelphia to bestir national political currents, placed Webster fully in the mainstream of counterrevolution from which he would never emerge.

The enormity of Webster's counterrevolutionary spirit was demonstrated in a telling pamphlet he titled *The Revolution in France, Considered in Respect to Its Progress and Effects*. Sent with a cover letter on April 20, 1794, to George Washington, stating that it "is intended to aid the cause of government and peace," the essay represented a thorough revision of *Sketches of American Policy*. It was to be a critical blueprint for the American nation. Of similar compass to *Sketches*, *The Revolution in France* revealed the ideological change that was occurring with thousands of Americans in the face of potential chaos in American society.[16]

Acknowledging that he discovered a "love of liberty" during the American Revolution and that his "pen has often advocated her cause," Webster from the outset of *The Revolution in France* condemned "the sanguinary proceedings of the Jacobins" who had subverted the French cause. The moment had arrived to sound the alarm that "an introduction of their principles and practice into this country, will prove dangerous to government, religion and morals." He then described the rise of Jacobin societies in France and how they succeeded in supplanting the National Convention as the controlling force in the nation's governance. In economics, agriculture, manufacturing, commerce, arts and science, and religion, these misguided and unprincipled people had destroyed one of the greatest nations on earth.

Webster castigated the dangerous "superstition" and "enthusiasm" that fueled the French nightmare. Both of these, unbridled, led directly to the destruction and enslavement of human beings. The impact on religion especially caught his interest, as he saw Notre-Dame converted into a temple of reason, "a colossal monument . . . in honor of the day, when reason triumphed over what they call fanaticism." This led him into a listing of the enormous sins of the National Convention: they abolished the Sabbath; they eradicated the monarchy; they dismantled the Church; they abrogated the use of "common titles of mere civility"; they canceled "the insignia of rank, civil and ecclesiastical"; and they annihilated "every ensign of royalty, nobility or priesthood." All order in France had vanished: "France now resembles a man under the operation of spasms, who is capable of exerting an astonishing degree of unnatural muscular force; but when the paroxysm subsides, languor and debility will succeed."

Webster paused to assess the ultimate import of his new thinking: "Let it not be thought that the writer of these sheets is an enemy to liberty or a republican government." He still wished "to see republican governments established over the earth, upon the ruins of despotism," but he had not "imbibed the modern philosophy, that rejects all ancient institutions, civil, social and religious, as impositions of fraud." Nor could he agree with French atheists who believed "that the universe is composed solely of matter and motion, without a Supreme Intelligence." He refused to accede to the practices of factional rule then regnant where "a mere adherence to a solemn oath, became high treason punishable with death."

"What had liberty and the rights of men to do with this second revolution?" asked Webster. Absolutely nothing, he rejoined as he listed lessons that must be applied to the American setting. "Party spirit is the source of faction and faction is death to the existing government" was his first conclusion. Second, private societies like the Jacobin societies "ought to be avoided like a pestilence in America." And, third, "nothing is more dangerous to the cause of truth and liberty than a party-spirit." Arguing that Americans should use the Constitution's provisions in making any changes in governance, Webster in a string of appended commentaries revisited such concepts as faction, reason, aristocracy, religion, and treason. "Americans! be not deluded," he proclaimed: "if you love liberty, adhere to your constitution of government. The moment you quit that sheet-anchor, you are afloat among the surges of passion and the rocks of error; threatened every moment with shipwreck." If Americans would do that, they "may be enabled to ride out the storm, and land . . . safely on the shores of peace and political tranquility." [17]

From the date Webster published *The Revolution in France,* he was a changed man. Like so many other counterrevolutionaries, he became obsessed with the French Revolution, in tracing its origins, in following its course, and in interpreting how it was playing itself out across the world and in America. In 1796, he asked Secretary of State Timothy Pickering for the right and privilege of reading official correspondence between France and the United States from the negotiation of the 1783 Articles of Peace to the present. "I intend to devote a considerable portion of time, this winter," he wrote to Pickering, "in developing the history and views of the French nation." He was convinced that the French "formed as early as 1792, the vast project of a general revolution, and have since added to their views the design of conquests as extensive as the Roman Empire in the plenitude of the greatness of her power." His mission was important since "there is no question that the great mass of citizens of the United States are utterly ignorant of the real views and character of the French government." [18]

Four months later, March 4, 1797, in a letter "To the Public" published in *The Minerva,* Webster revealed the results of his research. He traced the world's problems with the French Revolution back to November 19, 1792, when the National Convention issued the Decree of Fraternity, offering "fraternity and aid" to all subject peoples around the world who might wish to overthrow the yoke of their own ancien régime. To Webster, the decree was "a formal and solemn avowal of the most daring projects of throwing the world into confusion that have been exhibited since the incursions of the Goths and the Vandals." In recalling the Genet mission, Webster thought his actions "left no room to question that the insidious views of the French republicans extended to gain a control[l]ing influence over all nations and countries where they could obtain a footing, either by force or intrigue."

Revolutionary momentum came through "the establishment of popular clubs," whose purposes were "gradually and secretly to acquire numbers and strength till they were able to bid defiance to the constitutional authorities." Leagues of these societies were to be created across nations "disciplined to the orders of chiefs, whose views were concealed, even from the members themselves." Thus originated America's democratic-republican societies, which by 1797 had been scorned out of existence. They failed due to "the dispersed situation of the American people," the absence of "a sufficient quantity of combustible materials" in America, and "an explosion in the western country"—the Whiskey Rebellion—that "alarmed our unsuspecting yeomanry, unfolded to them the insidious wiles of our secret foes, and the societies." Webster declaired, "The period of delusion, is at last come to an end."[19]

At the same time Webster turned on the French Revolution, his support for equal rights and education for all vanished. His vision of an American utopia evaporated as well. During the four years he edited *The Minerva* and waged political wars, he came to see America much as he had described France in 1794. By 1797 he proclaimed, "From the date of Adam, to this moment, no country was ever so infested with corrupt and wicked men, as the United States. . . . We see now in our new Republic, the decrepitude of Vice; and a free government hastening to ruin, with a rapidity without example." While reviewing a copy of his *Sketches of American Policy* in 1797 Webster confided in a letter to Jedidiah Morse, "I was once a visionary and should now leave out a few ideas contained in it."[20]

The world had changed. Disgusted with partisan politics and with the bickering attendant to living in New York City, Webster retired to New Haven on April 1, 1798, hoping to have more time for reflection. By the time of his July 4 oration alongside Timothy Dwight's excoriation of the Bavarian Illuminati, Webster had given full form to his counterrevolutionary philosophy.

As with his other speeches or essays, Webster first had to grapple with what was the American Revolution and what was the French Revolution. Those two events became for him sine qua non of articulating social, political, and philosophical opinion. Despite all he had said in the past and all the rhetoric of his fellow Yale poets, the American Revolution became for Webster in 1798 nothing more than a war for independence from England. It was not for the rights of man; it was not for liberty; it was not for freedom. It was rather to throw off the yoke of a foreign power attempting to write laws for Americans. The American Revolution symbolized the orderly transfer of authority to where it belonged.

The French Revolution, by contrast, symbolized anarchy and chaos. Authority was transferred in a most disorderly fashion. It was done for spurious reasons and, as a result, France lay prostrate:

> Such are the inevitable consequences of that false philosophy
> which has been preached in the world of Rousseau, Condorcet,
> Godwin, and other visionaries, who sit down in their closets to
> frame systems of government, which are as unfit for practice,
> as a vessel of paper for the transportation of men on the trou-
> bled ocean.

Such people in any nation are "a greater scourge to society than a pestilence."

America, Webster believed, was faced with another war for independence in 1798. This time there were two enemies: France and anarchy. France was exporting revolution and intrigue, and those Americans who spouted ideas about liberty and equality were dividing the nation into warring factions. The only way to save America was to rid the country of "lawless democracy." What the nation needed was adherence to order and authority, respect for leaders and institutions, and a total eradication of factions: "Experience is a safe pilot, but experiment is a dangerous ocean, full of rocks and shoals." Quiet obedience was also necessary: "Let us never forget that the cornerstone of all republican governments is, that the will of every citizen is controlled by the laws or supreme will of the state."[21]

Webster was ready to burn bridges to anyone who continued to promote revolution or France. When Joel Barlow's letter to Abraham Baldwin criticizing the policies of John Adams became public, Webster publicly condemned his former Yale classmate and friend. In an extraordinary letter of November 16, 1798, Webster decried France, the French Revolution, and also Barlow in the severest of terms. France, he thought, "professes to be pursuing liberty while it is extending its territories" and that it "pretends great friendship for nations it intends to conquer." Returning again to the Decree of Fraternity of November 19, 1792, as the ideological root of this policy, Webster traced France's course with various nations and with the United States.

Although most of the letter was a rehash of views embraced as early as 1794, one new element of the counterrevolutionary style emerged. Webster, in support of his ideological position, rendered a stern judgment against revolutionaries— friend and foe. Writing to Barlow as "an old friend who once loved and respected you," Webster found Barlow's effusion to Baldwin "a striking proof of the effect of atheism and licentious examples on the civility and good manners of a well-bred man." Barlow had gone from America "with a good character for talents and for good breeding." But the impact of the French Revolution on him was clear: "No, Mr. Barlow, in divesting yourself of religion, you have lost your good manners, and like the French by the same process you have commenced a rude, insulting, dogmatical egotist."[22]

The tenor of Webster's verbal trouncing of someone once a close friend indicated that Americans were already severely divided on ideological as well as political lines. Webster and Barlow were not of different political parties. Rather one was a revolutionary; the other a counterrevolutionary.

WILLIAM COBBETT: COUNTERREVOLUTIONARY PROVOCATEUR

One reason Noah Webster fled the New York political heat was William Cobbett, known everywhere as Peter Porcupine. While Webster was fomenting a counter-revolution against France and the French Revolution, he also was charging Cobbett of covertly and, sometimes openly, attempting to reunite America with Britain. In the spring of 1797 Webster described his suspicions to Jedidiah Morse:

> Porcupine is evidently attempting to create or rally an English
> party in our country as violent and as devoted to foreign gov-
> ernment as the French party . . . But if he is not attempting this,
> his prejudices, his birth, and his violent principles will do great
> injury to the true American interests.

But then Webster concluded this analysis with his most perceptive comment on Cobbett: "Besides, he is a mere bully."[23]

"Bully" and verbal ruffian are entirely appropriate terms for Cobbett. Where he found the energy and art to write the books, pamphlets, and newspaper articles that bore his distinctively clever use of the English language is not clear. He was born into a peasant family, had little education, and served an eight-year tour of duty in Nova Scotia in the British army. Nothing in Cobbett's background suggested that he would become one of the most famous political writers in British and American history. Just as Webster has been more associated with revolution than with counterrevolution, Cobbett's role in history is even more misunderstood.

Cobbett exhibited contradictions in every facet of his life. By character and training he was devoted to authority, but also by nature he was an impulsive rebel. He loved nature, and in countless essays and books he described its perfection. But he delighted equally in finding the fatal flaws in humans, however famous. In America he was a monarchist and a friend of aristocracy. In Britain, by contrast, he was antimonarchical, proparliamentarian, and a friend of the poor. In America he has been viewed as a reactionary, while in Britain he has been identified as a radical reformer. Cobbett shattered every stereotype, but in doing so he revealed much about the character of the American Counterrevolution.

His contradictory career began when he brought charges of peculation in 1792 against officers with whom he had served in Nova Scotia. When it appeared that he might instead suffer prosecution, he fled with his wife to France. During his six months in France between March and September 1792, Cobbett witnessed the onset of the French war with Austria, the invasion of the Tuileries, and the suspension and arrest of Louis XVI by the National Assembly. Indeed, Cobbett was on his way to Paris when he heard of the king's predicament. He turned back toward Le Havre-de-Grace, and sailed from there with his wife to the United States on September 1.[24]

Arriving as a twofold refugee from both Britain and France, but possessing a newly acquired command of the French language, Cobbett settled in Wilmington, Delaware, as a tutor among new arrivals from St. Domingue. Although he bore a

William Cobbett (c. 1797). Counterrevolutionary provoca-
teur and enemy of liberty, he was the scourge of liberators.

letter from American Minister William Short introducing him to Thomas Jefferson, the secretary of state took no notice of Cobbett's appeal for help. Cobbett remained in relative obscurity for fifteen months, teaching English to French-speaking boarders and students. By early 1794, however, Cobbett was eager for action and moved his family into Philadelphia. There he hoped to write a couple of pamphlets and translate a few French works to English, enough to provide funds for passage to the West Indies. Enamored of his new West Indian friends, he dreamed of settling there permanently.[25]

He perhaps would have followed his modest plan if Joseph Priestley had not shown up in America as the oracle of the age. Priestley's parade across America provided Cobbett the kind of target the budding wordsmith could not resist. As if possessed, he spun out a pamphlet that he originally titled *The Tartuffe Detected.* The title and contents were too hot for Philadelphia publisher Mathew Carey. Thomas Bradford, however, changed the radical title to *Observations on the Emigration of Dr. Joseph Priestley,* and published it without an author's name in August 1794. The piece caused an immediate sensation both in Philadelphia and in Britain, where Priestley's detractors were many. It went through three editions in Philadelphia alone in six months.[26]

Basking in anonymous glory, Cobbett next attacked *Political Progress of Britain* by Scot James T. Callender. In *A Bone to Gnaw for the Democrats,* published in January 1795—still anonymously—it became clear that Cobbett planned to discredit all friends of liberty, especially those spilling out of Britain into America. That he did, including Benjamin Franklin Bache and the Democratic-Republican societies emerging in Philadelphia and across the country. His argument was that Callender, Bache, and other friends of liberty were advocating chaos in their radical preachments.[27]

He derided the inconsistencies of liberators who published ads for the sale of slaves. He observed that the meaning of the term "liberty" had gone awry. "Liberty, according to the Democratic Dictionary," he wrote, "does not mean freedom from oppression; it is a very comprehensive term, signifying, among other things, slavery, robbery, murder, and blasphemy." The extent to which liberty had lost its meaning to its friends was clear, Cobbett thought, from Jacques-Louis David's depiction of liberty as a dragon in one of his most recent paintings in support of revolution.[28]

In March 1795, Cobbett demolished yet another immigrant oracle of liberty, Susanna Rowson, author of best-selling *Charlotte, a Tale of Truth* (1791), a sentimental defense of women. In *A Kick for a Bite,* ostensibly a response to one of his critics, Cobbett kept his antidemocratic campaign going with a stinging rebuke against Rowson for her plays and novels proclaiming the rights of women. Arriving with her actor husband from England during 1793 to become part of Thomas Wignell's acting company at the New Chestnut Street Theater in Philadelphia, Rowson had produced one sensation after another as novelist, dramatist, and actress in the nation's capital.

On June 30, 1794, her opera *Slaves in Algiers* opened in Philadelphia, exploiting Americans' fascination with pirates, but also playfully touting women's superiority over men. The lines in the play, "Women were born for universal sway, / Men to adore, be silent and obey," sent Cobbett into convulsions. When, on January 21, 1795, Rowson's next play, *The Volunteers,* opened in Philadelphia, farcically making heroes out of Pennsylvania's whiskey rebels, Cobbett took full aim at a friend of liberty who, in his mind, could incite a bloody revolution in America.

In *A Kick for a Bite* Cobbett attacked Rowson's crusade to promote the rights of women. Describing her as "among the many treasures that the easterly winds have wafted us over, since our political emancipation [the American Revolution], I cannot hesitate to declare this lady the most valuable." He continued, "The inestimable works that she has showered . . . upon us, mend not only our hearts, but if properly administered, our constitutions." Continuing his satire, Cobbett made clear which constitutions he meant:

> A liquorish page from the Fille de Chambre [the novel *Rebecca,* 1792] serves me by way of a philtre, the Inquisitor [novel, 1788] is my opium, and I have ever found the Slaves in Algiers a most excellent emetic. As to Mentoria [novel, 1791] and Charlotte, it is hardly necessary to say what use they are put to in the chambre of the valetudinarian.

Having ridiculed every one of Rowson's works and provoked various Philadelphia women engaged in defining the rights of women, Cobbett for the first time used his pen name, Peter Porcupine.

Although Cobbett was attacked by various writers in pamphlets such as *A Rub from Snub* and *Epistle to Peter Porcupine,* he did not flinch. His counter-revolutionary sensibilities only grew when Rowson offered a new play, *The Female Patriot,* which opened in Philadelphia on June 19, 1795, and when she recited in Baltimore on October 29 a poetic address titled "The Standard of Liberty." She also published that year a four-volume novel titled *Trials of the Human Heart.* In the preface she called Cobbett "a kind of loathsome reptile" crawling all over the literary world. Refusing quarter, Cobbett described the attacks on him as "amazingly cruel, to accuse me of malice toward an authoress, when my only motive in so doing was to deliver her unfortunate play, 'the Slaves in Algiers,' from its dismal obscurity."

During the summer and fall of 1796, as he bashed Philadelphia's crusading women, he opened his own printshop and bookstore in a large house at 25 North Second Street. Strategically located across the street from Christ Church and near Benjamin Franklin's old printshop—then home to Benjamin Franklin Bache and his *Aurora*—Cobbett opened for business on July 11. Determined that he "must, at once, set all danger at defiance, or live in everlasting subjection to the prejudice and caprice of the democratical mob," he mounted in his windows an "exhibition" of things not seen in Philadelphia for more than twenty years:

> I put up in my windows . . . all the portraits that I had in my possession of <u>kings</u>, <u>queens</u>, <u>princes</u>, and <u>nobles</u>. I had all the English Ministry; several of the Bishops and Judges; the most famous Admirals; and in short, every picture that I thought likely to excite rage in the enemies of Great Britain.

At the center of the truculent scene was a portrait of George III.[29]

From this shop William Cobbett poured forth over the next two years a river of publications—books, pamphlets, translations, broadsides, and, finally, a newspaper—that shaped the way Americans thought about France and the French Revolution. Cobbett did much to turn Americans against their former notions of democracy, republicanism, and America's revolutionary course for the world. He translated French works that condemned the French revolution into English. He conspired with French expatriates in Philadelphia, including Talleyrand ("this modern Judas"), in publishing books discrediting all revolutions. It was he who issued Abbé Barruel's exposé of Illuminati and Freemasons.[30]

In such inviting titles as *The Scarecrow, Life and Adventures of Peter Porcupine,* and a series of documents titled *Censor,* Cobbett revealed a knowledge of events in France and Europe and a single-mindedness of purpose in turning back revolutionary ideas unrivaled by anyone, including Edmund Burke. Cobbett was rebutted by a host of friends of liberty—all writing anonymously—with equally suggestive titles: *Pill for Porcupine, The Imposter Detected, Tit for Tat,* and *A Roaster for Peter Porcupine.* These pamphlets focused on the person and works of Peter Porcupine, revealed during the summer of 1796 to be none other than

William Cobbett. Less and less did they focus on principles. Rather they raged against a tormentor whose wit they could not equal.[31]

Just as his critics focused ad hominem, Cobbett also took aim at the great icons of liberty. When Benjamin Franklin Bache published in 1795 a series of articles against Jay's Treaty titled *Letters of Franklin,* Cobbett attacked not only the anonymously written pieces but also Benjamin Franklin himself. Both in his formal response, titled *A Little Plain English,* and in future references to Franklin, Cobbett labeled Franklin as "the old Father Confessor on the banks of the Schuylkill," a "worthy" with Marat of the French Revolution, an "atheist" of the ilk of Voltaire, and an "old Lightning Rod" who used his positions in England and France to enrich himself. Accusations that he was "gnawing at the reputation of Dr. Franklin" bothered him not the least, for his agenda was to pull the underpinnings out from under liberty by demolishing one of its greatest patrons.[32]

In the summer of 1796 Cobbett savaged Thomas Paine. When Paine wrote his *Letter to Washington* that summer, controverting the Jay Treaty and Washington's attitude toward France, Cobbett used the occasion to bury Paine. In an open *Letter to Paine* (1796) he went for the jugular: "Your brutal attempt to blacken his [Washington's] character was all that was wanted to crown his honour and your infamy." When Paine dared to sully America's greatest emblem of independence, not even the "vilest democrats, not even Franklin Bache" would come to his defense. Arguing that Paine was writing "at the instigation of the despots of Paris," Cobbett scribbled Paine's obituary as a symbol of liberty: "Thus the great 'Rights of Man,' the sworn foe of corruption, and the reformer of nations, winds up his patriotic career: his being <u>bribed</u> is pleaded as an <u>alleviation of his crimes</u>."[33] Cobbett had successfully pushed Paine to the periphery of American moral consciousness.

Together with his attacks on friends of liberty, Cobbett provided Americans with the literature they needed to formulate their own counterrevolutionary philosophy. During 1796 he published the first American edition of Burke's *Letter to a Noble Lord.* Later in 1796, long before the Illuminati scare of 1798, he published an American edition of William Playfair's *History of Jacobinism,* including in it an appendix "Containing a History of the American Jacobins, commonly denominated Democrats." Charting the course of the French Revolution and of American revolutionary currents in a lengthy preface, Cobbett declared that notions of liberty, equality, and freedom were dead: "<u>the absurd and dangerous declaration of the rights of man must be exploded; and . . . to avoid the last excesses of Jacobins, it will be necessary to abandon and disclaim their first principles</u>."[34]

But Cobbett's most memorable and venomous weapon was his *Porcupine's Gazette,* launched on March 4, 1797, coincident with the inauguration of John Adams as president of the United States. It was in the *Gazette* that Cobbett slew the giants of liberty—Franklin, Bache, Priestley, Logan, Duane, Callender—and many lesser lights in and around Pennsylvania. His slashing editorials were reprinted and read almost as closely in Britain as they were in the United States. Everyone, friend or foe, acknowledged that he was without equal in literary warfare.

It was also through the *Gazette* that Cobbett for the first of several times in his life overstepped the bounds of legal propriety. During the yellow fever epi-

"The World of Revolutionary Chaos as Seen by William Cobbett" (1800). As Cobbett fled America, it seemed that the world had gone awry with the terrors of Despard and Robespierre, leading to the menacing rise of Napoléon from the ashes.

demic of 1797 Cobbett accused nearly everyone in sight of evil purpose or ineptitude. When Governor Mifflin issued a proclamation quarantining individuals struck by the disease, Cobbett attacked the policy as unjustifiable interference with the personal liberties of Pennsylvanians. It was also during that season that Cobbett destroyed Benjamin Rush. His venomous pen also provoked a lawsuit that would put *Porcupine's Gazette* out of business. Although litigation was delayed for two years, when it came in late 1799, Cobbett had angered so many Americans that there was little sympathy for his caustic methods. He withdrew to New York in October 1799, and from there he published issue after issue of the *Rush Light* defending his conduct. But Cobbett's career in America had ended.

Before he quit America for the second time, Cobbett was subjected to one of the typical onslaughts of the period. Benjamin Rush's son, John, angered by Cobbett's attacks on his father, headed in March 1800 to New York to confront the vitriolic journalist. Father Benjamin, fearful for what John might do, rushed a note to his New York attorney Brockholst Livingston asking for intercession to avoid potential violence. Although Livingston intercepted the young Rush, he was not able to stop him from issuing a challenge for a duel with Cobbett. Cobbett refused to accept the challenge. While young Rush went away unsatisfied, Cobbett published yet another issue of *Rush Light,* attacking the Rush family and defending his position.

As his legal entanglements unfolded in early 1800, Cobbett assaulted the Rush family, Pennsylvania, and America. His basic flaw, one that hounded him throughout his life, was that he could not disentangle his philosophy from his personal rancor. Bellowing like a wounded animal, he muddled brilliant insights with petty feuds until he left America for Britain on June 1, 1800.

As he departed, in the last of his *Rush Lights,* Cobbett wrote a letter to Joseph Priestley, feigning an apology for his 1794 attack on the scientist and philosopher. Focusing on the sad fates of Priestley and Cooper since their arrival in America, Cobbett suggested that they might wish to reconsider their brash statements of 1794 about exchanging "the tyranny of a king for the freedom of a republic." Indeed, expanding upon Priestley's experience in a last *Rush Light* intended as much for Britons as Americans, Cobbett hoped that "wayward and disaffected Britons may see a complete specimen of the baseness, dishonesty, ingratitude, and perfidy of Republicans, and of the profligacy, injustice, and tyranny of Republican governments."[35]

Cobbett had been sour about revolution and republicanism from the time he spent in 1792 in France. From the moment he arrived in America, he helped to build a mighty counterrevolution. His powerful voice was unmatched in a time of angry press fights. His popularity, even noted by Priestley in May 1800, was without rival. "At this time," wrote Priestley, "he is by far the most popular writer in this country, and, indeed, one of the best in many respects." Priestley thought Cobbett's "sarcastic humour" was "equal, if not superior to anything that I have ever seen." Rival editor Philip Freneau drew a bead on Cobbett's nature with a parting shot as Cobbett sailed from New York:

> Alack, alack, he might have stay'd
>
> And followed here the scribbling trade, . . .
>
> But democratic laws he hated
>
> Our government he so be-rated
>
> That his own projects he defeated.

Elizabeth Drinker in Philadelphia, meanwhile, reflected in her diary, "So there is an end of Peter Porcupine in this country . . . I don't know that I ever saw him, though I seem to know him well."[36]

William Cobbett's career in America was largely ended. Even though he returned for a quiet sojourn between 1817 and 1819, he had shifted his counterrevolutionary fervor from America to his native land. In the last *Rush Light,* he declared, "I depart for my native land, where neither the moth of Democracy, nor the rust of Federalism doth corrupt." Having experienced what he considered too much democracy in America, he eagerly anticipated seasons of order in a nation not in need of counterrevolutionary reform, not touched by flirtations with the chaos that characterized France and America. Congratulating himself for having "persisted in openly and unequivocally avowing my attachment to my native country" and for "being the first, and perhaps the only man, who, since the revolution, has . . . refused to take shelter under the title of <u>citizen</u>," Cobbett declared that "France, Frenchmen, republicanism and all their partisans" would henceforth "become the objects of my keenest satire." His surprising counterrevolutionary career was ready for new challenges.[37]

CHATEAUBRIAND: COUNTERREVOLUTIONARY DOCTRINAIRE

When François August-René de Chateaubriand put the finishing touches on his *Memoirs* in 1839, he capped his masterpiece with a "testamentary preface" telescoping the first seven decades of his life: "From my early youth [born 1768] until 1800, I was a soldier and traveller; from 1800 until 1814, under the Consulate and the Empire, my life was devoted to literature; from the Restoration down to the present day, my life has been political." He then capsulized his principal goal or "great task" in each of these distinctive periods. In the first, he "endeavoured to open up the polar regions." In the second, he "tried to rebuild religion on its own ruins." And in the third period "I have striven to give the nations the true system of constitutional monarchy with its various freedoms." He especially fought for "that freedom which is equal to all others . . . , freedom of the press."[38]

Although in later years he downplayed the importance of his activities prior to 1800, Chateaubriand, having seen a good deal of the world in his first twenty-five years, discovered the life of the mind that would be his during an exile in England that extended from 1793 until 1800. Penniless among a large community of émigrés on the outskirts of London, he worked as a translator of Latin and English literary works into French and as a schoolmaster for a girls' school. But his vocation work was as an author; he merely needed a cause to start him. That came with the grim deaths in April 1794, of his intellectual mentor, Malesherbes, and of his guardian brother Jean-Baptiste, along with the news that the rest of his family—his mother, sisters, and wife Celeste—had been under arrest for months.[39]

Stricken with grief and abhorrence of the French Revolution, Chateaubriand began writing meditations on revolutions that by 1797 resulted in two massive volumes titled *Essay Historical, Political and Moral on Revolutions Ancient and Modern Considered with Late Reports on the French Revolution*. Although published anonymously, Chateaubriand's authorship did not remain a mystery for long. In many ways a rambling exorcism of a personal demon, this massive work also reflected the kind of thinking Edmund Burke had been publishing since 1790. But whereas Burke's piercing essays were timely, prophetic tracts, Chateaubriand's provocative ruminations were an effort to come to grips with menacing realities.

Chateaubriand compared thirteen revolutions from antiquity to the present age with the French Revolution. None equaled the French experience, because none had the lofty goals later erased by total terror in France: "We note in the French Revolution excellent principles and baleful consequences. The former derive from an enlightened theory, the latter from a corruption of morals. This is the real reason for this incomprehensible mixture of crime grafted onto a philosophical trunk." Although he had once believed in the essential value of a social contract between peoples and their governments, he doubted the possibility in the case of most nations. The republic worked in the United States because Americans exhibited a virtuous character that was not replicated elsewhere.

Chateaubriand's *Essay on Revolutions* sounded enough like Burke's ruminations, and his next work, begun by 1799 titled *The Genius of Christianity* (1800), took a position strenuously argued by Burke. A difference, though, was that Chateaubriand came late to the conviction argued in the book that Christianity—in this case the Roman Catholic Church—was essential to civilization. From a strong anticlerical and deistic attitude on religion, Chateaubriand underwent a religious conversion in 1799 upon hearing of the mystical transformation of his sister Julie and the death of his mother. "I did not yield, I must admit," he wrote, "to a great supernatural illumination. My conviction came from the heart; I wept and I believed."

With his new enthusiasm he pored over church doctrine, Christian poetry and literature, and religious ceremony to argue that the Catholic Church was the most favorable on earth for the development of culture and liberty. Societal order demanded a moral order drawn from Christian tradition. Although Chateaubriand did not relate the necessity of moral order to one's personal life, he argued that the state could not exist without it.[40]

Chateaubriand's *Essay on Revolutions* (1797) and his *Genius of Christianity* (1800) set the stage for a counterrevolutionary career in France as he passed from Dover to Calais on May 8, 1800. The first solidified his opposition to all democratizing movements. The second brought him to the center of efforts in France to reunite church and state.

Chateaubriand returned to a France that was under the strong control of Napoléon as the First Consul. With the assistance of Madame de Staël and other female associates, he had his name struck from the list of outlawed émigrés and was himself restored as a full-fledged citizen of France. He firmly believed that order and liberty could be achieved in France only by the restoration of a constitutional monarchy and by the reestablishment of the Roman Catholic Church. Although Chateaubriand never met either Noah Webster or William Cobbett, the three individually discovered similar counterrevolutionary doctrines between 1793 and 1798, and they devoted their lives to preaching the necessity of order in society for any citizens to enjoy the fruits of liberty.[41]

CHAPTER 21

Friends of Order in the Land of Liberty: Poets and Luminaries

POETS OF LIBERTY, VOICES FOR ORDER

America's young poets, known historically as the Hartford Wits, worked assiduously in the early 1780s to put finishing touches on their Revolutionary War literary effusions. John Trumbull published his perfected celebration *M'Fingal* in
1782. Joel Barlow put a final gloss on his epochal *Vision of Columbus* (1787) that
same year. Timothy Dwight completed his massive *Conquest of Canaan* in
1785—which he brashly dedicated

> To his Excellency,
>
> George Washington, Esquire,
>
> Commander in chief of the American Armies,
>
> The Saviour of his Country,
>
> The Supporter of Freedom,
>
> And the Benefactor of Mankind.

Accepting appointment as secretary of America's Commission for Negotiating
Treaties of Commerce with Foreign Powers in 1784, David Humphreys also was
finishing a work honoring Washington in *A Poem on the Happiness of America:
Addressed to the Citizens of the United States of America* (1786).[1]

Even as they published their most memorable works, the poets were already
beginning to question the essence of liberty, and their answers set them on a
course that put them among the first Americans to part from the still fragile heritage of the American Revolution. The first indication that most of the Hartford
Wits were following the path charted by their Yale colleague Noah Webster was
the publication of a series of twelve poems between October 1786 and September
1787 known as *The Anarchiad*. Placed in fellow Yaleman Josiah Meigs's *New
Haven Gazette,* but written individually by at least four of the Wits, *The Anarchiad* revealed that by 1786 its writers were more concerned with finding order
than liberty.[2]

The Anarchiad, while attributed to four of the Hartford Wits—David
Humphreys, Joel Barlow, John Trumbull, and Lemuel Hopkins—was clearly the

idea of Humphreys. Son of a Congregational clergyman at Derby, Connecticut, and graduate of Yale in 1771, Humphreys cruised through several careers during his life of sixty-six years. After Yale he became a school teacher and tutor. In 1776 he joined the Connecticut militia, writing poetry about the Revolution and General George Washington. His poem "Adieu, thou Yale!" rang with patriotism. "Dear Columbia calls," he wrote, "Though fails this flesh devote to freedom's cause, / Can death subdue th' unconquerable mind? / Or adamantine chains ethereal substance bind?" The lines brought him fame. His praise of Washington brought him a job as aide-de-camp to Israel Putnam, then to Nathanael Greene, and finally in June 1780, to Washington himself.[3]

For the next twenty years his life was interblended with Washington's every whim. It was Humphreys that Washington chose in 1781 to deliver to Congress the surrender flags of the British army. It was with Humphreys that Washington shared his emotional moments at the resignation of his commission as general and the celebration at Mount Vernon of his victory over the British. Except when Washington sent him abroad on delicate diplomatic missions between 1784 and 1786 and after 1791 until 1802, Humphreys remained almost constantly in residence at Mount Vernon. Washington even commissioned the poet to write his official biography as the nation's Revolutionary War hero and first president.[4]

It came as no surprise that Humphreys was appointed in May 1784 as secretary to America's European Commerce Commission consisting of Benjamin Franklin, John Adams, and Thomas Jefferson. Humphreys used the two-year period in Paris and London to win the confidence of the three commissioners, to meet the world's great thinkers (including Edmund Burke and Richard Sheridan), and to learn the promise and perils of diplomacy. While in London furiously writing his own poetry, he promoted without success the publication of Timothy Dwight's *Conquest of Canaan* and Joel Barlow's *The Vision of Columbus*. He also read widely, including a mock epic satirizing the British government titled *The Rolliad*.

When he returned to America in the spring of 1786, Humphreys was astonished at the changed attitude of Americans. When he had gone abroad in 1784, America was filled with exuberance over the newly won liberty and independence. Indeed, he carried that effervescence to Europe, where he wrote a wildly enthusiastic poem "On the Happiness of America." Just after his return, however, he wrote to Thomas Jefferson about home conditions: "Many people appear to be uneasy and to prognosticate revolutions they hardly know how or why." When he arrived at Mount Vernon in July 1786 for a five-week visit, he and Washington spent long hours analyzing and lamenting the general unrest across the nation. A poem, "Mount-Vernon: An Ode," written during this visit revealed their growing concern.

As he traveled northward to his home in Derby, Connecticut, during the first days of September, he found the farmers' rebellion led by Daniel Shays underway in western Massachusetts. On November 1, Congress commissioned Humphreys to command a regiment of federal troops ostensibly to protect the frontier, but actually to counter the rebels. On that date he wrote Washington that "Gov-

"Con-g-ss Embarked on Board the Ship Constitution of America" (1790). The treacherous movement of the American government from new to the "Potowmack R." via Philadelphia, where it might be grounded on shoals of special interests.

ernment is prostrated in the dust. . . . [Nothing] but a good Providence can extricate us from our present difficulties & prevent some terrible convulsion." In another letter to Washington nine days later, he observed that "there is a licentious spirit prevailing among many of the people, a levelling principle."

As the threats of rebellion grew, Humphreys alerted the distressed Washington to the dire circumstances in Massachusetts and Connecticut. He remained in Hartford with his regiment, awaiting orders to march on Shays's band of twelve hundred men. When he at last was ordered to march on Springfield, Massachusetts, much of the rebellion had passed. From Springfield in February 1787 he wrote to Washington that, although "the spirit of Rebellion does not seem to be absolutely broken yet it is to be presumed with prudence and perseverance it may be utterly subdued." Without having actually engaged Shays's force, Humphreys's regiment was disbanded. He traveled next to Philadelphia and reported to Washington, the two then attending a general meeting of the Society of the Cincinnati.[4]

But all the while Humphreys served as Washington's point man at the rebellion, the warrior-poet labored on another project. In early November 1786, on the same day he took command of his regiment, Humphreys wrote to Benjamin Franklin in Philadelphia that he was engaged in a very different effort to counteract the rebellion: "Some of us [have] spoken & wrote, reasoned & ridiculed in conversation & in print as much as lay in our power." A week earlier there appeared in New Haven the first installment of *The Anarchiad: A Poem on the Restoration of Chaos and Substantial Night.* Drawing upon the power of *The Rolliad,* Humphreys united the team of four poets to copy its style in an extended analysis of America. In describing the project to Washington, he wrote, "In some instances the force of ridicule has been found of more efficacy than the force of argument, against the Anti-federalists & Advocates for Mobs."[6]

The title of *The Anarchiad* revealed the authors' perception of an America that had gone from glory to anarchy. Though individual authorship of the twelve installments was never revealed by the group, Humphreys almost certainly introduced the series on October 26 with No. I, "American Antiquities," and wrote much or all of five others: No. III, "Extracts from the Anarchiad, on Paper Money"; No. IV, "Extract from the Anarchiad, Book XXIII"; No. V, "Extract from Miscellaneous Papers Found in the Same Fort with the Anarchiad"; No. IX, "Extract from the Anarchiad, Book XXIII"; and No. X, "Extract from the Anarchiad, Book XXIV, The Speech of Hesper." These installments, bearing a consistent style and connected story, documented Humphreys's alarmed assessment of America.[7]

As he sat in Hartford ready to quash rebellion, Humphreys trumpeted that the American Revolution was dead. Writing anonymously to Meigs, editor and publisher of the *New Haven Gazette,* he assumed the role of an archaeologist who discovered in a fort in western Pennsylvania or Ohio "a folio manuscript which appeared to contain an epic poem." The poem, upon inspection, was found to be *The Anarchiad,* complete in twenty-four books. Claiming that Homer, Virgil, and Milton surely knew of this work and borrowed from it, Humphreys pledged to publish portions of it, for "the prophetic bard seems to have taken for the point of vision one of the lofty mountains of America, and to have caused, by his magic invocations, the years of futurity to pass before him."

The first installment was innocuous enough, only hinting that the times were ominous. But the second installment presenting the first fragments from the fictional *Anarchiad,* ended with the foreboding commentary

> But I draw the curtain; the picture is too melancholy to be viewed by a patriot eye without prompting the tear of sensibility, and forcing the sigh of sorrow, that THE GLORIOUS TEMPLE OF LIBERTY and happiness which had been erected in these ends of the earth, for an asylum to suffering humanity, should so soon be dissolved, and,
>
> "Like the baseless fabric of a vision,
>
> Leave not a wreck behind."

From that Humphreys and his colleagues then lamented the loss, not only of revolutionary spirit, but of aim. In turgid rhyme, they depicted the ruin that was America and searched for a new vision.

Humphreys first attacked "paper money," credited at the time with bankrupting many Americans:

> The crafty knave his creditor besets,
>
> And advertising paper pays his debts;
>
> Bankrupts their creditors with rage pursue,
>
> No stop, no mercy from the debtor crew.

He next decried the failure of America to arrange for payment of its wartime debts to Europe:

> Awake, my chosen sons, in folly brave,
>
> Stab Independence! dance o'er Freedom's grave!
>
> Sing choral songs, while conq'ring mobs advance,
>
> And blot the debts to Holland, Spain, and France—
>
> Till ruin come, with fire, and sword, and blood,
>
> And men shall ask where your republic stood.

Everywhere he looked, he saw failure, destruction, and loss of hope: "Behold the reign of anarchy, begun, / And half the business of confusion done."

Humphreys's lamentation nailed down to specifics. Writing six months after the death of his former general, Revolutionary War hero Nathanael Greene, he despaired of America's dearth of leaders. George Washington, "their great DEFENDER," was retired and

> No more to save a realm, dread GREENE appears,
>
> Their second hope, prime object of my fears;
>
> Far in the south, from his pale body riven,
>
> The deathful angel wings his soul to heaven.

In a bold speech by Hesper, one of the principal voices in the grand epic, he declared, "Where is the spirit of bold freedom fled? / Dead are my warriors; all my sages dead!" He went on, "Bid other Greenes and Washingtons arise! Once more, in arms, to make the glorious stand, / And bravely die, or save their natal land."

Amid the invocation of new heroes there arose a new vision, one that countermanded the spirit that had liberated the land. Hesper, speaking directly to Anarch, the fiend of disorder, proclaimed:

> Yes, they shall rise, terrific in their rage,
>
> And crush the factions of the faithless age;
>
> Bid laws again exalt th' imperial scale,
>
> And public justice o'er her foe prevail;
>
> Restore the reign of order and of right,
>
> And drive thee, howling, to the shades of night.

Humphreys's brief speech, written in anticipation of battle against Shays's army, combined the principal themes of America's rejection of its own Revolution.[8]

Counterrevolutionary Americans feared anarchy, believing it just as threatening as Humphreys's mythic Anarch. They deplored factions, partisanship, and political parties because these seemed to bring on anarchy. The faithlessness of the age demanded a return to religious institutions. Order's proponents lauded the rule of law over political whims and legislating institutions. Exalting laws to an "imperial scale" and demanding "public justice" over those who disagreed with the laws of the land became hallmarks of counterrevolutionary thought. Restoring the "reign of order" over anarchy and chaos became the central theme of the Counterrevolution. Humphreys's stark counterrevolutionary pronouncement was the most revealing ideological flip-flop of all. Not only would he restore the hegemony of order, he also wanted a new reign of "right," a set of moral absolutes that would replace rights. There plummeted the supremacy of the rights of man five years before Thomas Paine declared their sanctity.[9]

Humphreys headed in early May 1787 to Philadelphia and the assembly of the Society of the Cincinnati. There, meeting with a George Washington not very eager to participate in the impending Constitutional Convention, Humphreys demanded that the former commander in chief attend. He also decided to provide the assembled delegates with a massive chunk of his counterrevolutionary philosophy. Resurrecting Hesper, Humphreys published on the eve of the Convention, May 24, Hesper's "last solemn address to his principal counselors and sages, whom he had convened at Philadelphia."[10]

Through Hesper's praise of the sacrifices of the martyrs of the American Revolution—John Laurens, Joseph Warren, Hugh Mercer, and Richard Montgomery—he lamented that "In vain they conquer'd! and they bled in vain!" Their lives had been wasted, "For, see! proud Faction waves here flaming brand, / And discord riots o'er the ungrateful land." He asked, "Yet, what the hope? The dreams of Congress fade, / The federal UNION sinks in endless shade." No one was caring for the nation, neither citizens nor states:

> Nor less abhor'd, the certain woe that waits
> The giddy rage of democratic States,
> Whose pop'lar breath, high-blown in restless tide,
> No laws can temper, and no reason guide . . .
> Yet feel no reverence for one general sway;
> For breach of faith, no keen compulsion feel,
> And find no interest in the federal weal.

Arguing to delegates charged with writing a new federal constitution that "YE LIVE UNITED, OR DIVIDED DIE!" Hesper gave as his prescription for ending anarchy, "But know, ye favor'd race, onc potent head / Must rule your States, and strike your foes with dread, / The finance regulate, the trade control, / Live through the empire, and accord the whole."[11]

To classify *The Anarchiad* as but a call for a new constitution is to miss the power of the ideological shift that was beginning to occur. Humphreys's plea was not just for new government. His was a call to overrule anarchy and to install right. Even before the world's flirtation with revolution reached its climax between 1789 and 1793, Humphreys canted words and ideas that would in a few years be enshrined by Burke, Webster, Cobbett, Chateaubriand, and a myriad of counterrevolutionary voices across the world.

So did fellow poet and lifelong friend Timothy Dwight at the same time. Barely had he published his epic of liberty, *The Conquest of Canaan* (1785) when he also shifted direction. In *The Triumph of Infidelity* (1788), his next epic poem, he threw aside the spirit that reigned in the land of Canaan. The trend was obvious in 1785 in a poem he titled "Epistle to Colonel Humphreys," while Humphreys was departing for his mission to Europe. Dwight warned Humphreys to beware of "that foul Harlot Europe" that might defile and corrupt him. Already Dwight dreamed of making America a Kingdom of God against an otherwise devious world.[12]

Just as Humphreys became embroiled in the political scene surrounding Shays's Rebellion and tried to address America's troubles in *The Anarchiad,* Dwight also took to poetry to explain what was happening on the cosmic plane. He parodied the victory of infidelity over the world—equating its triumph with abject social and political disorder. He even addressed the piece to "Mons. de Voltaire," claiming that the French philosopher devoted his entire life to "a single purpose" of elevating himself over God: "You opposed truth, religion, and their authors, with sophistry, contempt, and obloquy; and taught, as far as your example or sentiments extended their influence, that the chief end of man was, to slander his God, and abuse him forever." Anticipating the avalanche of denunciation that would greet Thomas Paine's *The Age of Reason,* Dwight told Voltaire that "Reasoning is an unhappy engine to be employed against christianity; as, like elephants in ancient war, it usually . . . turns upon those who employ it."

In the poem Dwight soared through ethereal realms as he depicted the rise of rationalism in Europe and its eventual distressing migration to America. Claiming that when "the Briton left our happy shore" at the end of the American Revolution, America was where "the realms of freedom, peace, and virtue lay." At that same moment Europe lay in waste. Dwight, then, through the voice of Satan, chronicled the spread of infidelity from the death of Constantine the Great (reigned 306–337 C.E.) through the onslaughts of the Huns and Goths, through the Reformation, to the Enlightenment, when it "mushroom'd o'er Europa's putrid courts; / To deist clubs familiar dar'd retire, / Or howl'd, and powaw'd, round the Indian fire; / Such feats my sons atchiev'd, such honors won." Many philosophers helped him along the way, until Satan proclaimed, "I found my best Amanuensis, Hume, / And bosom'd in his breast." And with Hume's words registered, Satan continued, "To France I posted, on the wings of air, / and Fir'd the labors of the gay Voltaire."[13]

Hume inspired endless "corruptions of christianity," including those of Joseph Priestley. In a note included by Dwight, he joked that Priestley "has advanced so far, as to form a whole system of divinity out of fixed air." In America issued forth social, political, and religious miscreants. For example, financial magnate, Jeremiah Wadsworth, alleged villain in the death of Eliza Whitman (told in Hannah Foster's *The Coquette*) and real scoundrel in the life of Catherine Greene, was depicted by Dwight as "more hard than flint, in sin grown old, / Clinch'd close his claws, and grip'd his bags of gold." Dwight continued, "In vain, he [Wadsworth] cried, their woes let orphans tell; / In vain let widows weep; there is no hell / Six, six per cent, each month, must now be given, / For pious usury now's the road to heaven."[14]

Dwight's issue with America was the disorder, factionalism, and iniquity he saw enveloping the young nation. But in the last half of *The Triumph of Infidelity* he floated into obscure theological speculations as he tried to explain the origins of the nation's problems. He became obsessed with Charles Chauncy's theories of Universalism in religion, mimicking Chauncy's efforts to make Christianity warm and friendly and deriding such claims as "Hell is no more, or no more to be fear'd" and "Less fear'd Jehovah, and less valued heaven." But as he rejected Chauncy's godless and Christless religion, he also deposed the evangelical religion of his grandfather, Jonathan Edwards. Both approaches, Dwight believed, sapped religion of its ability to compel social order.[15]

The Triumph of Infidelity petered out without enunciating prescriptions for America's ills. Having articulated the terms "infidel" and "infidelity" in the sense they would be used to discredit the French Revolution, Dwight desisted in his dissection of America's condition. Though he was not yet ready to explain what was right for America, he was completely convinced that democracy was wrong, that kindly religion was misguided, that individualistic evangelicalism was mistaken, and that factionalism would destroy the nation. By the time he wrote his poem in 1787, his flirtation with liberty and equality was over.

Dwight echoed David Humphreys, who had already lectured the Constitutional Convention gathering in Philadelphia in *The Anarchiad*. Following Humphreys's example, Dwight pinpointed what was troubling him in two pieces published in the spring of 1787. In "An Essay on the Judgment of History Concerning America" (April) and in an "Address of the Genius of Columbia to the Members of the Continental Convention" (June), he decried the political, social, and moral chaos of America, blaming it all on an excess of democracy. The nation was rife with too many elections, too many public officials, too many lawsuits, and too much liberty in the press. As a reward for his wisdom in advising the nation, the College of Princeton that year awarded him a Doctor of Divinity degree, showing clearly that others shared his perspective.[16]

Dwight was already prepared in 1787 to put a cap on democracy and to head in the other direction of order. He followed up his advice to the delegates in Philadelphia with an "Address to the Ministers of the Gospel of Every Denomination in the United States" in July 1788, reiterating his retreat from liberty. By that time, he had begun formulating his own approach toward bringing order to America. With little faith in the constitution that came out of Philadelphia, he concluded that a firmer foundation for American governance was adherence to religious institutions. Even before the onset of the French Revolution and its assault on church and clergy, Dwight concluded that religion had to be the glue— social, moral, and political—to hold together American society.[17]

Despite the reservations of his colleagues—including Yale president Ezra Stiles and Noah Webster—Dwight launched into a career to christianize America. By 1790 he had effected a plan of formally associating New England Congregational and Presbyterian churches. In 1791, when he was chosen to give Connecticut's annual Election Sermon on May 12, he formally announced his ambitious goal. In a sermon afterward published with the title, *Virtuous Rulers a National*

Blessing, governments and churches should be brought closer together than ever: "The first duty of a ruler, and the first concern of a virtuous ruler, is the support of religion." [18]

Though Dwight would always be a proponent of a state-sanctioned church and would have established Congregationalism throughout America if he could have, that was not the idea he began enunciating in 1788. "Let not my audience . . . imagine," he proclaimed in his Election sermon, "that I wish a revival of that motley system of domination which in Europe has so long, so awkwardly, and so unhappily blended civil and spiritual objects." He was not thinking of "spiritual courts, laws prescribing faith, . . . or magistrates usurping the throne of the Creator, and claiming the prerogatives of the supreme head of the church." Rather those who were elected to and who assumed public office had a duty to promote religion "by steadfastly opposing immorality, by employing and honouring the just, by contemning the vicious, by enlarging the motives to righteousness, by removing the temptations to sin, and . . . [by calling] up a new creation of beauty, virtue, and happiness."

The ruler who thereby supported religion would support proper religious education and would "act always in such a manner, as to allure others to virtue, and not to vice; . . . uphold religion, and not licentiousness; . . . support the righteous, and not the enemies of righteousness." Religion in a community was "essentially necessary for its wellbeing," and a virtuous ruler would clearly acknowledge that. A "wicked" or "profligate" ruler, by contrast, would bring a community to destruction: "Corruption and ruin [will] spread through the members of a community, and poison the streams of health and life." Historical examples from scriptures proved this, as did others from classical history and the history of England and France. Though not mentioning George Washington by name, he invoked as an example "the first Magistrate of the United States of America." As "the present period" was not a time "of the most absolute declension," Americans could hope that the promotion of religion by other virtuous rulers would restore harmony and order. [19]

Having enunciated a proper religion as the glue to mesh America, Dwight went to work, while others flirted with liberty, to define a way in which churches together with virtuous rulers could structure American society. Taking advantage of his twelve-year sojourn from 1783 to 1795 as the Congregational pastor at Greenfield Hill in Fairfield, Connecticut, he delineated his plan for America in yet another poem titled *Greenfield Hill.* Published in 1794 in 168 pages of tumid rhyming couplets, the poem turned out to be a blueprint for the reorganization of America from stem to stern. Completed three days after the onset of the Great Terror in Paris, Dwight provided Americans a diversion from the madness being experienced by their compatriots in France.

Dwight's vision was to analyze what made a quiet New England village work and then to employ the same principles in the nation itself. Surely what had worked for generations in New England was timeless and true, far preferable than revolutions in the name of liberty. It took him four cantos to do the analysis and three to lay out his prescription. In "The Prospect" and "The Flourishing Village," he described the happy scenes of village governance and life. In "The

Burning of Fairfield" and "The Destruction of the Pequods," he depicted the effects of the American Revolution—especially the invasion of alien armies—and lamented somewhat sentimentally the execution of the native tribe. Though neither of these cantos reflected the impending doom that would appear in later Dwight productions, there was enough evidence of human irrationality for him to call for a new world order.

In the fifth canto, titled "The Clergyman's Advice to the Villagers," Dwight gave "his last advice, and blessing, to his Parishioners," ostensibly on how they could achieve their salvation. In reality, however, Dwight's notion of parish was America; of parishioners, all Americans; and of salvation, not that of one soul, but that of the nation:

> Let order round your houses reign,
>
> Religion rule, and peace sustain;
>
> Each morn, each eve, your prayers arise,
>
> As incense fragrant, to the skies;
>
> In beauteous group, your children join,
>
> And servants share the work divine:
>
> The voice, as is the interest, one,
>
> And one the blessing wrestled down.

Dwight had enunciated the rule of order in all its particulars, and the key to order was religion.

Rather than have a clergyman, with obvious self-interest, explain how this related to life in the American village, Dwight in Part VI introduced "a Farmer plain." Although a man of the soil and husbandry, the farmer, from the outset, sounded much like the clergyman:

> Let order o'er your time preside,
>
> And method all your business guide.
>
> Early begin, and end, your toil;
>
> Nor let great tasks your hands embroil.
>
> One thing at once, be still begun,
>
> Contriv'd, resolv'd, pursued, and done.

Reverberating with the simple advice of Benjamin Franklin's *Poor Richard's Almanak,* Dwight's avowed intention of unifying religion and life, church and society, worship and public meeting, sermon and public oratory, moral principle and popular aphorism was fulfilled.

So went the Farmer's speech:

> 'Tis folly in th' extreme, to till
>
> Extensive fields, and till them ill." . . .
>
> Your herds feed well, increase, amend,
>
> And from the wintery storm defend. . . .

> When first the market offers well,
> At once your yearly produce sell. . . .
> Neat be your farms: 'tis long confess'd,
> The neatest farmers are the best. . . .
> With punctual hand your taxes pay
> Nor put far off the evil day. . . .
> In merchants' books, from year to year,
> Be cautious how your names appear."

The Farmer covered nearly every responsibility from birth to death. He propounded on the care and education of children—both boys and girls. But girls were to be treated differently: "With gentler hand, your daughters train, / The housewife's various arts to gain." Children were to be taught "always to obey." Ruling over a home was the same as over a government:

> On uniformity depends
> All government, that gains its ends.
> The same things always praise, and blame,
> Your laws, and conduct, be the same.
> "Habits alone thro' life endure,
> Habits alone your child secure. . . .

Order, uniformity, habit, the Farmer taught. But, why?

> Thus taught, in every state of life,
> Of child, of parent, husband, wife,
> They'll wiser, better, happier, prove;
> Their freedom better know, and love;
> More pleasures gain, more hearts engage,
> And feast their own dull hours of age.

Order was the way to freedom, while liberty was the way to chains: "To habit bid the blessings grow; / Habits alone yield good below." Dwight's prescription for Greenfield Hill, for Connecticut, and for America was to find salvation through constancy and restraint.

His guiding principle—order—firmly established through the speech of the Farmer, Dwight in Part VII presented his version of "The Vision, or Prospect of the Future Happiness of America." The speaker in this part was the "Genius of the Sound," located somewhere off the Connecticut shore, looking at America. "See this glad world remote from every foe, / From Europe's mischiefs, and from Europe's woe!" he proclaimed. Assessing the wonders of Creation, the landscapes, and the American Eden he portrayed the nation as "O happy state! the state, by HEAVEN design'd / To rein, protect, employ, and bless mankind." Europe he described, by contrast, as "Thrice wretched lands! where, thousands of slaves to one, / Sires know no child, beside the eldest son; / Men know no rights; no justice nobles know; / And kings no pleasure, but from subjects' woe."

After describing the hell that was Europe, he turned to the heaven, in comparison, that was America:

> Here first shall man, with full conviction, know
> Well-system'd rule the source of bliss below;
> Invent, refine, arrange, the sacred plan,
> Check pride, rein power, and save the rights of man!

In Europe, by the rule of liberty, the rights of man had been lost. In America, by "well-system'd rule," the rights of man would be secured.

> Whence, men forgotten, Law supremely reigns,
> And justice flows, a river, o'er the plains! . . .
> In this bright mansion, all my sons shall find
> Whatever rights their God has given mankind;
> To rich, and poor, alike, th' avenues clear;
> Its gates, like Salem's, open round the year;
> Hence justice, freedom, peace, and bounty, flow,
> Redress for injuries, and relief for woe.

The word liberty had disappeared from Dwight's vocabulary; its coordinates, freedom and rights, appeared only when they were won by obedience, justice, and order.[20]

What is even more amazing about Dwight's transformation to the philosophy of order was that it was complete before he knew of the Terror in France, before the onset of America's Whiskey Rebellion, and before the appearance of Thomas Paine's *The Age of Reason*. In *Greenfield Hill* one would assume that he had these calamities in mind when he wrote near its conclusion:

> For soon, no more to philosophic whims,
> To cloud-built theories, and lunar dreams,
> But to firm facts, shall human faith be given,
> The proofs of Reason, and the voice of HEAVEN.
> No more by light Voltaire with bubbles fed,
> With Hume's vile husks no longer mock'd for bread,
> No more by St. John's lantern lur'd astray,
> Through moors, and mazes, from the broad highway.

Dwight's refutation of the Age of Reason was complete even before Paine's tome prompted him, as it did thousands of others in America and abroad, to reject the Enlightenment, the cult of rationalism, the courtship with liberty, and the love of revolution. That he was aware of rejecting the liberative principles of the American Revolution became clear in the pages of notes appended to *Greenfield Hill,* where he brooded about ever more alarming reports from France.[21]

COUNTERREVOLUTION IN VERSE

David Humphreys and Timothy Dwight were reacting to the Age of Reason, not to Paine's *The Age of Reason,* to the will to revolution and not specifically to the French Revolution, and to a sense of disorder and not to chaos itself in their poetry. Their associates, perhaps less attuned to universal truth, responded more to philosophical and political currents of the day. While Dwight, at least, was reconceiving the social order of America, his colleagues and students were advancing the rising counterrevolution by satirizing friends of liberty.

Richard Alsop, wealthy classmate of Noah Webster and Joel Barlow, began to set the tone for this rough-and-tumble satire with the launching of "The Echo" on August 8, 1791, soon after the Sheffield riots that destroyed Joseph Priestley's home and just after Louis XVI's ill-fated flight to Varennes. Appearing first in *The American Mercury* at Hartford, but republished in newspapers throughout the land, "The Echo" became a popular tool for commenting on current political events. Alsop, a Hartford businessman who dabbled in poetry, was the principal author of eighteen or so poems appearing under this title during the next three years, although some were most likely written by Theodore Dwight, pugnacious and politically embattled brother of Timothy Dwight.

The first issue of "The Echo" originated as a parody on a wordy description of a thunderstorm in a Boston newspaper published on July 14, 1791. Alsop "echoed" the story in couplets so popular that demands for more of his entertaining rhymes poured forth. He complied but turned to the ongoing French Revolution for his topic. Typical of Alsop's tone was one of his characterizations of French Jacobins in 1793:

> The Jacobins—I dwell upon the name,
>
> My admiration and my homage claim—
>
> To wondering nations do they not display
>
> A noble generous spirit every day?
>
> With much politeness and with equal skill,
>
> Do they not torture whom they mean to kill?
>
> And fired with zeal to render man humane,
>
> Bear high on pikes the heads of children slain?

Relentlessly accusing Jacobins of overturning society in the name of liberty, Alsop tellingly asked, "Have they not filled Old Freedom so with fire / That the good Dame is ready to expire?" His view on their treatment of Louis XVI was scathing. Tongue deep in cheek, he wrote, of their "love and loyalty" to their king, "In cutting off his head, to save his life / From scenes of woe, of horror, and of strife; / And thus by certain means, to keep away / Old age, that mournful period of decay."

Alsop's scorn was not only for the excesses of the French Revolution. There were lessons to be learned all the world over. In an "Echo" titled "Égalite" he satirized all ideas about equality. Equality was to his mind "O cursed thirst of absolute controul, / The youngest offspring of Hell's fiery hole!" Its pursuit in France was a lesson for the world:

> And France has proved that what mankind abhor,
> Fire, murder, rapine, Jacobins and war,
> Are far more useful, than that truth and peace,
> Should bid the jarring world from slaughter cease.

Applying this lesson to what he described as "the celebrated Equality Ball" given for blacks in Boston by Governor John Hancock in December 1792, Alsop decried the event to "treat the Negroes to a royal dance." The result of Hancock's benevolent act was sure: "And loud to Anarchy their voices raise / In hallelujahs and in hymns of praise, / To the sweet Tune of Freedom born anew; / That Tune so charming and so novel too." While Boston blacks were singing equality, freedom "took her flight, / And bade her ancient friends a long Good Night."

Commenting as he did almost exclusively on everyday events, Alsop's allusions to the loss of order in the name of equality were nevertheless clear. He even suggested that freedom of the press was a doubtful blessing: "'Tis therefore clear we cannot get along, / Unless We shackle every Federal tongue, / Our fame in garb inviolable dress, / And bind in chains the Freedom of the Press." He worried, given the partisanship of most newspapers, that "The Echo" would be "considered as a party production" and thereby "considerably lessen its reputation." Though Alsop's concentration on the moment's political squabbles assured that his outpourings would be inconsequential to history, the counterrevolutionary bent of his mind became evident with each installment in "The Echo."[22]

The attribution of three embattled poems similar to "The Echo" that appeared between 1795 and 1799 is not totally clear. *The Democratiad, A Poem in Retaliation, for the "Philadelphia Jockey Club"* (1795) and *The Guillotina, or a Democratic Dirge: A Poem* (1796) are sometimes attributed to Alsop, but also to Lemuel Hopkins, a Litchfield, Connecticut, physician and friend of Alsop. A third political satire, *The Political Green-House, for the Year 1798* (1799), is usually ascribed to Hopkins as well. But whatever their authorship, these three lengthy poems continued the rejection of liberty, freedom, and the rights of man as had been assumed by Americans as a legacy of the American Revolution.[23]

The Democratiad was written in response to a pamphlet titled *The Philadelphia Jockey Club,* published in Philadelphia in the style of "an English pamphlet," but commenting on American political affairs. Attacking the radical nature of Benjamin Franklin Bache's journalism, the author assaulted both Bache's freedom of speech and the practice of freedom in America itself. Calling Bache "Thou great descendant of that wondrous man, / Whose genius wild thro' all creation ran," the author picked Bache for attack due to "Thy grandsire's memory, and thy knack at lies." The satire continued, "That good old man behind

"The Looking Glass for 1787." Three members of the Hartford Wits stand on Mount Parnassas (left foreground), read from their Anarchiad, *describing the chaos of American polity in 1787. Two leaders of the Connecticut factions, pants lowered (right foreground), spray each other with defecation.*

him left a name, / Unmatch'd in <u>lustre</u> on the rolls of fame." But it was Bache's recently published copy of John Jay's hitherto secret treaty with Britain that made him an open enemy of America and good order.

The poet ridiculed every notion of democracy in somersaults of illogic: "In pure Republics secrets ne'er exist, / Knowledge, like wind, should blow where e'er it list" and "by the rules of Democratic lore, / Twenty is less than ten by three or four," in reference to the ten "democratic" members of the United States Senate. In a note explaining his stab at the ten senators, the poet explained,

> These <u>patriotic</u> Democrats would persuade us that we ought to obey <u>one third</u>, let <u>two thirds</u> say what they may. It is this kind of majority that the Democrats in the United States compose. However what they want in numbers <u>they say</u> they have in <u>merit</u>.

Commenting on one of the democrats, he wrote,

> Thy colleague is a decent sort of man,
> But tinctured with the Jacobinic plan;
> And thinks that every thing the Frenchmen do,
> No matter what—we ought to do so too. . . .

> Full well I see, how democrats will meet,
>
> And drink seditious toasts at every treat,
>
> Roar out to liberty to save the land,
>
> And damn a treaty they don't understand."

The poet next accused the democrats of having as their main support "Irish Whigs, accomplish'd in the art, / To take of other's property a part." Three quarters of the democrat's "patriot band" were Irish immigrants just arrived who "Sold for their passage, from the gallows sav'd, / That this vile country [the U. S.] need not be enslav'd." These "sons of Liberty and Equality," manipulated by a few resident "sons of sedition and anarchy—the Jacobins, or Democrats," threatened the very existence of America:

> A dismal proof of this we lately saw,
>
> When Faction yielded, and when triumph'd Law;
>
> When boldly rang'd along Rebellion's field,
>
> Our Whiskey-brethren rais'd the daring shield,
>
> While all our Clubs with expectation view'd,
>
> The hopeful prospect of a time of blood;
>
> When low in dust our Government should lie,
>
> And peace and safety from our country fly—

The rebels represented "true French Freedom, from the abyss of hell." Just when they were about to bring anarchy, "soon appeared great Freedom's awful form— / Still grew the thunder, disappeared the storm." Freedom, in this case, was a federal army that restored order. Finishing his twist on freedom, he concluded "Now I'm for living free, entirely free, / God never made a man to govern me." It was, by implication, laws, arms, and orderly government that brought freedom, not mobs.[24]

Despite its tortured logic, *The Democratiad* openly declared counterrevolution against what the author considered were misguided friends of liberty, dangerous immigrants, and blacks careening out of control. *The Guillotina,* appearing a year later and allegedly written by the author of *The Democratiad,* intensified the counterrevolution. "Come sing again!" he wrote, "since Ninety-Five, / Has left some Antis still alive; / Some Jacobins as pert as ever, / Tho' much was hop'd from Yellow-fever." America was still threatened by the activities of "a host of unhang'd Democrats, / And Speculators thick as rats." Grabs for land and wealth had brought forth "the anarchial powers that dwell, / In unform'd wilds 'twixt earth and hell."

Again charging Benjamin Franklin Bache with receiving political bribes to stir up democrats, the author wrote, "For here the deadly secret's told, / Who 'tis that fingers foreign gold." For the author, "patriots" like Bache when "stripp'd to state of nature, / Bear strong resemblance to the traitor." Such turncoats "yearn to enthrall this favour'd land" and "your Constitution to o'erturn." Bache and his colleagues, "fed with lies from day to day, / From venal presses in French pay, /

Fell Faction broods, and scents afar, / Predestin'd fields of civil war." But just as "The French have beat all other elves, / And now are beating fast themselves," the author feared the same for America: "New suns shall wake the blaze of day, / Where Chaos holds Eternal sway."

Praying for calm in America, the author concluded the frightening *Guillotina* with a prayer that America could remain a "land of peace, / Of Virtue, Law, and Happiness." Calling for all to return to productive work, he compared conditions in America and Europe, where anarchy had done its work:

> How safe <u>we</u> tend the fields for food,
> While Europe tills the fields of blood,
> Our sons how tranquil o'er the main,
> But their's in hostile navies slain,
> Their Anarchists still prowl for prey,
> But ours are held, like wolves, at bay,
> Their towns, while Emigrations drain,
> Rise in our wilds and bloom again,
> The Isles rejoice to heap their stores,
> In plenty on our smiling shores.

"Bold FREEDOM feeds her vestal fires" in America, he concluded, but only because Hamilton, Wolcott, and, most of all, Washington preserved order against the nation's would-be anarchists.[25]

Although counterrevolutionary fervor marked the rhetoric of *The Democratiad* and *The Guillotina,* their 1798 companion, *The Political Green-House,* completed the counterrevolutionary transformation of American values. "Most of all," began the author, "has Ninety Eight, / Outstripp'd the years of former date." Why? Because "while a Jacobin remains, / While Frenchmen live, and Faction reigns, / Her voice, array'd in awful rhyme, / Shall thunder down the steep of Time." He then reviewed the antics of Matthew Lyon, of Jeffersonian politicians in New England, and of American ministers in France who "had to deal with scurvy fellows, / With Autun, and the five-head Beast, / And half the Alphabet at least."

From that moment forward chaos absorbed America:

> Next from the press the tidings ran,
> From state to state, from man to man,
> In Freedom's cause they all combine. . . .
> The warlike spirit fills the presses,
> And teems the nation with addresses,
> Answers, Resolves, and Toasts in throngs,
> Orations, Sermons, Prayers, and Songs.
> The spirit freed of righteous hate,
> Like wild-fire spreads from state to state,

"Zion Besieged" (1787). The Articles of Confederation (Zion) and the principles of "Franklin & Liberty" fall under the attack of sinister forces—bankers, merchants, and other "moneyed people."

> And made thy sons, Columbia, see
> The extreme of insult heap'd on thee.

In the moment of crisis, as had happened twice before, "from Vernon's sacred hill," came George Washington to take charge of America's military: "He comes!—he comes! to re-array / Your hosts, ye heroes, for the affray!"

But also in this fearful situation, Thomas Jefferson ran for cover to Monticello: "Left from the tottering chair of state, / The storm should hurl him to his fate!" From there he began sending out sometimes innocent, often evil emissaries to do his dirty work, among them "foolish" George Logan," "spitting" Matthew Lyon, Benjamin Franklin Bache, and Tom Greenleaf, editor of the *New York Argus.* To bring them under control, it was necessary to "cloud the Jacobinic sky" with the Alien and Sedition Acts, placing them under some form of indictment:

> The dungeon walls shall teach thee reason,
> At least shall make thee sick of Treason.
> From these dread scenes of wild affright,
> Bache and Tom Greenleaf took their flight.

> The Yellow Fever clos'd their date,
>
> And sav'd two halters [i.e. nooses] to the State.

But while the fever took foes of order, it also took friends, including doctors and nurses. Benjamin Rush was one of the few left by the end of 1798 to challenge the "Hydra" and "how from earth to make him flee, / Is left, O learned Rush! with thee."

The author's greatest scorn was saved for errant fellow poet Joel Barlow. Whether *The Political Green-House* was written by Lemuel Hopkins, Richard Alsop, Theodore Dwight, or a combination among them, the poem's disparagement of their former friend revealed the extent to which they were committed to counterrevolution. Barlow, the author concluded, was a hopelessly insane traitor.

> Train'd in Illumination's school,
>
> And hir'd by rogues to play the fool, . . .
>
> This ever-changing, Proteus mind,—
>
> In all his turns, thro' every wind;
>
> From telling sinners where they go to,
>
> To speculations in Scioto,
>
> From pleading law, and taxing crimes,
>
> To stealing Colonel Humphrey's rhymes,
>
> From morals pure, and manners plain,
>
> To herding with Monroe and Paine,
>
> From feeding on his country's bread,
>
> To aping X, and Y, and Z,
>
> From preaching Christ, to Age of Reason
>
> From writing psalms, to writing treason.

In footnotes explaining some of the obscure references in this indictment, the author elucidated Barlow's poetic "stealing" by observing that it was "a prominent trait in the Jacobinical character, to take what belongs to others, without leave, and without paying for it." Another note told that Jacobins suffered from "a distemper among horses, called the POLL-EVIL, or as it is sometimes spelt POLE-EVIL. . . . This disease attacks the head; and when spelt in the former manner, means (among men) a strong propensity to obtain votes, no matter how; in the latter, as a strong disposition to erect Liberty Poles."

What worried the author was that America might be filled with Barlows who would wreck the nation: "this happy land, / Nurses a Jacobinic band, / Who, their united force employ, its richest blessings to destroy." For proof of their destructiveness, one needed only to look across the Atlantic to France:

> There a whole Nation sinks deprav'd,
>
> Corrupted, plunder'd, and enslav'd,
>
> Its dignity forever flown,

> Its manners lost, its honour gone,
> High on the ruins of a throne,
> Behold the base-born tyrants frown,
> Rapacious, cruel, proud, and vain,
> Far spreads the mischief of their reign.
> Of each inherent right bereft,
> Not Freedom's name, nor semblance left.

The contagion was also the work of "the *Illuminated* band accurs'd" of Adam Weishaupt: "Behold! this dark mysterious Band, / In myriads spread thro' every land, / Steal slyly to the posts of state, / And wield unseen the Nation's fate." In response, Jedidiah Morse and Timothy Dwight argued that Americans had to intercept the Illuminati and "Change their dark purpose ere too late, / Or else prepare to meet their fate."

Further proof of the spread of chaos could be seen in the French use of Theobald Wolfe Tone and James Napper Tandy to invade Ireland and William Tate to storm into Britain. They sought "Among the Irish Bulls, to teach / 'The rights of man,' and powers of speech." Evidence abounded in the course of Napoléon Bonaparte's victories in Italy and Austria and with his invasion of Egypt, northern Africa, and Turkey in search of the empire of Alexander the Great. The French Jacobins were

> Intent to sow the seeds of strife,
> To mar each bliss of human life,
> Spread wide Corruption's putrid flood,
> And bathe the nations round in blood,
> Extinguish Freedom's last remains,
> And rivet Slavery's galling chains.

And they were looking toward America: "O then, Columbia!" the poet proclaimed, "A warning draw ere yet too late; / For, from Destruction's lurid sky, / The *Fiend* has mark'd thee with his eye." Calling for Britain, Russia, Germany, and Switzerland to rise up and militarily "brave the Buccaniers of France," he also called upon Americans to resist the ideas arriving from "THE TERRIBLE GREAT NATION."[26]

By the time the trilogy of political poems had appeared, it was clear that a growing number of Americans had left behind aspirations for liberty, freedom, and human rights. They came to think of liberty as a misguided philosophical ideal incapable of practical achievement; of freedom as the independence of America to make its own social, political, and economic choices; and of rights, not as a set of guarantees, but as the prerogative of Americans to pursue property, wealth, home, and happiness. Concerns for the social and political conditions of Americans were set aside as counterrevolutionary ideologues—such particularly as the Hartford Wits redefined the heritage of the American Revolution they had once glorified.

The extent of the change was accentuated by the very different paths taken by Joel Barlow and the rest of the Hartford Wits. By 1799 Barlow was almost alone in talking about liberty, freedom, and rights. Only Josiah Meigs, about to be ejected by Timothy Dwight from Yale's faculty for lauding the French Revolution, sided with Barlow. The rest of the Wits had joined the growing counterrevolution. Even David Humphreys, who remained abroad through the 1790s in England and then as American minister to Spain, broke with Barlow. Although the two of them worked together, especially in 1796 and 1797 to free American prisoners being held in the Barbary states, their formerly prolific correspondence ended in 1798.[27]

While Barlow promoted revolution from Paris in 1798, Humphreys from Spain began sounding like his fellow authors of *The Democratiad, The Guillotina,* and *The Political Green-House.* In "A Poem on the Love of Country," completed in 1799, he called upon Americans to recognize that Barlow was a dangerous demagogue: "While demagogues, to gain a boundless sway, / The people flatter first, and next betray; / With false professions real slavery bring, / The guileful regents of the people-king!" Without uttering the word, he proclaimed that Americans must reject any further absorption with liberty:

> To save th' endanger'd state—unveil their guile!
> Man's rights and obligations reconcile!
> The demon-fury of the mob restrain,
> And bind licentiousness in law's strong chain! . . .
> Though great the plagues, though horrible the curse
> Of despotism! still anarchy is worse—
> Undup'd by popular names, shall we not shun
> The tyranny of MANY as of ONE?

In a sonnet written about the same time "On the Murders committed by the Jacobin Faction in the early Period of the French Revolution," he charged that the "blood-stain'd Jacobins" were "murd'rers of millions under freedom's name!" Not for another generation would it be possible for anyone in America to freely preach liberty, freedom, and the rights of man.[28]

CHAPTER 22

Friends of Order in the Land of Liberty: Political Philosophers

THE AMERICAN BURKE

Timothy Dwight's march from the worship of liberty to that of order was poignantly revealed in the personal dedications of his major poetic works following the American Revolution. *The Conquest of Canaan* (1785), celebrating American victory, liberty, and independence was dedicated to George Washington. *The Triumph of Infidelity, A Poem* (1788), his refutation of the Enlightenment, was inscribed satirically to Voltaire, an enemy of religion. *Greenfield Hill* (1794), his blueprint for a well-ordered America, was devoted to John Adams, then vice president of the United States. Adams, at that time, symbolized for Dwight the very essence of social and political order.

Despite the characteristic absence of the nation's vice presidency from the center of political struggles—a precedent he had the misfortune to establish—John Adams did not shroud his long career as political philosopher. Like Edmund Burke in Britain, Adams was driven to philosophize on human nature, political foibles, and social currents. In essays, pamphlets, books, and both published and unpublished letters, Adams ruminated about past history, current circumstances, and future worries. His ideas, beliefs, and preachings were remarkably similar to Edmund Burke's, although at almost every instance he preceded Burke in enunciating them.

But whereas Burke was a Jeremiah, trumpeting ideas in brilliant rhetoric, John Adams was an Ezekiel, cloaking his ideas in a maze barely decipherable to prose. However clear his voice during the American Revolution, after the war Adams became a theoretician who mostly muttered insights to himself and to a small circle of relatives and friends. Isolating himself from the scene of political, diplomatic, or social action, but brooding over events of his day, Adams persistently dissected human depravity and weaknesses; and, like Yahweh, pronounced judgment upon them.

Following Benjamin Franklin across the Atlantic in 1779 to become part of America's efforts to win European support against Britain and then to secure a permanent peace, Adams fretted while Franklin reigned as the American Über hero on the world stage. After observing Franklin's popular antics in France for more than three years, Adams commented in letters to fellow peace commissioner Arthur Lee and to Abigail Adams, "I expect Soon to See a proposition to name the 18th Century, the Franklinian Age, le Siècle Franklinnien." So oppressive did Adams find Franklin's presence in Paris, he was euphoric when he was able to make incursions into Holland and Britain and, finally, when he was appointed in 1785 as minister to the court of George III.

Adams entered into a decade of leisurely observation of world events. From his arrival in London in June 1785 until his inauguration as president of the United States in March 1797, Adams was sufficiently underemployed to spend nearly all of his waking hours writing letters, reading literature on liberty and government, and making his own contributions to philosophical and political thought. Observing the limitations of America's Confederation, Adams began what would eventually be a three-volume work titled *A Defence of the Constitutions of Government of the United States of America* (1787). The first volume appeared in both Britain and America just as the Constitutional Convention was forming to write the U.S. Constitution and as the Assembly of Notables was seated in France paving the way for a 1788 gathering of the Estates-General. By the time he left London to return to Massachusetts in February 1788, he had finished the other two volumes, which dribbled out with little fanfare during 1788 and 1789.[1]

Considered his magnum opus on the nature of republican governments, Adams sifted through all of the political philosophers and historians of Western history. But he did not do it very selectively or critically, copying elongated passages into his text with little explanation of the reason for their inclusion. It was clear, though, that he did not think that America should follow the British model of governance—even though he would be charged by his contemporaries with being a monarchist and British sympathizer. Fearful of the unicameral legislatures and central governments espoused by Turgot, Thomas Paine, and Benjamin Franklin, he also resented the implication that America's colonial constitutions were so rigidly British that they should be thrown out. He espoused the need for checks and balances in a republican government, and he hinted often on proper constitutionalism so much so that Benjamin Rush and others praised the effects of Adams's book on the 1787 Constitutional Convention.

Whatever the demerits of *Defence of the Constitutions,* the work was significant as Adams's reassessment of the meaning of liberty, freedom, and equality in a world spawned by the American Revolution. Adams made a variety of important judgments in 1786 that separated him as diametrically from the friends of liberty as would Burke's *Reflections on Revolution* four years later. By uttering his sentiments during the relatively calm atmosphere of constitution-making and placing them in an obscurantist tract, Adams's separation of himself from the revolutionary tides of Europe and America made not even a ripple at the moment.

Arguing that in governing societies man had to follow "the simple principles of nature," Adams laid out a new analysis of humanity that denied the democratizing tendencies of the American Revolution. Just as the architect Palladio proposed a plan of design "founded in nature," Adams argued that social governance flowed from "ordinary arts and sciences." Americans, when they wrote their state

John Adams (1783). Preparing to write his counterrevolutionary vision, Defence of the Constitutions of the United States.

constitutions, proved that "authority in magistrates and obedience of citizens can be grounded on reason, morality, and the Christian religion, without the mockery of priests, or the knavery of politicians."

What was true in forming governmental strictures, Adams argued, also applied to society. Logic proved that while one might construct a balanced republic, no democracy ever existed or could exist. In every society one found "a variety of orders" among humans due to the different "offices" or roles they played. Although Adams held that in America there were "different orders of <u>offices</u>, but none of <u>men</u>" and that in America "out of office, all men are of the same species, and of one blood," he soon qualified even that distinction when he came to the concept of equality. Almost deriding the very idea, he asked:

> Are the citizens to be all of the same age, sex, size, strength, stature, activity, courage, hardiness, industry, patience, ingenuity, wealth, knowledge, fame, wit, temperance, constancy, and wisdom? Was there, or will there ever be, a nation whose indi-

viduals were all equal, in natural and acquired qualities, in virtues, talents, and riches?

His reply could not be misunderstood: "The answer of all mankind must be in the negative. It must be acknowledged, that in every state . . . there are inequalities which God and nature have planted there, and which no human legislator ever can eradicate."

Even if laws eliminated hereditary titles, special crosses and ribbons, and all artificial inequalities of condition, Adams continued, "there are, nevertheless, inequalities of great moment . . . because they have a natural and inevitable influence in society." Adams cited two typical and ineradicable forms of inequality. First, there was "an inequality of wealth . . . whether by descent from their ancestors, or from greater skill, industry, and success in business." And the second was that of "birth." He was insistent on this point: "Let the page in history be quoted where any nation, ancient or modern, civilized or savage, is mentioned, among whom no difference was made between the citizens on account of their extraction." Confounding theoreticians of republics and democracies, he claimed "the truth is that more influence is allowed to this advantage [birth] in free republics than in despotic governments." To prove his idea he pointed at what was supposed to be the haven of freedom—the New England village. "Go into every village in New England," he charged, "and you will find that the office of justice of the peace, and even the place of representative . . . have generally descended from generation to generation, in three or four families at most."

As Adams pondered constitutions, he delved ever more deeply into human nature. He looked at a world which, to him, seemed on the brink of marching into chaos. From his vantage point in London, he viewed the world in a more detached manner than could Edmund Burke, who was forever locked in partisan warfare. Thus when Adams wrote that "it is weakness rather than wickedness which renders men unfit to be trusted with unlimited power," he observed the sad examples of Britain and France. And when he posited that "the nation that commits its affairs to a single assembly will assuredly find that its passions and desires augment as fast as those of a king," he had the model of Parliament before him and imagined, as would Burke four years later, what would happen in France if the ideas of French philosophers were put into practice. Addressing himself specifically to recent observations by Richard Price, Turgot, and the Abbé de Mably and publishing his works first in London merely proved that he was addressing himself to the fragile world of Europe, not America.

That Adams was looking at a world stage (while, yes, always concerned about how world affairs played themselves out in America) was further evident in the way he brought his *Defence of the Constitutions* to completion. Volume 2 was a belabored analysis of medieval Italian republics that further showed that unrestrained power could not be given to any individual or group. Volume 3 openly assaulted every theory of democracy and every notion that citizens in a republic can be expected ever to operate in the public interest. Taking on every friend of liberty in the civilized world, Adams pronounced democracy, equality, and freedom as chimeras without any possibility of becoming realities on earth. Even the discussion of them, he finally concluded, was a colossal waste of time.

Adams's pronouncement confronted Montesquieu's notion in his *The Spirit of Laws* that human beings had within them a basic love of democracy and of equality and that they would act out of virtue and frugality to preserve these states. After analyzing Montesquieu's ideas and conjecturing what form of madness could ever have brought him to such conclusions, Adams issued his own series of self-evident truths.

"No democracy ever did or can exist," Adams wrote. Even if you admitted that a democracy could theoretically exist, "no such passion as a love of democracy, stronger than self-love . . . ever did, or ever can prevail in the minds of citizens in general." And, in such a state, even if some citizens "preferred the public to their private interest, . . . it would not be from any such passion as love of the democracy, but from reason, conscience, a regard to justice, and a sense of duty and moral obligation." Or it might derive "from a desire of fame, and the applause, gratitude, and rewards of the public." Just as no democracy ever existed, also "no love of equality, at least since Adam's fall, ever existed in human nature." Nor was there ever a love of frugality. Adams concluded that "the democracy of Montesquieu, and its principle of virtue, equality, frugality, &c., . . . are all mere figments of the brain, and delusive imaginations.[2]

It was not Adams's purpose merely to enunciate a philosophical rebuttal to a popular theoretician of democracy. Rather he aimed to persuade the world that a pursuit of liberty, equality, and democracy would bring chaos. He concluded, "The word democracy signifies nothing more nor less than a nation of people without any government at all." Although he spoke not a word about the rights of human beings, he both anticipated and overreached Burke in condemning governments based on principles of democracy or equality. He continued throughout to use political terminology, but it became clear that he was talking about more than politics, constitutions, or governments. He was addressing the condition of humanity itself and whether it would be possible to keep the peoples of the world from marching down a path to inevitable destruction.[3]

Bored in London and frustrated as a diplomat, Adams paralleled the writing and publishing of his *Defence of the Constitutions* with an effort to return to America. Finally, in February 1788 his recall papers arrived, permitting his return to Massachusetts. Assuming that he would take a position in the Massachusetts government or practice law with his son John Quincy, he instead was drafted and elected the first vice president of the United States in November 1788. Not knowing quite what was a vice president, but wishing to be of assistance to his nation, he accepted the election. But when he arrived in New York in March 1789 for the inauguration of George Washington, he also learned of his responsibilities. His description of it to Abigail Adams has long endured: "My country has in its wisdom contrived for me the most insignificant office that ever the invention of man contrived or his imagination conceived."[4]

The prospect of four years, and eventually eight, as vice president could not have been a worse circumstance for John Adams. Just as the revolution he feared began to emerge in France, he was thrust into a position where he could speak for no one but himself. If he spoke, he was almost certain to disagree with the policies of President Washington, Treasury Secretary Alexander Hamilton, or Secretary of State Thomas Jefferson. Although he actively presided over Senate deliberations, he soon found himself engaged in attempting to understand the meaning of events in France for humanity, as he had in London tried to fathom the human condition in the post-Revolutionary era.[5]

While Americans hailed the actions of French revolutionaries, Adams found himself in a position akin to that of Burke's in Britain. He was in office, but not in power. He could not affect the direction of America—unless there was a fugitive tie vote in the Senate. He was of no party or faction and, in fact, deplored schemers and factions. He was a man with plenty of words to write in a nation still susceptible to the influence of prophetic judgment.

His actions over the coming months closely paralleled Edmund Burke's. Just as Burke was driven upon the receipt of Richard Price's prorevolutionary sermon of November 4, 1789, to launch into an antirevolutionary tirade, so was Adams. After saying to Price that he "admire[d] the general sentiments" of the address, Adams admitted that he had "learned by awful experience to rejoice with trembling" at news of such evens as were happening in France:

> I know that encyclopedists and economists, Diderot and
> D'Alembert, Voltaire and Rousseau, have contributed to this
> great event more than Sidney, Locke, or Hoadly, perhaps more
> than the American revolution; and I own to you, I know not
> what to make of a republic of thirty million atheists.

Already he saw a fatal flaw in the new French constitution, the same defect that would later be identified by Edmund Burke: "If the sovereignty is to reside in one assembly, the king, princes of the blood, and principal quality, will govern at their [the assembly's] pleasure as long as they can agree; when they differ, they will go to war."[6]

Compelled to explain to Price how the French constitution differed so fatally from those of Britain and America, he patiently explained the nature of sovereignty. Without a perfect allocation of power, France was sure to "act over all again the tragedies" of past regimes, because what was at work in France was not a dispute over governance, but a struggle for property: "Too many Frenchmen, after the example of too many Americans, pant for equality of persons and property. The impracticability of this, God Almighty has decreed, and the advocates for liberty, who attempt it, will surely suffer for it." Here Adams exercised, like Burke, his prophetic abilities: "I sincerely wish and devoutly pray, that a hundred years of civil wars may not be the portion of all Europe for want of a little attention to the true elements of the science of government."[7]

Just as Burke threw himself into writing his memorable *Reflections* during the remainder of 1790, Adams—working independently, but brooding over the same reports from France—engaged himself in writing his inscrutable and mostly forgotten *Discourses on Davila*. Each document reflected the very different character of its author. Burke's was filled with passionate fervor; Adams's with academic jargon. Burke's, although it addressed immediate political circumstances, elucidated his formerly vague principles; Adams's, although largely eschewing America's political conundrums, beclouded his own clear principles. Burke's, published as a single tract in November 1790, became an instant sensation and a lightning rod for counterrevolution; Adams's, published during 1790 as installments in the *Gazette of the United States* in Philadelphia and New York, went unnoticed except by political observers who either respected Adams or who loathed his prickly ideas.

While Burke's *Reflections* and Adams's *Discourses* were dissimilar as literary productions, they were almost identical in their analyses of the French Revolution, of the condition of humanity, and of the principles they enunciated for the future of both liberty and order. Burke blasted the ruling order in France; Adams castigated the order that ruled in France five hundred years earlier and that had failed to determine for all French history whether sovereignty lay with the king or with the people. Burke used his own voice to condemn practices in France; Adams used the contrivance of Davila, an early Italian historian, to tell the story of Pharamond, a king elected to power and from whom Louis XVI was descended, whose very election proved that all power derived from the governed in France and not from the monarch.

In spite of Adams's obscurantism, those who read *Discourses* closely (and many important individuals did) could not mistake his counterrevolutionary message. He focused on leadership—national, state, community—and how a person could be selected to lead a people and then be entrusted to provide honest direction. Looking at the desire of French leaders to select only the most qualified individuals to govern the nation, he asked, "Shall the whole nation vote for Senators? Thirty millions of votes, for example, for each Senator of France!" Such would be impossible: "The voters then must be exposed to deception, from intrigues and manoeuvres, without number . . . from all the chicanery, impostures and falsehoods imaginable, with scarce a possibility of preferring real merit." To avoid electoral chaos, he continued, "Will you divide the nation into districts, and let each district choose a Senator?" Though that made great sense in America, Adams responded, "this is giving up the idea of national merit, and annexing the honor and the trust to an accident, that of living on a particular spot."

Here was Adams, one of the great theoreticians of American republicanism, ridiculing democracy. Adams concluded that "the chance of having wisdom and integrity in a Senator by hereditary descent would be far better" than any electioneering mechanism that could be devised. And he abhorred even more the notion that supposedly democratically elected senators would then govern the nation through a single nationally elected assembly. He believed that all these democratically elected people, when gathered in one forum, "will act as arbitrarily and tyrannically as any despot." He continued, "It is a sacred truth that a sovereignty in a single assembly must necessarily, and will certainly be exercised by a majority, as tyrannically as any sovereignty was ever exercised by Kings or

Nobles." If the theories then espoused by the duc de la Rochefoucauld, Condercet, and, yes, Benjamin Franklin, would be followed "the present struggle in Europe will be little beneficial to mankind, and produce nothing but another thousand years of feudal fanaticism, under new and strange names."[8]

After eleven essays in which he meandered through French history, political theories antithetical to democracy, and analyses of the psychology of leadership, Adams, finally, in his twelfth essay moved from critic to prophet. He had a clear prescription for the world's ills. A brief poetic epigram suggested what would follow:

> Order is Heaven's first law—and this confess'd,
>
> Some are, and must be, greater than the rest:
>
> More rich, more wise—But who infers from hence,
>
> That such are happier, shocks all common sense.

Adams was ready to overthrow all of the dreams of those seeking liberty to secure order in the world. Long before the Reign of Terror, before Louis XVI's flight to Varennes, before Paine's *The Rights of Man,* and prior to Burke's *Reflections on the French Revolution,* Adams laid out a philosophy of counterrevolution that would sweep the world over the next eight years.

Adams minced no words. Citing long poetic passages to make his point, he continued:

> The Heaven's themselves, the Planets and this centre,
>
> Observe degree, priority and place,
>
> Insisture, course, proportion, season, form,
>
> Office and custom, in all line of order:
>
> And therefore is the glorious planet Sol,
>
> In noble eminence, enthron'd and spher'd. . . .

For Adams it was when the planets, people, and nations moved out of their given spheres that disorder arose:

> What plagues and what portents! what mutiny!
>
> What raging of the sea! Shaking of earth!
>
> Commotion in the winds! Frights, changes, horrors,
>
> Divert and crack, rend and deracinate,
>
> The unity and married calm of States.

Order depended entirely upon the adherence of all parties to their place.

Order also derived from the recognition and maintenance of degrees among people. By degrees Adams meant honors from schools and among brotherhoods, "primogenitive and due of birth," "prerogative of age, crowns, sceptres, laurels," and anything else that gave a person an "authentic place" in society. There *must* be degrees in society, he declared:

> Take but Degree away; untune that string
> And hark! what discord follows! each thing meets
> In meer oppugnancy: the bounded waters
> Should lift their bosoms, higher than the shores,
> And make a sop, of all this solid globe.

Without the orderliness of degrees, "Force should be right; or rather right and wrong / Should lose their names, and so should justice too." Without degree there is anarchy: "This chaos, when Degree is suffocate / Follows the choaking. The General's disdain'd, / By him one step below: he by the next; / That next by him beneath." The world without degree would disintegrate from "an envious fever / Of pale and bloodless emulation."

Adams was not merely becoming crotchety and conservative at the ripe age of fifty-five. He was changing the rules of politics, modifying the goals of human achievement, and redefining the way people operate in a republican society. As he looked into the crucible that was revolutionary France, he realized that the train of liberty on which most of the world was boarded was headed toward collision, where governments would fail and whole societies would demolish themselves. Not only could democracies not exist, he concluded, nations and societies could not survive if their reason for being was to deliver liberty, freedom, and equality. They could only survive if their central purpose was to protect and preserve order.

He thrashed his conclusion over and over in the next twenty Davila essays, sometimes couching his invective in one of his contorted historical stories and other times directly berating French and American claims of having achieved liberty for all citizens. In one essay on "emulation" in France and America, he argued that both nations were filled with rivalries, contests, and backstabbings to give individuals, cities, and whole states ascendancy over their competitors. He asked Americans

> Whether ttere [there?] are not emulations, of a serious complexion among ourselves? between cities and universities? between North and South? The Middle and the North? The Middle and the South? between one state and another? betwccn the governments of States and the National Government? and between individual patriots and heroes in all these?

As for France, "we are told that our friends, the National Assembly of France, have abolished all distinctions." Nothing could be more foolish, he claimed:

> But be not deceived, my dear countrymen. Impossibilities cannot be performed. Have they levelled all fortunes, and equally divided all property? Have they made all men and women equally wise, elegant, and beautiful? . . . Have they not still Princes of the first and second order, Nobles and Knights? Have they no record nor memory who are the men who com-

> pose the present National Assembly? Do they wish to have that
> distinction forgotten? Have the French officers who served in
> America melted their Eagles, and torn their ribbons?

While America praised the brilliant actions of the National Assembly, Adams ridiculed not only France, but also notions of liberty and democracy anywhere in the world.

He was not merely opposed to the regnant politics in France or to anti-Federalist contentiousness in America. He was proposing a fundamental rewriting of those verities that undergirded the Declaration of Independence and the American Revolution itself: "God, in the constitution of nature, has ordained that every man shall have a disposition to emulation, as well as imitation, and consequently a passion for distinction, and that all men shall not have equal means and opportunities of gratifying it." Any government that attempted to legislate equality where there was none or to impose democracy upon societies was doomed to failure. No party could alter "the constitution of human nature."

Just as Edmund Burke was able during 1790 to project the direction of the French Revolution, so was Adams. With incredible prescience Adams analyzed the tortuous makeup of the National Assembly. He saw "an aristocratical party, a democratical party, an armed neutrality, and most probably a monarchial party: besides another division . . . who are equal friends to monarchy, aristocracy, and democracy." Further,

> Each of these parties has its chief, and these chiefs are or will be
> rivals. Religion will be both the object and the pretext of some:
> liberty, of others; submission and obedience of others; and lev-
> eling, downright leveling, of not a few. . . . Contests and dis-
> sentions will arise between these runners in the same race.

Like Burke, Adams anticipated not only partisan dissension, but a devolution to chaos: "From sophistry and party spirit, the transition is quick and easy to falsehood, imposture, and every species of artificial evolution and criminal intrigue." Then would follow, he foretold, a raid on the press "as unbalanced parties . . . can never tolerate a free enquiry of any kind."[9]

And, just as Burke thought France would move inevitably into chaos and emerge under the aegis of a new dictator, Adams offered his own original version of the same future in 1790:

> A writer . . . may first be burnt in effigy: or a printer may have
> his office assaulted: cuffs and kicks, boxes and cudgels, are
> heard of, among plebeian statesmen; challenges and single
> combats among the aristocratic legislators—Riots and seditions
> at length break men's bones. . . . Lives are lost: and when blood
> is once drawn, men, like other animals, become outrageous: If
> one party has not a superiority over the other . . . a civil war
> ensues. When the nation arrives at this period of the progres-
> sion, every leader . . . will find himself compelled to form them

> into some military arrangement; . . . to build castles and fortify
> eminences. . . . If this should be the course in France, the poor,
> deluded, and devoted partizans would soon be fond enough of
> decorating their leaders . . . or doing any thing else, to increase
> the power of their commander over themselves . . . or to give
> him weight with their enemies.

While in the process of ridding France of one feudal system, Adams was certain that the National Assembly was laying the foundation for another: "A legislature in one assembly, can have no other termination than in civil dissention, feudal anarchy, or simple monarchy."[10]

Having telescoped the destruction of France if its course in 1790 remained unchanged, Adams, for a brief moment in the fifteenth of his thirty-two *Davila* essays, preached a clear message to both the French and the Americans. Whereas the Enlightenment savants thought the increase in knowledge was such that governments and societies could be perfected with liberty and equality for everyone, all that learning actually made it more difficult to control passions and rivalries among men: "Bad men increase in knowledge as fast as good men, and science, arts, taste, sense and letters, are employed for the purposes of injustice and tyranny, as well as those of law and liberty; for corruption as well as for virtue." "FRENCHMEN!" Adams thundered, "Act and think like yourselves! confessing human nature, be magnanimous and wise." Instead of denying man's nature, "consider that government is intended to set bounds to passions which nature has not limited: and to assist reason, conscience, justice and truth in controuling interests, which, without it, would be as unjust as uncontroulable."

He then reiterated the centerpiece of his message for both the French and Americans: "It becomes the more indispensable, that every man should know his place and be made to keep it." That was Adams's realization as he studied societies and governments and the nature of man throughout the 1780s. That was the core of his *Defence of the Constitutions*. That was what informed the process of constitution making in the states and what America was about: "AMERICANS! rejoice, that from experience, you have learned wisdom: and instead of whimsical and fantastical projects, you have adopted a promising essay, towards a well ordered government." The U.S. Constitution had begun the process of defining a place for every human being and of establishing controls to make sure that every being stayed in that place. Only by founding those controls and assuring universal adherence to them could Americans achieve and protect those rights to life, liberty, and property that sent them into rebellion against Britain.

By practicing a carefully designed system of control, Adams proclaimed, his fellow Americans "will not only secure freedom and happiness to yourselves and your posterity, but your example will be imitated by all Europe, and in time perhaps by all mankind." The heritage of the American Revolution was to establish constitutions that checked human passions, not to inaugurate freedom, to unleash liberty, to promise equality, or to play at democracy. According to Adams, the American approach provided a proper modicum of liberty to every member of society, even the downtrodden African:

> Liberty, led by philosophy, diffuses her blessings to every class of men; and even extends a smile of hope and promise to the poor African, the victim of hard impenetrable avarice. Man, as man, becomes an object of respect. Tenets are transferred, from theory to practice. The glowing sentiment, the lofty specula-tion, no longer serve "but to adorn the pages of a book:" they are brought home to men's business and bosoms.

In America, "what some centuries ago, it was daring but to think, and dangerous to express, is now realized and carried into effect."

Regrettably, Adams continued, the French, in looking toward America as a model, were attempting to copy the results of American constitution making without paying attention to the true "maxims, principles and example" of the Americans: "There is reason to fear she has copied from you errors, which have cost you very dear." While Americans struggled to build a workable system of protecting rights and providing liberties, the French simply proclaimed liberty, freedom, and equality without creating institutions to deliver them. Adams warned, "Amidst all their exultations, Americans and Frenchmen should remem-ber, that the perfectibility of man, is only human and terrestrial perfectibility. Cold will still freeze, and fire will never cease to burn; disease and vice will con-tinue to disorder, and death to terrify mankind." Only constant attention to bal-ance and control in government and society would check the tendency of human viciousness from "degenerating into dangerous ambition, irregular rivalries, destructive factions, wasting seditions, and bloody civil wars."

Adams's message was obvious—at least in this fifteenth *Davila* essay. Like Burke, he proclaimed that the only way to achieve liberty was first to secure order in government and society. There had to be a defined place and a clear role for every person—a station in life. The critical operations of government, the church, and educational institutions had to be carefully crafted—scientifi-cally, they both said—in the light of history. Government's role was to enforce order, the church's to preach virtue, and school's to teach proper behavior and responsibilities.

In one respect Burke and Adams, at first glance, looked very different. Burke stressed the central role of tradition in preserving order in society. Adams, on the other hand, assigned that crucial responsibility to civil constitutions. Burke harped on understanding the past. Adams, by contrast, emphasized the creative process of constitution making and of fine-tuning those constitutions to assure order.

Although their terminology was different and their descriptions of tradition and constitution making conjure up different images, they were describing the same processes. To make use of tradition, in Burke's terms, philosophers, histo-rians, and politicians would need to examine the historical record, determine precedent, and establish policy. Those same steps were involved in making and implementing constitutions in Adams's world plan. The instructive difference was that Americans, without their own established traditions, over the period of a dozen years or so from the onset of the American Revolution until the ratification of the Bill of Rights defined as comprehensively as possible what would be recognized then and in the future as the American tradition. Thereafter, accessing the American tradition became enormously easier than in those nations—such as Britain and France—without written and corporately ratified constitutions.

After his fifteenth *Davila* essay, Adams retreated again with Davila to a dissection of sixteenth-century French civil wars. He did not return to a direct analysis of affairs in France until his thirty-second essay. These intervening essays exhibit Adams's typical tortured story-telling style, but they have a certain planned coherence absent from the first fifteen essays. In those earlier essays Adams was reacting to daily headlines arriving from France with his own interpretations of the course of humanity.

Adams did not again reflect a consciousness of current affairs until mid-April 1791, on or about the first anniversary of Benjamin Franklin's death. Having observed acts of the National Assembly as it abolished titles of nobility, declared the church a civil institution and the clergy civil officers, and established various taxation schemes as civil unrest surged in France, and as open slave rebellion surfaced in St. Domingue, Adams could not restrain himself from blaming Benjamin Franklin for the mess in France. It was "upon Franklin's authority," he noted, that "the French adopted their government in one assembly." And that "one uncontrolled assembly" was producing in France a colossal Saint Bartholomew's Day: "the natural, necessary and unavoidable effect and consequence of diversities in opinion, the spirit of party, unchecked passions, emulation and rivalry, where there is not a power always ready and inclined to throw weights into the lightest scale, to preserve or restore the equilibrium." For all his brilliance as a scientist in the realms of electricity, heat, and weather, Adams might have said, Benjamin Franklin was naive when it came to political science.[11]

The same prickliness that impelled Adams to throw a dart at Benjamin Franklin's memory caused him just a few days later to make a comment so controversial that the *Davila* series had to be discontinued. In that essay he asked theoretically why humans so often had chosen to live under the rule of kings. He then proceeded to answer that "they had almost unanimously been convinced that hereditary succession was attended with fewer evils than frequent elections." He concluded, "This is the true answer, and the only one, as I believe."

His affirmation of the practicability of monarchy caused such a firestorm of protest that the editor of the *Gazette of the United States* had to stop the series. The attendant odium of Adams as a closet monarchist remained with him for the remainder of his life and in many histories thereafter.

That a promonarchist statement should be the immediate cause of silencing Adams after years of unabashed political commentary was understandable given the sensitivities of Americans in establishing an elective presidency. But that Adams could have driveled on, endlessly blasting every other principle of the American Revolution was remarkable. He had systematically discredited notions of democracy, equality, freedom, virtue, republicanism, and even liberty itself, for years without hindrance.

But these counterrevolutionary doctrines, it should be noted, had more to do with values than with partisan politics. Though he could not tamper with the nature of Washington's presidency, he was free to articulate counterrevolutionary philosophy, rhetoric, values, and a set of goals that countermanded the American Revolution. And he circulated those ideas to take root where they would.

John Adams was by 1790 America's most articulate counterrevolutionary. He did for America what Edmund Burke did for Britain and what Chateaubriand would do for France. In the guise of putting forth an international debate about sovereignty and forms of government, Adams introduced a whole new set of social and political values at variance with the derived philosophy and direction of the American Revolution. Brooding endlessly over these values through four large tomes—mainly unread at the time, but introduced by discussion, letters, reviews, and reference into American consciousness—Adams worked out a full-scale counterrevolutionary body of thought that he embraced between 1786 and 1790 as a more authentic philosophy for the American nation. He then spent the rest of this life as vice president, as president, and as elder statesman arguing vehemently that his version of the Revolutionary heritage—actually counter-revolutionary through and through—should be adopted as America's guiding national vision.

And he won. Although Adams failed as a politician, as a diplomat, and as president, he succeeded as a philosopher, as a political scientist, and as an arbiter of human foibles. His self-absorbed contemporaries overlooked the counter-revolution quietly being launched by Adams, the Hartford Wits, and by hundreds of others concerned more with the fabric of American society than with politics. Adams's bumbling acts as a politician, his identification as a monarchist, and his attacks upon everyone who disagreed with him obscured the fact that he had introduced a counterrevolutionary course.

The extent to which his contemporaries missed the essence of Adams's con-tributions to American thought became clear just two months after the last aborted *Davila* essay. By late spring 1791 both Edmund Burke's *Reflections on the Revolution in France* and Thomas Paine's *Rights of Man, Part 1* had appeared in American editions and were being widely read as two distinctive interpretations of events in France. The American edition of the *Rights of Man* was prefaced with a letter from Thomas Jefferson commending it to the pub-lisher and implying that Paine's work refuted John Adams as well as it did Edmund Burke. Although Jefferson later declared that he did not intend for the letter to be published (he said it was a transmittal letter only) or to publicly endorse Paine's book, the letter appeared to everyone as a political stab at Adams.[12]

A few weeks later, on June 8, 1791, a new series of essays began to appear in the *Columbian Centinel* under the pseudonym of "Publicola." The first essay began with the note that "the late Revolution in France has opened an extensive field of speculation to the philosopher and to the politician." Among the "friends of liberty" and "friends of humanity" whose ideas had been drawn forth, the author observed, none surpassed those of Edmund Burke and Thomas Paine. But before proceeding with a full-scale review of those works, the author cited the offensive passage in Jefferson's printed letter. Jefferson wrote:

> I am extremely pleased to find that it [*Rights of Man*] is to be re-printed here, and that something is at length to be publicly said against the <u>political heresies</u> which have sprung up among us. I have no doubt our citizens will <u>rally</u> a second time round the standard of <u>Common Sense</u>.

The author then attacked Jefferson: "I confess, sir, I am somewhat at a loss to determine what this very respectable gentleman means by <u>political heresies</u>." Wondering if Jefferson saw Paine's tract as "the canonical book of political scripture" or the book of "<u>Islam</u> of democracy," he asked if Jefferson wished "to compel all their countrymen to cry out, 'There is but one Goddess of Liberty, and Common Sense is her prophet?'"[13]

Before Paine should "be adopted as the holy father of our political faith" and his pamphlet "as his Papal Bull of infallible virtue," the author promised a sharp review of its contents. Stating also that it was "not my intention to defend the principles of Mr. Burke," the author then delved into questions of sovereignty, constitutions, representative assemblies, rights of succession, and rights to revolution. The author sharply differed with Paine's interpretation of the rights of man, revolutions, and government. The analysis was so thorough, so cogently drawn, so Adamsesque, that nearly everyone in America—except Adams himself and the true author—was sure that the author was the vice president.[14]

A counterattack against Adams ensued, engineered at least in part by Jefferson himself. Its fallout was such that Adams and Jefferson remained estranged for more than twenty years, although they formed a philosophical dialectic that would continue for over thirty years. Adams, for his part, knew not who was Publicola—at least not in the beginning. When the last essay appeared, the anonymous author acknowledged that his series had "called forth a torrent of abuse, not upon their real author nor upon the sentiments they express, but upon a supposed author, and supposed sentiments." The obloquy had been directed toward John Adams and his presumed monarchist views.

"With respect to the author," Publicola continued, "not one of the conjectures that have appeared in the public prints has been well grounded." He denied that the vice president wrote, corrected, sanctioned, or knew of their contents. And for those who presumed that the essays supported monarchy, he challenged anyone "to produce a single passage . . . which has the most distant tendency to recommend either a monarchy or an aristocracy to the citizens of these States."[15]

Once again a brilliantly written group of essays setting forth the tenets of what was becoming the American Counterrevolution were laid forth, only to be obscured by a set of political circumstances. Jefferson was correct when he described those doctrines as "political heresies." They sought nothing less than turning the liberative energy of the American Revolution upside down.

But Jefferson was wrong about the authorship of the Publicola essays. They were actually written by John Quincy Adams, who, already an accomplished scholar and world traveler at the age of twenty-three, had absorbed his father's counterrevolutionary philosophy and fervor. While there was ahead of him a long, varied, and—not unlike his father—ill-fated political career, he was in Publicola launching a public life in which he would be driven by principles shared with his discredited father.

VOICES OF THE OTHER ENLIGHTENMENT

In the early months of 1790 when America's great liberator, Benjamin Franklin, passed from the scene, James Madison, a member of Congress from Virginia, wrote one of the most definitive letters of his career. Under the date of February 4, 1790, Madison began a careful response to one of the most famous letters in the history of liberty and revolutions, Thomas Jefferson's epistle on the notion that "the earth belongs always to the living generation."

The letter in question was a private letter to Madison written while Jefferson was American minister in Paris. It was composed on September 6, 1789, at the end of that sweet summer of liberty Jefferson had just witnessed in the French capital—a season that intoxicated not only Jefferson, but also millions of people in the Western world. There had been the opening of the Estates-General in May, the creation of the National Assembly in June, the storming of the Bastille in July, the issuance of the Declaration of the Rights of Man and the Citizen in August.

This succession of incredible events provoked Jefferson to write Madison, "we seem not to have perceived that, by the law of nature, one generation is to another as one independent nation to another." Since generations, according to Jefferson's analysis exhausted every nineteen years, he observed, "On similar ground, it may be proved that no society can make a perpetual constitution, or even a perpetual law."

James Madison, a member of the Virginia Assembly, a decisive member of the U.S. Constitutional Convention of 1787, a participant in the Virginia ratification convention of 1788, and virtual author of the American Bill of Rights, calmly responded to Jefferson with a question: "Would not a Government so often revised become too mutable to retain those prejudices in its favor which antiquity inspires, and which are perhaps a salutary aid to the most rational Government in the most enlightened age?" He also thought that such constant revisionism would "engender pernicious factions that might otherwise not come into existence."

*James Madison (1796). Father of the American Constitution
and theorist of the American Counterrevolution.*

Madison was astonished at the naïveté exhibited by an individual whom he considered his closest ally and friend from Virginia and who, as author of the American Declaration of Independence, qualified as one of the great political philosophers of the age. Jefferson, for once in his astonishing political career, seemed to make no sense. Jefferson, enamored with French idealism and French architecture, believed for a moment that wisdom derived from the Enlightenment could fix every problem, could make efficient governments, and could build perfect societies. Madison, on the contrary, used this occasion to school his friend and mentor in some basic principles of republican order.

First of all, if every generation made its own government, rights in property would be endangered and perhaps lost. Second, the world would be robbed of the lessons of precedent, tradition, and history. Third, generations of people would feel no obligation to their fathers or to their heirs to make the world a safe haven. Indeed, Madison, like Edmund Burke, saw "a partnership not only between those who are living, but between those who are living, those who are dead, and those who are to be born."[16]

Madison, in responding to a momentarily wild-eyed Jefferson, must have felt that he was placed in a position of chiding his friend and political ally. But this was not new. From the moment of his election to the Virginia Convention that wrote the state's first constitution in 1776 until 1790, when he helped to launch the world's first national constitutional government, he had found himself constantly in the position of channelling Jefferson's enthusiasm for liberty. He had helped to implement Jefferson's hopes for freedom of religion in Virginia. He had promoted various schemes of taxation, the settlement of land claims, and commercial interaction among the states enabling America's confederation to work. And it was he who paved the way for a Constitutional Convention in 1787 to create a strong national government.

It was in that last effort—the writing of a new constitution—that Madison took greatest pride and through which Jefferson had caused him the most grief. Thirty-seven at the time, Madison had labored to draw up a governing document that could stand the test of time; that would give greater authority to states with larger populations; that would provide for national executive, legislative, and judicial branches of government controlled with appropriate checks and balances; that secured national defense and commercial operations; and that would be ratified by the people of the nation. Through the summer months of 1787 he had worked to guide discussions, to influence specific provisions, and to create a thorough record of the confidential sessions of the Convention. More than any other participant, Madison had shaped its final product.[17]

No sooner had the Convention finished its business than Jefferson, away in France, began to question its conception, many of its provisions, and, especially, the way it came about. That it was written in secret, that it limited states' rights, that it provided no limits on the reelection of the president, and that it contained no declaration of individual rights bothered Jefferson so much that he told Madison the document ought to be rejected by the states. Throughout the ratification process, Jefferson was quoted from afar as an ardent anti-Federalist who believed the constitution too sweeping in its assumption of authority and who called for additional conventions—as frequently as needed—to revise and rewrite whole sections of the charter.[18]

Madison listened patiently to Jefferson's biting and sometimes tactless criticisms. And, although he was chagrined to have to bear Jefferson's opposition in a close Virginia ratification convention, he pressed on, certain in his course. He collaborated secretly with Alexander Hamilton and John Jay to produce the *Federalist Papers,* not revealing to Jefferson his role in writing them. In one of those papers, number forty-nine, Madison actually refuted Jefferson's call for frequent constitutional conventions. Madison thought habit, custom, and precedent were more important in creating support for a constitution than in providing a mechanism for constant change. To submit constitutional issues to popular decision making was to risk reckless policy shifts. So profoundly different were their ideas about the republican governance, Madison constantly had to correct Jefferson's whimsical disrespect for history, institutions, and tradition throughout their careers.[19]

How had these two sons of the Enlightenment, neighbors, political collaborators, and friends come to such fundamentally different positions on republicanism, governance, and society? How was it that Jefferson in 1790 so much feared tradition and favored letting the popular voice constantly speak, while Madison sanctioned history and precedent as a safer instrument in a republic? The difference between the two was that, while both of them were sons of the Enlightenment, Jefferson responded to one flange of it—the French reasonings of Voltaire, Rousseau, and Condorcet—and Madison resonated to another—the Scottish philosophies of Thomas Reid, David Hume, and Adam Smith. The first of these

Enlightenment traditions held that man was sufficiently reasonable to choose always what was best for him and his society; the second was skeptical that man could ever know enough to understand all of the forces of nature, history, and human passions.

And, in that Jefferson could not in 1790 or thereafter grasp the necessity of harnessing the irrational forces of human passions, he would be buffeted during the 1790s and after between lip service to the values of the American Revolution and the use of partisan force to seize power and quell opposition. Madison, on the other hand, understanding the limits of human ability to always act rationally, was liberated in the 1780s and 1790s to direct along with John Adams and many others an American counterrevolution that brought permanent shape to America as a land devoted first and foremost to order.

Although both Jefferson and Madison grew up in Virginia, Madison very early fell under the influence of Scottish and religious instructors. Although he did not attend college until the rather late age of nineteen, he entered at a time, in a place, and under an influence that put him in a world wholly apart from that of Thomas Jefferson. The school was the College of New Jersey (Princeton). The year was 1769. And the towering figure under whose spell he came that year was John Witherspoon, president of the College of New Jersey.

Product and practitioner of the Scottish Enlightenment, Witherspoon at age forty-five was at the height of his powers of remaking the world in the image of all things Scottish. He was beginning his second year in America and as president at Princeton. Despite his still brief tenure, he was already deep into the process of converting the College of New Jersey into America's first national school for training in republicanism.

Son of a minister of the Church of Scotland, Witherspoon was challenged from birth educationally and religiously to become a moral educator. He received a Master of Arts degree from the University of Edinburgh in 1739 at age sixteen. He then studied theology until his ordination as a Scottish clergyman in 1745. During 1746 he raised a militia to resist the invasion of Charles Stuart. At the Battle of Falkirk he was captured and imprisoned for several months. From 1745 until his departure for America in 1768 he served as pastor of two Scottish churches, and in 1753 he made a name for himself with the publication of *Ecclesiastical Characteristics,* an assault on the sinful ways of eighteenth-century society. Although he was elected president of Princeton in 1766, it took the constant urgings of trustee Richard Stockton and of Edinburgh medical student Benjamin Rush to persuade Witherspoon to go to America in 1768.

From the outset Witherspoon did not restrict his activities to the academic environment of Princeton. He traveled extensively through New England, New York, Pennsylvania, and Virginia in pursuit of funds and students. It was Witherspoon's ever-expanding net that brought James Madison to Princeton in a class that also included Hugh Henry Brackenridge and Philip Freneau, poets of the American Revolution. His introduction of the philosophical principles of the Scottish Enlightenment transformed Princeton into a center of revolutionary activity. It was Witherspoon who introduced Francis Hutcheson's *System of*

Moral Philosophy (1755), Thomas Reid's *Inquiry into the Human Mind on the Principles of Common Sense* (1764), and James Oswald's *Appeal to Common Sense in Behalf of Religion* (1766).[20]

In his *Lectures on Moral Philosophy* and *Lectures on Eloquence* Witherspoon introduced to American education a new system of civic humanism that told students their place was in the world at large, not merely in the pulpit, in the academy, or in the counting house. He stressed the practicalities of life rather than mere aesthetics; he connected classical authors with living authorities; and he directly addressed the political and social concerns of the day. Witherspoon taught a system of ethics separated from the heart and translated into a science.[21]

More importantly, Witherspoon introduced a set of philosophical principles directly concerned with preserving social, political, and religious stability. He taught obedience to rulers and the importance of government as a voluntary compact among humans to protect liberty. Liberty was a precious commodity, prized especially by him and other Scots who had fought for centuries against English tyranny. But the love of order did not signify for Witherspoon the acceptance of tyranny. The historic Scottish distrust of England easily transferred to America and made Witherspoon one with other American patriots. It was the philosophy coming out of the Scottish Enlightenment that informed a whole generation of Americans not only to sue for their independence, but also to establish a sturdy and conservative constitutional government.[22]

Witherspoon's teachings and his promotion of virtuous republican leadership made Princeton a principal source of America's Revolutionary leaders and statesmen. Of the 335 students who attended Princeton between 1769 and 1783, only five became Loyalists. Despite the strong religious affiliation of the school, fewer than a fourth of the graduates during that period became ministers. But every graduate was well stocked with convictions that conformed with republican ideals and with a burning belief that America needed a constitution. Nine of the fifty-five delegates to the Constitutional Convention of 1787 were Princeton graduates. Thirty-one of those 335 students who came to Princeton in the era of the American Revolution played roles, often large, in the thirteen state conventions that ratified the Constitution. While Yale stocked the young nation with poets and moral philosophers, Princeton provided the country's political philosophers.[23]

Witherspoon provided for James Madison an indelible structure of thought that informed all his actions, policies, and beliefs developed or undertaken during his long career as lawmaker, government executive, and elder statesman. Madison was so taken by Witherspoon that he remained an extra year at the school studying theology, Hebrew, and ethics under his direct tutelage. Even then Madison could not relinquish the contemplation of the interstices between theology, human polity, and eternity. He remained in a state of self-analysis until he was aroused by the great struggle that ensued between the colonies and Britain.

Even as he was swept into service in the Committee of Safety for Orange County in 1775 and into the 1776 Virginia Convention that wrote a state constitution and a declaration of rights, Madison was also enraptured with endless theological speculations. During 1778 while he served on the Governor's Council in

Virginia, he corresponded with Princeton classmate Samuel Stanhope Smith on the nature of free will, the liberty of moral action, and salvation.

Between 1780 and 1783, Witherspoon and Madison—mentor and student—served together as members of the Continental Congress. Madison, while methodically at work translating his teacher's lessons into policies and laws, also resonated Witherspoon's declarations that the American Revolution was a providential event and that separation from Britain was ordained by God. Madison heard Witherspoon declare on April 19, 1783, a national day of thanksgiving set by Congress, that

> Nothing appears to me more manifest than that the separation of this country from Britain, has been of God; for every step the British took to prevent, served to accelerate it, which has generally been the case when men have undertaken to go in opposition to the course of Providence, and to make war with the nature of things.

Madison heard Witherspoon repeatedly express similar sentiments between June and November 1783, as Congress moved its meetings to Princeton, away from the shouts of disgruntled Pennsylvania veterans.

It was there, under Witherspoon's careful guidance, that George Washington laid down arms and acknowledged the supremacy of America's civil government. Witherspoon, searching over the annals of English and Scottish history, surely conspired with Elias Boudinot, chairman of Princeton's trustees and president of Congress, to plan the event. When Washington arrived, Boudinot remained seated with hat on his head to demonstrate the supremacy of civil over military power. A British spy in attendance at the scene reported to London that, through this scripted ceremony, Witherspoon poisoned "the minds of his young Students and through them the Continent." The influence of Princeton over the formation of the new government was enhanced by the prominence of Witherspoon and Boudinot, not to mention Madison, in the first days of American government following the war and the Treaty of Paris.

Although Witherspoon did not participate in the Constitutional Convention during 1787, his Scottish Enlightenment philosophy found expression through those nine Princeton graduates in attendance. The crucial committee on representation that blended the Virginia and New Jersey plans into a Senate and a House of Representatives contained five Witherspoon students. By the time the Constitution was in finished draft it resonated with the centuries of experience of Scottish skepticism about the abilities of man to govern wisely and for any government to exist when preponderant powers threatened the sovereignty of a people to govern themselves.[24]

The strength of Witherspoon's philosophical influence through his students explained the presence of an ideological consensus that could so effectively rewrite a national government in a direction far different from the democratizing currents swirling throughout the world at the time. Witherspoon's instincts left little room for faith in the ability of humans to make rational choices. This perspective blended beautifully with the similar predispositions of John Adams and set the stage for the United States to frame a counterrevolutionary governing charter at the same time the rest of the world was still marching toward revolution.

James Madison was driven by the spirit of Witherspoon throughout the 1780s to convert the ideals of the Scottish Enlightenment as transmitted by his mentor and a host of vigorous new writers—David Hume, Adam Smith, Adam Ferguson, William Robertson, James Beattie, and Dugald Stewart, among others—into concrete institutions of government. He worked between 1783 and 1786 to perfect Virginia's government and saw that the Confederation was not designed to provide those essential national services required for the states to work efficiently. Hardly had excitement over the Treaty of Paris cooled when Madison already was pushing for the establishment of interstate conferences and conventions to augment national authorities.[25]

It was not merely a sense of governmental efficiency that drove him. Linked to John Adams's way of looking at the world even more, Madison saw in the wake of the American Revolution that American ideas about republicanism and democratic government had gone awry. He was alarmed at the emergence of majoritarianism (the notion that majority votes in legislative assemblies determine everything) that had suddenly emerged. Majority rule rudely practiced was, he believed, debilitating and destructive to stable government. Changing majorities, he agreed with Adams, "forfeited the respect and confidence essential to order and good Government, involving a general decay of confidence and credit between man and man." There had to be stability, protection of property, standards of conduct and justice, continuity, and love of order for a republic to survive.

Madison, in promoting the convening of a convention to write a new national constitution, was as radical as the leaders of the National Assembly a few years later. Whereas it would become the end of French legislators to institutionalize majority rule in their national constitution, Madison's driving aim during 1786 in Annapolis and during 1787 in Philadelphia was to establish institutions that would ensure that America could never fall into the chaos of strict majority rule.

The complicated form of government devised by Madison and his fellow delegates during the summer of 1787 gave no pretense of being a democracy. It was, instead, a system of checks and balances, of delegated but encompassed powers, and of segmented authorities, not to assure that the will of the majority would prevail in America, but rather to guarantee that no one in the United States—especially a majority of citizens—should ever be in a position to control the nation.

Madison confirmed that such was his purpose just a few months after the Constitutional Convention when Edmund Randolph of Virginia suggested that there should be another convention to correct the antidemocratic tendencies of the Philadelphia document. In January 1788, Madison wrote to Randolph:

> Whatever respect may be due to the rights of private judgment,
> . . . there can be no doubt that there are subjects to which the
> capacities of the bulk of mankind are unequal, and on which

> they must and will be governed by those with whom they hap-
> pen to have acquaintance and confidence.

Writing more than a year prior to the storming of the Bastille and reflecting the same principles he would employ to rebut Jefferson's theory on the autonomy of generations, Madison showed that he was guided by a well-formed set of values, not by revolutionary events in France.[26]

Just as John Adams became a counterrevolutionary through his study of the science of government in the 1780s, James Madison underwent a conversion as he sought to apply the principles of the Scottish Enlightenment to American governance during those same years. Both of them discovered that democratic governments could not work, that there were profound inequalities among human beings, and that liberty could be achieved only by providing for order in government and society.

As Adams was guided by the principles he had unearthed, so Madison operated within the framework of ideas first taught to him by James Witherspoon and tested in the shaping of republican governments. Despite his personal friendship with Jefferson and their alliance in partisan politics, Madison was a full participant in America's counterrevolution from the 1780s until his dying days.[27]

CURIOUS SOUNDS OF FEDERALISTS

On a chilly fall morning in early November 1798, there appeared alongside one of the main roads in the town of Dedham, Massachusetts, a liberty pole—a popular form of political expression from the American Revolution forward. Beautifully crafted, the pole was topped with a liberty cap and a placard with a longer than usual inscription:

> Liberty and Equality—No Stamp Act—No Sedition—No
> Alien Bills—No Land Tax—Downfall to the Tyrants of Amer-
> ica—Peace and Retirement to the President—Long Live the
> Vice-President and the Minority—May Moral Virtue be the
> basis of Civil Government.

Mixing ideological principles and political sentiments, the author(s) of the charged label left few bases uncovered. Liberty, equality, and virtue were the energizing symbols. But everything else constituted a transitory political position; that is, no taxes, down with Federalists, away with John Adams, and up with Thomas Jefferson and his followers. And, yes, down with the Alien and Sedition Acts!

Unlike the hundreds of other liberty poles erected during the late 1790s that went unnoticed, this particular one from the first moment drew intense local and national attention. Federalist newspapers charged that this pole indicated an "outbreak of sedition," a "rallying point for the enemies of a Free Government." Another paper saw it as a harbinger "of insurrection and civil war" and "a sink of sedition and infamy." Finally, U.S. District Judge for Massachusetts, John Lowell, ordered the federal marshal "to demolish the above mentioned Symbol of

Sedition." But before the marshal arrived, "the honest zeal of the well-disposed people of the neighborhood prompted them to effect its destruction."

The dismantling of the politically offensive object was not enough to satisfy a national government that had just recently passed the Alien and Sedition Acts to silence American enemies. Under orders from John Adams and Timothy Pickering, federal attorneys laid out a vast net to identify and arrest the nay-saying culprits. Soon one Benjamin Fairbanks was arrested, charged with the crime of mounting the Dedham pole, and bound over after posting a large bail of $4,000 for trial in June 1799. Since Fairbanks was a respected citizen of Dedham, a property owner, and former town selectman, it was clear that the government was intent on demonstrating that even upstanding members of the community could be seduced into "deluded sedition."

Federal officials soon learned that the principal instigator in erecting the pole was an outside agitator by the name of David Brown. In March 1799 Brown was located in Andover, Massachusetts. There he was arrested; but when he could not post a similar bail of $4,000 he was taken to Salem, Massachusetts, where he remained in jail until trial. Brown, as it turned out, was a self-confessed political firebrand, a Connecticut native and a laborer. But he was also a Revolutionary War veteran who traveled into hundreds of communities preaching Republican politics, condemning taxes, and promoting candidates opposed to the reigning Federalists.

When Fairbanks and Brown came to trial in June 1799, Fairbanks presented "a paper to the Court in which he freely confessed his fault, stated that he had been present at the erection of the pole, but had been misled and had not known 'how serious an offence it was.'" As a result of beseeching the court for clemency, Fairbanks, upon entering a guilty plea was fined five shillings, court costs of ten shillings, and six hours of imprisonment. Brown, on the other hand, as the outside provocateur, received a severe tongue lashing from the presiding judge, Justice Samuel Chase of the U.S. Supreme Court, who,

> made some very impressive observations to Brown on the nature, malignity and magnitude of his offenses; on the vicious industry with which he had circulated and inculcated his disorganizing doctrines and impudent falsehoods, and the very alarming and dangerous excesses to which he attempted to incite the uninformed part of the community.

Although Brown proved barely literate and his political writings a jumble of inanities, Chase found Brown guilty of seditious conduct in that he used "vicious ingenuity" to "create discontent and to excite among the people hatred and opposition to their Government." He was sentenced to eighteen months in prison and fined $480.

Sixteen months after Brown had been imprisoned and a year after accomplice Fairbanks had served his six hours, he, in July 1800, appealed directly to John Adams for a pardon. Adams refused. Unable to pay his fine when he finished his full sentence in December 1800 Brown remained in prison. In February 1801, approaching two years in prison—the longest for anyone sentenced under the Sedition Law—Brown again appealed to Adams, arguing that he would never be able to pay the fine unless he was released from prison to find gainful employment. Adams again refused.[28]

On the surface it seemed that David Brown was the unfortunate victim of a national witch-hunt to stamp out insurrection, agitation, and even legitimate political opposition. John Adams appeared as a tyrant who would brook no criticism. Operating through henchmen Timothy Pickering, Samuel Chase, and even John Lowell, Adams conducted an American reign of terror to stamp out opposition or sedition—depending upon who was judging; to quiet a dangerous or hapless political agitator—depending upon the observer; and stamp out a helpless veteran of the American Revolution or an evil conspirator—depending, again, upon the adjudicator.

But there was more to the strange ordeal suffered by David Brown. During the course of his preparations for the trial, Benjamin Fairbanks asked Federalist politician and retired U.S. Senator Fisher Ames to serve as his legal counsel. Ames declined, but agreed to appear as a character witness. In court Ames testified that Fairbanks's acts resulted from a "warm and irritable temperament." All blame for the offensive liberty pole Ames placed on Brown, whom he described as a "wandering apostle of sedition." Justice Chase surely warmed to Ames, perhaps the nation's most articulate Federalist theoretician, and issued the lightest possible punishment for Fairbanks's guilty plea.[29]

But Fisher Ames was not the only Dedham Ames to testify in the Fairbanks-Brown case. Ames's older brother Nathaniel was also subpoenaed, but to testify instead on David Brown's behalf. Nathaniel Ames proved to be not so willing a witness. Twice he was summoned during the trial, and both times he refused on the grounds that the summons was not correctly served. Four months later in October 1799, he was arrested for contempt of court. Nathaniel Ames was carried kicking and screaming before the U.S. Circuit Court in Boston on October 22, as he described it, "like a felon, for pretended contempt of its process that I am not guilty of."

Nathaniel Ames, a feisty physician and considerably older brother of Fisher, was incensed by the treatment he received at the hands of Federalist judges and attorneys. After being refused copies of documents being used in his indictment, he wrote:

> I have more reason to suppose that Tiptoe novel Courts will become like the Inquisition by secreting their process and dark arbitrary vexations—the citizens ought to know how they proceed, but they yet fear the public eye. I was set among pickpocks at the Bar and was spunged of 8 dollars.

When Ames appealed the decision three weeks later, he wrote, "Judge Cushing here, refuses redress for gross injury and adds insult by referring me [for legal counsel] to F[isher] A[mes]."[30]

Fisher Ames (c. 1807). Counterrevolutionary idealogue for responsible speech in the American Republic.

The deeper one delves into the Fairbanks-Brown sedition case, the clearer it becomes that the entire case was little more than a political tug-of-war between two brothers who hated each other and among individuals choosing sides, with one of two available factions to vie for elective office. As it turned out, Nathaniel Ames loathed his brother and his Federalist associates. Although the elder Ames rarely ran for any office himself, he covertly worked with Fairbanks and Brown to advance an opposition party to unseat the very people—Adams, Pickering, Chase, Lowell, Davis, and even brother Fisher—who stomped, he believed, upon the rights of Americans.

Both Fisher and Nathaniel Ames, although principled people, were willing to overthrow their ideals to achieve political victory. That Fisher Ames should use the Alien and Sedition Acts in 1798 and 1799 to extinguish political threats contradicted his previous career of concentrating on the basic principles of governance. That Nathaniel Ames should exploit such victims as David Brown to politically upstage his brother and other hated Federalists also contravened his desire to see liberty reign supreme in America. The extent to which the older Ames toyed with Brown and left him to suffer was revealed thirteen years later when an article in the *Columbian Centinel* revealed that it was Nathaniel Ames himself who conceived the erection of the ill-fated pole and that it was he, not Brown, who wrote the offensive inscription![31]

But the Ames brothers were not alone in this struggle for power. Countless others of all political shades were trying to figure out the relationship between principles and politics, between responsibility and power, and how those dilemmas related to the desire for personal liberty and opportunity in a republic.

John Adams and James Madison found their resolutions, even though they did not necessarily make them better politicians. So did Fisher Ames and his successor in the Senate, Harrison Gray Otis. In that Nathaniel Ames spent so much of his long life—described in a diary extending from 1758 to 1822—playing essentially the dirty tricks of ward politics, it is doubtful that he made any significant contribution to the destiny of American liberty.

The first Nathaniel Ames lived only to see the first eight years of his son Fisher's life. The senior Ames, also a physician, became famous in America in 1725 as the first publisher of an American almanac—three years before James Franklin's and eight years before Benjamin Franklin's *Poor Richard's* series. Nathaniel Ames Jr. studied at Harvard, then returned to Dedham to practice medicine and publish the almanac. Always a close observer of events from the French and Indian Wars through the War of 1812, the cranky Nathaniel Ames opposed every government.[32]

Fisher Ames was the opposite: open, oratorical, always campaigning for causes or public offices. Viewed from his earliest years as gifted, he entered Harvard at age twelve and graduated at sixteen in 1774. During the stormy years of the American Revolution, he intermittently taught school, read the classics, and developed his writing skills. His only service in the war was a fifteen-day noncombatant tour of duty near home in March 1778. Between 1779 and 1781 he studied law with William Tudor, himself a student of John Adams. Launching into practice in 1781, Ames was by 1784 presented by John Lowell of the Fairbanks-Brown case, then one of Massachusetts's leading attorneys, to practice before the state supreme court.[33]

Given Fisher Ames's verbosity, it is odd that he waited until 1786 to issue his first public writing, inspired by Shays's Rebellion. Under the pseudonym of Lucius Junius Brutus, Ames addressed for the first time a topic that would absorb his interest for the entirety of his career; that is, how a republic secures the general interests of its citizens in the face of noisy factions constantly arguing that their rights had been violated. Daniel Shays's army was but the first such group to emerge following the American Revolution. Over the next twenty years, Ames witnessed many others. As a full participant in America's counter-revolution, he would explore a variety of solutions for this special problem of republics.

In his first essay Ames insisted that Daniel Shays and his followers had jeopardized the nation's governing bylaws:

> In a free government, the reality of grievances is no kind of justification of rebellion. It is hoped that our rulers will act with dignity and wisdom; that they will yield every thing to reason, and refuse every thing to force; . . . and that they will not descend to the injustice and meanness of purchasing leave to

> hold their authority by sacrificing a part of the community to
> the villainy and ignorance of the disaffected.

Ames detected a certain dishonesty on the part of the Shaysites that he hoped would be recognized by governing authorities.[34]

Observing that the "insurgents have refused the payment of taxes" and "have instituted conventions to find fault with government . . . to interfere between the precept of lawful authority, and the obedience of individuals," Ames concluded that "the existence of society is at hazard." What bothered him most was that "the insurgents, like the Hottentots, when it has been found impracticable to tame, seem prepared to renounce the institutions and duties of cultivated life." Addressing his words to the Massachusetts General Court Ames urged immediate action to quell the riot and to preserve the Constitution.

"Everything depends upon your wisdom and firmness," he charged, since the fact "cannot be concealed—our constitution is in jeopardy." The Constitution was the "work of philosophy and patriotism—it is the glory of our age and country" and the General Court had a sacred obligation to protect it. In his third essay, he concluded, "It is for you to say whether man shall fall a second time—from glory to infamy—from liberty to anarchy—from the rank of a citizen, to the wretchedness of the savage."[35]

Just as John Adams and James Madison feared anarchy arising from the abuse of power within the framework of government, Ames focused on the problem of power being exerted by factions outside government. Four months later he joined Adams, Madison, Webster, and Dwight calling for a constitutional convention. In five additional essays published between February 15 and March 15, 1787, under the pseudonym of Camillus, Ames focused on noisy minorities while calling for decisive action in Massachusetts.

In the second Camillus essay he addressed the issue of how a government that is of the people can restrain those same people. Acknowledging that "all lawful government is derived from the people" by consent, Ames argued that "if there is any government which can legitimate, and even sanctify force, it is the government which is founded on consent." He therefore argued, the "right of the Governour and General Court to suppress the rebellion, is as evident, as the right of taking a debtor's goods by execution." Indeed, the very act of establishing a constitution made "our rulers mere citizens." "They are disarmed," he continued, "by the constitution."[36]

Having addressed the matter of the people's sovereignty and the authority of constitutions and the governments that operate under them, Ames described just what was liberty. Characterizing Shays's followers as "returning to barbarism, and threatening to become fiercer than the savage children of nature," he asked how a "philosophic observer" should interpret their behavior?

> He will see them weary of liberty, and unworthy of it, arming
> their sacrilegious hands against it, though it was bought with
> their blood, and was once the darling pride of their hearts;

complaining of oppression because the law, which has not forbidden, has not also enforced cheating; endeavoring to oppose society against morality, and to associate freemen against freedom.

The philosophic observer would conclude that they had chosen anarchy: "He will call this a chaos of morals and politics, in which are floating and conflicting, not the first principles and simple elements out of which systems may be formed; . . . not the embryo, but the ruins of a world." [37]

The greatest imperfection of the American government, according to Ames—echoing Adams, Madison, Webster and others—was that it had to be operated by mortals. The revolutionary heroes "had anticipated a system of government too pure for a state of imperfection": "When they found that for the first time in the history of man, a nation was allowed by Providence to reduce to practice the schemes which Plato and Harrington had only sketched upon paper, they expected a constitution which should be perfect and perpetual." They found that they had made the constitution too democratic to work: "their admired plan of freedom of election had produced a too faithful representation of the electors." When, as governors, they had to make unpopular choices, "they were thrown into absolute despair, when they found, that not only individuals, but conventions, and other bodies of men, unknown to the Constitution, presumed to revise, and in effect to repeal, the acts of the legislature." [38]

In calling for a national constitutional convention to "amend" the Confederation, Ames was looking for a new instrument that would solve ahead of time one of the great weaknesses of the French government during the French Revolution. Not only did the revolutionary constitution not separate and place checks on the powers of branches of government or overcome the problem of faddish majoritarianism in the National Assembly, there were no shields to protect the government from being held hostage to the latest mob gathering on the streets of Paris. The Philadelphia draft constitution contained so many checks on the ability of branches of government to operate that a mob would have great difficulty deciding on whom to take hostage—the President, the Senate, the House, the Supreme Court, the secretary of war.

At the Massachusetts ratifying convention, Fisher Ames emerged as orator. His performance at the convention, combined with his probing political essays, won him a seat in 1788 in the Massachusetts General Court and in 1789 in Congress. As he moved from political philosopher to politician, he soon found that philosophy did not necessarily translate into power, law, or even governance. Just before heading into his public political career, he brawled with brother Nathaniel over their father's estate. Nathaniel, executor of the estate, had delayed settlement for twenty-three years. Their snarling agreement signed in June 1787 left them bitter enemies for life. As Fisher Ames headed to Congress, he had unwittingly just anointed the leader of his most steadfast political opposition.

When he arrived in Congress on March 4, 1789, he soon discovered that politicians rarely submitted to philosophical rules. Although their values were similar, Ames found Madison unduly cautious in taking action, fearful of upending Virginia political order (that is, not crossing Jefferson), and "very much Frenchified in his politics." The two found themselves often at odds on the details of issues differently affecting the economies of Virginia and New England.

But both Ames and Madison thought that the Philadelphia constitution of 1787 was a "comparatively perfect" document. They agreed that a bill of rights, though not essential, might be a fine addition. Ames marveled at Madison's diligence in "hunt[ing] up all the grievances and complaints of newspapers, the articles of conventions, and the small talk of their debates" to draw up potential amendments. Ames concluded that "upon the whole, [the amendments] may do some good towards quieting men, who attend to sounds only, and may get the mover [Madison] some popularity, which he wishes." His principal assistance to Madison in getting a short slate of amendments approved was in persuading the House not to sit as a committee of the whole in judgment upon them. Ames and Madison both feared a national convention that would begin to redraft the Philadelphia document.[39]

Even as the debate over a bill of rights continued in that sweet summer of liberty, Ames was whittling away at just how rights were protected and liberty might be preserved. On June 23, 1789, just a few weeks before the storming of the Bastille, Ames wrote to one of his regular correspondents about the powers of America's new national executive. In response to those opposed to giving the president any new powers, Ames flashed:

> I am commonly opposed to those who modestly assume the rank of champions of liberty, and make a very patriotic noise about the people. It is the stale artifice which has duped the world a thousand times, and yet, though detected, it is still successful. I love liberty as well as anybody. I am proud of it, as the true title of our people to distinction above others; but so are others, for they have an interest and a pride in the same thing. But I would guard it by making laws strong enough to protect it.

He favored giving the president the authorities he needed to protect liberty, because "I have no doubt of the tendency to a true aristocracy." Liberty's best chance was in the careful order wrought by an enlightened executive.[40]

The development of America's first political parties in the 1790s sent Ames and Madison in different directions politically, but their philosophical compatibility became evident—even if they were not in a position to acknowledge it. In 1793 and at the height of the French Revolution, Fisher Ames penned his most devastating critique of the position maintained by Thomas Jefferson in the earliest stages of ratifying the American constitution and in the coterminous phases of developing a French constitution. In "To Aristides" from "Bifrons Janus," Ames blamed Jefferson for the destructive direction of the French Revolution.[41]

Using public documents, Ames noted that Jefferson had "opposed the present Constitution of the United States." Citing a speech by Edmund Pendleton at the Virginia Ratification Convention in which he quoted from a Jefferson letter, Ames noted Jefferson's equivocation about the necessity of a new convention: "In short, this sagacious politician either meant to write such a letter as he thought would please both parties, not knowing then which was likely to preponderate, which indeed acounts [sic] for its having been quoted by both parties like a convenient law case." Ames charged, however, that Jefferson was explicit in his advice to the National Assembly, "who ignorant themselves of every principle of free and rational government swallowed greedily every project of our American politician and by their intemperance and fury drove out of France all those enlightened and patriotic citizens . . . who fought for a well-poised government, properly checked."

"At that time," Ames continued, "he countenanced one branch of legislation and if consistent he must have recommended the same policy to the United States in his amendments." Waxing ever more philosophical, Ames concluded, "this charge therefore is well maintained that Mr. J[efferson] is the promoter of national dissension, national insignif[ic]ance, public disorder and discredit. For the factions he has originated will, if not soon checked, end in all that." Though Ames had not the consistent logic and the irrefragable charm of Madison, he scoured Jefferson in the same manner and placed himself squarely on the counterrevolutionary side of America's political ledger.[42]

Ames in late 1793 returned to his favorite theme in a piece titled "Against Jacobins." "We have a noisy party who call themselves republicans—democrats—equality men," he proclaimed. But "they are anti-republicans, the real and truly dangerous aristocrats of our country, the very men who hate equality, and who try to rule and domineer in spite of the laws." And "they are united and they are industrious in mischief, whereas the citizens are dispersed . . . and they have other things besides politics to mind." He further wrote, "They pretend to be the advocates and watchmen for the people" and they "affect to make it an object to increase the popular influence on our government, because the will of the people is the sovereign power." But these very people "in contempt of their own declamations are the opposers of the authority of the people as expressed in their laws."[43]

The only flaw in Fisher Ames's brilliant insight was that he tended to apply it everywhere throughout his political career. At every stage from 1786 until his death in 1808, Ames identified one group after another to be discounted. First were Daniel Shays and his banditti. Next came the anti-Federalists who opposed the Constitution. Then arrived the friends of liberty in the Democratic Societies, along with Jefferson and his political following. Finally came David Brown and the emissaries of an evil conspiracy devoted to the overthrow of America.

Ames's career in politics ended in 1795 when he developed "lung fever," probably tuberculosis. He fell ill for weeks and suffered recurrences for the remainder of his life. The blow to his body and spirits was such that he had to retire from Congress in 1796 and restrict his life to Dedham. There he came under the care, at least partially, of his troublesome brother Nathaniel, who served as his faithful physician.

Despite the doctor-patient relationship, Fisher Ames's presence in Dedham merely sent brother Nathaniel into new paroxysms of political chicanery. Nathaniel took the occasion of the 1796 political campaign to announce his support of Jeffersonian Republicanism. Still bearing a hatred for Britain deriving from bitter days of the American Revolution, the older Ames began to champion Jefferson and all of those friends of liberty who stepped forward to promote democracy, freedom, and equality—Benjamin Franklin Bache, Matthew Lyon, George Logan, Thomas Cooper, and many more. His course against that of his brother was firmly set with news of Jay's Treaty, championed by the ailing Fisher Ames in virtually his last speech in Congress, but hated by Nathaniel Ames as an abandonment of the principles and purposes of the American Revolution.[44]

Though just able to write letters and occasional brief essays, Fisher Ames was not about to allow his brother or Jefferson to have free rein with the voters of Dedham. To counter his Jeffersonian brother, Ames planned a 1798 July Fourth gathering that would rekindle Federalist aspirations. He invited sixty "respectable" men to a dinner where there would be orations, songs, and toasts in honor of President John Adams and Federalism. At the elite gathering Ames presented a laudatory written address for everyone to sign and to send to Adams. Ames believed he saw the beginnings of a resurgence of Federalism in Dedham.

Nathaniel Ames was incensed by the dinner and by the actions of President Adams and Congress. Nathaniel Ames must have attended the dinner, for in his diary he wrote on the matter of signing an address to Adams, "I told them I chose to consider yet if the Gag bill etc. is cram'd down our jaws as well as Stamp Act etc.: direct taxes . . . by squeezing teazing greasing the Fed band obtain the signature of a few deluded people to a flattering address to J. Adams president—they soon repent." He considered the dinner's promoters to be "tools of F.A." He saw the Alien and Sedition Acts as the culmination of a rejection of the American Revolution: "It is amazing to see the apathy of the People under worse usurpation than that which once excited them to war." He wrote in his diary two weeks later, "Because I decently exercise the right of speech and press, like an independent Republican, my friends fear for me, while I am in no danger of being hanged for treason!"[45]

For all his brilliant political philosophy and for all of his literary and oratorical genius in alerting Americans to noisy minorities, the practical effect of Fisher Ames's constant bashing of those groups was to foment real political opposition. His endless seeking to discredit the claims of one group or another—done in the interests of protecting American liberty, but rendered with such ruthlessness—merely brought forth counterinvective and organized opposition. When the sheer force of his attack failed to bring silence, he and his colleagues were not averse to rejecting that very freedom of speech that was so preciously won in the American Revolution. The feud between Fisher and Nathaniel Ames was symptomatic of all America in 1798. Their nasty struggle for village power illustrated just how far the nation had retreated from the heritage of the American Revolution.

RIGHT AND RIGHTS IN THE REPUBLIC

Probably no one in America had a greater knowledge of the correct heritage of the American Revolution than Fisher Ames's successor in Congress, Harrison Gray Otis. When it came to pedigree and preparation for leadership, it would have been difficult for anyone to match Otis's qualifications. His first and middle names came from his maternal grandfather, Harrison Gray, one of Boston's most successful merchants and long-term treasurer of Massachusetts. The only problem was that Grandfather Gray, at the outset of the American Revolution, sided with Parliament and departed with the large flotilla of Loyalists who fled Boston on March 17, 1776.

But whatever shortage of revolutionary ardor there was on the Gray side of the family was more than accounted for on the Otis column. His grandfather, Col. James Otis, served from 1748 as Massachusetts attorney general and was an opposition member of the Governor's Council at the time of the American Revolution. His son, James Otis Jr., "The Patriot," was Harrison's famous uncle who in 1764 and 1765 published two critical pamphlets that played directly into the oncoming revolution. *The Rights of the British Colonies Asserted and Proved* and *Vindication of the British Colonies* set the stage for Americans to claim their rights in the Stamp Act Congress of 1765. James Jr. represented Massachusetts at that meeting, which opened on October 7, one day prior to Harrison Gray Otis's birth.

Otis's own father, Samuel Allyne Otis, a Harvard graduate who eschewed law to become a merchant, and another uncle, Joseph Otis, contributed not so much to the coming of the American Revolution as to its prosecution. Samuel employed his ships and mercantile expertise to carry goods to support, equip, and clothe the American army. Joseph maintained the family estate at Barnstable, while also serving as fighting brigadier general of the local militia. Joseph was decorated and awarded a permanent sinecure as collector of the port of Falmouth, on Cape Cod. Samuel was elected to Congress in 1787 and, while serving there, fell in love with legislative proceedings. With the help of Vice President John Adams in his capacity as president of the Senate, Samuel Otis was appointed secretary of the Senate in 1790, a post he retained until his death in 1814.

If Harrison Gray Otis was linked directly to the coming of the American Revolution and to its successful prosecution, he also was directly connected to the memory of the war and its causes. Through his father's sister, Mercy Otis Warren, he was united with an individual who made it her lifelong business to remember and to record every detail of the Revolution. It was as if Harrison Gray Otis had inherited an encyclopedia of the war and its living conscience. Many knew the swift justice of history meted out by Mercy Warren—including John Adams, Thomas Jefferson, and even nephew Harrison Gray Otis.

Although his father Samuel aspired to send Harrison to Middle Temple in London to study law, Harrison had to settle for an American education. He entered Boston Latin School at age eight in 1773. All was well until the family had to evacuate from Boston in 1775 during nearly a year of British occupation.

Harrison Gray Otis (1809). Boston Brahmin attorney
and scourge of alien Americans.

In the fall of 1776 he returned to school until 1779, when his mother died suddenly, brokenhearted over the loss of her father in the clash of loyalties aroused by the war. Before the boy could recover from that blow, his father enrolled him at age thirteen at Harvard.

Following on a track remarkably similar to that of Fisher Ames, Otis completed his four-year stint at Harvard in 1783. Though classes were small and resources limited, Otis received a solid grounding in history, philosophy, literature, science, and the languages. Indeed, his French instructor during his senior year was Albert Gallatin, a twenty-one-year-old graduate of the University of Geneva who rose to become one of America's most powerful leaders alongside Jefferson, Madison, and Monroe. Just as Ames graduated with top honors in his class, so did Otis, giving him the right to present the graduating address, which he titled, "An English Oration upon the American Revolution, and the Happy Prospects Arising from the Peace now Restored to these United States."

From 1783 to 1786, Otis studied law under the tutelage of the same John Lowell who ordered the arrest and trial of Benjamin Fairbanks and David Brown in Dedham, Massachusetts. Lowell took Otis along on trips to New York and Philadelphia, introducing him to people who would become his colleagues and adversaries in a meteoric political career. At the end of his training, Otis entered the realm of admiralty and maritime law, areas that pervaded the courts in ports such as Boston.

In January 1785, he and several of his friends formed an association called the "Sans Souci Club," devoted to monthly bouts of card playing, dancing, and carousing. It soon drew the attention of those who thought they had rather won America for reading, contemplation, work, and rational discussion. When Samuel Adams published an attack on the club, calling it a gambling hall and an affront to republican institutions, Otis responded under the pseudonym of Sans Souci, drawing the direct fire of Mercy Otis Warren, who described him as "a youth of genius and fire, and I hope he will always have self command to temper discretion with wit."

Like Fisher Ames, Harrison Gray Otis was rocked by the rebellion of Daniel Shays and his followers. He first offered to lead, as their captain, a volunteer militia company, the Independent Light Infantry. In January 1787 he volunteered his company to serve as long as needed to suppress the rebellion, but they were never called to serve. Unlike Ames, he left no record of his reaction to the rebellion. Given to expressing his opinions in public, however, he was invited to present the July Fourth address in 1788 in Boston. In New York on April 30, 1789, he witnessed the inauguration of George Washington as president and his father as secretary to the Senate.[46]

Between 1789 and 1796, Otis was busy earning a living from law and real estate transactions and establishing himself as one of Boston's leading business and social leaders. He was not directly engaged in politics until 1794, when he ran for a seat in the Massachusetts General Court. In April 1796 he made a strong appearance at a Boston town meeting in favor of Jay's Treaty. In an animated speech at the end of the turbulent meeting, Otis openly attacked his former French instructor, Albert Gallatin, then Republican leader in Congress, as "a vagrant foreigner" who "ten years ago came to this Country without a second shirt to his back." That speech won him an appointment a month later as U.S. district attorney for Massachusetts.

Although Otis was not an insider in the ultraconservative Essex Junto—a group of politically active merchant-shipowners and lawyers from Essex County who dominated Federalist politics until 1815—he was unanimously selected by Massachusetts Federalists to be Ames's successor. He was elected on November 7, 1796, on the same ballot that made John Adams president. The political and historical fates of Adams and Harrison Gray Otis became inextricably intertwined.

Although the Essex Junto doubted that Otis could live up to Fisher Ames's standards, Otis did not delay long in demonstrating his firm adherence to the counterrevolutionary principles preached by Ames. Just a week after the opening of his first session in Congress, Otis jumped headlong into the political fray. In debates on America's relations with France and French attacks on American ships, Otis set forth his attitude on recent history:

> There was a time when I was animated with enthusiasm in favor of the French Revolution, and I cherished it, while civil liberty appeared to be the object; but I now consider that Revolution as completely achieved, and the war is continued—not

for liberty, but for conquest and aggrandizement, to which I do
not believe it is the interest of this country to contribute.

The French Revolution, Otis continued, had launched a subversive "tide of conquest" that "may swell the great Atlantic and roll towards our shores, bringing upon its troubled surface the spirit of revolution." He feared that the revolution might "spread like a pestilence, possibly in the Southern States, and excite a war of the most dreadful kind—of slaves against their masters, and thereby endanger the existence of that Union so dear to my constituents."

In that speech Otis made such a splash that one observer, Supreme Court Justice James Iredell from North Carolina, wrote to Oliver Wolcott, "Mr Otis' speech has excited nearly as warm emotions as Mr. Ames' celebrated one, on the treaty. . . I confess, much as I expected from him, [it] far exceeds my expectations."[47]

But there was something ominous about his words and his style. Whereas Ames had talked about disruptive minorities dishonestly seeking power, Otis was pursuing something completely different. He was talking about subversive forces operating in silence. And for some reason that does not fit with any of his background, he linked the potential for revolutionary subversion in America with an uprising of slaves. It is true that news had just recently arrived of American William Tate's ill-fated invasion of Britain while in a French uniform. And there were rumors that Tate's forces just as easily could have been directed to the West Indies or to Louisiana. But Otis's graphic unity of subversion, conspiracy, and slave uprising brought a new element into the national consciousness.[48]

These became defining themes in his speeches, letters, and writings from that moment to the end of his long political career fifty years later. In a pamphlet issued a few months later, Otis continued on the theme that France "shall be confirmed in the belief that our internal divisions, and blind infatuation in her favor, will enable her, if not to conquer, at least to divide the Union." And "in the manufacture of the rights of man" France seemed to be willing to use every conceivable tool: "Spies, emissaries, exclusive patriots, and the honest but deluded mass of the people, are the tools with which, in other countries, she carves revolutions out of the rough material."

"Already their Geographers, with the scale and dividers," Otis continued, "mark out, on the Map of America, her future circles, departments and municipalities." Already the Bonapartes and Bernadottes of France were "planning future triumphs; here with the army of the Mississippi and Ohio; there with the army of the Chesapeake and Delaware." He was convinced that the end for America was near: "Can you, Sir, seriously doubt of their [French] hopes and expectations that Georgia, the Carolinas and Virginia will pass under their yoke? That they have an eye upon a Cis Appalachian as well as upon a Trans Appalachian Republic?" Otis wrote to his wife about the same date that the only hope for America lay with Great Britain. "Should Great Britain be compelled to yield," he scribbled, "it is my opinion that our liberties and independence would fall a sacrifice. She is the only barrier to the dreadful deluge."

Whereas Fisher Ames had ranted from 1786 through 1796 about irresponsible factions and made Americans alert to their character, he did not during his term in office propose measures for silencing them. It became the task of his successor to define means for controlling not only irresponsible factions, but also individuals and groups perceived as being subversive against the nation and its government. For the first of two moments, Harrison Gray Otis stepped onto the firing line and joined forces with John Adams and Thomas Pickering.

There were major drawbacks to defining controls over subversion during the years of the Adams presidency. The chief problem was the charged nature of the atmosphere—politically, diplomatically, militarily, and economically. Emotions ran so high, fears were so great, and perceptions so distorted that the sanest of individuals would have had difficulty charting a path. A second problem was that John Adams was a poor administrator. His laissez-faire approach to the presidency left cabinet officers and vice presidents wreaking havoc with national policy, laws, and administrative implementation.

A third problem was James Madison's absence from the nation's capital. Without Madison there to guide the development of new laws and uses of the Constitution in the manner he had conceived—protecting rights within bounds and allowing authorities to balance each other—the nation lacked the careful and experienced architect of the American republic. Just as Madison was the honored father of the Constitution, he was also heart of the counterrevolution that was reacting to the French Revolution and the military chaos in Europe.

Otis rushed into the vacuum. His first charges about the subversive French influence were issued only a week after Madison left Philadelphia. Two months later he projected that France would sever the union and foment slave revolts. On July 1, 1797, he proposed a tax of twenty dollars on each certificate of naturalization issued by the U.S. State Department. Such a plan, he urged, would augment the nation's revenues and bring order to the process.

In a letter to his wife, however, Otis acknowledged his real intent: "If some means are not adopted to prevent the indiscriminate admission of wild Irishmen & others to the right of suffrage, there will soon be an end to liberty and property." When members of the House revealed the bill's purpose, Otis responded:

> The Amendment will not affect those men who already have lands in this country, nor the deserving part of those who may seek an asylum in it. Persons of that description can easily pay the tax; but it will tend to foreclose the mass of vicious and disorganizing characters who can not live peaceably at home, and who, after unfurling the standard of rebellion in their own countries, may come hither to revolutionize ours. . . . I do not wish to invite hordes of wild Irishmen, nor the turbulent and disorderly of all parts of the world, to come here with a view to disturb our tranquility, after having succeeded in the overthrow of their own Governments.

Otis's bill failed to pass. But it revealed the tenor of his mind at a critical moment in American history. And it excited an angry reaction from Irish-Americans and other friends of liberty. One of them, "Citizen" John D. Burk, wrote: "Mr. Otis, if you can succeed in overthrowing the wild English government in Ireland, I will engage that sufficient charms will be found in Ireland to keep its wild men at home."

The tension-filled 1798 Congressional session opened with House member Matthew Lyon from Vermont spitting in fellow-member Roger Griswold's face. As Lyon befitted the kind of wild Irishman he considered anathema in America, Otis supported Lyon's expulsion from Congress. Otis charged that he "would challenge anyone to show so shameful an act of assault and battery committed without provocation at any former period or in any country. . . . It would not be suffered in a brothel or in a den of robbers!" The expulsion vote, of course, failed the two-thirds majority needed, handing Otis a second, but momentary setback.

Lyon's attempted expulsion and the following scuffle on the floor of the House opened one of the most bizarre years in the history of America. During 1798 the counterrevolutionary spirit then in ascendancy promoted the most extravagant measures in American history to secure order in government and society. The Naturalization Act enacted in June by Congress far surpassed Otis's bill from a year earlier. Although it required immigrants to wait nineteen years before they could become citizens, Otis pressed unsuccessfully to include a provision that would preclude the foreign-born from ever becoming eligible to hold elective office or to vote.

Feeling under siege, Otis led the way in getting control of America's alien population. In Congress he thundered:

> In my humble opinion, there is greater danger from this source
> [aliens] than from any other. I believe that it has been owing to
> this cause that all the Republics in Europe have been laid pros-
> trate in the dust; it is this system which has enabled the French
> to overleap all natural and artificial obstructions; to subjugate
> Holland and Italy, to destroy the Helvetic Confederacy, and to
> force a passage through rocks and mountains, which have been
> for ages sacred to the defense of liberty.

Throughout Europe "secret corruptions and foreign influence had completed their work." Whole nations "upon the slightest shock . . . crumbled into fragments" as "foreign agents and domestic traitors vaulted into place and power."

Otis savored the Sedition Act of July 14 that gave the federal government authority to bring charges against persons speaking or writing "with intent to defame" the president or Congress or to bring them "into contempt or disrepute." Otis gave the principal Federalist rationale for the strange measure that openly mocked the First Amendment of the Constitution. With regard to whether the Constitution allowed Congress to enact such a law, Otis argued:

> It must be allowed that every independent government has a
> right to preserve and defend itself against injuries and outrages
> which endanger its existence; for, unless it has this power, it is
> unworthy of the name of a free government, and must either
> fall, or be subordinate to some other protection.

Otis further argued that the law would not affect freedom of the press other than
to curb its excesses. The law would not censor speech; it would only make the
speaker liable for what he or she said or wrote.[49]

Otis was plying some of the most treacherous waters in the construction and
operation of a republic. He was attempting to deal with a matter that society
could not overlook. And the solution he and his fellow Federalists developed was
as messy as those employed by later Congresses in other seasons athwart Civil
War, World War, and Cold War.

But it was the first instance under the Constitution with a gloriously won Bill
of Rights, and it seemed, both in concept and with certainty, in execution to scorn
American pretensions of liberty. It dealt with a critical definition of constitutional
powers, but the timing of the debate, the flow of international events, and the
method of implementation assured that it would be remembered as one of the
saddest days in the history of American liberty.

It did not help that Otis's predecessor in office used the Sedition Act to stab
at a spiteful brother and his friends who thought a liberty pole in Dedham, Massachusetts, was a good way to express their opinions. It did not help that Otis and
his associates used the same law to put Matthew Lyon in prison when they could
not put him out of Congress. Nor did it help that the law was used to silence a
group of editors and friends of liberty—Benjamin Franklin Bache, Thomas
Cooper, and others—who were identified with the matter of liberty itself. The
Federalists, in their ardor to bring order to society, mixed too much political philosophy and raw power with politics. And as a result they reaped the whirlwind.

The clearest indication that Otis and his colleagues had gone astray was that
James Madison—heart and soul of the American Counterrevolution—disagreed
with this latest effort to define the operations of the new American republic.
Prompted in part by Vice President Thomas Jefferson, Madison drafted a resolution for the consideration of the Virginia Assembly declaring the Alien and Sedition Acts to be unconstitutional. Madison wrote anonymously for the use of Virginia that both acts were "a deliberate, palpable, and dangerous exercise of
powers not granted by the said compact." In the resolution he also argued that the
states "who are parties thereto, have the right and are in duty bound to interpose
for arresting the progress of the evil, and for maintaining within their respective
limits the authorities, rights, and liberties appertaining to them." He concluded
his draft with an invitation for other states to join Virginia in declaring the acts
unconstitutional and in "maintaining unimpaired the authorities, rights and liberties reserved to the States respectively, or to the people."[50]

Interestingly, his resolution, quickly adopted and published as the position
of Virginia, promised to be another useful tool for the official expression of

opinion in the republic. But before its effect could be played out, Jefferson drafted his own resolution on the same subject for the Kentucky General Assembly. Jefferson wanted to use the new constitutional ploy to have Kentucky declare the Alien and Sedition Acts "unauthoritative, void, and of no force" in the state of Kentucky—as he described it, "a nullification of the act." Jefferson had actually attempted to add similar wording to Madison's Virginia draft, but Madison had caught the changes between the introduction and the final passage of the resolution.

Madison did not see Jefferson's Kentucky resolution until after it was passed, considerably tempered by the Kentucky Assembly. But the language about nullification muddied a brilliant strategy on Madison's part to devise another check on an abuse of power by Congress and the president. When other states did not follow the examples of Virginia and Kentucky, Jefferson planned a second round of protests for those two states: They would threaten to detach themselves from the Union if the offensive laws were not annulled. Hearing indirectly of Jefferson's new tactic—politically inspired through and through—Madison raced to Monticello to dissuade the vice president from endorsing either nullification or secession as legitimate recourses under the Constitution.[51]

Recognizing "a habit in Mr. Jefferson, as in others of great genius, of expressing in strong and round terms impressions of the moment," Madison spent the next year trying to keep Jefferson from repeating the Federalists' political blunders. When the angry Federalists learned of Jefferson's authorship of the Kentucky Resolution, they roundly trashed his protest and threw out Madison's cautious plan with it. Sensing that the political jumble was such that his constitutional stratagem would be lost to history and would instead be read as an appendix to Jefferson's second great defiance, Madison explained his ploy in the *Virginia Report of 1800*. There he described in great detail what was wrong with the Alien and Sedition Acts and the meaning and purpose of the Virginia Resolution. Thirty years later he would have to explain it again, making excuses for Jefferson's brashness on matters constitutional.[52]

Regrettably for the American Counterrevolution, the matter of how to deal with dissenters—political, social, ideological, behavioral—was handled very badly during the first years of the republic under the Constitution. Even the clearest thinking and the foremost philosophers of the Counterrevolution could not be turned from the practice. Eventually organized political parties absorbed much of the venom, but the inability of the nation's first leaders to distinguish between opposition and subversion, consultation and conspiracy, protest and revolution, rent a gaping hole in the fabric of the republic.

Harrison Gray Otis stumbled his way through 1798 and beyond. Upon seeing the way his legislative handiwork was being used by the Essex Junto and other hardline Federalists, he began to moderate the differences between his political philosophy and practice of politics. In October 1798 the Essex Junto dispatched him to visit his most exceptional constituent, John Adams, to explain to the president "how much his frankness exposes himself and his friends." This Otis did on October 28 to useful effect.[53]

Through the visit a new bond was developed between the congressman and the president. When Adams chose peace, not war, with France in 1799, Otis was one of few Federalists to endorse the president. He also wrote a series of articles in April 1799 under the title "The Envoy," published in *J. Russel's Gazette,* promoting Adams's policy of peace.

For all of his odd behavior—acting on the basis of philosophy and beliefs, not political popularity—Adams was skewered by the Federalist Party at reelection time in 1800. Federalists threw their support to Charles Cotesworth Pinckney, almost assuring the election of their greatest enemy, Thomas Jefferson, as president.

As for Otis, he had had enough of politics, enough of the national capital, and enough internecine political warfare. He headed home to Boston. While defeated neighbor John Adams brooded for the next quarter century over his victories and failures, Otis had another half century in which to examine the relationship between his principles and his politics and in which to show that time little changed his devotion to the American Counterrevolution.

CHAPTER 23

The Most Radical Counterrevolutionary

In early May 1791, Thomas Paine's pirated copy of *The Rights of Man* was published in Philadelphia bearing what appeared to be the warm endorsement of Thomas Jefferson, the author of the Declaration of Independence.[1] In a letter extracted as a preface to the first American edition of *The Rights of Man,* Jefferson congratulated the publisher for printing the piece so that "something is at length to be publicly said against the political heresies which have sprung up among us. . . . I have no doubt [that] our citizens will rally a second time round the standard of Common Sense." Just as Jefferson had transferred some of the rhetoric of Paine's *Common Sense* into the Declaration of Independence in 1776, the two crusaders for liberty, freedom, and equality here seemed again united.[2]

The endorsement was characteristic of Thomas Jefferson, who was always championing calls for liberty. Wherever he lived and no matter his circumstance, he could be counted upon to endorse those who spoke the language of liberty, freedom, and equality. He did so in the context of the American Revolution, as lead attorney in revising the laws of Virginia between 1777 and 1779, and as governor of Virginia between 1779 and 1781. Laws of entail were repealed, primogeniture abolished, the establishment of religion ended, and trial by jury guaranteed. In his "Autobiography" written late in life, but from contemporary letters, he recounted the hundreds of times he reinforced revolutionary efforts.[3]

During his five-year tenure as American minister to France from 1784 until 1789, he observed the failures of the Confederation Congress and called for a constitutional convention to strengthen the national government and to establish executive and judiciary functions to balance against the legislative authorities of the Congress. Yet when he obtained a copy of the draft constitution in November 1787, he blasted James Madison for allowing a document with such fundamental flaws to be produced. It did not contain an enumeration of individual rights. Nor did it provide term limits for presidents and other officers of the new government. His expressed concerns about the absence of a "bill of rights" to Madison and to George Washington contributed significantly toward the way Virginia handled its ratification of the constitution and to Madison's creation of such a manifesto in the first Congress under the constitution.[4]

But he was also working with French leaders—particularly Lafayette—to secure for France its own constitution and bill of rights. He thought that "the American Revolution seems first to have awakened the thinking part of the French nation in general, from the sleep of despotism." Jefferson was enthralled by the passage from the Assembly of Notables to the creation of provincial assemblies, from the meeting of the Estates-General to the creation of the National Assembly, and by the transition from general reform to revolution itself.

Jefferson raced from Paris to Versailles daily to attend the debates of the Estates-General, and he was alarmed by Louis XVI's actions, locking out the National Assembly and forcing a showdown between the Third Estate and the entrenched nobles and clergy. Jefferson, "much acquainted with the leading patriots of the Assembly," intervened and "urged, most strenuously, an immediate compromise to secure what the government [of Louis XVI] was now ready to yield." He enumerated the rights that the king should recognize, among them, habeas corpus, freedoms of conscience and the press, trial by jury, and representative legislature.

The crisis was averted when Louis XVI urged the clergy and nobles to join the Third Estate, and the National Assembly continued with the business of making a constitution. But whereas the United States received a constitution and then a bill of rights, the National Assembly, with Jefferson's encouragement, started "first, and as Preliminary to the whole, [with] a general Declaration of the Rights of Man." A draft declaration, prepared with Jefferson's assistance, was introduced into the Assembly by Lafayette. Between July 8, when the Assembly began its constitutional work, and August 26, when it issued a completed Declaration of the Rights of Man and Citizen, Jefferson did for France what his friend Madison was doing simultaneously for the United States.

Jefferson, as American minister to France, could not intervene directly in the proceedings of the National Assembly. He therefore declined an invitation from the archbishop of Bordeaux, chairman of the Assembly's Committee on the Constitution, "requesting me to attend and assist at their deliberations." But he did not refuse on August 25 when Lafayette informed him "that he should bring a party of six or eight friends to ask a dinner of me the next day" to resolve some of the main principles of the constitution. The discussions began around Jefferson's dinner table at four in the afternoon and continued until ten at night. As Jefferson recalled it, he sat as

> a silent witness to a coolness and candor of argument, unusual in the conflicts of political opinion; to a logical reasoning and chaste eloquence, disfigured by no gaudy tinsel of rhetoric or declamation, and truly worthy of being placed in parallel with the finest dialogues of antiquity, as handed to us by Xenophon, by Plato and Cicero.

"This Concordate," Jefferson later wrote, "decided the fate of the Constitution." Earlier on that very day the Declaration of the Rights of Man and the Citizen— perhaps the crowning achievement of the French Revolution—had emerged

Thomas Jefferson (c. 1785). Patron of American liberty; father of American inequality.

bearing distinct shadows of Jeffersonian influence. Before the gathering at Jefferson's house ended, he and his guests had come to an agreement on the principles of a constitution that would convert France into a republic.[5]

Jefferson's persistent championing of the rights of man did not end with his sojourn in France. Upon his arrival in the United States in November 1789, he learned that George Washington wished him to become America's first secretary of state. Although Jefferson had hoped to participate further in the dramatic events in France, he accepted the office—one of only three cabinet posts in the new American government. No sooner had he arrived in New York in March 1790 than he found that the nation's governing elite had departed from or perhaps had forgotten the American Revolution. "Politics were the chief topic," he wrote, "and a preference of kingly over republican government was evidently the favorite sentiment." He continued, "I found myself, for the most part, the only advocate on the republican side of the question."

Alexander Hamilton, virtually in charge of the government, "was not only a monarchist, but for a monarchy bottomed on corruption." Vice President John Adams "had originally been a republican, [but] the glare of royalty and nobility, during his mission to England, had made him believe their fascination a necessary ingredient in government." Nor could President Washington be depended upon to promote republicanism and the rights of man. He merely kept the Hamiltons and the Adamses in check by "the dread of his honesty, his firmness, his patriotism, and the authority of his name."

It was left to Jefferson—as he portrayed it to his dying day—to save the nation from what he called "liberticide"—the abolition of the rights of man. He did it as best he could inside the Washington administration. But when he left, "the federalists got the unchecked hold of General Washington." And when Washington retired, leaving the American government in the hands of Adams, they "mounted on the car of State and free from control . . . drove headlong and wild" to destroy American liberties. They used the "horrors of the French Revolution, then raging . . . as a raw head and bloody bones" to justify "their stratagems of X. Y. Z. . . . their tales of tub-plots, ocean massacres, bloody buoys, and pulpit lyings and slanderings, and maniacal ravings . . . to spread alarm into all but the firmest breasts."

Through it all, however, Jefferson led an "unyielding opposition of those firm spirits who sternly maintained their post in defiance of terror, until their fellow citizens could be aroused to their own danger, and rally and rescue the standard of the constitution." Operating as an outsider, even though he was vice president of the nation, Jefferson joined hands with like minds to vanquish "federalism and monarchism" from America. Looking back years later, Jefferson savored his victory of 1800 by stating that "we may now truly say, we are all republicans, all federalists" and "that the motto of the standard to which our country will forever rally, will be, 'federal union, and republican government.'" By this he meant that the rights of man had been saved by the rise—or, as he would say, the preservation of republicanism. Through such republicanism—by which he became president in 1800—the rights of man fought for in the American Revolution could be savored by its citizens.[6]

But as Jefferson issued new and more powerful declarations of the rights of man, he began in 1785 to publish a different set of declarations that had an equally decisive effect on modifying who in America could enjoy those inalienable rights. His preparation of these declarations began in 1780, just four years after the Declaration of Independence, when he enthusiastically responded to a questionnaire circulated among the states by François Barbe-Marbois, secretary of the French legation at Philadelphia.

It was Barbe-Marbois's purpose to gather useful information about individual American states to expand French commerce among them. Jefferson took the questionnaire as "a good occasion" to assess the history, culture, racial composition, resources, problems, and opportunities of his native state—in the light of the Revolution and in the context of a newly independent nation. "I am at present busily employed for Monsr. Marbois," Jefferson reported on November 30, 1780, "and have to acknolege [sic] to him the mysterious obligation for making me much better acquainted with my own country than I ever was before."

Due to further events of the Revolution and to Jefferson's penchant for revision, the project extended over a period of four years. He did not return to it until the end of his governorship of Virginia in June 1781. By December he wrote Barbe-Marbois a letter with "imperfect" answers to the queries. At the same time he circulated copies among his friends, asking for comments and suggestions for improvements. As many of these expressed interest in having a copy of the final revision, Jefferson in the winter of 1783–1784 further revised it while in Philadelphia at the Confederation Congress. When he left for France in the summer of 1784, he carried a final version "swelled nearly to treble bulk" over the version he had sent to Barbe-Marbois.

His intent was to have a limited edition printed to be circulated among friends and selected diplomats in France and Europe. With Benjamin Franklin's help, he persuaded famous French printer Philippe-Denis Pierres to print the piece for one-fourth the cost of doing it in Philadelphia. By early May 1785 the manuscript titled *Notes on the State of Virginia* appeared in a modest "private" edition of two hundred copies without the author's name on the title page. He quietly distributed it to friends and colleagues, although he wrote to Madison that he hoped to place a copy in the hands of every student at the College of William and Mary.

His efforts to keep the project private—at least initially—were lost when some of his recipients declared their intentions of printing versions to be distributed publicly in both Europe and America. Jefferson averted the plans of one French bookseller to publish a translation by commissioning Abbé Morellet to prepare an authorized French version. Morellet's text, which Jefferson ultimately thought was a "bad French translation," appeared in February 1787, with Jefferson's initials on the title page. Jefferson had already selected London publisher John Stockdale to do the "definitive" English version of the work. When it was completed in July 1787, in a print run of a thousand copies, Jefferson was already contemplating a private distribution and a public sale of the book in the United States. Although American newspaper editors soon published excerpts from the Stockdale English edition, the entire manuscript was not printed until a pirated edition appeared in 1788 in Philadelphia.[7]

Since no complete American edition was available to the general public until 1788, *Notes on Virginia* had little or no effect on discussions of the slave trade or slavery at the Constitutional Convention. Nor was it widely available during the state ratification debates that occurred during the winter and spring of 1787 and 1788. But between June 25, 1788, when Virginia became the ninth and deciding state to ratify the Constitution, and February 1790, when the first Congress discussed slavery and the slave trade, *Notes on Virginia* achieved a wide circulation.[8]

Thus when Jefferson arrived in New York in March 1790 to take up his post as the first secretary of state of the United States, his views on slavery and race as articulated in *Notes on Virginia* were being hailed from every corner. As he walked into the halls of Congress, James Jackson of Georgia and William Loughton Smith from South Carolina were holding forth, citing letter and verse from the *Notes on Virginia* to uphold slavery.

"On the principle of emancipation this question arises," shouted Jackson. "What is to be done with the slaves when freed? Two propositions present themselves. Either by incorporating them with the class of citizens or by colonizing them—one or the other of those alternatives must be carried into execution."

And, why must they, Jackson continued:

> Mr. Jefferson, our secretary of state (speaking in his notes on Virginia) on the first head, declares it to be impolitic. I know not, Sir, whether I accurately deliver his words; but as well as my memory serves me they are, that 'deep rooted prejudices entertained by the whites—ten thousand recollections by the blacks of injuries they have sustained—new provocations—the real distinctions which nature has made, and many other circumstances would divide us into parties, and produce convulsions which would never end but with the extermination of the one or the other race.' To these he adds, physical and moral objections, as the difference of colour, and so forth.

"Sir," Jackson concluded his citation, "the observations of this learned gentleman are not merely theoretical—We are taught the truth and justice of them by experience." [9]

Smith made equally good use of the recently published views of Jefferson. He read extracts directly from *Notes on Virginia* "proving that negroes were by nature an inferior race of beings; and that the whites would always feel a repugnance at mixing their blood with that of the blacks." Thus, Smith deduced, "that respectable author [Jefferson], who was desirous of countenancing emancipation, was on a consideration of the subject induced candidly to avow that the difficulties appeared insurmountable." Besides, Smith harangued, "the author already quoted, has proved that they are an inferior race even to the Indians." [10]

The next speaker, Elias Boudinot of New Jersey, expressed shock at the sentiments voiced by Jackson and Smith. He admonished Congress to remember the principles of the American Revolution, still not seven years past: "When gentlemen attempt to justify this unnatural traffic, or to prove the lawfulness of slavery, they should advert to the genius of our government and the principles of the revolution." He then cited Jefferson's words, but from a different writ. He reminded the members of Congress of "the language of America in [its] day of distress," July 4, 1776: "We hold these truths to be self-evident: that all men are created equal; that they are endowed by their creator, with certain unalienable rights; that among these are life, liberty, and the pursuit of happiness." [11]

In the space of twenty-four months since its first public appearance in America, a new text of literature had taken its place as a permanent fixture in the imaginations of leaders. Written by the man revered everywhere as the author of the most inspired words about liberty, *Notes on the State of Virginia* would achieve in America as it did abroad the same kind of instant authority that early Christians gave a new epistle from St. Paul.

As obscurantist-sounding as was its title, *Notes on Virginia* had the potential of inspiring the revolution that grew out of the former American colonies and was presently being played out in France and Europe or of subverting the march of liberty. Or, like Burke's *Reflections on the Revolution in France,* Noah Webster's *Sketches of American Policy,* Adams's *Defense of Constitutions,* or Chateaubriand's *Genius of Christianity,* it could have ordained a counterrevolutionary course to achieve liberty through order.

Just as those treatises established the positions of their authors in an age of revolution, *Notes on Virginia* defined where Jefferson—alongside Franklin, America's most renowned friend of liberty—ultimately fit in the broader scale of American and world revolution.

A clue for understanding the impact of *Notes on Virginia* on future discussions of liberty—and particularly on race and slavery—was evident in the first Congress in March 1790. Having heard three speakers quote Jefferson to promote and then attack liberty, to oppose and then defend slavery, to prove black racial inferiority and then praise the abilities of blacks as long as they were slaves, Pennsylvania representative Thomas Scott spoke prophetically: "What is finally done in Congress at this time, will in some degree form the political character of America on the subject of slavery. What is said will form the characters of the speakers, and what is done will in a degree form the character of the American people on this subject." He added ruefully, "I perceive that most of the arguments advanced on this occasion have gone against the emancipation of such as are already slaves in America."

Scott could not help noting the strange character of these proceedings against the backdrop of the American Revolution:

> An advocate for slavery, in its fullest latitude, at this age of the world, and on the floor of the American Congress too, is, with me, a phenomenon in politics; yet such advocates have appeared, and many arguments have been advanced on that head, to all which I will answer only by calling upon . . . every person who has heard them, to believe them if they can! With me they defy, yea, mock all belief.

As much as he could not believe it, the fervor of the American Revolution—when it came to the matter of slavery and the rights of black Americans—was coming to an abrupt end.[12]

And why would these proceedings have such a profound effect on America's dealings with slavery and race and, indeed, on the future of liberty itself? They came less than a month before the death of Benjamin Franklin, when it first could be seen that the pendulum of liberating revolution was giving sway to a counterrevolution toward order. Behind this universal sweep of history, two particulars held ominous forebodings for liberty in America. First, after all of the gnashing of teeth in Congress that March of 1790, the body acting as a Committee of the Whole concluded "That Congress have no authority to interfere in the emancipation of slaves, or in the treatment of them within any of the States; it remaining with the several States alone to provide any regulations therein, which humanity and true policy may require." In other words, the national deliberative body in the United States, the Congress, did not have the authority—as did the British Parliament or the French National Assembly (both of which would outlaw slavery)—either to regulate or to abolish slavery. This meant in practice that there would be at least as many systems of slavery in America as there were states.[13]

The second particular was in many ways more ominous than the first. Into these debates was introduced Jefferson's *Notes on Virginia* as a new authority that would, as Congressman Scott feared, establish the terms of nearly all future debates about slavery, race, and liberty itself in America. Coming as it did, *Notes on Virginia*, in essence, gave a blessing to discussions, views, and beliefs that were contrary to the liberating principles of the American Revolution. Before the appearance of the odd little book, opinions on race and slavery were discussed mainly in hushed terms, guardedly kept in the bounds of liberating principles. After the book appeared, the boundaries of liberty had been broken. License was given to the free expression of opinions that contradicted the brief history of liberty, freedom, equality, and the rights of man unleashed by the American Revolution.

Notes on the State of Virginia was counterrevolutionary through and through. It was without a doubt the most important treatise of the American Counterrevolution, and Jefferson became the most influential character of that counterrevolution. Once known as one of the firmest friends of liberty, after publishing the book, Jefferson could be viewed only as the world's leading doubter of the "self-evident truths" he himself had set forth. He not only questioned those truths, he dared to articulate his views publicly and to teach Americans for generations to come exactly how to articulate those doubts themselves.

What precisely did Jefferson say in *Notes on Virginia* that helped launch and fuel the American Counterrevolution? And how did he come to say it?

While the American Revolution was still raging in 1780 and 1781, Jefferson began gathering the data for his report on Virginia. But as he examined the colony-become-state more closely, he realized that he was looking at America in all of its richness, textures, and opportunities. By the time he had answered the original questions posed by the French legate Barbe-Marbois, he had become so fascinated with the project that he could not put it aside. One revision followed another until by 1784 he had charted out a course for the entire country, under the guise of a little report on his native Virginia.

When Jefferson published his private edition of *Notes on Virginia* in Paris in early 1785 he unleashed a new plan for America that preceded Adams's *Defence of Constitutions* and Webster's *Sketches of American Policy* by two years. Already Jefferson was obsessed with the problem that confronted all of America's counterrevolutionary thinkers: How can one bring order to an amorphous land, settled by many peoples in separate colonies with a variety of traditions? What form of governance must prevail in such a commonwealth and across its society?

To answer this question, Jefferson, following the scientific methodologies of the Enlightenment, examined many realms. The boundaries, the rivers, the mountains, and all of the natural wonders of Virginia. Its minerals, fauna, and flora. The climate. Colleges, buildings, and roads. Religion, commerce, manufactures. Weights and measures. Tax revenues and budgets. Constitutions, laws, histories, memorials, and state papers. All was rich opportunity, abundant resources, shrewd business practices, and enlightened governance—the kind of propaganda written about Virginia and America from the days of Sir Walter Raleigh and Capt. John Smith forward.

Jefferson then came to the subject of "population." On this heading the pen that enumerated the self-evident truths of liberty disclosed a new set of equally self-evident truths of order. He addressed this topic in several chapters, the first in which he also described animal life in North America; the second under the heading of population; and the last, in a chapter on laws.

The most remarkable discussion was a digression from his description of animal life, a response to a theory put forth by the French Count Buffon that animals and humans beings in the North American habitat tended to degenerate physically and lacked "ardor" and "genius." Jefferson vigorously refuted the theory, praising the swiftness, tenacity, and wise counsels of American Indians and tabulating American geniuses equal to the most distinguished Europeans: "In war we have produced a Washington; . . . In physics we have produced a Franklin; . . . We have supposed Mr. Rittenhouse second to no Astronomer living." While still investigating the animal kingdom, he revealed his fascination with the development or degeneracy of races in America by listing seven cases "of an anomaly of nature, taking place sometimes in the race of negroes brought from Africa, who, though black themselves, have in rare instances, white children, called Albinos."

In his chapter on population, Jefferson expressed a deep fear of "great importations of foreigners" to stock Virginia. Presenting projections of population growth proceeding "on our present stock" or "on a double stock," he argued that immigration should be closed except for "the importation of useful artificers." The doors should be shut to others because "they will bring with them the principles of the governments they leave, imbibed in their early youth; or, if able to throw them off, it will be in exchange for an unbounded licentiousness, passing, as is usual, from one extreme to another." By keeping out troublemakers and extremists, Jefferson asked, "May not our government be more homogeneous, more peaceable, more durable?"

Before leaving population and his concern for social homogeneity, Jefferson approached the subject that would spotlight *Notes on Virginia* as an extraordinary counterrevolutionary document. As he enumerated the number of free inhabitants in Virginia compared to slaves, he made two important observations. First, "under the mild treatment our slaves' experience, and their wholesome, though coarse, food, this blot in our country increases as fast, or faster, than the whites." Next he noted that "in the very first session held under the republican government [of Virginia], the assembly passed a law for the perpetual prohibition of the importation of slaves." His conclusion was that "This will in some measure stop

"The Providential Detection" (1800). Thomas Jefferson depicted as a counter-revolutionary and traitor burning Bache's Aurora, *Paine's* Age of Reason, *and the writings of Rousseau, Voltaire, Godwin, and Helvetius; the American eagle snatches the Constitution from his hand before he can burn that as well.*

the increase of this great political and moral evil, while the minds of our citizens may be ripening for a complete emancipation of human nature."

At first glance it would appear that the "blot" and the "great political and moral evil" were the institution of slavery. In his later chapter on laws, however, it became unclear whether the greater evil in Jefferson's mind was slavery or the enslaved black population. Outlining his proposed revision of the Virginia laws developed during the Revolution, Jefferson included his plan "to emancipate all slaves born after passing the act." Newborn slaves would remain with their parents until women were eighteen and men twenty-one. When those ages were attained, "they should be colonized to such place as the circumstances of the time should render most proper . . . and to send vessels at the same time to other parts of the world for an equal number of white inhabitants."

What was this? An exchange of one part of the American population for a new group of immigrants! Had Jefferson not just expressed his concerns about dangerous foreigners among the American population? Yes, but in his mind, homogeneity had more to do with national origin than it did with racial origin.

If there was any doubt about the greater evil—slavery or a black population—Jefferson clarified it. "It will probably be asked," he continued, "Why not

retain and incorporate the blacks into the state, and thus save the expence of supplying, by importation of white settlers, the vacancies they will leave?" His
answer was the classic statement cited by James Jackson in the congressional
debate of 1790: "Deep rooted prejudices . . . [that] will divide us into parties, and
produce convulsions which will probably never end but in the extermination of
the one or the other race."

Boldly and in print for all to read for the ages: The black race had to be
removed from America because of the dangers of civil "convulsions." Jefferson
then turned again to the theme of homogeneity, this time racial. He outlined all
of the ways in which blacks were inferior to whites and Native Americans:
physical inferiority, moral weakness, hair color, body odor, mental incapacity.
"But never yet could I find that a black had uttered a thought above the level of
plain narration; never seen even an elementary trait of painting or sculpture,"
Jefferson continued in his relentless catalog. He even belittled Phillis Wheatley's
rhymes as religion, not poetry; and Ignatius Sancho's letters as effusions of emotion, not intellect. He concluded that "blacks, whether originally a distinct race
or made distinct by time and circumstances, are inferior to the whites in the
endowments both of body and mind."

This inferiority of blacks, in Jefferson's mind, justified "an effort to keep
those in the department of man as distinct as nature has formed them." The possibility of racial mixture was again Jefferson's principal fear: "This unfortunate
difference of colour, and perhaps of faculty, is a powerful obstacle to the emancipation of these people." Comparing American slavery with that of Rome, where
he assumed all the slaves were white, Jefferson wrote, "Among the Romans
emancipation required but one effort. The slave when made free, might mix with,
without staining the blood of his master. But with us a second is necessary,
unknown to history. When freed, he is to be removed beyond the reach of mixture." For Jefferson, then, the illusion that "all men are created equal" was broken. Because they were not equal—at least in the instance of blacks—they did
not have unalienable rights. Indeed, because of their inequality, they should not
be permitted to mix.[14]

This reanalysis of the rights of man less than a decade after the Declaration
of Independence and before the formulation of the American Bill of Rights was
the most radical formulation of the American Counterrevolution. It provided a
blueprint for establishing and maintaining a counterrevolutionary America with a
homogeneous white population, bereft of blacks and thereby of slavery. Or alter-
natively, if the black population could not be removed, slavery would remain to
avoid the potential of mixing a white population with an inferior race.

Is it possible that this could be a misreading of Jefferson's intentions or that
his ruminations were temporary aberrations? Hardly. On this matter Jefferson
himself was the most reliable witness. On February 4, 1824, Jefferson responded
to a letter he had just received from Jared Sparks, editor of the *North American
Review.* Sparks had recently moved back to his native Boston after a four-year
sojourn as pastor of the First Unitarian Church of Baltimore. While there he met
many of the first families of Virginia, including Jefferson, whose views he often

sought. Sparks had sent Jefferson a copy of the January 1824 issue of his *North American Review*, inviting the former president's attention to an article that included the sixth annual report of the American Colonization Society.

Jefferson read the article "with great consideration" and informed Sparks that he learned more "than I had before known" about the progress of African colonization, an activity he had been promoting for more than forty years. He liked the article for two reasons: First, he thought that a colony of blacks from America in Africa might "introduce among the aborigines the arts of cultured life, and the blessings of civilization and science." Second, and as Jefferson proclaimed—"the most interesting to us, as coming home to our physical and moral characters, to our happiness and safety, was that it provided an asylum to which we can, by degrees, send the whole of that population from among us, and establish them under our patronage and protection, as a separate, free and independent people, in some country & climate friendly to human life and happiness."

And what was that whole population to which Jefferson referred? Free blacks? No. Slaves? No. He meant the entire black and partially black population of the United States. Noting that the American Colonization Society's method probably was too expensive to reach his goal, Jefferson reminded Sparks that he had outlined the best solution forty years earlier. "It was sketched in the *Notes on Virginia*," he wrote, that "by emancipating the after-born, leaving them . . . with their mothers, until their services are worth their maintenance, and then putting them to industrious occupations, until a proper age for deportation."

Jefferson recommended not free and willing departure, but rather "deporture." Removal and banishment as an alien race whose presence was neither lawful nor wanted. "No particular place of asylum was specified" in *Notes*, Jefferson continued, because he had thought "in the revolutionary state of America, then commenced, events might open to us some one within practicable distance." He told Sparks, "This has now happened. . . . St. Domingo has become independent and with a population of that color only; and . . . their Chief offers to pay their passage, to receive them as free citizens, and to provide them employment." According to Jefferson's calculations, with a small tax, with "voluntary surrenders" on the part of masters, and with fifty vessels "constantly employed in that short run . . . to be continued about twenty or twenty-five years," the "final extinction" of a black population from America would be accomplished.[15]

Not just exported or expatriated; rather eradicated, eliminated, extinguished. These were not the rantings of an old man, although he was approaching his eighty-second birthday at the time. They were ideas he had formulated four decades earlier, only a few years after he had written the most stirring words in human history about the rights of man and the equality of all human beings. At that early date, he had solemnly concluded that blacks had no place in the United States and their presence had to be eliminated. He cared not how it would happen, only that it had to happen.

Before *Notes on Virginia*, it was generally presumed by nearly everyone North and South that the principles of the American Revolution dictated the eventual eradication of slavery from the United States. It was also generally presumed that the elimination of slavery meant the extension of the rights of citizenship to freed blacks. Though there might have been occasional hopes from the fringes that both slavery and blacks could be abolished, Jefferson was the first to propose this as a stated public policy. And he remained openly consistent on this subject throughout his long career.

His *Notes on Virginia* changed the way Americans thought and talked about liberty, freedom, equality, and the rights of man. From the day the book hit the streets people, preachers, and politicians talked openly and without censure about eliminating slavery, eliminating blacks and mulattoes from America, eliminating the rights of free blacks, and keeping those blacks not eliminated in slavery—and they could call upon the blessings of the author of the Declaration of Independence to support their arguments. Of all the visions of the American Counterrevolution this was the most fundamental, the most radical, and possibly the most permanent. For it would take generations of black activists, abolitionists, Reconstruction Republicans, Supreme Court Justices, civil rights marchers, and reconstructed southerners to battle this counterrevolution that Jefferson baptized and placed in America's holy writ.

CHAPTER 24

Black American Friends of Order

BLACK AMERICAN BURKE

Benjamin Banneker was not the only African American to participate in the surge of learning and production of belles lettres that was the Enlightenment. There was another African poet—besides Phillis Wheatley—Jupiter Hammon, who published the earliest known poem by an African American. Titled *An Evening Thought. Salvation by Christ, with Penitential Cries,* the piece was written by Hammon for December 25, 1760. One would not distinguish it as the work of an African American had its title not been subjoined with a statement that the poem had been "Composed by Jupiter Hammon, a Negro belonging to Mr. Lloyd, of Queen's-Village, on Long-Island." Its eighty-eight lines looked for salvation in much the same manner of hymns and prayerful effusions from many a Christian of the period.[1]

That is what made Jupiter Hammon, although an African slave, a part of the learned culture of the period—however simple his poetry. Born in 1711 on Long Island to a slave belonging to Henry Lloyd, he remained a slave throughout his ninety-five years, serving three generations of Lloyds. But Henry Lloyd afforded Hammon an education alongside his own children and among the other children in the area known as Lloyd's Neck. And Hammon was cared for by Lloyd as evidenced by bits of information concerning his medical history, a provision for him to have his own books, and Lloyd's admonition in his will that "my old Negroes are to be provided for." That stipulation was written in 1763, the year Lloyd died, and Hammon was passed on to the service and care of son Joseph Lloyd, an American patriot in the coming Revolution.[2]

Like Benjamin Banneker, Jupiter Hammon's intellectual qualities did not bear fullest fruit until he was an older man. Hammon's poetic outpouring began when he was sixty-seven, spurred to production in 1778 when Joseph Lloyd fled Long Island and the occupying British to Hartford. Though Hammon had written his first poem in the cultural isolation of agricultural Long Island, he came to a city where the Hartford Wits were currently giving America its first native corpus of poetry. As he read the patriotic works of Barlow, Dwight, and Humphreys, he was inspired by them as they were by each other to use poetic form to express the hopes, fears, and passions that accompanied the American Revolution.[3]

Over the next four years Hammon issued at least four poems published individually and in the Hartford Wits' favorite medium, the *Connecticut Courant*. He also penned three prose works during this period, also published at Hartford, making him the most prolific African-American author of the Revolutionary era alongside Phillis Wheatley. When Hammon's young master committed suicide in 1780 upon receiving the incorrect news that American forces had surrendered to the British army, Hammon passed to his third Lloyd master, Joseph's grandson John. Whether Hammon was legally transferred to John or whether Hammon chose to bind himself to John Lloyd was not clear, since rumors abounded two years later that Hammon at age sixty-nine had forfeited manumission in favor of continued enslavement.[4]

Fittingly, he devoted his first Hartford poem in 1778 to Phillis Wheatley, praising the youthful poet, also a slave, "That thou a pattern still might be, / To youth of Boston town." Titled "An Address to Miss Phillis Wheatley," the 104-line poem blended salvation with the belief that America was becoming the land of freedom. "Adore / The wisdom of thy God, / In bringing thee from distant shore, / To learn His holy word," Hammon wrote, describing Africa as "a dark abode." "God's tender mercy brought thee here, . . . God's tender mercy set thee free," clearly not of slavery, but rather of Africa. "Among the heathen live no more, / Come magnify thy God," he proclaimed, while also exhorting: "Dear Phillis, seek for heaven's joys, / Where we do hope to meet." Hammon bespoke the widespread notion that Africans in America, though slaves, enjoyed freedom far greater than their unenlightened past relatives in Africa. Hammon most likely was unaware that Phillis Wheatley, by the sudden death of both master and mistress, had become free of slavery, but was no longer alive.[5]

Although his next two pieces, *An Essay on Ten Virgins* (1779) and *A Poem for Children* (1782), concentrated on religious themes, a prose work titled *A Winter Piece* reflected a growing concern with matters temporal. Urged by fellow blacks to address the treatment of Africans in America, Hammon wrote, "My brethren, seeing I am desired by my friends to write something more than poetry, give me leave to speak plainly to you." There followed a lengthy exhortation on the scriptural passage, "Come unto me all ye that labour and are heavy laden," urging all blacks, slave or free, to concentrate on achieving religious salvation. All humans were equal before God: "Come my dear fellow servants and brothers, Africans by nation, we are all invited to come."

Within the twenty-four pages of devotional thought came a stark acknowledgment that Africans in America had asked Hammon to specifically address the subjects of liberty and freedom. Noting that there was a rumor afloat that he had forfeited freedom, Hammon blurted:

> My dear Brethren, as it hath been reported that I had petitioned
> to the court of Hartford against freedom, I now solemnly
> declare that I never have said, nor done any thing, neither

> directly nor indirectly, to promote or to prevent freedom; but my answer hath always been I am a stranger here [on earth] and I do not care to be concerned or to meddle with public affairs, and by this declaration I hope my friends will be satisfied, and all prejudice removed.

He then returned to religious themes, "Let us all strive to be united together in love, and to become new creatures, for if any man be in Christ Jesus he is a new creature." Nowhere did he deny that, faced with the reality that destroyed Phillis Wheatley—loss of master and freedom from slavery—he freely chose continued enslavement.[6]

Stung by criticism that he was setting a bad example for Africans yearning for freedom, Hammon composed a larger prose and poetic work, also published in 1782, titled *An Evening's Improvement. Shewing, the Necessity of Beholding the Lamb of God. To which is Added a Dialogue, Entitled, The Kind Master and Dutiful Servant.* The purpose of this work was both to respond to his critics and to enlarge upon his theme that the eyes of all humans—black or white, servant or master, woman or man—should be on heaven and not on earth. The prose essay in the form of a sermon preceded the 121-line poem.

He acknowledged that *A Winter Piece* was elicited by requests from "my superiors, gentlemen, whose judgement I depend on, and [by] my friends in general [that] I would write something more for the advantage of my friends." Indeed, he had received "an invitation to give a public exhortation," but declined because he "did not think it my duty at that time." As in *A Winter Piece* he then returned to the subject of salvation. Near the end of the piece he again spoke candidly to his fellow slaves:

> My dear brethren we are many of us seeking for a temporal freedom, and I pray that God would grant your desire; if we are slaves it is by the permission of God; if we are free it must be by the power of the most high God; be not discouraged, but cheerfully perform the duties of the day, sensible that the same power that created the heavens and the earth and causeth the greater light to rule the day and the lesser to rule the night, can cause a universal freedom.

Hammon admitted, "But as I am advanced to the age of seventy-one years, I do not desire temporal freedom for myself." He did not want to experience what America's other black poet was undergoing—misery, starvation, death.[7]

Certain that most African slaves were not prepared to deal with freedom, he appended to *An Evening's Improvement* a poetic dialogue between *The Kind Master and the Dutiful Servant* that lauded virtuous reciprocal responsibilities within the slave system itself. Establishing an almost idyllic relationship between master and slave, Hammon had the master set the stage: "Come my servant, follow me, / According to thy place; / And surely God will be with thee, / And send thee heav'nly grace." The servant faithfully responded, "Dear Master, that's my whole delight, / Thy pleasure for to do; / As for grace and truth's in sight, / Thus far I'll surely go."

The dialogue of kindness and reciprocity continued until Hammon introduced "A Line on the Present War." It was a prayer for peace so that virtue could "make a show." "Then we shall see the happy day, / That virtue is in power" and "When ev'ry Nation acts like friends, / Shall be the sons of God." Hammon concluded the poem as he did the essay with a message to his fellow slaves: "Believe me now my Christian friends, / Believe your friend call'd Hammon: / You cannot to your God attend, / And serve the God of Mammon." If everyone placed his or her eye upon heaven, even slavery would be bearable. The achievement of liberty in life came in the practice of virtue, whatever one's status.[8]

Whence came these outpourings of America's earliest black poet? Was Hammon a pawn of those "superiors, gentlemen, whose judgement I depend on?" After all, he wrote in Hartford, in the midst of New England states already debating the abolition of slavery. Pennsylvania had already adopted a gradual emancipation law, and the subject was being debated in Massachusetts, New Jersey, and Connecticut, where he continued to reside with his master to the end of the American Revolution.

Was he afraid that at age seventy-one he would be thrown upon the world without any means of support? He surely knew that Phillis Wheatley was destitute in Boston, unable to find publishers or supporters for the new poems she had written and held ready for the press. But there had to be more energizing Hammon's pen. If dependent slaves were set free without training in the skills of independent living, there was a good chance that many would falter; and by stumbling, they would fuel the prejudices already expressed by white Americans toward Africans. Hammon understood the need for an orderly transition. Those ready for freedom should be given it; those not yet ready, prepared for it; and those, like he, in the twilight of his years, allowed to spend his last days in peace and security.

In his last and most passionate essay completed in September 1786, titled *An Address to the Negroes in the State of New York* (1787), Hammon focused on the construction of the nation. Just as John Adams questioned the practical operation of democratic governments, Hammon doubted the ability of peoples who had been deprived of public or personal responsibility to operate successfully in a republican society. He was the first African American to understand the difficult construction of republican order and to propound that blacks needed preparation to participate effectively.

Dedicating his *Address* to the newly formed African Society in New York City, he opened with "the tenderness of a father and friend" and with the assumption that other blacks "will be more likely to listen to what is said, when you know it comes from a negro, one of your own nation and colour." Indicating that he was in his seventies and that "my lot has been so much better than most slaves have had," he established several basic principles. First he argued that slaves should obey their masters, that they should practice honesty and faithfulness, and that they should avoid profaneness. They should, he preached, "make religion the great business of your lives."

Liberty, he argued, was something to be achieved, not conferred: "Now I acknowledge that liberty is a great thing, and worth seeking for, if we can get it honestly; and by our good conduct prevail on our masters to set us free." He reiterated "for my own part I do not wish to be free," yet "I should be glad if others, especially the young Negroes, were to be free; for many of us who are grown up slaves, and have always had masters to take care of us, should hardly know how to take care of ourselves; and it may be more for our own comfort to remain as we are." Nevertheless, liberty was a great thing as evidenced by "the conduct of the white people in the late war." He noted, "How much money has been spent, and how many lives have been lost to defend their liberty!" He had hoped "that God would open their eyes, when they were so much engaged for liberty, to think of the state of the poor blacks, and to pity us."[9]

It was true that some had formed manumission societies, abolition societies, and societies to protect the liberty of free blacks. Some states had adopted gradual abolition laws, although the one proposed for New York had just been defeated and would not come back for consideration for almost a decade. As the day of fulfilled liberty seemed postponed, Hammon underscored the need for slaves to regulate their own conduct and to look toward heaven: "If we should ever get to Heaven, we shall find nobody to reproach us for being black, or for being slaves. . . . Let me beg of you, my dear African brethren, to think very little of your bondage in this life; for your thinking of it will do you no good."[10]

Despite Hammon's heavenward gaze he constantly returned to the theme of earning liberty on earth. After instructing slaves on proper deportment, he turned "with a few words to those Negroes who have their liberty." Those who were free were under obligation to work constantly to "improve your freedom," both for their own sakes and for those who remained in slavery: "If you are idle, and take to bad courses, you will hurt those of your brethren who are slaves, and do all in your power to prevent their being free." Hammon urged them to "take care to get an honest living by your labour and industry" and "to lead quiet and peaceable lives in all Godliness and honesty" for the sake "of your own good and happiness, in time, and for eternity, and for the sake of your poor brethren."[11]

Hammon's analysis of American society and of the role of Africans—slave or free—within it set him apart from the other two giants of the African-American Enlightenment—Phillis Wheatley and Benjamin Banneker. Whereas Wheatley created beautiful, even lofty rhymes, Hammon used his prose and poetic powers to laud the merits of religion while also probing the human condition. Whereas Banneker pursued his personal curiosities and demonstrated the results of painstaking calculations, Hammon strung together words and rhymes to illuminate human behavior. By exploring the liberating powers of religion, by prescribing the behavior of Africans in society, by probing the human condition and preaching hard work among his fellows, he believed he would ultimately contribute more to the achievement of liberty for black Americans.

BLACK COUNTERREVOLUTION

Benjamin Rush described in his commonplace book for August 22, 1793, the happiest moment in the search of blacks for liberty, freedom, and rights in post-Revolutionary America. A most unusual scene it was, the placing of the roof beam on the African Episcopal Church of St. Thomas in the city of Philadelphia:

> Attended a dinner a mile below the tower in 2nd Street to celebrate the raising of the roof of the African Church. About 100 white persons, chiefly carpenters, dined at one table, who were waited upon by Africans. Afterward about 50 black people sat down at the same table, who were waited upon by white people. Never did I see people more happy. Some of them shed tears of joy. An old black man took Mr. [John] Nicholson by the hand and said to him, "May you live long, and when you die, may you not die eternally." I gave them two toasts, viz: "Peace on earth and good will to man," and "May African Churches everywhere soon succeed African bondage." The last was received with three cheers.[12]

Wholly unique in the annals of early America, no event like this would be seen again until the days of the abolitionists; and then not again until the civil rights struggles of the 1950s and 1960s. "To me," Rush wrote to his wife, "it will be a day remembered with pleasure as long as I live."[13]

But why was Rush so happy? Why did those present consider this the erection of the first separate church for blacks a turning point in the history of black American struggles for freedom? Were not the rights of Americans already guaranteed by the Declaration of Independence, the Constitution, and the Bill of Rights? Why did the celebrants lament the necessity for black Americans to build their own churches? After all, the entire movement to build this first African Episcopal church began with a widely noted racial incident at Old St. George's Methodist Episcopal Church in Philadelphia less than a year earlier in 1792.

Richard Allen, founder of the African Methodist Episcopal Church in America, remembered the Old St. George's story well when he put it in writing for the first time in 1817 in the first edition of the *Doctrines and Discipline of the African Methodist Episcopal Church*. He later embellished it in his brief autobiography, *Life Experience and Gospel Labors of the Rt. Rev. Richard Allen*. But when he wrote the account in 1817 he was a fifty-seven-year-old man who had been fighting for at least thirty years to gain control over the religious lives, services, property, and institutions of black Americans. In his autobiography completed near the end of his life, he acknowledged that "a great part of this work [was] . . . written many years after events actually took place" and that "my memory could not point out the exact time of many occurrences."[14]

From the vantage of 1817, Allen placed the incident—the touchstone for separate black denominations in America—in November 1787, five years before it actually happened:

*Richard Allen (c. 1793). Counterrevolutionary propo-
nent of free black cohesiveness.*

A number of us usually attended St. George's church in Fourth
street; and when the colored people began to get numerous in
attending the church, they moved us from the seats we usually
sat on, and placed us around the wall, and on Sabbath morning
we went to church and the sexton stood at the door, and told us
to go in the gallery. He told us to go, and we would see where
to sit. We expected to take the seats over the ones we formerly
occupied below, not knowing any better. We took those seats.
Meeting had begun, and they were nearly done singing, and
just as we got to the seats, the elder said, "Let us pray." We had
not been long upon our knees before I heard considerable scuf-
fling and low talking. I raised my head up and saw one of the
trustees, H—— M——, having hold of the Rev. Absalom
Jones, pulling him up off of his knees, and saying, "You must
get up—you must not kneel here." Mr. Jones replied, "Wait
until prayer is over, and I will get up and trouble you no more."
With that he beckoned to one of the other trustees, Mr. L——
S—— to come to his assistance. He came, and went to William
White to pull him up. By this time prayer was over, and we all
went out of the church in a body, and they were no more
plagued with us in the church. This raised a great excitement
and inquiry among the citizens, in so much that I believe they
were ashamed of their conduct.

Allen concluded his rendition of a classic racial incident: "But my dear Lord was with us, and we were filled with fresh vigor to get a house erected to worship God in."[15]

Only Allen's last sentence hinted that what happened at Old St. George's in 1792, not 1787, was not an exercise of power over innocent victims so much as a showdown of colossal wills. Allen and his closest partner in the incident, Absalom Jones, far from being innocent bystanders, had long prepared for that very moment when the black members of Old St. George's would go "out of the church in a body." Indeed, the event, while not necessarily staged to happen at that precise moment, was inevitable and was as much induced by Allen, Jones, and their fellow black parishioners as by the white trustees who herded them to the new church gallery. It was the culmination of the first phase of black Americans' search for liberty.

Allen and Jones, although they moved to separate church denominations, were the great power brokers of black freedom during the early years of the American republic. Jones was born in 1746 into Sussex County, Delaware, as a slave. In 1762 his master, Benjamin Wynkoop, sold Jones's mother and six brothers and sisters and brought the boy to Philadelphia to work in his store. Wynkoop also allowed young Jones to attend school. At twenty-three Jones married at St. Peter's Anglican Church and purchased his wife's freedom so that their children would be born free. Although he could have escaped slavery when the British Army evacuated Philadelphia, he and his family remained behind. Finally, Jones's desires for freedom were granted when Wynkoop in 1783 allowed Jones to purchase his freedom.[16]

Richard Allen followed a slightly different route to freedom. He, too, was born in slavery in 1760 to Philadelphia lawyer, Benjamin Chew. When Chew's law practice went sour in 1767, Allen's entire family—father, mother, and four children—was sold to Delaware farmer Stokely Sturgis near Dover. Sturgis sold Allen's parents and several siblings, leaving the teenage boy without his family. Some time in the late 1770s both Allen and his master succumbed to Methodist evangelism, which also persuaded Sturgis that the evil practice of slavery would keep any slaveholder outside of God's grace. Sturgis then proposed that Allen and his brother purchase their freedom, which they did. Allen's manumission came on January 25, 1780, just before his twentieth birthday. "We left our master's house," Allen later wrote, "and I may truly say it was like leaving our father's house; for he was a kind, affectionate and tenderhearted master."[17]

Over the next six years Allen was a peripatetic woodcutter, brickmaker, wagon driver, and Methodist gospeler moving about Delaware, New Jersey, Maryland, and Pennsylvania. He traveled extensively with various white Methodist itinerants, preaching to both blacks and whites with considerable approval. So impressive was he that Francis Asbury, the father of American Methodism, invited Allen to become his traveling companion as he crisscrossed America. Allen declined, though, after Asbury told him that "in the slave countries, Carolina and other places, I must not intermix with the slaves."[18]

In 1784 Allen participated in a national and international connection that brought together all Methodist ministers in America at Baltimore to organize an American Methodist Episcopal Church and to forbid the "buying or selling the bodies and souls of men, women and children with an intention to enslave them." Although not an official delegate at the famous Christmas Conference that established American Methodism, Allen saw the handiwork of God and the American Revolution when the Conference declared slavery to be

> contrary to the golden law of God on which hangs all the law and the prophets, and the unalienated rights of mankind, as well as every principle of the Revolution, to hold in the deepest debasement, in a more abject slavery than is perhaps to be found in any part of the world except America so many souls that are capable of the image of God.

Not only did the Conference condemn slavery, it also called upon all Methodists to emancipate their slaves within twelve months unless prohibited by state law.[19]

Why make such a requirement? It had worked in the case of Stokely Sturgis and his slave Richard Allen. Did not the Revolution and Christian compassion require such a step? And it certainly was in step with efforts all about America to correct a practice incongruous with the principles of the Revolution. Throughout much of New England, blacks had been suing successfully for their freedom. Such judicial findings in Massachusetts had practically abolished slavery there without the passage of a law. The Vermont constitution outlawed slaveholding. New Hampshire allowed slaves to sue for freedom. Pennsylvania in 1780 had passed a gradual emancipation act, which, although it freed no slaves immediately, provided for the end of slavery. The subject was being debated in New Jersey, Connecticut, and Rhode Island just as the Christmas Conference convened in Baltimore.[20]

Moreover, in Philadelphia the Pennsylvania Abolition Society, originally formed as the Pennsylvania Society for the Relief of Free Negroes Unlawfully Held in Bondage in 1775, reconstituted itself in 1784 and resumed its work of entering court actions to free blacks illegally held as slaves. Although the first society had been dominated by Quakers, the new group quickly diversified to reflect the broad spectrum of religious interests and individuals opposed to slavery and illegal enslavement. By 1787 the universal abolition of slavery had become its goal as its name changed to the Pennsylvania Society for the Abolition of Slavery, the Relief of Free Negroes, and for Improving the Condition of the African Race.[21]

Indeed, it was Benjamin Rush's reawakening in 1787 that boosted the Pennsylvania Abolition Society into its abolition mode. The sudden start was spurred by a dream in which Rush found himself in a beautiful country inhabited only by blacks who were at the moment in the midst of religious services. At Rush's approach, they paused as if disturbed. A venerable leader, speaking for the whole group, expressed their fear at the sight of a white man, since white, which was "the emblem of innocence in every other creature of God, is, to us, a sign of guilt in man."

When Rush identified himself, the man embraced him and welcomed him to this place "called the Paradise of Negro Slaves"—a temporary "residence till the general judgment." Then, one by one, the individuals living there asked Rush about their former masters. One bore the ax mark where his master had killed him for saddling the wrong horse. Another had been sold by his master after sixty years of faithful service at age eighty, separating him from his twenty-eight children and grandchildren. Another, a woman, had been sold to pay a gambling debt by a young master she had nursed from birth—to the detriment of her own child. Another woman had been sold at thirty-three and shipped to Hispaniola when she asked her master if she could buy her freedom.

The parade of mistreated slaves was suddenly interrupted by the approach of another white man. Silence ensued as "the eyes of the whole assembly were turned" from Rush "and directed to a little white man who advanced toward them." Rush continued his vision:

> His face was grave, placid, and full of benignity. In one hand he carried a subscription paper and a petition; in the other he carried a small pamphlet on the unlawfulness of the African slave-trade, and a letter directed to the King of Prussia, upon the unlawfulness of war. While I was employed in contemplating the venerable figure, suddenly I beheld the whole assembly running to meet him; the air resounded with the clapping of hands, and I was awakened from my dream by the noise of a loud and general acclamation of—"ANTHONY BENEZET!"

This dream, admitted Rush, was evoked by his reading of Thomas Clarkson's 1786 *Essay on the Slavery and Commerce of the Human Species*. "Mr. Clarkson's ingenious and pathetic essay" made "so deep an impression upon my mind, that it followed me in my sleep, and produced a dream of so extraordinary a nature, that I have communicated it to the public."[22]

It was as if the spirit of Anthony Benezet had been directly transferred to Benjamin Rush, who assumed the gentle, but relentless drive to reform the world that had marked the Quaker's American career. Although Benezet, a native of France whose family suffered religious persecution, had not originated Quaker opposition to slavery, he had launched the world's crusade against the institution. His Quakerism came from a fifteen-year residence among Friends in London and his pulpit was the classroom where he served as a teacher of females in Germantown and Philadelphia for more than forty years. He taught all day, then operated an evening school for blacks. He spent all night writing hundreds of reformist books and pamphlets on education, Indians, religion, war, the Acadians' plight, as well as on slavery.[23]

An anonymous poem published in Philadelphia in 1790 captured well Benezet's significance. Americans and Europeans heard not African groans, "Until thy meeker spirit, [John] Woolman, rose, / Aiming to soften rather than oppose; / And thou, lov'd Benezet, of kindrid mind, / The World thy country, and thy Friends mankind." His caring for mankind was shown through his extensive publications on slavery from *An Epistle of Caution and Advice Concerning the Buying and Keeping of Slaves* (1754) to *The Case of Our Fellow-Creatures, the Oppressed Africans* (1783), published just months before his death. Almost single-handedly he set off a worldwide crusade against both the slave trade and slaveholding. His essays and letters elicited responses from such diverse people as Granville Sharp, John Wesley, Benjamin Franklin, and Abbé Raynal.[24]

It was Anthony Benezet who in 1772 first recruited Benjamin Rush to speak out against slavery. In a pamphlet titled *An Address to the Inhabitants of the British Settlements on the Slavery of the Negroes in America* (1772), Rush issued one of the most noted antislavery tracts to appear before the American Revolution. It drew a bitter response from a West India planter in *Slavery Not Forbidden in Scripture; or a Defence of the West India Planters* (1773), which caused Rush to issue another attack. Of Rush's efforts, a Virginian, Robert Pleasants wrote in 1774, "I think the Phisition [*sic*] has handled the subject of slavery in a masterly manner." Granville Sharp found Rush's essay compelling, even though he could not find a London publisher to reprint it. He attributed that to "the Backwardness of the Booksellers" for not "undertaking publications of Books, which <u>are not on entertaining Subjects,</u> suited to the Depravity of the generality of Readers."[25]

It was in part the continued presence of Anthony Benezet that helped bring the Pennsylvania Abolition Society back into existence in February 1784. Although he died three months later on May 3, he lived long enough to see a revival of his antislavery witness—but with a major change. Whereas in the 1760s he had been a lone witness to the evils of slavery and the slave trade, by 1784 the central thrust of the American Revolution fell on the side of emancipation and the recognition of the equal rights of all humans. No longer did he have to argue the logic of freedom; liberty was at hand and needed only to be seized.

In such an atmosphere evangel Richard Allen arrived in Philadelphia in 1786 and soon linked himself with the revivified Pennsylvania Abolition Society. Allen, whose fame as a preacher was spreading, was called by the presiding elder at St. George's Methodist Church to provide special services to the large number of free blacks who were beginning to crowd into Philadelphia. Whereas Philadelphia had fourteen hundred slaves and a hundred free blacks in 1765, by 1783 the numbers had nearly reversed to four hundred slaves and a thousand free blacks. By 1790 the number of free blacks increased to two thousand, giving Philadelphia the largest free black community in America.[26]

Allen held services for blacks at 5:00 A.M. at St. George's, but he also preached at other places around the city. He soon had a black membership of forty-two and his services became popular gatherings for Philadelphia blacks. Absalom Jones joined the class, abandoning for a time the Episcopal Church, as did a number of other former slaves recently arrived in Philadelphia. Very soon, admitted Allen, "I saw the necessity of erecting a place of worship for the colored people." He proposed the idea to "the most respectable people of color in this city," but he found acceptance in only three individuals—Jones, William White, and Dorus Ginnings. As a consequence, he set aside the idea temporarily, but not away altogether.[27]

Instead, Allen, Jones, and others formed the Free African Society of Philadelphia on April 12, 1787, a mutual aid society that attracted an increasing number of black religious leaders as well as black businessmen, including Cyrus Bustill, William Gray, Robert Douglas, and James Forten.

Forten was a particularly important addition to the group. He had just returned from England where he had sought out Granville Sharp, the British antislavery legend. Trained in Benezet's school for blacks, the twenty-year old was fully conversant on all subjects relating to liberty, equality, and the rights of man. Forten had also been trained in sailmaking, a business in which he would excel in Philadelphia.[28]

The Free African Society became in a short time the most important tool in transforming Philadelphia's black community. From the outset the organizers wanted to form "some kind of religious society," but it was to "be formed without regard to religious tenets, provided the persons lived an orderly and sober life, in order to support one another in sickness and for the benefit of their widows and fatherless children."

In addition, each member was required "for the benefit of each other, to advance one shilling in silver Pennsylvania currency a month." This money would be pooled "to hand forth to the needy of this society, if any should require, the sum of three shillings and nine pence per week of said money." Self-discipline and self-help increased in importance as the society grew in numbers and its members in wealth.[29]

At the same moment Benjamin Rush reorganized the Pennsylvania Abolition Society to combat slavery and foster the rights of free blacks. By making Benjamin Franklin president and by recruiting Tench Coxe, Philadelphia entrepreneur, and James Pemberton, wealthy Quaker, Rush quickly transformed the society into a strong operation. The expanded membership included many of the city's leading merchants, shopkeepers, professionals, and artisans. With Benjamin Franklin as an articulate spokesman on the subject of slavery, with Rush working behind the scenes, with the existence of a new organization of energetic free blacks, and in a nation still aglow with its liberating Revolution, the prospects for eliminating slavery and extending rights to black Americans could not have looked brighter in the spring of 1787 in Philadelphia.

When the Constitutional Convention came to Philadelphia during the summer of 1787, the Pennsylvania Abolition Society petitioned it to ban the slave trade and worked assiduously to persuade the delegates that the day of liberty had arrived, that the world was moving to abolish both the slave trade and slavery, and that free blacks were ready to take their proper place in American society. Samuel Stanhope Smith in his *Essay on the Causes of the Variety of Complexion and Figure in the Human Species* questioned notions of racial inferiority for the benefit of delegates. Benjamin Rush produced examples of black geniuses. Achievements of Philadelphia free blacks were touted in the local press. And, of course, the Convention had within its membership the president of the Pennsylvania Abolition Society, Benjamin Franklin.[30]

Despite all the preparations, the public relations campaign, and Franklin's presence, the Convention reported a draft that both permitted slavery and the slave trade to continue, albeit the latter was slated to end in twenty years. Despite his presidency of the Pennsylvania Abolition Society and despite the fact that he had in hand a petition hand-delivered by society secretary Tench Coxe on June 2, 1787, Franklin never mentioned slavery or the slave trade at the Convention, according to the records of the deliberations. When a firestorm arose later concerning his failure to present the petition, its contents were published in the *Pennsylvania Gazette* with the explanation that it was "withheld upon an assurance being given by a member of the convention that the great object of the memorial [abolition of the slave trade] would be taken under consideration."[31]

The delegates at the Convention did not consider it the right moment to deal with imperfections in American society. Nor were those blemishes to be addressed two years later when the first Congress under the Constitution spent the better part of three months drawing up the Bill of Rights. Petitions to Congress, including one from Benjamin Franklin still as president of the Pennsylvania Abolition Society, were ignored by Congress in 1790. America's national government would not deal with the matter of slaveholding itself (it dealt only with where slaves could be held in territories and new states) until the end of the Civil War, three-quarters of a century later.[32]

The failure of the national government to address slavery confirmed and solidified a direction already evident. The idealistic action of the Methodist Christmas Conference of 1784 proved to be a chimera. A twelve-month deadline for disposing of slaves by all church members was not realistic; after only six months the rule had to be suspended when it became clear, in Virginia at least, that Methodists would not follow the mandate. Bishops Asbury's and Thomas Coke's preachments of instant emancipation and threats to eject noncomplying Methodists from the new Church mainly fell on deaf ears—even those of George Washington, who politely declined to sign their antislavery petition directed to the Virginia General Assembly.

Although the Methodist Episcopal Church adopted antislavery resolutions until 1800, it never again sought the wholesale emancipation of slaves by Methodists. By 1787, Bishop Coke, the church's most outspoken antislavery leader, had changed his approach. To overcome the objections of Virginia slaveholders, he wrote, "Here I bore a public testimony against slavery and have found a method of delivering it without causing tumult; and that is, by first addressing the Negroes in a very pathetic manner on the Duty of Servants to Masters, and then the whites will receive quietly what I have to say." He and other Methodist ministers urged the signing of antislavery petitions, but they no longer condemned slavery from the pulpit.[33]

By the end of 1787 Richard Allen, Absalom Jones, and their colleagues in the Philadelphia Free African Society had to wonder about the commitment of white Americans to bring to all men—particularly enslaved blacks—the blessings of liberty so hotly contested in the late Revolution. Despite the continued activity of various state abolition societies and the action of some states to outlaw the slave trade within their borders, the momentum to abolish slavery and to expand the rights of black Americans ground to a halt. Abolition societies instead absorbed themselves with legal actions seeking to establish the freedom of kidnapped free blacks. Ironically, the drive to end the slave trade in many states was an effort to stop the system of selling free blacks back into slavery and to halt the illicit transfer of those already enslaved.[34]

As time passed free blacks came to recognize that it was not only the institution of slavery that took away black rights. If one happened to be kidnapped, his or her testimony would not automatically be considered as having legal standing—even if a hearing could be obtained before a constable, a judge, or a court. Only when white lawyers recruited by abolition societies intervened would cases be scheduled and heard.

The new federal government also chipped away at black citizenship. In 1790 Congress limited naturalization to white aliens and forbade the issuance of passports for travel abroad by free blacks. In 1792, when Congress organized the militia nationally, enrollment was restricted to white male citizens—despite the fact that black warriors had helped to win American independence.[35]

Reports circulated across the land that the true home for blacks who were not otherwise lodged in slavery was Africa, not America. Quaker William Rotch Sr., a Westport, Massachusetts, merchant and partner of black sea captain Paul Cuffe, returned from a trip abroad in January 1787 with glowing reports of Granville Sharp's plans to colonize Sierra Leone with former American slaves. Sharp had just sent three shiploads of former slaves who had been residing in relative squalor in the city of London to the new Province of Freedom. Rotch traveled about New England praising the idea, which he saw as a simple solution to the problem of black citizenship in America. To his thinking it provided an opportunity for blacks to make a home in a place where they could both live in freedom and teach the principles of liberty to others.

Two individuals who heard Rotch's preachments about African colonization willingly embraced his lessons. One was Paul Cuffe; the other was the wealthy, Edinburgh-educated physician William Thornton, a self-appointed gadfly who had many careers in America, including as architect of the U.S. Capitol and superintendent of the U.S. Patent Office. Both Cuffe and Thornton shared Rotch's enthusiasm for African colonization and spent the rest of their lives promoting the idea.

Cuffe initially did a lot of listening and thinking about the subject as he saw dozens of New England blacks clamor to join the movement to Africa. In December 1787, he received a request from seventy-three free blacks in Boston for passage to Sierra Leone. Prince Hall, writing for these unhappy residents, described the "very disagreeable and disadvantageous circumstances, most of which attend us so long as we and our children live in America." He also heard from blacks in Newport, Rhode Island, and Wilmington, Delaware—regular ports of call for him—requesting his assistance. Newport blacks saw their circumstances in

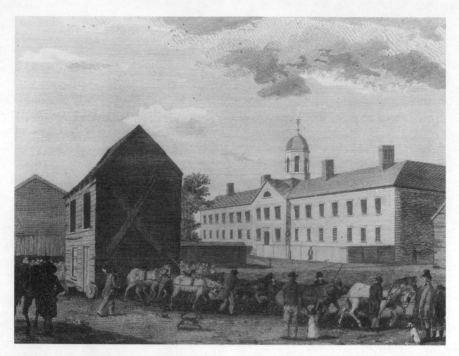

"Gaol, in Walnut Street, Philadelphia" (c. 1794). A former blacksmith's shop is hauled in front of the Walnut Street Jail to Sixth Street in Philadelphia to be converted into the first African Methodist Episcopal meeting house in America— "Mother Bethel"—by Richard Allen and his followers.

America as a "calamitous state" and themselves as "strangers and outcasts in a strange land." Samuel Hopkins, Newport Congregational minister and strong proponent of African colonization, pleaded with Cuffe on their behalf. Cuffe listened, but took no immediate action. He instead tied himself financially more closely with America.[36]

Thornton, on the other hand, promoted colonization everywhere he went. When he inherited his father's sugar plantation on Antigua in 1785, he decided to add his own large cadre of slaves to the experiment. He then barnstormed across U.S. cities urging blacks to join the migration and whites to assist blacks in escaping from an increasingly unfriendly America. From his point of view there could be "no sincere union between the whites and the Negroes" in America or elsewhere. Moreover, blacks could take Christian religion and Western civilization to dark Africa.

Thornton won the interest of blacks everywhere he went until he arrived in Philadelphia. He was surprised to discover at the Free African Society of Philadelphia meeting not a soul interested in joining the migration. Indeed, the society sent one of its members, Henry Stewart, to Newport and Boston to find out why blacks there were so eager to quit America. Stewart brought back pained letters lamenting the sufferings of blacks in both places; the society in response sent back letters of cheer and encouragement.[37]

Something was happening among these Philadelphians. A new approach to liberty was evolving among them as early as 1789. By that time Philadelphia black leaders had found that rights were not going to be extended merely because they were enunciated during the course of the American Revolution. They concluded instead that liberty would have to be secured through confrontation, challenge, and negotiation. And they deliberately set out to create institutions that would enable them to do exactly that.

Following Benjamin Franklin's death in April 1790, the Pennsylvania Abolition Society, recharged by Benjamin Rush, moved aggressively to oppose slavery and to protect free blacks. Its black-controlled counterpart, the Free African Society, acted just as decisively to solve problems facing black Americans and the Philadelphia black community. In May 1790 it secured a burial ground for free blacks. By the end of 1790 the society's coffers used to assist needful members were bulging; an ample surplus was held in the Bank of North America. The society also urged its members to marry and began that year to issue marriage certificates to qualified members.

Although the society encouraged and assisted its members, Richard Allen and Absalom Jones wanted desperately to establish an independent African church for Philadelphia blacks. But they differed strongly about its proper religious affiliation and principal audience. That was likely the discussion on November 15, 1788, when Allen bolted from a meeting of the society in an "abrupt manner." For the next six months members of the society attempted to woo him back, but he refused to participate unless the organization focused on establishing a church.

A committee appointed to meet with him reported on June 20, 1789, that in view of his behavior "he is accordingly disunited until he shall come to a sense of his conduct, and request to be admitted a member according to our discipline." Allen never returned. But when the society eventually pursued his cherished goal of a separate black church, he worked assiduously to make it happen.[38]

In September 1790 the society decided to hold religious services for black Philadelphians independent of the various religious denominations. The first service in the form of a Quaker meeting was held on January 1, 1791. Promoted especially by Absalom Jones with Benjamin Rush's encouragement, the society hoped, Rush wrote to Granville Sharp, to unite "the scattered and unconnected appendages of most of the [black] religious societies in the city." With such an inauspicious beginning, it is astonishing how quickly the idea of a separate church was transformed into a counterrevolutionary movement.[39]

From the outset, Rush, Jones, and Richard Allen knew that the project would redefine American society and the role of black Americans within it. By separating one defined group of Americans from others for special services and for particular treatment, they were going against the spirit of the American Revolution.

In attempting to bring order to the black American community in this manner they were launching a counterrevolutionary tactic to deal with the failure of the American Revolution to deliver freedom, equality, and rights to a vast segment of the American population. They knew, at least subconsciously, that they were substituting for the fundaments of the American Revolution a new approach to organizing American society.

The enterprise proceeded just as the earliest stirrings of counterrevolution were emerging around the world. Edmund Burke's *Reflections on the Revolution in France* had just been published. Austria had just retaken Belgium, setting the stage for a new territorial struggle. Unhappy mulattoes in St. Domingue led by Vincent Ogé had just demanded their rights in the French empire. The Pope was preparing his condemnation of the French civil constitution. And, in Philadelphia, Congress was developing a national bank to organize finances and introducing a whiskey tax that would generate a new type of revolutionary heat in America.

Rush and Allen were aware that they were launching a counterrevolutionary maneuver. Six months after the first religious services began, on July 25, 1791, Benjamin Rush met with twelve free blacks, for the purpose of drawing up "sundry articles of faith and a plan of church government which I had composed for them." He continued, "They appeared well satisfied with it, and agreed to deliberate upon it previously to its being adopted and laid before the public." Rush invited Robert Ralston, wealthy merchant, Presbyterian layman, and generous philanthropist to sit in on this meeting. While Rush advised the group on philosophy and governance, Ralston provided guidance on finances.

Just one week after this secret meeting, on August 1, William White, Episcopal bishop and rector of Christ Church, accosted Rush and "in very strong terms expressed his disapprobation to the proposed African church." On the same day, Absalom Jones raced to Rush's house to report that "the Quakers were much displeased with them." Rush assured him that they were headed in the right direction and sent him home.[40]

But then Rush reflected for a moment on the significance of launching a separate church just for black Philadelphians:

> The objections from both these quarters satisfied me more than ever of the necessity of an African church and of the advantages to be expected from it. I conceive it will collect many hundred Blacks together on Sundays who now spend that day in idleness. It may be followed by churches upon a similar plan in other States, and who knows but it may be the means of sending the gospel to Africa, as the American Revolution sent liberty to Europe? Then perhaps the Africans in America may say to those who brought them here as slaves, what Joseph said to his brethren when they condemned themselves for selling him into Egypt.[41]

It was not merely a matter of providing a place where blacks could gather; it was the launching of a new order whereby black Americans could declare themselves

Americans, not Africans, They could speak in unity, care for each other, and praise God together. This nondenominational church was to be called the African Church of Philadelphia. For two years Richard Allen had opposed the reticence of the Free African Society and the heavy Episcopal and Quaker influence over its deliberations. But when it became clear that the church was to be for all blacks and would be nondenominational, he joined the small group of counterrevolutionaries.

The first public appeal, issued on August 27, 1791, downplayed its intent by promising that it would gather together those blacks who did not at the time worship in any of the existing white churches. But it highlighted one of its counterrevolutionary purposes by commenting that "men are more influenced by their moral equals than by their superiors" and that they "are more easily governed by persons chosen by themselves for that purpose, than by persons who are placed over them by accidental circumstances."[42]

After the subscription paper was issued, the battle to stop the project or to gain control of it began. According to Allen, the local elder, John McClaskey, "called upon us and told us if we did not erase our names from the subscription paper, and give up the paper, we would be publicly turned out of meeting." When Allen asked if he had "violated any rules of discipline by so doing," McClaskey replied, "I have the charge given to me by the Conference, and unless you submit I will read you publicly out of meeting." McClaskey's threats failed. Allen wrote years later that the interview ended thus: "We told him if he turned us out contrary to the rule of discipline [Methodist church law], we should seek further redress . . . we were determined to seek out for ourselves, the Lord being our helper."[43]

Benjamin Rush and Robert Ralston did much to help with the campaign. Allen recalled, "I hope the name of Dr. Benjamin Rush and Robert Ralston will never be forgotten among us." Rush was the behind-the-scenes mover; Ralston was the public treasurer for the project. Wrote Allen: "They were the first two gentlemen who espoused the cause of the oppressed, and aided us in building the house of the Lord for the poor Africans to worship in. Here was the beginning and rise of the first African church in America." With these two behind the project contributions came from George Washington, Thomas Jefferson, Granville Sharp, the Free African Union Society of Newport. But Allen and Jones also raised funds, Allen reporting that the two of them garnered $360 on the first day they solicited.[44]

Allen's devotion to fundraising sidelined him when it came to the matter of where the church would be located. Representing a committee of four appointed to search for a lot for the new church, Allen entered into a purchase agreement for a lot at the corner of Lombard and Sixth Street. The committee then found a better lot on Fifth Street, just a block from the State House, and decided to spend collected funds on that parcel. "The first lot they threw upon my hands," Allen wrote, "and wished me to give it up. . . . I thought it was hard that they would throw it upon my hands. I told them I would sooner keep it myself than to forfeit the agreement I had made. And so I did." Was it irritation, honor, or spite that caused Allen to keep the lot? Perhaps he was holding the lot as a trump card until the matter of religious affiliation was firmly established. Whatever the case, the committee settled on its preferred site and made the purchase on February 17, 1792.[45]

News about the purchase of this lot and of Allen's resolve to hold on to a second building site undoubtedly generated acrimony between Allen and Jones and the ministers and trustees of St. George's Church. After the project languished for eight months, Benjamin Rush appealed to Welsh immigrant and land speculator John Nicholson for a loan to underwrite construction of the church. Rush's letter, hand-carried to Nicholson by Absalom Jones and William Gray, implored the tycoon's support "for the sake of Religion & Christianity and as this is the first Institution of the kind." Nicholson responded promptly with a handsome loan.[46]

One or both of these fortuitous events set the stage for the encounter at St. George's related by Richard Allen as the critical counterrevolutionary moment in American black history. The upper galleries to which Allen, Jones, and other black worshipers were consigned were completed at St. George's in May 1792, so that the incident occurred sometime after that date, probably in late November or December, when the Nicholson loan assured that the first African church would be built.

Given this tableaux of events, it becomes much easier to see the built-up venom that led to the reseating of black worshipers at St. George's and the heated exchanges between Allen and Jones and the presiding elder at the church. The reseating was an angry move against a group of blacks who had publicly and widely announced their intentions of building a separate church for blacks. And from the point of view of the Methodist elder, it was far worse that the new church would be owned by a group of black Methodists and not by the Methodist Episcopal Church itself. This was indeed contrary to Methodist church law, a disciplinary provision that from the founding of the Methodist Episcopal Church in 1784 prevented Methodist clergymen from providing services in churches not owned by the national church itself.

When elder John McClaskey attacked Allen and Jones, then, it was not as if they were first wronged and then set out to build their own church in retort. Rather they were regular attendees at St. George's, even as they planned to build a separately owned African Church. Allen and Jones's dramatic departure from St. George's was as much an announcement of victory as of defeat; it was a rallying cry to consolidate Philadelphia's free blacks. When McClaskey urged them not to proceed with the church, Allen and Jones proudly stated: "We told him we had no place of worship; and we did not mean to go to St. George's church any more, as we were so scandalously treated in the presence of all the congregation."[47]

In March 1793 ground was broken for the African Church building. Not merely a symbolic turning of a spade of dirt, the activity of the day was to dig the cellar. Allen brought two or three teams of workers and "as I was the first proposer of the African church, I put the first spade in the ground to dig a cellar for the same." The event may have been witnessed by Paul Cuffe, whose ship *Mary* sailed into Philadelphia for the first time that month. He was then met by James Forten, master sailmaker and strong supporter of the Free African Society. When Cuffe learned of the ambitious plans of Philadelphia free blacks to make this counterrevolutionary statement, he surely reevaluated his plans to colonize black Americans in Africa.[48]

Although groundbreaking day was festive, there were cost overruns in constructing a building designed to seat eight hundred individuals. Work soon had to be halted for more fund-raising. By August John Nicholson loaned another $1,000, matching his earlier advance. Thus on August 22, 1793, when finally the roof beam was lifted into place, Philadelphia whites and blacks enjoyed one of the happiest, though little-remembered moments in American history.[49]

BLACK SAMARITAN TRAGEDY

Three days earlier Benjamin Rush discovered a tragedy that would vitally affect the completion of the African church and the direction of the counterrevolutionary crusade being waged by the free black community of Philadelphia. At 77 Water Street, Rush entered the home of Peter and Catherine LeMaigre, a French importer and his vivacious wife of thirty-three. Rush's purpose in going to the home was to join two other medical colleagues, Hugh Hodge and John Foulke, in evaluating a strange ailment suffered by Catherine. That day they diagnosed one of the first noted cases of the great yellow fever epidemic of 1793, and they determined that the disease arose from a cargo of rotted coffee that had arrived on the ship *Amelia,* which also carried a load of refugees fleeing the revolution in St. Domingue.[50]

Two days later twelve Philadelphians died of the disease. On August 22, as Rush attended the roof raising of the African Church, thirteen died. Two days later, seventeen. At the request of Mayor Mathew Clarkson and Gov. Thomas Mifflin, the Philadelphia College of Physicians assembled its members on August 25 to advise government officials on the nature and treatment of the disease. Much was discussed, many ideas proposed. Rush and three other doctors were appointed as a committee to draw up a report to be issued the following day. The committee proposed eleven measures, the first being "Avoid every infected person, as much as possible."

Mifflin doubted Rush's analysis and report that the disease came from the rotted coffee. He instead thought that it came from the West Indians on the same ship and other ships from St. Domingue. Two thousand refugees had arrived during the two months before the plague began. Among them were a variety of French physicians with considerable experience treating yellow fever, who refuted both Mifflin's prejudices and Rush's theories as to the origins of the disease. As a group they counseled that patients suffering the disease should be strengthened, not weakened by bleedings and purges.

To Rush's credit, he sought out perhaps the most eminent of these physicians, Dr. Edward Stevens, originally from St. Croix and at the time occasionally teaching in New York, but practicing medicine in Philadelphia. Stevens advised Rush that only mild remedies were used in the West Indies: cold baths, gentle herbs and barks, and wine. Although this sounded perhaps logical to Rush, he abandoned the system within days, when he saw no improvement in his patients. Based on his reading of a description of a yellow fever epidemic in Virginia in

*Benjamin Rush (c. 1800). Champion of liberty for men,
women, and blacks; discredited as a medical quack.*

1741, he returned to a system of purges and bleeding prescribed in ever greater
amounts than had ever been used before.[51]

That Rush would countermand Stevens's advice was strange, for Stevens
was a credible authority on yellow fever. Not only did he derive from the West
Indies and had spent most of his life there, he was, like Rush, a graduate of the
medical school at the University of Edinburgh and had practiced medicine in
London. There he had studied gastrointestinal disorders and had received prizes
for twenty-five experiments on digestion. He had even served briefly as president
of the Royal Medical Society in London. Most importantly, he had practiced
medicine for the decade from 1783 to 1793 in St. Croix and had handled countless cases of yellow fever. He had even referred West Indian patients to Rush
when he thought the famous Philadelphian was better suited to handle a case.[52]

Rush nevertheless began to employ his radical treatment on August 29. He
informed every physician he met about his divinely inspired cure. On September 3
he described the treatment to the Fellows of the College of Physicians. The next
day he declared that he had saved nine out of ten patients with the cure. On September 7 he claimed that he had saved twenty-nine out of thirty. The befuddled
Fellows of the College of Physicians met and, after discussions presided over by
Dr. John Redman, Rush's first medical instructor, reluctantly accepted, but did not
endorse, Rush's radical approach.[53]

Still concerned about getting the African church built and paid for, Rush conceived a daring strategy that would make Philadelphia's free blacks the saviors of

the city-wide panic. City services had come to a halt. There were no people available to carry the sick to hospitals or dead bodies to their burial. There were no nurses to care for the sick. There were none available to remove garbage, empty toilets, or dig graves. And, most important, there were no interns available to apply Rush's treatment of purging and bleeding the sick. What if the black community came forth as volunteers to provide these services, thought Rush. Would that not place Philadelphia's blacks on a pedestal that would be long remembered?

His scheme rested on an assumption that he expressed in a letter to Richard Allen and William Gray. Writing on the day that he publicly declared the discovery of a cure for yellow fever, he observed that the illness killing the white population "passes by persons of your color." In view of this God-given immunity, Rush noted, Philadelphia's black community was "under an obligation to offer your services to attend the sick."[54]

The leaders and members of the Free African Society took everything written or said by Benjamin Rush seriously. His plea (or was it a generous offer?) they received solemnly. The leaders of the society met on September 5 and, after discussion, surveyed the city for themselves. They spread out across the city two by two and found devastation and death wherever they went. When the surveyors reconvened that evening, they concluded that serve they must.

Absalom Jones and Richard Allen waited for Mayor Mathew Clarkson the next morning. The beleaguered mayor was ecstatic. He quickly sent notices to newspapers announcing that members of the Free African Society could be called upon for assistance. Jones, Allen, and William Gray dispatched black Samaritans across the city. And true to their word, before the next day ended, they had recruited nurses for every one of Rush's patients, and Rush had trained the three leaders as assistants in purging and bleeding. Moreover, Jones and Allen asked Mayor Clarkson to release a select list of black prisoners from Walnut Street Jail to serve as a nursing corps at Bush Hill, an emergency hospital set up to deal with sufferers. The grateful mayor happily granted their wish.[55]

Within days Philadelphia's free blacks were carrying away bodies to be buried. "Our services were the production of real sensibility," wrote Allen; "we sought not fee nor reward, until the increase of the disorder rendered our labor so arduous, that we were not adequate to the service we had assumed." The Free African Society then hired additional blacks, not among those willing to volunteer their time, to handle some of the work. Their fees were recovered through payments to the society from families served. Soon the only people moving about the streets of Philadelphia were the inspired free blacks who felt called to a God-given mission to save the city.

In addition to carrying bodies, digging graves, and nursing the ill, the blacks carried out Rush's radical treatment. Eight hundred individuals were repeatedly bled and purged. And for each patient they kept careful records of their treatments, the results, and, if death ensued, the appearance of the body at death. Armed with sharp lancets and emetic laudanum, the workers carried out their orders, dictated by their patron Dr. Rush. "This has been no small satisfaction to us," wrote Allen, "for we think that when a physician was not attainable, we have been the instruments in the hands of God, for saving the lives of some hundreds of our suffering fellow mortals."[56]

All was well for the space of a week, when suddenly a letter arrived at the College of Physicians from Alexander Hamilton, U.S. secretary of the treasury, addressing not economies, but rather treatments for yellow fever. Writing, he said, out of "motives of humanity and friendship to the citizens of Philadelphia," Hamilton revealed that "I have myself been attacked with the reigning putrid fever, and with violence." But thanks to God and "the skill and care of my friend Doctor Stevens," he wrote, "I trust that I am now completely out of danger." Stevens's "mode of treating the disorder varies essentially from that which has been generally practiced—And I am persuaded, where pursued, reduces it to one of little more than ordinary hazard." Hamilton concluded his letter by urging the College of Physicians to consult directly with Stevens, who "has been detained several days on my account" from a journey to New York.[57]

Hamilton's letter caused great consternation across Philadelphia. Just when Rush had his treatment plan in place, politics intruded. Or so he firmly believed as long as he lived. But was Hamilton's letter a political attack on Rush? Probably not, for on September 16, Stevens, in a letter of his own, outlined West Indian practices in treating yellow fever. He was, he said, "dictated solely by a philanthropic desire of checking the ravages of disease, and of restoring tranquillity to the dejected minds of the public."[58]

Stevens wrote "This disorder arises from contagion. . . . In the first stage of the disorder, a little attention, and the well directed efforts of a skilful practitioner, may generally prove successful in mitigating the violence of future symptoms, and preventing either much danger or long confinement." Avoid fatigue, "remain at perfect rest," take "a few extraordinary glasses of old Madeira," and ingest "a few doses of good genuine bark." He continued, "When the disorder has gained ground and become violent," patients should receive "an infusion of camomile flowers . . . small doses of a cordial mixture," and cold baths. More "old Madeira," a tea-spoon only of laudanum, and a few grains of powdered rhubarb. "All drastic cathartics do injury when the disease is in its advanced state," Stevens noted. Indeed, he counseled "the use of the tonic plan in its fullest extent, and by warning against the ill consequences of debilitating applications, or profuse evacuations in every period of the disease."[59]

Rush was shocked. He filed his own letter with the College of Physicians the next day, noting, "It is with extreme regret that I have read Dr. Stevens's letter to our College in one of the news-papers." Stevens's "theory of the disease in the West Indies, is as erroneous, as the practice he has recommended has been fatal, in Philadelphia." After analyzing briefly where Stevens went wrong, Rush wrote, "I shall make no apology for thus publicly dissenting from his opinions and practice."

Rush instead called for sufferers to "be visited by physicians as often, and attended by nurses as carefully, as in other acute diseases." Such attention to his system of treatment would "soon reduce it in point of danger and mortality, to a level with a common cold." Rush wrote days later to his wife Julia lamenting, "I think it probable that if the new remedies had been introduced by any other person than a decided Democrat and a friend of Madison and Jefferson, they would have met with less opposition from Colonel Hamilton."[60]

Even as he wrote that, another desideratum devastated him more than Hamilton's supposed political challenge and Stevens's medical imputations. At just about the time Stevens's letter appeared, Richard Allen fell ill to the fever. By September 26, Rush acknowledged that "the Negroes are everywhere submitting to the disorder." Suddenly another of his blindly accepted principles—that blacks were immune to the disease—came into question [61]

By September 26 Benjamin Rush had lost three of his five students and two black servants to yellow fever, and his mother and sister were both leveled by the disease. Yet, he continued to attack anyone who doubted his treatments. He also urged his susceptible free black nurses to redouble their efforts. "Dr. Rush," wrote Allen, "called us more immediately to attend upon the sick, knowing that we could both[?] bleed." Bleed they did, until they were threatened when they appeared carting bodies, removing vats of black vomit, and preparing for new bleedings.[62]

Rush and his good Samaritans fought on with their grisly treatment even while nearly everyone in Philadelphia defected to the West Indian method of treating the disease. Stephen Girard, French merchant and hero of the epidemic, struggled for control of the Bush Hill hospital where hundreds of sick people were taken. He placed the hospital under the direction of Dr. John Deveze, another West Indian who was well versed in the Stevens method. Deveze had in St. Domingue suffered the fever himself and had treated patients there for eighteen years. A refugee from Le Cap François, he took over Bush Hill and made it a model treatment center. While Rush would in future years lament the political battering he received, Deveze would receive world acclaim for his treatment system and his report on the 1793 epidemic.

INSTITUTIONALIZING THE COUNTERREVOLUTION

By the middle of October, when the disease finally declined and when the Bush Hill successes became clear, Philadelphia's free blacks were dealt an incredible blow. Throughout the epidemic a volunteer citizens' committee formed on September 14 "to transact the whole of the business relative to the sick" kept careful records on every aspect of the plague. They appointed members to investigate rumors of waste, misdeeds, pilfering, and mistreatment of the sick and dying. Mathew Carey, immigrant publisher and bookseller, was frequently called upon to make these investigations.

And a good investigator was Carey. He listened to laments and complaints, wishes and needs. In October, he was asked by Mayor Clarkson and the committee to compile the records of their campaign against the epidemic. He began writing what he titled *A Short Account of the Malignant Fever, Lately Prevalent in Philadelphia; with a Statement of the Proceedings That Took Place on the Subject in Different Parts of the United States.* By November 4, when the number of deaths in the city had reduced to four, he hurried to finish the first published account of the siege.[63]

The next day, Benjamin Rush rounded out the story of the epidemic. Enraged at physicians who had discredited his medical treatments, Rush sent his letter of resignation to the College of Physicians. He addressed his letter to his first mentor, Redman: "I beg you would convey by means of this letter my resignation of my fellowship in the College of Physicians. I request at the same time that their acceptance of a copy of Dr. Wallis's edition of the works of Dr. Sydenham." As he explained a few years later, "I intended, by the present of Dr. Sydenham's works, to convey to the College a defense of the principles which had regulated my practice in the yellow fever, and a rebuke of the ignorance of many of the members of the College, of the most common law of Epidemicks which are recorded in almost every page of that author."

Rush was bitter and brokenhearted. His career as a practicing physician was ruined. But his chagrin was slight compared to what happened when the first edition of Mathew Carey's *Short Account of the Malignant Fever* appeared on November 14. The sensational piece sold out within days. Nine days later, Carey issued a second edition, expanded and with more history. A third edition appeared in five days with a necrology of the "Names of the Persons Buried in the Several Graveyards of the City and Liberties of Philadelphia from August 1st, to November 9th, 1793." A fourth edition followed in December and an improved fourth edition in January. Four French editions appeared. German editions surfaced in Chestnut Hill and Lancaster. There were immediate London reprints of the English editions and a Dutch translation in Haarlem.

What made the Carey report one of the best-selling publications of 1793? First was the enormity of the epidemic in the New World's best-known city, a place blessed with advanced physicians and health care facilities. A tenth of the population died. A third of the population fled. Second was the controverted story of how the plague was identified and how physicians thought best to treat it. Here figured the account of the battle between Dr. Rush and the French doctors from St. Domingue under Stephen Girard's leadership to promote alternative forms of treatment, one bloody and gruesome, the other a "tonic" and comforting.[64]

Neither of them compared to the devastating effect of a third story. In the second edition, Carey folded into his account "a partial, censorious paragraph" that "asperses the blacks alone, for having taken the advantage of the distressed situation of the people." At least that was the way Absalom Jones and Richard Allen described the passage in which Carey suggested that Philadelphia's free black volunteers stole from homes of the sick, looted homes of the dead, and charged exorbitant prices to nurse or deliver bodies.

Jones, Allen, and Gray were devastated. They had worked for six years to organize and uplift Philadelphia's free blacks—mutual aid, schools, relief of the poor, and the building of a first African meetinghouse. In a moment of great civic need, under the promise that they were immune to a rampant disease, they devoted their energies to assisting whites. For more than two months they had risked their lives at filthy and disgusting tasks, only to learn that they were far from safe from the disease. Indeed, three hundred of their number fell to the same horrible death. And, yet, at Rush's insistence, and as seventeen thousand whites departed the city, they persisted in their grim project, out of a love of mankind and to prove that black Americans could perform dangerous missions.

Jones and Allen rose up in moral outrage and defended their actions. In a pamphlet responding to Carey's *Short Account of the Malignant Fever,* they cried out, "We feel ourselves sensibly aggrieved by the censorious epithets of many who did not render the least assistance in the time of necessity, yet are liberal of their censure of us, for the prices paid for our services, when no one knew how to make a proposal to anyone they wanted to assist them." The demand had been greater than the supply of volunteers. Within days of beginning their mission, the Free African Society found that white Philadelphians were willing to pay a premium if more help could be found. As Jones and Allen solicited other blacks to work on a paying basis: "We set no price until the reward was fixed by those we had served."

Furthermore, wrote Jones and Allen, "We do assure the public that all the money we received for burying and for coffins, which we ourselves purchased and procured, has not defrayed the expense of wages which we had to pay those whom we employed to assist us." In a financial statement "for the truth of which we solemnly vouch," they showed that they had incurred expenses of £411 and had received payments of £233 against those expenses. "We are out of pocket" a total of £178 wrote the two leaders, and they did not expect to recover as much as £110 of that amount. Nor had Jones, Allen, or Gray charged for their time; their own families, in fact, went without support for seventy days.

"That some extravagant prices were paid we admit," wrote Jones and Allen. But these payments went to workers not associated with the benevolent effort. "Had Mr. Carey been solicited to such an undertaking, for hire, query—what would he have demanded?" asked the black leaders. But, of course, they noted, Carey was gone from the city during the worst of the plague (September 16ff.). They also charged that Carey's lightning speed editions were exploitative: "We believe he has made more money by the sale of his 'Scraps' than a dozen of the greatest extortioners among the colored nurses." They asked, "Is it a greater crime for a black to pilfer, than for a white to privateer?"[65]

Continuing with one of the first great counterattacks in defense of black honor, Jones and Allen wrote: "We wish not to offend; but when an unprovoked attempt is made to make us blacker than we are, it becomes less necessary to be over-cautious on that account." They, recounted instance after instance of white exploitation during the epidemic. There followed even more cases of black sacrifices. They then addressed the heart of the issue:

> We have many unprovoked enemies who begrudge us the liberty we enjoy, and are glad to hear of any complaint against our color, be it just or unjust; in consequence of which we are more

earnestly endeavoring all in our power, to warn, rebuke and
exhort our African friends to keep a conscience void of offense
towards God and man; and at the same time, would not be
backward to interfere, when stigmas or oppression appear
pointed at or attempted against them unjustly.

There were those, in short, who wanted to see the black reformers fail and who
would criticize their every action. Henceforth, Jones and Allen would not shrink
from the challenge, "and we are confident we shall stand justified in the sight of
the candid and judicious for such conduct."[66]

Their attempts to lead the black community in a time of crisis had ended in
tragedy. It was partly due to the nature of the disaster, but also due to the misguided beliefs of their patron, Benjamin Rush, and to the gruesome task he
assigned them. But it was also because they were blacks who contradicted the
stereotype of blacks in America. They were organized; they did good where others faltered; and they persisted despite threats to their health.

When Carey renewed the tendency of white Americans to dehumanize their
fellow blacks, Jones and Allen blasted their detractors. Already black Americans
had helped to win the American Revolution. Here they had attempted to save life
in the nation's capital. Neither won credit for them in winning that liberty and
equality promised by the Revolution and by the American nation.

But in the Free African Society, Philadelphia blacks had blazed a counterrevolutionary path at odds with the principles of the American Revolution and the
assumptions of the Constitution and Bill of Rights. They separated themselves
from white American society to bring order to the black community. They used the
collective needs of black Americans to establish mutual assistance. They did, on
their own, for black Americans what white Americans neither encouraged nor permitted. Even if they could not secure all of their liberties as Americans, they would
prepare for the day when they could be accepted alongside white Americans.

The key to achieving their vision was to produce a religiously uplifted black
community. They had to have black churches with black ministers. Black
churches would be the building blocks of this new black America. And into this
endeavor Jones and Allen and many other Philadelphia and American blacks
threw themselves after they had finished with the yellow fever epidemic of 1793.
No sooner had they finished with their defenses than they drove with new passion
and conviction to secure those institutions that would enable them to enjoy a
measure of freedom in a society increasingly making them unfree.

In December 1793 construction, which had ended virtually the day the roof
beam was raised in the opening days of the epidemic, resumed on the African
Church. The building was enclosed by the end of the year. More money was
raised during the spring of 1794. But two other obstacles intruded to stall the
completion of this first step of black counterrevolution.

The first was the opposition of existing churches and clergy to the project.
Over the previous ten years, black membership in white churches had grown dramatically. Whether Episcopal, Methodist Episcopal, or Presbyterian, black mem-

bership had expanded with the rise in free black population. Existing churches held the keys to the Kingdom of God, including the power to ordain, to administer sacraments, and to perform marriage vows and burial rites. Without the ability to ordain a minister or perform religious rites, the African church could not operate legally. From the outset, it was dependent on affiliation with another church.

The second obstacle grew out of the first. The Free African Society *had* to choose a denominational affiliation. Sometime late in 1793 or perhaps in early 1794, a special meeting of the society was held to consider three possibilities— Quaker, Episcopalian, and Methodist. After much wrangling, an election was held. "At the election it was determined," Richard Allen later wrote, "there were two in favor of the Methodist, the Rev. Absalom Jones and myself, and a large majority in favor of the Church of England. The majority carried." The group had chosen Episcopal affiliation because at that moment only the local Episcopal Church was willing to see the establishment of a semi-independent black church with a black presiding minister.[67]

According to Allen it was at that point that "a committee was appointed from the African Church to solicit me to be their minister, for there was no colored preacher in Philadelphia but myself." Allen wrote later, "I informed them that I could not be anything else but a Methodist." Allen then decided to do what in his heart he had wanted to do all along: build his own Methodist Church.

This was not a bit of capricious denominationalism. This was for Allen a fundament of the counterrevolution: "I was confident that there was no religious sect or denomination would suit the capacity of the colored people as well as the Methodist." He had seen for himself over many years why "the Methodist is so successful in the awakening and conversion of the colored people." It was due to "the plain doctrine and having a good discipline." Once aroused, whether free black or slave, black converts would "toil in their little patches many a night until midnight to raise their little truck and sell to get something to support" Methodist ministers.[68]

Allen knew firsthand that "the Methodists were the first people that brought glad tidings to the colored people." They unleashed among blacks, not only the gospel, but hopes for liberty. "I am well convinced that the Methodist has proved beneficial to thousands and ten times thousands," he noted. And, thereby, he raised a plan that probably was all along in the back of his mind. The lot he had purchased for the first African Church he had reserved as a potential site for his own church—not just a church where he would preach as he wished, but one that he would literally own. He would also take with him almost all of the blacks who had been fund-raising for the other church (nine of ten black contributors to the other church joined in Allen's endeavor).[69]

So as not to interfere with the progress of the other church, Allen created his own Methodist church with his own resources. On May 5, 1794, he assembled a group of ten black Methodists to help. He bought a small frame building that had been used as a blacksmith shop, then had it hauled to his waiting lot on Sixth Street. Again, with his own funds, he hired carpenters to repair the structure and to convert it into a place of worship. By early July the church was ready to be dedicated.[70]

During July 1794, just twelve days apart, not one, but two black-controlled institutions were dedicated in Philadelphia. On July 17, just weeks after Toussaint-L'Ouverture had taken control of Hispaniola, Philadelphia blacks of all persuasions (and many of their white patrons) gathered to open the African Church of Philadelphia for worship.

Although the audience was subjected to a paternalistic sermon from a white minister, only days passed before Absalom Jones, the new black minister of the first church in America built specifically for black Americans, declared that "the people that walked in darkness have seen a great light." Just as Toussaint was bringing order to an island filled with anarchy, Jones gave witness to the promise that blacks in America would use their churches to do the same.[71]

Ten days later Robespierre and Saint-Just were arrested in Paris and were held overnight to be executed on July 28, 1794. After a yearlong Reign of Terror had resulted in thousands of senseless deaths, the pendulum was swinging in the direction of order. The next day, Bishop Francis Asbury rode into Philadelphia and, at the request of Richard Allen, presided over the dedication of Bethel, first African Methodist Episcopal Church in America. "My dear Lord was with us," wrote Allen much later, "so that there were many hearty 'amen's' echoed through the house."[72]

Allen's little church opened a new epoch. Although Allen and his congregation immediately returned to disputes with white Methodist ministers over the control of this beachhead and over who could preach there, the war for freedom was joined. Allen had a vision for black Americans, and from Bethel—it would forever be known as Mother Bethel—he pursued his vision of making all blacks in America into black Americans.

While other black Americans saw their rights and destiny better achieved through a migration to Africa, Allen, Jones, and many others like them in Philadelphia, Boston, New York, Baltimore, Norfolk, Wilmington, and Charleston chose America as home. And they had to depart from many of the assumptions of the American Revolution to do it. They had to foment a counterrevolution among black Americans and contend with increasing repression in the land of liberty against both free and enslaved blacks. But they were in America to stay.

CHAPTER 25

Order in America's Other Land of Liberty

ADAMS FEDERALISTS AS HAITIAN LIBERATORS

On September 10, 1800, Dr. Edward Stevens, American consul general to St. Domingue, wrote a remarkable letter from Cap François to the American secretary of state assessing the situation on that volatile island. This was the same Edward Stevens who had bedeviled Benjamin Rush during the great Philadelphia yellow fever epidemic of 1793. In 1800 he was serving as diplomatic liaison and observer for the United States in a land nominally a French colony, but that was daily becoming more independent of France and drawing closer to Britain and the United States.

The indomitable Haitian general Toussaint L'Ouverture had just consolidated power over enemies foreign and domestic when Stevens wrote:

> . . . the most perfect Tranquility has been restored to this Colony. The Cultivators of the South have been recalled to their respective Plantations, the various civil Administrations reorganized, and the most effectual Measures adopted for the future Peace and good order of that Department. Agriculture and Commerce begin to revive. . . . the Attention of the General in Chief [Toussaint] has been, altogether, turn'd towards the Establishment of such wise and salutary Regulations as must, eventually, tend to promote the Happiness and Prosperity of St. Domingo [St. Domingue].

Addressing a consideration of importance to American merchants and business leaders, Stevens continued:

> As General Toussaint has been invested by the Inhabitants of this Colony with the supreme Power, both civil and military, and has always evinced the most friendly Sentiments towards America, I should imagine that the present Moment is very favourable for obtaining from him such additional Privileges as would place our Commerce on a permanent and advantageous Footing.

Written to John Marshall, brief replacement for John Adams's mainstay, Timothy Pickering, as secretary of state, Federalist Stevens's statement was astonishing. Nothing so positive was ever written about the Adams administration—even by an Adams relative![1]

How was it that the conservative Stevens—agent of a Federalist administration—came to describe Toussaint L'Ouverture—history's goblin of slave insurrection—in such glowing terms? After a bloody decade of invasions, massacres, and executions prompted by the mother country, Toussaint had answered in kind with former slaves turned warriors. Toussaint had just carried out years of genocidal warfare against André Rigaud, another military genius, and head of the mulatto minority on the island. For five years Toussaint had fought to expel a British invasion begun in 1793 with the intent of bringing the rich sugar island into the British orbit.

On the other hand, Toussaint was entering into conventions and treaties with Britain and the United States to foster new and expanded commerce. He sent marauding black warriors back to plantations, where they were being employed as wage laborers. Toussaint invited fleeing whites back to conduct the fledgling nation's business and to rebuild productive plantations with free labor. Toussaint also singlehandedly cornered the white revolutionary Sonthonax and derailed his active plans to exterminate the white populace of the island.[2]

Following the defeat of British and French armies and the expulsion of Sonthonax in August 1797, Toussaint set about establishing institutions of a republican government. Not only did he begin to form a stable government for the island, he also lectured the French Directory about its responsibilities in protecting liberty. In November 1797, he wrote:

> It is your duty, citizen directors, to help us weather the storm that is being brewed in the shadows of silence by the eternal enemies of liberty. It is your duty to put laws in effect that truly enlighten. It is your duty to keep the enemies of our new order from swarming again over the coasts of our unfortunate island and defiling them with new crimes.

In response the French Directory sent a new special agent in early 1798 with secret orders to draw Toussaint into an invasion of either the British island of Jamaica or the United States. The goals of such an invasion were twofold: first, to harass Britain or the United States and perhaps to seize some territory for France; and, second, to assure the destruction of Toussaint's troublesome but formidable black army.[3]

As the new French agent, Théodore Hédouville, headed to St. Domingue, Toussaint's troops overwhelmed the last forts in British possession around Port-au-Prince and annihilated the last two helpless regiments. Over five years Britain had spent ten million pounds and lost ten thousand casualties attempting to seize the island. But, due to Toussaint's fighting skills, not an inch of the island had been converted into British territory. British generals, filled with European pride, had failed to reckon with the tropical island's disease-infested environment, and they

Toussaint L'Ouverture (n.d.). Indefatigable warrior, he was an enemy of slavery and a crusader for peace.

did not appreciate the fighting abilities of Toussaint's well-trained warriors.[4]

Most of all, they did not recognize that from the fiery uprising of black slaves in 1791 through the abolition of slavery (albeit as a desperate war measure) in 1793, the Haitian love of liberty was stronger than any force that could be assembled by European powers. The British had wasted five years and leaders of the French Revolution made the same mistake, too, for decades. Not long after the arrival of Theódore Hédouville, Toussaint realized the absence of French interest in equality either in France or in St. Domingue. After his triumphal entry into Port-au-Prince, the self-made general began his meteoric campaign to throw all enemy forces off the island and to maneuver his homeland in the direction of an independent republic.

As Hédouville tried to persuade Toussaint to undertake foolhardy invasions of Jamaica and the United States, Toussaint instead entered into agreements with newly arrived British General Thomas Maitland to introduce British commerce across the island. And as Hédouville then conspired with the rival mulatto general André Rigaud to invade Jamaica or to engage Toussaint for the control of St. Domingue, Toussaint came up with a brilliant new strategy. He accepted the title of supreme governor of the island and began exercising powers reserved to the heads of nations, entering into a treaty with another grateful sovereign, George III.[5]

When Hédouville and Rigaud combined their forces in September 1798, the wily general employed the surest winning tactic in his arsenal of special weapons. He spread the rumor that Hédouville with the assistance of Rigaud planned to restore slavery. A force of thousands marched once again with knives, clubs, and vengeance on Cap François. As waves of freed plantation workers descended on the city, Hédouville and a thousand of his collaborators took to waiting ships and fled to France. The result of the frantic stampede neutralized, at least momentarily, a second enemy of independence for the troubled island, namely, the mother country.[6]

A new French agent also was powerless against Toussaint's might. Toussaint faced yet one more domestic enemy and another foreign power in his drive to bring independence to the revolutionary island. But to bolster his drive, Toussaint, in November 1798, opened direct communications with the United States. Fervently believing that the United States had succeeded where France had failed, he addressed a formal letter to that individual who, to him, was the current leader of the free world: John Adams, president of the United States.

It did not matter that Adams had just presided over the enactment of the Alien and Sedition Acts and, through his cabinet, was attempting to wipe out political opposition both among American citizens and resident aliens. It did not matter that Adams was at war with an opposition press and its editors, with Congressional opponents and with Joseph Priestley, Thomas Cooper, and Thomas Paine. It did not matter that Adams was depicted internally as an enemy to the American Revolution, as a latter-day royalist, and as a traitor to liberty itself. Adams also was an elected president soon to be retested at the polls again; he was at the moment for Toussaint the very king of liberty.

What *did* matter to Toussaint was that when the United States closed off commercial relations with France in June 1798, the growing trade between St. Domingue and America also had been disrupted. Toussaint's fervent letter, bearing above his title as "Général en chef de l'Armeé de Saint Domingue" the words *Liberté* and *égalité* and dated November 6 requested America to reopen trade with his land and thereby to come to the assistance of the peoples of St. Domingue. Toussaint wanted aid that, in the Haitian quest for that same liberty, had been so beautifully achieved in the United States.

Adams and Secretary of State Pickering promptly took two actions that caused the United States to do just what Toussaint requested. An act of Congress passed on February 9, 1799, permitted the president to reopen trade with St. Domingue by proclamation—when he was satisfied that American ships would be protected against privateers. Second, on the same date, Adams appointed Dr. Edward Stevens consul general to the island to assist in determining when and if those safe conditions were met.[7]

Secretary of State Pickering declared that the Adams administration would reopen trade with St. Domingue as soon as Stevens's certification had been received. But the president brooded over the matter in self-reflective memoranda to Pickering. In the first of these Adams concluded that "independence is the worst and most dangerous condition they [the West Indian Islands] can be in, for the United States." In the second, he wrote, "It is my earnest desire . . . to do nothing without the consent, concert, and cooperation of the British government in this case."

In the third, after receiving affirmative dispatches from Stevens suggesting that a resumption of trade might be favorable, Adams advised Pickering:

> The result of the whole is, in my mind, problematical and precarious. Toussaint has evidently puzzled himself, the French government, the English cabinet, and the administration of the United States. All the rest of the world know as little what to do with him as he knows what to do with himself.

By July 1799, despite Adams's natural penchant for caution, he and his cabinet were enthralled by the colorful Haitian general. Toussaint had somehow greased his way into the American orbit and had already opened St. Domingan ports to America ships with guarantees for their protection.[8]

All of this was confirmed in a tripartite treaty between Toussaint, Britain, and the United States signed on May 22, 1799, protecting Anglo-American trade in those portions of St. Domingue controlled by Toussaint, guaranteeing that Toussaint would not attack either Jamaica or the United States, and providing, that neither Britain nor America would interfere with a small navy being developed by Toussaint. At the request of both Britain and the United States—nations that unlike France and St. Domingue still recognized the institution of slavery—an amendment was added on June 13 wherein Toussaint agreed not to promote the indoctrination of slaves in either nation or their possessions with "dangerous principles." By giving a little and by demanding quite a lot from Britain and the United States—both paranoid about the potentials of slave revolts and racial warfare—Toussaint obtained the solid backing he needed to take his next carefully calculated steps toward a single government for the island and independence from France.[9]

The emboldened Toussaint made another direct appeal to President Adams on August 14, 1799. Earlier he wanted American shipping. This time he wanted the support of armed American ships as he wiped out the only remaining faction not under his control—André Rigaud's mulatto army in the south and west of St. Domingue. The alternative was that he would expand his fledgling navy to challenge an armada of attack barges possessed by Rigaud. He reiterated that only the defeat of Rigaud would make it possible for American shippers to begin trading, under protection, in that part of the island.[10]

Adams obliged. When Toussaint launched his struggle to the death with Rigaud in October, he had the guaranteed firepower of a strong American naval fleet. As he sent General Dessalines against Grand and Petit Goave and General Christophe against the mulatto stronghold of Jacmel, heavily armed American ships bombarded mulatto fortifications and destroyed Rigaud's transport barges. When the British navy intercepted and seized a small naval squadron built secretly against British wishes by Toussaint early in 1800, the American navy emerged again in March to reinforce Toussaint's final push on Jacmel. The American ships *Boston, Connecticut, Constitution,* and *General Greene*—apt symbols of the American Revolution—stood by, bombarding where needed and attacking mulatto vessels. The display of American force and the fierce fighting of Toussaint's troops brought victory.[11]

André Rigaud fled to the mulatto capital of Les Cayes, where he again defied Toussaint's rule. Although Toussaint offered Rigaud and his officers clemency to lay down their arms, the general refused. When Toussaint sent Dessalines against the city in late July with orders to silence all resistance, Rigaud boarded a waiting ship and fled to France by way of Cuba. With Rigaud's departure on July 29, 1800, Toussaint marched triumphantly into Les Cayes on August 1. Finally, all St. Domingue had come under the control, not of a European, but a Haitian. Although there had been no formal declaration of independence, Toussaint was on the verge of accomplishing what only George Washington had done before.[12]

The action secured the French end of the island of Hispaniola, but Toussaint's sights were set higher. He aspired to consolidate the entire island by eliminating any colonial power that might control the eastern end. In early January 1801

Toussaint attacked Spanish Santo Domingo and walked without resistance across the eastern end of the island. By January 24 he made a triumphal entry into the city of Santo Domingo as the conqueror of the colony, issuing a proclamation giving freedom to the fifteen thousand slaves living there. He also planned to consolidate the former Spanish dominion into a model republic for the Western world.

Taking a cue perhaps from the constitutionalist Adams, Toussaint on February 5 established a Central Assembly of ten members to draft a constitution for the consolidated St. Domingue. Just as in the case of the American constitution, Toussaint wanted the document to reflect the wisdom of history, political philosophy, and the special character of his unique island. Rather than stacking the Central Assembly with individuals chosen to represent the various factions and racial groups on the island, he appointed seven white and three mulatto citizens—all selected for their knowledge and commitment to constitutionalism.[13]

The Central Assembly's work behind closed doors extended over a period of several months. As they worked Toussaint issued the most important letter of his inspired career. Under the date of February 12, 1801, he addressed his aims to the sole remaining obstacle in his course toward an independent Haitian republic, the first consul of France, Napoléon Bonaparte. His request of Napoléon was simple and direct, but fraught with symbolic power. He wrote:

> Now that peace has been restored to the colony and it has been rid of enemies, it is my duty to write and ask you to confirm the promotions that you had promised to the courageous soldiers who helped me during the difficult campaigns. They are all deserving officers who are worthy of the confidence and the gratitude of the nation. Citizen Consul, the soldiers of Haiti have indeed earned their right to be recognized by the government of France.

The rest of his letter justified his invasion of Santo Domingo against the advice of the current French agent in St. Domingue, but the key to any future connection between France and the consolidated island lay, in Toussaint's mind at least, in the full recognition of the Haitian army and its generals as officers in the French national army.

While he awaited word as to whether the French consul, soon to become emperor, would incorporate Haitians fully into French citizenship, Toussaint continued working with his handpicked Central Assembly to write a Haitian constitution. Led by Bernard Borgella, former mayor of Port-au-Prince and once a royalist, the assembly studied the American constitution as its model. Encouraging petitions from towns and villages across the island, it then moved into confidential sessions. Toussaint bade the assembly to declare emphatically that slavery in any form would be banned from Haiti forever, but also that the rights of whites, mulattoes, and blacks would be protected. "All people shall live, worship and die on this island as free Frenchmen," he demanded.[14]

When the assembly turned over its final draft of the constitution on May 9, Toussaint still had not heard from Napoléon—even though the First Consul had drafted, but had not released, a cordial response on March 4. He would never send it.[15]

In the absence of guidance or notice from France, Toussaint accepted the draft constitution and entered into consultations with Borgella and the assembly that lasted four weeks. He reviewed every detail with Borgella, asking shrewd questions and wanting revisions that stressed the importance of religion and morals in the nation and—unlike in the American model inspired by Adams—the absolute executive power of the governor-general (himself!) for life, with the right to designate his successor.

Although his model for a constitution was that of the United States, his vision for governance under that constitution was that of the French first consul. The final version of the constitution was approved by the Central Assembly on July 7, and he promulgated it as the law of the land on July 16, 1801, reading it before a gathering of thousands in Cap François. Toussaint swore his allegiance to the new constitution so long as he should serve as governor-general or live.[16]

By now Haiti was midway through the first year of peace the island had known in a decade. The Haitian population had returned to work in villages and on plantations as free laborers. Plantation production and commerce had been restored, with the help of American ships and merchants, almost to the level achieved before the night of fire in 1791. Once again ships were arriving from Africa with a fresh labor force of free immigrants to a free land. All of this had been engineered by the farseeing Toussaint, but it also was a product of the direct encouragement of perhaps America's most conservative administration prior to the Civil War, that of John Adams, the American Burke.

TOUSSAINT, THE HAITIAN BURKE

The cupid in the love affair between John Adams and Toussaint L'Ouverture was Edward Stevens who had been sent in early 1799 to determine when it would be safe for American ships to call on former French ports in St. Domingue. From the moment of Stevens's arrival in Cap François, he reported that Toussaint wanted to do business with America. In his first dispatch on May 3, 1799, he wrote:

> He [Toussaint] received me very favorably—expressed much satisfaction, at the attention which had been paid to his letter by the Executive of the United States, and seemed particularly pleased, with the Presidents humane Permission to afford a temporary supply to the Colony, at a moment when it was reduced to the extremest Distress, by a total want of all the articles usually imported from America.

"His penetration and good sense, enabled him to see the Justice and Propriety of the President's Demands," wrote Stevens, "and after lengthy conversation . . . was convinced that nothing was asked, but what was conducive to the prosperity of the Colony." And what was asked was the safe arrival and departure from St.

Domingue. Stevens also claimed, "He will be responsible for every-thing that happens to American Vessels trading to the different ports contained in it." [17]

On the subject of the suspected Haitian invasion of Jamaica, he wrote to British General Maitland assuringly, "Toussaint is determined to prevent this Expedition, in Conformity to his Treaty with you." Just a month later in June 1799, as Toussaint was preparing to take on André Rigaud, Stevens forwarded to Pickering the secret convention of June 13 between Toussaint, Maitland, and Stevens outlining "every essential point respecting the Safety of American Commerce." Things were going so well with Toussaint that Stevens admitted he had unilaterally provided some of "the Pressing Wants of Gen: Toussaint," namely "a small temporary Supply of Provisions" from Jamaica. These items were to feed Toussaint's "Army of 12000 Men in this Neighborhood [at Arcahaie, central Haiti], and [with] not a single Pound of Flour or Salt Provisions to give them." Stevens justified his direct intervention in this manner: "I thought it advantageous to the Interests of America to consent to the Supply, especially as it is intended entirely for the Use of Toussaint's Army, is small and limited and will be consumed before the Ports are open'd, and, of course, will have no Influence on the Market." [18]

The next day Stevens further defended his action by describing the well-provisioned army of André Rigaud, while "Toussaint's Army, on the contrary, is in want of every Thing." He also described for Pickering and John Adams just what was at stake: "Toussaint has on his Side most of the Blacks, and all of the Whites of the Colony. His humane and mild Conduct has render'd him respectable to the latter, and they now look up to him as their only Shield against the cruel Tyranny of Rigaud." In fact, when Rigaud took possession of Petite Goave, near Port-au-Prince, the whites of that city counterattacked. But, Stevens wrote, "Toussaint objected to it, observing that they had already suffered Misfortunes enough by the Revolution, and that he had Men enough to finish the Contest, and protect them, without subjecting them again to the Horrors of War."

Stevens then contrasted Rigaud and Toussaint. Rigaud, "proud, haughty and cruel, and agitated by a restless Ambition, views with Impatience a Negro at the Head of Affairs and in Possession of that Power which he thinks is due alone to his superior Talents." Toussaint, by comparison, was "more mild and humane [and] thinks that the Interests of human Nature require this Man to be deposed." Stevens believed Rigaud "would deluge the Country with Blood to accomplish his favourite Point, and slaughter indiscriminately whites, blacks, and even the leading Chiefs of his own Colour." Toussaint, on the contrary,

> is desirous of being confirmed in his Authority by the united Efforts of all the Inhabitants, whose Friend and Protector he wishes to be consider'd, and, I am convinced, were his power uncontroled he wd: exercise it in protecting Commerce, encouraging Agriculture and establishing useful Regulations for the internal Government of the Colony.

With regard to fighting abilities between Toussaint and Rigaud, Stevens wrote, "as soon as the former has furnished his Army with what it wants and taken to the Field, the latter must yield." [19]

The more Stevens observed Toussaint, the clearer was his judgment that the general had firm principles and clear goals for his homeland. Even as Toussaint contended with Rigaud—one of the great veterans of the 1779 siege of Savannah—another Haitian veteran of that experience, Martial Besse, arrived in Cap François with orders from the French Directory to command the French invasion of Jamaica. Stevens intercepted a copy of the plan as it was presented by Besse to Toussaint with pleas for the general to join in the scheme. Pickering and Adams must have shivered to read Stevens's commentary: "I shall make no Comments on this diabolical Attempt to extend the destructive Influence of french Principles and to add another Million to those which already crouch under the Iron Sceptre of modern Liberty, and Equality." But they surely breathed easier when Stevens added, "Toussaint on the other Hand is determined that the Invasion shall not take Place. He appears to encourage it that he may the more certainly prevent it." Toussaint not only had character, principles, and goals, he could outwit the best of them, including Martial Besse, who from the days at Savannah had a long history of fomenting revolution to secure the rights of mulattoes, not of all Haitians. [20]

Stevens's dispatches on events in St. Domingue poured in to Pickering and Adams with glorious depictions of the amazing Toussaint. As Toussaint opened his assault to rout Rigaud from the island, he took time to address details concerning the arrival and departure of American ships. After one such session, Stevens wrote, "I have the most perfect Confidence in the Attachment of Toussaint to the Government of the U.S. and in his sincere Desire to establish a beneficial and permanent Commerce between the two Countries." And as soon as Toussaint sent General Christophe against Jacmel, Stevens proposed a plan "to make the necessary Provision for opening the Ports of the South, in Proportion as they are surrender'd by Rigaud." This was possible because "as soon as they are in Toussaint's Possession the commercial Relations may be renewed between them and the U. States with Safety and Advantage." To promote this end Stevens again gave Toussaint the use of "a small american Schooner that I keep here chiefly as a Packet Boat." [21]

Stevens's next dispatch was written from aboard the armed American vessel *Experiment* in January 1800, as the American fleet encountered André Rigaud's armada of barges "strongly armed and manned with upwards of 500 Negroes and Mulattoes." During the encounter, two American ships were captured by Rigaud's forces. Toussaint's cruisers retook one of them, while the other escaped. Although Toussaint was discouraged that British and American naval commanders would not let him expand his own fleet, he was grateful for the American support from sea. Again Stevens stood out as a strong and independent arm acting out American policy in the field. During and after these engagements, he served as link among Toussaint, British agents and commanders, and American naval officers, defining policy and directing military support for Toussaint's crusade, all the while faithfully reporting his actions to the eager Pickering and the always nervous Adams.[22]

Stevens spent the next six months sending Pickering and Adams dispatches with evidence of the wisdom of his course. On February 13 he wrote that the "Command of the Treasury and a control of the civil as well as military Departments has been openly assumed by the Genl. in Chief and his subordinate Officers." In fact, he thought, "Every Thing announces a speedy Dissolution of those Ties, which once connected this important Colony with the Mother Country."

Toussaint revealed to the American agent his "real Intentions." Stevens, writing immediately to Pickering, declared "it is my Duty to announce them to you," as follows: "He is taking his measures slowly but securely. All connection with France will soon be broken off. If he is not disturbed he will preserve appearances a little longer. But as soon as France interferes with this colony he will throw off the mask and declare it independent." True to his word, Toussaint closed down the operations of the latest agent of France (Philippe Roume), but kept him under house arrest with the knowledge that, if allowed to depart the island, he would surely "intrigue against him in France." Reported Stevens, "he will keep him a close Prisoner, and take all <u>power civil and military</u> into his own Hands."[23]

By the middle of April 1800, the peoples of the island began to speak out. The heads of municipalities and armed forces, Stevens faithfully reported, began clamoring for Toussaint "to assume the Command and administer the Affairs of Government." When Toussaint demurred, "a respectable Deputation was sent from hence [Cap François] with an Address signed by at least 2500 of the principal Inhabitants . . . soliciting the Genl. in Chief to supercede" the French Agent. "It is no difficult Matter to foresee how this Business will terminate," wrote Stevens: "<u>He will accept of the unanimous Invitation of the Colony, and from that Moment it may be considered as forever separated from France.</u>"[24]

The Stevens portrait of Toussaint was becoming ever more compelling, as he described the rise of a true Spartacus. Stevens pictured a military genius with diplomatic cunning devoted to a clear set of causes—liberty for the peoples of Haiti from slavery and liberty of Haiti from foreign manipulation—the same worthy goals that had driven the course of John Adams from the onset of the American Revolution until its conclusion.

But what a strange circumstance during those heady months that brought the eighteenth century to a close, that saw liberty among Americans challenged through internal dissensions and by alien and sedition laws, and that presented Americans with their first divisive electoral campaign to depose a sitting president. As those fewer and fewer Americans who had the right to vote went to the polls in December 1800 to cast votes for electors who would chose a president, Toussaint in St. Domingue was consolidating his government, uniting his island, and beginning work on a new constitutional government.

By the middle of February 1801, as American electors were deadlocked in what would be remembered as one of the most politically savage presidential selections in American history, Toussaint was sending off a letter to the first consul of France announcing the vanquishment of enemies against France and the onset of peace across his land. In that letter and in other speeches, letters, and the constitution he would promulgate in July 1801, Toussaint made it clear that he was not a minister of revolution, but rather of order. Every action he took made him one of the world's most accomplished proponents of the counterrevolution that was sweeping through the Western world.

Under his constitution he maintained the army as his principal instrument of order, but he installed a system of individual identification and of employment that gave work to the able-bodied across the island. The supportive place of the Roman Catholic Church was restored, and priests were given a prominent role in eliminating voodoo practice, prostitution, and concubinage—practices Toussaint identified with slavery. He also urged the Church to expand its system of education and committed state support—second only to the army—to the effort. Hence, a year before Chateaubriand would publish his second call, *The Genius of Christianity* (April 1802), to restore the Church in France, Toussaint had already done so in his black republic.

In instructions issued to his officers he insisted upon the teaching of the catechism and religious services. In one of his orders he wrote,

> the army commanders shall be ordered to lead the men in morning or evening prayers, to the extent their service activities allow this. At the very next parade, the commanding generals must have a High Mass celebrated and a *Te Deum* sung in all municipalities of their province as a manifestation of gratitude to the Lord for having led us in our campaigns, for the enemy's departure without blood having been shed and for a safe return of thousands of people of all skin colors who had gone astray.

He threw himself into building schools, roads, and parks in a land of careful order, of political hierarchy, and of devotion to God.[25]

From the point of view of Edward Stevens, this Toussaint was a godsend. And he sent that message to Pickering, to Marshall, to Adams. Stephen Girard, millionaire merchant of Philadelphia with vast investments in St. Domingue, heard the message and happily expanded his business there. Even George Washington, having read Toussaint's orders to open ports to Americans, shipped a load of flour there that would not keep long in "the approaching heats."[26]

It was not that Stevens was intentionally making the world safe for American business and commerce. He was, of course, doing that. Nor was it that Stevens and Alexander Hamilton, both deriving from the West Indies, had a special agenda among those islands. It was rather that Toussaint was consciously carrying out a counterrevolution in St. Domingue to bring order to the island for the first time in a decade. He was doing it so that he and his fellow citizens—black, mulatto, and white—could enjoy the liberty often promised, but always taken away by revolution and ideology. Adams and his fellow Federalists, swept from office through an electoral logjam and a backroom deal worked out by Alexander Hamilton, could only marvel in early 1801 that Toussaint, the Haitian Burke, was doing a better job than they in securing both liberty and order.

CHAPTER 26

The Judgment of History

Just as Macaulay's *History of England* was as much a history of liberty as of England, Mercy Otis Warren's *History of the Rise, Progress, and Termination of the American Revolution,* published in 1805—but begun during the war in the 1770s—was a stern assessment of human devotion to the progress of freedom. Human actions were black or white, rarely gray. Human actors, be they innocent Americans, corrupt loyalists, or tyrannical Britons, played their parts to produce in America a divinely inspired republic. Despite all of the muddle of foreign diplomacy, ruined economies, starving armies, and civil strife, the outcome was never in question. American goodness was certain, due to God's guidance, to win in the end. American soldiers fought with righteous spirit; British troops harassed and raped women and children. But in the end America's revolution was the first great act of a world striving to bring liberty to all peoples.[1]

Although Warren's *History of the American Revolution* would not be published until 1805, the basic text remained little changed from the euphoric hopes for liberty she spread in her poems and plays during and after the Revolution. Stirring descriptions of social and political events, the movement of armies, and the character of America's revolutionary leaders filled thirteen hundred pages of her work. And since she was "connected by nature, friendship, and every social tie, with many of the first patriots, and most influential characters on the continent" and had from before the revolution maintained "epistolary intercourse with several gentlemen employed abroad in the most distinguished stations," her history was, she argued, a faithful eyewitness account. Because men were the ones who spilled blood and whose blood was let, she purposely left out descriptions of "the blood-stained field" and "of slaughtered armies," abdicating the responsibility of describing those acts to male authors.

Through her plays, her poems, and her history, Warren attested to the power of liberating revolutions in bringing freedom to men and women throughout the world. She also established herself as an enviable American role model for women who wished to establish their independence and take their place in careers and society. Alongside Catherine the Great, Suzanne Necker, and Catharine

Macaulay, she inspired generations of women hoping to enjoy the fruits of liberty promised by the American Revolution.

From the Stamp Act controversy in chapter 2 of the first volume through chapter 30 of George Washington's resignation of his commission, liberty marched brashly and beautifully on. But in that the *History* was not published until 1805, Warren could not resist the opportunity of bringing the story of liberty to the end of the century. In a ninety-page chapter 31, she offered "Supplementary Observations on succeeding Events, after the Termination of the American Revolution." She forecasted its contents in the work's preface, signed March 1805: "As a new century has dawned upon us, the mind is naturally led to contemplate the great events that have run parallel with, and have just closed the last." Claiming that the United States should adhere to "those principles which obtained their independence," she observed that "these [principles] have indeed, at certain periods, appeared to be in the wane." But, she continued, "let them never be eradicated, by the jarring interests of parties, jealousies of the sister states, or the ambition of individuals!"[2]

The interests of parties, jealousies of states, and ambition of individuals subsumed her appended chapter. Although America at the end of the Revolution was "possessed of a prize, replete with advantages seldom thrown into the hand of any people," vicious forces soon emerged. Factions, economic interests, and "various other combinations caused a cloud of chagrin to sit on almost every brow, and a general uneasiness to pervade the bosoms of most of the inhabitants of America." Massachusetts "seemed to be the seat of sedition," with its troublesome Shays's rebellion. Fearful men gathered in Philadelphia in 1787 in secrecy to contemplate a restoration of monarchy: "The greatest happiness of the greatest number was not the principal object of their contemplations."

The resulting document "was thought by many to be too strongly marked with the features of monarchy." It was further flawed by the absence of any guarantee of human rights. It was so antirepublican that "the philosophic doctor Franklin observed, when he lent his signature to the adoption of the new constitution, 'that its complexion was doubtful; that it might last for ages, involve one quarter of the globe, and probably terminate in despotism.'" Whereas most accounts of Franklin's views on the Constitution cast him as hopeful, Warren concluded, "he signed the instrument for the consolidation of the government of the United States with tears, and apologized for doing it at all, from the doubts and apprehensions he felt, that his countrymen might not be able to do better, even if they called a new convention."

America's yeomanry "who had tasted the sweets of mediocrity, equality, and liberty" greeted the ratification of the Constitution "in silent anguish, folded the solemn page with a sigh, and wept over the names of the native sons of America, who had sold their lives to leave the legacy of freedom to their children." Only the addition of the Bill of Rights and the placement of George Washington, "the favorite of every class of people," at the head of the new government saved America from annihilation. Despite Washington's character and judgment, "a struggle

*"The Triumph of Liberty" (1796). A reminder in 1796 that the Liberty (tall col-
umn) achieved by American revolutionaries (listed on the shorter column) had
brought Plenty, Justice, and Peace (the goddesses in the center) and the overthrow of kings (fleeing, suicidal figures on the right).*

began to take place between monarchists and republicans." A class of men soon
appeared who "imbibed ideas of distinguished rank and ostentatious titles, incom-
patible with republican principles."

Washington shockingly entered into a treaty with America's archenemy, England, thereby obliterating America's amity with a French people struggling "for
freedom and the equal rights of man." He then unleashed armies to crush unhappy
farmers in Pennsylvania. Washington's record was so defective, wrote Warren, "that
further strictures on his character and conduct shall be left to future historians."

Washington's successor, John Adams—Warren's lifelong friend and correspondent—came to the presidency tainted by "a partiality for monarchy" taken
on while he lived in London in the 1780s. Although Adams "was undoubtedly a
statesman of penetration and ability, . . . his prejudices and his passions were
sometimes too strong for his sagacity and judgment." Warren could not decipher
how someone who had been so sound on republicanism during the American
Revolution could have strayed so far.

Without actually listing Adams's "mistakes or changes in political opinion, or errors in public conduct," Warren assumed that her readers shared her judgment. Hence, she refrained from

> any further strictures . . . on the character of a gentleman, whose official stations, abilities and services, amidst the revolutionary conflict, may probably excite some future historian to investigate the causes of his lapse from former republican principles, and to observe with due propriety on his administration and its consequences while president of the United States.

Adams, she knew directly, was in private life of "unimpeachable character" and "beloved by his neighbours"; as president of the United States he was a decided enemy of liberty.

Having championed liberty throughout her life, Warren, like every friend of liberty, had to grapple with the realities of revolution and chaos, rights and responsibilities, freedom and order. As she surveyed from the vantage point of 1801, the surges for liberty and rights that circled the globe in the early 1790s she observed that "Authority and obedience are necessary to preserve social order, and to continue the prosperity or even the existence of nations. But it may be observed, that despotism is not always the certain consequence of monarchy, nor freedom the sure result of republican theories." Having condemned the failures of Washington and Adams to pursue liberty correctly, she again called all Americans to the original aspirations of their Revolution.

America, she firmly believed, lived through "a revolution that will be ever memorable, both for its origin, its success, and the new prospects it has opened both at home and abroad." Despite the foibles of politicians and misguided monarchists

> the consequences of this revolution have not been confined to one quarter of the globe, but the dissemination of more liberal principles in government, and more honorable opinions of the rights of man, and the melioration of his condition, have been spread over a considerable part of the world.

Though Warren lost faith in human actors—including the closest of her friends—she preached to her last breath the providential blessings of the American Revolution and the eternal opportunities it offered for the liberty, freedom, and rights of all humans—women and men. And she preached it all in the context of a set of principles and practices that would bring order.[3]

PART V

THE VICTORY OF ORDER

CHAPTER 27

Friends of Liberty in the Land of Order

LIBERATORS REPUDIATED

On Wednesday, August 30, 1797, Mary Wollstonecraft, author of *A Vindication of the Rights of Woman,* entered into labor for the second time in her short life. She was in perfect health and even ridiculed the practice of women of remaining in their bedchambers for up to a month after giving birth. Determined to bear her second child the way nature intended, she eschewed doctors and nurses and engaged an experienced midwife. From five in the morning until two in the afternoon, she chatted with friends in her parlor and wrote notes to her husband William Godwin and her friends. At 11:20 P.M. she gave birth to her second daughter, later known as Mary Wollstonecraft Shelley.

Godwin waited in the parlor below, awaiting the moment when he would be presented with his first child. When the midwife descended, she instead gave him the alarming news that the afterbirth had not emerged from the uterus as it should have. Godwin raced to the residence of Dr. Poignand, physician at the Westminster Lying-in Hospital. Poignand came immediately and began the delicate process of removing the afterbirth piece by piece until he was satisfied that no residue remained.

During the ordeal Wollstonecraft lost so much blood that she remained most of the next day in a state of semiconsciousness. In one of her conscious moments she asked Godwin to call in Dr. George Fordyce, a close friend. Poignand scoffed at the idea during his visit to Wollstonecraft that day. "Dr. Fordyce," he quipped, "was not particularly conversant with obstetrical cases." Godwin, nevertheless, summoned Fordyce, who found Wollstonecraft to be properly on the mend; he even commended her for the use of a midwife.

Thursday, Friday, and Saturday saw constant improvement in Wollstonecraft's condition. On Sunday, September 3, Godwin went about business as usual the entire day. When he returned late in the evening to have dinner with his wife of only five months, he learned that she had suffered a "shivering fit" during the day. Poignand was called in again. Upon examination, he proclaimed that some portion of the placenta must have remained in Wollstonecraft's womb. He was dismissed and Fordyce was put solely in charge of the increasingly ill patient.

Fordyce's daily ministrations could not avert puerperal infection. On September 4 Fordyce took the baby from Wollstonecraft's breast. The next day, he called a surgeon to consider another removal procedure, then ordered that she be plied freely with wine to numb her growing pain. Godwin fed her wine for three hours until a Mr. Carlisle, an expert in wine diets for the dying, could be brought in. Carlisle ministered his liquid sedatives while Fordyce, the surgeon, and nurses provided constant care. Four of Godwin's closest friends consoled the melancholy husband. Wollstonecraft seemed to improve after the flow of wine began. But within a day, Carlisle reported with great alarm that he thought death was near. Wollstonecraft spoke of death, but lingered. At six in the morning of Sunday, September 10, Carlisle called Godwin from his bed to experience what would surely be the last moments. At 7:40 A.M., Godwin observed Wollstonecraft's last breath. She expired having entrusted her two daughters to Godwin.

Few were called to her funeral and burial. These occurred on the morning of September 15 at 10:00 A.M. in the parish of St. Pancras, Middlesex. Over her tomb Godwin erected a monument bearing the inscription:

MARY WOLLSTONECRAFT GODWIN,

Author of

A Vindication

of the Rights of Woman:

Born 27 April, 1759

Died 10 September, 1797

At the tender age of thirty-eight she lay dead, one of the most important individuals in the history of women's rights.[1]

At the same moment that Godwin memorialized his late wife as the champion of women's rights, he also began a project that destroyed her as a credible spokesperson for either liberty or women. In a mysterious and unvarnished narrative that covered every episode in Wollstonecraft's life—published in 1797 just months after her death—Godwin dismantled the heroine, declared her to be emotionally unstable, and stated that she had violated every convention of polite society.

He showed that her family life was troubled from birth to adulthood. She had supported a cantankerous father and her underemployed siblings. Striving for "usefulness," she received help from Richard Price, Samuel Johnson, and Mrs. Burgh, widow of the famous author of *Political Disquisitions*. But it was the publisher Joseph Johnson who in 1787 set her up in a new career of editing, translating French texts, and writing essays for his journal, the *Analytical Review*. With the income provided to her, she was finally able to place her sisters and brothers in suitable schools or work positions and to send one brother to America.

Disentangling herself from family, Godwin continued, allowed Wollstonecraft to assume a lifestyle heretofore unknown in the annals of womanhood. The onset of the French Revolution produced "a conspicuous effect in the progress of Mary's reflections," he wrote. Indeed, "her respect for establishments was undermined." Then "full of sentiments of liberty," she "seized her pen in the full burst of indigna-

Mary Wollstonecraft (c. 1797). She authored A Vindication of the Rights of Woman, *but was often victim to the whims of self-righteous men.*

tion" and attacked Edmund Burke's *Reflections on the Revolution in France.* According to Godwin, her attack was "a too contemptuous and intemperate treatment of the great man against whom its attack [was] directed." Next came *A Vindication of the Rights of Woman,* which he denominated as "a very unequal performance and eminently deficient in method and arrangement," but which, nevertheless, "will be read as long as the English language endures." It would be read because Wollstonecraft would "be found to have performed more substantial service for the cause of her sex, than all the other writers, male or female, that ever felt themselves animated in the behalf of oppressed and injured beauty."

Godwin's strangely mixed critique of his wife then took an inexplicable turn. He prefaced it with some of his characteristic but ominous brackets: "[The remainder of the story I have to relate is less literary, than personal. For the rest of her life Mary was continually occupied by a train of circumstances, which roused all the prepossessions and passions of her mind.]" What demon caused Godwin to move from scathing critique to a tell-all narrative of Wollstonecraft's most intimate feelings and actions? And once he started, nothing was too sacred to hold back.

First, he recounted Wollstonecraft's efforts to snare a married man, the artist Henry Fuseli. "She conceived a personal and ardent affection for him," Godwin wrote. "What she experienced in this respect, was no doubt heightened, by the state of celibacy and restraint in which she had hitherto lived, and to which the rules of polished society condemn an unmarried woman." But Wollstonecraft chose not to follow those rules, believing, "that whatever related to the gratification of the senses, ought to arise, in a human being of a pure mind, only as the consequence of an individual affection." The chase died when Fuseli's wife turned Wollstonecraft away.

No sooner had her efforts to lure Fuseli failed than "she entered into that species of connection for which her heart secretly panted"—"an affair of the heart." For four months in 1793, Wollstonecraft and the American adventurer Gilbert Imlay explored sensuality in every manner possible: "Her confidence was entire; her love was unbounded. Now, for the first time in her life, she gave loose to all the sensibilities of her nature." When the four-month affair concluded,

Wollstonecraft was madly in love with Imlay and found "reason to suppose herself with child." Before Imlay departed on business, she had determined they would not be married. She thought the institution superfluous to human needs. She did take the American Imlay's name, however, to avoid arrest in revolutionary France.

Wollstonecraft bore Imlay's illegitimate daughter. When Imlay deserted her, she chased after him to Le Havre, to London, and across England. She twice attempted suicide. In another bracketed interruption to the narrative Godwin pondered Wollstonecraft's sanity, concluding that she had "deluded" herself into a position where she was "willing to consign all these [life, motherhood, and happiness] to premature destruction."

In a final bracketed message covering the period of April 1796, Godwin delved into the subject of Wollstonecraft's morals when he and she came together as lovers. "Her visit [to his quarters], it seems, is to be deemed a deviation from etiquette; but she had through life trampled on those rules which are built on the assumption of the imbecility of her sex." He then observed that until Wollstonecraft had taken up with him "calumny itself had not dared to utter an insinuation against her." But he admitted that "in the latter part of her life, she departed from the morality of vulgar minds too decidedly to be forgiven by its abettors." This judgment he rendered even though both of them favored an open relationship and opposed marriage; that is, until April 1797 when they wedded due to "the circumstance of Mary being in a state of pregnancy."[2]

This intimate picture of Mary Wollstonecraft was sprung upon the world in December 1797. Until its appearance in book form in London, Wollstonecraft, both in Britain and in America, had been received as a prophet of liberty and of a new age for women. Her articles, translations, and even *A Vindication of the Rights of Woman* had been praised and frequently reprinted in the United States for American readers. While some editors considered her a severe critic of Edmund Burke, most in both Britain and America found her treatise on women sensible and appropriate. In Britain the *Monthly Review,* the *Critical Review,* and Johnson's *Analytical Review* carried warm appraisals of her calls to establish the rights of men and women. In the United States the major urban magazines—*The New-York Magazine, The Columbian Centinel* (Boston), *The Philadelphia Monthly, The Massachusetts Magazine,* and *Lady's Magazine and Repository of Entertaining Knowledge* (Philadelphia)—praised her proposals. Most of these published generous obituaries during the first three months after her death.[3]

But lightning struck her fame and legacy when Godwin's *Memoirs* appeared first in London, then in excerpts in the same magazines that had lauded her, and, finally, in book reprints in America in 1799. The *European Magazine* in early 1798 derided her life as an ugly example of the new order she had called for and "a philosophical wanton, breaking down the bars intended to restrain licentiousness." The *British Critic* now found her to be "in the strongest sense, a voluptuary and sensualist but without refinement." The editors noted particularly from

Godwin's detailed account of her death that "during her last illness, no religious expression escaped the author's lips." The *Anti-Jacobin Review* also scored her morals, questioned her principles, and judged her behavior as illustrations of Jacobinism in action. Two books appeared in London expanding the attack: Richard Polwhele's satirical poem, *The Unsex'd Females* (1798) and George Walker's novel, *The Vagabond: Or Practical Infidelity* (1799).[4]

And when excerpts of the *Memoirs* appeared in the United States, American readers were stunned. In a six-page correspondence to *The Monthly Magazine and American Review* one reviewer acknowledged, "In the memoirs of her life, and her Wrongs of Woman, I felt shocked, and even disgusted, at the licence she seems to allow to the unrestrained indulgence of the feelings." The same writer concluded:

> I stand aghast at the dismal spectacle! my soul shudders at
> the terrific ruin!—a creature so noble!—a genius so towering!
> . . . Oh! Mary, thou who couldst speak with such sublime emo-
> tion of the God who formed thee, couldst thou think thou
> hadst a right to destroy his workmanship? . . . What mist
> obscured thy judgment?—What demon chained thy prudence
> and palsied thy activity?—Where slept thy reason, whither
> wandered thy philosophy at this momentous crisis?

The same journal soon published a playful dialogue between two young women in which they discussed their reading of Wollstonecraft's *A Vindication of the Rights of Woman*. The conclusion was that a young woman "should never qualify herself to judge correctly of so coarse a performance."

The denunciations continued after the American printings of Godwin's *Memoirs* appeared in 1799. Sarah Wood in a novel titled *Dorval: or the Speculator* charged that Wollstonecraft in her treatise "endeavored to shake the foundation of female happiness; . . . to rob them of their honor, probity, and integrity; . . . to trample upon duty and virtue; [and to] laugh at the institution of marriage." George Walker's *Vagabond* and Richard Polwhele's *Unsex'd Females* appeared in Boston and New York. The former was a thinly veiled rendition of Wollstonecraft's life as recounted by Godwin. The Philadelphia *Port-Folio* praised the book whose "object is to expose the moral deformity of modern philosophers."

The latter poem by Polwhele was reprinted by William Cobbett in New York, who prefaced his edition with a charge that Wollstonecraft and other "liter-ary ladies in Great Britain had thrown aside that modesty, which is the best char-acteristic . . . of their sex, and . . . with unblushing front, had adopted the senti-ments and the manners of the impious amazons of republican France." Polwhele's poem was graphic in detail, everywhere filled with allusions to sex:

> See Wolstonecraft [*sic*], whom no decorum checks,
> Arise, the intrepid champion of her sex;
> O'er humbled man assert the sovereign claim
> And slight the timid blush of virgin fame.

A review of this edition of Polwhele's work in the Boston *Columbian Centinel and Massachusetts Federalist* in June 1800 openly attacked "the moral deformity of those arrogant and audacious, literary, political, philosophical courtezans, who emulous of the fame of MRS. WOOLSTONECRAFT [*sic*], have striven to divest the sex of their ancient character." The reviewer thought that Wollstonecraft, in particular, "invited women to become amazons and statesmen, and directors, and harlots, upon philosophical principles."[5]

These reactions to Godwin's story of Wollstonecraft were the beginning of a floodtide of letters, articles, poems, and satires mocking her as a liberator of either men or women. Though some female correspondents praised her call for the rights of women, none defended her moral behavior. By 1800 her reputation had been destroyed; she became for the next half-century a subject for derision.[6]

A satiric poem in the *Columbian Centinel* in 1801 reflected the standard outlook on Wollstonecraft as mediated to history by Godwin:

> When Godwin can prove that thieving is just,
>
> That virtue is pleasure, and pleasure is lust,
>
> That marriage is folly, and wh-r-ing is wise,
>
> And Wollstonecraft pure in Philosophy's eyes.
>
> Though logical Godwin new morals may preach,
>
> That ends sanctify means though he artfully teach,
>
> The world will still call a robber a knave
>
> And his lecherous Mary of passion a slave.[7]

Thanks to Godwin's *Memoirs* Wollstonecraft's search for love overshadowed her great contributions to the promotion of liberty and equality. The heroine of liberty for both women and men had been repudiated.

REASON REJECTED

But it is clear that Godwin can be convicted only of distorting the life of Mary Wollstonecraft. He cannot bear full blame for causing her philosophy to be negated. Even as renunciation fell against her lifestyle and her claims of equality between men and women, there surfaced a much broader rejection of the entire liberating tendencies of the eighteenth century. Nothing demonstrates more clearly that a massive counterrevolution was underway in the 1790s than the banishment of revolutionary liberators throughout the Western world.

Various critics who lambasted Godwin's version of Wollstonecraft's life linked their judgment of her with other liberators as well. Sarah Wood, American author of *Dorval,* had one of her characters after attacking Wollstonecraft say, "but really I consider Mrs. Wollstonecraft's *Rights of Women* as injurious to female happiness as Tom Paine's *Age of Reason* is to the cause of religion." The *Anti-Jacobin Review* also in 1798 blasted Wollstonecraft's connections with Thomas Paine:

Her doctrines are almost all obvious corollaries from the theo-
rems of Paine. If we admit his principle, that all men have an
equal right to be governors and statesmen, without any regard
to their talents and virtues, there can be no reason for excluding
women or even children.

Although Wollstonecraft's fate as a woman and as a proponent of the rights of
women was determined at the time by Godwin's biography, her fate as a liberator
suffered the same destiny as that of other liberators—especially that of the arch-
liberator Thomas Paine.[8]

By 1798 Thomas Paine—one of the architects of American liberty, the preeminent friend of liberty in Britain, and in France a revolutionary member of the
National Convention—had also fallen on ill times. Given his transatlantic antics
from 1789 through the Reign of Terror (in which he barely survived the guillotine), his popularity and acceptance among Britons and the French suffered a
severe decline. *The Age of Reason,* written with Joel Barlow's assistance in 1794,
and *The Age of Reason, Part II* in 1795 placed him at sharp odds with most
Americans as well.

In *The Age of Reason* Paine went to war with Christianity, with Holy Scriptures, and with Christian institutions. At the outset, he declared his credo: "I
believe in one God, and no more; and I hope for happiness beyond this life. I
believe in the equality of man; and I believe that religious duties consist in doing
justice, loving mercy, and endeavoring to make our fellow creatures happy." If
that sounded innocuous enough, it opened up whole lines of attack. According to
Paine, the only God around was the Creator. In fact, the only time and place God
spoke was in the Creation itself. Jesus Christ was merely man. The Old and
New Testaments did not record God's revelations but merely were mythology
and paltry tales. Indeed, the Bible recorded a "history of wickedness" and led
people astray from the use of "reason" to order their lives. Christianity was as
near to "atheism as twilight is to darkness" and served as a form of despotism
over human beings to serve the avarice of priests. Christianity, in fact, had inaugurated an "age of Ignorance" that needed to be replaced by a new age ruled by
Reason.[9]

Those were fighting words in a world that was trying desperately to find
order, authority, and an understanding of the role of religion in society. Though
Paine had found the right words—*Common Sense*—to frenzy Americans into a
war for independence in 1776 and the right phrase—*The Rights of Man*—to fuel
a search for liberty in the Western world, his new call—*The Age of Reason*—was
ill-timed and misplaced. Inadvertently fanning the flames of a counterrevolution
against every sentiment he spoke, it counteracted everything for which he had
stood during all of his crusading years.

In America the repudiation of Paine's call for a national religion was thorough. Uzal Ogden, rector of Trinity Church in Newark, New Jersey, helped initi-
ate an instantaneous anti-Paine campaign in 1795 with two volumes titled *Antidote to Deism,* a "refutation of all the objections of Thomas Paine against the

Christian religion; as contained in a pamphlet, entitled, *The Age of Reason.*"
Ogden, dedicating his volumes to George Washington, pledged to challenge the
deism that seemed to reign in France and Italy. The "design" of the publication
was "not only to refute Mr. Paine's objections against Christianity, but to be a
general defence of divine revelation against the attacks of deists of every description." Ogden traced the history of French and English deism and declared Paine's
brand of liberation virtually dead in the Western world—because it offended
every principle of religion.[10]

If Ogden opened the counterrevolutionary campaign against Paine's *The Age
of Reason,* he was soon joined by others: the counterrevolutionary editors John
Fenno, William Cobbett, and Noah Webster; the Congregational clerical leaders
Timothy Dwight and Jedidiah Morse; and a host of Presbyterian leaders including
Elias Boudinot, Alexander McWhorter, and Samuel Miller.[11]

The universality of the renunciation could be seen in microcosm in Virginia,
where in the space of a few months a multitude of voices drowned out Paine's
effort to direct the energies of humanity. Andrew Broaddus, a popular Baptist
minister and leader in Caroline, King and Queen, and King William Counties,
Virginia, published in Richmond *The Age of Reason & Revelation* before the end
of 1795. The Scottish-born Presbyterian cleric in Alexandria, James Muir, published in Baltimore in 1795 an even larger critique titled *An Examination of the
Principles Contained in the Age of Reason.* Between March 10 and May 5,
1795, an anonymous author using the pseudonym "Common Sense" published a
series of nine articles attacking Paine in the *Virginia Gazette and Richmond
Chronicle.*

During 1796 two intrepid warriors for Christian orthodoxy, Presbyterian
leader Moses Hoge and Episcopalian book peddler Mason Locke "Parson" Weems,
published editions of Anglican bishop Richard Watson's two anti-Paine essays,
Apology for the Bible and *An Address to Scoffers at Religion.* With these editions
Hoge and Weems subjoined their own brief essays lambasting Paine's credibility
on the subject of religion, Hoge titling his essay "The Sophist Unmasked." By the
end of 1796 denunciations of Paine filled Virginia's press, labeling him not only as
an enemy of religion, but also of basic American values.[21]

Broaddus, Muir, Hoge, and Weems countered both Paine's views on religion
and his political philosophy. They rejected his ideas about God. They loathed his
effort to deify Reason as the new godhead. And they refused to accept his charge
that the ills of humanity in the Western world resulted from the illogical creeds of
Christian churches—especially Protestant churches.

Even more fundamentally they objected to the effect of his ideas on political
order. Although Paine's theories had fomented the American Revolution and had
led to the disestablishment of the church in America, the same ideas in France
had led to religious and political chaos. Churches had been destroyed and clergy
defrocked. Political order had devolved into chaos. His continued campaign
against religious and political institutions in *The Rights of Man* and *The Age of
Reason* would bring similar anarchy to the United States. Hence their efforts to
discredit his very character as a moral being.[12]

By the end of 1798 the world's two most important liberators—Paine and Wollstonecraft—had been repudiated. The principles of liberty they had inspired and the supremacy of reason they espoused had been rejected. The texts they had written simultaneously in London during 1791 would be spurned for generations to come. *The Age of Reason* never received reading among a general public. Godwin's revelations about Wollstonecraft's life and rumors about Paine's debauched behavior derided their characters as well. But even though their critics found them easy targets, much more was at work than character assassination. The most fundamental counterrevolution of the modern world was fully underway.

THE POWER OF ORDER

Thomas Jefferson and St. George Tucker were both students, a few years apart, of George Wythe, professor of law at the College of William and Mary. Jefferson made a name for himself as a politician, a governor, and as author of the Declaration of Independence. As American minister to France, secretary of state, vice president, and even president of the United States he made an indelible mark on world history. Tucker succeeded Wythe as professor of law at William and Mary in 1789 and spent the next thirty years teaching law to young Virginians and as a jurist exploring Blackstone's legal systems and trying to explain the logic of what had been done to Virginia's legal systems by the likes of Patrick Henry, George Mason, Jefferson, Madison, and other authors of Virginia law.[13]

Both in the appreciation of law and in devotion to Virginia, Wythe, Jefferson, and Tucker shared a common bond. It was in collaboration with Wythe that Jefferson revised the laws of Virginia in 1779 and wrote his draft bill to emancipate Virginia slaves and to remove them to a realm outside the United States. It was Wythe who told Jefferson in 1786 that he thought it rash to put a copy of his *Notes on the State of Virginia* (1785) in the hands of every student at the College of William and Mary. With Wythe, Jefferson continued to promote law reform and education in Virginia even while he was away in France.[14]

But it was left to Tucker, nine years Jefferson's junior and Wythe's successor, to deal with the legal, political, and moral impact of Jefferson's counterrevolutionary treatise. Almost ten years to the day after Jefferson issued the first copies of *Notes on Virginia* Tucker revisited the central issues of the book in search for alternatives not so counterrevolutionary as those presented by the sage of Monticello. Coming as it did after the framing and ratification of the Constitution, adoption of the Bill of Rights, and formation of the federal government, Tucker had the advantage of knowing the basic shape of America's permanent government. The results of his researches were presented to the General Assembly of Virginia and published in Williamsburg on May 20, 1796, with the impressive title, *A Dissertation on Slavery with a Proposal for the Gradual Abolition of It, in the State of Virginia.*[15]

Tucker's *Dissertation on Slavery* was a frontal assault on slavery and a jeremiad on America's declension from the principles of the American Revolution. On the title page Tucker quoted Montesquieu's famous statement that "Slavery not only violates the Laws of Nature, and of civil Society, it also wounds the best Forms of Government: in a Democracy, where all Men are equal, Slavery is contrary to the Spirit of the Constitution." He then declared that he would "consider the nature of slavery, its properties, attendants, and consequences" in order "to demonstrate the incompatibility of a state of slavery with the principles of our government, and of that revolution upon which it is founded, and to elucidate the practicability of its total, though gradual, abolition."[16]

He castigated the young nation for its treatment of black residents, slave or free:

> Whilst America hath been the land of promise to Europeans and their descendants, it hath been the vale of death to millions of the wretched sons of Africa. The genial light of liberty, which hath here shone with unrivalled lustre on the former, hath yielded no comfort to the latter, but to them hath proved a pillar of darkness, whilst it hath conducted the former to the most enviable state of human existence.

Furthermore, this harsh treatment was accorded as Americans fought for their own freedom:

> Whilst we were offering up vows at the shrine of Liberty, and sacrificing hecatombs upon her altars . . . we were imposing upon our fellow men, who differ in complexion from us, a slavery, ten thousand times more cruel than the utmost extremity of those grievances and oppressions, of which we complained.

After this vigorous condemnation of American hypocrisy, Tucker was ready to provide a solution to the greatest evil of the age.

But first came his promised analysis of slavery. Under this heading Tucker astutely observed the realities of life in post-Revolutionary America. In between discussions of political slavery and domestic slavery, Tucker described a new form of slavery that had emerged since the Revolution. He called it "civil slavery," a condition that arises when the natural liberty of any citizen is "by the laws of the state, further restrained than is necessary and expedient for the general advantage." It also arises "whenever there is an inequality of rights, or privileges, between the subjects or citizens of the same state." In such an instance "a state of civil slavery commences immediately."

Civil slavery existed in Virginia in 1796, Tucker proclaimed, and in virtually all of the other American states—"notwithstanding the maxims of equality which have been adopted in their several constitutions . . . in the persons of our free Negroes and mulattoes." In Virginia these individuals were "excluded from the right of suffrage," from holding elective office, and from serving as a witness "in any prosecution, or civil suit in which a white person is a party." They could be whipped for offering "resistance to a white person." Free blacks had to be registered to labor or to "go at large in any county." Free blacks could be sold back into slavery to pay the debts of a former master or be hired out to pay their taxes. Free blacks from other states were prohibited from moving to Virginia. All of the foregoing disabilities also applied to mulattoes (defined as one-fourth black or more).

Although he listed the legal disabilities for Virginia's free blacks and mulattoes, he had communicated with authorities in Massachusetts, Connecticut, and other states to determine that a whole new form of legalized "slavery" separate from ownership by another person was emerging across America. And though many of these laws originally had been enacted during the restrictive colonial era, what so alarmed Tucker was that in Virginia and in other states, they had been recodified by the new state governments. Even more distressing, they were yearly being expanded and extended, tightening the reins on free blacks and taking away their natural rights.

Having identified this realm in which citizen rights were being abolished contrary to the principles of the Revolution, Tucker next ranted about the practice of domestic slavery itself:

> That a people who have declared, "That all men are by nature equally free and independent," and have made this declaration the first article in the foundation of their government . . . should tolerate a practice incompatible therewith, is such an evidence of the weakness and inconsistency of human nature, as every man who hath a spark of patriotic fire in his bosom must wish to see removed from his own country. . . . If ever there was a cause . . . in which all hearts should be united, every nerve strained, and every power exerted, surely the restoration of human nature to its inalienable right is such."

Tucker then demonstrated the disposition of rights. He divided civil (natural) rights into three realms: "the right of personal security; the right of personal liberty; and the right of private property." And in the case of slavery,

> the two last are wholly abolished, the person of the slave being at the absolute disposal of his master; and property, what he is incapable, in that state, either of acquiring or holding in his own use. Hence it will appear how perfectly irreconcilable a state of slavery is to the principles of a democracy, which form the basis and foundation of our government.

But since the Virginia bill of rights declared that "all men are by nature equally free and independent," Tucker concluded, it would be hard "to reconcile reducing the Negroes to a state of slavery to these principles, unless we first degrade them below the rank of human beings, not only politically, but also physically and morally."

This he did not wish to do—even though it already had been done in Jefferson's *Notes on Virginia*—since it would interfere with the eradication of slavery. He admitted that "at no period since the revolution, could the abolition of slavery in this state have been safely undertaken until the foundations of our newly established governments had been found capable of supporting the fabric itself, under any shock, which so arduous an attempt might have produced." Perhaps it was not possible when Jefferson looked over the American landscape in the early 1780s. But Tucker thought times had changed by 1796: "But these obstacles being now happily removed, considerations of policy, as well as justice and humanity, must evince the necessity of eradicating the evil, before it becomes impossible to do it, without tearing up the roots of civil society with it." He concluded, "It only remains, to consider the mode by which slaves have been or may be emancipated."

To this point in his *Dissertation on Slavery* Tucker was embattled, judgmental, and driven. Slavery was inconsistent with the principles of the Revolution and should have been eradicated. Instead, new barriers had been erected and a new form of slavery had been created for free blacks. Even though he did not condemn Jefferson directly for this moral and political aberration, he made it clear that no one could defend slavery given the principles of equality undergirding the Revolution and America's form of government. This was harsh judgment against Jefferson and all the other leaders of the Revolution who had failed to correct this blemish in the American firmament.

Yet when the moment arrived for Tucker to unveil his promised solution, he turned to the Jefferson writ to obtain authority for his modest proposal. First, even though he condemned the emerging system of civil slavery for free blacks throughout America, he, like Jefferson, accepted it as a norm to be expected for any black in America who was not a slave: "With us, we have seen that emancipation does not confer the rights of citizenship on the person emancipated; on the contrary, both he and his posterity, of the same complexion with himself, must always labour under many civil incapacities." Like Jefferson, he concluded that it was the free black's "choice to submit to that civil inferiority, inseparably attached to his condition in this country, or seek some more favorable climate, where all the distinctions between men are either totally abolished, or less regarded than in this."

The closer he approached his solution, the more Jeffersonian he became. Quoting from Jefferson's *Notes on Virginia,* he argued that "human prudence forbids that we should precipitately engage in a work of such hazard as a general and simultaneous emancipation." He agreed with Jefferson that the experience of slavery, "the early impressions of obedience and submission," tended to "unfit" slaves for freedom. With Jefferson he held that "to retain them among us [after manumission], would be nothing more than to throw so many of the human race upon the earth without the means of subsistence: they would soon become idle, profligate, and miserable." And, Tucker continued on a slightly different note, "the recent history of the French West Indies exhibits a melancholy picture of the probable consequences of a general, and momentary emancipation in any of the states, where slavery has made considerable progress."

Given these obstacles, Tucker asked, "Must we then quit the subject, in despair of the success of any project for the amendment of their, as well as our own condition?" His answer was "I think not." Then came his plan: "The abolition of slavery may be effected without the emancipation of a single slave; without depriving any man of the <u>property</u> which he <u>possesses</u>, and without defrauding a creditor who has trusted him on the faith of that property." It would be accomplished, of course, by instituting in Virginia a plan of gradual abolition such as the Pennsylvania plan drawn up, he thought, "under the auspices of the immortal Franklin" or that of Connecticut, or New York, or that plan drawn up by "Mr. Jefferson" and "the committee of revisors" as described in *Notes on Virginia.*

Tucker next addressed the subject of what to do with those blacks who would under any of these systems be emancipated. He covered the same territory as Jefferson—sending them to Africa, colonizing them beyond the Mississippi, or retaining them in Virginia. Quoting Jefferson's answer that freed blacks must be sent abroad to avoid "the extermination of one or the other race," Tucker agreed in view of "the recent scenes transacted in the French colonies in the West Indies," which were "enough to make one shudder with the apprehension of realizing similar calamities in this country." The costs of transporting freed blacks to Africa or anywhere else was prohibitive, however.

Tucker's solution to this dilemma was also implicit in Jefferson's *Notes on Virginia,* although the jurist wanted to find a legal basis for it. Slavery would be abolished gradually by letting "every female born after the adoption of the plan be free, and transmit freedom to all her descendants, both male and female." Such persons would serve their masters until the age of twenty-eight, thus compensating the masters and not becoming wards of the state. When they became free they would enter into that other form of citizenship earlier described somewhat negatively by Tucker as "civil slavery." They would remain in "civil slavery" so long as they lived or until they chose to leave Virginia for another state or nation.

But in a nation where all citizens were promised equal rights, how could the institution of civil slavery be justified? Tucker mildly castigated Jefferson's solution to this problem: "Mr. Jefferson seems to suppose, that the Africans are really an inferior race of mankind." Such a conclusion was not entirely acceptable to Tucker. His alternative simply was not to extend rights to a people who did not seem to be interested in those rights in any case: "The experiment [manumission] so far as it has been already made among us, proves that the emancipated blacks are not ambitious of civil rights." Why give rights to blacks, he continued, when they have not been requested:

> We must therefore endeavor to find some middle course, between the tyrannical and iniquitous policy which holds so many human creatures in a state of grievous bondage, and that which would turn loose a numerous, starving, and enraged banditti, upon the innocent descendants of their former oppressors.

Rather, he concluded, "<u>nature, time,</u> and <u>sound policy</u> must co-operate with each other to produce such a change."

Tucker then listed the details of his system of gradual abolition and the confirmation of the condition of civil slavery. He recognized that in Virginia and throughout America free blacks were not being accorded equal rights of citizenship. Even though this was contrary to the principles of the American Revolution, it was in his mind less offensive than the perpetuation of slavery. But like Jefferson and many other veterans of the American Revolution, the central problem for the new nation was the existence of people who did not fit into white American society. Strive as they might, there seemed to be no solution.

Tucker's *Dissertation on Slavery* offered an alternative to Jefferson's stern plan of removing all blacks from America. His scheme recognized the realities of life for free blacks throughout America and—as antithetical to equality as it was—it was the policy and practice already embraced by states North and South. In a sense, this part of his plan was a sociological recognition of what was already at work. The other part of his treatise, the gradual abolition of slavery by freeing newborn females, when it was presented to the Virginia General Assembly, was tabled without action.

Try as he might, Tucker was unable to break out of the counterrevolutionary march toward a new order that had already been blessed by Jefferson in his *Notes on Virginia.* Jefferson had embraced a theory of the inequality of blacks that authorized, even in the land of liberty, unequal treatment. And that unequal treatment included Tucker's civil slavery for free blacks and slavery itself so long as blacks should remain in America.

Tucker was just as counterrevolutionary as Jefferson. After concluding his case for the recognition of civil slavery, he restated his prejudices:

> Though I am opposed to the banishment of the Negroes, I wish not to encourage their future residence among us. By denying them the most valuable privileges which civil government affords, I wished to render it their inclination and their interest to seek those privileges in some other climate. . . . By excluding them from offices, the seeds of ambition would be buried too deep, ever to germinate: by disarming them, we may calm our apprehensions of their resentments arising from past sufferings; by incapacitating them from holding lands, we should add one inducement more to emigration and effectually remove the foundation of ambition. . . .

Although he berated Jefferson and the other founding fathers for not ridding the new nation of slavery, nothing could have been more counterrevolutionary than his call for institutionalizing civil slavery. Tucker, who died just a year after Jefferson in 1827, followed the Jeffersonian model to the end. He, too, chose not to free his own slaves either during his lifetime or in his last will and testament.[17]

WOMEN DEFLECTED

On March 22, 1802, at the Federal Street Theater in Boston, an audience of 150 people arrived long before the curtain time for a scheduled production of Shakespeare's *King Henry IV,* to witness a spectacle that had been advertised in the *Columbian Centinel and Massachusetts Federalist* as a unique opportunity. Thirty minutes before the Shakespearean players took the stage, a lone person in the military garb of George Washington's Continental Army marched across the platform making sharp turns and twirling a rifle on orders barked out by a drill sergeant located offstage. Complete with boots, spats, and ammunition pouch, the soldier deftly demonstrated twenty-seven manual-of-arms maneuvers. Upon completion of the martial arts display, the drillmaster announced that the soldier would present an oration to the growing audience.

In the introduction it was revealed that the audience had just witnessed a performance by none other than Deborah Sampson, "whose life and character are peculiarly distinguished—being a Continental soldier for nearly three years, in the late American [Revolutionary] War, during which time, she performed the duties of every department, into which she was called, with punctual exactness, fidelity and honor, and preserved her chastity inviolate, by the most artful concealment of her sex."

They would hear a presentation from the only woman who served as a regular foot soldier in the American Revolution, albeit in disguise as a man. This most unusual heroine of the Revolution broke all convention in order to fight for those liberating principles spelled out in the Declaration of Independence. How wonderful that a woman had contributed in the field to the victory of liberty over tyranny! Under the assumed name of Robert Shurtliff, she served at West Point, at White Plains, at Fort Meigs, and in other skirmishes across Massachusetts, New York, New Jersey, and Pennsylvania.

Deborah Sampson, an authentic American Revolutionary, came to a special Boston podium—one of dozens she frequented in New England and New York during 1802 and 1803—to discuss her experiences in the war for independence. Her first words introduced the tone of all that would follow: "My achievements are a breach in the decorum of my sex, unquestionably." She quickly continued, "I must frankly confess I recollect them [the achievements] with a kind of satisfaction, which no one can better conceive and enjoy than him who, recollecting the good intentions of a bad deed, lives to see and to correct any indecorum of his life."

How odd! Here was a unique heroine who risked identity, personal safety, and life itself to wage the war for liberty, informing her audience that she had betrayed her sex. While every other warrior of the Revolution celebrated his service to the nation, this lone woman condemned her career as an aberrant act that somehow shamed her in the world of women.

She explained her actions to some degree: "my mind became agitated with the enquiry—why a nation, separated from us by an ocean . . . should endeavor to enforce on us plans of subjugation, the most unnatural in themselves, unjust, inhuman . . . and unpracticed even by the uncivilized savages of the wilderness?" It was, then, to right a wrong played out by the tyrannical mother country:

> Wrought upon at length . . . by an enthusiasm and phrenzy that
> could brook no control—I burst the tyrant bonds, which held
> my sex in awe, and clandestinely, or by stealth, grasped an
> opportunity, which custom and the world seemed to deny, as a
> natural privilege. [And thus] did I throw off the soft bailments

*Deborah Sampson (1797). Hero in soldier's uniform during
the Revolution, she became a clown in soldier's clothing
during the counterrevolution.*

of my sex, and assume those of the warrior, already prepared
for battle.

Although these words were less apologetic than her opening lines, she continued
to focus on the transgression of bursting out of her role as woman rather than
upon her brave accomplishment.[18]

Her words to the audience contrasted sharply with public reactions to her
performance and with those she recorded in her diary. The critic who covered the
performance of *King Henry IV* commented favorably on Sampson's soldiering
that night: "She almost made the gun talk." And Sampson, in her diary, after a
similar showing in Providence two months later, wrote: "I was much pleased at
the appearance of the audience. It appeared from almost every countenance that
they were full of unbelief—I mean, in Regard to my being the person that served
in the Revolutionary Army." Her reaction to the audience when she rose to speak
was candid: "I think I may say with much candor I applauded the people for their
serious attention and peculiar Respect, <u>especially the Ladies</u>."

If her audiences were attentive and respectful, particularly the women, why
did Sampson refer to her Revolutionary service as deviant behavior? The answer
lay in her sensational biography. In July 1796 a little-known printer and editorial
writer for the *Village Register* in Dedham, Massachusetts, finished a startling lit-

tle book that illustrated the views of at least white American men on the subject
of the role of women in the new land of order. Herman Mann, just twenty-four
when he wrote *The Female Review: or, Memoirs of an American Young Lady*
(signed July 1796, published 1797), revealed in his detailed biography of America's only female Revolutionary War veteran the extent to which the American
Counterrevolution was discouraging women from lives of independence, urging
instead that they should confine themselves to lives of domestic duty. In 257
pages, ostensibly written as a memorial to Sampson, Mann actually bade women
not to follow her example.[20]

Just as Jefferson in his *Notes on Virginia* and Tucker in his *Dissertation* had
stressed the elimination of rights and liberty for blacks, Mann spoke directly to
women, telling them never to waver from proper female character and demeanor.
He dedicated his *Female Review,* not to Sampson, not to women, and not to liberty, but rather to "the Patrons and Friends of Columbia's Cause." He made it
clear that he wrote the piece not to extol any of those ideals and

> not with intentions to encourage the like paradigm of Female
> Enterprise [Sampson's example]—but because such a thing, in
> the course of nature, has occurred; and because every circum-
> stance, whether natural, artificial, or accidental, that has been
> made conducive to the promotion of our Independence, Peace,
> and Prosperity . . . must be sacredly remembered. . . .

No liberty, freedom, equality, or unalienable rights here. Mann launched his review
of the great "accident" that was Deborah Sampson to preach order, not liberty.

In his preface Mann elucidated the duality of his purpose: "My first business
. . . with the public is to inform them, that the Female, who is the subject of the
following Memoirs, does not only exist in theory and imagination, but in reality."
His second bit of business grew out of his belief "that every subject intended for
public contemplation, should be managed with intentions to promote general
good." He continued, "I have taken the liberty to intersperse, through the whole, a
series of moral reflections."

Since much of what he planned to describe about Deborah Sampson's life as
a soldier "would be a subject as delicate, especially for the Ladies, as it is different from their pursuits; I have studiously endeavored to meliorate every circumstance, that might seem to[o] much tinctured with the rougher, masculine
virtues." He promised that he would write "with a diction softened and com-
ported to the taste of the virtuous female." This because, "although I am a well-
wisher to their whole circle [women], it is the cause of this class only [virtuous
women], I wish to promote."[21]

The early years of Sampson's life were filled with great difficulties. Born
near Plymouth, Massachusetts, she was a direct descendant of Gov. William
Bradford, Myles Standish, and John Alden. But there were too many children,
and her father was intemperate and abusive. Placed in a foster home at age five,
she was bound as a servant with a nearby farmer at age ten. There she remained

until she was eighteen. How did Mann characterize these years? "She had stronger propensities for improvement, and less opportunities to acquire it."

When she was fourteen the battles of Lexington and Concord and Bunker Hill occurred. Throughout the war years Sampson followed every battle, every troop movement, every ounce of information she could gather. Wrote Mann: "Miss Sampson is the one, who not only listened to the least information relative to the rise and progress of the late American War; but her thoughts were, at times, engrossed with it."

On April 15, 1775, just before the battles of Lexington and Concord, she had a dream about a serpent that presaged her later conviction that she must join the American effort to destroy the dragon that was Great Britain. Agonizing over the implications of her dream and her compulsive focus on the war, she asked herself,

> shall I swerve from my sex's sphere for the sake of acquiring a
> little useful acquisition; or, shall I submit . . . to a prison where
> I must drag out the remainder of my existence in ignorance:
> where the thoughts of my too cloistered situation must forever
> harass my bosom with listless pursuits, tasteless enjoyments,
> and responsive discontent?

Amazingly, Mann put these words into the mind and mouth of Sampson so he could use the female hero of the Revolution to describe women's condition as being just as useless and humdrum as Jefferson's and Tucker's descriptions of Virginia blacks.[22]

Soon after this dream Sampson "privately dressed herself in a handsome suit of man's apparel and visited a prognosticator." The fortune teller "considered her as a blithe and honest young gentleman." Having so easily fooled one who was supposed to predict the future, Sampson concluded that she could pass herself off as a soldier. Mann there paused in his story to present one of his lessons: "Females! you have resolutions, and you execute them. And you have, in a degree the trial of the virtues and graces, that adorn your sex . . . I cannot desire you to adopt the example of our Heroine, should the like occasion again offer." Nevertheless, eager to recount what he considered the mildly off-color story of Sampson, Mann told his female readers, "Let your imagination, therefore, travel with me through the toils and dangers she has passed . . . I am sure, I shall never be tired with your company."[23]

Mann had Sampson leave family, friends, and a potential suitor in April 1781 to join the Continental Army. She would then have been twenty. She actually left almost precisely one year later. Either way, she had to make sacrifices and deceits that would establish a unique record. She signed up for three years of service in Massachusetts on May 20, 1782, under the name of Robert Shurtliff. Once she was in her red, white, and blue Continental Army uniform, neither friends, family, nor suitor could recognize her.[24]

She was mustered into service at Worcester, Massachusetts, on May 23, 1782, in the 4th Massachusetts Regiment commanded by Capt. George Webb, which was part of the First Brigade of the Continental Army under the command of Gen. John Paterson, one of George Washington's most faithful and productive generals. And he proved a dutiful friend to both Robert Shurtliff and Deborah Sampson.[25]

Having enlisted Sampson into the army, Mann had to explain how she was able to play the role of man and fool everyone around her. He described "her stature" as "more than middle size; that is, five feet and seven inches." As for her face and figure, she was "not what a physiognomist would term the most beautiful." As he detailed in several instances, however, "ladies of taste considered them handsome, when in the masculine garb."

Mann further explained how the well endowed Sampson made herself bosomless: "She wore a bandage about her breasts, during her disguise, for a very different purpose from that which females wear round their waists." Mann could not resist a speculation: "It is not improbable, that the severe pressure of this bandage served to compress the bosom, while the waist had every natural convenience for augmentation."

Next came her military record. She passed muster with her French rifle and bayonet, knapsack, cartridge box, and thirty cartridges. She drilled with her comrades by morning and joined the grand parade by evening. She marched with her company from Worcester to West Point in New York and from thence to Harlem and back to White Plains. At White Plains her company encountered a Hessian cavalry unit, and a skirmish ensued in which three of the companions by her side were killed as "she escaped with two shots through her coat, and one through her cap."

Mann probably had Sampson enter the army in 1781 rather than 1782 because he wanted to report her presence at Yorktown for the surrender of Cornwallis to the armies of Washington and Lafayette. Upon Sampson's arrival by ship at Williamsburg, he wrote, she found herself "much indisposed." It was at that moment that she "experienced the inconveniences of the concealment of her sex." Mann wrote, "She puked for several hours without much intermission," Mann wrote, although "the lustre and august maneuvring [*sic*] of the army seemed to perfect a cure beyond the reach of medicine."

This was the perfect setup for Mann to toy with a subject unmentionable in polite print. Sampson and her unit were ordered to attack and take a heavily armed redoubt two hundred yards away and to take no prisoners. When they "marched to the assault with unloaded arms, but with fixed bayonets," they were shocked to find two women in the trenches with the enemy guards. Sampson heard one of the women pronounce the word "yankee" just as she "saw a bayonet plunged into her breast and the crimson, vital liquid, that gushed from the incision, prevented her further utterance!"

As Sampson and her fellows left the scene of carnage, one of them "clapped her on the shoulder, and said—'Friend, fear not; you are only disfigured behind.'" Not making it clear whether Sampson's disfigurement resulted from a wound or her menstruation, Mann concluded the scene by saying, "Methinks I see the crimson cheek of the female turning pallid, her vigorous limbs relaxing and tottering in the rehearsal of this eventful scene." He continued toyingly, "The proper coloring is left for those peculiar inmates of the female benevolent and heroic breasts.—I hasten to drop the scene."

Following this drama of contrived double entendres, Mann placed Sampson back in New York, where she was involved in several skirmishes. In one of them she was wounded in the head and on one leg. As she found her right boot filled with blood, Mann took the occasion to distinguish this from the earlier bloody scene: "Females! this effusion was from the veins of your tender sex, in quest of that Liberty, you now so serenely possess." But fearful of being discovered should she be taken to a doctor, she refused treatment as "with a penknife and needle, she extracted the ball from her thigh." The wound, while it slowed her, did not deter her from further service in caring for another wounded soldier or from an expedition to subdue a group of warring Indians near Saratoga.

In April 1783, as prospects of peace were in the offing, General Paterson chose Sampson to be his personal aide. She thus moved into Paterson's family quarters as a servant. Her fighting days ended, Mann took a pause to draw another lesson about female behavior: "Thus, Females, whilst you see the avidity of a maid in her teens confronting dangers and made a veteran example in war, you need only half the assiduity in your proper, domestic sphere, to render your charms completely irresistible." And to underscore his point, he then addressed another trial Sampson had met and conquered—that of being forced to bathe with the other soldiers. When her unit received orders to disrobe and "clean their bodies" in the Hudson, she had to devise a dodge to avoid "unbosoming the delicate secret." She found a thicketed rivulet that "answered every purpose of bathing a more delicate form." In a curious afterthought, Mann added, "Nor were there any old, lecherous, sanctified Elders to peep through the rustling leaves to be inflamed with her charms."[26]

Though her days of war were over, she was still vulnerable to discovery. In the summer of 1783 she was sent as part of a detachment of fifteen hundred troops from West Point to Philadelphia to help quell rebellious veterans who were threatening Congress and the fledgling Confederation government. An epidemic fever struck Sampson's encampment on the outskirts of the city. She was one of the first victims.

Removed to Pennsylvania Hospital for treatment, she was examined alongside other dying patients by Dr. Barnabas Binney, chief surgeon of the hospital. Mann described Dr. Binney's discovery: "Putting his hand in her bosom to feel her pulse, [he] was surprised to find an inner waist-coat tightly compressing her breasts. Ripping it in haste, he was still more shocked, not only on finding life, but the breasts and other tokens of a female." Binney did not at that moment betray her. He ordered that she be taken to a private residence to be cared for in confidence.[27]

Before finishing his story, Mann threw in a love affair between Dr. Binney's niece from Baltimore and the recovering soldier still known as Robert Shurtliff. Then an exploration trip to the west with Col. Benjamin Tupper was arranged by Binney. Sampson won the release of an "unfortunate sister sufferer"—a white female captive—held by a group of Indians and about "to be burnt, after they should have one court and a pawaw [pow wow]." Shurtliff delivered the young woman safely to Philadelphia after stopping by Baltimore to visit Binney's love-struck niece. These stories added little luster, only more adventure to the claims of Sampson and the sermon Mann continued to preach on female behavior.[28]

One more adventure awaited Deborah Sampson when she reached the home of her benefactor, Dr. Binney. He provided her with a letter to General Paterson attesting, he said, to her illness, survival, and valor; and he gave her money for her trip back to West Point. She, in turn, feared that Binney's letter revealed her identity as a woman. In this inventive adventure her ferry from Elizabethtown, New Jersey, to New York City, foundered, and she almost drowned. As she fought the watery depths, she saved the letter against her better judgment out of respect for her patron. As Mann managed the story, she became more pathetic as her female identity returned. As long as she paraded as a man, she was valorous. When she returned to her female identity, she became helpless and dependent on men.[29]

Back at West Point, Mann wrote: "Her next business was, to deliver the letter. Cruel task! Dreading the contents, she delayed it some days." The letter finally delivered, she awaited a call from Paterson. It came in less than an hour. Meeting General Paterson then became "harder than facing a cannonade." Paterson put forth the prickly question, "Does that martial attire, which now glitters on your body, conceal a female's form!" The next moment was predictable: "The close of the sentence drew tears in his [Paterson's] eyes; and she fainted." Poor girl! Concealed as a male soldier she could deal with any man. Revealed as a woman, she could only faint. As Paterson said, "Can it be so!" Sampson admitted her feminine Achilles' heel: "Her heart could no longer harbor deception. Banishing all subterfuge . . . she confessed herself—a female."

No longer could she remain unattended among men. Paterson promised her that she could "think herself safe, while under his protection." Then "he would quickly obtain her discharge, and she would be safely conducted to her friends." And "immediately she had an apartment assigned to her own use." She, in turn, "requested, as a pledge of her virtue, that strict enquiry should be made of those, with whom she had been mess-mate" to validate her total chastity. This "accordingly done" she was honorably discharged on October 25, 1783, by Gen. Henry Knox at West Point on "recommendations from Gens. Paterson and Shepard." As Mann concluded, "Thus she made her exit from the tragic stage . . . to close the last affecting scene of her complicated, woe-fraught revolution of her sex!"[30]

The grand deception over, Sampson returned to Massachusetts, where she resumed life as a woman. On September 3, 1782, she was expelled from the Third Baptist Church of Middleborough, Massachusetts, for "Dressing in men's Clothes, and inlisting as a soldier in the army and [for being] strongly suspected of being guilty and for sometime before behaved very loose and unchristian like." On January 10, 1784, a New York newspaper reported

> An extraordinary instance of virtue in a FEMALE SOLDIER, has occurred, lately in the American army, in the Massachusetts line, viz. a lively, comely young nymph, nineteen years of age, dressed in man's apparel, has been discovered; and what

redounds to her honor, she has served in the character of a soldier for nearly three years, undiscovered.

On April 7, 1785, she married a farmer, Benjamin Gannett, and bore three children. On January 20, 1792, the Massachusetts General Court found that Deborah
Gannet "did actually perform the duties of a soldier, in the late Army of the
United States" and ordered that she be paid for this service "the sum of thirty four
pounds, bearing interest from October 23, 1783."[31]

Why, then, did Sampson in 1802 before audiences in thirty or forty cities
belittle her record and apologize to women for her deviation from female character? It was because Herman Mann, entrepreneur and promoter, organized her tour
and scripted her orations in every city. He prescribed that she, like a prize fighter,
should put on her Revolutionary garb, take a rifle, and march as an automaton
across the stage. It was Mann who put the self-deprecating words in her mouth
and puppeted her on stage before grand dramas as a caricature. No longer a heroine of the Revolution, she would instead be presented as a sideshow freak.

In his *Female Review* of 1797, Herman Mann argued that any woman who
followed Sampson's example would also be viewed as a freak. Frail and weak-
minded, women, he remonstrated, belonged in the home. Their energies should
be directed toward building the home and fulfilling their domestic duties. The
rights, privileges, and opportunities for women to become equal citizens of the
United States—for a few years possible to many other sisters who had marched
forth not as soldiers, but as actresses, novelists, and persons of business—had
been abolished.

AFRICANS AMERICANIZED

June and July 1798 were among the darkest hours in America's rejection of the
principles of its Revolution. It was during those months that the U.S. Congress
passed the most repressive laws in American history: the Naturalization Act, June
18; the Alien Act, June 25; the Alien Enemies Act, July 6; the Sedition Act, July
14. Even as these acts were impending or just passed, the last champions of liberty were being expelled. Volney departed Philadelphia to France on June 7 to
avoid the terror; so did thousands of other French émigrés during July after the
American treaty with France was annulled on July 7. Benjamin Franklin Bache
was arrested on June 26 and charged with sedition in Philadelphia; so was John
Daley Burk in New York on July 6. James Callender fled Philadelphia on July 13
rather than face the same fate.

The sudden departure of so many French nationals from the United States
and the indictment of newspaper editors opposed to the Adams administration
has led many later historians to view the events of these months and the surrounding years as a part of the evolution of America's first party system or as the
consequence of having the young nation pincered between two superpowers. But
the revulsion from revolutionary heroines and heroes such as Mary Wollstonecraft and Thomas Paine, the victory of Thomas Jefferson's racist doctrines

as articulated in his *Notes on Virginia* and reconfirmed in St. George Tucker's *Dissertation on Slavery,* and the deflection of women as in Herman Mann's *Female Review* revealed some of the harsh realities that were beginning to emerge from beneath the surface of the Counterrevolution.

The doctrines laid out in rejecting the liberating principles of the American Revolution and in implementing these new doctrines that appeared by 1798 produced a counterrevolutionary America that was committed to order, not liberty. And the effects of the counterrevolution were best seen in its impact on free blacks and the free black community in the United States of the 1790s.

During June 1798, while John Adams and Congress were dealing with troublesome French aliens and with oppositional newspaper editors, Congress also took the occasion to exclude free blacks from service in the U.S. Navy and the Marine Corps. Already, thanks to the Naturalization Act of 1790, blacks could neither willingly immigrate to the United States from another nation nor become naturalized citizens. Citizenship was restricted to "free white persons" who resided in the United States for one year and had taken an oath of allegiance to their new land. Emigrants could flee from any nation in the world to the land of liberty as long as they did not come from Africa or were not of black or mulatto complexion. The only Africans permitted into the United States during the early years of the liberated republic were those brought to America as slaves.[32]

The extent to which blacks were not welcome in the land of liberty was made abundantly clear in that same June 1798 in Pennsylvania. When word arrived in America that British generals had given up their fight to capture or defeat Toussaint in St. Domingue that year, fears spread across Philadelphia that it would again be overrun, as it had been in 1793, with hordes of blacks—free and slave—fleeing the conflagration. When two ships arrived at Philadelphia in mid-June jammed with white and black refugees from the island, Gov. Thomas Mifflin acted.

On June 27, Mifflin issued an order prohibiting the landing of "any French negroes" in Philadelphia. At the same time, he requested Adams's assistance in preventing the landing of French blacks in nearby states and in stopping the entry of all blacks—whether slave or free. The two suspect ships and others entering the Delaware River were halted and quarantined.

Nevertheless, the next day, new word arrived in Philadelphia that hundreds of French slave masters and their slaves had left their ships and were dispersing across adjacent lands. Fears increased as the commandant of Fort Mifflin on the Delaware south of Philadelphia announced that 250 or 300 blacks, "well-armed, trained to war" and who "know no laws and count their lives as nothing," were making ready to march through New Jersey to Philadelphia."[33]

The crisis subsided when clarification came four days later that the ships contained, not 300 but rather 55 slaves, and that none of them were armed. But the new data about the number of blacks and their status did nothing to take away the resolve of Pennsylvanians and other Americans to stem the flow of Africans slave or free into the United States and across state borders into their states.[34]

Nor did it slow or halt other practices, public and private, that restricted the rights of free blacks and threatened the liberty of many blacks who had recently won their freedom from slavery. The Fugitive Slave Act of 1793—intended to facilitate with minimal legal obstacles the recovery of escaped slaves by masters— unleashed, instead, a wave of kidnapping of free blacks. Because masters or their agents could seize without warrant any black person claimed as their property, no free black was safe. Once seized, the captive could not testify as to his status as free, fugitive, or slave, because blacks either by law or local court practice were not permitted to give testimony in cases involving whites.[35]

Protecting kidnapped free blacks had been one of the purposes of the Pennsylvania Abolition Society. Although the society intervened legally to assist some free blacks who were kidnapped and sold into slavery, the real problem was the legal status and rights of all blacks in America. Their deteriorating status came to the fore in 1797 when sixteen recently freed blacks from North Carolina arrived in Philadelphia and learned that due to the Fugitive Slave Act their liberty could be jeopardized. Although they had earned their freedom primarily through manumission by North Carolina Quakers, state and national laws gave leeway for unscrupulous slave traders to target them for capture.

Recognizing the threat to their legal status, the sixteen frightened men appealed directly to the leaders of Philadelphia's developing black community for assistance. Richard Allen and Absalom Jones stepped forth in January 1797—just as they had ten years earlier in founding Philadelphia's Free African Society and as they had four years earlier in establishing the first independent African churches—to ask the national Congress directly, without white intermediary, to bring an end to slavery and to repair or repeal the odious Fugitive Slave Act of 1793. They were joined by sailmaker James Forten, an articulate layman and business leader.

On behalf of the endangered sixteen and, also, all the other blacks—slave and free—in the United States, they wrote to their national government: "To the President, Senate, and House of representatives of the—most free and enlightened nation in the world!!!" Referring to the "unconstitutional bondage in which multitudes of our fellows in complexion are held," they argued that natural rights should be extended to Americans held in bondage. Comparing the effects of the Fugitive Slave Act to the capture of American sailors by the Barbary States, they stated that worse treatment occurred daily in the United States to emancipated men who had "tasted the sweets of liberty," but who were "again [being] reduced to slavery by kidnappers and man-stealers." The first editor who published the petition asked, "whether, instead of being the most free and enlightened nation in the world, America is not rivalling Algiers in barbarity and oppression?"

Despite their reasoned and justifiable grievance, the petition was set aside, when James Madison in the House of Representatives stated for the record that appeals from blacks "have no claim on their attention" since "the Constitution

Absalom Jones (c. 1808). Preacher for the rights of free blacks, he was also a patron of order among black Americans.

gives them no hopes of being heard here." In this snub from Congress, a message was delivered to all those blacks torn from Africa and sprinkled across the Atlantic rim: A land of liberty, freedom, and equality had been created in North America, but blacks were systematically and purposefully excluded from that land.[36]

Prince Hall, founder of the first black Masonic lodge in America in Boston, analyzed the alarming situation in "A Charge, Delivered to the African Lodge, June 24, 1797." Referring to a charge he had given his lodge five years earlier in June 1792, Hall noted that he had then said "we must be good subjects to the laws of the land in which we dwell" and that we must "have no hand in any plots or conspiracies or rebellion." He also in 1792 had asked whether in "the largest Christian church on earth [America] . . . if they were all whites, they would refuse to accept them [Africans] as their fellow Christians."

In his 1797 speech Hall displayed a very different tone. He wrote that "it is our duty to sympathize with our fellow men [other blacks] under their troubles." He bemoaned the slave trade that "dragg'd them from their native country by the iron hand of tyranny and oppression . . . to bear the iron yoke of slavery and cruelty till death as a friend shall relieve them." Whereas in 1792 he spoke of the opportunities of liberty, in 1797 he wrote:

> Patience I say, for if we were not possess'd of a great measure of it you could not bear up under the daily insults you meet in the streets of Boston; . . . how are you shamefully abus'd, and that at such a degree that you may truly be said to carry your lives in your hands, and the arrows of death are flying about your heads. . . .

An observer of "that filthy behaviour in the [Boston] common" stated that "he never saw so cruel behaviour in all his life . . . in the West-Indies" where a slave "on Sunday or holidays enjoys himself and friends without any molestation."

Acknowledging considerable awareness of events in St. Domingue, Hall continued, "let us not be cast down under these and many other abuses we at present labour under." Indeed, he said, "let us remember what a dark day it was with our African brethren six years ago, in the French West-Indies." He then noted, "But blessed be God, the scene is changed, they now confess that God hath no respect of persons, and therefore receive them as our friends, and treat them as brothers." At least in St. Domingue freedom was at hand: "Thus doth Ethiopia begin to stretch forth her hand, from a sink of slavery to freedom and equality."

But while liberty was emerging in St. Domingue, it was conspicuously absent from America: "You are deprived [here] of the means of education." And threats against every black easily caused a "slavish fear of man." Counseling meditation and "war against fear," Hall praised the American republic, which brought "cheer [to] the heart of those our poor unhappy brethren, to see a ship commissioned from God . . . that all men are free and are brethren." But he called for the nation's leaders "to see them in an instant deliver such a number from their cruel bolts and galling chains, and to be fed like men and treated like brethren." America had secured the release of American seamen from the Barbary States. "How sudden were they delivered by the sympathizing members of the Congress of the United States, who now enjoy the free air of peace and liberty," Hall wrote. The same should happen for black residents in the United States.[37]

If there was a will in America to extend rights to blacks, it could be legislated, Prince Hall argued. That was also the theme of a petition from Philadelphia's "Absalom Jones and others. 73 subscribers." As they had done two years earlier, Jones and his fellows addressed the president, the Senate, and the House of Representatives with a "Petition of the People of Colour, free men, within the City and Suburbs of Philadelphia." They were grateful "to the Government under which we live, for the blessings and benefits granted to us in the enjoyment of our natural right to liberty."

But there was a problem, they continued: "We cannot be insensible of the condition of our afflicted brethren, suffering under various circumstances, in different parts of these states." The Constitution of the United States was being "violated by a trade carried on in a clandestine manner, to the coast of Guinea, . . . and another equally wicked, practised openly by citizens of some of the southern states, upon the waters of Maryland and Delaware." Jones and his fellows asked, "Can any commerce, trade, or transaction, so detestably shock the feeling of man, or degrade the dignity of his nature equal to this?" Wrote Jones and his cosigners, "volumes might be filled with the sufferings of this grossly abused part of the human species, seven hundred thousand of whom . . . are now in unconditional bondage in these states."

They noted dutifully that "we address you as guardians of our rights, and patrons of equal and national liberties, hoping you will view the subject in an impartial, unprejudiced light." Making it clear that they were not asking "for an immediate emancipation of all, knowing that the degraded state of many, and their want of education, would greatly disqualify [them] for such a change," they yet "humbly" desired that Congress "may exert every means in your power to undo the heavy burdens, and prepare the way for the oppressed to go free." Harking back to the founding of the American nation by the American Revolution and its philosophy, they wrote:

> In the Constitution and the Fugitive Bill, no mention is made of
> black people, or slaves: therefore, if the Bill of Rights, or the
> Declaration of Congress [Declaration of Independence] are of
> any validity, we beseech, that as we are men, we may be admit-

ted to partake of the liberties and unalienable rights therein held forth.

The practice of liberty, freedom, and equality promised by the American Revolution, if extended "to all classes" living in the United States, would be "a means of drawing down the blessing of Heaven upon this land."[38]

This petition, too, was spurned by Congress. Presented in the Congress by Robert Waln of Philadelphia, the petition prompted the same reaction as the 1797 petition of Jones, Allen and Forten; that is, a petition from a people deemed noncitizens was unworthy of Congress's time. The various pronouncements of senators and representatives revealed the extent to which Jefferson's counter-revolutionary rhetoric on slavery had taken hold.

Waln stated that he was not advocating emancipation of the slaves but rather was seeking adjustments of federal law to regulate the kidnapping of free blacks for reenslavement or sale in the international slave trade. John Rutledge Jr. of South Carolina thought that the petition contained dangerous intimations of the anarchical principles of the French Revolution. Citing the fundamental principle of Jeffersonian doctrine, he said, "I thank God" that most blacks in America are held in slavery; "if they were not, dreadful would be the consequences."

Harrison Gray Otis of Massachusetts, noting that the Jones petition bore marks rather than signatures, charged that it came from a group of illiterates who were "incapable of digesting the principles" contained therein. The acknowledgment of such a document, Otis argued, could have baleful consequences: "It would teach them the art of assembling together, debating, and the like, and would soon, if encouraged, extend from one end of the union to the other." In other words, black Americans might just start acting like the revolutionaries who effected the American Revolution!

The reference to the seven hundred thousand humans being held in "unconditional bondage in these states" pricked the most vociferous opinions. George Thacher of Massachusetts called slavery "a cancer of immense magnitude" and those held in bondage as "700,000 enemies" within the boundaries of the United States. Although his demand that Congress consider the elimination of slavery has been viewed as evidence of abolitionist opinion in Congress, it was nothing of the kind. What he actually proposed was for Congress to consider the plan for the elimination of slavery authored by the "second man" of the United States, that is, Jefferson. Far from being an emancipationist, Thacher, true to Jefferson doctrine, proposed the elimination of slavery and the black population from the United States.

John Brown of Rhode Island also reflected Jeffersonian doctrine when he argued that the petition's contents should not be further discussed: "No subject surely was so likely to cause a division of the states as that respecting slaves." No one wanted to encourage southern slaves to escape from bondage and migrate to northern states, where they would "reside as vagabonds and thieves." It was better that the "700,000 enemies" of America be held in slavery. There were "five million [whites] to withstand them; they can at any time subdue them."[39]

So persuasive was the Jeffersonian approach to the problem of race in America that no group of politicians could break out of the stranglehold of Jefferson's counterrevolutionary logic that the protection of order was more important than the pursuit of liberty. Thacher's proposal that Congress should have a "full, free and deliberate discussion" on eliminating slavery (and blacks) from America was overridden by a vote of 85 to 1. Thus in early 1800 the subject of race was brushed away once again with America's regnant counterrevolutionary fidelity to order—there to remain until a Civil War forced a revival of some of the principles of the American Revolution.

The fate of liberty in America was captured in a letter written by James Forten to George Thacher after the little-noticed vote was taken. Noting that only Thacher had spoken up for any of the provisions of their petition, Forten wrote, "We, therefore, sir, Africans and descendants of that unhappy race, respectfully beg leave to thank you for the philanthropic zeal with which you defended our cause when it was brought before the General Government, by which only we can expect to be delivered from our deplorable state." The "deplorable state" intended by Forten was the prospects that free blacks living in Philadelphia "ere long . . . might be reduced to slavery."

Angry about what was happening to blacks in America, Forten argued that "by principles of natural law our thraldom is unjust." He continued, "Judge what must be our feelings, to find ourselves treated as a species of property, and levelled [in this land] with the brute creation, and think how anxious we must be to raise ourselves from this degraded state." Forten prefaced this complaint with one of the most poignant statements written by anyone about America's rejection of the equalitarian principles of the American Revolution:

> Though our faces are black, yet we are men; and though many
> among us cannot write, yet we all have the feelings and pas-
> sions of men, and are as anxious to enjoy the birth-right of the
> human race as those who from our ignorance draw an argument
> against our Petition, when that Petition has in view the diffusion
> of knowledge among the African race, by unfettering their
> thoughts, and giving full scope to the energy of their minds.

Forten concluded his lament that in America in 1800 too many people "consider us as [so] much property, as a house, or a ship, and would seem to insinuate that it is lawful to hew down the one as to dismantle the other."

Forten then thanked Thacher for taking at least one position that was contrary to the Jeffersonian convention on slavery: "You, sir, more humane, consider us part of the human race." [40]

The irony of Forten's reference to this indictment of Jefferson is that even as the theorists of the American Counterrevolution held forth about how to achieve order in America, America's black leaders were doing precisely the same thing in their own communities. While Adams, Webster, Jefferson, Madison, Ames, Otis, Dwight, and Morse formulated counterrevolutionary principles, Allen, Jones, and Forten developed their ideas about how to bring order in the emerging Philadelphia black community. As were Prince Hall in Boston, Paul Cuffe in Rhode Island, and Daniel Coker in Baltimore. It was even the thrust of Jupiter Hammon's advice to blacks in New York in 1787—not to leap from slavery too soon.

The quest for order in the black community had called forth the Free African Society in Philadelphia in 1787. It had spurred the formation of black masonic lodges in Boston in 1787 and another one in Philadelphia in 1797. It had driven the movement to form black churches in Philadelphia, New York, Boston, Baltimore, Charleston, and Savannah in the 1790s. It had led blacks in Boston in 1796 to come together as "African Members" to "form ourselves into a Society . . . for the mutual benefit of each other, which may from time to time offer." Underscoring their commitment to order, they pledged to act "as true and faithful citizens of the Commonwealth in which we live; and that we take no one into the Society, who shall commit any injustice or outrage against the laws of their country."[41]

This was the power behind those who gathered in Philadelphia in 1797, to form the Friendly Society of St. Thomas's African Church. "Frequently conversing on that most amiable of all the social virtues, Charity, and feeling a desire to promote it in the most consistent manner," they concluded "to associate and unite ourselves together." And what structure did they give this society? A membership with officers consisting of a president, a vice president, a treasurer, a secretary, and a "Committee of Seven Members" as a board of directors. Every member of the society "shall deposit one quarter of a dollar into the hands of the President, who shall cause the Secretary to credit each member for every such payment, in a book to be kept fair and correct for that purpose." The funds thus produced "shall be disposed of only for the relief and support of the orphans and widows of deceased members . . . and for the relief of necessitous members."[42]

Black Americans had quickly understood the drift of white Americans away from the stated principles of the American Revolution. The implications of calls for order; of a new constitution vague on the question of black citizenship and on the future of slavery; of laws permitting the naturalization only of free white residents; of laws regulating the movement of blacks from state to state and forbidding their testimony in courts of law were thoroughly counterrevolutionary.

America's black leaders dealt with this dilemma by organizing the black community. They coalesced meager funds for mutual assistance and community action. They educated themselves, studied the public prints. They preached orderliness, clean living, and service to community, state, and nation.They provided assistance in times of peril, famine, and disease. And they condemned violations of law and human decency when committed by members of the black community. They made use of the justice system to secure the release of free blacks who had been kidnapped and sold into slavery, enlisting white lawyers to aid them. They petitioned and protested for the enjoyment of the unalienable rights promised to them, they fervently believed, in the Declaration of Independence.

Even though Paul Cuffe and others debated whether blacks were better off in America or in Africa, as the American Counterrevolution unfolded, black leaders increasingly embraced the shift in direction between 1783, when the Revolution ended, and 1800, when the Counterrevolution had taken full force.

They disagreed with the Jeffersonian doctrines on the inferiority of blacks and the necessity of slavery in America, but they accepted much else of the theories and implications of a worldwide counterrevolution, using those very teachings to demand that they deserved equal rights as American citizens.

They shifted their attentions from dreaming about a new African land of promise to the promised land of America. They used counterrevolutionary tactics to move America back to the principles of its Revolution; no longer Africans living tentatively in America, they became fully Americanized. And they could play the politics of the counterrevolution as well as anyone else.

OTHER ENDINGS IN THE LAND OF ORDER

Hannah Adams (1755–1831). With the successful publication of her *Alphabetical Compendium of the Various Sects* (1784) in seven American and British editions, she eked out a career for a time as a writer. Following her publication of another work titled *Summary History of New-England* (1799), Jedidiah Morse pirated it in an abridged school book on New England. Morse denied her accusation of plagiarism in a series of letters. In 1809 the dispute was placed before a group of arbitrators approved by both parties, and Morse published a 190-page defense of his actions in 1814. Adams's defenders provided her with a financial stipend in lieu of Morse's refusal to acknowledge financial damages.

Richard Allen (1760–1831). After organizing the Free African Society in Philadelphia in 1787 and the second African church there in 1794, he fought for independence of the church from the Methodist connection. Ordained a deacon by Bishop Francis Asbury in 1799, he created a separate African Methodist Episcopal Church by 1816.

James Lafayette Armistead (1760–1832). An honored slave and spy who infiltrated Cornwallis's headquarters in 1781 and who provided information to defeat British forces at Yorktown, he was emancipated by the Virginia Assembly in a special dispensation in 1786 that gave freedom to black soldiers. Not until 1816 was he given the right to buy land. When Lafayette returned in 1824, Armistead was briefly honored with Lafayette as a hero of the Revolution.

Sarah Franklin Bache (1743–1808). After returning from her European fling, she and husband Richard retired to an estate they called "Settle" on the Delaware River. Occupied with constant recreation, music, and river outings they lived off income from the sale of the elder Franklin's silver, furnishings, and real estate—including his home.

Benjamin Banneker (1731–1806). With the publication of almanacs in 1792 and 1793 bearing his name and the ephemerides he had calculated, he became a widely known free black mathematician. After retiring from tobacco farming, Banneker devoted his attention to preparing ephemerides for twenty-nine editions of his almanacs published through the year 1797. Although he continued to prepare them annually until 1804, he could not find a publisher for his works from 1798 forward. He lived alone in his cabin at Ellicott's Lower Mills until his death. His cabin burned to the ground during his funeral, destroying his papers and scientific equipment. The location of his grave has been lost to history.

Andrew Bryan (1737–1812). His efforts in Savannah, Georgia, paralleled the work of Richard Allen and Absalom Jones in Philadelphia, by organizing the free black communities in Savannah and Augusta into fledgling Baptist churches. In the wake of the revolution in St. Domingue, he and his deacons were attacked by white patrols objecting to their free assembly. In one such arrest they were "inhumanly cut and their backs were so lacerated that their blood ran down to the earth, as they, with uplifted hands, cried unto the Lord." Under the protection of sympathetic whites, Bryan organized three black churches in Savannah and one in Augusta.

Oliver Cromwell (1752–1853). Having traveled the Revolution as a lone black in the 2nd New Jersey Regiment in the service of George Washington over a period of six years, he received a Badge of Merit from Washington and an annual federal pension of $96 per year. He settled on a New Jersey farm, where he reared six children.

Paul Cuffe (1759–1817). He expanded his shipping business throughout the 1790s, but became convinced that many African Americans would find their best home in Africa. Though he found opposition to his plan, especially among the Americanized black community in Philadelphia, he continued to promote the idea and transported shiploads of free blacks to Africa until his untimely death.

Austin Dabney (1760?–1834). A wounded hero at Kettle Creek, Georgia, in 1779, he was crippled for life. He was emancipated by the Georgia legislature in 1786 under the auspices of a law stipulating that he could not be reenslaved by his former master. Passed over for land grants given to Revolutionary War veterans, he worked as a servant for a Georgia family who had nursed his wounds. An act granting him a 112-acre farm in 1821 touched off a firestorm among Georgia politicians.

Elizabeth Sandwith Drinker (1735–1807). She continued until her death the detailed diary she had begun in 1758 reflecting the values of prominent Philadelphia Quakers. Though the Drinkers freed their slaves and assisted fugitive slaves in their home, she continued to believe that there should be class distinctions and a separation of races. She first thought Wollstonecraft "in very many of her sentiments . . . speaks my mind, in some others, I do not, altogether coincide with her— I am not for quite so much independence." By 1798 Drinker wrote, "I dont like her, or her principles, 'tho amused by her writings." On Paine's *The Age of Reason,* she concurred with the friends of order, "Much may be said in answer to his blasphemies, but the misfortune is, that all who read his poisoned discourses, do not take the pains to look for the antidote." She called Richard Allen "a black man of consequence." In December 1797 she reported that husband Henry "and seven others went this forenoon to wait on Congress, with a petition for the poor blacks [written by Allen and Jones]. Our society has done much in this business with good effect—but not as much as could have been desired." Yet, when the Drinkers had to

"Washington's Funeral Procession on High Street from the Country Market, Philadelphia" (1799). Philadelphians pay homage to the nation's founding father and first president as the American Counterrevolution reached its culmination.

have the contents from their overflowing sewer removed by a group of blacks, she wrote, "If liberty and equality which some talk much about, could take place, who would they get for those, and many other hard and disagreeable undertakings."[43]

Jean Baptiste Pointe Du Sable (1745?–1818). As a Haitian free black, he continued to operate his trading post on Lake Michigan from 1784 until 1800, when he sold the later Chicago site for a handsome sum of $1,200. Although married to a Potawatomi woman, he failed at business when his horses were shortly thereafter stolen. He died penniless in St. Charles, Missouri, eighteen years later.

William Flora (?–c. 1818). Following his heroics at the Battle of Great Bridge in 1775 as a lone black against Lord Dunmore's "black regiment," he served out the Revolution valiantly. Returning to Portsmouth, Virginia, after the war, he prospered, bought the freedom of his wife and children, and established a business hauling freight between merchants and farmers in the area.

James Forten Sr. (1766–1842). He became the first black foreman of a sailmaking loft in Philadelphia in 1786 and owner of the place by 1798. As a prominent Philadelphia businessman he promoted equal rights for blacks throughout the 1790s and beyond. He wrote eloquent defenses of the rights of black Americans in 1799 and at other critical junctures in American history until his death.

Amos Fortune (1710?–1801). He prospered as a black tanner with his wife Violate at the loom in Jaffrey, New Hampshire, after the Revolution. Although forced to sit in black pews in the town church, he donated from his meager income to local causes, including the town library and the local school. He left his estate to Violate until her death and thence as an endowment to the local school. The endowment continues to the present.

Hannah Webster Foster (1758–1840). Although her anonymously published *The Coquette* (1797) was reprinted dozens of times into and through the nineteenth century, her name did not appear on the title page until 1866. Her only other publication in the balance of her long life was *The Boarding School* in 1798, setting forth in moral lessons the proper life of young women in the counterrevolutionary American republic.

William Temple Franklin (1762–1823). As the other principal heir of Benjamin Franklin's estate with Sarah Bache, he inherited the Franklin manuscripts, the vast library, and money. Following the example of Aunt Sarah, he sold the library and used the proceeds to travel to England, where he lived a life of idleness until 1798. Moving then to Paris he did not undertake the responsibility of publishing his grandfather's *Autobiography* until 1817, when he finally issued his first and quite faulty edition of Franklin's famous book. His reason for publishing after twenty-seven years: he needed the money to maintain his dissolute lifestyle.

Elizabeth Freeman (c. 1742–1829). Freed by a court order in 1783 based on the bill of rights in the Massachusetts constitution, she spent the balance of her life as housekeeper and nurse for two generations of Sedgwicks. She was buried with the Sedgwick family in the burial ground at Stockbridge, Massachusetts.

Catharine Littlefield Greene (1755–1814). Having used funds from her hard-won settlement from Congress of Nathanael Greene's estate to finance the development, sales, and protection of Eli Whitney's cotton gin, in 1803, she found herself deeply in debt to the partnership. Having also lost heavily in the Yazoo Company land fraud of 1796, she remained deep in debt and in persistent litigation for the rest of her life, a virtual prisoner in her endangered "Dungeness" on Cumberland Island, Georgia.

Prince Hall (1735?–1807). After seeking to absolve black participation in Shays's Rebellion in 1786, arguing that blacks were "peaceable subjects to the Civil powers where we reside [and would not] participate in any plot or conspiracies against the state," and establishing black masonry in Boston in 1787 and in Philadelphia in 1797, Hall was utterly frustrated in getting the state of Massachusetts or the selectmen of Boston to permit the establishment of a school in Boston to educate black students. In protest he started a school in his own home in 1800.

Jupiter Hammon (1711–1806?). America's first black poet continued to write his poems after the Revolution and remained, by choice, a slave on Long Island until his death. When attacked for turning his back on the principles of the American Revolution, Hammon proclaimed to fellow blacks in New York "for my part I do not wish to be free." He concluded, "For many of us, who are grown up slaves, should hardly know how to take care of ourselves, and it may be more for our own comfort to remain as we are."

Agrippa Hull (1759–1848). He served as devoted orderly to Gen. Tadeusz Kościusko for four years until discharged by Washington in 1783. He farmed thereafter and served as a butler in Stockbridge, Massachusetts, marrying a fugitive slave and adopting another fugitive as his daughter. As a village elder, he recounted for visitors and children his experiences in the service of Washington and Kościusko during the war.

Absalom Jones (1746–1818). Ordained the first black deacon in the American Episcopal Church in 1794 and to the priesthood in 1804, Jones led the first independent African church in Philadelphia and authored many of the early petitions seeking to secure rights for black Americans. He established a society for mutual assistance and a school for blacks in his own semi-independent church and sought to exercise strict order in his black Episcopal community.

Salem Poor (1758–?). Although a hero in the capture of Col. James Ambercrombie at the Battle of Bunker Hill in 1775, he was not allowed to reenlist in the Continental Army until Lord Dunmore opened the British Army to free blacks. Finally readmitted, his role in history was lost after the Revolution.

Lucy Terry Prince (1733–1821). Despite her modest fame as a poet and the honor of her two sons' valiant service in the American Revolution, she was unable to persuade the trustees of Williams College, Williamstown, Massachusetts, to admit another son, Abijah Jr., as a student.

Joseph Ranger (1760–?). Serving as a black sailor on Virginia naval vessels during the Revolution, he was captured with the seizure of the *Patriot* by British forces and held as a prisoner until the surrender of Lord Cornwallis at Yorktown. Thereafter, he served on Virginia vessels until 1787. Not until 1832 was he granted one hundred acres of land and a pension of $96 per annum.

Peter Salem (1750–1816). Like Salem Poor and other blacks, he was briefly not allowed to reenlist in the Continental Army despite his heroics at Bunker Hill. Salem settled in a cabin near Leicester, Massachusetts, weaving cane for a living until he entered the Framingham poorhouse, where he died.

Deborah Sampson (1760–1827). Following her 1802 tour recreating her talents as a marching soldier from Washington's brigades, she appealed in 1804 to Paul Revere to assist her in recovering compensation for her Revolutionary War service. Revere wrote the appeal, stating that he expected to encounter "a tall, masculine female, who had a small share of understanding, without education, and one of the meanest of her sex." Instead, "I was agreeably surprised to find a small, effeminate, and conversable woman, whose education entitled her to a better situation in life." With his letter she received a pension for life of four dollars a month. In 1831 her widower, Benjamin Gannett, petitioned Congress for a continuation of her pension. Although championed by John Quincy Adams, it was not approved until July 7, 1838, three weeks after Gannett's death. The act, nevertheless, was the first instance in which the United States granted a pension to a man for his wife's military service.

Jack Sisson (c. 1743–1821). Following his heroics in capturing British General Prescott in 1777, his act, but not his name, was immortalized in a popular ballad. Angry that his name was absent, he spent the rest of his life dressing in his uniform on holidays and singing the ballad, clarifying that it was he who led the capture.

Caesar Tarrant (?–1798). A slave who "entered very early into the service of his country and continued to pilot the armed vessels of the state [Virginia] during the late war," Tarrant was freed by the Virginia General Assembly in 1789. He worked until his death as an artisan at Hampton, Virginia. Finally, in 1833 his wife was granted a parcel of land in Ohio as compensation for his service.

Denmark Vesey (1767–1822). He bought his freedom from slavery by winning the triennial lottery in Charleston, South Carolina, in 1799. The rest of his money he used to open a shipbuilding shop in Charleston, where he developed a career that enabled him to study the revolutions in St. Domingue and other West Indian islands. He shared his reflections with fellow blacks—free and slave—in Charleston and far beyond. He used his knowledge and charisma to organize a conspiracy of nine thousand blacks—slave and free—to take over Charleston, South Carolina, on July 14, 1822—the thirty-third anniversary of the storming of the Bastille.

PILGRIMAGE

1. Simon Schama, *Citizens: A Chronicle of the French Revolution* (New York: Alfred A. Knopf, 1989).

2. Heinrich Fichtenau, *The Carolingian Empire: The Age of Charlemagne* (New York: Harper & Row, 1964), 71–75; Einhard, *The Life of Charlemagne* (Ann Arbor: Univ. of Michigan Press, 1960), 56–57.

3. Colin Jones, *The Longman Companion to the French Revolution* (London: Longman, 1988), 114–21.

4. For Charlemagne's attention to architectural detail see Fichtenau, *Carolingian Empire,* 54–56, 68–71; for Napoleon's renowned orderliness see Georges Lefebvre, *Napoleon from 18 Brumaire to Tilsit, 1799–1807* (New York: Columbia Univ. Press, 1969), 77–92.

5. Michael Paul Driskel, *As Befits a Legend: Building a Tomb for Napoleon, 1840–1861* (Kent, Ohio: Kent State Univ. Press, 1993), 51–53, 60.

6. Most of the details here are also in *Encyclopaedia Britannica* (11th edition, 1910), 3:555–56.

7. Franklin probably wrote "An Address to the Public from the Pennsylvania Society for Promoting the Abolition of Slavery," issued by that society under the date of November 9, 1789, and did write a burlesque attack *On the Slave Trade* under the date of March 23, 1790—three weeks prior to his death. Wesley's last letter, written on February 14, 1791, a week before his death, was a stirring call for William Wilberforce to persist in his fight against slavery and the slave trade.

8. I am grateful to Peter Jones for countless discussions on the Scottish Enlightenment and for rendering to me, in view of my enthusiasm, his personal copy of *A Hotbed of Genius: The Scottish Enlightenment, 1730–90,* edited by himself with David Daiches and Jean Jones (Edinburgh: Edinburgh Univ. Press, 1986) to accompany an exhibition of this title at the National Museum of Scotland that same year.

PROLOGUE

1. A description of Franklin's last days issued by his physician, John Jones of the Pennsylvania Hospital, was published contemporaneously throughout the

world. See, for example, *American Museum, or Universal Magazine* 7 (May 1790): 266; for a standard secondary account of Franklin's death and funeral, see Carl Van Doren, *Benjamin Franklin* (New York: Viking Press, 1938), 778–81.

2. This touching story of the Mifflin dinner party appears in Horace Wemyss Smith, *Life and Correspondence of the Rev. William Smith, D.D.,* 2 vols. (1880; reprint, New York: Arno Press, 1972), 324–25.

3. Ibid., 779–80.

4. The somewhat tangled, but intriguing story of tributes to Franklin is told in considerable detail by Julian Boyd in "Death of Franklin: The Politics of Mourning in France and the United States," in *Papers of Thomas Jefferson* (Princeton, N.J.: Princeton Univ. Press, 1974): 19:78–106.

5. "Of Dr. Franklin," *Massachusetts Magazine* 2 (May 1790): 259–62.

6. Ibid., 309; "Memoirs of the Late Benjamin Franklin," *American Museum, or Universal Magazine,* 8 (July and November 1790): 12–20, 210–14.

7. The story of the French reaction to Franklin's death is told in considerable detail in Gilbert Chinard, "The Apotheosis of Benjamin Franklin: Paris, 1790–1791," *Proceedings of the American Philosophical Society,* 99 (December 1955): 440–73. Boyd's "Politics of Mourning," 78–106, makes some corrections to Chinard's interpretation and adds some detail to the account.

8. Boyd, "Politics of Mourning," 79–81; Chinard, "Apotheosis of Franklin," 440; "National Assembly of France," *Massachusetts Magazine* 2 (August 1790): 509.

9. Boyd, "Politics of Mourning," 80–81; Chinard, "Apotheosis of Franklin," 440–42.

10. Chinard, "Apotheosis of Franklin," 442–50.

11. Boyd, "Politics of Mourning," 78–79.

12. Ibid., 97–98.

13. Ibid., 80–90, 110–11.

14. Ibid., 95–97.

15. It is Boyd's conclusion, as well, that Hamilton was operating behind the scenes; see Ibid., 90–91, 95–99.

16. William Smith, D.D., *Eulogium on Benjamin Franklin . . . Delivered March 1, 1791, in the German Lutheran Church of the City of Philadelphia, before the American Philosophical Society* (Philadelphia: Benjamin Franklin Bache, 1792), iii–iv. Smith generously acknowledged the assistance he received.

17. Ibid., 1–40 passim.

18. Ibid., iv and postscript. For more about Smith and his delivery of the *Eulogium,* see Smith, *William Smith,* 344–45, where a story is related about the reaction of Smith's daughter Rebecca. When Smith asked his daughter's opinion of his performance, she responded, "Only—papa—now you wont be offended—will you? I don't think you believed more than one-tenth part of what you said of old Ben Lightning-rod."

CHAPTER 1: Friends of Liberty

1. Helen E. Veit, Kenneth R. Bowling, and Charlene Bangs Bickford, eds., *Creating the Bill of Rights: The Documentary Record from the First Federal Congress* (Baltimore: Johns Hopkins Univ. Press, 1991), 77–79, covering Madison's opening address on the amendments, June 8, 1789.

2. The foregoing narrative is informed by the treatment of the French Revolution in Schama's *Citizens* 428–70; see also Jones, *Longman Companion* 6–13.

3. For the story of the London Revolution Society, see Albert Goodwin, *The Friends of Liberty: The English Democratic Movement in the Age of The French Revolution* (Cambridge: Harvard Univ. Press, 1979), 106–10.

4. Richard Price, "A Discourse on the Love of Our Country, Delivered on Nov. 4, 1789, at the Meeting-House in the Old Jewry, to the Society for Commemorating the Revolution in Great Britain," *Political Sermons of the American Founding Era, 1730–1805,* Ellis Sandoz, ed. (Indianapolis: Liberty Press, 1991), 1005–28.

5. Goodwin, *Friends of Liberty,* 106–111.

6. Ibid., 113–16.

7. Van Doren, *Benjamin Franklin,* 419–20. Franklin thought so much of Price's knowledge of economics and accounting that he recommended that the American Congress bring him to America to take charge of the nation's early financial systems. Though Price was flattered by the invitation, he respectfully declined.

8. Derek Jarrett, *The Begetters of Revolution: England's Involvement with France, 1759–1789* (Totowa, N.J.: Rowman and Littlefield, 1973), 127–30.

9. Goodwin, *Friends of Liberty,* 99–103; Jarrett, *Begetters of Revolution,* 130–35. Included among the Bowood Circle, in addition to Franklin, Price, Priestley, and Morellet, were such renowned figures as Anne-Robert-Jacques Turgot and Honoré-Gabriel Riqueti, Mirabeau Comtede, architects of the French Revolution; Jeremy Bentham and Samuel Romilly, British reformers; Pierre-Étienne Dumont, Genevan publicist and reformer; and Jacques-Pierre Brissot de Warville and Simon-Nicolas-Henri Linguet, central figures in the French Revolution. The Bowood group also launched the careers of British reformers James Townshend, John Horne Tooke, Maj. John Cartwright, Charles Stanhope, Henry Beaufoy, and Benjamin Vaughan. Biographical information compiled also from various sources, including François Furet and Mona Ozouf, eds., *A Critical Dictionary of the French Revolution* (Cambridge: Harvard Univ. Press, 1989); Bernard Peach and D. O. Thomas, eds., *The Correspondence of Richard Price,* 2 vols. (Durham, N.C.: Duke Univ. Press, 1983); and *Concise Dictionary of American Biography* (New York: Charles Scribner's Sons, 1964).

10. These and other examples are mentioned in Goodwin, *Friends of Liberty,* 102–104.

11. Ibid., 103–6; Jarrett, *Begetters of Revolution,* 252–61; Furet and Ozouf, *Dictionary of French Revolution,* 265–71.

12. Jarrett, *Begetters of Revolution,* 263–83.

13. Peter Brown, *The Chathamites: A Study in the Relationship between Personalities and Ideas in the Second Half of the Eighteenth Century* (New York: St. Martin's Press, 1967), 168–74, 184–86; see also *Dictionary of National Biography,* s.v., "Price, Richard" (hereafter cited as *DNB*).

14. Jarrett, *Begetters of Revolution,* 284–86. See also *DNB,* s.v. "Petty, William."

15. Anne Holt, *A Life of Joseph Priestley* (London: Oxford Univ. Press, 1931), 1–23; Joseph Priestley, *The Memoirs of Dr. Joseph Priestley* (Washington, D.C.: Barcroft Press, 1964), 9–36.

16. Holt, *Life of Priestley,* 38–41; Priestley, *Memoirs,* 41–52.

17. Peach and Thomas, *Correspondence of Price,* 1:132–38. Priestley, *Memoirs,* 53–74; Holt, *Life of Priestley,* 66–82, 95–97.

18. Holt, *Life of Priestley,* 80–82. Priestley, *Memoirs,* 70–74.

19. Priestley, *Memoirs,* 77–82.

20. Goodwin, *Friends of Liberty,* 136–79 passim; John Binns, *Recollections of the Life of John Binns: Twenty-Nine Years in Europe and Fifty-Three in the United States, Written by Himself* (Philadelphia: Printed by the Author, 1854), 36–71.

21. *Dictionary of American Biography,* s.v., "Rhees, Morgan John" (hereafter cited as *DAB*).

22. Michael Durey, *"With the Hammer of Truth": James Thomson Callender and America's Early National Heroes* (Charlottesville: Univ. Press of Virginia, 1990), 1–28.

23. Kenneth Wyer Rowe, *Mathew Carey: A Study in American Economic Development* (Baltimore: Johns Hopkins Press, 1933), 9–15.

24. Charles Campbell, ed., *Some materials to Serve for a Brief Memoir of John Daly Burk* (Albany, N.Y.: Joel Munsell, 1868), 9–12.

25. Wolfe Tone's brief, but fantastic career, has been well told in Frank MacDermot, *Theobald Wolfe Tone: A Biographical Study* (London: Macmillan and Co., 1939), 68–89, and in Marianne Elliott, *Wolfe Tone: Prophet of Irish Independence* (New Haven: Yale Univ. Press, 1989), 134–59.

26. Kim Tousley Phillips, "William Duane, Revolutionary Editor" (Ph.D. diss.; Univ. of California, Berkeley, 1968), 4–12.

27. David Freeman Hawke, *Paine* (New York: Harper & Row, Publishers, 1974), 160–187 passim.

28. I would like to acknowledge the usefulness of Michael Durey's article "Thomas Paine's Apostles: Radical Émigrés and the Triumph of Jeffersonian Republicanism," *William and Mary Quarterly* 44, series 3 (October 1987); 661–88, in helping to focus the following story of the emigration of particular journalists to the United States. Though I did not come upon this stimulating piece until late in my research, it proved helpful to compare his findings with my own. Holt, *Life of Priestley,* 145–154.

29. Schama, *Citizens,* 561–68.

30. Holt, *Life of Priestley,* 145–78.

31. Dumas Malone, *The Public Life of Thomas Cooper, 1783–1939* (1923; reprint, Columbia: Univ. of South Carolina Press, 1961), 34–67.

32. Ibid., 67–72; *DAB,* s.v. "Cheetham, James."

33. Durey, *With Hammer of Truth,* 40–47.

34. *DAB,* s.v. "Rhees, Morgan John."

35. W. H. G. Armytage, "The Editorial Experience of Joseph Gales, 1786–1794," *North Carolina Historical Review,* 27 (July 1951): 332–61; Robert Neal Elliott, Jr., *The Raleigh Register, 1799–1863* (Chapel Hill: Univ. of North Carolina Press, 1955), 8–13. The Gales's family experience was beautifully described in an autobiography written in the early 1830s by Joseph Gales's wife Winifred in "Reminiscences," Joseph Gales Papers, Southern Historical Collection, Univ. of North Carolina, Chapel Hill, N.C.

36. Goodwin, *Friends of Liberty,* 323–24; William H. Furness, *A Discourse Delivered on the Death of John Vaughan* (Philadelphia: J. Crissy, Printer, 1842), 3–17.

37. Elliott, *Wolfe Tone,* 246–254; see also *DNB,* s.v., "Jackson, William."

38. Campbell, *Memoir of John Daly Burk,* 9–12, 25–26.

39. Phillips, "William Duane," 13–21, 22–32, 36–42, 43–47.

40. Binns, *Life of John Binns,* 36–166 passim. On the settlement for friends of liberty in Northumberland, Pennsylvania, see Priestley, *Memoirs,* 103; also Malone, *Thomas Cooper,* 80–82.

41. Priestley, *Memoirs,* 122–23; Malone, *Thomas Cooper,* 31–32; Elliott, *Raleigh Register,* 7; Durey, *With Hammer of Truth,* 41; Phillips, "William Duane," 24–28.

42. Goodwin, *Friends of Liberty,* 207, 215, 271; Hawke, *Paine,* 238–55.

43. Hawke, *Paine,* 277–96.

44. Frances Sergeant Childs, *French Refugee Life in the United States, 1790–1800: An American Chapter of the French Revolution* (Baltimore: Johns Hopkins Press, 1940), 9ff.

45. Childs, *French Refugee Life in the U. S.,* 30–35, 37–39.

46. James Morton Smith, *Freedom's Fetters: The Alien and Sedition Laws and American Civil Liberties* (Ithaca, N.Y.: Cornell Univ. Press, 1956), 164–65.

47. Childs, *French Refugee Life,* 39–41.

48. [Duff Cooper, *Talleyrand,* (1932; Stanford: Stanford Univ. Press, 1967), 47–72 passim]

49. Alfred N. Hunt, *Haiti's Influence on Antebellum America: Slumbering Volcano in the Caribbean* (Baton Rouge: Louisiana State Univ. Press, 1988), 23–39; Childs, *French Refugee Life,* 10–16.

50. Childs, *French Refugee Life,* 51–55.

51. Hawke, *Paine,* 291–306; A. J. Ayer, *Thomas Paine* (Chicago: Univ. of Chicago Press, 1988), 125–31.

52. Hawke, *Paine,* 307–18; Ayer, *Thomas Paine,* 131–39.

53 Hawke, *Paine,* 318–20.

CHAPTER 2: Joseph Priestley and American Liberty

1. Edgar F. Smith, *Priestley in America, 1794–1804* (Philadelphia: P. Blakiston's Son, 1920), 12–19.

2. Ibid., 20–22.

3. Ibid., 22–34; Holt, *Life of Priestley,* 182–83; see also Philip S. Foner, *The Democratic–Republican Societies, 1790–1800* (Westport, Conn.: Greenwood Press, 1976), 182–83.

4. Smith, *Priestley in America,* 35–40.

5. Ibid., 48–51.

6. Joseph Priestley, Jr., "A Continuation of the Memoirs of Dr. Joseph Priestley," in *The Memoirs of Dr. Joseph Priestley,* ed. John T. Boyer (Washington, D.C.: Barcroft Press, 1964), 129–32; Malone, *Public Life of Thomas Cooper,* 75–78.

7. Priestley, Jr., "Continuation of Memoirs," 143; Holt, *Life of Priestley,* 188–90; Malone, *Public Life of Thomas Cooper,* 81–83, 226. The story of the Joseph Priestley House in Northumberland, Pennsylvania, is a fascinating one. Although Priestley bequeathed the house to his children, it escaped the family's hands in the nineteenth century. Many times renovated and subdivided to provide tenant housing, it was acquired by the Commonwealth of Pennsylvania to be used as a historic house museum in the twentieth century. It was my pleasure while executive director of the Pennsylvania Historical and Museum Commission during 1981–87 to oversee historical research that located an original plan for the house at the Royal Society in London and to supervise extensive archaeological investigations that pinpointed the landscape plan, recovered artifacts from Priestley's laboratory, and architectural analysis that discovered the long-covered-over laboratory hood.

8. Binns, *Recollections,* 169–76.

9. Holt, *Life of Priestley,* 193–97; Smith, *Priestley in America,* 71–73.

10. Smith, *Priestley in America,* 98–102; Priestley, Jr., "Continuation of Memoirs," 144–48.

11. Mary Elizabeth Clark, *Peter Porcupine in America: The Career of William Cobbett, 1792–1800* (Philadelphia: Times and News Publishing, 1939), 21–27; George Spater, *William Cobbett: The Poor Man's Friend,* (Cambridge: Cambridge Univ. Press, 1982), 1, 39–51.

12. Malone, *Public Life of Thomas Cooper,* 83–87.

13. Joseph Priestley, *Letters to the Inhabitants of Northumberland* (Northumberland, Pa.: Andrew Kennedy, 1799), 45–46; Malone, *Public Life of Thomas Cooper,* 91, 106–8.

14. Thomas Cooper, *Political Essays* (Northumberland, Pa.: Andrew Kennedy, 1799), 3–4; Malone, *Public Life of Thomas Cooper,* 92–100.

CHAPTER 3: Friends of Liberty in the Land of Liberty

1. On the origin and spread of the Jacobin Club movement, see the article on "Jacobinism" in Furet and Ozouf, *Critical Dictionary of French Revolution,* 704–715.

2. Eugene Perry Link, *Democratic–Republican Societies, 1790–1800* (Morningside Heights, N.Y.: Columbia Univ. Press, 1942), 6–15; see also Philip S. Foner, *The Democratic Republican Societies,* (Westport, Conn.: Greenwood Press, 1976), 3–10.

3. Link, *Democratic–Republican Societies,* 6–10; Foner, *Democratic–Republican Societies,* 53, 345–46.

4. Link, *Democratic–Republican Societies,* 10–12; Foner, *Democratic–Republican Societies,* 64–68, 411–14.

5. Foner, *Democratic–Republican Societies,* 64–110 passim; see also James Tagg, *Benjamin Franklin Bache and the Philadelphia Aurora* (Philadelphia: Univ. of Pennsylvania Press, 1991), 205–31.

6. Foner, *Democratic–Republican Societies,* 102–4, 417.

7. Link, *Democratic–Republican Societies,* 13–15.

8. Ibid., 71–99.

9. Ibid., 381–82, 436; see also biographical note on Tate in E. H. Stuart Jones, *The Last Invasion of Britain* (Cardiff: Univ. of Wales Press, 1950), 275–77; Tate's group is also characterized in Meade Minnigerode, *Jefferson Friend of France, 1793: The Career of Edmond Charles Genet 1763–1834* (New York: G. P. Putnam's Sons, 1928), 256–57.

10. Carl Binger, *Revolutionary Doctor: Benjamin Rush, 1746–1813* (New York: W. W. Norton, 1966), 32–48.

11. Ibid., 70–111 passim.

12. Binger, *Revolutionary Doctor,* 177–202; Link, *Democratic–Republican Societies,* 81–82.

13. Daniel Marder, *Hugh Henry Brackenridge* (New York: Twayne Publishers, 1967), 17–31; Daniel Marder, ed., *A Hugh Henry Brackenridge Reader, 1770–1815* (Pittsburgh: Univ. of Pittsburgh Press, 1970), 56–60.

14. Marder, *Brackenridge,* 31–48; Foner, *Democratic–Republican Societies,* 129–30, 419.

15. Jacob Axelrad, *Philip Freneau: Champion of Democracy* (Austin: Univ. of Texas Press, 1967), 3–42, 43–78.

16. Ibid., 75–79, 105–15.

17. Ibid., 139–57.

18. Ibid., 209–34; Foner, *Democratic–Republican Societies,* 3–12, 411, 437.

19. Aleine Austin, *Matthew Lyon: "New Man" of the Democratic Revolution, 1749–1822* (University Park: Pennsylvania State Univ. Press), 7–29, 30–44.

20. Ibid., 45–82, 167.15.

21. Bache's brief but dramatic life is beautifully told by Tagg, *Benjamin Franklin Bache,* 1–18.

22. Ibid., 23–32; for Franklin's ideas on how to educate boys, especially William Temple and Bennie Bache, see Jeffrey A. Smith, *Franklin and Bache* (New York: Oxford Univ. Press, 1990), 45–62.

23. Tagg, *Benjamin Franklin Bache,* 32–35.

24. Ibid., 35–47; Smith, *Franklin and Bache,* 76–79; Rowe, *Mathew Carey,* 12–13.

25. Tagg, *Benjamin Franklin Bache,* 56–78.

26. Ibid., 86–109. This distinction has been well confirmed by Rosenfeld, Richard, *American Aurora: A Democratic–Republican Returns* (New York: St. Martin's Press, 1997).

27. Ibid., 205–31.

28. Ibid., 122–27.

29. Smith, *Franklin & Bache,* 111–33; Tagg, *Benjamin Franklin Bache,* 127–38.

30. Tagg, *Benjamin Franklin Bache,* 138–42.

31. Both James Tagg and Jeffrey Smith, the most thorough biographers of Bache, connect him to the radical Enlightenment ideas of Franklin and portray him as I have here as an ardent, well-meaning revolutionary; see Tagg, *Benjamin Franklin Bache,* 140–49 and Smith, *Franklin & Bache,* 128–33.

32. Rowe, *Mathew Carey,* 16–28.

33. Durey, *Hammer of Truth,* 50–73.

34. *DAB,* s.v. "Morgan John Rhees."

35. Elliott, *Raleigh Register,* 12–16.

36. MacDermot, *Theobald Wolfe Tone* 167, 170–75.

37. Ibid., 168–69, 177–78; Elliott, *Wolfe Tone,* 266, 269; Durey, *Hammer of Truth,* 42, 50, 76–77.

38. MacDermot, *Theobald Wolfe Tone,* 169–70, 176–79; Elliott, *Wolfe Tone,* 262–66, 275–77.

39. Elliott, *Wolfe Tone,* 271–72, 277–78; Edmund Berkeley and Dorothy Smith Berkeley, *John Beckley: Zealous Partisan in a Nation Divided* (Philadelphia: American Philosophical Society, 1973), 130–31.

40. MacDermot, *Theobald Wolfe Tone,* 177–78; for the Bache connection, see Elliott, *Wolfe Tone,* 269, 279, 455n.72.

41. Kenneth Roberts and Anna M. Roberts, *Moreau de St. Mery's American Journey, 1793–1798* (Garden City, N.Y.: Doubleday & Company, 1947), xv–xvii, 34, 90–92, 143–44, 176, 206.

42. Roberts, *American Journey,* xv–xvii. The confused history of the first English and French editions of Volney's *The Ruins* is somewhat imperfectly outlined in C. F. Volney, *The Ruins* (1913 edition), iii–xii.

43. Roberts, *American Journey,* 176, 214–16; Green, *Talleyrand,* 72–77.

44. *DNB,* s.v. "Vaughan, Benjamin;" *DAB,* s.v. "Vaughan Benjamin; also William H. Furness, *A Discourse, Delivered on the Occasion of the Death of John Vaughan, in the First Congregational Unitarian Church, Sunday, Jan. 16, 1842* (Philadelphia: J. Crissy, Printer, 1842), 3, 10–17.

45. Campbell, *Materials of John Daly Burk,* 14–15, 19–30.

46. Smith, *Freedom's Fetters,* 204–7.

47. Michael Durey, "Thomas Paine's Apostles," *W&M Quarterly* 44 (October 1987): 667. Although he did not play a role in the battle for liberty in the United States in the 1790s, John Binns, the long-suffering and frequently imprisoned president of the London Corresponding Society throughout the 1790s joined his colleagues Joseph Priestley and Thomas Cooper in Northumberland, Pennsylvania.

Arriving by ship in Baltimore, the impoverished Binns walked to Harrisburg, Pennsylvania, and then on to Northumberland. He addressed a July 4 crowd in 1802 and soon started up a weekly paper called *The Republican Argus,* bearing the motto, "Equal and exact justice to all men, of whatever sect or persuasion, religious or political." Binns also served as printer and publisher for Priestley and Cooper. Remote central Pennsylvania had an extraordinary voice on the side of liberty. C. Binns, *Recollections,* 167–73, 176–77, 180–82.

48. Phillips, "William Duane," 46–52.

CHAPTER 4: Sarah Franklin's Declaration of Independence

1. Franklin's will as it appears in Albert Henry Smyth, ed., *The Writings of Benjamin Franklin* (New York: 1905, 1907) 10: 493–510. Substantial files on the history of the will also reside at the Benjamin Franklin National Memorial of the Franklin Institute in Philadelphia and at the American Philosophical Society. It was my distinct pleasure shortly after I arrived at the Franklin Institute to assist Mayor Wilson Goode of Philadelphia in appointing a committee of historians and citizens to determine what should be done with Philadelphia's portion of Franklin's trust fund on the occasion of the bicentennial of his death, April 17, 1990. Philadelphia was the first of the four receiving entities to select a disposition for its funds. Our committee recommended that the funds be transferred to the Philadelphia Foundation to make loans and guarantee credit for students of the trades, to make grants to strengthen trades training programs, and to give awards to individuals demonstrating outstanding proficiency in the various trades. The Commonwealth of Pennsylvania followed this plan in part by making half of its funds available to community foundations for the same purposes as the Philadelphia initiative. The other half was granted to the Franklin Institute of Philadelphia to continue its program of training students and citizens of Philadelphia in science, technology, and the mechanical arts.

2. Ibid., 593–94, 598–600.

3. Sheila L. Skemp, *William Franklin: Son of a Patriot, Servant of a King* (New York: Oxford Univ. Press, 1990), 273–74.

4. The respective careers of Franklin's heirs are richly detailed in Claude-Anne Lopez and Eugenia W. Herbert, *The Private Franklin: The Man and His Family* (New York: W. W. Norton, 1975), 305–11.

5. I am grateful to colleague Claude-Anne Lopez for additional insights on the Bache trip to England, during a phone conversation, December 3, 1993; see also Lopez and Herbert, *Private Franklin,* 306–7. According to Sheila Skemp, *William Franklin,* 274–75, William Franklin provided similar services to Sally's second son and his namesake, William Franklin Bache, when he went to London to study medicine.

6. Information on activities of the Baches in England provided by Lopez, telephone conversation; descriptions of the portraits are inspired by Lopez and Herbert, *Private Franklin,* 307.

7. Information on Sally's correspondence with Le Veillard from Lopez; infor-

mation on Franklin's friends and their fate from Lopez and Herbert, *Private Franklin,* 277–78.

8. Lopez, telephone conversation; for Le Veillard, see J. A. Leo Leman and P. M. Zall, eds., *Benjamin Franklin's Autobiography: An Authoritative Text, Backgrounds, Criticism* (New York: W. W. Norton, 1986), 188.

9. Lopez, telephone conversation.

10. Skemp, *William Franklin,* 8–21, 28–29.

11. Lopez and Herbert, *Private Franklin,* 70–76, 82–83.

12. Ibid., 100–42 passim.

13. Ibid., 215–16.

14. Ibid., 143, 287–88, 304–5.

CHAPTER 5: Liberty and the Rights of Women

1. *Notable American Women,* s.v. "Rowson, Susanna Haswell."

2. Susanna Rowson, "Sketches of Female Biography," in *A present for Young Ladies; Containing Poems, Dialogues, Addresses, &c, as Recited by the Pupils of Mrs. Rowson's Academy, at the Annual Exhibitions* (Boston: John West, 1811), 83–86, 90–97, 98–101, 105–17.

3. Ibid., 87–88, 101–5; for Deborah Sampson's odd career, see Lucy Freeman and Alma Bond, *America's First Woman Warrior: The Courage of Deborah Sampson* (New York: Paragon House, 1992).

4. Rowson, "Sketches of Female Biography," 101–2; Sidney Harcave, *Russia: A History,* 5th ed. (Philadelphia: J. B. Lippincott, 1964), 97, 99, 114–15.

5. Rowson, "Sketches of Female Biography," 102–3; Harcave, *Russia,* 119–20.

6. Rowson, "Sketches of Female Biography," 104–5.

7. See also Priscilla Mason, "The Salutatory Oration," in *The Rise and Progress of the Young Ladies Academy of Philadelphia: Containing an Account of a Number of Public Examinations & Commencements; the Charter and Bye-Laws; Likewise, a Number of Orations Delivered by the Young Ladies, and Several by the Trustees of Said Institution* (Philadelphia: Stewart & Cochran, 1794), 90–95. Ms. Mason also mentioned Elizabeth Carter, Jane Elizabeth Moore, and Elizabeth Singer Rowe. See Sharon M. Harris, ed., *American Women Writers to 1800* (New York: Oxford Univ. Press, 1996), 69–73.

8. John T. Alexander, *Catherine the Great: Life and Legend* (New York: Oxford Univ. Press, 1989), 20–23.

9. Ibid., 25–57 passim.

10. Harcave, *Russia: A History,* 125–26.

11. The story follows closely the narrative given by Alexander, *Catherine the Great,* 3–16.

12. Harcave, *Russia,* 127–35.

13. Alexander, *Catherine the Great,* 100–2, 132–33.

14. Harcave, *Russia,* 140–42, 176–77; Alexander, *Catherine the Great,* 277–79.

15. Alexander, *Catherine the Great,* 279–80, 283–84.

16. Ibid., 296–304.

17. Harcave, *Russia,* 180–81; Alexander, *Catherine the Great,* 304–6.

18. J. Christopher Herold, *Mistress of an Age: A Life of Madame de Staël* (Indianapolis: Bobbs-Merrill, 1959), 10–11.

19. Ibid., 12–13; Patricia B. Carddock, *Edward Gibbon, Luminous Historian, 1772–1794* (Baltimore: Johns Hopkins Univ. Press, 1989), 51, 61, 83–88.

20. Herold, *Mistress to an Age,* 9–21.

21. Herold, *Mistress to an Age,* 22–24.

22. Dena Goodman, "Enlightenment Salons: The Convergence of Female and Philosophic Ambitions," *Eighteenth-Century Studies* 22 (Spring 1989): 329–50.

23. Herold, *Mistress to an Age,* 24–25.

24. Goodman, "Enlightenment Salons," 335–37.

25. Dena Goodman, "Governing the Republic of Letters: The Politics of Culture in the French Enlightenment," *History of European Ideas,* 13, no. 3, 183–99.

26. Herold, *Mistress to an Age,* 24, 26–27.

27. Ibid., 44–51, 84–85.

28. DNB, s.v. "MaCaulay, Catharine."

29. Catharine Macaulay, *The History of England from the Accession of James I to That of the Brunswick Line,* 8 vols., (London, 1763–1783); Bridget Hill, *The Republican Virago: The Life and Times of Catharine Macaulay, Historian* (Oxford: Clarendon Press, 1992), 25–51.

30. Catharine Macaulay, *Observations on a Pamphlet Entitled "Thoughts on the Cause of the Present Discontents"* (London: E. and C. Dilly, 1770); *An Address to the People of England, Scotland and Ireland on the Present Important Crisis of Affairs* (Bath and London, 1775; New York: John Holt, 1775).

31. Hill, *Republican Virago,* 207–11, 214–18.

32. Jones, *Longman Companion,* 317, 326, 385.

33. Hill, *Republican Virago,* 224–30.

34. Emily Sunstein, *A Different Face: The Life of Mary Wollstonecraft* (New York: Harper & Row, 1975), 188–89.

35. Catharine Macaulay, *Letters on Education with Observations on Religious and Metaphysical Subjects* (London: C. Dilly, 1790), 203–8.

36. Ibid., 208; Mary Wollstonecraft, *Vindication of the Rights of Woman* (London: Joseph Johnson, 1792) was an expansion and vast elaboration of Macaulay's brief essay. Both terminology and contents reflect Macaulay's influence. The first sentence where she tagged a note referring to Macaulay sounded as if it were Macaulay's words: "Man, taking her [woman's] body, the mind is left to rust; so that while physical love enervates man, as being his favourite recreation, he will endeavour to enslave woman:—and, who can tell, how many generations may be necessary to give vigour to the virtue and talents of the freed posterity of abject slaves?" In her note listing the great heroines of history—Sappho, Eloisa, Catherine the Great, Madame d'Eon, and Macaulay—she added "I wish to see women neither heroines nor brutes; but reasonable creatures."

When she reviewed the literature on the topic of educating women, she soon came to Macaulay's *Letters on Education* and departed from her analysis and made the great historian her subject. "The very word respect brings Mrs. Macaulay to my remembrance," she wrote:

> The woman of the greatest abilities, undoubtedly, that this country has ever produced.—And yet this woman has been suffered to die without sufficient respect being paid to her memory. Posterity, however, will be more just; and remember that Catharine Macaulay was an example of intellectual acquirements supposed to be incompatible with the weakness of her sex. In her style of writing, indeed, no sex appears, for it is like the sense it conveys, strong and clear.

Having come back to Macaulay's *Letters on Education* following a year and a half of revolutionary development in her own thinking, Wollstonecraft chose this spot to undo her previous application of "masculine" in describing Macaulay's work. "I will not call hers a masculine understanding," she wrote. Rather, "her judgement, the matured fruit of profound thinking, was a proof that a woman can acquire judgment, in the full extent of the word." Before getting on with the rest of her revolutionary work, Wollstonecraft paid Macaulay, whom she never met, the highest possible respect: "When I first thought of writing these strictures I anticipated Mrs. Macaulay's approbation, with a little of that sanguine ardour, which it has been the business of my life to depress; but soon heard with the sickly qualm of disappointed hope; and the still seriousness of regret—that she was no more!" Wollstonecraft added a note indicating the extent to which she borrowed directly from Macaulay: "Coinciding in opinion with Mrs. Macaulay relative to many branches of education, I refer to her valuable work, instead of quoting her sentiments to support my own."

37. Wollstonecraft, *Vindication* 77n.8.

38. Hill, *Republican Virago,* 105–7.

39. *DNB,* s.v. "Macaulay, Mrs. Catherine," for the story of the statue and vault. The statue is depicted in Hill, *Republican Virago,* 114.

40. Hill, *Republican Virago,* 107.

41. Ibid., 107, 210–11.

42. Ibid., 108–25.

43. Mercy Otis Warren, *Poems, Dramatic and Miscellaneous* (Boston: I. Thomas and E. T. Andrews, 1790). For evaluations of the book, see the introduction by Benjamin Franklin in *The Plays and Poems of Mercy Otis Warren* 5 (Delmar, N.Y.: Scholars' Facsimiles & Reprints, 1980), xxiii–xxviii.

44. Warren, *Poems,* iii–v.

45. Ibid., vii–xxiii.

46. Katharine Anthony, *First Lady of the Revolution: The Life of Mercy Otis Warren* (Garden City, N.Y.: Doubleday, 1958), 19–40; Jean Fritz, *Cast for a*

Revolution: Some Friends and Enemies, 1728–1814 (Boston: Houghton Mifflin, 1972), 3–12.

47. Fritz, *Cast for a Revolution,* 69–73; Anthony, *First Lady of the Revolution,* 41–47.

48. Anthony, *First Lady of the Revolution,* 123–24; Fritz, *Cast for a Revolution,* 108–9.

49. Fritz, *Cast for a Revolution,* 109–10.

50. Mercy Otis Warren, *The Adulateur. A Tragedy, as it is Now Acted in Upper Servia* (Boston: New Printing-Office, 1773); "The Defeat" appeared in Boston newspapers and is reprinted in *Plays and Poems of Warren.*

51. Mercy Otis Warren, *The Group* (Boston: Edes and Gill, 1775); idem, *The Blockheads: or, The Affrighted Officers. A Farce* (Boston: Printed in Queen-Street, 1776); idem, *The Motley Assembly, a Farce. Published for the Entertainment of the Curious* (Boston: Nathaniel Coverly, 1779). I have accepted the arguments of Benjamin Franklin in his introduction to *Plays and Poems of Mercy Otis Warren,* viii–xxiii, as to Warren's authorship of these five plays.

52. Lester H. Cohen, "Mercy Otis Warren: The Politics of Language and the Aesthetics of Self," *American Quarterly,* 35 (Winter 1983): 481–98; Jean B. Kern, "Mercy Otis Warren: Dramatist of the American Revolution," in *Curtain Calls: British and American Women and the Theater, 1660–1820* (Athens: Ohio Univ. Press, 1990), 247–59; Joan Hoff Wilson and Sharon L. Bollinger, "Mercy Otis Warren: Playwright, Poet, and Historian of the American Revolution (1728–1814)," in *Female Scholars: A Tradition of Learned Women before 1800* (Montreal: Eden Press Women's Publications, 1980), 161–82.

53. Warren, *Poems,* 189, 205, 214.

54. Hill, *Republican Virago,* 126–27.

55. Ibid., 127–28; Anthony, *First Lady of the Revolution,* 134–35; Fritz, *Cast for a Revolution,* 225–26.

56. Warren, *Poems,* 9–12.

57. Ibid., 99–101.

58. Alice Brown, *Mercy Warren* (New York: Charles Scribner's Sons, 1896), 238–43; Anthony, *First Lady of the Revolution,* 187–89.

59. Anthony, *First Lady of the Revolution,* 157–62; Mercy Otis Warren, *Observations on the New Constitution, and on the Federal and State Conventions. By a Columbian Patriot* (Boston: n.p., 1788).

60. Anthony, *First Lady of the Revolution,* 186–87; Fritz, *Cast for a Revolution,* 273–74.

61. Mercy Warren, *History of the Rise, Progress and Termination of the American Revolution. Interspersed with Biographical, Political and Moral Observations,* 3 vols (Boston: Manning and Loring, 1805). Macaulay told Warren in March 1787 that she was relinquishing any thoughts of writing such a history herself (Hill, *Republican Virago,* 128–29).

62. This characterization of Warren's *History of the American Revolution* is informed, in part, by the following: William Raymond Smith, *History as Argument:*

Three Patriot Historians of the American Revolution (The Hague: Mouton, 1966), 73–119, and Nina Baym, "Mercy Otis Warren's Gendered Melodrama of Revolution," *South Atlantic Quarterly,* 90 (Summer 1991): 531–54.

63. Warren, *History of the American Revolution,* 1: iii–v.

CHAPTER 6: Phillis Wheatley and African Liberty

1. Merle A. Richmond, *Bid the Vassal Soar: Interpretive Essays on the Life and Poetry of Phillis Wheatley (ca. 1753–1784) and George Moses Horton (ca. 1797–1883)* (Washington, D.C.: Howard Univ. Press, 1974), 31–34.

2. Ibid., 24–25, 34.

3. Dorothy Porter, ed., *Early Negro Writing, 1760–1837* (Boston: Beacon Press, 1971), 532–34.

4. Richmond, *Bid the Vassal Soar,* 27–29, 31–32.

5. Letter, Benjamin Franklin to Jonathan Williams, Sr., 7 July 1773 and Jonathan Williams, Sr., to Benjamin Franklin, 17 October 1773, in *Papers of Benjamin Franklin,* 19, 291–92, 445–46.

6. Lopez and Herbert, *Private Franklin,* 296–98, 299–303.

7. "The Somerset Case and the Slave Trade," *Papers of Benjamin Franklin,* 19: 187–88.

8. "The Somerset Case and the Slave Trade," *The London Chronicle,* June 18–20, 1772, *Papers of Benjamin Franklin,* 19: 187–88; Lopez and Herbert, *Private Franklin,* 304–7.

9. On Wheatley's business dealings with Williams and Franklin, see Williams to Franklin, 19 September 1771; Franklin to Williams, 13 January 1772, 7 July 1773; Williams to Franklin, 17 October 1773, *Papers of Benjamin Franklin,* 17: 219–21; 19: 32–34, 291–92, 445–46.

10. This interpretation is also that of the editors of the *Papers of Benjamin Franklin,* 19: 291–92.

11. Richmond, *Bid the Vassal Soar,* 32–33, 36. Almost all biographies and biographical sketches of the life of Phillis Wheatley argue that the haste in heading back to America was so Phillis Wheatley could care for her ailing mistress. Although Susannah Wheatley died nine months later in March 1774 after a long illness, this seems an unlikely explanation for a mission planned, arranged, and financed so thoroughly by the mistress herself.

12. Ibid., 34–36.

13. Ibid., 7–8. The navy poems are referenced in *Dictionary of American Negro Biography,* s.v. "Wheatley, Phillis" (hereafter cited as *DANB*).

14. Richmond, *Bid the Vassal Soar,* 4–7.

15. Ibid., 3.

16. Ibid., 39–40, 41–42.

17. Ibid., 43–47. Peters is uniformly depicted as a shiftless charlatan and evil character, although virtually no contemporaneous records exist; Jupiter Hammon, "An Address to Miss Phillis Wheatley, Ethiopian Poetess, in Boston . . .," in *Early Negro Writing,* 535–37.

18. Richmond, *Bid the Vassal Soar,* 47–48.

19. Ibid., 50–52.

CHAPTER 7: Liberty and the Rights of Africans

1. According to David Brion Davis, Wilberforce's "great speech of May 13, 1789 . . . initiated the abolitionist campaign"; see Davis, *The Problem of Slavery in the Age of Revolution, 1770–1823* (Ithaca, N.Y.: Cornell Univ. Press, 1975), 115. Wilberforce's long speech was handily summarized in *The Enormity of the Slave-Trade; and the Duty of Seeking the Moral and Spiritual Elevation of the Colored Race* (New York: American Tract Society, 1846), 5–19; see also Ellen Gibson Wilson, *Thomas Clarkson: A Biography* (New York: St. Martin's Press, 1990), 50–51.

2. Sidney Kaplan, *The Black Presence in the Era of the American Revolution, 1770–1800* (Greenwich, Conn.: New York Graphic Society Ltd., 1973), 204–6. Careful analysis of Equiano's *Narrative* and similar writings by blacks in the eighteenth century have revealed replication of stories and considerable distortion or inaccuracy of dates, places, and names. One particularly good edition of many of these narratives is Vincent Carretta, ed., *Unchained Voices: An Anthology of Black Authors in the English–Speaking World of the 18th Century* (Lexington: Univ. Press of Kentucky, 1996), 1–14. Despite the overlap and exaggeration, these narratives provide a valuable description of a world that otherwise could not be fathomed.

3. Kaplan, *Black Presence,* 206. Olaudah Equiano [Gustavus Vassa], *Equiano's Travels: His Autobiography,* ed. Paul Edwards (Oxford: Heinemann Educational Books, 1967), xi–xiii, 176–77. This is not meant to detract from the fundamental work being done at the same time by Thomas Clarkson and the Committee for the Abolition of the Slave Trade; see Wilson, *Thomas Clarkson,* 13–65. The point here is that the efforts of black abolitionists in these early stages of the antislavery movement have been almost totally overlooked.

4. *Equiano's Travels,* 1–34, 35–44, 45–65.

5. Ibid., 77–80, 85–87, 91, 93.

6. Ibid., 86–93. According to Carretta, *Unchained Voices,* 306n.180, Equiano must have been mistaken about hearing Whitfield in Philadelphia. He probably heard him in Savannah in February 1765, as the ship on which he served was there at the same time as was Whitfield.

7. *Equiano's Travels,* 93–97, 98–101.

8. Ibid., 105–21.

9. Ibid., 84–85.

10. Gustavus Vassa to Dr. Revd. & Worthy friends, 27 February 1792, *Equiano's Travels,* 176–77.

11. *Equiano's Travels,* 124–31.

12. Ibid., 132–48; Carretta, *Unchained Voices,* 308–9n.224, has confirmed that Equiano was likely on the polar expedition and was listed on the muster roll as Gustavus Weston.

13. *Equiano's Travels,* 148–56. The elusive Irving has been tied down a bit in the researches of Vincent Carretta for his Penguin Classic edition of Equiano's

The Interesting Narrative (New York: Penguin Group, 1995), 285–86n.485; and for his very useful *Unchained Voices* 308–9n.224. Irving's probable dates are derived from Carretta's data.

14. Because of a last–minute dispute with the expedition organizers, Granville Sharp ordered Equiano left ashore at Plymouth when the colony departed in April 1787. This led to a long and bitter public dispute between Equiano and the Sierra Leone board. In the end his behavior was exonerated, and he was paid for several months of services; see appendix to *Equiano's Travels,* 162–71; also Kaplan, *Black Presence,* 205–6.

15. *Equiano's Travels,* 158–61.

16. Ibid., xii–xiii, 157.

17. Ibid., xiii.

18. Briton Hammon, "A Narrative of the Uncommon Sufferings, and Surprising Deliverance of Briton Hammon, a Negro Man,—Servant to General Winslow, of Marshfield, in New England; Who Returned to Boston, after Having Been Absent Almost Thirteen Years" in *Early Negro Writing,* 522–28.

19. *DAB,* s.v. "Winslow, John."

20. Hammon, "A Narrative of the Sufferings" 522–28.

21. James Albert Ukawsaw Gronniosaw, *A Narrative of the Most Remarkable Particulars in the Life of James Albert Ukawsaw Gronniosaw, an African Prince* (London: R. Groombridge; Manchester: J. Gadsby; Glasgow: David Robertson, 1840), 2–9.

22. Ibid., 10–13; for Frelinghuysen's tough character see James Tanis, *Dutch Calvinistic Pietism in the Middle Colonies: A Study in the Life and Theology of Theodorus Jacobus Frelinghuysen* (The Hague: Martinus Nijhoff, 1967), 42–56. It is interesting that, although Frelinghuysen had such a great impact upon Gronniosaw, he is not even mentioned in this fairly thorough biography. Gronniosaw called his teacher "Vanosdore," probably Hendrick Visscher who joined Frelinghuysen as helper, teacher, and catechist in 1736 (Tanis, *Dutch Pietism,* 66–67).

23. Tanis, *Dutch Pietism,* 90–93.

24. Gronniosaw, *Narrative,* 13–16.

25. Ibid., 18–20. Frelinghuysen had remained very close to his colleagues and friends in the Netherlands (Tanis, *Dutch Pietism,* 57–71).

26. Gronniosaw, *Narrative,* 18–24.

27. Venture Smith, "A Narrative of the Life and Adventures of Venture, a Native of Africa: But Resident Above Sixty Years in the United States of America" *Early Negro Writings,* 538–58.

28. Ibid., 552–56.

29. Lamont D. Thomas, *Rise to Be a People: A Biography of Paul Cuffe* (Urbana: Univ. of Illinois Press, 1986), 3–11.

30. Kaplan, *Black Presence* 144–46.

31. John Marrant, "A Narrative of the Lord's Wonderful Dealings with John Marrant, a Black, (Now Gone to Preach the Gospel in Nova Scotia)," *Early Negro Writings,* 427–47.

32. Ibid., 444–46. Carretta, *Unchained Voices,* 130–31n.47, concluded that Marrant may have fabricated his service on the *Scorpion* and the *Princess Amelia.*

33. *DANB,* s.v. "Marrant, John," and Kaplan, *Black Presence* 97.

34. *DANB,* s.v. "Hall, Prince," and Kaplan, *Black Presence* 97.

35. John Marrant, *Sermon Preached on the 24th Day of June 1789, Being the Festival of St. John the Baptist, at the Request of the Right Worshipful the Grand Master Prince Hall, and, the Rest of the Brethren of the African Lodge of the Honorable Society of Free and Accepted Masons in Boston* (Boston: Bible and Heart, 1789), 3–9.

36. Ibid., 10–24.

37. Kaplan, *Black Presence* 97–99.

38. Ibid., 76; *DANB,* s.v. "Liele, George."

39. Kaplan, *Black Presence* 75–76. *DANB,* s.v. "George, David." I have used here the corrected dates, places, and names provided by Carretta in *Unchained Voices,* 347–50nn.

40. Kaplan, *Black Prescence,* 75–76; *DANB,* s.v. "Bryan, Andrew."

41. Kaplan, *Black Presence* 76–77.

42. Ibid., 75–76; *DANB,* s.v. "George, David."

43. Kaplan, *Black Presence* 77–79; *DANB,* s.v. "Bryan, Andrew." 77.

44. John Lofton, *Denmark Vesey's Revolt: The Slave Plot that Lit a Fuse to Fort Sumter,* (2d. ed.; Kent: Kent State Univ. Press, 1983), xiii–xiv, 5–7, 10–15. Although Lofton, 14–15, states that in the trip from St. Thomas to St. Domingue "the captain and his officers were struck with the appearance and intelligence of the youngster from the Danish slave market" and "made a pet of him by taking him into the cabin and giving him presentable clothes" and named him "Denmark Vesey," to me this has all of the marks of apocrypha.

45. Ibid., 16–17.

46. Ibid., xiii–xiv, 19–23.

47. Ibid., 28–31, 40–41, 76–77.

48. See Gary B. Nash, *Forging Freedom: The Formation of Philadelphia's Black Community, 1720–1840* (Cambridge: Harvard Univ. Press, 1988) 42–65, for an excellent depiction of the dilemmas facing black slaves during the Revolution.

49. Kaplan, *Black Presence* 7–10.

50. *DANB,* s.v. "Salem, Peter" and "Poor, Salem;" Kaplan, *Black Presence* 15–19.

51. *DANB,* s.v. "Salem, Peter."

52. Kaplan, *Black Presence* 20–21; *DANB,* s.v. "Flora, William."

53. Kaplan, *Black Presence* 47; *DANB,* s.v. "Cromwell, Oliver."

54. *DANB,* s.v. "Whipple, Prince;" *DAB,* s.v. "Whipple, William;" Kaplan, *Black Presence* 44–46.

55. Kaplan, *Black Presence* 36–39, 65–66.

56. *DANB,* s.v. "Dabney, Austin."

57. *DANB,* s.v. "Ranger, Joseph" and "Tarrant, Caesar."

58. *DANB*, s.v. "Armistead, James."

59. *DAB*, s.v. "Jones, John Paul."

60. Franklin's detailed involvment in these plans is described by Van Doren, *Benjamin Franklin*, 607–23.

61. On d'Estaing, see Alexander A. Lawrence, *Storm over Savannah: The Story of Count d'Estaing and the Siege of the Town in 1779* (Athens: Univ. of Georgia Press, 1951), 14–16.

62. Charles C. Jones, Jr., *The Siege of Savannah, in 1779, as Described in Two Contemporaneous Journals of French Officers in the Fleet of Count D'Estaing* (Albany, N.Y.: Joel Munsell, 1874), 39–40. The force eventually consisted of 4,456 in the French Army and 2,127 in the American Army for a total of 6,583 troops. Among the proud officers were Louis-Marie, Vicomte de Noailles, brother-in-law of Lafayette and career soldier; Arthur, Count Dillon, of twelve generations of nobility and favorite of Marie Antoinette; the Marquis de Ponde-vaux, nephew of the French Prime Minister Vergennes; and a full roster of offi-cers from the great families of France, including the Vicomte de Fontanges, the Comte d'Hervilly; the Vicomte de Bethisy; the Marquis de Rouvray; the Comte de Villeverd; and the Marquis de la Roche-Fontenilles; and Baron Curt von Sted-ingk, later favorite of Catherine the Great.

63. "Journal of a Naval Officer in the Fleet of Count D'Estaing, 1782," in *Siege of Savannah*, 58–59. There seems to be some confusion on Chavannes's first name: Thomas O. Ott, *The Haitian Revolution, 1789–1804* (Knoxville: Univ. of Tennessee Press, 1973) 36–36, calls him "Marc," while Carolyn E. Fick, *The Making of Haiti: The Saint Domingue Revolution from Below* (Knoxville: Univ. of Tennessee Press, 1990), 83, calls him "Jean–Baptiste;" Martin Ros, *Night of Fire: The Black Napoleon and the Battle for Haiti* (New York: Sarpedon Publish-ers, Inc., 1994), 26, 27, 106, also uses "Jean-Baptiste."

64. Alexander, *Storm over Savannah*, 15–20.

65 . Jones, *Siege of Savannah*, 18; Alexander, *Storm over Savannah*, 46–53.

66. Alexander, *Storm over Savannah*, 43–45, 54–55.

67. Ibid., 64–65. The vital link between this battle and the later revolution in St. Domingue is recognized also by Sylvia R. Frey in *Water from the Rock: Black Resistance in a Revolutionary Age* (Princeton: Princeton Univ. Press, 1991), 95–98.

68. Jones, *Siege of Savannah*, 23–25.

69. Ibid., 26–27; Alexander, *Storm over Savannah*, 76–79.

70. Alexander, *Storm over Savannah*, 81–82.

71. Jones, *Siege of Savannah*, 28–31. Although d'Estaing's narrative was irri-tatingly translated into English in the present tense, I have throughout my quota-tions translated it into the past tense so as not to alter the flow of the narrative.

72. Ibid., 30–35.

73. Sylvia R. Frey, *Water from the Rock: Black Resistance in a Revolutionary Age* (Princeton: Princeton Univ. Press, 1991), 97–98.

74. Jones, *Siege of Savannah*, 35–38.

75. John W. Vandercook, *Black Majesty: The Life of Christophe, King of Haiti* (New York: Harper & Brothers, 1928), 10–17.

CHAPTER 8: Yale College and World Revolution
1. Biographical information from a variety of sources, particularly the *DAB*. I depart from traditional interpretations of the Hartford Wits, which, taking a cue from Vernon L. Parrington, treat the group as monolithic, one-dimensional Federalist conservatives (excepting the renegade Barlow, of course); see Vernon L. Parrington, *The Colonial Mind, 1620–1800* orig. 1927 (Norman: Univ. of Oklahoma Press, 1987), 357–67; but cf. Robert E. Spiller *et al.*, eds. *Literary History of the United States: History,* 4th ed., (New York: Macmillan Publishing, 1974), 162–68.
2. Richard M. Rollins, *The Long Journey of Noah Webster* (Philadelphia: Univ. of Pennsylvania Press, 1980), 14–15, 17–18.
3. Timothy Dwight, "A Valedictory Address to the Young Gentlemen, who Commenced Bachelors of Arts at Yale College, July 25th, 1776" in Stephen E. Berk, *Calvinism versus Democracy: Timothy Dwight and the Origins of American Evangelical Orthodoxy* (Hamden, Conn.: Archon Books, 1974), 21–23.
4. Parrington, *Colonial Mind,* 248–52.
5. Principal sources for the foregoing are respective entries in *DAB*; also Rollins, *Long Journey,* 18.
6. James Woodress, *A Yankee's Odyssey: The Life of Joel Barlow* (New York: Greenwood Press, 1958), 50–53, 76–77, 85.
7. Rollins, *Long Journey,* 23–33.
8. Berk, *Calvinism versus Democracy,* 26–28.
9. William M. Meigs, *Life of Josiah Meigs* (Philadelphia: n.p., 1887) 24–27.

CHAPTER 9: American Liberators and World Revolution
1. On Webster's relationship with Franklin, see Rollins, *Long Journey,* 47, 51, 54, 59, 62, 64; on the subject of language and phonetics, see Harry R. Warfel, ed., *Letters of Noah Webster* (New York: Library Publishers, 1953), 49–53; Parrington, *Colonial Mind,* 359–60.
2. *DAB,* s.v. "Humphreys, David."
3. Meigs, *Life of Josiah Meigs,* 27–32.
4. Woodress, *Yankee's Odyssey,* 53–59, 66, 76, 77, 82, 90–98.
5. Ibid., 94–100, 110–16, 117–18.
6. Emily W. Sunstein, *A Different Face* 192–97.
7. Ibid., 218–20; Woodress, *Yankee's Odyssey,* 117–19; Ayer, *Thomas Paine,* 72–73.
8. Sunstein, *Different Face,* 179–86, 200–6, 218–20; Woodress, *Yankee's Odyssey,* 126–27.
9. Sunstein, *Different Face,* 206–7; Mary Wollstonecraft, *Vindication of the Rights of Woman,* ed. by Carol H. Poston (New York: W. W. Norton, 1975), vii–ix, 3–6.
10. Woodress, *Yankee's Odyssey,* 118–19; Joel Barlow, *Advice to the Privileged*

Orders, in the Several States of Europe, Resulting from the Necessity and Propriety of A General Revolution in the Principle of Government, Part I (New York: Childs and Swaine, 1792), 1–3.

11. Hawke, *Paine,* 229–30, 232–34.

12. Ibid., 205; Sunstein, *Different Face,* 207–8.

13. Woodress, *Yankee's Odyssey,* 118–19.

14. Hawke, *Paine,* 238–39.

15. Virginia Sapiro, *A Vindication of Political Virtue: The Political Theory of Mary Wollstonecraft* (Chicago: Univ. of Chicago Press, 1992), 25–26.

16. Hawke, *Paine,* 239–40; Sunstein, *Different Face,* 213–14; Woodress, *Yankee's Odyssey,* 119.

17. Hawke, *Paine,* 240; Wollstonecraft, *Vindication of Rights of Woman,* vii; Victor Clyde Miller, *Joel Barlow: Revolutionist, London, 1791–92* (Hamburg, Germany: Friederrichsen, de Gruyter, 1932), 6–7, 51–52.

18. Miller, *Joel Barlow,* 24.

19. Ibid., 17, 25, 26, 45–46; Barlow, *Advice to the Privileged Orders. Part I,* [119]; Joel Barlow, *Advice to the Privileged Orders in the Several States of Europe, Resulting from the Necessity and Propriety of A General Revolution in the Principle of Government. Part II* (Paris: English Press, 1793), [4]. For full citations of Barlow's other pieces: Joel Barlow, *The Conspiracy of Kings, a Poem: Addressed to the Inhabitants of Europe, from another Quarter of the World* (London: J. Johnson, 1792); Joel Barlow, *A Letter to the National Convention of France, on the Defects in the Constitution of 1791, and the Extent of the Amendments which Ought to Be Applied* (London: J. Johnson, 1792).

20. Woodress, *Yankee's Odyssey,* 123; Miller, *Joel Barlow,* 46–47.

21. Barlow, *Advice to the Privileged Orders Part 1,* 1–2, 7, 14–15.

22. Ibid., 23–24, 28, 53.

23. Barlow, *Conspiracy of Kings,* 101–13.

24. Barlow, *Letter to the National Convention,* 4–5, 20, 23–24; Miller, *Joel Barlow,* 74–81.

25. Miller, *Joel Barlow,* 16–21; Woodress, *Yankee's Odyssey,* 124–27.

26. Woodress, *Yankee's Odyssey,* 127–28.

27. Miller, *Joel Barlow,* 26–30, 34–37, 38–42.

28. Woodress, *Yankee's Odyssey,* 130–33; Miller, *Joel Barlow,* 42–43.

29. Joel Barlow, *A Letter Addressed to the People of Piedmont, on the Advantages of the French Revolution, and the Necessity of Adopting Its Principles in Italy* (New-York: Columbian Press, 1795), iii–iv, 6, 8.

30. Wollstonecraft, *Rights of Woman,* 3–5, 140–50; Sapiro, *Vindication of Political Virtue,* 227–30, 237–40.

31. Wollstonecraft, *Rights of Woman,* viii–ix; Sunstein, *Different Face,* 217.

37. Sunstein, *Different Face,* 219–20, 221–25, 229–34.

33. Ibid., 235–36; also *DAB,* s.v. "Imlay, Gilbert."

34. *DAB,* s.v. "Imlay, Gilbert;" Sunstein, *Different Face,* 235–36.

35 Minnigerode, *Career of Edmond Genet,* 247–49, 257.

36. Sunstein, *Different Face,* 236–44.

37. Ibid., 245–49; Woodress, *Yankee's Odyssey,* 145–46.

38. Sunstein, *Different Face,* 252–75.

39. Mary Wollstonecraft, *Letters Written during a Short Residence in Sweden, Norway, and Denmark* (Lincoln: University of Nebraska Press), vii–xii; Mary Wollstonecraft, *Letters to Imlay* (reprint of 1879 edition; New York: Haskell House Publishers, 1971), 119–45.

40. Wollstonecraft, *Letters to Imlay,* 185–89; Sunstein, *Different Face,* 290–92.

41. Sunstein, *Different Face,* 294–96; *DNB,* s.v. "Godwin, Mary Wollestonecraft" and "Godwin, William."

42. Sunstein, *Different Face,* 352. Imlay's death, however, was recorded in a church record on the Island of Jersey as November 20, 1828. His inscrutable tombstone inscription there reads, "Stranger intelligent! Should you pass this way / Speak of the social advances of the day."

43. Schama, *Citizens,* 498, 530, 657, 802; Jones, *Companion to French Revolution,* 264, 351.

44. J. Christopher Herold, *Mistress to an Age: A Life of Madame de Staël* (Indianapolis: Bobbs-Merrill, 1958), 57–70. This biography and many other accounts of Germaine de Staël dwell on the sexual mores of her society to the extent that her influence as a thinker and politician is frequently obscured; Morroe Berger's *Madame de Staël on Politics, Literature, and National Character* (Garden City, N.Y.: Doubleday, 1964) reveals her considerable range of thought.

45. Noel Parker, *Portrayals of Revolution: Images, Debates and Patterns of Thought on the French Revolution* (Carbondale: Southern Illinois Univ. Press, 1990), 117–20.

46. Herold, *Mistress to an Age,* 69–70.

47. Ibid., 92–102; Cynthia Owen Philip, *Robert Fulton: A Biography* (New York: Franklin Watts, 1985), see esp. 102–18 on the lifestyle and sexual orientation of the Barlows and Robert Fulton.

48. Berger, *Madame de Staël,* 10–12; Herold, *Mistress to an Age,* 79–91.

49. Berger, *Madame de Staël,* 12–13; Herold, *Mistress to an Age,* 124–25, 128, 158–60, 161–62, 201–3.

50. Herold, *Mistress to an Age,* 123–27, 130–31.

51. Stephen Holmes, *Benjamin Constant and the Making of Modern Liberalism* (New Haven: Yale Univ. Press, 1984), 5–10.

52. Herold, *Mistress to an Age,* 174–78; Holmes, *Benjamin Constant,* 10–12.

53. Elliott, *Wolfe Tone,* 281–86; E. H. Stuart Jones, *The Last Invasion of Britain* (Cardiff: Univ. of Wales Press, 1950), 53.

54. Jones, *Last Invasion,* 53–55; Elliott, *Wolfe Tone,* 281–86.

55. Elliott, *Wolfe Tone,* 286–90; Harry Ammon, *James Monroe: The Quest for National Identity* (New York: McGraw–Hill, 1971), 135–36.

56. Elliott, *Wolfe Tone,* 313–15.

57. Jones, *Last Invasion,* 54–56; Elliott, *Wolfe Tone,* 315–16.

58. Jones, *Last Invasion,* 56–60, 61–71, 73–78, 83–101.

59. Ibid., 101–13, 122–26, 131–33.

60. Ibid., 134–39. In 1809, almost eighty years old and sorely in debt, he asked to be released from military duty. He was granted indefinite leave to travel to the United States. In July 1809, he left from Dunkirk for the land of liberty and of his birth. Following an uneventful arrival in Washington, his name no longer appeared in historical records.

61. Elliott, *Wolfe Tone,* 324–33, 335–38, 362–66, 374–86.

62. *DNB,* s.v. "Tandy, John Napper."

63. *DNB,* s.v. "Tone, Theobald Wolfe Tone."

64. *DNB,* s.v. "Tandy, John Napper." While Theobald Wolfe Tone died a martyr to Irish independence, Tandy pursued a rather messy escape. Three days after the death of his compatriot, Tandy arrived in Hamburg and took up residence at the American Arms, a tavern and inn. British officials obtained a warrant from the city of Hamburg for his arrest. When the police arrived at the American Arms at 4:00 A.M. on the morning of November 24, Tandy presented a pistol, but before he could discharge it, the police wrested it from him and took him and three companions into custody. After months of wrangling between France and England over Tandy's legal citizenship, authorities transferred him on September 29, 1799, to British custody. On February 12, 1800, he was brought to trial in Dublin on charges of high treason. When he pleaded guilty of involvement in the invasion of Rutland Island, he was immediately convicted and sentenced to be executed on May 4. The conviction, achieved with a high degree of legal awkwardness, ignited an international incident. Napoléon Bonaparte demanded Tandy's extradition as a French citizen. Through Bonaparte's exertions, Tandy was eventually released in early 1802. When he arrived in Bordeaux on March 14, 1802, he was treated as a hero of the Revolution. A banquet was given in his honor, at which he was promoted to a full general. He basked in both French and Irish glory for another year until he died on August 24, 1803, from dysentery.

65. Philip, *Robert Fulton* (New York: Franklin Watts, 1985), 3–7. Philip's data on Fulton's early years disagrees substantially with information in the normally reliable *DAB.*

66. Ibid., 8–15.

67. Ibid., 15–25; *DAB,* s.v. "West, Benjamin."

68. Philip, *Robert Fulton,* 28–46, 49–61.

69. Ibid., 28–29; Goodwin, *Friends of Liberty,* 86, 106, 122, 127, 312, 361, 362.

70. Philip, *Robert Fulton,* 63–68.

71. These documents are extensively quoted and outlined by Philip, *Robert Fulton,* 68–72.

72. Ibid., 72–74, 76–77, 79–84.

73. Ibid., 85–88, 102–18. Philip discusses the strong likelihood of the Barlows' and Fulton's three–way affair gently, but convincingly.

74. Ibid., 89–91, 94–95.

75. Ibid., 95–96. None of these claims is intended to diminish the significant achievement of another American engineer, David Bushnell (1740–1826), who in 1774 built and tested a similar diving vessel that he called the *American Turtle*. This device also could surface and dive, using a propeller for lift and pull, an air chamber for rise and descent, and much more. The *American Turtle* was tested, it is claimed, before Benjamin Franklin off Ayer's Point in the Connecticut River in 1775 and was taken into battle at Fort Lee on the Hudson River in 1776. Several attempts to attach mines to the underside of British warships were failures. The device was lost as the sloop carrying it was sunk during the bombardment of Fort Lee. An operating replica of the *American Turtle* built in 1976 is on exhibit at the Connecticut River Museum, Essex, Connecticut. Bushnell's vessel was an engineering curiosity; Fulton's *Nautilus* was a military marvel. Marion Hepburn Grant, *The infernal Machines of Saybrook's David Bushnell* (Old Saybrook, Conn.: Bicentennial Committee, 1976).

76. Ibid., 96–101.

77. Ibid., 109–18.

CHAPTER 10: Citizenesses in the Land of Liberty

1. The story of Priscilla Mason told here derived from a single source: "The Salutatory Oration Delivered by Miss Mason," in *The Rise and Progress of the Young-Ladies Academy of Philadelphia: Containing an Account of a Number of Public Examinations & Commencements; The Charter and Bye-Laws; Likewise, a Number of Orations Delivered by the Young Ladies, and Several by the Trustees of Said Institution* (Philadelphia: Stewart & Cochran, 1794), 89–95.

2. Most of the general biographical information about this group of eight, except as otherwise documented, derives from biographical sketches included in the *DAB* and the *Dictionary of Notable American Women,* (hereafter cited as *DNW*) except in the case of Elizabeth Drinker, who is not included in either work. Information on her comes from the introduction, Elaine Forman Crane, ed., to *The Diary of Elizabeth Drinker: The Life Cycle of an Eighteenth–Century Woman.* 3 vols. (Boston: Northeastern Univ. Press, 1991) 1: ix–xxxviii.

3. William Franklin to Elizabeth Graeme, 26 February, 25 April, 2 May, 16 May, 1757, "Some Material for a Biography of Mrs. Elizabeth Ferguson, nee Graeme," Simon Gratz, ed. *Pennsylvania Magazine of History and Biography* 39 (1915): 260–63.

4. Franklin to Graeme, 24 October 1758, in Gratz, "Some Material for Biography of Elizabeth Ferguson," 263–68.

5. John F. Stegeman and Janet A. Stegeman, *Caty: A Biography of Catharine Littlefield Greene* (Athens: Univ. of Georgia Press, 1977), 5–7, 12.

6. *Diary of Elizabeth Drinker,* 1: xii.

7. Vena Bernadette Field, *Constantia: A Study of the Life and Works of Judith Sargent Murray, 1751–1820* (Orono, Maine: University Press, 1931), 19–26.

8. The odd circumstances of the marriage partly showed through in a letter from Mary Redman to Elizabeth Ferguson, 2 October 1772, "Some Material for Biography of Mrs. Elizabeth Ferguson," 283–85.

9. Stegeman, *Caty,* 112–24, 170, 180.

10. Hannah Adams in her *A Memoir of Miss Hannah Adams, Written by Herself. With Additional Notices, by a Friend* (Boston: Gray and Bowen, 1832) described herself as timid, poverty-stricken, and frequently ill. Although she had many male friends and supporters and wrote in one of her publications on the nature of marriage, her own personal interests were not addressed; see 2–3, 6, 12, 65–67.

11. *Diary of Elizabeth Drinker,* xxviii.

12. Field, *Constantia,.* 20–22; Adams, *Memoir of Hannah Adams,* 11–12.

13. Stegeman, *Caty,* 14–124 passim.

14. *DNW,* s.v. "Ferguson, Elizabeth Graeme."

15. Petition to the Assembly, 1 March 1781; William Smith to Elizabeth Ferguson, 2 March 1781; Henry Hill to Elizabeth Ferguson, 11 April 1781, "Some Material for a Biography of Ferguson," 305–10.

16. The revolutionary era experiences of Hannah Webster are unknown. She presumably was living with her father in Boston in 1771. By the latter days of the Revolution she was writing newspaper articles, for Rev. John Foster noticed the articles and took an interest in the author; see *DNW,* s.v. "Foster, Hannah Webster."

17. Richard Peters to Elizabeth Graeme, 20 November, 4 December, 14 December 1764; 9 July, 22 September 1765, "Some Material for Biography of Ferguson," 273–83.

18. *DNB,* s.v. "Ferguson, Elizabeth Graeme."

19. Jones, *Pair of Lawn Sleeves,* 137–39; *DAB,* s.v. "Hopkinson, Francis," and "Reed, Joseph."

20. Smith was in London at the same time as Graeme and named a daughter born at the time after her; Hopkinson was in London in 1766 looking for, but not receiving, a political appointment; Rush was in Edinburgh and London from 1766 to 1769 studying medicine; Reed studied law at Middle Temple in 1764 and 1765.

21. See Jones, *Pair of Lawn Sleeves,* 137–39, 172–73; see also *The Autobiography of Benjamin Rush: His "Travels Through Life" Together with His Commonplace Book for 1789–1813,* George W. Corner, ed. (Princeton: Princeton Univ. Press, 1948), 116, 167.

22. *DAB,* s.v. "Evans, Nathaniel," "Ferguson, Elizabeth Graeme," and "Smith, William"; *DNW,* s.v., "Ferguson, Elizabeth Graeme."

23. *Autobiography of Rush,* 320–21; Jones, *Pair of Lawn Sleeves,* 172–73; William Smith to Elizabeth Fergusson, 9 November 1791, "Some Material for Biography of Ferguson," 315–16.

24. *Diary of Elizabeth Drinker,* 1, xiv–xxviii.

25. Adams, *Memoir,* iii–iv, 1–3; cf. Franklin, *Autobiography,* Norton edition, xiii–xv, 1–5. The similarity between the two autobiographies also has been noted by Nina Baym, "Between Enlightenment and Victorian: Toward a Narrative of American Women Writers Writing History," *Critical Inquiry* 18 (Autumn 1991): 35–36; see William Temple Franklin, *Memoirs of the Life and Writings of Benjamin Franklin* 3 vols. (London: Colburn, 1818).

26. Franklin, *Autobiography* 6–20; Adams, *Memoir,* 5–9.

27. Franklin, *Autobiography* 34; Adams, *Memoir,* 13–15.

28. Adams, *Memoir,* 19–21.

29. Ibid., 22–27; Arthur H. Shaffer, *To Be an American: David Ramsay and the Making of the American Consciousness* (Columbia: Univ. of South Carolina Press, 1991), 89–90.

30. Field, *Constantia,* 18, 24–25.

31. Judith Sargent Murray, "On the Equality of the Sexes," in Field, *Constantia,* 68–69.

32. Field, *Constantia,* 26–29.

33. Judith Sargent Murray, *The Gleaner* (Schenectady, NY: Union College Press, 1992), vii; Field, *Constantia,* 24–26.

34. Constantia [Judith Sargent Murray], *The Gleaner. A Miscellaneous Production. In Three Volumes* (3 vols. Boston: I. Thomas and E. T. Andrews, 1798), 1, 13–17.

35. Ibid., 3, 313–18; cf. Nina Baym's insightful introductory essay to Murray, *The Gleaner* (Schenectady, NY.: Union College Press, 1992), iii–xx.

36. Constantia, *The Gleaner,* 1: Chaps. ii, vii–xi, xiii, xx–xxii, xxviii–xxix; 2: Chaps. xxxviii–liii; 3: Chaps. xcviii; see Field, *Constantia,* 53–59, for an analysis of the Margaretta story.

37. Constantia, *The Gleaner,* 2: 115–24.

38. Ibid., 188–89, 192–223.

39. Field, *Constantia,* 30–32, 43–44.

40. Constantia, *The Gleaner,* 1: iii–x; 3: 313–28.

41. Ibid., 3: 262.

42. Judith Sargent Murray to Sarah Franklin Bache, 19 June 1795, Sarah Franklin Bache Papers, American Philosophical Society, Philadelphia. I am grateful to Mary Kelley, History Department, Dartmouth College for bringing this letter to my attention.

43. *DNW* s.v. "Rowson, Susanna;" Mary Anne Schofield, "The Happy Revolution: Colonial Women and the Eighteenth-Century Theater," in *Modern American Drama: The Female Canon,* June Schluetev, ed. (London: Associated Univ. Presses, 1990), 33–35.

44. *DNW,* s.v. "Rowson, Susanna," *DAB,* s.v. Rowson, Susanna."

45. *DNW,* s.v. "Rowson, Susanna."

46. Schofield, "The Happy Revolution," 29–30. Schofield lists Margaretta Bleecker Faugeres (1771–1801), and a Mrs. Marriott (n.d.) as additional women playwrights.

47. Constantia, *The Gleaner,* 3: 260–64.

48. Ibid., 1: 224–40.

49. Field, *Constantia,* 32–36.

50. Constantia, *The Gleaner,* 3: 12–14.

51. Ibid. 3: 14; Field, *Constantia,* 74–79.

52. Field, *Constantia,* 37–38, 79–84.

53. Ibid., 38–43.

54. Cathy N. Davidson, introduction to *The Coquette* by Hannah Webster Foster (reprint, New York: Oxford Univ. Press, 1986), vii–viii.

55. Woodress, *Yankee's Odyssey,* 64.

56. Davidson, introduction to *Coquette,* viii–ix.

57. *DAB,* s.v. "Wadsworth, Jeremiah." My assessment of Wadsworth's potential complicity grows out of his similar treatment of Catherine Littlefield Greene. (Stegeman, *Caty,* 132–33).

58. Davidson, Introduction to *Coquette,* ix–x, xix–xx, xxii.

59. *DNW,* s.v. "Rowson, Susanna."

60. *DAB,* s.v. "Rowson, Susanna," and *DNW,* s.v. "Rowson, Susanna."

61. Stegeman, *Caty,* 123–24.

62. Greene's tangled affairs are well-described in Stegeman, *Caty* passim.

63. The foregoing interpretation is but a slight twist on the much briefer version told by the Stegemans in *Caty,* 132–33. Though they do not suggest that Wadsworth was indeed the missing figure in the Eliza Whitman case, I believe his ill treatment of Catherine Greene strongly suggests that he was the culprit.

64. Ibid., 134–55.

65. Jeannette Mirsky and Allan Nevins, *The World of Eli Whitney* (New York: Macmillan, 1960), 54–55.

66. Ibid., 4–10, 22–27, 38–44, 46–48, 55–57.

67. Stegeman, *Caty,* 156–59.

68. M. B. Hammond, "Correspondence of Eli Whitney Relative to the Invention of the Cotton Gin," *American Historical Review* 3 (October, 1797–July 1798): 99–100, 122–23.

69. Stegeman, *Caty,* 160–63.

70. Mirsky, *World of Whitney,* 95–96.

71. Ibid., 58–59, 68–70; Hammond, "Correspondence of Eli Whitney," 99–101.

72. Hammond, "Correspondence of Eli Whitney," 100.

73. Mirsky, *World of Whitney,* 109–18, 119–20; Stegeman, *Caty,* 166–69.

74. Hammond, "Correspondence of Eli Whitney," 105–7.

75. These cases I have had the pleasure of studying personally. Each has piles of public and private documentation.

76. Stegeman, *Caty,* 172–73.

CHAPTER 11: Africans in the Land of Liberty

1. F. Alexander Magoun, *Amos Fortune's Choice: The Story of a Negro Slave's Struggle for Self-fulfillment* (Freeport, Maine: Bond Wheelwright, 1964), 1, 74, 94–95, 108, 113–17.

2. Ibid., 123–24, 127, 133–34, 138, 146–47.

3. Ibid., 149–52, 158, 173–74, 200–1, 208, 211–13.

4. Ibid., 152, 163, 195, 217–37. According to Magoun (236) a gift of $100 was given in 1805 to the Jaffrey church and a cash balance of $233.85 was set aside for the school endowment. The fund as of 1964 stood at $1500 and by act

of the state legislature was being used to fund public speaking prizes for local school students.

5. Jon Sensbach, *African–Americans in Salem* (Winston–Salem, N. C.: Old Salem, n.d.), 1–8, 10–12, 14–15, 16–21.

6. Kaplan, *Black Presence in the Era of the American Revolution,* 209–11.

7. Ibid., 210–11; also *DANB,* s.v. "Prince, Abijah" and "Prince, Lucy Terry."

8. Kaplan, *Black Presence* 216–17.

9. Thomas, *Rise to Be a People,* 9–21.

10. Esther M. Douty, *Forten the Sailmaker: Pioneer Champion of Negro Rights* (Chicago: Rand McNally, 1968), 66–68.

11. Nash, *Forging Freedom* 51–52; Douty, *Forten the Sailmaker,* 28–32.

12. Douty, *Forten the Sailmaker,* 51–65, 77–81.

13. Ibid., 72–77.

14. Silvio A. Bedini, *The Life of Benjamin Banneker* (New York: Charles Scribner's Sons, 1972), 152–66.

15. Banneker's principal interests and achievements are nicely summarized in *DANB,* s.v. "Bannecker, Benjamin."

16. Summarized from Bedini, *Benjamin Banneker,* 3–42, 43–45, 49–75, 76–85.

17. Ibid., 85–89. In fact, Banneker did prepare ephemerides for the years 1798 to 1804 without payment or publication.

18. Ibid., 99–102, 147–49, 181–82.

19. Ibid., 146–47, 176–83, 184–92, 193–94.

CHAPTER 12: Liberty in America's Other Land of Liberty

1. Commander de Puech, *My Odyssey: Experiences of a Young Refugee from Two Revolutions, by a Creole of Saint Domingue,* Althea de Puech Parkahm, ed. and trans. (Baton Rouge: Louisiana State Univ. Press, 1959), 27–28. Although the name of the author of these moving letters is not known, he is known to have been an ancestor of the family of James Amedee de Puech of New Orleans. So as not to encumber the following account unduly with references to the unnamed but very real author of this work, I refer to him as "Commander de Puech."

2. All of the foregoing is drawn variously from the following works: Thomas O. Ott, *The Haitian Revolution, 1789–1804* (Knoxville: Univ. of Tennessee Press, 1973), 40–42, 47–49; Martin Ros, *Night of Fire: The Black Napoleon and the Battle for Haiti* (New York: Sarpedon Publishers, 1994), 1–6; Carolyn E. Fick, *The Making of Haiti: The Saint Domingue Revolution from Below* (Knoxville: Univ. of Tennessee Press, 1990), 92–104.

3. The story of Ogé and Chavannes in varying, sometimes conflicting, detail appears in Fick, *Making of Haiti,* 82–84; Ott, *Haitian Revolution,* 29–30, 36–38; Ros, *Night of Fire,* 25–27. Other details also appear in Hubert Cole, *Christophe: King of Haiti* (London: Eyre & Spottiswoode, 1967), 32–33 and Vandercook, *Black Majesty,* 23–25.

4. Ott, *Haitian Revolution,* 20–21, 26–27 n.96, 28–31.

5. Fick, *Making of Haiti,* 82.

6. Ott, *Haitian Revolution,* 36–37; Fick, *Making of Haiti,* 83.

7. Fick, *Making of Haiti,* 83–84; Ros, *Night of Fire,* 26–27; Cole, *Christophe,* 33; Ott, *Haitian Revolution,* 37–38.

8. It is Cole's suggestion that Christophe served in the militia against Ogé and Chavannes in *Christophe,* 32–33, 43–44; Vandercook, *Black Majesty,* 16–26.

9. Ott, *Haitian Revolution,* 38–39; Fick, *Making of Haiti,* 120–21, 125.

10. Fick, *Making of Haiti,* 118–25; Ros, *Night of Fire,* 27–28.

11. Ott, *Haitian Revolution,* 54–55, 65.

12. Ros, *Night of Fire,* 43–48.

13. Ibid., 48–49; Ott, *Haitian Revolution,* 65–66.

14. Ros, *Night of Fire,* 50–51; Ott, *Haitian Revolution,* 66–67

15. Ros, *Night of Fire,* 49, 51–52; Fick, *Making of Haiti,* 315 n.3.

16. Ros, *Night of Fire,* 50–51; Fick, *Making of Haiti,* 312 n.3. Ott, *Haitian Revolution,* 67–68.

17. Fick, *Making of Haiti,* 158–59, 315 n.8; Ros, *Night of Fire,* 52–53; Ott, *Haitian Revolution,* 69–70.

18. Parham, *My Odyssey,* 84–92.

19. Ros, *Night of Fire,* 53–54; Ott, *Haitian Revolution,* 71–72; Fick, *Making of Haiti,* 159–60.

20. Puech, *My Odyssey,* 92–96.

21. Ott, *Haitian Revolution,* 76–78.

22. Fick, *Making of Haiti,* 161–68, for an excellent analysis of the messiness of the process.

23. Ros, *Night of Fire,* 8–9.

24. Ibid., 9–10; Ott, *Haitian Revolution,* 57–58.

25. Ros, *Night of Fire,* 40–44, 51, 57–60.

26. Fick, *Making of Haiti,* 184–85.

27. Ros, *Night of Fire,* 66–68; Ott, *Haitian Revolution,* 79–80.

28. Ros, *Night of Fire,* 61–66.

29. The various secondary accounts of this session of the National Convention differ dramatically in almost every detail—the number of delegates, who presented resolutions, who spoke, and where such key figures as Danton and Robespierre stood on the resolution of abolishing slavery. I am following principally those authors citing original sources: Ros, *Night of Fire,* 76–80; James, *Black Jacobins,* 138–42; Ott, *Haitian Revolution,* 82–83. The usually solid Fick, *Making of Haiti,* skips over the action of the National Convention.

30. James, *Black Jacobins,* 139–40, 141–42.

31. Ros, *Night of Terror,* 63–64, 71–73, 75, 83–85.

CHAPTER 13: Annus Mirabilis I—1793

1. Minnigerode, *Career of Genet,* v, 337–341.

2. Ibid., 3–24, 67–79, 100–18, 119–39.

3. Ibid., 257, 358–59; Foner, *Democratic–Republican Societies,* 6–7, 411.

4. Minnigerode, *Career of Genet,* 195–97, 201–11; Foner, *Democratic––Republican Societies,* 55–56, 411.

5. Binger, *Revolutionary Doctor,* 203–5, 207–8, 209–13.

CHAPTER 14: Liberty and Revolution in America

1. Jones, *Companion to French Revolution,* 30–36.

2. Axelrad, *Philip Freneau,* 209–22, 275–85.

3. Hugh Henry Brackenridge, "Oration on the Celebration of the Anniversary of Independence, July 4th, 1793," *A Hugh Henry Brackenridge Reader, 1770–1815,* Daniel Marder, ed. (Pittsburgh: Univ. of Pittsburgh Press, 1970), 147–48, 149–50.

4. Link, *Democratic–Republican Societies,* 13–15; Foner, *Democratic–Republican Societies,* 123–27.

5. Foner, *Democratic–Republican Societies,* 127–35.

6. Leland Baldwin, *Whiskey Rebels: The Story of a Frontier Uprising* (Pittsburgh: Univ. of Pittsburgh Press, 1939), 56–75; Raymond Walters, Jr., *Albert Gallatin: Jeffersonian Financier and Diplomat* (Pittsburgh: Univ. of Pittsburgh Press, 1957), 65–71.

7. Marder, *Hugh Henry Brackenridge,* 105–8.

8. Walters, *Albert Gallatin,* 65–75. Gallatin described his course in the Whiskey Rebellion as "my only political sin."

9. Henry Hugh Brackenridge, "Incidents of the Insurrection in Western Pennsylvania in the Year 1794," in *Brackenridge Reader,* 267–69, 272–82, 283–301.

10. Baldwin, *Whiskey Rebels,* 220–25, 227–31.

11. Brackenridge, "Incidents of the Insurrection," 303–4, 312–21.

12. Baldwin, *Whiskey Rebels,* 248–52; for Gallatin's similar ordeal, see Walters, *Albert Gallatin,* 76–86.

13. Austin, *Matthew Lyon,* 81–84, 85–89, 90–98.

14. Griswold's description is in a letter of February 25, 1798, from Yale University Library, cited in Austin, *Matthew Lyon,* 98–100.

15. Tagg, *Benjamin Franklin Bache,* 234–42.

16. Smith, *Freedom's Fetters,* 188–92.

17. Tagg, *Benjamin Franklin Bache,* 328–29; Smith, *Freedom's Fetters,* 192–93.

18. Smith, *Freedom's Fetters,* 194–95.

19. Ibid., 195–202; Tagg, *Benjamin Franklin Bache,* 367–70.

20. Tagg, *Benjamin Franklin Bache,* 370–75.

21. Goodwin, *Friends of Liberty,* 266, 387–88; for the fascinating trials of Thomas Hardy, Horne Tooke, and John Thewall, see 343–58.

22. Durey, *With Hammer of Truth,* 76–82, 91–92, 95–96, 97–109.

23. Elliott, *Raleigh Register,* 15–17; Ames, *History of National Intelligencer,* 73–76.

24. Volney, *The Ruins,* xviii–xx; Smith, *Freedom's Fetters,* 159–60; Childs, *French Refugee Life in the U. S.,* 119–21.

25. Priestley, *Memoirs,* 143, 146–47.

26. Volney, "Volney's Answer to Dr. Priestly," appended to *The Ruins,* 211–214, 219. This piece was published, among other places, in the *Anti–Jacobin Review* (March/April 1799).

27. Volney, "Answer to Dr. Priestly," 214–19.

28. Smith, *Freedom's Fetters,* 164–69.

29. Childs, *French Refugee Life,* 54–56.

30. Smith, *Freedom's Fetters,* 169–70; Moreau, *American Journey,* 252–53.

31. Moreau, *American Journey,* 252–53; Smith, *Freedom's Fetters,* 160–61, 170.

32. Smith, *Freedom's Fetters,* 206–9; Burk, *Brief Memoir of John Daly Burk,* 30.

33. Smith, *Freedom's Fetters,* 208–11, 212–18.

34. Austin, *Mathew Lyon,* 104–17, 119–25, 126–30.

35. Tagg, *Benjamin Franklin Bache,* 395–96.

36. Smith, *Franklin and Bache,* 158–63.

37. Tagg, *Benjamin Franklin Bache,* 396.

38. Ibid., 376–77.

39. Binger, *Revolutionary Doctor,* 236–37.

40. Spater, *William Cobbett,* 1, 100–101; Rowe, *Mathew Carey,* 23–24.

41. Binger, *Revolutionary Doctor,* 240–41; Spater, *William Cobbett,* 99–100.

42. Spater, *William Cobbett,* 1, 101.

43. Binger, *Revolutionary Doctor,* 236–37, 242.

44. Ibid., 237–39; Page Smith, *John Adams* 2 vols. (Garden City, N.Y.: Doubleday & Company, 1962), 2, 899–900, 910, 942–43.

45. Spater, *William Cobbett,* 2, 101–09.

46. Smith, *Franklin and Bache,* 162–63; Jacob E. Cooke, *Tench Coxe and the Early Republic* (Chapel Hill: Univ. of North Carolina Press, 1978), 344–46.

CHAPTER 15: American Liberators as Outcasts

1. Woodress, *Yankee's Odyssey,* 153–86, 187–94.

2. Frederick B. Tolles, *George Logan of Philadelphia* (New York: Oxford Univ. Press, 1953), 3–26, 27–42.

3. Deborah Norris Logan, *Memoir of Dr. George Logan of Stenton,* Frances A. Logan, ed. (Philadelphia: Historical Society of Pennsylvania, 1899), 9–17, 42–49, 78–85. This volume is a moving account of the world of the 1790s from a bright and reflective woman's point of view.

4. Tolles, *George Logan,* 68–79.

5. Ibid., 105–28.

6. Logan, *Memoir of Dr. Logan,* 53–54; Tolles, *George Logan,* 129–44; Ammon, *James Monroe,* 150–54.

7. Tolles, *George Logan,* 144–48, 149–52, 153–56, 157–69.

8. Logan, *Memoir of Dr. Logan,* 57–60.

9. Ibid., 72–75; Tolles, *George Logan,* 172.

10. Logan, *Memoir of Dr. Logan,* 72–80.

11. Tolles, *George Logan,* 172–73.

12. Ibid., 174–75; Logan, *Memoir of Dr. Logan,* 84–85.

13. Tolles, *George Logan,* 174–76; Gerard H. Clarfield, *Timothy Pickering and*

American Diplomacy, 1795–1800 (Columbia: Univ. of Missouri Press, 1969), 188–89, concludes that Pickering and John Adams placed absolutely no faith in the words of George Logan.

14. Tolles, *George Logan,* 176–180.

15. Ibid., 179, 183–84; Page Smith, *John Adams,* 2 vols. (Garden City, N.Y.: Doubleday & Company, 1962), 2, 990–91, 994–95, report Murray's favorable assessment, "The *nature* of the affairs of the U.S. and the direction of her [France's] views are changed very much. At least great objects present themselves that were dormant a year since."

16. Tolles, *George Logan,* 184, 194.

CHAPTER 16: Liberty Abolished in America

1. Tolles, *George Logan,* 185–202.

2. See Logan, *Memoir of Dr. Logan,* 89–93, for the entire text of Logan's touching letter.

3. Woodress, *Yankee's Odyssey,* 193–96, 197, 198–99.

4. Webster to Barlow, 16 November 1798, *Letters of Noah Webster,* Harry R. Warfel, ed. (New York: Library Publishers, 1953), 187–90, 191–94.

5. Hawke, *Paine,* 314–39.

6. Phillips, "William Duane," 52–56, 59–62; Smith, *Freedom's Fetters,* 277–79.

7. Phillips, "William Duane," 66–69, 70–75.

8. Smith, *Freedom's Fetters,* 282–83, 284–97, 298–301.

9. Ibid., 301–6, 316–17, 328.

10. Ibid., 307–11; Malone, *Public Life of Cooper,* 104–6.

11. Smith, *Freedom's Fetters,* 312–28.

12. Smith, *Priestley in America,* 109–11, 122–28; Joseph Priestley, *Letters to the Inhabitants of Northumberland and Its Neighborhood, on Subjects Interesting to the Author, and to Them* (Northumberland: Andrew Kennedy; Philadelphia: Printed by John Bioren, 1801).

13. Smith, *Priestley in America,* 125–28, 142–47; Holt, *Life of Priestley,* 209–12, 214–15.

14. Smith, *Priestley in America,* 166–68.

15. Cooper soon launched his own attack on the land of liberty. Although he initiated a correspondence with Jefferson that would continue until the former president's death—sometimes on matters of science and policy, but frequently on the subject of Cooper's need for employment—Cooper was angry with America. He continued to be attacked in the press, and he maintained a steady barrage of counterattacks on hundreds of subjects until his own death in 1839. The one topic that absorbed his venom more than any other was his imprisonment for sedition in 1799. He sought Jefferson's help in petitioning Congress to repay the fine he had been charged when he went to prison. But the petition went nowhere. With every new president and Congress, he brought up the issue. Mahlon Dickerson, a personal friend in Congress from New Jersey, handled the petition in the 1820s.

Martin Van Buren championed the cause for a time. When Cooper later moved to South Carolina, the cause was taken up by a very interesting string of southern senators—James Hamilton, Jr., Robert Y. Hayne, and James Henry Hammond. Though they were not successful during Cooper's lifetime, he exacted a promise from them and from his wife to pursue the matter—out of principle—until it should be settled properly and correctly. On July 18, 1850, the U.S. Senate concurred with the House of Representatives on an act authorizing the U.S. Treasury to pay Cooper's heirs an amount of $400 plus 6 percent interest accumulated from November 1, 1800, to the date of repayment—approximately $1,600. This unusual act was taken by Congress in the midst of the greatest debate ever held on the fate of the American Union, just weeks before the Compromise of 1850. Though Cooper, through a whole generation of devoted disciples, finally won his battle for the principle of free speech, he failed in another concurrent last desire— to provide a financial legacy for his family. A battle among his heirs over the proper distribution of the windfall could not be resolved. As a consequence, the repayment was never made.

CHAPTER 17: Edmund Burke, Friend of Order

1. Conor Cruise O'Brien, *The Great Melody: A Thematic Biography and Commented Anthology of Edmund Burke* (Chicago: Univ. of Chicago Press, 1992), 586–87.

2. Ibid., 566–67.

3. For the story of Tate's "last invasion" of England, see chapter 10.

4. Burke to Lord Charlemont, 9 August 1789, *Great Melody*, 387.

5. Burke to William Windham, 27 September 1789, *Great Melody*, 388.

6. Burke to Richard Burke, 10 October 1789, *Great Melody*, 389.

7. O'Brien, *Great Melody*, 394–96, but the emphases here are mine; on Price and the Revolution Society, see chapter 2.

8. O'Brien, *Great Melody*, 389–91, 394–97.

9. Ibid., 405–9. All of the foregoing is carefully cited and analyzed in O'Brien.

10. Ibid., 402–5, makes much of Burke's prophetic style in the *Reflections* and other writings. The following discussion is also informed by Russell Kirk, *The Conservative Mind from Burke to Eliot*, 7th ed. (Chicago: Regnery Books, 1986), esp. 3–71; Frank O'Gorman, *Edmund Burke: His Political Philosophy* (Bloomington: Indiana Univ. Press, 1973), esp. 107–47; and Steven Blakemore, ed., *Burke and the French Revolution: Bicentennial Essays* (Athens: Univ. of Georgia Press, 1992), passim.

11. All of these and many other topics are helpfully outlined by Oskar Piest in a useful edition of *Reflections on the Revolution in France*, Thomas H. D. Manoney, ed. (Indianapolis: Bobbs–Merrill Company, 1955), xxix–xxxviii.

12. Ibid., 39–51, 77–79.

13. Ibid., 66–72.

14. Ibid., 55–59, 214–17.

15. Ibid., 56–57, 286–90; Kirk, *Conservative Mind*, 64–69.

16. Burke, *Reflections*, 98–101, 113–15.

17. Ibid., 102–4, 111–13, 176–78.

18. Ibid., 34–35, 39–45.

19. Biographical information provided here is drawn heavily from Russell Kirk, *Edmund Burke, a Genius Reconsidered* (New Rochelle, N.Y.: Arlington House, 1967), 1–25.

20. For excellent coverage of these topics, see O'Brien's *Great Melody*, where Burke's four great involvements are the center of attention.

21. Ibid., 409–12.

22. For Wollstonecraft and Paine, see chapter 6; Mackintosh is mentioned briefly by O'Brien, *Great Melody*, 413–14.

23. O'Brien, *Great Melody*, 414–31.

24. Edmund Burke, "A Letter to a Member of the National Assembly" [May 1791] in *Further Reflections on the Revolution in France*, Daniel E. Ritchie, ed. (Indianapolis: Liberty Fund, 1992), 29–72, with quoted material on 38–39, 43–44. According to Ritchie's note, Bajazet was "the eponymous hero of a tragedy by Racine" who "was executed by his brother, Sultan Murad IV of Turkey, who was an Ottoman Nero, in the words of one commentator" (44n.8).

25. Burke, "An Appeal from the New to the Old Whigs" (August 1791) in *Further Reflections*, 75–201.

26. For Franklin and Burke's friendship, see Van Doren, *Benjamin Franklin*, 331, 335, 467, 473, 487, 508, 521, 529, 534, 627–29, 669.

27. Burke, *Further Reflections*, 106–7.

28. Ibid., 104–5, 208–9.

29. O'Brien, *Great Melody*, 494–95, 496–500, 571–75.

30. Ibid., 509–11, 570.

31. Ibid., 469–71, 473, 570–71; Elliott, *Wolfe Tone*, 169–71, 187, 336.

32. O'Brien, *Great Melody*, 550–51; *The Works of the Right Honorable Edmund Burke*, rev. ed., 12 vols; (Boston: Little, Brown, 1867), 6, 413–29.

33. O'Brien, *Great Melody*, 557–58, 570–75; *Works of Burke*, 6, 428–29.

34. O'Brien, *Great Melody*, 589–92.

CHAPTER 18: Friends of Order

1. Schama, *Citizens*, 98, 822–27; Jones, *Longman Companion to French Revolution*, 369.

2. Schama, *Citizens*, 825–26.

3. Ibid., 96–103, 294–97, 655–69, 822–23.

4. R. R. Palmer, ed. and trans., *The Two Tocquevilles Father and Son: Hervé and Alexis de Tocqueville on the Coming of the French Revolution* (Princeton, N.J.: Princeton Univ. Press, 1987), 3–6, 35–37.

5. Ibid., 7–13, 21–23.

6. Joan Evans, *Chateaubriand: A Biography* (London: Macmillan, 1939), 32–53, 81–93.

7. Ibid., 1–34, 35–53, 54–68, 69–72, 73–80, 82–93.

8. Jacques Godechot, *The Counter-Revolution: Doctrine and Action, 1789–1804* (Princeton: Princeton Univ. Press, 1971), 3–22, 24–27, 32–49, 67–83, 84–101, 108–19.

9. Freidrich von Gentz, "The French and American Revolutions Compared," in *Three Revolutions,* Stefan T. Possony, ed. (Westport, Conn.: Greenwood Press, 1959), v–vii, 5–9.

10. Von Gentz, "French and American Revolutions Compared," 35–37, 48–50, 52–53, 62–63, 67–68, 79, 82–83, 86–88.

11. Ibid., 69–75, 83–84, 93 95.

12. Stefan T. Possony, Introduction to *Three Revolutions,* vi–ix.

13. Vernon Stauffer, *New England and the Bavarian Illuminati* (New York: Columbia Univ. Press, 1918), 142–47, 148–52, 153–77, 178–80, 181–85, 186–92, 215–27.

14. David Daiches, "The Scottish Enlightenment," in David Daiches, Peter Jones, and Jean Jones, editors, *A Hotbed of Genius: The Scottish Enlightenment, 1730–90* (Edinburgh: Univ. Press, 1986), 1–2. I am grateful to Peter Jones, director of the Institute for Advanced Studies in the Humanities at the University of Edinburgh, for many lively discussions on the nature of the Scottish Enlightenment and its influence on the modern world and especially in America.

15. Ibid., 3–10, 11–16, 17, 18–40.

16. Van Doren, *Benjamin Franklin,* 281–82.

17. John Playfair, "Biographical Account of the Late John Robison, LL.D, F.R.S Edin. and Professor of Natural Philosophy in the University of Edinburgh," in *Transactions of the Royal Society of Edinburgh* (Edinburgh: Archibald Constable, 1814), 7, 495–531.

18. Patrick O'Leary, *Sir James Mackintosh: The Whig Cicero* (Aberdeen: Aberdeen Univ. Press, 1989), 1–13, 15–23.

19. James Mackintosh, *Vindiciae Gallicae: Defence of the French Revolution and Its English Admirers Against the Accusations of the Right Hon. Edmumd Burke: Including Some Strictures on the Late Production of Mons. de Calonne* (London: G. G. J. and J. Robinson, 1791); the 351-page work was condensed into a smaller edition of 175 pages, published at Philadelphia in 1792 by William Young, a bookseller.

20. O'Leary, *Sir James Mackintosh,* 22–25; James T. Boulton, "James Mackintosh: *Vindiciae Gallicae,*" *Renaissance and Modern Studies* 21 (1977): 106–18; Lionel A. McKenzie, "The French Revolution and English Parliamentary Reform: James Mackintosh and the *Vindiciae Gallicae,*" *Eighteenth-Century Studies* 14 (Spring 1981): 264–82.

21. O'Leary, *Sir James Mackintosh,* 25–31.

22 Boulton, "James Mackintosh," 115–16; O'Leary, *Sir James Mackintosh,* 35–36.

23. Boulton, "James Mackintosh," 116–17; O'Leary, *Sir James Mackintosh,* 36–38.

24. O'Leary, *Sir James Mackintosh,* 48–49.

25. McKenzie, "French Revolution and English Parliamentary Reform," 264–65, 279–82.

26. O'Leary, *Sir James Mackintosh,* 49–51, 55–56.

27. Stauffer, *Bavarian Illuminati,* 199–203, 204–8, 212–14, 227–28.

CHAPTER 19: Annus Mirabilis II—1798

1. Charles E. Cuningham, *Timothy Dwight, 1752–1817: A Biography* (New York: Macmillan, 1942), 171–73; Meigs, *Life of Josiah Meigs,* 31–33.

2. Meigs, *Life of Meigs,* 33–39; Cuningham, *Timothy Dwight,* 197–99.

3. Josiah Meigs, "To the Honorable and Reverend Corporation of Yale College," Records of the Corporation of Yale College, Yale University Library; Meigs, *Life of Meigs,* 39–41.

4. Woodress, *Yankee's Odyssey,* 197–98.

5. Chandos Michael Brown, *Benjamin Silliman: A Life in the Young Republic* (Princeton: Princeton Univ. Press, 1989), 83; Meigs, *Life of Josiah Meigs,* 42–45.

6. Timothy Dwight, *The Duty of Americans at the Present Crisis, Illustrated in a Discourse, Preached on the Fourth of July, 1798* (New-Haven: Printed by Thomas and Samuel Green, 1798), 5–11, 12–14, 17–19.

7. Dwight, *Duty of Americans,* 19–32.

8. Stauffer, *Bavarian Illuminati,* 252–54.

9. Joseph W. Phillips, *Jedidiah Morse and New England Congregationalism* (New Brunswick, N.J.: Rutgers Univ. Press, 1983), 13–38.

10. On Dobson, see Robert D. Arner, *Dobson's Encyclopedia: The Publisher, Text, and Publication of America's First Britannica, 1789–1803* (Philadelphia: Univ. of Pennsylvania Press, 1991), 15–17; Phillips, *Jedidiah Morse,* 73–75.

11. Phillips, *Jedidiah Morse,* 73–82; Stauffer, *Bavarian Illuminati,* 261–93; Jedidiah Morse, *A Sermon, Exhibiting the Present Dangers, and Consequent Duties of the Citizens of the United States of America. Delivered at Charlestown, April 25, 1799, the Day of the National Fast* (Charlestown: Samuel Etheridge, 1799), 15–17.

12. Stauffer, *Bavarian Illuminati,* 297–308, 309–12; Phillips, *Jedidiah Morse,* 82–85.

13. Phillips, *Jedidiah Morse,* 86–87; Christoph Ebeling to William Bentley, 13 March 1799, in *American Antiquarian Society Proceedings,* n.s., 35 (1925): 307–33.

14. Joseph G. Wateus, "Biographical Sketch of William Bentley," in *The Diary of William Bentley, D.D., Pastor of the East Church, Salem, Massachusetts* 4 vols, (1907; reprint, Gloucester, Mass.: Peter Smith, 1962), 1: ix–xxii.

15. Bentley, *Diary,* 2: 32 (June 1793), 64, 70–71 (October 1793), 164 (November 1795).

16. *Diary of Bentley,* 2: 278 (August 1798), 291 (December 1798), 296 (February 1799), 302 (May 1799).

17. Woodress, *Yankee's Odyssey,* 150–51; Bentley, *Diary of Bentley,* 2: 194 (August 1796), 283 (September 1798), 338 (May 1800); see also Gordon McNett

Stewart, *The Literary Contributions of Christoph Daniel Ebeling* (Atlantic Highlands, N.J.: Humanities Press, 1978), 27–28.

18. William Coolidge Lane, "Letters of Christoph Daniel Ebeling," *American Antiquarian Society Proceedings,* 272–95; Stewart, *Literary Contributions of Ebeling,* 35–37.

19. Lane, "Letters of Ebeling," 297, 299, 300, 310–11.

20. *Diary of Bentley,* 2: 290 (December 1798), 296 (February 1799); Stauffer, *Bavarian Illuminati,* 313–14.

21. Phillips, *Jedidiah Morse,* 86–87; Stauffer, *Bavarian Illuminati,* 314–16.

22. Lane, "Letters of Ebeling," 307 33 (13 March 1799). In a postscript to this long letter, Ebeling revealed that he had sent the same views not only to Morse, but also to Eliphalet Pearson and David Tappan, Morse's panel of impartial judges, 337.

23. Lane, "Letters of Ebeling," 344–47 (26 July 1800), 351–53 (16 April 1801), 354–55 (12 July 1801), 358 (14 July 1801); see also Jean-Joseph Mounier, *On the Influence Attributed to Philosophers, Free-Masons, and to the Illuminati on The Revolution of France* (1801; reprint, Delmar, N.Y.: Scholars' Facsimiles & Reprints, 1974), iii–iv.

24. Lane, "Letters of Ebeling," 358–59 (14 July 1801); DiPadova, *Introduction to Influence Attributed to Philosophers,* v–vi.

25. DiPadova, *Introduction to Influence Attributed to Philosophers,* iv–v, vi–vii. Although still a monarchist, he was provided with appointments and preferments by Napoléon until his untimely death in 1806.

26. Mounier, *Influence Attributed to Philosophers,* vi–vii, ix–xiii, 5–7, 10–13, 20, 27–28, 31–32, 40–41, 120–24.

27. Ibid., 168–71, 172–73, 215–18, 223, 227–30.

28. Phillips, *Jedidiah Morse,* 93–97.

29. Until his death in 1817, Ebeling continued to be baffled by Morse's constant references to the subject. Morse simply would never let it go. Dwight, in his informal discussions with the senior class at Yale, spoke as if the Illuminati were a near and present danger. In stenographic notes taken of Dwight's discussion on January 5, 1814, Dwight spoke as follows:

> Illuminism began in Germany, but was carried to perfection in France. It was the most cunningly devised project that the world ever saw. The fundamental principles of the society were, to bind the members to do whatever was determined to be expedient for the fraternity; and to choose out for their own service all persons remarkable for genius or any thing else that could be turned to advantage. The members, by the training to which they were subjected, were led to murder their own friends in cold blood. Every thing done by the society was done in a masterly way. They communicated whatever they chose all over the world; they got hold on the courts, the church, the press. The only way to oppose an association like this, would

be to establish a society in opposition to it, founded on good principles. The Illuminees would have got possession of the world, if they had not been too certain of success.

See Theodore Dwight, Jr., *President Dwight's Decisions of Questions Discussed by the Senior Class in Yale College, in 1813 and 1814* (New York: Jonathan Leavitt; Boston: Crocker & Brewster, 1833), 135–36.

30. Phillips, *Jedidiah Morse,* 97–98. For Ebeling's incredulity over the behavior of Morse and Dwight, see Lane, "Letters of Christoph Ebeling," 368–69 (19 November 1804), 392 (25 October 1809), 401 (2 April 1810), 407 (27 August 1810), 415 (17 April 1812).

31. Lane, "Letters of Ebeling," 333–34 n.62, 362 n.5, 362–63.

32. Playfair, "Biographical Account of John Robison," 7, 522–31.

33. Bernard Faÿ, *Revolution and Freemasonry, 1680–1800* (Boston: Little, Brown, 1935), 216–85 passim; Bernard Faÿ, *Franklin, the Apostle of Modern Times* (Boston: Little, Brown), 929.

34. Faÿ, *Revolution and Freemasonry,* 286–305.

35. "U.S. Is Held in Danger of Going Communist," *New York Times,* 12 March 1937; Stanley J. Kunitz and Howard Haycraft, eds., *Twentieth Century Authors* (New York: H. W. Wilson, 1942), 294–95.

36. *New York Times,* 28 August 1944; 26 November, 6 December 1946; Stanley J. Kunitz, ed., *Twentieth Century Authors: First Supplement* (New York: H. W. Wilson, 1955), 318. For Faÿ's obituary, see *Le Monde,* (Paris) 4 January 1979. Faÿ was a prolific writer with a hundred books and articles in French and English by 1931, and with an additional dozen or so books after his imprisonment. I am grateful to Claude-Anne Lopez of New Haven, Connecticut, editor emerita of *The Papers of Benjamin Franklin* (New Haven: Yale Univ. Press, 1959) and to amateur historian Daniel Jouve of Paris, France, for their unstinting assistance in tracing down the mysterious life of Faÿ.

CHAPTER 20: Course of Counterrevolution

1. Noah Webster, *An Oration, Pronounced before the Citizens of New Haven, on the Anniversary of the Declaration of Independence of the United States, July 4th, 1798* (New Haven: T. and S. Green, 1798).

2. *The Autobiographies of Noah Webster: From the Letters and Essays, Memoir, and Diary,* Richard M. Rollins, ed. (Columbia: Univ. of South Carolina Press, 1989), 5–7.

3. Rollins, *Long Journey* 34–37.

4. Webster to Franklin, 1786 *Letters of Noah Webster,* 44–45.

5. Van Doren, *Benjamin Franklin,* 424–28.

6. Franklin and Webster's meetings are noted in Webster's diary published in Rollins, *Autobiographies of Webster,* 224–48.

7. "Memoir of Noah Webster," in Rollins, *Autobiographies of Webster,* 145–47.

8. "Diary of Noah Webster," in Rollins, *Autobiographies of Webster,* 224–48, noting, as examples, entries for 27 February, 25 May 1786; 1 February, 9 February, 28 July, 4 August, 7 August, 17 September, 18 September, 17 October, 28 December 1787.

9. Noah Webster, *Sketches of American Policy (1785)* (1785; reprint, New York: Scholar's Facsimiles & Reprints, 1937), i–iii, 2–29, 30–48.

10. "Memoir of Noah Webster," 147–48, 185; and "Diary of Noah Webster," 243–46 (esp. 18 July, 4 August, 5 August, 17 September, 18 September) in Rollins, *Autobiographies of Webster.*

11. Noah Webster, *A Collection of Essays and Fugitive Writings on Moral, Historical, Political and Literary Subjects* (Boston: I. Thomas and E. T. Adams, 1790), 22–36; Warfel, *Letters of Noah Webster,* 118–23; Rollins, *Long Journey of Webster,* 55–68.

12. Rollins, *Long Journey,* 65–66, 74–75.

13. Ibid., 76–77; other Webster biographers have Genet and Webster meeting and dining together on August 12. Webster's affidavit on Genet's threats places the dinner on August 26. See Minnigerode, *Career of Genet,* 317–29; see also "The Affidavit" in "Memoir of Noah Webster," 158.

14. "Affidavit," in "Memoir of Noah Webster," 158.

15. "Memoir of Noah Webster," 157–59.

16. Warfel to Washington, 20 April 1794, *Letters of Noah Webster,* 117–18.

17. Noah Webster, "The Revolution in France, Considered in Respect to Its Progress and Effects" Ellis Sandoz, ed. *Political Sermons of the American Founding Era,* (Indianapolis: Library Press, 1991) 1239–99.

18. Webster to Pickering, 8 December 1796, *Letters of Webster,* 143–44.

19. "To the Public," 4 March 1797, *Letters of Noah Webster,* 145–46.

20. Rollins, *Long Journey,* 82–83.

21. From extracts included in Rollins, *Long Journey,* 86–88.

22. Webster to Barlow, 16 November 1798, *Letters of Noah Webster,* 187–94.

23. Webster to Morse, 15 May 1797, *Letters of Noah Webster,* 47–48.

24. Lewis Melville, *The Life and Letters of William Cobbett in England & America,* 2 vols. (London: John Lane, 1913) 1: 81–83.

25. *Peter Porcupine in America* 5–17.

26. Ibid., 18–23. This essay and Cobbett's other American essays have been nicely gathered and edited in William Cobbett, *Peter Porcupine in America: Pamphlets on Republicanism and Revolution,* David A. Wilson, ed. (Ithaca: Cornell Univ. Press, 1994), 50–86.

27. Clark, *Peter Porcupine in America,* 21–27; for the text see Cobbett, *Peter Porcupine in America,* 87–118.

28. Cobbett, *Peter Porcupine in America,* 95, 106–7.

29. Clark, *Peter Porcupine in America,* 28–35, 60–65.

30. Ibid., 36–42.

31. For example, *Pill for Porcupine,* attributed to James Callender, accused Cobbett of seducing and virtually kidnapping his wife; the author of *The Imposter*

Detected accused Cobbett of dirty dealings with his first publishers, the Brad-fords; see Clark, *Peter Porcupine in America,* 70–73.

32. Clark, *Peter Porcupine in America,* 50, 64, 76, 83.

33. Ibid., 76–79.

34. William Playfair, *History of Jacobinism: Its Crimes, Cruelties and Perils, Comprising an Inquiry into the Manner of Disseminating, under the Appearance of Philosophy and Virtue, Principles which Are Equally Subversive of Order, Virtue, Religion, Liberty and Happiness* 2 vols (Philadelphia: Printed for William Cobbett, 1796) 1: 5–11; Clark, *Peter Porcupine in America,* 84–85.

35. Clark, *Peter Porcupine in America,* 94–97, 144–54, 160–65, 167–70.

36. Ibid., 166, 170–71.

37. Melville, *Life of William Cobbett,* 1: 113–16.

38. *The Memoirs of Chateaubriand,* Robert Baldick, trans. (New York: Alfred A. Knopf, 1961), xx–xxi.

39. Ibid., 94–108.

40. Godechot, *Counter-Revolution* 120–33, 134–35.

41. Evans, *Chateaubriand,* 114–17, 134–41, 325–60 passim.

CHAPTER 21: Friends of Order in the Land of Liberty—Poets and Luminaries

1. William J. McTaggart and William K. Bottorff, *The Major Poems of Timothy Dwight (1752–1817)* (Gainesville, Fla.: Scholars' Facsimiles & Reprints, 1969), 15; Edward M. Cifelli, *David Humphreys* (Boston: Twayne Publishers, 1982), 45–55.

2. Luther G. Riggs, ed., *The Anarchiad: A New England Poem (1786–1787)* (1861; reprinted Gainesville, Fla: Scholars' Facsimiles & Reprints, 1967), v–vii.

3. Cifelli, *David Humphreys,* 1–12.

4. Ibid., 12–14, 54–56. Humphreys never completed the biography.

5. Ibid., 52–53, 56–61, 68–70.

6. Ibid., 60–61.

7. The attribution of the foregoing installments to Humphreys is the judgment of Cifelli, *David Humphreys,* 62–68.

8. Riggs, *The Anarchiad,* 3–7, 8–12, 13–20, 21–24.

9. My view here is similar to William Dowling in his *Poetry & Ideology in Revolutionary Connecticut* (Athens: Univ. of Georgia Press, 1990), 63, who wrote as follows:

> Perhaps nothing so vividly reveals the degree to which the American Revolution had been based on an imaginary or illu-sory consensus, or the degree to which the illusion had been sustained by Country ideology as a mainly negative or demys-tifying strategy without concrete content of its own, as the speeches made by Patrick Henry against the United States Con-stitution. For when the Revolution is over and the time has ar-

rived to declare what positive vision of the new republic has animated their struggle, its leading spirits discover again and again that the vision to which they have appealed has all along meant different things to different people.

10. Riggs, *The Anarchiad,* 54; Cifelli, *David Humphreys,* 70.

11. Riggs, *The Anarchiad,* 54–61.

12. The poem is in Timothy Dwight, "A Discourse Delivered at New-Haven, February 22, 1800 on the Character of George Washington, Esq., at the Request of the Citizens" in Berk, *Calvinism versus Democracy* 43–44.

13. Timothy Dwight, *The Triumph of Infidelity: A Poem* (n.p.: Printed in the World, 1788), iii–iv, 5–17.

14. Ibid., 21–27; the contemporary identification of the figure "W******" in *Triumph of Infidelity* as Jeremiah Wadsworth is explained by Kenneth Silverman, *Timothy Dwight* (New York: Twayne Publishers, 1969), 89, 93.

15. This is also the thesis of Silverman, *Timothy Dwight,* 83–91, in attempting to explain this inscrutable, but farseeing work of Dwight: "Actually, the poem attacks not only skeptics or liberal Calvinists, but all the forces of social instability. Its subject is political. . . . Dwight specifies that Christianity and political order have the same basis; to mock God is to mock all governance."

16. Timothy Dwight, "An Essay on the Judgment of History Concerning America," *New-Haven Gazette and Connecticut Magazine* (12 April 1787): 60; Timothy Dwight, "Address of the Genius of Columbia to the Members of the Continental Convention," *American Museum,* (1 June 1787): 483.

17. Timothy Dwight, "Address to the Ministers of the Gospel of Every Denomination in the United States," *American Museum,* (4 July 1788): 30–33; both Silverman, *Timothy Dwight,* 83–93, and Berk, *Calvinism versus Democracy,* 107–11, pursue the foregoing themes in Dwight's career and writings.

18. Timothy Dwight, *Virtuous Rulers a National Blessing: A Sermon Preached at the General Election, May 12th, 1791* (Hartford: Hudson and Goodwin, 1791), 18; on the plan of association between Congregational and Presbyterian churches, see "Memoir of the Life of President Dwight," in Timothy Dwight, *Theology Explained and Defended in a Series of Sermons,* 4 vols. (New-York: Harper & Brothers, 1850) 1: 19.

19. Dwight, *Virtuous Rulers* 18–19, 20–37.

20. Timothy Dwight, *Greenfield Hill: A Poem in Seven Parts* (New York: Childs and Swaine, 1794), 26–37, 101–57 passim.

21. Ibid., 163–64, 169–84nn, in which he laments widespread violence in France (169), infidelity (170), the ill effects of and ill treatment of slaves in Virginia and the West Indies (171–72, 173–74), and in which he comments on the basis of real liberty ("The foundation of all equal liberty is the natural and equal descent of property to all the children of the proprietor. Republics cannot long exist, but upon this basis." [180]) and on the "lovely" and "respectable" character of the women of New England ("They blend the useful, and the pleasing, the re-

fined, and the excellent, into a most delightful, and dignified union; and well deserve, from the other sex, that high regard, and polite attention, which form a very respectable branch of our national manners." [182–83]).

22. Karl P. Harrington, *Richard Alsop: "A Hartford Wit"* (Middletown, Conn.: Wesleyan Univ. Press, 1969), v–vi, 48–50, 60–69.

23. Ibid., briefly addresses the confused attribution to Alsop, Hopkins, and others, v–vi, 48, 69–74.

24. [Lemuel Hopkins?], *The Democratiad, A Poem, in Retaliation for the "Philadelphia Jockey Club"* (Philadelphia: Thomas Bradford, Printer, 1795), iii–iv, 5–6, 7–19.

25. [Lemuel Hopkins?], *The Guillotina, or a Democratic Dirge, A Poem* (Philadelphia: The Political Book-Store, [1796], 3–7, 8–14.

26. [Lemuel Hopkins?], *The Political Green–House, for the Year 1798. Addressed to the Readers of the Connecticut Courant, January 1st, 1799* (Hartford: Hudson & Goodwin, [1799]), 3–5, 6–7, 8–12, 13–14, 15–16, 17–24.

27. Woodress, *Yankee's Odyssey,* 153–86; Samuel Bernstein, *Joel Barlow: A Connecticut Yankee in an Age of Revolution* (Cliff Island, Me.: Ultima Thule Press, 1985), 130–32.

28. Cifelli, *David Humphreys,* 92–95, 99.

CHAPTER 22: Friends of Order in the Land of Liberty—Political Philosophers

1. Peter Shaw, *The Character of John Adams* (Chapel Hill: Univ. of North Carolina Press, 1976), 164–200, 206–7.

2. *The Selected Writings of John and John Quincy Adams* Adrienne Koch and William Peden, eds. (New York: Alfred A. Knopf, 1946), 77–86, 88–97, 98–100, 106–10.

3. Ibid., 111; Shaw, *Character of John Adams,* 216–24.

4. The letter to Abigail Adams is quoted in *DAB,* s.v. "Adams, John."

5. Shaw, *Character of John Adams,* 225–30, describes well Adams's predicament as vice president.

6. Adams to Richard Price, 19 April 1790, *The Works of John Adams, Second President of the United States* (Boston: Little, Brown, 1854), 9, 563–64.

7. Adams to Price, 17 April 1790, *Works of John Adams,* 9, 564–65.

8. An American Citizen [John Adams], *Discourses on Davila. A Series of Papers, on Political History. Written in the Year 1790, and then published in the Gazette of the United States* (Boston: Printed by Russell and Cutler, 1805), 5, 7, 9–15, 48–52, 53–54.

9. Ibid., 71, 73, 76–79, 80–82.

10. Ibid., 82–83. Adams, on the matter of the emergence of a dictator, gloated in a footnote on this passage in the 1805 edition of *Discourses on Davila,* "This has all been accomplished in the new Emperor Napoleon, 1804."

11. Ibid., 84–91, 242–43.

12. Shaw, *Character of John Adams,* 236–37, 239–40.

13. *Selected Writings of John and John Quincy Adams,* 225–27.

14. Ibid., 227–31; Shaw, *Character of John Adams,* 239–40; Ellis, *Passionate Sage,* 191–97.

15. *Selected Writings of John and John Quincy Adams,* 232–34.

16. I am, in the foregoing analysis of Madison's response to Jefferson, deeply indebted to Drew R. McCoy and his fascinating biographical essay, *The Last of the Fathers: James Madison & The Republican Legacy* (Cambridge: Cambridge Univ. Press, 1989), 39–64.

17. These generally known facts on Madison's influence at the Constitutional Convention listed in *DAB,* s.v. "Madison, James."

18. McCoy, *Last of the Fathers,* 39–47

19. Ibid., 47–52; McCoy's entire book is a story of Madison's many differences from Jefferson on issues relating not only to the Constitution, but also to the role of Congress and the executive, the powers of the Supreme Court, nullification, slavery, and much more.

20. Mark A. Noll, *Princeton and the Republic, 1768–1822: The Search for a Christian Enlightenment in the Era of Samuel Stanhope Smith* (Princeton: Princeton Univ. Press, 1989), 16–17, 22–27, 36–41.

21. Ibid., 41–47; Thomas P. Miller, "Witherspoon, Blair and the Rhetoric of Civic Humanism," in *Scotland and America in the Age of Enlightenment,* Richard B. Sher and Jeffrey R. Smitten, eds. (Princeton: Princeton Univ. Press, 1990), 100–14.

22. Peter J. Diamond, "Witherspoon, William Smith and the Scottish Philosophy in Revolutionary America," *Scotland and America in the Age of the Enlightenment,* 115–32; Noll, *Princeton,* 47–49. See also the pathbreaking work that first charted the significance of the Scottish Enlightenment in America, Henry F. May, *The Enlightenment in America* (New York: Oxford Univ. Press, 1976), 307–62.

23. Noll, *Princeton,* 50, 53, 90–91.

24. Ibid., 62–72, 80–84, 89–91.

25. May, *Enlightenment in America,* 341–46.

26. McCoy, *Last of the Fathers,* 39–45, 61–63.

27. McCoy in *Last of the Fathers* demonstrates clearly Madison's adherence to a set of principles frequently contrary to beliefs expressed and policies pursued by Jefferson.

28. Charles Warren, *Jacobin and Junto or Early American Politics as Viewed in the Diary of Dr. Nathaniel Ames, 1758–1822* (Cambridge: Harvard Univ. Press, 1931), 105–6, 108–10, 109n.

29. Winifred E. A. Bernhard, *Fisher Ames: Federalist and Statesmen, 1758–1808* (Chapel Hill: Univ. of North Carolina Press, 1965), 299–300.

30. Warren, *Jacobin and Junto,* 110–11.

31. This is Warren's evidence and conclusion in *Jacobin and Junto,* 110 n.3.

32. Ibid., 15–41.

33. Bernhard, *Fisher Ames,* 20–43.

34. "Lucius Junius Brutus I," 12 October 1786, in *Works of Fisher Ames,* Seth Ames, ed., 2 vols. (reprint 1854; Indianapolis: Liberty Classics, 1983), 1: 38–45.

35. "Lucius Junius Brutus II," 19 October 1786, and "Lucius Junius Brutus III," 26 October 1786, in *Works of Fisher Ames,* 1: 45–56.

36. "Camillus I," 15 February 1787, and "Camillus II," 22 February 1787, in *Works of Fisher Ames,* 1: 56–69.

37. "Camillus III," 1 March 1787, in *Works of Fisher Ames,* 1: 69–73.

38. "Camillus IV," 8 March 1787, in *Works of Fisher Ames,* 1: 81–86.

39. Bernhard, *Fisher Ames,* 52–54, 55–75, 81–94, 104–7.

40. Ames to George Richards Minot, 23 June 1789, *Works of Fisher Ames,* 1: 676–78.

41. "To Aristides," ca. 1793, and "Against Jacobins," ca. 1794, in *Works of Fisher Ames,* 2: 966–84.

42. "To Aristides," ca. 1793, in *Works of Fisher Ames,* 2: 966–74.

43. "Against Jacobins," ca. 1794, in *Works of Ames,* 2: 974–80.

44. Bernhard, *Fisher Ames,* 252–54, 255–56, 268–74; Warren, *Jacobin and Junto,* 112–15.

45. Bernhard, *Fisher Ames,* 297–99; Warren, *Jacobin and Junto,* 103.

46. Samuel Eliot Morison, *Harrison Gray Otis, 1765–1848: Urbane Federalist* (Boston: Houghton Mifflin, 1969), 1–11, 17–22, 30–32, 39–43, 49–53.

47. Ibid., 83–85, 94–96, 100–102.

48. See sup. for Tate's invasion of Britain.

49. Morison, *Harrison Gray Otis,* 102–5, 107–9, 110–11, 116–17, 118–20.

50. McCoy, *Last of the Fathers,* 143–45; excerpts from Madison's Virginia Resolution are in *DAB,* s.v. "Madison, James."

51. McCoy, *Last of the Fathers,* 144–46.

52. The foregoing is my elaboration of McCoy's revision of the collaboration between Jefferson and Madison in *Last of the Fathers,* 130–51.

53. Morison, *Harrison Gray Otis,* 153–56.

CHAPTER 23: The Most Radical Counterrevolutionary

1. Pauline Maier's pathbreaking book *American Scripture: Making the Declaration of Independence* (New York: Alfred A. Knopf, 1997), showing Jefferson to be more of a compiler in producing the Declaration of Independence, does not alter the fact that Jefferson always enjoyed the title and was understood historically to be the author of this fundamental treatise on the rights of man. He wore this title with great authority throughout his career and long retirement.

2. Quoted in Noble E. Cunningham, Jr., *In Pursuit of Reason: The Life of Thomas Jefferson* (Baton Rouge: Louisiana State Univ. Press, 1987), 167.

3. Thomas Jefferson, "Autobiography," in *The Life and Selected Writings of Thomas Jefferson* Adrienne Koch and William Peden, eds. (New York: Random House, 1993), 10–59.

4. Ibid., 75–77; Cunningham, *In Pursuit of Reason,* 116–18.

5. "Autobiography," *Selected Writings of Jefferson,* 67–70, 81–86, 87–91, 97–100.

6. "The Anas," *Selected Writings of Jefferson,* 112–13, 117–20.

7. Thomas Jefferson, *Notes on the State of Virginia,* William Peden, ed. (John Stockdale's London text of 1787; reprint Chapel Hill: Univ. of North Carolina Press, 1955), xii–xix.

8. Ibid., xxi–xxiii. It is interesting that in all of the documents compiled by John Kaminski in his thorough *A Necessary Evil? Slavery and the Debate Over the Constitution* (Madison: Madison House, 1995), Jefferson's name never appeared in any discussions, letters, editorials, or ratification debates until the Congressional debates of 1790. From that time forward, however, his views became part of nearly every discussion of slavery and race.

9. Kaminski, *Necessary Evil,* 214, from debates in the House of Representatives on March 16, 1790.

10. Ibid., 215–20; Smith spoke on the following day, March 17, 1790.

11. Ibid., 224–25.

12. Ibid., 225–26; Scott spoke immediately after Boudinot on March 22, 1790.

13. Ibid., 229.

14. Jefferson, *Notes on Virginia,* 58–65, 70–71, 82–87, 137–43.

15. Kaminski, *Necessary Evil,* 264, 265–67.

CHAPTER 24: Black American Friends of Order

1. *America's First Negro Poet: The Complete Works of Jupiter Hammon of Long Island,* Stanley Austin Ransom, Jr., ed. (Port Washington, N.Y.: Kennikat Press, 1970), 44–47.

2. Oscar Wegelin, "Biographical Sketch of Jupiter Hammon," in Ransom, *Complete Jupiter Hammond,* 21–24.

3. Vernon Loggins, "Critical Analysis of the Works of Jupiter Hammon," in *Complete Jupiter Hammon,* 35–37.

4. *Complete Jupiter Hammon,* 14–15, 19. The sad story of Joseph Lloyd's demise is told in Nathan Perkins, *A Sermon Occasioned by the Unhappy Death of Mr. Lloyd: a Refuge from Long Island, June 18, 1780* (Hartford: Hudson & Goodwin, 1780).

5. "An Address to Miss Phillis Wheatly," in *Complete Jupiter Hammon,* 49–53.

6. "A Winter Piece: Being a Serious Exhortation, with a Call to the Unconverted: And a Short Contemplation on the Death of Jesus Christ" in *Complete Jupiter Hammon,* 67–85.

7. Jupiter Hammon, *An Evening's Improvement. Shewing, the Necessity of Beholding the Lamb of God. To which is Added a Dialogue, Entitled, The Kind Master and Dutiful Servant* (Hartford: Printed for the Author, 1782), 100–101.

8. "A Dialogue, Entitled, The Kind Master and Dutiful Servant," in *Complete Jupiter Hammon,* 59, 60–64.

9. "An Address to the Negroes in the State of New-York" in *Complete Jupiter Hammon,* 103–7, 112–13.

10. Ibid., 117; for circumstances surrounding efforts to get an abolition law passed in New York, see Arthur Zilversmit, *The First Emancipation: The Abolition of Slavery in the North* (Chicago: Univ. of Chicago Press, 1967), 146–52.

578 THE AMERICAN COUNTERREVOLUTION

11. "Address to the Negroes of New–York" in *Complete Jupiter Hammon,* 117–18.

12. *The Autobiography of Benjamin Rush: His "Travels Through Life" together with his Commonplace Book for 1789–1813,* George W. Corner, ed. (Princeton: Princeton Univ. Press for the American Philosophical Society, 1948), 228–29; Gary Nash also emphasizes this incident in the introduction to his *Forging Freedom: The Formation of Philadelphia's Black Community, 1720–1840* (Cambridge: Harvard Univ. Press, 1988), 1.

13. Quoted by Nash, *Forging Freedom,* 1.

14. The traditional date for the Old St. George's incident, given by Allen himself, was November 1787. That date was accepted uncritically by church historians and scholars alike until Milton C. Sernett, *Black Religion and American Evangelicalism: White Protestants, Plantation Missions, and the Flowering of Negro Christianity, 1787–1865* (Metuchen, N.J.: Scarecrow Press, 1975), 117–18, 219–20, provided evidence that the incident could not have occurred until after May 1792, when the new galleries described by Allen were completed and when the individuals cited by Allen by initials held the church positions he mentioned. This corrected dating is essential to understanding the actual relationship between liberty, order, and the establishment of separate black religious denominations. See Nash, *Forging Freedom,* 118–19, 310; Richard Allen, *The Life Experience and Gospel Labors of the Rt. Rev. Richard Allen to Which is Annexed the Rise and Progress of the African Methodist Episcopal Church in the United States of America* (reprint, Nashville: Abingdon Press, 1960), 13.

15. Allen, *Life Experience and Gospel Labors,* 25–26.

16. Nash, *Forging Freedom,* 66–70.

17. Allen, *Life Experience and Gospel Labors,* 17–18; Nash, *Forging Freedom,* 94–96; Charles H. Wesley, *Richard Allen, Apostle of Freedom* (Washington, D.C.: Associated Publishers, 1961), 9–12.

18. Allen, *Life Experience and Gospel Labors,* 18–23; Wesley, *Richard Allen,* 26–35.

19. Wesley, *Richard Allen,* 41–42.

20. Zilversmit, *First Emancipation* 110–14, 116, 120–23, 130–31, 134, 142–44.

21. Ibid., 162–64; Nash, *Forging Freedom,* 55, 92–94, 103–4.

22. Wilson Armistead, *Anthony Benezet: From the Original Memoir* (Philadelphia: Lippincott, 1859), 139–44; Nash, *Forging Freedom,* 104–5, 306.

23. Benezet's vast production of writings are listed in George S. Brookes, *Friend Anthony Benezet* (Philadelphia: Univ. of Pennsylvania Press, 1937), 193–203; biographical data here also from Brookes's excellent brief biography, 1–175 -passim.

24. Ibid., 77, 86–93, 196–98.

25. Ibid., 93–95.

26. Population figures for free blacks and slaves are from Nash, *Forging Freedom,* 38, 65, 134.

27. Allen, *Life Experience and Gospel Labors,* 23–25.

28. Julie Winch, *Philadelphia's Black Elite: Activism, Accommodation, and the Struggle for Autonomy, 1787–1848* (Philadelphia: Temple Univ. Press, 1988), 4–7; Douty, *Forten the Sailmaker,* 51–65.

29. Wesley, *Richard Allen,* 59–65.

30. Nash, *Forging Freedom,* 105–7, 307.

31. See Kaminski, *Necessary Evil,* 42, 147–48 (text of the memorial) and for the firestorm surrounding Franklin's failure to take a stand on slavery at the Convention, 119, 121, 131, 132.

32. Zilversmit, *First Emancipation,* 156, 164–65, 174.

33. Wesley, *Richard Allen,* 42–45.

34. Carol Wilson, *Freedom at Risk: The Kidnapping of Free Blacks in America, 1780–1865* (Lexington: Univ. Press of Kentucky, 1994), passim.; Nash, *Forging Freedom,* 108–09; Zilversmit, *The First Emancipation,* 156–59.

35. Wilson, *Freedom at Risk,* 68; Leon Litwack, *North of Slavery: The Negro in the Free States, 1790–1860* (Chicago: Univ. of Chicago Press, 1961), 30–31; 54–57.

36. Thomas, *Rise to be a People,* 19–21.

37. Nash, *Forging Freedom,* 101–3.

38. Wesley, *Richard Allen,* 65–68.

39. Nash, *Forging Freedom,* 109–12; Winch, *Philadelphia's Black Elite,* 5–7.

40. *Autobiography of Rush,* 202.

41 Ibid., 202–3; Joseph's words in Genesis 45:5 were, "Now, therefore be not grieved, nor angry with yourselves, that ye sold me hither: for God did send me before you to preserve life."

42. Quoted in Nash, *Forging Freedom,* 113–14.

43. Allen here confuses the story by placing this interview after the St. George's incident late in 1792. It had to have happened a year earlier in the fall of 1791; see Allen, *Life Experience and Gospel Labors,* 26–27.

44. Nash, *Forging Freedom,* 116–17; Allen, *Life Experience and Gospel Labors,* 26–28.

45. Allen, *Life Experience and Gospel Labors,* 27–28; Nash, *Forging Freedom,* found the date of the purchase, 310n.58.

46. Quoted in Nash, *Forging Freedom,* 119.

47. Allen, *Life Experience and Gospel Labors,* 27.

48. Ibid., 28; Thomas, *Rise to be a People,* 20–21; Douty, *Forten the Sailmaker,* 66–71.

49. Nash, *Forging Freedom,* 119–21; Allen, *Life Experience and Gospel Labors,* 28.

50. The story here told closely follows selected elements of the history of the 1793 epidemic written by J. H. Powell, *Bring out Your Dead: The Great Plague of Yellow Fever in Philadelphia in 1793* (1949; reprint, Philadelphia: Univ. of Pennsylvania Press, 1993).

51. Ibid., 74–78.

52. Stacey B. Day, *Edward Stevens: Gastric Physiologist, Physician and*

American Statesman (Montreal: Cultural and Educational Productions, 1969), 18–23, 42–61, 91.

53. Powell, *Bring out Your Dead,* 78–80, 84–89. It was Rush who declared himself an instrument of God in the epidemic as he commented in his autobiography about "the success which attended the remedies which it pleased God to make me the instrument of introducing into general practice in the treatment of the fever of 1793," See *Autobiography of Rush,* 96.

54. Powell, *Bring out Your Dead,* 94–95; Nash, *Forging Freedom,* 122.

55. Powell, *Bring out Your Dead,* 96–98; Nash, *Forging Freedom,* 122–23.

56. Absalom Jones and Richard Allen, "A Narrative of the Proceedings of the Colored People During the Awful Calamity in Philadelphia in the Year 1793; and a Refutation of Some Censures Thrown upon Them in Some Publications" in *Life Experience and Gospel Labors,* 48–65.

57. Alexander Hamilton to College of Physicians, 11 September 1793, *Edward Stevens,* 82–83.

58. *Autobiography of Rush,* 97, 99–101; Stevens to Dr. Redman at College of Physicians, 16 September 1793, *Edward Stevens,* 84–86.

59. Stevens to Redman, 16 September 1793, *Edward Stevens,* 85–86.

60. Benjamin Rush to Redman, 17 September 1793, *Edward Stevens,* 87.

61. Rush to Mrs. Rush, 3 October 1793, *Edward Stevens,* 81–82; Nash, *Forging Freedom,* 123–24.

62. Jones and Allen, *Narrative of Proceedings,* 50, 62–64; Powell, *Bring out Your Dead,* 117–21.

63. Powell, *Bring out Your Dead,* 153–64, 174–94, 270–71, 280.

64. *Autobiography of Rush,* 98, 280–82.

65. Jones and Allen, *Narrative of Proceedings,* 50–53; Powell, *Bring out Your Dead,* 293–94.

66. Jones and Allen, *Narrative of Proceedings,* 57–58.

67. Wesley, *Richard Allen,* 70–72; Allen, *Life Experience and Gospel Labors,* 28–29; Nash, *Forging Freedom,* 116–17.

68. Allen, *Life Experience and Gospel Labors,* 29–30.

69. Much of the foregoing is my interpretation of a confusing spate of data resulting from Allen's conflation of events leading to the creation of both churches; for the count on the free black contributors, see Nash, *Forging Freedom,* 117–18 and 310 n.59.

70. Allen, *Life Experience and Gospel Labors,* 30–31; Nash, *Forging Freedom,* 130.

71. Nash, *Forging Freedom,* 128–29.

72. Allen, *Life Experience and Gospel Labors,* 30–31.

CHAPTER 25: Order in America's Other Land of Liberty

1. "Letters of Toussaint L'Ouverture and of Edward Stevens, 1798–1800," *American Historical Review,* 16 (October 1910): 64–66, 101.

2. Ott, *Haitian Revolution,* 88–91; Ros, *Night of Fire,* 91–94.

3. Ros, *Night of Fire,* 146–47; Ott, *Haitian Revolution,* 102–4.

4. Ros, *Night of Fire,* 94–98; Ott, *Haitian Revolution,* 92–93, 100–101.

5. Ott, *Haitian Revolution,* 103–5; Ros, *Night of Fire,* 95, 99–101.

6. Ott, *Haitian Revolution,* 106–8.

7. "Letters of Toussaint and Stevens," 67–68; Stacey B. Day, ed., *Edward Stevens: Gastric Physiologist, Physician and American Statesman* (Montreal: Cultural and Educational Productions, 1969), 94–99.

8. John Adams to Timothy Pickering, 17 April, 15 June, 2 July, 1799, *Edward Stevens,* 100–2, 105–6.

9. Ott, *Haitian Revolution,* 110–11.

10. Toussaint to President Adams, 14 August 1799, "Letters of Toussaint and Stevens," 81–82.

11. Ott, *Haitian Revolution,* 112–15; Ros, *Night of Fire,* 105–13.

12. Ott, *Haitian Revolution,* 115–16.

13. Ros, *Night of Fire,* 117–19, 124–25; Ott, *Haitian Revolution,* 118–19.

14. Ros, *Night of Fire,* 123–26.

15. Ibid., 151–60, describes the contents of Napoléon's unsent letter and why it was never delivered.

16. Ibid., 125–26, 133–37; Ott, *Haitian Revolution,* 119–20.

17. Stevens to Pickering, 3 May 1799, "Letters of Toussaint and Stevens," 67–72.

18. Stevens to General Maitland, 23 May 1799, and Stevens to Pickering, 23 June 1799, "Letters of Toussaint and Stevens," 74–76.

19. Stevens to Pickering, 24 June 1799, "Letters of Toussaint and Stevens," 76–81.

20. Stevens to Pickering, 30 September 1799, "Letters of Toussaint and Stevens," 82–85.

21. Stevens to Pickering, 3 December 1799, "Letters of Toussaint and Stevens," 87–88.

22. Stevens to Pickering, 16 January 1799, "Letters of Toussaint and Stevens," 88–93. Adams's nervousness about independent action—especially by the U.S. Navy—in these waters is reflected in two letters he sent to Secretary of the Navy B. Stoddert, 7 June 1799 and 23 July 1800, reprinted in *Edward Stevens,* 104–5, 106–7.

23. Stevens to Pickering, 13 February and 16 March 1800, "Letters of Toussaint and Stevens," 93–94.

24. Stevens to Pickering, 19 April 1800, "Letters of Toussaint and Stevens," 94–96.

25. Ros, *Night of Fire,* 122–32, 140–43.

26. Bd Hanlon to Stephen Girard, 6 May 1799; Cassarrouy to Stephen Girard, 6 June 1799; George Washington to Clement Biddle, 6 June 1799; George Washington to Secretary of State and to Secretary of War, both 11 August 1799, *Edward Stevens,* 102–4, 154–56.

CHAPTER 26: The Judgment of History

1. This characterization of Warren's *History of the American Revolution* is informed, in part, by the following: *History as Argument* 73–119 and Nina Baym, "Mercy Warren's Melodrama," 531–54.

2. Warren, *History of the American Revolution,* 1: iii–v, vi–viii.

3. Ibid., 338–57, 363–64, 366, 369–71, 375–89, 391–95, 397, 401.

CHAPTER 27: Friends of Liberty in the Land of Order

1. William Godwin, *Memoirs of Mary Wollstonecraft* (1797; reprint New York: Richard R. Smith, 1930), with the original text and annotations on the second London edition of 1802. Godwin's *Memoirs of Wollstonecraft* were quickly published in America with Philadelphia editions of 1799 (James Carey) and 1804.

2. Ibid., 8–49, 50–56, 57–62, 68–76, 77–88, 98–103.

3. The reaction to Wollstonecraft's writings prior to the appearance of Godwin's *Memoirs* has been carefully documented by three historians: R. M. Janes, "On the Reception of Mary Wollstonecraft's *A Vindication of the Rights of Woman,*" in *Journal of the History of Ideas,* 29 (Spring 1978): 293–302; Marcelle Thiebaux, "Mary Wollstonecraft in Federalist America, 1791–1802," in *The Evidence of the Imagination: Studies of Interactions between Life and Art in English Romantic Literature,* Donald Redman, Michael Jaye, and Betty Bennett, eds. (New York: New York Univ. Press, 1978), 195–235; and Patricia Jewell McAlexander, "The Creation of the American Eve: The Cultural Dialogue on the Nature and Role of Women in Late Eighteenth-Century America," in *Early American Literature,* 9 (Winter 1975): 253–66.

4. Janes, "Reception of Wollstonecraft's *Vindication,*" 297–99.

5. Thiebaux, "Wollstonecraft in Federalist America," 207–15.

6. Ibid., 215–28; see also Janes, "Reception of Wollstonecraft's *Vindication,*" 298–302.

7. McAlexander, "Creation of the American Eve," 262–63.

8. Thiebaux, "Wollstonecraft in Federalist America," 209–10; Janes, "Reception of Wollstonecraft's *Vindication,*" 298–99.

8. These arguments and the circumstances of the publication of *The Age of Reason* are nicely summarized in James H. Smylie, "Clerical Perspectives on Deism: Paine's *The Age of Reason* in Virginia," in *Eighteenth-Century Studies,* 6 (Winter 1972–73): 206–9.

10. Uzal Ogden, *Antidote to Deism: The Deist Unmasked; or and Ample Refutation of All the Objections of Thomas Paine, Against the Christian Religion; as Contained in a Pamphlet, Entitled, "The Age of Reason"; addressed to the Citizens of these States* 2 vols. (Newark: John Woods, 1795) 1: iii–ix, 16, 20, 23; 2, 94, 221, 234, 270.

11. Smylie, "Clerical Perspectives on Deism," 203–5.

12. Ibid., 210–17.

13. The following is informed by a paper I wrote for the 1996 meeting of the

Society for Historians of the Early American Republic on papers by Anthony Iaccarino on St. George Tucker and by Daniel W. Stowell on Zephaniah Kingsley.

14. Jefferson, *Notes on Virginia,* xvii, 286–87 nn. 4–6. *The Portable Thomas Jefferson,* Marrill D. Peterson, ed. (New York: Penguin Books, 1975), 398–400.

15. St. George Tucker, *A Dissertation on Slavery: With a Proposal for the Gradual Abolition of It, in the State of Virginia* (1796; reprint, Westport, Conn.: Negro Univ. Press, 1970).

16. Ibid., i, 9.

17. Ibid., 7–8, 15–20, 25–28, 47–49, 65–67, 73–78, 80–88.

18. Lucy Freeman and Alma Halbert Bond, *America's First Woman Warrior: The Courage of Deborah Sampson* (New York: Paragon House, 1992), 189–92.

19. Ibid.,190, 192. My emphasis added in the last quotation.

20. [Herman Mann], *The Female Review: Or, Memoirs of an American Young Lady. By a Citizen of Massachusetts* (Dedham, Mass.: Printed by Nathaniel and Benjamin Heaton, for the Author, 1797). Although Mann's name was not printed in the first edition, everyone knew he was the author; he had recruited the 191 subscribers who paid for publication of the book.

21. Ibid., iii, v–xiii.

22. Ibid., 17–56, 57–108, with quotes from 62, 108.

23. Ibid., 110–17.

24. Ibid., 117–24; it is not clear how Mann could have confused the dates of Sampson's service since he drew his information from documents in her possession and from interviews directly with her; for the correct dates, see Freeman and Bond, *America's First Woman Warrior,* 16.

25. Patterson's career in army, state, and Congress is outlined in *DAB,* s.v. "Patterson, John."

26. Mann, *Female Review,* 131–33, 141–45, 147–54, 173–85, 186–90.

27. Ibid., 192–95; Freeman and Bond, *America's First Woman Warrior,* 120–23. Mann, working from interviews with Sampson fourteen years later, identified the attending physician as Dr. Bana.

28. Mann, *Female Review,* 195–227.

29. Ibid., 228–31; Freeman and Bond, *America's First Woman Warrior,* 145–51.

30. Mann, *Female Review,* 231–35.

31. Ibid., 253–56; Freeman and Bond, *America's First Woman Warrior,* 182–83.

32. Donald L. Robinson, *Slavery in the Structure of American Politics, 1765–1820* (New York: Harcourt Brace Jovanovich, 1971), 253–54.

33. This story of the 1798 debacle at Philadelphia was researched and well told by Gary Nash in *Forging Freedom* 175–76, 322.

34. Ibid., 176.

35. Carol Wilson, *Freedom at Risk,* 9–39 for kidnappings and 40–66 for those who seized free blacks within the framework of the 1793 law; also Kaminski, *A Necessary Evil,* 238–39.

36. Nash, *Forging Freedom,* 186–87; Robinson, *Slavery in Structure of American Politics,* 288–90.

37. Prince Hall, "A Charge Delivered to the Brethren of the African Lodge on the 25th of June, 1792," in *Early Negro Writing,* 63–69, 73–77.

38. Jones, "Petition of the People of Colour," in *Early Negro Writing,* 330–32.

39. Robinson, *Slavery in American Politics,* 313–14, 315.

40. "A Letter from James Forten," in *Early Negro Writing,* 333–34.

41. "Laws of the African Society, Instituted at Boston, Anno Domini 1796," in *Early Negro Writing,* 9–12.

42. "Constitution and Rules to be Observed and Kept by the Friendly Society of St. Thomas's African Church," in *Early Negro Writing,* 28–32.

43. *The Diary of Elizabeth Drinker,* 22 April 1796 (187–88), 30 November 1797 (195), 3 July 1798 (199), 28 August 1798 and 25 November 1798 (204).

BIBLIOGRAPHICAL NOTE

The sources used to write *The American Counterrevolution* are listed in the endnotes of the foregoing pages. As already stated, primary sources are biographies and original texts—many of which have been reprinted in those sources cited. I will, therefore, not repeat that data in this bibliographical note.

My purpose here is to share with readers the evolution of this book through the reading and contemplation of various works. I include here those works that contributed to the conception of this book and that fired my thinking about some of the important themes within it.

The project began concurrently with my move to the Benjamin Franklin National Memorial in Philadelphia in the summer of 1989. There I had to figure out who was this Benjamin Franklin who figured so prominently in the American Revolution, the French Revolution, the Industrial Revolution, and a dozen other revolutions in science, diplomacy, and literature. Fortunately for me the bicentennial of Benjamin Franklin's death in 1790 was on the immediate horizon. Franklin's bequests of £1,000 each to Boston and Philadelphia were about to reach their two hundredth anniversary, the time at which those invested funds should be dispersed. What a pleasure it was to participate in discussions in both Philadelphia and Boston about how those funds would be allocated.

Mayor Wilson Goode in Philadelphia asked me to join a committee of historians to divine Franklin's wishes. The gathered group recommended that Franklin's funds should go to the Philadelphia Foundation to continue Franklin's expressed interest in and concern for new "artificers" (skilled workers and craftsmen) appearing on the scene. Those funds, which had grown to many millions of dollars in both Philadelphia and Boston, were for the most part reinvested.

I needed to know Benjamin Franklin the man and went quickly to the sources. I found that the best place of all to find him was in *The Papers of Benjamin Franklin* (50 volumes projected), edited by Leonard Labaree, Whitfield Bell, Jr., Claude-Anne Lopez, Barbara Oberg, and many assistant editors from 1959 forward; (New Haven: Yale Univ. Press, 1959 to approx. 2006) [the tricentennial of Franklin's birth]).

When I arrived at the National Memorial, Leo Lemay, Franklin scholar from the University of Delaware, was planning a symposium on Franklin. That event resulted in a book titled *Reappraising Benjamin Franklin: A Bicentennial*

Perspective, edited by J. A. Leo Lemay (Newark: Univ. of Delaware Press, 1993). The papers for the book were presented in various Franklin-related Philadelphia and Delaware settings in April 1990, capturing the essence of the perennial Franklin.

Two older works about Franklin raised interesting and useful ideas about the multifaceted man. The best book about Franklin is *The Private Franklin: The Man and His Family,* writted by Claude-Anne Lopez and Eugenia W. Herbert (New York: W. W. Norton, 1975). Lopez and Herbert arrive at the essence of Franklin—without flattering him out of recognition. The most distressing book about Franklin is Bernard Faÿ's *Revolution and Freemasonry, 1680–1800* (Boston: Little, Brown, 1935), wherein Faÿ argues that Franklin was the secret Masonic purveyor of revolution in America and France. Both of these books reveal sides of Franklin that are sometimes dark and somewhat troubling.

But it was through his grandson, Benjamin Franklin Bache, that some of Franklin's more radical ideas became manifest. Bache was largely overlooked in American history until this same Bernard Faÿ pulled him out for large treatment in *The Two Franklins: Fathers of American Democracy* (Boston: Little, Brown, 1938). Bache still remained little noticed until the 1990s, when he has become a major figure in a number of works. The most important are these: Jeffrey A. Smith, *Franklin and Bache: Envisioning the Republic* (New York: Oxford Univ. Press, 1990); James Tagg, *Benjamin Franklin Bache and the Philadelphia Aurora* (Philadelphia: Univ. of Pennsylvania Press, 1991); and the most extravagant, but difficult to understand book on Bache is that of Richard Rosenfeld, *American Aurora: A Democratic-Republican Returns* (New York: St. Martin's Press, 1997).

The principal object of my interest was post-revolutionary America. Regrettably there was not much available in either American or European literature that helped explain how the age of revolution played itself out in America. R. R. Palmer's *The Age of Democratic Revolution: A Political History of Europe and America, 1760–1800* (2 vols.; Princeton: Princeton Univ. Press, 1959, 1964)—one of the great classics of modern history—did much for Europe, but little for America. These volumes gladly drove me to the European scene for a better glimpse of America.

Several other volumes provided important insights, but did not get at the heart of the phenomena I noticed in my research. John Fiske's classic, *The Critical Period of American History, 1783–1789* (Boston: Houghton, Mifflin, 1899), focused as it is on politics, provided little help. The little book of lectures *Revolutions: Reflections on American Equality and Foreign Liberations* (Cambridge: Harvard Univ. Press, 1990), by David Brion Davis fueled me to look deeper into the revolutionary character of the period. Noel Parker's *Portrayals of Revolution: Images, Debates and Patterns of Thought on the French Revolution* (Carbondale: Southern Illinois Univ. Press, 1990), provided other perspectives.

Gordon S. Wood's award-winning and renowned *The Radicalism of the American Revolution* (New York: Alfred A. Knopf, 1992) appeared after this project was well on its way. As noble as is the theme of this important work, it does not help us understand the counterrevolution against freedom and equality that emerged in America and the rest of the Western world in the late 1780s and 1790s. But I do agree with Wood that the American Revolution put the issues of freedom and equality irrevocably on the front burners of virtually every nation from 1776 to the present.

That many historians did not agree with Wood's idealistic perspective was confirmed at a session I attended at a meeting of the Organization of Historians in 1993—just after Wood's book received the National Book Award and the Pulitzer Prize—where historians such as Michael Zukerman, Joyce Appleby, and Barbara Clark-Smith heatedly rebutted the thesis of the book.

I next moved to the literature on the French Revolution that was emerging on the bicentennial of the fall of the Bastille. Simon Schama's *Citizens: A Chronicle of the French Revolution* (New York: Alfred A. Knopf, 1989) was my emotive introduction. But that was just the beginning of a vast and growing literature on this fundamental event in the history of Western culture.

I examined dozens of histories of the French Revolution written by such luminaries as Edmund Burke, Mary Wollstonecraft, and Madame de Staël. I concluded that the French Revolution was such a distressing event in Western culture that almost no one could get a start in public service without writing a history of the event. The most dramatic and persuasive documents I found were Thomas Carlyle's moving *The French Revolution: A History* (1837; reprint New York: Modern Library, 1959); Alexis de Tocqueville's brilliant *The Old Regime and the French Revolution,* translatd by Stuart Gilbert (1836; reprint Garden City, N.Y.: Doubleday & Co., 1955); and François René Chateaubriand's masterful *Memoirs,* translated by Robert Baldick (1848; reprint New York: Alfred A. Knopf, 1961).

Reading these classic texts was like walking with the giants of human history. But they were supplemented on the bicentennial of the French Revolution by a variety of new works that were helpful to me in keeping straight information on the events and people of the French Revolution. François Furet and Mona Ozouf, editors of *A Critical Dictionary of the French Revolution* (Cambridge: Harvard Univ. Press, 1989) proved useful—although, not indexed, it was a bear to use. Much more accessible was Colin Jones's *The Longman Companion to the French Revolution* (London: Longman, 1988). *The Legacy of the French Revolution,* edited by Ralph C. Hancock and L. Gary Lambert (Lanham, Md.: Rowman & Littlefield Publishers, 1996), also helped in the chase of historial figures and events.

Once I found that Alexis de Tocqueville's father had been nearly on the chopping block during the French Revolution, I began to understand how that Revolution—like the Holocaust—invigorated strong passions in families closely affected. These Tocquevilles—father and son—had profound understandings of what was happening in their world. My sources were *The Recollections of Alexis de Tocqueville,* translated by Alexander Teixeira de Mattos and edited by J. P. Mayer (London: Harvill Press, 1948); *The Two Tocquevilles, Father and Son: Herve and Alexis de Tocqueville on the Coming of the French Revolution,* edited and translated by R. R. Palmer (Princeton: Princeton Univ. Press, 1987); and

André Jardin, *Tocqueville, a Biography,* translated by Lydia Davis (New York: Farrar Straus Giroux, 1988).

Early in the project I became interested in the prospects and shape of "counterrevolution," which became one word without a hypen in the last twenty or thirty years in the various dictionaries. Unfortunately, the concept of counterrevolution has been little studied or discussed by historians. The best source on the French Counterrevolution is Jacques Godechot, *The Counter-Revolution: Doctrine and Action, 1789–1804,* translated by Salvator Attanasio (Princeton: Princeton Univ. Press, 1971).

But on the subject of counterrevolution itself, there is little help. The available sources deal only with counterreactions to Communist revolutions of the twentieth century: Seymour Martin Lipset, *Revolution and Counterrevolution: Change and Persistence in Social Structures* (1970; revised New Brunswick, N.J.: Transaction Books, 1988); and Herbert Marcuse, *Counterrevolution and Revolt* (Boston: Beacon Press, 1972). Given the paucity of discussion, there was not much for me to use in this work that mainly addresses the overthrow of ideas and values, not governments.

Since my main subject throughout this book is liberty and what happened to it as a concept, I pored through various discussions of liberty during that period. And what I discovered was a rancorous debate about what liberty really meant and to whom. Some of the works I consulted in this large cacophony of discordant voices were these: Joyce Appleby, *Capitalism and a New Social Order: The Republican Vision of the 1790s* (New York: New York Univ. Press, 1984) and *Liberalism and Republicanism in the Historical Imagination* (Cambridge: Harvard Univ. Press, 1992); J. C. D. Clark, *The Language of Liberty, 1660–1832: Political Discourse and Social Dynamics in the Anglo-American World* (Cambridge: Cambridge Univ. Press, 1994); Maldwyn A. Jones, *The Limits of Liberty: American History, 1607–1992* (New York: Oxford Univ. Press, 1993); Joseph Klaits and Michael H. Haltzel, editors, *Liberty/Liberté: The American and French Experiences* (Baltimore: Johns Hopkins Univ. Press: 1991); Isaac Kramnick, *Republicanism and Bourgeois Radicalism: Political Ideology in Late Eighteenth-Century England and America* (Ithaca: Cornell Univ. Press, 1990); J. G. Merquior, *Liberalism, Old and New* (Boston: Twayne Publishers, 1991); Thomas L. Pangle, *The Spirit of Modern Republicanism: The Moral Vision of the American Founders and the Philosophy of Locke* (Chicago: Univ. of Chicago Press, 1988); and Barry A. Shain, *The Myth of American Individualism: The Protestant Origins of American Political Thought* (Princeton: Princeton Univ. Press, 1994).

Probably few books ever written have depended more on biographical sources than this one. Early in the project I obtained copies of the following worthy directories so they could be available for ready consultation: *The Dictionary of National Biography*, edited by Leslie Stephen (63 vols. and supplements; New York: Macmillan and Co., 1885); *Chamber's Biographical Dictionary of All Times and Nations,* edited by David Patrick and Francis Hindes Groome (London: W & R Chambers, 1912); *Dictionary of American Biography,* edited by

Allen Johsnon (20 vol. and supplements; New York: Charles Scribner's Sons, 1928); *Notable American Women, 1607–1950: A Biographical Dictionary,* edited by Edward T. James (3 vols.; Cambridge: Harvard Univ. Press, 1971); *Dictionary of American Negro Biography,* edited by Rayford W. Logan and Michael R. Winston (New York: W. W. Norton, 1982); *Black Women in America: An Historical Encyclopedia,* edited by Darlene Clark Hine, Elsa Barkley Brown, and Rosalyn Terborg-Penn (Bloomington: Indiana Univ. Press, 1993); and *Biographical Directory of the American Congress, 1774–1961* (Washington, D.C.: Government Printing Office, 1961).

Though I cite hundreds of biographies, I used many of them for a greater purpose than to provide biographical data. A few of those that helped particularly in understanding the period under consideration (some of which are not mentioned in the notes) were these: Joseph J. Ellis, *Passionate Sage: The Character and Legacy of John Adams* (New York: W. W. Norton, 1993); Steven Blakemore, *Burke and the French Revolution: Bicentennial Essays* (Athens: Univ. of Georgia Press, 1992); Conor Cruise O'Brien, *The Great Melody: A Thematic Biography and Commented Anthology of Edmund Burke* (Chicago: Univ. of Chicago Press, 1992), not for O'Brien's interpretation, but because he made so much core Burke easily accessible; Hubert Cole, *Christophe: King of Haiti* (New York: Viking Press, 1967); Warren Roberts, *Jacques-Louis David, Revolutionary Artist: Art, Politics, and the French Revolution* (Chapel Hill: Univ. of North Carolina Press, 1989); Douglas R. Egerton, *Gabriel's Rebellion: The Virginia Slave Conspiracies of 1800 and 1802* (Chapel Hill: Univ. of North Carolina Press, 1993); Patricia B. Craddock, *Edward Gibbon, Luminous Historian, 1772–1794* (Baltimore: Johns Hopkins Univ. Press, 1989); John F. and Janet A. Stegeman, *Caty: A Biography of Catharine Littlefield Greene* (Athens: Univ. of Georgia Press, 1977); George Green Shakelford, *Thomas Jefferson's Travels in Europe, 1784–1789* (Baltimore: Johns Hopkins Univ. Press, 1995), more revealing of Jefferson's character than a dozen other biographies; Drew R. McCoy, *The Last of the Fathers: James Madison and the Republican Legacy* (Cambridge: Cambridge Univ. Press, 1989); Moreau de St. Mery, *Moreau de St. Mery's American Journey, 1793–98,* translated and edited by Kenneth Roberts and Anna M. Roberts (Garden City: Doubleday & Co., 1947); Chandos Michael Brown, *Benjamin Silliman: A Life in the Young Republic* (Princeton: Princeton Univ. Press, 1989); Marianne Elliott, *Wolfe Tone: Prophet of Irish Independence* (New Haven: Yale Univ. Press, 1989); and Richard M. Rollins, *The Long Journey of Noah Webster* (Philadelphia: Univ. of Pennsylvania Press, 1980).

In addition to using biography as primary source material, I also used many other original and contemporary sources that I do believe have not been mined enough for the insight they provide into the lives of people from this period. Dorothy Porter's (ed.) invaluable compilation in *Early Negro Writing, 1760–1837* (Boston: Beacon Press, 1971) opened up uncharted territories for me, as did Vincent Carretta, (ed.) in his copiously documented *Unchained Voices: An Anthology of Black Authors in the English-Speaking World of the Eignteenth Century* (Lexington: Univ. Press of Kentucky, 1996).

Too few scholars have taken seriously the poetry of the Hartford Wits, which served almost as a barometer of the counterrevolutionary changes occurring in America after the Revolution. From their *Anarchiad: A New England Poem,* published serially in the *New Haven Gazette and Connecticut Magazine* from October 1786, until September 1787, through the 1790s in such pieces as *The Democratiad, A Poem in Retaliation for the "Philadelphia Jockey Club"* (Philadelphia: Bradford, 1795), *The Guillotina, or a Democratic Dirge* (Philadelphia: [Bradford], 1796), and *The Political Green-House* (Hartford: Hudson & Godwin, [1799]), they reflected graphically the tides of reaction.

Fortunate for me, a number of topical compilations of documents or chronologies appeared while I was writing that aided immeasurably in tracking ideas, influences, and currents. The most useful were these: *Creating the Constitution: The Convention of 1787 and the First Congress,* edited by Thornton Anderson (University Park: Pennsylvania State Univ. Press, 1993); *Creating the Bill of Rights: The Documentary Record from the First Federal Congress,* edited by Helen E. Veit, Kenneth R. Bowling, and Charlene Bangs Bickford (Baltimore: Johns Hopkins Univ. Press, 1991); and, the most invaluable of all—particularly in detecting the power of Jefferson's *Notes on Virginia* in debates on slavery and race—was John P. Kaminski's *A Necessary Evil? Slavery and the Debate Over the Constitution* (Madison, Wisc.: Madison House, 1995). Another important tool was Philip S. Foner's useful *The Democratic-Republican Societies, 1790–1800: A Documentary Sourcebook of Constitutions, Declarations, Addresses, Resolutions, and Toasts* (Westport, Conn.: Greenwood Press, 1976).

Three other primary sources elated me when I encoutered them fully for the first time. Edmund Burke proved to be such a great prophet of revolution and counterrevolution that I decided to dig deeper into his long career of powerful preachments. One excellent Philadelphia bookstore found for me a well-preserved twelve-volume set of *The Works of the Right Honorable Edmund Burke* (revised ed.; Boston: Little Brown, 1866). It did not matter that it was a revised edition, since when I opened the fly leaf, I found it inscribed as set "No. 79" in an edition of only one hundred copies.

I felt much the same as I plied my own copy of Mercy Otis Warren's *History of the Rise, Progress and Termination of the American Revolution* (2 vols.; Boston: Manning and Loring, 1805). Here was a woman who wrote with all of the fervor of Burke, but who was just as much a champion of liberty as was he of order. I also discovered a copy of John Robison's wildly fanatical *Proofs of a Conspiracy* (1798; reprint Boston: Western Islands, 1967). This book, ridiculed by critics almost from the day it first appeared in 1798, cloaked a mysterous power over gullible people that I felt had to be understood. Thus I did what I think probably few have done: I read it.

Certain secondary works one uses prove to be helpful in knitting together essential bodies of data. I was struck while reading Albert Goodwin's *The Friends of Liberty: The English Democratic Movement in the Age of the French Revolution* (Cambridge: Harvard Univ. Press, 1979) to find that there were radical political upheavals in Britain at about the same time as in America. But then I was dumbfounded when I reread James Morton Smith's classic *Freedom's Fetters: The Alien and Sedition Laws and American Civil Liberties* (Ithaca, N.Y.: Cornell Univ. Press, 1956) to find that the very people described as "friends of liberty" in Britain were in many cases the same individuals bashed by John Adams's alien and sediton laws in America. A vital connecting link had been found. Jeffrey A. Smith's *Printers and Press Freedom: The Ideology of Early American Journalism* (New York: Oxford Univ. Press, 1988) also helped to clear some of the mists of this most contentious period of American history.

We have only just begun to understand how profoundly African Americans were isolated from equal rights in America. I hope that *American Counterrevolution* will further assist in clarifying what actually happened shortly after the American Revolution. My views on this phenomenon about the nature of liberty in America were strongly influenced by both some classic works and some newer studies: Leon F. Litwack, *North of Slavery: The Negro in the Free States, 1790–1860* (Chicago: Univ. of Chicago Press, 1961); Arthur Zilversmit, *The First Emancipation: The Abolition of Slavery in the North* (Chicago: Univ. of Chicago Press, 1967); Sidney Kaplan, *The Black Presence in the Era of the American Revolution, 1770–1800* (Washington, D.C.: Smithsonian Institution Press, 1973); and Gary B. Nash, *Race and Revolution* (Madison, Wisc.: Madison House, 1990).

Part of the problem has been a context in which to understand the power of race and enslavement in the Western world. Revealing new perspectives on the vastness of the problem and how dangerous it was to be black in America appear in three outstanding studies: Robin Blackburn, *The Overthrow of Colonial Slavery, 1776–1848* (London: Verso, 1988)—the big picture; Gary B. Nash, *Forging Freedom: The Formation of Philadelphia's Black Community, 1720–1840* (Cambridge: Harvard Univ. Press, 1988)—the discouraging record in the birthplace of liberty; and Carol Wilson, *Freedom at Risk: The Kidnapping of Free Blacks in America, 1780–1865* (Lexington, Ky.: Univ. Press of Kentucky, 1994)—the disturbing losses of freedom by free blacks.

We are also just beginning to understand what happened to the rights of women after the Revolution. Many provocative articles provided to me by Mary Kelley, as well as her important book *Private Woman, Public Stage: Literary Domesticity in Nineteenth-Century America* (New York: Oxford Univ. Press, 1984), helped me think about the comparative experiences of women in this period. Also helpful were Mary Beth Norton, *Liberty's Daughters: The Revolutionary Experience of American Women, 1750–1800* (Boston: Little, Brown, 1980); *French Women and the Age of Enlightenment,* edited by Samia I. Spencer (Bloomington: Indiana Univ. Press, 1984); and *American Women Writers to 1800,* edited by Sharon M. Harris (New York: Oxford Univ. Press, 1996).

One of the discoveries that helped me understand the causes and nature of the American Counterrevolution was the profound but little-known Scottish Enlightenment. The power of the Scottish Enlightenment over what became the United States is becoming more known through these sources: *A Hotbed of*

Genius: The Scottish Enlightenment, 1730–1790, edited by David Daiches, Peter Jones, and Jean Jones (Edinburgh: Edinburgh Univ. Press, 1986); Henry F. May *The Enlightenment in America* (New York: Oxford Univ. Press, 1976); David Dobson, *Scottish Emigration to Colonial America, 1607–1785* (Athens: Univ. of Georgia Press, 1994); Mark A. Noll, *Princeton and the Republic, 1768–1822: The Search for a Christian Enlightnment in the Era of Samuel Stanhope Smith* (Princeton: Princeton Univ. Press, 1989); and *Scotland and America in the Age of the Enlightenment,* edited by Richard B. Sher and Jeffrey R. Smitten (Princeton: Princeton Univ. Press, 1990).

When I concluded that I should include revolutionary St. Domingue in this study, I was surprised to discover the paucity of secondary literature on the Haitian Revolution. And then I was distressed to discover the many discrepancies, as well as errors of names and facts in the few sources that are available. Despite their limitations I made the best use I could to understand this third great revolution of the eighteenth century: Thomas O. Ott, *The Haitian Revolution, 1789–1804* (Knoxville: Univ. of Tennessee Press, 1973); Alfred N. Hunt, *Haiti's Influence on Antebellum America: Slumbering Volcano in the Caribbean* (Baton Rouge: Louisiana State Univ. Press, 1988); Carolyn E. Fick, *The Making of Haiti: The Saint Domingue Revolution from Below* (Knoxville: Univ. of Tennessee Press, 1990); and Martin Ros, *Night of Fire: The Black Napoleon and the Battle for Haiti,* trans. by Karin Ford-Treep (New York: Sarpedon, 1991).

When it came to the considerably important matter of illustrating this book—what is a book with only words?—I found several print sources to be of considerable assistance: *The American Revolution in Drawings and Prints: A Checklist of 1765–1790 Graphics in the Library of Congress,* edited by Donald H. Cresswell (Washington, D.C.: Library of Congress, 1975); *National Portrait Gallery: Permanent Collection Illustrated Checklist* (Washington, D.C.: Smithsonian Institution Press, 1987); Bernard Reilly, *American Political Prints, 1766–1876: A Catalog of the Collections in the Library of Congress* (Boston: G. K. Hall, 1991); Benjamin Lewis, *Engravings in American Magazines, 1741–1810* (New York: New York Public Library, 1959); and for those extremly rare images of blacks in the eighteenth century, Sidney Kaplan's extraordinary *Black Presence in the Era of the American Revolution,* already mentioned above. Since most available images do not appear in print, a number of illustrations that appear in this book were located during visits to the various repositories cited in the illustration credits and to a rich portrait index maintained by National Portrait Gallery on its website.

I am grateful to the authors of the works listed here for stimulating my thinking or helping me find some additional needed data. I am also beholden to dozens, nay hundreds, of other authors whose works I consulted along the way, but which, for the sake of brevity, I have not mentioned. The world of learning is broad indeed, and many are our debts to the words and wisdom of others.

ACKNOWLEDGMENTS

If it were not for F. B. M. Hollyday, Joel Colton, and Robert F. Durden, three of my undergraduate history teachers at Duke University, there would not be these pages. Hollyday presented the "defenestration of Prague" in such compelling terms that I fell in love with history. Joel Colton, with Robert R. Palmer, coauthor of a great textbook on modern Europe, made it clear to me during intense discussions in his office that if I did not understand Europe, I could not understand America. Bob Durden made American history so exciting that I could not study any other subject. He showed that one cannot understand the present without figuring out the past. Exhilarating! That it was, and now it is.

During my first class with Durden, he strode to the front of the room and chalked two words on the blackboard. They were "liberty" and "order." Said he, with his provocative playfulness, "If you can understand the relationship between liberty and order in American history, then you can comprehend the course of American history." It is not that I have in this book set out to explore what he meant in that first lecture. Rather, that profound juxtaposition proved illuminating as I looked at the many characters who strove to enjoy their rights to life, liberty, and equality after the American Revolution.

I am indebted to Lewis Perry for relaunching me into scholarly research when I substituted for him at Vanderbilt during 1987 and 1988. Two semesters of teaching a class on the culture of the Civil War era at Temple University allowed me to test my theory of interpreting American history without words, but rather with artifacts, music, art, architecture, tourist sites, drama, and furniture. Devoted librarians immeasurably aided this project: Richard Dunn of the Philadelphia Center for Early American Studies, University of Pennsylvania; Shelkron and Joseph Benford of the Free Library of Philadelphia; Roy Goodman and Elizabeth Carroll-Horrocks of American Philosophical Society; John Van Horne, James Green, and Jennifer Sanches of the Library Company of Philadelphia; Stephen Urice of Rosenbach Library and Museum; Arnold Thackray of the Chemical Heritage Foundation; and the libraries of the Historical Society of Pennsylvania, the National Portrait Gallery, the Library of Congress, and Duke University.

Much research was done while I served as executive director of the Benjamin Franklin National Memorial at The Franklin Institute. There I must thank Chairman Charles Andes for bringing me into a position where I could think history, do research, and sometimes write; Joel Bloom and James L. Powell for supporting my pursuit of a fellowship from the National Endowment for the Humanities that gave me more than a period of fifteen months, the equivalent in hours of a six-month leave to work on the project. My faithful assistants Kathleen DeLuca, Berrie Torgan, and Wendy Ellis Green withstood "the thing" and ceaselessly encouraged me. Institute librarians Irene Coffey and Virginia Ward found for me fugitive articles and books and surfed the internet to find much else I needed. Robert Kuss was my computer guru throughout this project.

The NEH fellowship was critical and would not have been had without the generous support of William Freehling, Eugene Genovese, and Bertram Wyatt-Brown. I met them many years ago while a graduate student. Though they have all been unmerciful in their criticism of my work (and I of theirs), it has never been driven by personal animus, only by a desire for understanding. I count these three historians as my intellectual godfathers, demanding much, giving more.

Fugitive characters often spark the greatest illuminations. Among these have been a host of great raconteurs: Martin Meyerson, President Emeritus of the University of Pennsylvania; Peter Jones, Director of the Institute for Advanced Studies in the Humanities at the University of Edinburgh; Guy Ourisson, President of the French Academy of Sciences in Paris and chemistry professor at the University of Strasbourg; Pablo Rudimon, Principal Investigator at the Institute for Advanced Studies at the University of Mexico, Mexico City; Thomas Odhaimbo, Director of the Center for Insect Physiology and Ecology in Nairobi, Kenya; Ann Boulton, Secretary of the Manchester Literary and Philosophical Society in Manchester, England; Michael Dawes, Senior Editor for Elsevier Science Publishers, Oxford, England; David and Margaret McGovern, American citizens long in Paris, and Danielle Prevot, railroad promoter and personal tour guide there.

Special American storytellers, too, led me to sources and characters that otherwise would have been missed. These include: Donald Mathews, who planted the seeds of many topics covered here while I was in graduate school at the University of North Carolina; Claude-Anne Lopez and Barbara Oberg of the Benjamin Franklin Papers Project at Yale University—colleagues, confidants, and friends; Charles Blockson, Director of the Blockson Collection on black American history at Temple University; Gretchen Worden, Director of the Mutter Museum at the Philadelphia College of Physicians. William S. Price, Jeffrey Crow, and Brent Glass served as valued advisers since our first ritual lunches at the Upstairs and the Mecca Restaurants in Raleigh, North Carolina in 1975. Although the gathering was physically disrupted in 1981 by my departure to Pennsylvania, they have not ceased to influence my thoughts. The same goes for Mary Kelley of Dartmouth College, who in 1993 took pity on a guy who had just realized that he knew nothing about women's history.

That last thank you deserves explanation. Halfway through my NEH fellowship, Richard Dunn, founder of the Philadelphia Center for Early American Studies, kindly scheduled me for a presentation on my work in progress before one of the biweekly seminars of the Center. I presented an outline of my project, two chapters in the work, and my findings. I was stared down by the ample group of women present, who suggested that I would have a stronger work if I could do the same examination of women seeking liberty in the eighteenth century that I had done for men. I spent a year doing that.

Next I spent a good year looking at black men and women seeking liberty. Thanks, Charles Blockson. My research drove me to St. Domingue and the West Indies, because it seemed that we had not yet figured out that the Haitian thirst for liberty was every bit as strong as that of the Americans.

Friends Malcolm Call at the University of Georgia Press and John Easterly of the Louisiana State University Press pushed and encouraged me. Vivian Weyerhaeuser Piasecki asked me systematically where I was in this project and made me explain exactly why more and more characters had to be added to the story. For three years Mary Gregg spoke to me not at all without exacting an accounting of my precise location in my work. Nancy Kolb read most of the words and eliminated those that seemed excessive. Marsha Jagodich continually asked for a projected ending date and introduced me early in the project to the restful hotel run by her daughter Diane and son-in-law Peter in Ocean Grove, New Jersey.

Marian Godfrey of the Pew Charitable Trusts, encourager of much that is intellectual in Philadelphia, provided advice professional and personal, throughout most of the research and writing. She, too, offered a great place to work and to think at the remote Godfrey compound on Vinalhaven Island, Maine. In Colorado, Cape Cod, aboard the *Etoile de Champagne* south from Paris, and even on a bicycle from Orléans to Perpignan, I have had plenty of inspiring retreats; just too little connected time. As the conclusion neared, the England clan of Boston became very encouraging—especially Albert England, former Harvard neuroscientist, daughter Jean England Brubaker, and little Alexander Charles England who arrived when I was dealing with the insulting effects of prostate surgery.

But this book would never have come to fruition were it not for a group of history colleagues who generously took the time to read a 1,300-page manuscript from beginning to end and who gave me a rich assortment of good suggestions. They proved that historical works are the product of fertile interaction. These stars, to whom I will be endlessly grateful, are as follows: William C. "Jack" Davis, of Mechanicsburg, Pennsylvania; Douglas R. Egerton, Le Moyne College, Syracuse, New York; Mary Kelley, Dartmouth College; Peter Kolchin, University of Delaware; and Randall M. Miller, Saint Joseph's University, Philadelphia. Additionally, William W. Freehling of the University of Kentucky read enough to provide me with his greatest compliment: "Tise, you are outrageous!"

I am doubly grateful to Jack Davis for not only reading the manuscript, but also for introducing me to Stackpole Books. This fine press and the skilled editor with whom I have had the privilege to work, Michelle Simmons, spared no time or expense in producing a good product.

Many contributed to this book ideas and insights too abundant to enumerate. My apologies to you for not being able to list everyone who added texture and richness to this tapestry. Please know that without your help, I could not have ended this volume with, like Cyrano, my panache.

Note: Illustration credits for portraits are arranged alphabetically by the surname of each subject. Credits for other images are arranged by year of creation. Illustrations used as chapter logos are listed among nonportrait images. To find individual credits refer to the subject or year key under the illustration.

All illustrations are reproduced courtesy of the institutions indicated below. Special appreciation for assistance in finding these illustrations is hereby extended to Kenneth Finkel of the William Penn Foundation, Jennifer Ambrose of the Library Company of Philadelphia, and Joseph Benford of the Free Library of Philadelphia.

ABBREVIATIONS

APS   American Philosophical Society, Philadelphia

BVP   *The City of Philadelphia, in the State of Pennsylvania, North America; As It Appeared in the Year 1800* (Philadelphia: Wiliam R. Birch & Son, 1800)

CAB   *Appleton's Cyclopedia of American Biography* (6 vols.; New York: D. Appleton and Co., 1888)

CHF   Chemical Heritage Foundation, Philadelphia

FLP   Free Library of Philadelphia, Philadelphia

LAL   *Library of American Literature* (11 vols.; New York: Charles L. Webster & Co., 1891)

LC   Library of Congress, Washington, D.C.

LCP   Library Company of Philadelphia, Philadelphia

MMCP   Mutter Museum, College of Physicians, Philadelphia

NPG   National Portrait Gallery, Smithsonian Institute, Washington, D.C.

NYHS   The New-York Historical Society, New York City

PC   Private Collections (including those of the author)

RS   The Royal Society, London, U.K.

RIHS   Rhode Island Historical Society

SPNEA   Society for the Preservation of New England Antiquities, Boston

YUAG   Yale University Art Gallery, New Haven

Portraits

Adams, John   Engraving based on 1783 portrait by John Singleton Copley (LCP: P.8911.40)

Allen, Richard   "Revd. Richard Allen. Bishop of the First African Methodist Episcopal Church. Of the U.S.," lithograph by P. S. Duval, Philadelphia, n.d. (NPG.79.93)

Ames, Fisher   Gilbert Stuart, c. 1807, oil on panel (NPG. 79.215)

Bache, Benjamin Franklin
Detail of cartoon, anonymous, 1798, titled *The Times: A Political Portrait* (NYHS negative #2737)

Bache, Sarah Franklin
Wood engraving, artist unknown, n.d. (FLP, Lewis Collection)

Benneker, Benjamin
Wood engraving from *Benjamin Bannaker's Pennsylvania, Delaware, Maryland, and Virginia almanac for the Year of our Lord 1795* (Baltimore, [1794]), frontispiece (PC)

Barlow, Joel   Engraving, 1793, Louis Charles Ruotte (NPG.76.42)

Brackenridge, Hugh Henry
Etching by Albert Rosenthal, n.d., based on contemporaneous drawing by Robert Smith (FLP: Lewis Collection)

Burke, Edmund   Stipple engraving, by H. W. Smith from portrait by Sir Joshua Reynolds, 1866, in *The Works of the Right Honorable Edmund Burke* (revised edition; Boston, 1866), I, frontispiece (PC)

Carey, Matthew   Engraving, "Mr. Matthew Carey, Printer" from Mathew Carey, *The Plagi-Scurriliad* (Philadelphia, 1786) (FLP, Lewis Collection)

Cobbett, William   Engraving, "Mr. Cobbett," n.d., artist unknown (LCP 5750.F.956)

Cooper, Thomas   Oil on canvas, "Thomas Cooper," by Charles Wilson Peale, 1819, Mutter Museum, College of Physicians, Philadelphia

Cuffe, Paul   Engraving, "Captain Paul Cuffe, 1812," by Mason & Mass "from a drawing by John Pole, M.D. of Bristol, Eng." (NPG.77.161)

Duane, William   Engraving, "Duane, 1802" by Charles Balthazer Julien F'evret de Saint-Memin (NPG.74.39.159)

Dwight, Timothy
Oil on canvas, "Timothy Dwight," by John Trumbull, ca. 1804 (YUAG 1817.1)

Equiano, Olaudah
>Engraving, "Olaudah Equiano, or Gustavus Vassa, the African. Publish'd March 1, 1789 by G. Vassa," by D. Orme from painting by W. Denton (NPG.78.82)

Ferguson, Elizabeth Graeme
>Stipple engraving, n.d. (FLP, Lewis Collection)

Forten, James   Oil on paper, n.d. (FLP, Lewis Collection)

Franklin, Benjamin
>Engraving, "B. Franklin, L.L.D., F.R.S. Born at Boston in New England, Jan. 6th, 1706. Died at Philadelphia April 17th, 1790," in *Massachusetts Magazine* (1790), II, no. 5 (LC USZ—31,139)

——— Engraving, "Benjamin Franklin," by H. B. Hall from original oil portrait by J. A. Duplessis, 1783 (PC: LAL, III, frontispiece)

Freneau, Philip   Engraving, by P. Halpin (PC: LAL, III, facing p. 446)

Fulton, Robert   Stipple engraving, "R. Fulton," by H. B. Hall, Jr., from original oil painting by Benjamin West (PC: CAB, II, facing p. 563)

Genet, Edmond   Engraving, "Citizen Genet," by Gilles-Louis Chretien, 1793 (FLP, Lewis Collection)

Greene, Nathanael
>Engraving, "Nathaniel [*sic*] Greene, Major General in the American armies, a Patriot, a hero, and a Friend," by Justus Chevillet after Charles Wilson Peale, c. 1780 (NPG.80.43)

Jefferson, Thomas
>Engraving, "Th. Jefferson," by A. B. Hall (PC: CAB, II, facing p. 415)

Jones, Absalom   Liverpool ware jug, "Rev. Absalom Jones of the African Church, Philada," ca. 1808 (NPG.71.61)

Logan, George   Etching, "George Logan, M.D., by Albert Rosenthal, 1889," based on an original painting from the period (FLP, Lewis Collection)

Macaulay, Catharine
>Engraving, "Catharina Macaulay," 1769, from Macaulay, *History of England from James I* (London, 1769), vol. 1 (LCP negative collection)

Madison, James   Stipple and line engraving, "Jas. Madison," by unidentified artist, after Charles Willson Peale, 1796; and published in Charles Smith, *The Gentleman's Political Pocket Almanack for 1797* (New York, 1796) (NPG.77.211)

Morse, Jedediah   Oil painting, "Jedediah Morse and His Son Samuel F. B.

Morse, said to be by a Mr. Sargent" in Edward Lind Morse, ed., *Samuel F. B. Morse: His Letters and Journals* (2 vols.; Boston: 1914) (PC)

Otis, Harrison Gray
Oil painting, "Harrison Gray Otis," by Gilbert Sutart, 1809, Society for the Preservation of New England Antiquities

Paine, Thomas   Engraving, "Thomas Paine"—secretary of the U.S. Congress, author of *Common Sense* and of responses to Burke, and deputy of the National Convention—, by A. Sandos after painting by Peale [?] of Philadelphia, ca. 1792 (NPG.84.167)

Priestley, Joseph Pastel on paper, by James Sharples, ca. 1797 (NPG.77.160)

Rowson, Susanna
Engraving, "S. Rowson," unidentified artist, n.d. (FLP, Lewis Collection)

Rush, Benjamin   Engraving, "Dr. Benjamin Rush," by J. Wiggin after Jeremiah Paul, Jr., 1800 (NPG.77.253)

Sampson, Deborah
Oil painting, "Deborah Sampson," by Joseph Stone, Framingham, Mass., 1797 (RIHS—[X3] 2513)

Tone, Theobald Wolfe
Engraving, "The Unfortunate Theobald Wolfe Tone, Esq.," in *Walker's Hibernian Magazine* (October, 1798) (PC)

Toussaint L'Overture
Stipple lithograph, "Toussaint L'Overture," by Delpech, n.d. (LC USZ62—7862)

Volney, Constantin
Stipple and line engraving, "M. le Cte. de Volney, Pair de France," artist unknown, n.d. (FLP, Lewis Collection)

Warren, Mercy Otis
Steel engraving, "Mercy Warren" (LAL, III, facing p. 122) (PC)

Webster, Noah   Relief cut, "Noah Webster, Jun., Esq.," by unidentified artist, 1789, published in Noah Webster, *The American Spelling Book* (Boston, 1789) (NPG.78.90)

Weishaupt, Adam
Engraving, "Adam Weishaupt," by C. W. Bock, after painting by C. V. Mansinger, 1788, in *Verbessertes System der Illuminaten* (Frankfurt & Leipzig, 1788)

Wheatley, Phillis Engraving, "Phillis Wheatley, Negro Servant to Mr. John Wheatley of Boston," by unidentified artist after Scipio Moorhead, 1773, published in Phillis Wheatley, *Poems on Various Subjects, Religious and Moral* (London, 1773) (NPG.77.2)

Wollstonecraft, Mary
> Stipple engraving, "Mary Wollstonecraft Godwin," by S. Clayton (LCP negative file)

Caricatures, Cartoons, and Other Illustrations

1778   Mixed method print, "The Tea-Tax-Tempest, or the Anglo-American Revolution," by [Carl Guttenburg of Nuremberg], 1778. (LC USZ62-1523)

1779.1   Wash drawing, "Vue de la Ville de Savannah, du Camp, des Tranchees et de L'attaque, Octobre, 1779," artist unidentified. (LC USZ62—11,898)

1779.2   Text, "The Allied Army at the Siege of Savannah," in *The Siege of Savannah, in 1779* (Albany, N.Y., 1874), p. 40. (PC)

1783   Etching, map cartouche of Washington and Franklin founding the United States of America on a map titled "The United States of America laid down from the best Authorities, Agreeable to the Peace of 1783. Published April 3d. 1783 by the Proprietor John Wallis, at his Map-Warehouse, Ludgate Street, London." (LC G&M Neg. 709757 #438)

1786.1   Etching, "Venerate the Plough" by JT, 1786, in "Plan of a Farm Yard" in *The Columbian Magazine, or Monthly Miscellany* (October, 1786), facing p. 77. (LC USZ62—31,153)

1786.2   Etching, "While Commerce Spreads Her Canvass O'er the Main" in *The Columbian Magazine, or Monthly Miscellany* (1787), frontispiece. (LC USZ62—30,932)

1787.1   Etching, "Illuminaten & Englische Freymauerey," in *Religions Begebenheiten* (1787), p. 62. (PC)

1787.2   Engraving, "The Looking Glass for 1787. A House Divided Against Itself Cannot Stand. Mat. chap. 13th verse 26," by Amos Doolittle [?], 1787, New Haven, Connecticut. (LC USZ62—96,402)

1787.3   Etching, "Zion Besieged & Attacked," unidentified artist, 1787. (LCP 5760.F.3)

1788   Etching, "Behold! a Fabric now to Freedom rear'd" by Trenchard, 1788, in *The Columbian Magazine, or Monthly Miscellany* (1788), frontispiece. (LC USZ62—45,513)

1789.1   Mixed method, "America! with Peace and Freedom blest," unidentified artist, 1789, in *The Columbian Magazine, or Monthly Miscellany* (1789), frontispiece. (LC USZ62—45,573)

1789.2   Woodcut, ornament for title page, *The Columbian Magazine, or Monthly Miscellany* (1789). (LC USZ62—45,574)

1790.1   Etching, "Con-g-ss Embark'd on board the Ship Constitution of America bound to Conogocheque by way of Philadelphia," unidentified artist, 1790. (LC USZ62—1552)

1790.2 Mixed method, Two women celebrate the birth of America, by S. Hill, 1790, in *The Massachusetts Magazine* (1790), frontispiece. (LC USZ62 —45,522)

1790.3 Mixed method, ornament for title page, *The Universal Asylum and Columbian Magazine* (1790), by Thackara & Vallance after Charles Wilson Peale. (LC USZ62—46,096)

1791.1 Etching, "A Birmingham Toast, as given on the 14th of July, by the — ———- Revolution Society," by James Gillray, published July 23, 1791 by S. W. Fores, Picadilly, London. (CHF Collection)

1791.2 Engraving, "Attaque et Combat de Leogane, St. Dominigue," by Couche after Martinet, 1791. (LC USZ62—32,395)

1791.3 Hand-colored engraving, "Burke's Pair of Spectacles for Short Sighted Politicians," by James Sayer, published May 12, 1791, by Thomas Cornell, Bruton Street, London. (CHF Collection)

1792 Oil on canvas, "Liberty Displaying the Arts and Sciences," by Samuel Jennings, 1792. (LCP Collection)

1793 Etching, "A Peep into the Antifederal Club," unidentified artist, published at New York, August 16, 1793. (FLP, Lewis Collection)

1794 Engraving, "Gaol in Walnut Street," by William Birch, ca. 1794, BP. (FLP-BVP)

1795 Engraving, "Triumph of Liberty. Dedicated to its Defenders in America," by P. C. Verger, N. York, November, 1796, and drawn by John Francis Renault, September 1795. (LC USZ62—40,969)

1796 Stipple engraving and mezzotint, "Liberty. In the form of the Goddess of Youth; giving Support to the Bald Eagle," by Edward Savage, published June 11, 1796. (LC USZ62—15,369)

1798.1 Etching, "Congressional Pugilists," unidentified artist, February, 1798 (first state). (LC USZ62—1551)

1798.2 Engraving, "Congress Hall & New Theater, Chestnut Street, Philadelphia," by William Birch, ca. 1798. (FLP-BVP)

1798.3 Engraving, "Library & Surgeons Hall in Fifth Street, Philadelphia, Pennsylvania," by William Birch, ca. 1798. (FLP-BVP)

1798.4 Engraving, "Norris House, Philadelphia" by William Birch, ca. 1798. (FLP-BVP)

1798.5 Engraving, "Pennsylvania Hospital in Pine Street, Philadelphia," by William Birch, ca. 1798. (FLP-BVP)

1798.6 Engraving, "Preparation for War to defend Commerce," by William Birch, ca. 1798. (FLP-BVP)

1798.7 Engraving, "The Times: A Political Portrait," unidentified artist, 1798. (NYHS, negative #2737)

1799   Engraving, "Washington's Funeral Procession. High Street from the Country Market," by William Birch, ca. 1799. (FLP-BVP)

1800.1   Cartoon etching, "Return to England from America," by James Gillray, n.d., in *The Life and Letters of William Cobbett in England and America* (2 vols.; London, 1913), I, pp. 84–85 (PC)

1800.2   Cartoon etching, "The Providential Detection," 1800. (LCP 7898.F)

1800.3   Water color, "Plan of Dr. Priestley's House at Northumberland in the State of Pennsylvania . . . As also a View of the Vicinity, July 1800, Plans & Drawn by T. Lambourne, Survr., Luzerne County," in *Joseph Priestley in America, 1794–1804* (N.p., 1994), p. 24 (RS—MS.654,f.66)

1803   Engraving, "Battle of Serpents' Ravine between Troops of Toussaint and France," by Outhwaite based on drawing by Karl Girardet, ca. 1803. (LC USZ62—17,250)

INDEX

This index has been constructed to be a combination of finding aid for names, place names, organizations, and topics appearing in the text—and a biographical directory of individuals who are examined in the book. Readers may track topics and individuals by referring to subject and biographical data contained in this index.